Econometrics
Volume 2:
Econometrics and the Cost
of Capital

Econometrics
Volume 2:
Econometrics and the Cost
of Capital: Essays in Honor of
Dale W. Jorgenson

Edited by Lawrence J. Lau

The MIT Press
Cambridge, Massachusetts
London, England

Library of Congress Cataloging-in-Publication Data

Jorgenson, Dale Weldeau, 1933–
  Econometrics / edited by Lawrence J. Lau.
   p. cm.
  Includes bibliographical references and index.
  ISBN 0-262-10083-5 (v. 2: hc: alk. paper)
  1. Production (Economic theory)—Econometric models. I. Title.
HB241.J67 2000
330′.01′5195—dc21   99–046138

Contents

List of Tables

Preface

Lawrence J. Lau

1. Introduction

Dale W. Jorgenson introduced the concept of the cost of capital in his celebrated article, "Capital Theory and Investment Behavior" (1963; reprinted in Jorgenson, 1996a). This volume provides a comprehensive overview of the applications of the cost of capital in the many diverse areas in economics. In chapter 1 we review the historical origins of the concept of capital as a factor of production with a rental price given by the cost of capital. (It is important to note that the "cost of capital" is used in a different sense in the literature on financial economics. For example, Modigliani and Miller (1958) use this term to denote the weighted average rate of return to equity and debt, one component of the rental price of capital services.)

The unifying theme of Jorgenson's many contributions to economics is a model of the cost of capital and investment. This consists of a forward-looking model of future asset prices and a backward-looking model of past accumulations of capital. At each point of time these models are linked through the quantity of investment and the rental price of capital services or the cost of capital. In chapter 1 we consider the role of the cost of capital in modeling investment behavior, technology and productivity measurement, consumer behavior and welfare measurement, and intertemporal general equilibrium modeling. We review Jorgenson's contributions to each of these areas chronologically. Finally, we outline the research opportunities still remaining.

2.   Investment Demand, Capital Income Taxation, and the Cost of Capital

Jorgenson (1963) introduced all the important features of the econometric models of investment behavior summarized in his survey paper, "Econometric Studies of Investment Behavior: A Review" (1971; reprinted in Jorgenson, 1996a). Prior to Jorgenson's work the modeling of investment behavior had been based on various *ad hoc* principles, such as the capacity principle, the profits principle, and the like. His work initiated the cumulative progress in modeling of investment that has continued up to the present.

Jorgenson's key innovations are the derivation of investment demand from a model of capital as a factor of production, the incorporation of the tax treatment of income from capital into the rental price of capital services, and new econometric methods for modeling gestation lags in the investment process. Recent research surveyed by Ricardo Caballero (1999, p. 821) has confirmed the continuing empirical validity of the long-run relationship between investment and the cost of capital. Current research concentrates on capturing the features of more detailed data sets now available, especially the short-run dynamics of investment behavior at the firm and establishment level.

The relationship between investment and the cost of capital remains an important focus of the empirical literature on the dynamics of investment demand. Similarly, the theory of investment proposed by Jorgenson (1967) has retained a central role. The econometric methodology for modeling gestation lags based on rational distributed lags, introduced by Jorgenson (1966; reprinted in Jorgenson, 1996a), has been assimilated into the statistical literature through the "transfer function" approach of Box and Jenkins (1970).

Jorgenson (1963) originated the cost-of-capital approach to the taxation of income from capital. This approach makes complex tax provisions for capital income much more transparent. The special strength of the cost-of-capital approach lies in its ability to absorb almost unlimited detail on the features of specific tax policies. This approach has had important practical consequences by providing a precise instrument for achieving horizontal equity in capital income taxation.

The principle of horizontal equity holds that taxpayers in the same circumstances should have the same tax liabilities. The appeal of this principle is threefold. First, it achieves fairness in the sense of equitable treatment of citizens before the law. Second, under the rubric of "tax neutrality," it eliminates any possibilities for increasing economic efficiency by redistributing the tax burden. Finally, it leads to simplicity by expunging from tax statutes the detailed specifications of transactions subject to special provisions.

The principle of horizontal equity for capital income taxation was embodied in the Tax Reform Act of 1986 in the United States. This legislation reversed decades of piecemeal creation of specific incentives for particular classes of taxpayers. Similar reforms have now been adopted in industrialized countries around the world, broadening the base for capital income taxes and reducing tax rates. These reforms have contributed greatly to more efficient allocation of capital within market economies.

The article by Robert Hall and Jorgenson, "Tax Policy and Investment Behavior" (1967; reprinted in Jorgenson, 1996b) makes the concept of the cost of capital more exact and employs this concept in the analysis of alternative tax policies. Jorgenson's cost of capital had been incorporated into all major forecasting models in the United States by the early 1980s. And simulations of the short-run economic impacts of alternative tax policies had become the staple fare of debates over specific tax proposals. Simulations of the long-run impacts of tax policy based on the cost of capital, surveyed by Yolanda K. Henderson (1991), made their appearance in tax policy debates by the end of the 1980s.

Alan Auerbach and Jorgenson augment the cost of capital framework by introducing the marginal effective tax rate in their article, "Inflation-Proof Depreciation of Assets" (1980; reprinted in Jorgenson, 1996b). Jorgenson's cost of capital summarizes the information about future consequences of investment decisions essential for current decisions about capital allocation. The marginal effective tax rate characterizes the tax consequences of investment decisions in a way that is particularly suitable for comparisons among alternative tax policies. Efficient capital allocation requires equalization of marginal effective tax rates among all assets.

The cost of capital and the marginal effective tax rate were employed in the design of reforms of capital income taxation in the United States and around the world during the 1980s and early 1990s. The reforms are described for nine countries—the G7 plus Australia and Sweden—by Jorgenson (1993) in his "Introduction and Summary" to *Tax Reform and the Cost of Capital* (Jorgenson and Ralph Landau,

1993). Marginal effective tax rates have been compiled for dozens of countries. King and Fullerton (1984), the OECD (1991), The Commission of the European Communities (1992), and Jorgenson (1993) have provided international comparisons.

Hall and Alvin Rabushka (1995) are the originators of the Flat Tax approach to implementation of a national consumption tax. In chapter 2 Hall considers the international consequences of three leading consumption tax proposals—the Flat Tax, the national sales tax, and the personal consumption tax. The analysis of tax reform in the open U.S. economy has to consider the general equilibrium in a world economy with heterogeneous tax systems. Tax systems in major industrialized countries, like the U.S. tax system today, rely on a mixture of consumption and income, including capital income, taxation.

3. Productivity and the Cost of Capital

In the area of productivity analysis and growth accounting, Jorgenson and Zvi Griliches take a crucial step beyond the aggregate production function employed by Robert M. Solow (1957). In "The Explanation of Productivity Change" (1967; reprinted in Jorgenson, 1995a), they allow for the joint production of consumption and investment goods from capital and labor services. This makes it possible to identify the embodiment of new technology with a constant-quality price index for investment goods. Jorgenson and Griliches construct constant-quality indices of capital and labor inputs by weighting the components of each input by their marginal products. The marginal products of the capital inputs are the rental prices of capital services.

Laurits Christensen and Jorgenson (1973; reprinted in Jorgenson, 1995a) extend the model of the cost of capital employed by Jorgenson and Griliches by distinguishing among different legal forms of organizations—corporate business, non-corporate business, and households and institutions. This makes it possible to represent the distinctive features of the taxation of capital income for each of these legal forms of organization. Christensen and Jorgenson imbed the production account employed in productivity measurement in a complete system of U.S. national accounts, including Jorgenson's cost of capital as the price of capital services. This system consists of accounts for production, income (including imputed incomes from consumer durables and owner-occupied residential housing) and expenditure (again including imputed expenditures on consumer durables and housing), capital formation and wealth.

Jorgenson, Frank Gollop, and Barbara Fraumeni (1987) dispense with the aggregate production function entirely in allocating the sources of U.S. economic growth to the level of individual industries. Their book contains by far the most detailed data ever compiled on investment and productivity in the U.S. economy. Industry outputs are represented as functions of capital, labor, and intermediate inputs, each defined in terms of a constant-quality index of the corresponding inputs. The innovations of Jorgenson, Griliches, Christensen, Gollop, and Fraumeni dramatically reduce the role of (total factor) productivity as a source of economic growth and greatly increase the relative importance of investments in human and non-human capital. These investments respond to changes in economic policies such as tax policies.

In chapter 3 Christensen summarizes his research on capital measurement for the U.S. and other industrialized countries, as well as numerous firms and industries in the U.S. economy. He then focuses on the measurement of productivity and provision of proper incentives for productivity improvement in regulated industries. He observes that regulatory agencies have adopted simplified measures of capital costs based on the nominal cost of capital, rather than the real cost implied by Jorgenson's concept of the cost of capital. This has distorted production and investment decisions in regulated industries, such as the electric power industry in the United States, especially during inflationary periods like the 1970s. Christensen describes a system for incentive regulation, based on the real cost of capital, that would provide appropriate incentives for regulated firms.

In chapter 5 Gollop compares the "production approach" to productivity measurement introduced by Jorgenson (1966b; reprinted in Jorgenson, 1995a) with the "welfare approach," employed by Solow (1957) and others, that preceded it. The welfare approach begins with the income and expenditure account, while the production approach starts from the production account. The production approach captures changes in technology and distinguishes movements along the production possibility frontier from shifts in the frontier, as proposed by Solow. The welfare approach, which is complementary rather than competing, is appropriate for allocating current income between present and future consumption in the form of saving. Gollop shows how this distinction has led to a resolution of the lengthy controversies that followed the introduction of the production approach.

In chapter 6 Fraumeni considers the features of the Jorgenson system of national accounts. This consists of three major components: the Christensen-Jorgenson (1973) national accounts, the Jorgenson-Gollop-Fraumeni (1987) sectoral production accounts, and the Jorgenson-Fraumeni (1989a; reprinted in Jorgenson, 1995a) human capital and non-market accounts. She points out that the main weakness of the U.S. national accounts is that stocks of reproducible, tangible assets are not linked to the services they produce. This deficiency is overcome by Jorgenson's system. Jorgenson and Fraumeni have extended the system to investment, stocks, and services of human capital and the associated market and non-market activities.

Data on the sources of growth at the industry level similar to those of Jorgenson, Gollop, and Fraumeni (1987) were constructed for Japan by Jorgenson, Masahiro Kuroda, and Mieko Nishimizu (1987; reprinted in Jorgenson, 1995b) and for Germany by Klaus Conrad and Jorgenson (1986; reprinted in Jorgenson 1995b). These data made it possible to compare productivity levels for individual industries in the three countries. The international comparisons required purchasing power parities for capital and labor inputs and outputs at the industry level, extending the purchasing power parities for aggregate outputs developed by Irving Kravis, Alan Heston, and Robert Summers (1982). The purchasing power parity for capital inputs is based on Jorgenson's cost of capital.

Jorgenson and his collaborators show that the U.S. began the postwar period with an enormous productivity advantage over its competitors. Although gains in productivity by Germany and Japan in the early postwar period were very dramatic, the gains slowed markedly after 1973 and these countries emerged as productivity laggards. Defining international competitiveness in terms of the relative prices of goods and services in a common currency, competitiveness has been driven primarily by depreciation of the U.S. dollar since the collapse of the Bretton Woods regime. Relative productivity levels between the U.S. and other industrialized countries have moved in the opposite direction from international competitiveness.

In chapter 7 Charles Hulten and Robert Schwab apply the conceptual framework for international comparisons employed by Jorgenson, Kuroda, and Nishimizu (1987) to regional comparisons within the United States. The key result of the article is that the path of productivity efficiency has been essentially parallel across U.S. regions in recent decades. This suggests that manufacturing technology and organizational practice had already diffused widely throughout the country by the beginning of the period. This leaves little room for explanations of convergence of regional growth based on technological diffusion, increasing returns to scale, or differential growth of public infrastructure capital.

4. Production and the Cost of Capital

In their article, "Transcendental Logarithmic Production Frontiers," Laurits Christensen, Jorgenson, and Lawrence Lau (1973; reprinted in Jorgenson, 2000) present econometric models of production for the U.S. economy based on transcendental logarithmic price and production possibility frontiers. The innovations embodied in these econometric models—price-quantity duality in production, statistical methods for estimation and inference in systems of nonlinear simultaneous equations, and flexible functional forms—define the standard for econometric modeling of producer behavior. The extensive and growing literature emanating from this approach is surveyed by Jorgenson (1986; reprinted in Jorgenson, 2000).

Price-quantity duality in the theory of production is especially critical in generating econometric models that provide flexible representations of technology. Jorgenson and Lau (1974; reprinted in Jorgenson, 2000) have linked the theory of producer behavior employed in these models to the technological opportunities faced by producers through price-quantity duality. Jean-Jacques Laffont and Jorgenson (1974; reprinted in Jorgenson, 2000) introduce the method of nonlinear three-stage least squares employed in estimating the unknown parameters. Generalizations of this method by Lars Hansen (1982) have become the basis for the Generalized Method of Moments, now the standard approach for estimation and inference in macroeconometric modeling.

In the model presented by Christensen, Jorgenson, and Lau, the economy supplies outputs of investment and consumption goods and demands inputs of capital and labor services. Myopic decision rules for econometric models of production are derived by identifying the rental price of capital input with Jorgenson's cost of capital. An increase in the output of investment goods requires foregoing a part of the output of consumption goods, so that adjusting the rate of investment is costly. However, costs of adjustment are external to the

producing unit and are fully reflected in the market price of investment goods. This price incorporates forward-looking expectations of
the prices of future capital services.

An alternative approach to introducing forward-looking expectations in modeling investment was introduced by William Brainard
and James Tobin (1968) and Tobin (1969). Tobin's Q is defined as the
ratio of expected profits to the market value of the firm's assets.
Fumio Hayashi (1982) provided a neo-classical interpretation of
Tobin's Q by showing how to identify internal costs of adjustment
from the Q-ratio under constant returns to scale in production. Internal costs of adjustment are an alternative to gestation lags in modeling
the short-run dynamics of investment behavior. If all costs of adjustment are external and returns to scale are constant, then Tobin's Q is
identically equal to unity, as in the model of Christensen, Jorgenson,
and Lau.

In chapter 4 Hayashi reviews the theory of investment demand
since the publication of Jorgenson (1963). He introduces the corporate
income tax and derives Jorgenson's cost of capital. He then presents
the Q theory of investment, the Euler equation approach to investment
theory, and surveys the complexities that arise from the introduction
of multiple capital goods. Finally, he introduces uncertainty and irreversibility of investment and discusses the connections between
investment and finance. His theme is the essential role played by Jorgenson's cost of capital in all the existing models of investment. He
also points out that the cost of capital is the sole channel through
which tax parameters exert incentive effects, which accounts for the
central role of this concept in the theory of capital income taxation.

5.   Welfare and the Cost of Capital

Christensen, Jorgenson, and Lau (1975, reprinted in Jorgenson, 1997a)
present econometric models of consumer demand for the U.S. economy that parallel their models of production. These models are based
on transcendental logarithmic direct and indirect utility functions and
combine flexibility in the representation of preferences with parsi-
mony in the number of parameters. Jorgenson's cost of capital plays a
critical role in modeling consumer demand for housing and consumers' durables. Demands for these commodities are represented in
terms of flows of capital services and the prices faced by consumers
are rental prices of the capital services. Investments in housing and

consumers' durables are derived from the accumulation equations for the stocks of these types of capital.

The models of Christensen, Jorgenson, and Lau (1975) retain the concept of a representative consumer employed in earlier models of consumer demand. This omits a crucial link between individual and aggregate demands arising from the fact the aggregate demands are sums of individual demands. Lau's (1977, 1982) theory of exact aggregation is the key to surmounting the limitations of the representative consumer model. The essential innovation is to incorporate the attributes of consumers, such as their demographic characteristics that reflect heterogeneity of preferences, into statistics of the joint distribution of attributes and total expenditures over the population.

The econometric model of aggregate consumer behavior presented by Jorgenson, Lau, and Thomas Stoker (1982, reprinted in Jorgenson, 1997a) successfully integrates the two principal streams of empirical research on consumer behavior by pooling aggregate time series data with cross section data for individual households. Moreover, the Jorgenson, Lau and Stoker model permits an exact decomposition of the estimated aggregate demand function into individual demand functions distinguished by demographic and other characteristics. Jorgenson and Stoker (1986; reprinted in Jorgenson, 1997a) have extended the econometric methodology of Jorgenson and Laffont (1974) to permit pooling of time series and cross section data. Stoker (1993) has summarized the extensive empirical literature emanating from the exact aggregation approach to modeling consumer behavior.

In chapter 8 Stoker summarizes Jorgenson's research on consumer behavior. The objective of this research is to analyze economic policy, ultimately, to see how the welfare of individuals is affected by a policy change. The model of aggregate consumer behavior constructed by Jorgenson, Lau, and Stoker (1982) has been used for this purpose in the general equilibrium modeling of Jorgenson, Mun Ho (1994; reprinted in Jorgenson, 1998b), and Peter Wilcoxen (1993; reprinted in Jorgenson, 1998b). This model of consumer behavior embodies important innovations in economic theory and econometric method, as well as econometric modeling that defined the research frontier in this area for nearly a decade. The model successfully captures price, income and demographic effects in a consistent fashion and has provided the foundation for the subsequent developments surveyed by Stoker (1993).

Jorgenson and Daniel Slesnick (1984, reprinted in Jorgenson, 1997b) introduce an approach to normative economics that exploits the econometric model of Jorgenson, Lau, and Stoker. Measures of welfare for each consumer are recovered from individual demand functions. These are combined into a single indicator of social welfare, reflecting concepts of horizontal and vertical equity. As Amartya Sen (1977) has persuasively argued, this requires dispensing with ordinal measures of welfare that are not comparable among individuals. Jorgenson and Slesnick meet this requirement by constructing cardinal measures of welfare that are fully comparable among individuals.

Jorgenson and Slesnick have constructed measures of the cost and standard of living, inequality in the distribution of individual welfare, and poverty. They have also compared their approach, based on the distribution of total expenditures on consumption, with approaches based on the distribution of income. The distribution of income is used for official measures of poverty, inequality, and the standard of living by statistical agencies in the U.S. and many other countries. Differences between these two approaches are mainly due to differences between the distribution of total expenditure and the distribution of income, but differences in the cost of living and changes in the composition of families are also important. Jorgenson (1990; reprinted in Jorgenson, 1997b) and Slesnick (1998) have surveyed empirical applications of the new approach to normative economics.

In chapter 9 Slesnick summarizes the innovations in applied welfare economics emanating from his research with Jorgenson. The measurement of individual well-being is tied explicitly to an econometric model of consumer behavior to obtain an exact welfare indicator that increases only if utility actually rises. This supersedes index number methods based on consumers' surplus that remain in common use, but provide an exact welfare indicator only for identical, homothetic preferences. The empirical evidence presented by Jorgenson, Lau, and Stoker (1982) and numerous predecessors contradicts these conditions. In addition, the measurement of social welfare is founded on the principles of social choice that have been the exclusive preserve of microeconomic theorists.

Slesnick reviews applications of the econometric approach to applied welfare economics. These include the consequences of changes in economic policy for the distribution of individual welfare, as well as cost of living indexes for individual households, and household equivalence scales. They also include the impact of changes in economic policy on social welfare. The measurement of social welfare also leads to a new approach to cost of living measurement and new measures of the standard of living, inequality, and poverty. Slesnick compares the results of the econometric approach, based on consumption, with the official income-based measures published in the United States by the Bureau of the Census.

Erwin Diewert (1976) was the first to link the flexible functional forms employed in econometric modeling to index number formulas used in productivity and welfare measurement. In chapter 11 Diewert and Denis Lawrence review the fundamentals of capital theory for productivity and welfare measurement. They point out that Jorgenson's concept of the cost of capital has become the standard for productivity measurement, as in the aggregate and sectoral productivity measures published by the Bureau of Labor Statistics (1983). They consider three alternative models of capital as a factor of production and the cost of capital, based on alternative accounting formulas for depreciation—declining balance, straight line, and one-hoss-shay. Finally, they implement these models for the private business sector in Canada for the period 1962–1996.

6.   Economic Growth, Intertemporal General Equilibrium, and the Cost of Capital

Edward Hudson and Jorgenson (1974; reprinted in Jorgenson, 1998a) originate the econometric approach to general equilibrium modeling. Their model of the U.S. economy incorporates econometric representations of technology and preferences as basic building blocks. Earlier approaches to general equilibrium modeling, going back to Leontief (1941), had "calibrated" the behavioral responses of producers and consumers to a single data point. While the calibration approach economizes radically on the use of data, it requires highly restrictive assumptions, such as fixed input-output coefficients. This assumption is contradicted by the massive evidence of energy conservation in response to changes in world energy prices, beginning in 1973.

The concept of an intertemporal price system provides the unifying framework for the econometric general equilibrium model of the impact of tax policy on U.S. economic growth constructed by Jorgenson and Kun-Young Yun (1986a, 1986b; reprinted in Jorgenson, 1996a). The model incorporates the econometric representations of technology and preferences introduced by Christensen, Jorgenson, and Lau (1973, 1975), as well as a forward-looking econometric model of consumer behavior, based on the "Euler equation" approach originated by Hall (1978). The model includes a rental price of capital services, based on Jorgenson's cost of capital, for each class of assets distinguished in the U.S. tax system.

Both macroeconometric models used to analyze the short-run impact of tax policy and applied general equilibrium models employed to analyze the long-run impact have omitted a forward-looking model of asset pricing. These models are subject to the critique of Robert Lucas (1976) that tax policies change future asset prices, but these changes are not taken into account in models of producer and consumer behavior. Jorgenson and Yun have overcome the Lucas critique by associating each tax policy with an intertemporal equilibrium. Both producers and consumers optimize, subject to an intertemporal price system. In this system asset prices are equal to rational expectations of the present values of future capital services.

In chapter 10 Yun describes the role of Jorgenson's cost of capital in intertemporal general equilibrium modeling of the effects of tax policy. Yun first extends the standard expressions for the cost of capital to incorporate the policy instruments employed in recent tax reform proposals. Second, he summarizes the current version of the Jorgenson-Yun model of U.S. economic growth and applies this to the 1981 and 1986 tax reforms in the U.S. Third, he considers an analytical framework for the welfare analysis of tax policy changes. Finally, he employs this in analyzing the consequences of tax policy reform in the U.S.

Jorgenson and Wilcoxen (1990; reprinted in Jorgenson, 1998b) and Ho and Jorgenson (1994; reprinted in Jorgenson, 1998b) have constructed highly detailed models of U.S. economic growth. These models are based on the detailed accounts for production at the level of individual industries presented by Jorgenson (1990; reprinted in Jorgenson, 1995b), including a price of capital services for each industry and each class of asset, based on Jorgenson's cost of capital. As a basic building block, the models incorporate an econometric representation of technology by industry, constructed by Jorgenson and Fraumeni (1984; reprinted in Jorgenson, 2000). Similarly, the models include the econometric representation of preferences for individual households by Jorgenson, Lau, and Stoker (1982).

In chapter 12 Ho simulates the elimination of tariff and non-tariff barriers to trade in the U.S. These simulations successfully capture the impact of trade policy on Jorgenson's cost of capital and the price of new capital goods. This gives rise to dynamic effects of trade policy changes through capital formation and economic growth. The magnitude of these effects depends critically on the values assigned to the key parameters. Ho demonstrates the value of the econometric approach to parameter estimation by considering the sensitivity of the results to alternative parameter values like those employed in models calibrated from a single data point.

In chapter 13 Wilcoxen describes a "quiet revolution" in the economic analysis of environmental policy during the 1990s. This is based on the observation that environmental regulation affects Jorgenson's cost of capital and economic growth. Regulations can raise the price of new capital goods, slow the rate of capital formation, and reduce the rate of economic growth. By contrast market-based environmental policies, such as emissions taxes and tradable permits, may raise sufficient revenue to reduce capital income taxes and lower the cost of capital, thereby stimulating growth. The evaluation of an environmental policy requires a model that can capture environmental regulations at a detailed level, trace the effects of these regulations through the economy to determine their impact on the cost of producing new capital goods, and determine the effect on saving and investment.

Wilcoxen analyzes the "double-dividend" hypothesis that market-based instruments for environmental policy have the potential for stimulating economic growth. The weakest form of this hypothesis is true by definition. Using revenue to lower a distorting tax is superior to returning the revenue to consumers through lump sum rebates. The strongest form of the hypothesis identifies possibilities for reducing preexisting distortions, mainly associated with taxes on incomes from labor and capital. This could improve economic welfare even before environmental benefits are considered, generating a double dividend. Wilcoxen employs the distribution of measures of social welfare derived from an econometric general equilibrium model to confirm the hypothesis that shifting to energy taxes in the U.S. would produce a double dividend.

The concept of an intertemporal price system provides the unifying framework for the econometric general equilibrium models of Jorgenson, Ho, Wilcoxen, and Yun. This price system balances demands and supplies for products and factors of production at each point of time. A forward-looking feature of this price system is that asset prices are rational expectations of present values of future capital services, based on Jorgenson's cost of capital. This is combined with backward link-ages among current capital services, the stock of capital, and past investments in modeling the long-run dynamics of economic growth. Jorgenson and Wilcoxen (1993, reprinted in Jorgenson, 1998b) provide a survey of the literature on econometric general equilibrium model-ing, including applications to energy, environmental, trade, and tax policies.

7. Acknowledgments

The papers included in this volume were presented at the Conference on the Cost of Capital in Economic Analysis, held in honor of Dale W. Jorgenson's sixtieth birthday at the John F. Kennedy School of Govern-ment, Harvard University, on May 7–8, 1993. It was my great privilege to have the responsibility of organizing this surprise conference on behalf of Jorgenson's Ph.D. thesis advisees. The indispensable advice and assistance of Dale's beautiful wife Linda Mabus Jorgenson are most gratefully acknowledged. I wish to take this opportunity, on behalf of his former students, to thank Dale Jorgenson once more for what he has done for us. What successes we may have as economists can be largely attributed to our experience as "apprentices" in his "shop." We could not have found a better teacher and mentor.

After the conference the papers were revised and updated for pub-lication. Erwin Diewert and Denis Lawrence substituted a new paper on capital theory and measurement for the one presented by Diewert at the conference; similarly, Charles Hulten and Robert Schwab substi-tuted a paper on regional growth for the paper presented by Hulten. Ten of the authors are former Ph.D. thesis advisees of Jorgenson—three at Berkeley and seven at Harvard. Two—Diewert and Barbara Fraumeni—were graduate students who benefited from Jorgenson's advice on their dissertations—and Robert Hall was an undergraduate thesis advisee.

The conference was attended by thirty-six of Jorgenson's fifty-six former Ph.D. thesis advisees at Berkeley and Harvard, as of the time of the conference. Three thesis advisees who have subsequently received their Ph.D.'s from Harvard participated in the conference. Many of Jorgenson's current and past research collaborators, profes-sional colleagues, and friends from around the world also attended the conference. Laurits R. and Dianne Cummings Christensen, Robert E. Hall, Charles R. Hulten and Nancy P. Humphrey, Ralph and Claire

Landau, and the Lau family sponsored the conference. The Asia/Pacific Research Center and the Technology and Economic Growth Program, Center for Economic Policy Research, Stanford University, and the Center for Business and Government at the Kennedy School, Harvard University, provided additional support. June Wynn of the Department of Economics at Harvard University assisted with the invitations and local arrangements.

Renate D'Arcangelo of the Editorial Office of the Division of Engineering and Applied Sciences at Harvard assembled the manuscripts, mainly in machine-readable form, and edited them, proofread the final versions, and prepared them for typesetting. William Richardson and his associates provided the index. Gary Bisbee of Chiron Incorporated typeset the manuscript and provided camera-ready copy for publication. The staff of the MIT Press, especially Terry Vaughn, Judy Feldmann, Jane Macdonald, and Michael Sims, was helpful at every stage of the project. To all of these individuals, we give our heartfelt thanks. Financial support for the publication was provided by the Program on Technology and Economic Policy of the Kennedy School of Government at Harvard.

References

Box, George, E.P., and Gwilym M. Jenkins. 1970. *Time Series Analysis: Forecasting and Control.* San Francisco, CA: Holden-Day.

Brainard, William C., and James Tobin. 1968. Pitfalls in Financial Model Building, *American Economic Review* 58, no. 2 (May): 99–122.

Bureau of Labor Statistics. 1983. Trends in Multifactor Productivity, 1948–1981, Bulletin no. 2178, Washington, DC: U.S. Department of Labor.

Caballero, Ricardo J. 1999. Aggregate Investment. In *Handbook of Macroeconomics*, eds. John B. Taylor and Michael Woodford, vol. 1B, 813–862. Amsterdam: North-Holland.

Commission of the European Communities. 1992. Report of the Committee of Independent Experts on Company Taxation, Luxembourg.

Diewert, W. Erwin. 1976. Exact and Superlative Index Numbers, *Journal of Econometrics* 4, no. 2 (May): 115–146.

Hall, Robert E. 1978. Stochastic Implications of the Life Cycle-Permanent Income Hypothesis. *Journal of Political Economy* 86, no. 6 (December): 971–987.

Hall, Robert E., and Alvin Rabushka. 1995. *The Flat Tax.* Stanford, CA: The Hoover Institution Press.

Hansen, Lars P. 1982. Large Sample Properties of Generalized Method of Moments Estimators. *Econometrica* 50, no. 4 (July): 1029–1054.

Hayashi, Fumio. 1982. Tobin's Marginal q and Average q: A Neo-Classical Interpretation, *Econometrica* 50, no. 1 (January): 213–224.

Henderson, Yolanda K. 1991. Applications of General Equilibrium Models in the 1986 Tax Reform Act in the United States, *The Economist* 139 (Spring): 147–168.

Jorgenson, Dale W. 1995a. *Postwar U.S. Economic Growth*. Cambridge, MA: The MIT Press.

———. 1995b. *International Comparisons of Economic Growth*. Cambridge, MA: The MIT Press.

———. 1996a. *Capital Theory and Investment Behavior*. Cambridge, MA: The MIT Press.

———. 1996b. *Tax Policy and the Cost of Capital*. Cambridge, MA: The MIT Press.

———. 1997a. *Aggregate Consumer Behavior*. Cambridge, MA: The MIT Press.

———. 1997b. *Measuring Social Welfare*. Cambridge, MA: The MIT Press.

———. 1998a. *Econometric General Equilibrium Modeling*. Cambridge, MA: The MIT Press.

———. 1998b. *Energy, the Environment, and Economic Growth*. Cambridge, MA: The MIT Press.

———. 2000. *Econometric Modeling of Producer Behavior*. Cambridge, MA: The MIT Press.

Jorgenson, Dale W., Frank M. Gollop, and Barbara M. Fraumeni. 1987. *Productivity and U.S. Economic Growth.* Cambridge, MA: Harvard University Press.

Jorgenson, Dale W., and Ralph Landau. 1993, eds. *Tax Reform and the Cost of Capital*. Washington, DC: The Brookings Institution.

King, Mervyn A., and Don Fullerton. 1984. *The Taxation of Income from Capital*. Chicago, IL: University of Chicago Press.

Kravis, Irving, Alan W. Heston, and Robert Summers. 1982. *World Product and Income: International Comparisons of Real Gross Product*. Baltimore, MD: Johns Hopkins Press.

Lau, Lawrence J. 1977. *Existence Conditions for Aggregate Demand Functions: The Case of Multiple Indexes*. Technical Report No. 248, October. Institute for Mathematical Studies in the Social Sciences, Stanford University (revised in 1980 and 1982).

———. 1982. A Note on the Fundamental Theory of Exact Aggregation. *Economics Letters*, vol. 9, no. 2 (February): 119–126.

Leontief, Wassily W. 1941. *The Structure of the American Economy, 1919–1929.* New York: Oxford University Press (second edition, 1951).

Lucas, Robert E., Jr. 1976. Econometric Policy Evaluation: A Critique. In *The Phillips Curve and Labor Markets,* eds. Karl Brunner and Alan H. Meltzer, 19–46. Amsterdam: North-Holland.

Modigliani, Franco, and Merton Miller. 1958. The Cost of Capital, Corporation Finance, and the Theory of Investment, *American Economic Review* 48, no. 3 (June): 261–297.

Organization for Economic Cooperation and Development. 1991. Taxing Profits in a Global Economy: Domestic and International Issues, Paris.

Sen, Amartya K. 1977. On Weights and Measures: Informational Constraints in Social Welfare Analysis, *Econometrica* 45, no. 7 (October): 1539–1572.

Slesnick, Daniel T. 1998. Empirical Approaches to the Measurement of Welfare. *Journal of Economic Literature* 36, no. 4 (December): 2108–2165.

Solow, Robert M. 1957. Technical Change and the Aggregate Production Function. *Review of Economics and Statistics* 39, no. 3 (August): 312–320.

Stoker, Thomas M. 1993. Empirical Approaches to the Problem of Aggregation over Individuals. *Journal of Economic Literature* 31, no. 4 (December): 1827–1874.

Tobin, James. 1969. A General Equilibrium Approach to Monetary Theory. *Journal of Money, Credit, and Banking* 1, no. 1 (February): 15–29.

United Nations, Eurostat, IMF, OECD, and the World Bank. 1993. *A System of National Accounts, 1993.* New York, Luxembourg, Washington, DC, and Paris.

About the Authors

Lawrence J. Lau (Editor) received his B.S. degree in Physics and Economics from Stanford University in 1964, and his M.A. and Ph.D. degrees in Economics from the University of California at Berkeley in 1966 and 1969, respectively. He is the author of *Farmer Education and Farmer Efficiency* with Dean T. Jamison, published by Johns Hopkins University Press, and *Models of Development: A Comparison of Economic Growth in South Korea and Taiwan*, published by the Institute of Contemporary Studies, San Francisco. He is a Fellow of the Econometric Society, a Member of Academia Sinica, Taipei, an Overseas Fellow of Churchill College, Cambridge, England, and an Honorary Member of the Chinese Academy of Social Sciences, Beijing. In 1999 the Hong Kong University of Science and Technology awarded him the honorary degree of Doctor of Social Sciences. He is the Kwoh-Ting Li Professor of Economic Development at Stanford University.

Laurits R. Christensen received his B.A. in economics from Cornell University in 1964. His graduate studies at the University of California, Berkeley, led to an M.A. in statistics in 1966 and a Ph.D. in economics in 1968. He was Professor of Economics at the University of Wisconsin-Madison from 1967 to 1987. He is Chairman of Laurits R. Christensen Associates, an economic research and consulting firm in Madison, Wisconsin.

Erwin R. Diewert received his Honours B.A. in 1963 and his M.A. in 1965, both in mathematics, from the University of British Columbia. He received his Ph.D. in economics from the University of California, Berkeley, in 1969. He is a Fellow of the Econometric Society, a Fellow of the Royal Society of Canada, a Research Associate of the National Bureau of Economic Research, and the Chairman of the Prices Advisory Committee, Statistics Canada. He is Professor of Economics at the University of British Columbia. Denis Lawrence received his Honours

B.Ec. from the Australian National University in 1977 and his Ph.D. from the University of British Columbia in 1987, both in economics. He is Director of Tasman Asia Pacific, an economics, management and policy consultancy in Canberra, Australia.

Barbara M. Fraumeni received her B.A. from Wellesley College in 1972 and her Ph.D. in 1980 from Boston College, both in economics. After graduating from Wellesley she served as a Research Assistant for Dale W. Jorgenson and began a collaboration that continues up to the present. She co-authored *Productivity and U.S. Economic Growth*, published by the Harvard University Press in 1987, with Jorgenson and Frank M. Gollop. She was a Professor of Economics at Northeastern University from 1982 through 1998 and a Research Fellow of the Program on Technology and Economic Policy, John F. Kennedy School of Government, Harvard University from 1988 through 1998. She is Chief Economist of the Bureau of Economic Analysis, U.S. Department of Commerce.

Frank M. Gollop received his A.B. degrees in economics in 1969 and philosophy in 1970 from the University of Santa Clara. He was awarded his Ph.D. in economics from Harvard University in 1974. In 1987 he co-authored *Productivity and U.S. Economic Growth* with Jorgenson and Fraumeni. He is Professor of Economics and the Director of Graduate Studies in the Economics Department at Boston College.

Robert E. Hall received his B.A. in economics from the University of California, Berkeley, where Jorgenson was his thesis adviser, in 1964 and his Ph.D. from Massachusetts Institute of Technology in 1967. He is the co-author with Alvin Rabushka of *The Flat Tax*, published by the Hoover Institution in 1995, *Booms and Recessions in a Noisy Economy*, published by the Yale University Press in 1991, and *The Rational Consumer*, published by the MIT Press in 1990. Hall is a Fellow of the American Academy of Arts and Sciences and a Fellow of the Econometric Society. He serves as Director of the Research Program on Economic Fluctuations and Growth of the National Bureau of Economic Research. He is the Robert and Carole McNeil Joint Professor of Economics at Stanford University and Senior Fellow at Stanford's Hoover Institution.

Fumio Hayashi received his B.A. from the University of Tokyo in 1975 and his Ph.D. from Harvard University in 1980, both in economics. He is the author of *Understanding Saving: Evidence from the U.S. and Japan*, was published by MIT Press in 1997, and *Econometrics,* published by Princeton University Press in 2000. In 1995 he was the first recipient of the Nakahara Prize in Economics, awarded annually by the Japanese Economic Association to the most outstanding Japanese economist under the age of 45. He is a Research Associate of the National Bureau of Economic Research and a Fellow of the Econometric Society. He was Carl Sumner Shoup Professor of the Japanese Economy at Columbia University from 1993–1997 and is Professor of Economics at Tokyo University.

Mun S. Ho received his B.A. in mathematics from Northwestern University in 1983 and his Ph.D. in economics from Harvard University in 1989. He taught at the State University of New York, Buffalo from 1989–1992. He is affiliated with the University Committee on the Environment, Harvard University, and is a Visiting Scholar at Resources for the Future, Washington, and Research Fellow at the John F. Kennedy School of Government, Harvard University.

Charles R. Hulten received his A.B. in statistics in 1965 and his Ph.D. in economics in 1973 from the University of California, Berkeley. He is the co-editor of *The Legacy of Reaganomics* with Isabel V. Sawhill and editor of *Depreciation, Inflation and the Taxation of Income from Capital*, both published by The Urban Institute Press, and editor of *Productivity in Japan and the United States*, published by the University of Chicago Press. He is Research Associate of the National Bureau of Economic Research and Chairman of the Conference on Research in Income and Wealth. He is Professor of Economics at the University of Maryland. Robert M. Schwab received his B.A. from Grinnell College in 1969 and his Ph.D. from Johns Hopkins University in 1980, both in economics. He is Professor of Economics and Director of Graduate Studies at the University of Maryland.

Daniel T. Slesnick received his B.S. in mathematics from the University of Washington in 1978 and his Ph.D. in economics from Harvard University in 1982. He is the author of *Consumption and Social Welfare: Living Standards and their Distribution in the United States*, published by the Cambridge University Press in 2000. He ranked first in applied econometrics publications in the Applied Econometricians' Hall of Fame, published the *Journal of Applied Econometrics*, in 1999. He is the Rex G. Baker, Jr. Professor of Political Economy at the University of Texas at Austin.

Thomas M. Stoker received his B.S. in mathematics from the University of Arizona in 1974 and his A.M. and Ph.D. in economics from

Harvard University in 1978 and 1979, respectively. Stoker is a Fellow of the Econometric Society and has served on the editorial boards of many professional journals, including Econometrica, the *Journal of Econometrics*, and the *Journal of the American Statistical Association*. He is the Gordon Y Billard Professor of Applied Economics at the Sloan School of Management, Massachusetts Institute of Technology.

Peter J. Wilcoxen received his B.A. in physics from the University of Colorado in 1982 and his A.M. and Ph.D. in economics from Harvard University in 1985 and 1989, respectively. He is the co-author of *Notes and Problems in Applied General Equilibrium Economics* with Peter B. Dixon, Brian R. Parmenter, and Alan A. Powell, published by North-Holland. He is Associate Professor of Economics at the University of Texas at Austin and a Nonresident Senior Fellow at the Brookings Institution.

Kun-Young Yun received his B.S. in Engineering in 1974 and his M.A. in Public Administration in 1976, both from Seoul National University, and his M.A. in Economics from the State University of New York at Binghamton in 1979. He received his A.M. and his Ph.D. in economics from Harvard University in 1983 and 1984, respectively. He is the co-author of *Tax Reform and the Cost of Capital* with Jorgenson, published by the Oxford University Press in 1991, and co-editor of *Public Finance in Korea* with Kwang Choi, Dong-Kun Kim, and Taewon Kwack, published by the Seoul National University Press in 1992. In 1990 he received the Chung Ram Award, awarded by the Korean Economic Association to the most outstanding Korean economist under the age of 40. He is Professor of Economics in the Department of Economics at Yonsei University, Seoul, Korea.

Dale W. Jorgenson
Photo copyright 1998 Rick Friedman

Biography

Dale W. Jorgenson is the Frederic Eaton Abbe Professor of Economics at Harvard University. He has been a Professor in the Department of Economics at Harvard since 1969 and Director of the Program on Technology and Economic Policy at the Kennedy School of Government since 1984. He served as Chairman of the Department of Economics from 1994 to 1997. Jorgenson received his Ph.D. in economics from Harvard in 1959 and his B.A. in economics from Reed College in Portland, Oregon, in 1955.

Jorgenson was elected to membership in the American Philosophical Society in 1998, the Royal Swedish Academy of Sciences in 1989, the U.S. National Academy of Sciences in 1978, and the American Academy of Arts and Sciences in 1969. He was elected to Fellowship in the American Association for the Advancement of Science in 1982, the American Statistical Association in 1965, and the Econometric Society in 1964. He was awarded honorary doctorates by Uppsala University and the University of Oslo in 1991.

Jorgenson is President of the American Economic Association. He has been a member of the Board on Science, Technology, and Economic Policy of the National Research Council since 1991 and was appointed to be Chairman of the Board in 1998. He is also Chairman of Section 54, Economic Sciences, of the National Academy of Sciences. He served as President of the Econometric Society in 1987.

Jorgenson received the prestigious John Bates Clark Medal of the American Economic Association in 1971. This Medal is awarded every two years to an economist under forty for excellence in economic research. The citation for this award reads in part:

Dale Jorgenson has left his mark with great distinction on pure economic theory (with, for example, his work on the growth of a dual economy);

and equally on statistical method (with, for example, his development of estimation methods for rational distributed lags). But he is preeminently a master of the territory between economics and statistics, where both have to be applied to the study of concrete problems. His prolonged exploration of the determinants of investment spending, whatever its ultimate lessons, will certainly long stand as one of the finest examples in the marriage of theory and practice in economics.

Jorgenson is the author of more than two hundred articles and the author and editor of twenty books in economics. His collected papers have been published in nine volumes by The MIT Press, beginning in 1995. The most recent volume, *Econometric Modeling of Producer Behavior*, was published in 2000.

Prior to Jorgenson's appointment at Harvard he was Professor of Economics at the University of California, Berkeley, where he taught from 1959 to 1969. He has been Visiting Professor of Economics at Stanford University and the Hebrew University of Jerusalem and Visiting Professor of Statistics at Oxford University. He has also served as Ford Foundation Research Professor of Economics at the University of Chicago.

Forty-two economists have collaborated with Jorgenson on published research. An important feature of Jorgenson's research program has been collaboration with students in economics at Berkeley and Harvard. This collaboration has often been the outgrowth of a student's dissertation research and has led to subsequent joint publications. Many of his former students are professors at leading academic institutions in the United States and abroad and several occupy endowed chairs.

Jorgenson was born in Bozeman, Montana, in 1933 and attended public schools in Helena, Montana. He is married to Linda Mabus Jorgenson, who is a partner in the law firm of Spero and Jorgenson in Cambridge, Massachusetts. Professor and Mrs. Jorgenson reside in Cambridge. Their daughter Kari, 25, is an honors graduate of Harvard College, Class of 1997, and is a law student at Columbia University. Their son Eric, 27, is a graduate of Duke University, Class of 1995, and is a graduate student in human genetics at Stanford University.

List of Publications

Books

Optimal Replacement Policy, Amsterdam, North-Holland, 1967 (with J.J. McCall and R. Radner); Italian Edition: *Politiche Ottimali di Sostituzione e Manuetezione dei Macchinari* (trans. Armando Brandolese), Milan, Franco Angeli Editore, 1969.

Measuring Performance in the Private Economy of the Federal Republic of Germany 1950–1973, Tübingen, J.C.B. Mohr, 1975 (with K. Conrad).

(Editor), *Econometric Studies of U.S. Energy Policy*, Amsterdam, North-Holland, 1976.

(Editor), *Technology and Economic Policy*, Cambridge, Ballinger, 1986 (with R. Landau).

Productivity and U.S. Economic Growth, Cambridge, Harvard University Press, 1987 (with F.M. Gollop and B.M. Fraumeni); reprint, iUniverse.com, 1999.

(Editor), *Technology and Capital Formation*, Cambridge, MIT Press, 1989 (with R. Landau).

(Editor), *General Equilibrium Modeling and Economic Policy Analysis*, Oxford, Basil Blackwell, 1990 (with L. Bergman and E. Zalai).

(Editor), *Technology and Agricultural Policy*, Washington, National Academy Press, 1990 (with C. Benbrook, K. Farrell, R. Landau, and V. Ruttan).

Tax Reform and the Cost of Capital, Oxford, Oxford University Press, 1991 (with K.-Y. Yun).

(Editor), *Tax Reform and the Cost of Capital: An International Comparison*, Washington, The Brookings Institution, 1993 (with R. Landau).

International Comparisons of Economic Growth, Cambridge, MIT Press, 1995 (Productivity, vol. 2).

Postwar U.S. Economic Growth, Cambridge, MIT Press, 1995 (Productivity, vol. 1).

Capital Theory and Investment Behavior, Cambridge, MIT Press, 1996 (Investment, vol. 1).

(Editor), *Improving the Performance of America's Schools: The Role of Incentives*, Washington, National Academy Press, 1996 (with Eric Hanushek).

Tax Policy and the Cost of Capital, Cambridge, MIT Press, 1996 (Investment, vol. 2).

Aggregate Consumer Behavior, Cambridge, MIT Press, 1997 (Welfare, vol. 1).

Measuring Social Welfare, Cambridge, MIT Press, 1997 (Welfare, vol. 2).

Econometric General Equilibrium Modeling, Cambridge, MIT Press, 1998 (Growth, vol. 1).

Energy, the Environment, and Economic Growth, Cambridge MIT Press, 1998 (Growth, vol. 2).

Econometric Modeling of Producer Behavior, Cambridge, MIT Press, 2000 (Econometrics, vol. 1).

Articles

"Growth and Fluctuations: A Causal Interpretation," *Quarterly Journal of Economics*, vol. 74, no. 3, August 1960, pp. 416–436; reprinted in S. Mittra (ed.), *Dimensions of Macroeconomics*, New York, Random House, 1971, pp. 410–423.

"On Stability in the Sense of Harrod," *Economica*, vol. 27, no. 107, August 1960, pp. 243–248.

"A Dual Stability Theorem," *Econometrica*, vol. 28, no. 4, October 1960, pp. 892–899. Growth 1, ch. 1, pp. 1–8.

"Stability of a Dynamic Input-Output System," *Review of Economic Studies*, vol. 27, no. 76, February 1961, pp. 105–116; reprinted in F.H. Hahn (ed.), *Readings in the Theory of Economic Growth*, London, Macmillan, 1971, pp. 264–275.

"Multiple Regression Analysis of a Poisson Process," *Journal of the American Statistical Association*, vol. 56, no. 294, June 1961, pp. 235–245.

"The Development of a Dual Economy," *The Economic Journal*, vol. 71, no. 282, June 1961, pp. 309–334.

"The Structure of Multi-Sector Dynamic Models," *International Economic Review*, vol. 2, no. 3, September 1961, pp. 276–291.

"Optimal Replacement and Inspection of Stochastically Failing Equipment," in K.J. Arrow, S. Karlin, and H. Scarf (eds.), *Studies in Applied Probability and Management Science*, Stanford University Press, 1962 (with R. Radner), pp. 184–206.

"Elementary Proofs of Propositions on Leontief-Minkowski Matrices," *Metroeconomica*, vol. 14, no. 3, December 1962 (with D.V.T. Bear and H.M. Wagner), pp. 59–64.

"The Structure of Multi-Sector Dynamic Models: Some Further Examples," *International Economic Review*, vol. 4, no. 1, January 1963, pp. 101–104.

"Optimal Replacement Policies for a Ballistic Missile," *Management Science*, vol. 9, no. 3, April 1963 (with J.J. McCall), pp. 358–379.

"Capital Theory and Investment Behavior," *American Economic Review*, vol. 53, no. 2, May 1963, pp. 247–259; reprinted in R.A. Gordon and L.R. Klein (eds.), *Readings in Business Cycles*, Homewood, Irwin, 1965, pp. 366–378; reprinted in *Bobbs-Merrill Reprint Series in Economics*, Econ-167. This article has been identified as a Citation Classic, based on 195 citations in the *Social Sciences Citation Index*, in *Current Contents*, vol. 14, no. 40, October 4, 1982. Investment 1, ch. 1, pp. 1–16.

"Stability of a Dynamic Input-Output System: A Reply," *The Review of Economic Studies*, vol. 30, no. 83, June 1963, pp. 148–149.

"Optimal Scheduling of Replacement and Inspection," *Operations Research*, vol. 11, no. 5, October 1963 (with J.J. McCall), pp. 732–746.

"Opportunistic Replacement of a Single Part in the Presence of Several Monitored Parts," *Management Science*, vol. 10, no. 1, October 1963 (with R. Radner), pp. 70–84.

"Principles of Efficiency: Discussion," *American Economic Review*, vol. 54, no. 3, May 1964, pp. 86–88.

"Minimum Variance, Linear, Unbiased Seasonal Adjustment of Economic Time Series," *Journal of the American Statistical Association*, vol. 59, no. 307, September 1964, pp. 681–724.

"Anticipations and Investment Behavior," in J.S. Duesenberry, G. Fromm, L.R. Klein, and E. Kuh (eds.), *The Brookings Quarterly Econometric Model of the United States*, Chicago, Rand McNally, 1965, pp. 35–92. Investment 1, ch. 2, pp. 17–76.

"Rational Distributed Lag Functions," *Econometrica*, vol. 34, no. 1, January 1966, pp. 135–149. Investment 1, ch. 3, pp. 77–93.

"The Embodiment Hypothesis," *Journal of Political Economy*, vol. 74, no. 1, February 1966, pp. 1–17. Productivity 1, ch. 2, pp. 25–49.

"Sources of Measured Productivity Change: Capital Input," *The American Economic Review*, vol. 56, No. 2, May 1966 (with Z. Griliches), pp. 50–61.

"Testing Alternative Theories of the Development of a Dual Economy," in I. Adelman and E. Thorbecke (eds.), *The Theory and Design of Economic Development*, Baltimore, Johns Hopkins Press, 1966, pp. 45–60; reprinted in *Bobbs-Merrill Reprint Series in Economics*, Econ-168; reprinted in condensed form in *Development Digest*, vol. 4, no. 2, July 1966, pp. 83–91; reprinted in Ian Livingstone (ed.), *Development Economics and Policy*, London, George Allen and Unwin, 1981, pp. 67–74.

"The Time Structure of Investment Behavior in United States Manufacturing, 1947–1960," *Review of Economics and Statistics*, vol. 49, no. 1, February 1967 (with J.A. Stephenson), pp. 16–27. Investment 1, ch. 4, pp. 95–122.

"Seasonal Adjustment of Data for Econometric Analysis," *Journal of the American Statistical Association*, vol. 62, no. 317, March 1967, pp. 137–140.

"Investment Behavior in U.S. Manufacturing, 1947–1960," *Econometrica*, vol. 35, no. 2, April 1967 (with J.A. Stephenson), pp. 169–220. Investment 1, ch. 5, pp. 123–180.

"Rational Choice and Patterns of Growth in a Monetary Economy: Discussion," *American Economic Review*, vol. 57, no. 2, May 1967, pp. 557–559.

"Tax Policy and Investment Behavior," *American Economic Review*, vol. 57, no. 3, June 1967 (with R.E. Hall), pp. 391–414; reprinted in *Bobbs-Merrill Reprint Series in Economics*, Econ-130. Investment 2, ch. 1, pp 1–26.

"The Explanation of Productivity Change," *The Review of Economic Studies*, vol. 34, no. 99, July 1967 (with Z. Griliches), pp. 249–280; reprinted in A.K. Sen (ed.), *Growth Economics*, Hammondsworth, Penguin Books, 1970, pp. 420–473; reprinted in *Survey of Current Business*, vol. 52, no. 5, part II, May 1972, pp. 3–63. Productivity 1, ch. 3, pp. 51–98.

"Surplus Agricultural Labour and the Development of a Dual Economy," *Oxford Economic Papers*, vol. 19, no. 3, November 1967, pp. 288–312. Growth 1, ch. 5, pp. 77–104.

"The Theory of Investment Behavior," in R. Ferber (ed.), *The Determinants of Investment Behavior*, Conference of the Universities—National Bureau Committee for Economic Research, New York, Columbia University Press, 1967, pp. 129–156; reprinted in Harold R. Williams and John D. Huffnagle (eds.), *Macroeconomic Theory: Selected Readings*, New York, Appleton-Century-Crofts, 1969, pp. 207–230; reprinted in S. Mittra (ed.), *Dimensions of Macroeconomics*, New York, Random House, 1971, pp. 161–178. Investment 1, ch. 6, pp. 181–207.

"Capital and Labor in Production: Comment," in M. Brown (ed.), *The Theory and Empirical Analysis of Production*, Studies in Income and Wealth, no. 31, New York, Columbia University Press, 1967, pp. 467–471.

"Linear Models of Economic Growth," International *Economic Review*, vol. 9, no. 1, January 1968, pp. 1–13.

"Industry Changes in Non-Labor Costs: Comment," in J. Kendrick (ed.), *The Industrial Composition of Income and Product*, Studies in Income and Wealth, no. 32, New York, Columbia University Press, 1968, pp. 176–184.

"A Comparison of Alternative Theories of Corporate Investment Behavior," *American Economic Review*, vol. 58, no. 4, September 1968 (with C.D. Siebert), pp. 681–712. Investment 1, ch. 7, pp. 209–243.

"Optimal Capital Accumulation and Corporate Investment Behavior," *Journal of Political Economy*, vol. 76, no. 6, November/December 1968 (with C.D. Siebert), pp. 1123–1151. Investment 1, ch. 8, pp. 245–279.

"Anticipations and Investment Behavior in U.S. Manufacturing, 1947–1960," *Journal of the American Statistical Association*, vol. 64, no. 325, March 1969 (with J.A. Stephenson), pp. 67–89. Investment 1, ch. 9, pp. 281–314.

"Tax Policy and Investment Behavior: Reply and Further Results," *American Economic Review*, vol. 59, no. 3, June 1969 (with R.E. Hall), pp. 388–401.

"Issues in the Development of the Neo-classical Theory of Investment Behavior," *Review of Economics and Statistics*, vol. 51, no. 3, August 1969 (with J.A. Stephenson), pp. 346–353.

"The Measurement of U.S. Real Capital Input, 1929–1967," *Review of Income and Wealth*, Series 15, no. 4, December 1969 (with L.R. Christensen), pp. 293–320.

"The Role of Taxation in Stabilizing Private Investment," in V.P. Rock (ed.), *Policy Makers and Model Builders*, New York, Gordon and Breach, 1969 (with R.E. Hall), pp. 73–96.

"The Demand for Capital Services," in K.A. Fox, G.V.L. Narasimham, and J.K. Sengupta (eds.), *Economic Models, Estimation, and Risk Programming: Essays in Honor of Gerhard Tintner*, New York, Springer-Verlag, 1969, pp. 35–57.

"The Role of Agriculture in Economic Development: Classical versus Neo-classical Models of Growth," in C.R. Wharton, Jr. (ed.), *Subsistence Agriculture and Economic Development*, Chicago, Aldine, 1969, pp. 320–348; reprinted in Italian as "Il Ruolo dell'Agricoltura nello Sviluppo Economico," *Revista Internazionale di Scienze Economiche e Commerciali*, vol. 14, no. 9, September 1967 (trans. G. Gaburro), pp. 837–856.

"A Programming Model for a Dual Economy: Comment," in E. Thorbecke (ed.), *The Role of Agriculture in Economic Development*, Conference of the Universities—National Bureau Committee for Economic Research, New York, Columbia University Press, 1969, pp. 231–234.

"U.S. Real Product and Real Factor Input, 1929–1967," *Review of Income and Wealth*, Series 16, no. 1, March 1970 (with L.R. Christensen), pp. 19–50.

"A Comparison of Alternative Econometric Models of Quarterly Investment Behavior," *Econometrica*, vol. 38, no. 2, March 1970 (with J. Hunter and M.I. Nadiri), pp. 187–212. Investment 1, ch. 10, pp. 315–343.

"The Predictive Performance of Econometric Models of Quarterly Investment Behavior," *Econometrica*, vol. 38, no. 2, March 1970 (with J. Hunter and M.I. Nadiri), pp. 213–224. 1, ch. 11, pp. 345–358.

"Econometrics," in N. Ruggles (ed.) *Economics*, Englewood Cliffs, Prentice-Hall, 1970, pp. 55–62.

"Recruitment, Training, and the Organization of Research," in T. Dalenius, G. Karlsson, and S. Malmquist (eds.), *Scientists at Work*, Uppsala, Almquist and Wiksells, 1970, pp. 66–71.

"Investment Behavior in U.S. Regulated Industries," *Bell Journal of Economics and Management Science*, vol. 2, no. 1, Spring 1971 (with S.S. Handel), pp. 213–264. Investment 1, ch. 12, 359–421.

"Divisia Index Numbers and Productivity Measurement," *Review of Income and Wealth*, Series 17, no. 2, June 1971 (with Z. Griliches), pp. 53–55.

"Econometric Research and the National Accounts," in *The Economic Accounts of the United States: Retrospect and Prospect, Survey of Current Business*, vol. 51, no. 7, July 1971, part II, pp. 99–102.

"Efficient Estimation of Simultaneous Equations by Instrumental Variables," *Review of Economics and Statistics*, vol. 53, no. 3, August 1971 (with J.M. Brundy), pp. 207–224.

"Econometric Studies of Investment Behavior: A Review," *Journal of Economic Literature*, vol. 9, no. 4, December 1971, pp. 1111–1147. Investment 1, ch. 12, pp. 423–478.

"Application of the Theory of Optimum Capital Accumulation," in G. Fromm (ed.), *Tax Incentives and Capital Spending*, Washington, The Brookings Institution, 1971 (with R.E. Hall), pp. 9–60. Investment 2, ch. 2, pp. 27–76.

"The Economic Impact of Investment Incentives," in Joint Economic Committee, *Long-Term Implications of Current Tax and Spending Proposals*, Washington, Ninety-Second Congress, First Session, 1971, pp. 176–192; reprinted in W.E. Mitchell, J.H. Hand, and I. Walter, *Readings in Macroeconomics*, New York, McGraw-Hill, 1974, pp. 174–183. Investment 2, ch. 4, pp. 101–123.

"Investment Behavior and the Production Function," *Bell Journal of Economics and Management Science*, vol. 3, no. 1, Spring 1972, pp. 220–251.

"Investment Incentives in the 1971 Tax Bill," *Business Economics*, vol. 7, no. 3, May 1972 (with Roger Gordon), pp. 7–13.

"Issues in Growth Accounting: A Reply to Edward F. Denison," *Survey of Current Business*, vol. 52, no. 5, part II, May 1972 (with Z. Griliches), pp. 65–94. Productivity 1, ch. 4, pp. 99–174.

"Issues in Growth Accounting: Final Reply," *Survey of Current Business*, vol. 52, no. 5, part II, May 1972 (with Z. Griliches), p. 111.

"The Econometrics of Price Determination: Discussion," in O. Eckstein (ed.), *The Econometrics of Price Determination*, Washington, Board of Governors of the Federal Reserve System, 1972, pp. 333–336.

"An Empirical Evaluation of Alternative Theories of Corporate Investment," in K. Brunner (ed.), *Problems and Issues in Current Econometric Practice*, Columbus, Ohio State University, 1972 (with C.D. Siebert), pp. 155–218.

"Transcendental Logarithmic Production Frontiers," *Review of Economics and Statistics*, vol. 55, no. 1, February 1973 (with L.R. Christensen and L.J. Lau), pp. 28–45. This article has been identified as a Citation Classic, based on 225 citations in the *Science Citation Index and the Social Sciences Citation Index, in*

Current Contents, vol. 17, no. 15, April 15, 1985. Econometrics 1, ch. 4, pp. 125–158.

"Technology and Decision Rules in the Theory of Investment Behavior," *Quarterly Journal of Economics*, vol. 87, no. 4, November 1973, pp. 523–543. Investment 2, ch. 3, pp. 77–99.

"U.S. Income, Saving and Wealth, 1929–1969," *Review of Income and Wealth*, Series 19, no. 4, December 1973 (with L.R. Christensen), pp. 329–362.

"Measurement of Macroeconomic Performance in Japan, 1951–1968," in K. Ohkawa and Y. Hayami (eds.), *Economic Growth: The Japanese Experience since the Meiji Era*, vol. 1, Tokyo, Japan Economic Research Center, 1973 (with M. Ezaki), pp. 286–361; reprinted in Japanese as "Makuro Seisansei Henka no Sokutei, 1951–1968," in K. Ohkawa and K. Hayami (eds.), *Nihon Keizai no Choki Bunseki*, Tokyo, Nikkei Newspaper Company, 1973, pp. 87–127. Productivity 2, ch. 2, pp. 99–177.

"Consistent and Efficient Estimation of Simultaneous Equation Systems by Means of Instrumental Variables," in P. Zarembka (ed.), *Frontiers in Econometrics*, New York, Academic Press, 1973 (with J.M. Brundy), pp. 215–244.

"The Economic Theory of Replacement and Depreciation," in W. Sellekaerts (ed.), *Econometrics and Economic Theory*, New York, MacMillan, 1973, pp. 189–221. Investment 2, ch. 5, pp. 125–155.

"Measuring Economic Performance in the Private Sector," in M. Moss (ed.), *The Measurement of Economic and Social Performance*, Studies in Income and Wealth, no. 37, New York, Columbia University Press, 1973 (with L.R. Christensen), pp. 233–351; reprinted in *IDA Economic Papers*, December 1973, pp. 154. Productivity 2, ch. 5, pp. 175–272.

"The Duality of Technology and Economic Behavior," *Review of Economic Studies*, vol. 41 (2), no. 126, April 1974 (with L.J. Lau), pp. 181–200; reprinted in Chinese as "Chi-shu Erh-Chung-Hsing yu Ching-chi Hsing-wei," *Academia Economic Papers*, vol. 2, no. 6, March 1974, pp. 13–43. Econometrics 2, ch. 5, pp. 159–188.

"Duality and Differentiability in Production," *Journal of Economic Theory*, vol. 9, no. 1, September 1974 (with L.J. Lau), pp. 23–42. Econometrics 1, ch. 6, pp. 189–208.

"U.S. Energy Policy and Economic Growth, 1975–2000," *Bell Journal of Economics and Management Science*, vol. 5, no. 2, Autumn 1974 (with E.A. Hudson), pp. 461–514; reprinted in International Institute for Applied Systems Analysis, *Proceedings of IIASA Working Seminar on Energy Modeling*, Laxenburg, IIASA, 1974, pp. 174–278, and in C.J. Ciccheti and W.K. Foell (eds.), *Energy Systems Forecasting, Planning, and Pricing*, Madison, Institute for Environmental Studies, University of Wisconsin, 1975, pp. 127–159.

"The Relative Efficiency of Instrumental Variables Estimators of Simultaneous Equations," *Annals of Social and Economic Measurement*, vol. 3, no. 4, October 1974 (with J.M. Brundy), pp. 679–700.

"Efficient Estimation of Non-Linear Simultaneous Equations with Additive Disturbances," *Annals of Social and Economic Measurement*, vol. 3, no. 4, October 1974 (with J.J. Laffont), pp. 615–640. Econometrics 1, ch. 7, pp 209–240.

"Investment and Production: A Review," in M. Intriligator and D. Kendrick (eds.), *Frontiers in Quantitative Economics*, vol. II, Amsterdam, North-Holland, 1974, pp. 341–366. Investment 2, ch. 6, pp. 157–180.

"Tax Policy and Energy Use," in Committee on Finance, United States Senate, *Fiscal Policy and the Energy Crisis*, Washington, Ninety-Third Congress, First and Second Sessions, 1974 (with E.A. Hudson), pp. 1681–1694.

"Economic Analysis of Alternative Energy Growth Patterns," in David Freeman *et al.*, *A Time to Choose*, Cambridge, Ballinger, 1974 (with E.A. Hudson), pp. 493–511.

"The Structure of Consumer Preferences," *Annals of Social and Economic Measurement*, vol. 4, no. 1, January 1975 (with L.J. Lau), pp. 49–101. Welfare 1, ch. 2, pp. 29–90.

"Transcendental Logarithmic Utility Functions," *American Economic Review*, vol. 65, no. 3, June 1975 (with L.R. Christensen and L.J. Lau), pp. 367–383. Welfare 1, ch. 1, pp. 1–28.

"The Integration of Energy Policy Models," *Computers and Operations Research*, vol. 2, no. 3, September 1975 (with B. Bernanke), pp. 225–249. Growth 1, ch.8, pp. 221–261.

"Policy Alternatives for the Investment Tax Credit," in Committee on the Budget, United States Senate, *Encouraging Capital Formation through the Tax Code*, Washington, Ninety-Fourth Congress, First Session, 1975 (with R. Gordon), pp. 15–84.

"Projections of U.S. Economic Growth and Energy Demand," in Robert W. Greenleaf (ed.), *Structural Change and Current Problems Facing Regulated Public Utilities*, Indianapolis, Graduate School of Business, University of Indiana, 1975 (with E.A. Hudson), pp. 75–128.

"U.S. Tax Policy and Energy Conservation," in D. Jorgenson (ed.), *Econometric Studies of U.S. Energy Policy*, Amsterdam, North-Holland, 1976 (with E.A. Hudson), pp. 7–94. Growth 1, ch. 6, pp. 105–189.

"The Investment Tax Credit and Counter-Cyclical Policy," in O. Eckstein (ed.), *Parameters and Policies in the U.S. Economy*, Amsterdam, North-Holland, 1976 (with R. Gordon), pp. 275–314. Investment 2, ch. 7, pp. 181–222.

"Economic and Technological Models for Evaluation of Energy Policy," *Bell Journal of Economics*, vol. 8, no. 2, Autumn 1977 (with K. Hoffman), pp. 444–466. Growth 1, ch. 9, pp. 263–289.

"Tests of a Model of Production for the Federal Republic of Germany, 1950–1973," *European Economic Review*, vol. 10, no. 1, October 1977 (with K. Conrad), pp. 51–75. Econometrics 1, ch. 8, pp. 241–266.

"Statistical Tests of the Theory of Consumer Behavior," in H. Albach, E. Helmstädter, and R. Henn (eds.), *Quantitative Wirtschaftforschung*, Tübingen, J.C.B. Mohr, 1977 (with L.J. Lau), pp. 383–394. Welfare 1, ch. 3, pp. 91–102.

"Consumer Demand for Energy," in W.D. Nordhaus (ed.), *International Studies of the Demand for Energy*, Amsterdam, North-Holland, 1977, pp. 309–328.

"The Structure of Consumer Preferences, Federal Republic of Germany, 1950–1973," *Zeitschrift für Nationalökonomie*, vol. 38, nos. 1–2, 1978 (with K. Conrad), pp. 1–28. Welfare 1, ch. 6, pp. 153–178.

"Energy Policy and U.S. Economic Growth," *American Economic Review*, vol. 68, no. 2, May 1978 (with E.A. Hudson), pp. 118–123. Growth 1, ch. 10, pp. 291–297.

"The Structure of Technology: Non-jointness and Commodity Augmentation, Federal Republic of Germany, 1950–1973," *Empirical Economics*, vol. 3, Issue 2, 1978 (with K. Conrad), pp. 91–113. Econometrics 1, ch. 9. pp. 267–290.

"The Role of Energy in the U.S. Economy," *National Tax Journal*, vol. 31, no. 3, September 1978, pp. 209–220. Growth 1, ch. 11, pp. 299–315.

"How Energy and its Cost Enter the Productivity Equation," *Spectrum*, vol. 15, no. 10, October 1978 (with E. Berndt), pp. 50–52.

"Energy Prices and the U.S. Economy, 1972–1976," *Natural Resources Journal*, vol. 18, no. 4, October 1978 (with E.A. Hudson), pp. 877–897; reprinted in W.J. Mead and A.E. Utton (eds.), *U.S. Energy Policy*, Cambridge, Ballinger, 1979, pp. 175–195. Growth 1, ch. 12, pp. 317–341.

"The Economic Impact of Policies to Reduce U.S. Energy Growth," *Resources and Energy*, vol. 1, no. 3, November 1978 (with E.A. Hudson), pp. 205–230; reprinted in B. Kursunoglu and A. Perlmutter (eds.), *Directions in Energy Policy*, Cambridge, Ballinger, 1979, pp. 141–164. Growth 1, ch. 13, pp. 343–369.

"U.S. and Japanese Economic Growth, 1952–1974: An International Comparison," *Economic Journal*, vol. 88, no. 352, December 1978 (with M. Nishimizu), pp. 707–726; reprinted in S. Tsuru (ed.), *Economic Growth and Resources, Problems Related to Japan*, vol. 5, London, MacMillan, 1980, pp. 35–60. Productivity 2, ch. 3, pp. 179–202.

"The Structure of Technology and Changes of Technology over Time, Federal Republic of Germany, 1950–1973," *Zeitschrift für Wirtschafts und Sozialwissenschaften*, Drittes Heft, 1978 (with K. Conrad), pp. 259–279. Econometrics 1, ch. 10, pp. 291–310.

"Productivity Growth, 1947–1973: An International Comparison," in W. Dewald (ed.), *The Impact of International Trade and Investment on Employment*, Washington, U.S. G.P.O., 1978 (with L.R. Christensen and D. Cummings), pp. 211–233.

"The Integrability of Consumer Demand Functions," *European Economic Review*, vol. 12, no. 2, April 1979 (with L.J. Lau), pp. 115–147. Welfare 1, ch. 4, pp. 103–136.

"Testing the Integrability of Consumer Demand Functions, Federal Republic of Germany, 1950–1973," *European Economic Review*, vol. 12, no. 2, April 1979 (with K. Conrad), pp. 149–169. Welfare 1, ch. 7, pp. 179–201.

"Energy and the Future of the U.S. Economy," *The Wharton Magazine*, vol. 3, no. 4, Summer 1979, pp. 15–21; reprinted in Committee on The Budget, United States Senate, *Second Concurrent Resolution on The Budget—Fiscal Year 1980*, Ninety-Sixth Congress, First Session, 1979, pp. 27–32.

"Statistical Inference for a System of Simultaneous, Nonlinear, Implicit Equations in the Context of Instrumental Variables Estimation," *Journal of Econometrics*, vol. 11, nos. 2/3, October/December, 1979 (with A.R. Gallant), pp. 275–302. Econometrics 1, ch. 11, pp. 311–340.

"Rates of Return by Industrial Sector in the United States, 1948–1976," *American Economic Review*, vol. 70, no. 2, May 1980 (with B.M. Fraumeni), pp. 326–330; reprinted in Committee on Commerce, Science and Transportation, United States Senate, *Industrial Innovation*, Ninety-Sixth Congress, First Session, 1979, pp. 110–120.

"Welfare Comparison and Exact Aggregation," *American Economic Review*, vol. 70, no. 2, May 1980 (with L.J. Lau and T.M. Stoker), pp. 268–272.

"Inflation-Proof Depreciation of Assets," *Harvard Business Review*, vol. 58, no. 5, September-October 1980 (with A. Auerbach), pp. 113–118; reprinted in Committee on Ways and Means, United States House of Representatives, *Tax Restructuring Act of 1979*, Washington, Ninety-Sixth Congress, First Session, 1980, pp. 66–76; and in Committee on Finance, United States Senate, *Tax Cut Proposals*, part 2, Second Session, 1980, pp. 803–828. Investment 2, ch. 8, pp. 223–234.

"U.S. Productivity Growth by Industry, 1947–1973," in J.W. Kendrick and B. Vaccara (eds.), *New Developments in Productivity Measurement, and Analysis*, Studies in Income and Wealth, vol. 41, Chicago, University of Chicago Press, 1980 (with F. Gollop), pp. 17–136.

"Economic Growth, 1947–1973: An International Comparison," in J.W. Kendrick and B. Vaccara (eds.), *New Developments in Productivity Measurement and Analysis*, Studies in Income and Wealth, vol. 41, Chicago, University of Chicago Press, 1980 (with L.R. Christensen and D. Cummings), pp. 595–698. Productivity 2, ch. 4, pp. 203–295.

"The Role of Capital in U.S. Economic Growth, 1948–1976," in G. von Furstenberg (ed.), *Capital Efficiency and Growth*, Cambridge, Ballinger, 1980 (with B.M. Fraumeni), pp. 9–250.

"Accounting for Capital," in G. von Furstenberg (ed.), *Capital Efficiency and Growth*, Cambridge, Ballinger, 1980, pp. 251–319.

"The Sectoral Sources of U.S. Economic Growth, 1948–1976," in J. Frohn and R. Staglin (eds.), *Empirische Wirtschaftsforschung*, Berlin, Duncker and Humblot, 1980 (with B.M. Fraumeni), pp. 27–40; reprinted in Committee on Commerce, Science, and Transportation, United States Senate, *Industrial Innovation*, Ninety-Sixth Congress, First Session, 1979, pp. 82–101.

"Investitions Theorie," in M. Beckmann, G. Menges, and R. Selten (eds.), *Handwörterbuch der mathematischen Wirtschaftwissenschaften*, Band 1, Wiesbaden, Verlag Dr. Th. Gabler KG, 1980, pp. 113–118.

"Capital Formation and U.S. Productivity Growth, 1948–1976," in A. Dogramaci (ed.), *Productivity Analysis*, Boston, Martinus Nijhoff, 1980 (with B.M. Fraumeni), pp. 49–70.

"The Impact of Restrictions on Electric Generating Capacity," in J.R. Moroney (ed.), *Advances in the Economics of Energy and Resources*, vol. 3, Greenwich, JAI Press, 1980 (with E.A. Hudson and D.C. O'Connor), pp. 111–157. Growth 1, ch. 14, pp. 371–423.

"Relative Productivity Levels, 1947–1973: An International Comparison," *European Economic Review*, vol. 16, no. 1, May 1981 (with L.R. Christensen and D. Cummings), pp. 61–94. Productivity 2, ch. 5, pp. 297–331.

"Energy Prices and Productivity Growth," *Scandinavian Journal of Economics*, vol. 83, no. 2, 1981, pp. 165–179; reprinted in Jerome Rosow (ed.), *Productivity: Prospects for Growth*, New York, Van Nostrand/Work in America Institute, 1981, pp. 35–53; reprinted in Paul Tempest (ed.), *International Energy Options*, Cambridge, Oelgeschlager, Gunn, and Hain, 1981, pp. 75–92; reprinted in L. Matthiessen (ed.), *The Impact of Rising Oil Prices on the World Economy*, London, Macmillan, 1982, pp. 65–79; reprinted in Sam H. Schurr, Sidney Sonenblum, and David O. Wood (eds.), *Energy, Productivity, and Growth*, Cambridge, Oelgeschlager, Gunn, and Hain, 1983, pp. 133–153.

"Taxation and Technical Change," *Technology in Society*, vol. 3, nos. 1–2, 1981, pp. 151–171; reprinted in Joint Economic Committee, United States Congress, *The Economy of 1981: A Bipartisan Look*, Ninety-Seventh Congress, First Session, 1981, pp. 166–184.

"Aggregate Consumer Behavior and Individual Welfare," in D. Currie, R. Nobay, and D. Peel (eds.), *Macroeconomic Analysis*, London, Croom-Helm, 1981 (with L.J. Lau and T.M. Stoker), pp. 35–61.

"Relative Prices and Technical Change," in E. Berndt and B. Field (eds.), *Modeling and Measuring Natural Resource Substitution*, Cambridge, MIT Press, 1981 (with B.M. Fraumeni), pp. 17–47; reprinted in W. Eichhorn, R. Henn, K. Neumann, and R.W. Shephard (eds.), *Quantitative Studies on Production and Prices*, Würzburg, Physica-Verlag, 1983, pp. 241–269. Econometrics 1, ch. 12, pp. 341–372.

"Inflation and Corporate Capital Recovery," in C.R. Hulten (ed.), *Depreciation, Inflation, and the Taxation of Income from Capital*, Washington, The Urban Institute Press, 1981 (with M.A. Sullivan), pp. 171–238, 311–313. Investment 2, ch. 9, pp. 235–298.

"The Transcendental Logarithmic Model of Aggregate Consumer Behavior," in R.L. Basmann and G. Rhodes (eds.), *Advances in Econometrics*, vol. 1, Greenwich, JAI Press, 1982 (with L.J. Lau and T.M. Stoker), pp. 97–238. Welfare 1, ch. 8, pp. 203–356.

"Econometric and Process Analysis Models for the Analysis of Energy Policy," in R. Amit and M. Avriel (eds.), *Perspectives on Resource Policy Modeling: Energy and Minerals*, Cambridge, Ballinger, 1982, pp. 9–62.

"An Econometric Approach to General Equilibrium Analysis," in M. Hazewinkel and A.H.G. Rinooy Kan (eds.), *Current Developments in the Interface: Economics, Econometrics, Mathematics*, Dordrecht, D. Reidel, 1982, pp. 125–157; reprinted in Institute of Economics, *Chung-Hua Series of Lectures*, no. 7, Taipei, Academia Sinica, 1984, pp. 41–71.

"Modeling Production for General Equilibrium Analysis," *Scandinavian Journal of Economics*, vol. 85, no. 2, 1983, pp. 101–112; reprinted in F.R. Forsund (ed.), *Topics in Production Theory*, London, Macmillan, 1984, pp. 1–12.

"The Accumulation of Human and Non-Human Wealth," in R. Hemming and F. Modigliani (eds.), *The Determinants of National Saving and Wealth*, London, Macmillan, 1983 (with A. Pachón), pp. 302–350.

"Sectoral Measures of Labor Cost for the United States, 1948–1978," in J.E. Triplett (ed.), *The Measurement of Labor Cost*, Studies in Income and Wealth, vol. 44, Chicago, University of Chicago Press, 1983 (with F. Gollop), pp. 185–235, 503–520.

"Lifetime Income and Human Capital," in P. Streeten and H. Maier (eds.), *Human Resources, Employment and Development*, vol. 2, London, Macmillan, 1983 (with A. Pachón), pp. 29–90.

"Individual and Social Cost of Living Indexes," in W.E. Diewert and C. Montmarquette (eds.), *Price Level Measurement*, Ottawa, Statistics Canada, 1983 (with D.T. Slesnick), pp. 241–323; reprinted in W.E. Diewert (ed.), *Price Level Measurement*, Amsterdam, North-Holland, 1990, pp. 155–234. Welfare 1, ch. 2, pp. 39–98.

"The Role of Energy in Productivity Growth," *American Economic Review*, vol. 74, no. 2, May 1984, pp. 26–30; expanded version reprinted in *The Energy Journal*, vol. 5, no. 3, July 1984, pp. 11–25; further expanded version reprinted in J.W. Kendrick (ed.), *International Comparisons of Productivity and Causes of the Slowdown*, Cambridge, Ballinger, 1984, pp. 279–323; reprinted in Italian as "Il Ruolo dell'Energia Nella Crescita della Produttivita," *Energia*, vol. 5, no. 4, Dicembre 1984, pp. 50–55; reprinted in S.H. Schurr and S. Sonenblum (eds.), *Electricity Use, Productive Efficiency and Economic Growth*, 1986, Palo Alto, Electric Power Research Institute, pp. 43–92. Econometrics 1, ch. 14, pp. 403–456.

"Aggregate Consumer Behavior and the Measurement of Inequality," *Review of Economic Studies*, vol. 51(3), no. 166, July 1984 (with D.T. Slesnick), pp. 369–392; reprinted in Institute of Economics, *Chung-Hua Series of Lectures*, no. 7, Taipei, Academia Sinica, 1984, pp. 3–39.

"Relative Price Changes and Biases of Technical Change in Japan," *Economic Studies Quarterly*, vol. 35, no. 2, August 1984 (with M. Kuroda and K. Yoshioka), pp. 116–138. Econometrics 1, ch. 13, pp. 373–402.

"Econometric Methods for Applied General Equilibrium Analysis," in H. Scarf and J. Shoven (eds.), *Applied General Equilibrium Analysis*, Cambridge, Cambridge University Press, 1984, pp. 139–203. Growth 2, ch. 2, pp. 89–155.

"Aggregate Consumer Expenditures on Energy," in J.R. Moroney (ed.), *Advances in the Economics of Energy and Resources*, vol. 5, Greenwich, JAI Press, 1984 (with T.M. Stoker), pp. 1–84. Welfare 1, ch. 9, pp. 357–448.

"Inequality in the Distribution of Individual Welfare," in R.L.Basmann and G. Rhodes (eds.), *Advances in Econometrics*, vol. 3, Greenwich, JAI Press, 1984 (with D.T. Slesnick), pp. 67–130. Welfare 2, ch. 3, pp. 99–164.

"The Contribution of Education to U.S. Economic Growth," in E. Dean (ed.), *Education and Economic Productivity*, Cambridge, Ballinger, 1984, pp. 95–162.

"Efficiency versus Equity in Petroleum Taxation," *The Energy Journal*, vol. 6, Special Tax Issue, 1985 (with D.T. Slesnick), pp. 171–188.

"Efficiency versus Equity in Economic Policy Analysis," *American Economist*, vol. 29, no. 1, Spring 1985, pp. 5–14; reprinted in M. Szenberg (ed.), *Essays in Economics: The John Commons Memorial Lectures*, Boulder, Westview Press, 1986, pp. 105–121.

"Efficiency versus Equity in Natural Gas Price Regulation," *Journal of Econometrics*, vol. 30, nos. 1/2, October/November 1985 (with D.T. Slesnick), pp. 301–316; reprinted in W.A. Barnett and A.R. Gallant (eds.), *New Approaches to Modeling, Specification Selection and Econometric Inference*, Cambridge, Cambridge University Press, 1989, pp. 301–316.

"General Equilibrium Analysis of Economic Policy," in J. Piggott and J. Whalley (eds.), *New Developments in Applied General Equilibrium Analysis*, Cambridge, Cambridge University Press, 1985 (with D.T. Slesnick), pp. 293–370. Welfare 2, ch. 4, pp. 165–218. "Microeconomics and Productivity," in R. Landau and N. Rosenberg (eds.), *The Positive Sum Strategy*, Washington, National Academy of Sciences Press, 1985, pp. 57–76.

"Sectoral Productivity Gaps between the United States, Japan and Germany, 1960–1979," in H. Giersch (ed.), *Probleme und Perspektive der weltwirtschaflichen Entwicklung*, Berlin, Duncker and Humblot, 1985 (with K. Conrad), pp. 335–347. Productivity 2, ch. 7, pp. 347–376.

"The Efficiency of Capital Allocation," *Scandinavian Journal of Economics*, vol. 88, no. 1, 1986 (with K.-Y. Yun), pp. 85–107; reprinted in V. Bergstrom, S. Honkapohja, and J. Sodersten (eds.), *Growth and Distribution*, Oxford, Basil Blackwell, 1986, pp. 85–107. Investment 2, ch. 10, pp. 299–320.

"The Oil Price Decline and Economic Growth in Japan and the U.S.," *Keio Economic Studies*, vol. 23, no. 1, 1986, pp. 1–19.

"The Great Transition: Energy and Economic Change," *The Energy Journal*, vol. 7, no. 3, July 1986, pp. 1–13; reprinted in National Energy Administration, *Energy—Economics and Politics*, Stockholm, Statens energiverk, 1985: 4, pp. 39–61; reprinted in T. Shishido and R. Sato (eds.), *Economic Policy and Development*, Dover, Auburn House, 1985, pp. 260–286.

"Tax Policy and Capital Allocation," *Scandinavian Journal of Economics*, vol. 88, no. 2, 1986 (with K.-Y. Yun), pp. 355–377; reprinted in V. Bergstrom, S. Honkapohja, and J. Sodersten (eds.), *Growth and Distribution*, Oxford, Basil Blackwell, 1986, pp. 109–131. Investment 2, ch. 11, pp. 321–364.

"Econometric Methods for Modeling Producer Behavior," in Z. Griliches and M.D. Intriligator (eds.), *Handbook of Econometrics*, vol. 3, Amsterdam, North-Holland, 1986, pp. 1841–1915.

"Nonlinear Three-Stage Least-Squares Pooling of Time Series and Cross-Section Data," in R.S. Mariano (ed.), *Advances in Statistical Analysis and Statistical Computing*, vol. 1, Greenwich, JAI Press, 1986 (with T.M. Stoker), pp. 87–115. Welfare 1, ch. 10, pp. 449–474.

"The Role of Capital in U.S. Economic Growth, 1948–1979," in A. Dogramaci (ed.), *Measurement Issues and Behavior of Productivity Variables*, Boston, Martinus Nijhoff, 1986 (with B.M. Fraumeni), pp. 161–244.

"Testing the Integrability of Consumer Demand Functions, United States, 1947–1971," in D. Slottje (ed.), *Advances in Econometrics*, vol. 5, Greenwich, JAI Press, 1986 (with L.J. Lau), pp. 3–48. Welfare 1, ch. 5, pp. 137–152.

"Japan-U.S. Industry-Level Productivity Comparisons, 1960–1979," *Journal of the Japanese and International Economies*, vol. 1, no. 1, March 1987 (with M. Kuroda and M. Nishimizu), pp. 1–30.

"Aggregate Consumer Behavior and Household Equivalence Scales," *Journal of Business and Economic Statistics*, vol. 5, no. 2, April 1987 (with D.T. Slesnick), pp. 219–232. Welfare 2, ch. 5, pp. 219–251.

"General Equilibrium Analysis of Natural Gas Price Regulation," in E.E. Bailey (ed.), *Public Regulation*, Cambridge, MIT Press, 1987 (with D.T. Slesnick), pp. 153–190. Welfare 2, ch. 6, pp. 253–289.

"Production and Cost Functions," in J. Eatwell, M. Milgate, and P. Newman (eds.), *The New Palgrave*, vol. 3, London, Macmillan, 1987, pp. 1002–1007.

"Vintages," In J. Eatwell, M. Milgate, and P. Newman (eds.), *The New Palgrave*, vol. 4, London, Macmillan, 1987, pp. 814–816.

"Two-Stage Budgeting and Consumer Demand for Energy," in J.R. Moroney (ed.), *Advances in the Economics of Energy and Resources*, vol. 6, Greenwich, JAI Press, 1987 (with D.T. Slesnick and T.M. Stoker), pp. 125–162. Welfare 1, ch. 11, pp. 475–522.

"Productivity and Economic Growth in Japan and the U.S.," *American Economic Review*, vol. 78, no. 2, May 1988, pp. 217–222. Productivity 2, ch. 8, pp. 377–385.

"Two-Stage Budgeting and Exact Aggregation," *Journal of Business and Economic Statistics*, vol. 6, no. 3, July 1988 (with D.T. Slesnick and T.M. Stoker), pp. 313–326.

"Productivity and Postwar U.S. Economic Growth," *Journal of Economic Perspectives*, vol. 2, no. 4, Fall 1988, pp. 23–42. Productivity 1, ch. 1, pp. 1–23.

"Investment in Education," *Educational Researcher*, vol. 18, no. 4, May 1989 (with B.M. Fraumeni), pp. 35–44.

"The Accumulation of Human and Nonhuman Capital, 1948–1984," in R.E. Lipsey and H.S. Tice (eds.), *The Measurement of Saving, Investment and Wealth*, Studies in Income and Wealth, vol. 52, Chicago, University of Chicago Press, 1989 (with B.M. Fraumeni), pp. 227–282. Productivity 1, ch. 6, pp. 273–331.

"Capital as a Factor of Production," in D.W. Jorgenson and R. Landau (eds.), *Technology and Capital Formation*, Cambridge, MIT Press, 1989, pp. 1–35.

"Redistributional Policy and the Measurement of Poverty," in D. Slottje (ed.), *Research on Economic Inequality*, Greenwich, JAI Press, 1989 (with D.T. Slesnick), pp. 1–48. Welfare 2, ch. 7, pp. 291–342.

"Inequality and the Standard of Living," *Journal of Econometrics*, vol. 43, nos. 1/2, January/February 1990 (with D.T. Slesnick), pp. 103–120. Welfare 2, ch. 8, pp. 343–360.

"Environmental Regulation and U.S. Economic Growth," *Rand Journal of Economics*, vol. 21, no. 2, Summer 1990 (with P.J. Wilcoxen), pp. 314–340. Growth 2, ch. 3, pp. 157–193.

"Aggregate Consumer Behavior and the Measurement of Social Welfare," *Econometrica*, vol. 58, no. 5, September 1990, pp. 1007–1040. Welfare 2, ch. 1, pp. 1–38.

"Tax Reform and U.S. Economic Growth," *Journal of Political Economy*, vol. 98, no. 5, part 2, October 1990 (with K.-Y. Yun), pp. 151–193; reprinted in L. Bergman, D.W. Jorgenson, and E. Zalai (eds.), *General Equilibrium Modeling and Economic Policy Analysis*, Oxford, Basil Blackwell, 1990, pp. 58–110. Investment 2, ch. 12, pp. 365–410.

"Intertemporal General Equilibrium Modeling of U.S. Environmental Regulation," *Journal of Policy Modeling*, vol. 12, no. 4, December 1990 (with P.J. Wilcoxen), pp. 1–30.

"Bilateral Models of Production for Japanese and U.S. Industries," in C.R. Hulten (ed.), *Productivity in the U.S. and Japan*, Studies in Income and Wealth, vol. 51, Chicago, University of Chicago Press, 1990 (with H. Sakuramoto, K. Yoshioka, and M. Kuroda), pp. 59–83. Econometrics 1, ch. 15, 457–498.

"Productivity and International Competitiveness in Japan and the United States, 1960–1985," in C.R. Hulten (ed.), *Productivity in the U.S. and Japan*, Studies in Income and Wealth, vol. 51, Chicago, University of Chicago Press, 1990 (with M. Kuroda), pp. 29–58; reprinted in B. Hickman (ed.), *International Productivity and Competitiveness*, Oxford, Oxford University Press, 1992, pp. 203–229; reprinted in *Journal of International and Comparative Economics*, vol. 1, no. 1, March 1992, pp. 29–54. Productivity 2, ch. 9, pp. 387–417.

"Productivity and Economic Growth," in E. Berndt and J. Triplett (eds.), *Fifty Years of Economic Measurement*, Studies in Income and Wealth, vol. 54, Chicago, University of Chicago Press, 1990, pp. 19–118. Productivity 2, ch. 1, pp. 1–98.

"Productivity Trends and the Cost of Reducing Carbon Dioxide Emissions," *Energy Journal*, vol. 12, no. 1, January 1991 (with W.W. Hogan), pp. 67–85.

"The Excess Burden of U.S. Taxation," Journal of Accounting, Auditing, and Finance, vol. 6, no. 4, Fall 1991, pp. 487–509 (with K.-Y. Yun); reprinted in Hungarian as "Az adozas tobbletterhei az Egyesult Allamakban," *Kozgazdasagi Szemle*, vol. 38, no. 5, May 1991 (trans. Julia Kiraly), pp. 481–499; reprinted in A. Heimler and D. Muelders (eds.), *Empirical Approaches to Fiscal Policy Modelling*, London, Chapman and Hall, 1992, pp. 9–24; reprinted in Italian as "l'Eccesso di Pressione della Tassazione negli Stati Uniti," *Sviluppo Economico*, vol. 1, no. 1, Gennaio-Aprile 1993, pp. 1–27; reprinted in A. Knoester (ed.), *Taxation in the United States and Europe*, London, Macmillan, 1993, pp. 117–136. Investment 2, ch. 13, pp. 411–433.

"Investing in Productivity Growth," in National Academy of Engineering, *Technology and Economics*, Washington, National Academy Press, 1991, pp. 57–64.

"Global Change, Energy Prices, and U.S. Economic Growth," *Structural Change and Economic Dynamics*, vol. 3, no. 1, March 1992 (with P.J. Wilcoxen), pp. 135–154.

"Productivity Growth in U.S. Agriculture," *American Journal of Agricultural Economics*, vol. 74, no. 3, August 1992 (with F.M. Gollop), pp. 745–750. Productivity 1, ch. 9, pp. 389–399.

"Carbon Taxes and Economic Welfare," *Brookings Papers in Economic Activity: Microeconomics 1992* (with D.T. Slesnick and P.J. Wilcoxen), pp. 393–431. Welfare 2, ch. 9, pp. 361–399.

"Investment in Education and U.S. Economic Growth," *Scandinavian Journal of Economics*, vol. 94, Supplement, 1992 (with B.M. Fraumeni), pp. 51–70. Productivity 1, ch. 8, pp. 371–388.

"Productivity and International Competitiveness: Introduction," *Economic Studies Quarterly*, vol. 43, no. 4, December 1992, pp. 291–297.

"Technology, Productivity, and Competitiveness of U.S. and Japanese Industries," in T.S. Arrison, C.F. Bergsten, E.M. Graham, and M.C. Harris (eds.), *Japan's Growing Technological Capability*, Washington, National Academy Press, 1992 (with M. Kuroda), pp. 83–97; reprinted in *Economic Studies Quarterly*, vol. 43, no. 4, December 1992, pp. 313–325.

"The Output of the Education Sector," in Z. Griliches (ed.), *Output Measurement in the Services Sector*, Studies in Income and Wealth, vol. 55, Chicago, University of Chicago Press, 1992 (with B.M. Fraumeni), pp. 303–338. Productivity 1, ch. 7, pp. 333–369.

"Reducing U.S. Carbon Dioxide Emissions: The Cost of Different Goals," in J.R. Moroney (ed.), *Advances in the Economics of Energy and Resources*, vol. 7, Greenwich, JAI Press, 1992 (with P.J. Wilcoxen), pp. 125–158. Growth 2, ch. 3, pp. 195–227.

"The Economic Impact of the Clean Air Act Amendments of 1990," *Energy Journal*, vol. 14, no. 1, January 1993 (with P.J. Wilcoxen), pp. 159–182. Growth 2, ch. 5, pp. 229–252.

"Reducing U.S. Carbon Emissions: An Econometric General Equilibrium Assessment," *Resource and Energy Economics*, vol. 15, no. 1, March 1993 (with P.J. Wilcoxen), pp. 7–26. Growth 2, ch. 6, pp. 253–273.

"Reducing U.S. Carbon Dioxide Emissions: An Assessment of Alternative Instruments," *Journal of Policy Modeling*, vol. 15, nos. 5 and 6, 1993 (with P.J. Wilcoxen), pp. 491–520. Growth 2, ch. 7, pp. 275–301.

"Energy, the Environment, and Economic Growth," in A.V. Kneese and J.L. Sweeney (eds.), *Handbook of Energy and Natural Resource Economics*, vol. 3, 1993 (with P.J. Wilcoxen), pp. 1267–1349. Growth 2, ch. 1, pp. 1–87.

"Energy Prices, Productivity, and Economic Growth," in R.H. Socolow, D. Anderson, and J. Harte (eds.), *Annual Review of Energy and the Environment*, vol. 18, Palo Alto, Annual Reviews, 1993 (with P.J. Wilcoxen), pp. 343–395.

"Introduction and Summary," in D.W. Jorgenson and R. Landau (eds.), *Tax Reform and the Cost of Capital: An International Comparison*, Washington, The Brookings Institution, 1993, pp. 1–56.

"Trade Policy and U.S. Economic Growth," *Journal of Policy Modeling*, vol. 16, no. 2, 1994 (with M.S. Ho), pp. 119–146; reprinted in J.C. Moore, R. Riezman, and J.K. Melvin (eds.), *Trade, Theory and Econometrics*, New York, Rautledge, 1999, pp. 17–43. Growth 2, ch. 8, pp. 303–330.

"Computers and Economic Growth," *Economics of Innovation and New Technology*, vol. 3, nos. 3–4, 1995 (with K. Stiroh), pp. 295–316.

"The Economic Effects of a Carbon Tax," in H. Lee (ed.), *Shaping National Responses to Climate Change*, Washington, The Island Press, 1995 (with P.J. Wilcoxen), pp. 237–260.

"Intertemporal Equilibrium Modeling of Energy and Environmental Policies," in P.-O. Johansson, B. Kristrom, and K.-G. Maler (eds.), *Current Issues in Environmental Economics*, Manchester, University of Manchester Press, 1995 (with P.J. Wilcoxen), pp. 171–191.

"Investment and Economic Growth," in Committee on Finance, United States Senate, *Importance of Savings in Our Economy*, One Hundred Fourth Congress, First Session, 1995, pp. 102–116.

"Empirical Studies of Depreciation," *Economic Inquiry*, vol. 34, no. 1, January 1996, pp. 24–42. Econometrics 1, pp. 73–96.

"The Agenda for U.S. Tax Reform," *Canadian Journal of Economics*, vol. 29, part 2, Special Issue, April 1996, pp. S649–S657.

"International Comparisons of the Sources of Economic Growth," *American Economic Review*, vol. 86, no. 2, May 1996 (with C. Dougherty), pp. 25–29.

"Capital Cost Recovery and U.S. Tax Reform," in Committee on Ways and Means, United States House of Representatives, *Contract with America— Savings and Investment*, One Hundred Fourth Congress, Second Session, 1996.

"The Economic Impact of Fundamental Tax Reform," in M. Boskin (ed.), *Frontiers of Tax Reform*, Stanford, Hoover Institution, 1996, pp. 181–196; reprinted in Joint Economic Committee, Congress of the United States, *Roundtable Discussion on Tax Reform and Economic Growth*, One Hundred Fourth Congress, First Session, 1996, pp. 98–112.

"The Economic Impact of Taxing Consumption," in Committee on Ways and Means, United States House of Representatives, *Replacing the Federal Income Tax*, vol. II, One Hundred Fourth Congress, Second Session, 1996, pp. 105–113; reprinted in Joint Economic Committee, Congress of the United States, *Roundtable Discussion on Tax Reform and Economic Growth*, One Hundred Fourth Congress, First Session, 1996, pp. 79–97.

"Technology in Growth Theory," in J.C. Fuhrer and J.S. Little (eds.), *Technology and Growth*, Boston, Federal Reserve Bank of Boston, 1996, pp. 45–77.

Final Report of the Advisory Commission to Study the Consumer Price Index, Committee on Finance, United States Senate, One Hundred Fourth Congress, Second Session, 1996 (with M. Boskin, E.R. Dulberger, R.J. Gordon, and Z. Griliches).

"Introduction," in E. Hanushek and D.W. Jorgenson (eds.), *Improving the Performance of America's Schools: The Role of Incentives*, Washington, National Academy Press, 1996, pp. 1–8.

"The CPI Commission: Findings and Recommendations," *American Economic Review*, vol. 87, no. 2, May 1997 (with M. Boskin, E.R. Dulberger, R.J. Gordon, and Z. Griliches), pp. 78–83.

"Implications of Overstating Inflation for Indexing Government Programs and Understanding Economic Progress," *American Economic Review*, vol. 87, no. 2, May 1997 (with M. Boskin), pp. 89–94.

"The Long-Run Dynamics of Fundamental Tax Reform," *American Economic Review*, vol. 87, no. 2, May 1997 (with P.J. Wilcoxen), pp. 126–132.

"Fundamental Tax Reform and Energy Markets," *Energy Journal*, vol. 18, no. 3, July 1997 (with P.J. Wilcoxen), pp. 1–30. Growth 2, ch. 11, pp. 413–441.

"There is no Silver Bullet: Investment and Growth in the G7," *National Institute Economic Review*, No. 162, October 1997 (with C. Dougherty), pp. 57–74; reprinted in Tsu-Tan Fu, Cliff J. Huang, and C.A. Knox Lovell, eds., *Economic Efficiency and Productivity Growth in the Asia-Pacific Region*, Northhampton, Edward Elgar, 1999, pp. 95–124.

"The Effects of Fundamental Tax Reform and the Feasibility of Dynamic Revenue Estimation," in Joint Committee on Taxation, Congress of the United

States, *The Modeling Project and 1997 Tax Symposium Papers*, Washington, U.S. Government Printing Office, November 20, 1997 (with P.J. Wilcoxen), pp. 130–151.

"Consumer Prices, the Consumer Price Index, and the Cost of Living," *Journal of Economic Perspectives*, vol. 12, no. 1, Winter 1998 (with M. Boskin, E.R. Dulberger, R.J. Gordon, and Z. Griliches), pp. 3–26.

"Did We Lose the War on Poverty?" *Journal of Economic Perspectives*, vol. 12, no. 1, Winter 1998, pp. 79–96.

"China's Economic Growth and Carbon Emissions," in M.B. McElroy, C.P. Nielsen, and P. Lydon (eds.), *Energizing China*, Cambridge, Harvard University Press, 1998 (with M.S. Ho and D.H. Perkins), pp. 301–342.

"Environmental Regulation and U.S. Trade," in D.W. Jorgenson, *Energy, the Environment, and Economic Growth*, Cambridge, MIT Press, 1998 (with M.S. Ho), pp. 331–372.

"Investment and Growth," in S. Strom (ed.), *Econometrics and Economic Theory in the 20th Century*, Cambridge, Cambridge University Press, 1998 pp. 204–237.

"Stabilization of Carbon Emissions and the Competitiveness of U.S. Industries," in D.W. Jorgenson, *Energy, the Environment, and Economic Growth*, Cambridge, MIT Press, 1998 (with M.S. Ho), pp. 373–412.

"Indexing Government Programs for Changes in the Cost of Living," *Journal of Business and Economic Statistics*, vol. 16, no. 2, April 1999 (with D.T. Slesnick), pp. 170–181.

"Special Section on Consumer Price Research: Introduction," *Journal of Business and Economic Statistics*, vol. 16, no. 2, April 1999 (with M.W. Watson), pp. 137–140.

"Information Technology and Growth," *American Economic Review*, vol. 89, no. 2, May 1999 (with K.J. Stiroh), pp. 109–115.

"Controlling Carbon Emissions in China," *Environment and Development*, vol. 2, part 4, October 1999 (with R. Garbaccio and M.S. Ho), pp. 493–518.

"Why Has the Energy-Output Ratio Fallen in China?" *Energy Journal*, vol. 20, no. 3, July 1999 (with R. Garbaccio and M.S. Ho), pp. 63–91.

"Productivity Growth in Taiwan's Manufacturing Industry," in Tsu-Tan Fu, Cliff J. Huang, and C.A. Know Lovell, (eds.), *Economic Efficiency and Productivity Growth in the Asia-Pacific Region*, Northampton, Edward Elgar, 1999 (with C.-Y. Liang), pp. 95–124.

"Qu'Est-il Advenu de la Croissance de la Productivite, *L'Actualite Economique, Revue d'Analyse Economique*, vol. 75, no. 4, 1999 (with Eric Yip).

"An Economic Theory of Agricultural Household Behavior," in D.W. Jorgenson, *Econometric Modeling of Producer Behavior*, Cambridge, MIT Press, 2000 (with L.J. Lau), pp. 97–124.

"U.S. Economic Growth at the Industry Level," *American Economic Review*, vol. 90, no. 2, May 2000 (with K. J. Stiroh), pp. 161–167.

Ph.D. Thesis Advisees

Dr. Joseph M. Anderson, Ph.D., Harvard University, 1977. "An Economic-Demographic Model of the United States Labor Market." President, Capital Research Associates

Dr. William J. Barger, Ph.D., Harvard University, 1972. "The Measurement of Labor Input: U.S. Manufacturing Industries, 1948–1966." President and Chief Executive Officer, High Point Academy

Dr. James M. Brundy, Ph.D., University of California, Berkeley, 1974. "The Relative Efficiency of Instrumental Variables Estimators." Assistant General Counsel, Bank of America

Dr. Timothy Buehrer, Ph.D., Harvard University, 1994. "Can Trade Losses Explain the Current Recession in Slovenia?" Resident Coordinator, Economic Analysis Project, Harvard Institute for International Development, Jakarta, Indonesia

Prof. Christophe Chamley, Ph.D., Harvard University, 1977. "Aggregate Capital Accumulation, Taxation, and the Public Debt." Professor of Economics, Boston University

Prof. Peter Chinloy, Ph.D., Harvard University, 1974. "Issues in the Measurement of Labor Input." Professor of Finance and Real Estate, American University

Dr. Laurits R. Christensen, Ph.D., University of California, Berkeley, 1968. "Saving and the Rate of Return." Chairman, L.R. Christensen Associates

Dr. Ronald Cooper, Ph.D., University of California, Berkeley, 1969. "Econometric Models of Cyclical Behavior." Business Consultant

Dr. Mansoor Dailami, Ph.D., Harvard University, 1978. "Measuring Labor and Total Factor Productivity." Lead Economist, The World Bank

Dr. Chrys Dougherty, Ph.D., Harvard University, 1992. "An Analysis of Productivity and Economic Growth in the G-7 Countries." Director, School Information Project, Just for the Kids

Dr. Steven I. Dym, Ph.D., Harvard University, 1981. "Supply Shocks and Macro-economic Dynamics." Business Consultant

Prof. Mitsuo Ezaki, Ph.D., Harvard University, 1974. "Quantitative Study of Japan's Economic Growth, 1958-1980: An Approach from the System of National Accounts." Professor, Graduate School of International Development, Nagoya University

Dr. John Fernald, Ph.D., Harvard University, 1993. "Explaining Productivity Growth: Essays in Infrastructure and Imperfect Competition." Senior Economist, Council of Economic Advisors (through June 2000, on leave from Board of Governors, Federal Reserve System)

Prof. Karen A. Fisher-Vanden, Ph.D., Harvard University, 1999. "Structural Change and Technological Diffusion in Transition Economies: Implications for Energy Use and Carbon Emissions in China." Assistant Professor of Environmental Studies, Dartmouth College

Dr. Robert C. Fry, Jr., Ph.D., Harvard University, 1985. "Differential Taxation of Capital at the Industry Level." Senior Associate Economist, DuPont

Prof. Frank Gollop, Ph.D., Harvard University, 1974. "Modeling Technical Change and Market Imperfections: An Econometric Analysis of U.S. Manufacturing, 1947-1971." Professor of Economics, Boston College

Dr. Sidney Handel, Ph.D., University of California, Berkeley, 1965. "Investment Behavior in the Regulated Industries." Psychotherapist

Prof. Michael Hanemann, Ph.D., Harvard University, 1978. "A Theoretical and Empirical Study of the Recreation Benefits from Improving Water Quality in the Boston Area." Professor of Agricultural and Resource Economics, University of California, Berkeley

Prof. Fumio Hayashi, Ph.D., Harvard University, 1980. "Utility Maximization, Rational Expectations, and Aggregate Consumption." Professor of Economics, University of Tokyo

Dr. Peter Higgs, Ph.D., Harvard University, 1986. "Applied General Equilibrium Economics: Data and Applications." Chief Executive Officer, Tactical Global Management Limited

Dr. Mun S. Ho, Ph.D., Harvard University, 1989. "The Effects of External Linkages on U.S. Economic Growth: A Dynamic General Equilibrium Analysis." Research Fellow, Kennedy School of Government, Harvard University

Prof. Charles Yuji Horioka, Ph.D., Harvard University, 1985. "Household Saving in Japan: The Importance of Target Saving for Education and Housing." Professor of Economics, Institute of Social and Economic Research, Osaka University

Dr. Edward A. Hudson, Ph.D., Harvard University, 1973. "Optimal Growth Policies." Managing Director, E-DEC Ltd.

Prof. Charles R. Hulten, Ph.D., University of California, Berkeley, 1973. "The Measurement of Total Factor Productivity in U.S. Manufacturing, 1948–1966." Professor of Economics, University of Maryland

Prof. Nazrul Islam, Ph.D., Harvard University, 1993. "Estimation of Dynamic Models from Panel Data." Assistant Professor of Economics, Emory University

Dr. Daehwan Kim, Ph.D., Harvard University, 2000. "The Stock Market Value of Research and Development Assets." Financial Economist, Folio[fn]

Prof. Sungwoo Kim, Ph.D., University of California, Berkeley, 1967. "Capital Appropriation and Investment Behavior of U.S. Manufacturing." Professor of Economics, Northeastern University

Prof. Eugene Kroch, Ph.D., Harvard University, 1978. "Economic Dynamics of Energy Resource Allocation." Professor of Economics, Villanova University

Prof. Taewon Kwack, Ph.D., Harvard University, 1983. "Taxation, Subsidy and Investment in Korean Manufacturing Industry." Professor of Economics, Sogang University

Prof. John Laitner, Ph.D., Harvard University, 1976. "The Role of Bequests in the Determination of the Steady-State Ratio of Capital to Labor." Professor of Economics, University of Michigan

Prof. Lawrence J. Lau, Ph.D., University of California, Berkeley, 1969. "Duality and Utility Structure." Kwoh-Ting Li Professor of Economic Development, Stanford University

Prof. Ronald D. Lee, Ph.D., Harvard University, 1971. "Econometric Studies of Topics in Demographic History." Professor of Demography and Economics, University of California, Berkeley

Dr. Randall Mariger, Ph.D., Harvard University, 1983. "Liquidity Constraints, Intergenerational Transfers, and Life-Cycle Consumption." Director, National Economic Consulting Group, PricewaterhouseCoopers LLP

Dr. Peter R. Merrill, Ph.D., Harvard University, 1982. "Adjustment Costs and Industry Investment." Partner, PricewaterhouseCoopers LLP and Director, National Economic Consulting Group

Prof. Jose Garcia Montalvo, Ph.D., Harvard University, 1993. "Essay on Growth and Productivity." Professor of Economics, Universitat Valencia and Universitat Pompeu Fabra

Prof. M. Ishaq Nadiri, Ph.D., University of California, Berkeley, 1964. "Predictive and Forecasting Ability of Econometric Investment Functions." Jay Gould Professor of Economics, New York University

Dr. David H. Nissen, Ph.D., University of California, Berkeley, 1968. "Consistent and Inconsistent Intertemporal Behavior." Manager of Strategic Consulting, Poten and Partners

Prof. Yoichi Okita, Ph.D., Harvard University, 1974. "The Domestic and International Impact of Japanese Fiscal Policy: 1951–1969." Professor, National Graduate Institute for Policy Studies, Japan

Dr. Robert J. Oster, Ph.D., University of California, Berkeley, 1967. "The Cost of Capital and Investment Behavior: A Study of the Opportunity Cost of Investment, its Determinants and its Determination of Business Investment Behavior." Private venture capitalist

Dr. Alvaro Pachón, Ph.D., Harvard University, 1981. "Integrating Human Capital in The National Accounts: Conceptual Framework and Empirical Implementation." General Manager, Alvaro Pachón and Associates

Prof. Richard W. Parks, Ph.D., University of California, Berkeley, 1966. "An Econometric Model of Swedish Economic Growth, 1861–1955." Professor of Economics, University of Washington

Prof. William Perraudin, Ph.D., Harvard University, 1989. "Essays in Portfolio Theory." Professor of Finance, Birkbeck College, University of London

Dr. William A. Pizer, Ph.D., Harvard University, 1996. "Modeling Long-Term Policy Under Uncertainty." Fellow, Resources for the Future

Dr. Rudy Pizzano, Ph.D., Harvard University, 1986. "An Integrated Approach to Promotional Pricing." President, Roadmap Technologies

Dr. C. Tait Ratcliffe, Ph.D., University of California, Berkeley, 1969. "Tax Policy and Investment Behavior in Postwar Japan." President, IBI, Inc., Tokyo

Dr. Lee W. Samuelson, Ph.D., Harvard University, 1972. "Portfolio Analysis and the Theory of the Firm: An Investigation of Asset Management Behavior Under Risk." Head, Computer and Communications Operations Division, Organization for Economic Co-operation and Development

Prof. N.E. Savin, Ph.D., University of California, Berkeley, 1969. "Log Grading and the Prediction of Lumber Grade Output: A Statistical Analysis." Professor of Economics, University of Iowa

Dr. Jaypee Sevilla, Ph.D., Harvard University, 1999. "An Econometric Implementation of the Mirrlees Theory of Optimal Taxation." Associate, Harvard Institute for International Development

Prof. C.D. Siebert, Ph.D., University of California, Berkeley, 1966. "A Comparison of Alternative Theories of Corporate Investment Behavior." Professor of Economics, University of Iowa

Prof. Ajit Singh, Ph.D., University of California, Berkeley, 1970. "Takeovers, the Stock Market and the Theory of the Firm." Professor of Economics, University of Cambridge

Prof. Daniel T. Slesnick, Ph.D., Harvard University, 1982. "An Axiomatic Approach to Applied Welfare Economics." Rex G. Barker, Jr., Professor of Political Economy, University of Texas

Prof. James A. Stephenson, Ph.D., University of California, Berkeley, 1965. "Investment Behavior in U.S. Manufacturing, 1947–1960." Emeritus Professor of Economics, Iowa State University

Dr. Kevin Stiroh, Ph.D., Harvard University, 1995. "Essays on Capital Accumulation." Economist, Federal Reserve Bank of New York

Prof. Thomas M. Stoker, Ph.D., Harvard University, 1979. "Aggregation Over Individuals and Demand Analysis." Gordon Y. Billard Professor of Applied Economics, Sloan School of Management, MIT

Dr. Eric Stubbs, Ph.D., Harvard University, 1992. "A Life Cycle Model of Household Portfolio Allocation." Director, Head of Analytical Tools Allocation, Credit Suisse First Boston Corporation

Dr. Lee Tsao Yuan, Ph.D., Harvard University, 1982. "Growth and Productivity in Singapore: A Supply Side Analysis." Director, Institute of Policy Studies, Singapore

Prof. Charlie G. Turner, Ph.D., Harvard University, 1981. "Quantitative Restrictions on International Trade of the United States and Japan." Associate Professor of Economics, Old Dominion University

Prof. Rafael B. Weston, Ph.D., Harvard University, 1972. "The Quality of Housing in the U.S., 1929–1970." Dean, School of Business, Adams State College, Colorado

Prof. Peter J. Wilcoxen, Ph.D., Harvard University, 1989. "The Effects of Environmental Regulation and Energy Prices on U.S. Economic Performance." Associate Professor of Economics, University of Texas

Prof. Frank A. Wolak, Ph.D., Harvard University, 1985. "Testing Inequality Constraints in Econometric Models." Professor of Economics, Stanford University

Prof. Brian D. Wright, Ph.D., Harvard University, 1976. "The Taxation of Petroleum Production." Professor of Agricultural and Resource Economics, University of California, Berkeley

Dr. Eric Yip, Ph.D., Harvard University, 2000. "Time-Series Evidence on Economic Growth." Associate, McKinsey & Company

Prof. Kunio Yoshihara, Ph.D., University of California, Berkeley, 1966. "An Econometric Study of Japanese Economic Development." Professor of Economic Development, Center for Southeast Asian Studies, Kyoto University

Prof. Kun-Young Yun, Ph.D., Harvard University, 1984. "Taxation of Capital Income, Allocative Efficiency and Welfare: A General Equilibrium Approach." Professor of Economics, Yonsei University

1 Research on the Cost of Capital: Past, Present, and Future

Lawrence J. Lau

1.1 Introduction

The celebrated article by Dale W. Jorgenson, "Capital Theory and Investment Behavior," immediately attracted the attention of the economics profession when it was published in the *American Economic Review*[1] for May 1963. In 1971, only eight years later, Jorgenson's research on investment behavior was cited as the basis for awarding him the prestigious John Bates Clark Medal of the American Economic Association for his contributions to economic research. Today the article has become a true classic and ranks among the most cited articles in economics.[2] In this article, Jorgenson recognizes capital explicitly as a factor of production and introduces the concept of the "cost of capital" (sometimes also referred to as the "user cost of capital") as the "*shadow* price or implicit rental of one unit of capital service per period of time."[3]

Jorgenson shows, in his article, that the formula for the "cost of capital" can be derived from the hypothesis of maximization of present value on the part of a firm. In the absence of taxation, the "cost of capital" formula is given by:

$$p \frac{\partial Q}{\partial K} = q \left(r + \delta - \frac{\dot{q}}{q} \right) \tag{1.1}$$

where Q is the quantity of output, K is the quantity of the capital stock, $\partial Q/\partial K$ is the marginal product of capital service, p is the price of output, q is the price of investment good, r is the rate of interest, and δ is the rate of exponential depreciation.[4] Equation (1.1) may be interpreted to mean that the implicit rental price of one unit of capital service is equal to the price of the investment good times the sum of the rate of interest and the rate of depreciation less the rate of appreciation of the investment good.[5] Thus, the "cost of capital" formula takes into account the price of the investment good, the rate of interest (the time value of money), the durability (life) and the mortality density (depreciation) of the investment good and the appreciation, if any, in the price of the investment good.

For a present-value maximizing firm, given an appropriately measured "cost of capital," the wage rate, and the price of output of the current period, the demands for capital service and labor input and hence the supply of output in the current period may be completely determined from a knowledge of the production function, without reference to the "cost of capital," the wage rate and the price of output of any future, or for that matter, past, period.[6] The "cost of capital" embodies, or summarizes, all of the information on future prices (or expectations of future prices) that may affect the current behavior of the firm (through the appreciation term). Thus, the behavior of a firm may be modeled as if it maximizes the profit of the current period given only the prices, including the cost (rental price) of capital, of the current period. The quantity of fixed investment in the current period may in turn be derived as the difference between the desired capital stock and the inherited capital stock (less depreciation and retirement, if any) and is thus a function of only the prices, including the "cost of capital," and the inherited, depreciated, capital stock of the current period. The producer may then be said to behave "myopically," that is, to look only at the present but not the future, and yet still be optimal in the long run.[7] The concept of the "cost of capital" makes possible the Fisherian separation of the current period from the future period and transforms a multi-period problem of dynamic present-value maximization into a sequence of single-period problems of static profit maximization. The "cost of capital" provides the link between static and dynamic behavior—between the present and the future—for producers.[8] In general, the demand for investment in the current period depends on the "cost of capital" (as well as the quantity of inherited capital stock) and the supply of saving in the current period depends on the rate of interest, r, and current and future (or expectations of future) prices of output and investment goods and wage rates (as well as the inherited stock of non-human wealth). Saving and investment are brought into equilibrium through adjustments in the rate of interest and current levels and rates (or expected rates) of change of prices.

The "cost of capital" formula may be modified to reflect the extent of tax-deductibility of depreciation, which may be faster or slower than physical depreciation or mortality, investment tax credit, and the taxability of capital gains on investment goods. With proportional income taxation, and under the assumption of static expectations, the "cost of capital" formula takes the form:[9]

$$p \frac{\partial Q}{\partial K} = q(r+\delta) \frac{(1-uz)}{(1-u)} \tag{1.2}$$

where Q is the quantity of output, K is the quantity of the capital stock, $\partial Q / \partial K$ is the marginal product of capital service, p is the price of output, q is the price of investment good, r is the after-tax rate of interest, δ is the rate of exponential depreciation, u is the rate of proportional taxation, and z is the present value of the depreciation deductions on one unit of new investment.

Thus, the after-tax "cost of capital" formula incorporates tax policy for capital income as a determinant of the demand for capital services and hence of investment. In empirical and in policy analysis, it is the after-tax "cost of capital" that is relevant. Jorgenson shows that the after-tax "cost of capital" is a primary determinant of the demand for the capital input for given output, and which, together with the inherited capital stock, in turn determine the demand for investment for given output. The Jorgensonian "cost of capital" is now a standard variable in the analysis of macroeconomics and of investment behavior at the firm, industry and economy-wide levels. It has also become the standard tool for the assessment of the economic impacts of changes in tax policy. The concepts of the "cost of capital" and its associated measure of a "marginal effective tax rate" have generated a voluminous literature in the economics of taxation. Marginal effective tax rates played an important role in the analysis of alternative tax proposals leading to the Tax Reform Act of 1986 in the United States. Measures of the "cost of capital" and "marginal effective tax rates" are now available for literally dozens of countries. The "cost of capital" has been incorporated into both conventional macroeconometric models and intertemporal general equilibrium models of the impacts of tax policy.[10]

It is a measure of Jorgenson's success in transforming the thinking of the profession that economists nowadays routinely use the Jorgensonian "cost of capital" formula, as well as its many derivatives, without citing the original article any more—this is the sign of a true classic.[11]

In addition to the "cost of capital" and the related analysis of investment behavior, Jorgenson has made highly important contributions to many diverse areas in economics: measurement of income and wealth; measurement of productivity and technical progress; technology and producer behavior; preferences and consumer behavior; econometric methodology; social welfare measurement; energy and environmental economics; and applied general equilibrium analysis. Jorgenson's achievements in each of the areas alone would have been the envy of many an economist, not to mention the immense breadth and depth of the entire corpus. However, in this seemingly unrelated ensemble, a design can in fact be discerned. Behind all of Jorgenson's work, there is a common thread—the goal of the construction of a theoretically consistent intertemporal general equilibrium macroeconomic model, estimated econometrically with the properly specified variables and measured data. The "cost of capital," which provides the intertemporal link, is the key to the realization of this goal.

The same 1963 article on the "cost of capital" also illustrates Jorgenson's characteristic style of economic research, which sets a standard for other economists to emulate. The hallmark of Jorgenson's work, regardless of the area of investigation, is the use of an integrated approach, combining theoretical rigor in modeling, sound statistical methodology, and exacting requirements on the measurement of economic variables in a consistent and unified framework. Jorgenson has a strong commitment to total excellence in all aspects of economic research. As his students, we have all learned that neither "econometrics without theory" nor "theory without econometrics" are likely to be sufficient to reveal the true state of the world.

1.2   Historical Origin of the "Cost of Capital"

Hotelling (1925) appeared to be the first economist to have written down the formula for the rental price of capital service, but for a world without intertemporal variations in prices and without taxation. Keynes (1935) introduced the term "user cost of capital" to distinguish it from the price of the capital asset (the investment good) itself. Subsequently, Haavelmo (1960) derived the formula in Equation (1.1), again, without regard for the effects of taxation. Jorgenson (1963)'s contribution is to incorporate the effects of changes in the price of the capital good, when new, and income taxation into the measurement of the "cost of capital" as well as to use the "cost of capital" as a factor price variable on a par with the wage rate in the integrated analysis of production and investment behavior. Thus, the supply of output and the demands for labor and capital services in a competitive market economy can be expressed as functions of the price of output, the wage rate, and the "cost of capital" (but not the price of the investment good). Under constant returns to scale, the demands for labor and capital services per unit of output can be expressed as functions of the wage rate and the "cost of capital" alone. (Alternatively, the price of output can be express as functions of the wage rate and the "cost of capital"—the dynamic analogue of the "factor-price frontier" of Samuelson (1953).)

Jorgenson's derivation of the "cost of capital" formula is based on the assumption of an exponential mortality density for capital in the aggregate, with a constant rate of depreciation, an assumption also employed by Hotelling (1925) and Haavelmo (1960). Arrow (1964) also derived "cost of capital" formulas for capital characterized by other forms of mortality density, e.g., the "one-hoss-shay" or "sudden-death" case. Finally, Hall and Jorgenson (1967) and Hall (1981) further refined the after-tax "cost of capital" formula to reflect the effects of modifications of the income tax laws.

1.3   The Quest—The Econometric Modeling of Intertemporal General Equilibrium

Jorgenson has pursued his goal of an econometrically estimated intertemporal general equilibrium model with determination and single-mindedness, organizing his efforts in phases in the three decades following the first publication of the "cost of capital" article. Why is it important to economists to have an econometric model of intertemporal general equilibrium? First, the proposition that partial equilibrium analysis can give incomplete and sometimes even misleading results is almost universally accepted by economists of every persuasion. A general equilibrium analysis is therefore essential. This means it is not enough to analyze the demand for a commodity in isolation from its supply, or to analyze the market for a commodity in isolation from the markets for other commodities. For example, in the analysis of the effects of an increase in the world price of oil, we need to trace through not only the decrease in the demand for oil in the first instance but also the increase in the domestic supply of oil that the increase in price may stimulate. In addition, the increase in price may induce the substitution of other forms of energy for oil as well as the substitution of other factor inputs, capital and labor, and other consumption goods for energy. The general equilibrium effects can therefore be quite complex.

However, a general equilibrium model that is static, that is, that applies to only one period, is not adequate because both the past history and the expectations about the future affect behavior in the present. For example, the inherited stocks of capital and wealth and their distribution, and past patterns of consumption affect current production and consumption behavior. Coupled with expectations about the future, they also affect current saving and investment behavior. However, expectations about the future cannot be arbitrary, they must also be consistent with general equilibrium in future periods. In other words, both the current and future periods must be simultaneously in "virtual" general equilibrium, in the sense that if all expectations are fulfilled in the future then the planned consumption, production and investment paths of all agents (firms and households) will in fact be consistent with general equilibrium of the economy in every future period. This is also referred to as a "rational expectations" general equilibrium. It is important to note the distinction between genuine intertemporal general equilibrium and a sequence of single-period general equilibria linked together by some kind of *ad hoc* transition dynamics, for example, by using an empirical aggregate savings function.

Intertemporal general equilibrium models are critical for the understanding of the entire process of economic growth. It requires an intertemporal general equilibrium model to take into account fully the mutual dependence of present and future. But more generally, only intertemporal general equilibrium models reflect the way in which the real economy operates, and are therefore necessary for the analysis of the full dynamic effects of alternative economic policies. For example, the Ricardian equivalence between taxes and bonds[12] is very much the consequence of intertemporal general equilibrium.

Finally, in order for an intertemporal general equilibrium model to be useful for applied economic analysis, it must bear some resemblance to the real world. For example, the demand function for capital in the model must be capable of tracking the actual demand for capital in the real economy fairly closely. The only way one can be assured that a demand function in a model reproduces relatively faithfully the actual behavior of the real economy is for the demand function to have been estimated or derived from actual empirical data. Many practitioners of computable (intertemporal or atemporal) general equilibrium (CGE) models use the "calibration" approach to derive their parameters. Very crudely, the "calibration" approach amounts to estimating the parameters of a demand, or supply, or for that matter any other kind of a function in the model by using the data from a single observation. The reliability of the parameters derived by the "calibration" approach is therefore greatly suspect. Moreover, because only a single observation is available, the modeler is necessarily limited to using highly specialized functional forms which may further bias the properties of the resulting general equilibrium model.[13]

Thus, the practice of using "calibration" rather than econometric estimation in deriving the parameters of a general equilibrium model is fine with an illustrative example but may lead to misleading and/or unreliable results if the general equilibrium model is to be used as a serious tool for economic policy analysis. Jorgenson never used the shortcut of "calibration."[14] Jorgenson insists on estimating the parameters of his intertemporal general equilibrium models econometrically from actual empirical data. Jorgenson's approach stands out from those of most practitioners of computable general equilibrium models. In deriving the parameters of a model econometrically, there is the additional advantage that the modeler is able to test, statistically, the validity of the underlying assumptions of the model. As applied general equilibrium analysis becomes more widely understood and taken more seriously by economic policy makers, interest will gradually shift away from the numerical computation of examples, using hypothetical parameters, to models that better mimic the real world. There will then be a premium for econometrically estimated intertemporal general equilibrium models that are based on sound theoretical as well as empirical analysis.

The Building Blocks of an Intertemporal General Equilibrium Model

What are the necessary building blocks for an intertemporal general equilibrium model? We may begin by considering a static (single-period) general equilibrium model with production. There are firms and households in the economy. Production (or supply) depends on the technology, behavior, and inherited endowments of the firms and demand depends on the preference and the distribution of the initial endowments of the households. General equilibrium is attained through the simultaneous clearing of the output and factor (capital and labor) markets, determining the equilibrium prices of goods and factors. Thus, as a minimum, one needs to model both production and consumption (including leisure) behavior in the economy. In a single-period model, investment may as well be treated as exogenous; alternatively, the "cost of capital" may be treated as exogenous.[15] The basic framework is not substantively different if there are more commodities distinguished. For example, one may wish to distinguish between consumption and investment outputs, as was done in Christensen, Jorgenson and Lau (1971, 1973). Or one may attempt to model explicitly the production of commodities with commodities, in an inter-industry setting. However, as long as one is only concerned with general equilibrium in a single period, the analytics remain the same, even though computationally the model may become more complex.

As one moves from a single-period to a multiple-period general equilibrium, investment and saving can no longer be taken as exogenous, and a serious effort must be made to model investment and saving behavior. This is where the "cost of capital" comes in—as a variable embodying the effects of the future on the present and thus providing the crucial link between the future and the present. The introduction of the "cost of capital" allows the decomposition of intertemporal general equilibrium into a sequence of single-period equilibria. One period is linked with the next, through capital accumulation by both firms and households. The "cost of capital" also provides the link between a theory of investment and a theory of production. In general equilibrium, the demand for investment is a derived demand that depends on the technology, the current and expected future relative prices of output and factors,[16] and not just simply determined through some macroeconomic consumption function or multiplier-accelerator mechanism. A theory of investment then becomes absolutely necessary for an intertemporal general equilibrium model. The "cost of capital" contains all of the necessary information that must be passed between one period and the next. It also enables the separation between the present and the future in the sense that given the "cost of capital," the production, investment behavior, and saving behavior in the present period may be modeled without reference to prices in the future periods.

The "cost of capital" also figures in the analysis of saving behavior, through the purchases and consumption of durables, most notably owner-occupied housing. Thus, the households invest directly, in the form of consumer durables, including housing, as well as indirectly, through their ownership, direct or portfolio, of the firms. Moreover, the households also invest directly in human capital, which also has finite useful lives. In general equilibrium, the equalization of the value of the marginal product of each type of capital and its corresponding "cost of capital" across the different sectors is a condition of efficiency of the economy.

The effects of government policies cannot be ignored in an intertemporal general equilibrium model, both in terms of their direct effects on the "cost of capital" and in terms of their indirect effects through public savings (which can be negative), which supplements (or competes with) household and firm savings. The after-tax "cost of capital," which is the relevant determinant for the investment behavior of firms and households, depends on the taxation of income and capital gains, investment tax credits, if any, and the tax treatment of depreciation. The supplies of savings and labor from the households also depend on the laws of individual income taxation. Government regulations, for example, on the environment, also have direct impacts on the economy that can be evaluated only in a general equilibrium framework.

The fundamental building blocks of an intertemporal general equilibrium model therefore consist of models for (I) Investment Behavior; (II) Technology and Producer Behavior; (III) The Effects of Government Policies; (IV) Preferences and Consumer Behavior; and (V) Saving Behavior.

Methodological Innovations for the Implementation of an
Intertemporal General Equilibrium Model

In addition to the five building blocks, methodological innovations are also necessary to enable the correct empirical implementation of an intertemporal general equilibrium model. These innovations can be grouped into three areas: (I) Aggregation; (II) Econometric Methods; and (III) The Measurement of Economic Variables. We discuss each area in turn.

Aggregation
In any model of the entire economy, at least two types of aggregation are necessary—the aggregation across commodities and aggregation across possibly heterogeneous economic agents (firms and households). Aggregation across commodities enables the modeler to repre-

sent the economy in terms of a finite and hopefully relatively small number of commodities. For example, automobiles, trucks, railroad cars, ships and airplanes may be aggregated into a single good referred to as transportation equipment. Labor, differentiated by age, education, and gender, may be aggregated into a single quantity index of labor. Aggregation across commodities typically depends on separability assumptions on the demand or preference side. On the supply side, a proportionality assumption is more likely. Jorgenson has pioneered the use of the Divisia index number in the aggregation across commodities. A discrete-time version of the Divisia index number is the Törnquist index number formula, which turns out to be exact if and only if the underlying aggregator function has the transcendental logarithmic functional form.

Aggregation across economic agents is also essential. On the production side, under constant or decreasing returns to scale, if all producers maximize profits, the marginal products of every output with respect to every input will be equalized across all the producers. There will be a single price for each commodity in the economy, subject to a normalization. Efficiency will prevail. The economy will therefore behave as if it were a single firm maximizing profits subject to an aggregate production function (with multiple outputs). Aggregation is therefore quite straightforward. However, on the consumption side, even if all households maximize utility, there is no assurance that in the aggregate the economy will behave as if it were a single consumer maximizing utility,[17] unless it can be assumed that income is continuously redistributed across the households so as to maximize some social welfare function. Thus, the "representative consumer model" is in general an over-simplification of the real world that may distort the analysis. The modeler may have to appeal to the theory of exact aggregation and employ the exactly aggregable aggregate consumer demand system developed by Jorgenson, Lau and Stoker (1980a), which is also based on a variant of the indirect transcendental logarithmic utility function.

Econometric Methods

In a general equilibrium system, both prices and quantities are endogenous variables, and we cannot assume that either set of variables are exogenous, as in a partial-equilibrium, microeconomic context. The equations of the general equilibrium systems are also more often than not nonlinear in parameters. This is because linearity in parameters, coupled with the restrictions imposed by the theory, often has observable implications that are at variance with known empirical regularities. For example, a system of constant-elasticity consumer demand functions leads to constant budget shares, which is inconsistent with the observed facts[18] and almost all linear-in-parameters system of consumer demand functions imply unitary income elasticities of demand for all commodities, a proposition that is well known to be false. What is needed, then, is an econometric methodology for the estimation and statistical inference in the context of a system of non-linear simultaneous equations. Jorgenson, together with his collaborators, James Brundy, Jean-Jacques Laffont, and Ronald Gallant, have indeed proceeded to develop such methods.

As previously discussed an alternative approach to the derivation of the parameters in a general equilibrium model, used by many practitioners of "computable general equilibrium (CGE)" models, is the calibration approach. However, the statistical reliability of such estimates of the parameters is suspect. Still another approach is that of sensitivity analysis—changing the values of the parameters systematically and assessing the resulting changes in the general equilibria. While the sensitivity analysis approach can be useful and informative, especially when the number of critical parameters is small, e.g., the elasticity of substitution between capital and energy, it becomes extremely cumbersome with a large general equilibrium model with a large number of unknown parameters.

Jorgenson insists on seeking parameters from empirical data, and that means estimating them econometrically, ensuring that the specified general equilibrium model as well as the underlying assumptions actually fit the real world. It is also for this reason that Jorgenson has pioneered the use of flexible functional forms such as the transcendental logarithmic function—to allow the empirical data to reveal the true state of the world. For example, if a nonflexible functional form such as the Cobb-Douglas function is used in the econometric analysis of technology, then the elasticities of substitution among the inputs are already pre-ordained to be unity, whatever values the empirical data may take. This will indeed bias or distort any conclusions to be drawn from the model. Under the econometric approach, the statistical reliability of the estimates of the parameters, and hence the model "predictions" of general equilibria, can also be readily assessed. The same is not true of the non-econometric approaches.

The Measurement of Economic Variables

Crucial to the construction of an intertemporal general equilibrium model is the appropriate measurement of the economic variables. Here, the most important distinction is that between stock and flow—between capital stock and capital service, and between consumer purchases, which include durables, most notably owner-occupied housing, and consumption of the services produced by these durables. The imputations of the service flows, which are not normally directly observed, are critical to the proper measurement of income and saving. The welfare of the households in the current period depends on its consumption and not on its purchases. Similarly, production plans in the current period depend on the "cost of capital" and not on the price of investment goods.[19]

The appropriate measurement of the "cost of capital" is therefore extremely important. Moreover, once the "cost of capital" is obtained, the value of the service flow can be simply calculated as the product of the "cost of capital" and the quantity of the capital stock. Thus, the correct measurement of outputs and inputs as well as their prices hinges on the correct measurement of the "cost of capital."

The Grand Synthesis—An Econometric Model of Intertemporal General Equilibrium

The ultimate goal of Jorgenson is to combine his research on the various building blocks, including his models of production, consumption, investment, saving, and effects of government policies, into a single econometrically estimated intertemporal general equilibrium model. The model will be characterized by theoretical rigor, statistical correctness, and conformity of the empirical measurements of the variables to the theoretical concepts. An example of such a model is that of Jorgenson and Yun (1986). Once an econometrically estimated intertemporal general equilibrium model is constructed, it can be used for the very much needed applied welfare analysis of changes in government policies or external environment.

The "cost of capital" provides the unifying common element that underlies Jorgenson's approach to intertemporal general equilibrium. It is, one could say, "a sufficient statistic" for the future. It allows the transformation of an intertemporal dynamic optimization problem into an equivalent sequence of single-period static optimization problems. However, the computation of an intertemporal general equilibrium model with a finite horizon typically depends on the terminal conditions as well as the initial conditions. While the initial conditions depend on past history, the terminal conditions can only be specified with some degree of arbitrariness.[20] But the solution to an intertemporal general equilibrium model is likely to be sensitive to the terminal conditions, especially as one moves close to the terminal time. There is also the possibility of "time-inconsistency." A feasible alternative is to do a full rational expectations (perfect foresight) solution of the intertemporal equilibrium, with all of the economic agents (firms and households) forward-looking, coupled with transversality conditions.[21]

In what follows, we shall analyze Jorgenson's progress towards his ultimate goal decade by decade, showing how he has assembled the different building blocks together, solving the theoretical problems, constructing the databases, and developing new methodology and statistical techniques on the way. Of course, there is also considerable independent interest in Jorgenson's research contributions in their own right—his pioneering work on productivity analysis, his corpus of work on stability and on the development of dual economies (which employs a general equilibrium approach) and his applied work on taxation and energy and more recently on the environment—and not solely in the context of intertemporal general equilibrium modeling.

1.4   The First Decade (1963–1973)

The First Decade following the publication of Jorgenson's first "cost of capital" article may be viewed as mostly preparatory towards the goal of constructing an econometrically estimated intertemporal general equilibrium model. Fundamental progress was made in many areas— the measurement of economic data; the perfecting of the models of investment and production; and the development of an econometric methodology for the estimation of a large, nonlinear system of simultaneous equations—during this decade. We shall review this progress building block by building block.

(BI)   Investment Behavior

Investment behavior plays a central role in any analysis of intertemporal allocation of resources. What is not consumed but invested today
augments the capital stock of tomorrow, which in turn increases the
feasible output (and hence consumption) tomorrow. Investment provides a link between current and future production and reflects the
tradeoff between current and future consumption. Jorgenson began
his work on the modeling of investment behavior with his justly
celebrated article (1963) on the "cost of capital" and investment
behavior.[22] In this article, capital is explicitly modeled as a factor of
production with its demand being derived from a production function, and the concept of a "user cost" of capital that incorporates the
structure of taxation on income and capital gains, is introduced. Thus,
the planned demand for investment in the current period is a function
of the price of output, the wage rate, the "cost of capital," the quantity
of expected or planned output, and the quantity of inherited capital
stock, all of the current period.

Empirically, this article also applies the concept of rational distributed lag functions, introduced in Jorgenson (1966a) to the modeling of time lags in the realization of investment plans. Jorgenson
(1963) lays the foundation of an extensive body of empirical econometric research on investment behavior, conducted jointly by Jorgenson and his various collaborators, R. E. Hall, C. D. Siebert and J. A.
Stephenson, to name only a few, at the levels of the individual firms as
well as industrial sectors of the U.S. economy.[23] The relationship
between the demand for investment and the "cost of capital" is
described in detail in Jorgenson (1967b). The effects of changes in tax
policy on the "cost of capital" are further studied in a series of joint
papers with Robert E. Hall, beginning with Hall and Jorgenson (1967).

This first phase of Jorgenson's research on investment behavior and
the "cost of capital" is reviewed and summarized in Jorgenson (1971),
which also presents comparisons of his model, derived from present-
value maximization subject to a production function constraint, with
capital being explicitly recognized as a factor of production, with
other alternative models of investment. It is also covered in the other
survey article by Jorgenson (1974) on this subject.

(BII)   Technology and Producer Behavior

The Measurement of Productivity and Technical Progress
Jorgenson's research on productivity was initiated in a joint article
with Zvi Griliches published in 1966. Their subsequent article, "The
Explanation of Productivity Change," published in 1967, represents
the first attempt to account for economic growth in the United States
on the basis of the growth of disaggregated capital and labor inputs.
They reached the important empirical conclusion that the growth of
inputs, appropriately measured, is much more important in the explanation of the growth of output than had been previously thought and
that technological change, as measured by the "residual," is an important but not the dominant source of growth, in contrast to earlier findings of Moses Abramovitz (1956) and Robert Solow (1957). In 1969
and 1970, Jorgenson published more detailed estimates of productivity growth for the U.S. with Laurits Christensen (1969, 1970). A joint
output of these studies of productivity and technical progress is a set
of estimates of the quantities and prices of the services rendered by
each of the inputs of production, capital and labor. The price of capital services is precisely given by the "cost of capital."

Technology and Producer Behavior
Jorgenson's research program in the modeling of the technology and
producer behavior was initiated in articles published in 1971 and 1973
with Laurits Christensen and Lawrence Lau.[24] These articles present
econometric methods for modeling technology and producer behavior, a fundamental building block of general equilibrium models of
economic systems. The important innovations embodied in Jorgenson's work with Christensen and Lau consist of the introduction of a
flexible functional form (the transcendental logarithmic, or translog,
functional form) for production, cost and profit functions, the development of statistical methods for the estimation of nonlinear systems
of simultaneous equations, and the application of duality theory to the
modeling of production. The translog functional forms have become
the standard tools for econometric modeling of not only producer but
also consumer behavior. Christensen, Jorgenson and Lau (1971, 1973)
also pioneer the joint output approach (consumption and investment
are modeled as jointly produced outputs) as an alternative to the custom of treating real GDP as a single output. However, if real GDP can

in fact be treated as a single output, separability between inputs and outputs is implied. If, in addition, it is assumed that separate production functions exist for consumption and investment goods, that is, production is non-joint, then the production functions of consumption and investment goods must be identical up to a constant of proportionality,[25] an implication that is theoretically unpalatable and empirically false.

Moreover, application of the dual approach (profit and cost functions and the demand functions derived from them) requires the proper specification of the "cost of capital"—the rental price of capital services. Christensen, Jorgenson and Lau (1971, 1973) employs data on the prices and quantities of outputs and input services generated within the accounting system developed in the work on productivity measurements by Christensen and Jorgenson (1969, 1970).

Christensen, Jorgenson and Lau (1971, 1973) has had great influence in the empirical analysis of production and spawned a large literature. The new functional form has facilitated the study of factor substitution, technological change and scale effects, enabling biases as well as levels to be empirically identified and estimated. In particular, it has become the workhorse for studies of production technologies that distinguish more than two inputs, for example, in "KLEM" K(Capital), L(Labor), E(Energy) and M(Material) models and in general equilibrium work.[26] However, users of the translog functional form nowadays typically do not cite the original article, just as the users of the Cobb-Douglas production function today hardly cite Cobb and Douglas any more, and spell translog with a lower case t because it has become so well known.

(BIII)   The Effects of Government Policies

The effects of changes in tax policy on the "cost of capital," such as the investment tax credit and accelerated depreciation, are studied by Jorgenson in a series of joint articles with Robert Hall (Hall and Jorgenson, 1967, 1969). Of course, what matters to producers in a private enterprise market economy is the after-tax "cost of capital." The after-tax "cost of capital" formula developed by Hall and Jorgenson has since become the standard of the profession.

(BIV)   Preferences and Consumer Behavior

During the first decade, preparatory work was done by Jorgenson, in collaboration with Laurits Christensen, on the data required for the estimation of consumer demand functions and the analysis of consumer behavior in a theoretically consistent way. The basic problem consists of estimating the value of consumption in the current period, which is in general not the same as consumer expenditures in the current period, because of the presence of consumer durables, including owner-occupied housing. In order to estimate the quantities of goods consumed in the current period, which is the object of the theory of consumer demand, it is necessary to impute the value of the consumption service flows from the consumer durables capital stock, in the same way as the capital stock used in production. Once again, the "cost of capital" for the consumer durables is indispensable for the construction of consumption data compatible with the received theory of consumer demand. It is in the next decade that a consumer demand model utilizing the same translog functional form used in Christensen, Jorgenson and Lau (1971, 1973) is introduced and estimated.

(BV)   Saving Behavior

The central importance of saving behavior for intertemporal general equilibrium models was recognized by Jorgenson right from the start. Jorgenson initiated his research on saving behavior as part of his work on his unpublished "Model of the Swedish Economy."[27] The Ph.D. dissertation of Laurits Christensen, one of Jorgenson's first graduate students, is on the subject of "Saving and the Rate of Interest." However, it is not until the third decade that Jorgenson returned to do research on this block.

(MI)   Aggregation

The theory of aggregation of economic variables is not a subject of central concern during this first phase. However, the groundwork was laid by Jorgenson for the exploitation of the theory of exact index numbers in the aggregation across commodities (both outputs and inputs) by his meticulous separation of prices and quantities for each disaggregated output and input in the construction of the database.

(MII)   Econometric Methods

Jorgenson (1964, 1966a, 1967a) presents statistical methods for modeling seasonal adjustment and rational distributed lags, which he employs in his econometric studies of investment behavior. In addition, Jorgenson and his collaborators, James Brundy (1971, 1973, 1974) and Jean-Jacques Laffont (1974), develop methods of estimation and statistical inference for a system of nonlinear simultaneous equations in a series of articles on instrumental variables, which are then applied to his models of technology and producer behavior.

(MIII)   The Measurement of Economic Variables

The Measurement of the Price and Quantity of Factor Inputs
Jorgenson strongly believes that economic variables must be measured in precisely the same way as they are specified in the theoretical model. For his research on productivity, initiated in 1966, Jorgenson constructed a database for the factor inputs with the novel features that the quantities of the inputs, including capital and labor, are available in both current and constant prices and that there are detailed imputations of the quantities and values of service flows of capital, including residential housing and consumer durables. Thus, there is a separate price and a separate quantity for every separately distinguished factor input. The concept of the "cost of capital" is embodied in Jorgenson's accounting systems as the price of capital services. In addition, the before and after-tax "costs of capital" are explicitly distinguished. These systems underlie the econometric modeling of producer and consumer behavior in the general equilibrium models described below.

The database thus constructed also lends itself to aggregation across inputs in accordance with the underlying functional structure (e.g., homotheticity or separability), based on either Divisia-type indexes or other exact index number formulas.

The Measurement of National Income
In collaboration with Laurits Christensen (1969, 1970), Jorgenson extended his productivity database to develop systems of national income and product accounts compatible with the theoretical requirements of a general equilibrium model. The result was a completely new set of national income and product accounts data for the United

States. The critical innovation in this accounting system is the integration of accounts for investment, capital stock, and capital services into production and income and expenditure accounts, in both current and constant prices. This feature is essential to econometric modeling of technology and producer behavior and consumer behavior. Conventional accounting systems, such as the United Nations System of National Accounts and the U.S. National Income and Product Accounts, do not successfully integrate capital accounts with income and production accounts. For example, the production account in conventional national accounting systems provides only the output side in constant prices.

The Econometric Modeling of Intertemporal General Equilibrium

In this first, essentially preparatory phase, there is no attempt to put together a general equilibrium model as yet. Methods for the computation of general equilibrium are also not yet a central focus. The emphasis is on the assembly of a correctly specified database and the construction of the component blocks of the intertemporal general equilibrium model. Jorgenson's progress towards his goal of an intertemporal general equilibrium model during the First Decade is presented in Figure 1.1.

1.5   The Second Decade (1973–1983)

(BI)   Investment Behavior

Jorgenson's research on investment behavior was essentially completed during the First Decade. During the Second Decade, Jorgenson focused on the other building blocks, only to return to the investment behavior block in the Third Decade.

(BII)   Technology and Producer Behavior

The Measurement of Productivity and Technical Progress
Jorgenson extended his research on productivity measurements in two directions—to other industrialized countries, including Japan and West Germany, and to individual industrial sectors. He also refined his measurements of the labor input by taking into account the quality of the labor input, as reflected by its characteristics and their changes

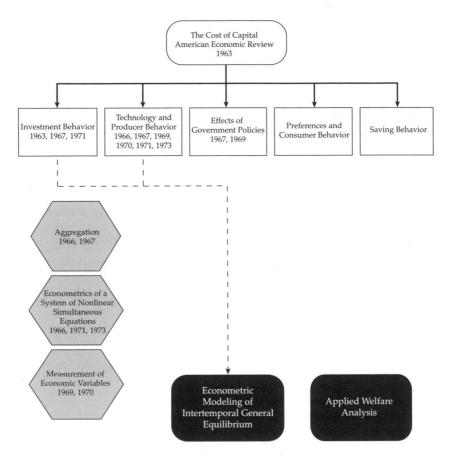

Figure 1.1
The First Decade (1963–1973).

over time, thereby distinguishing between labor hours and human capital. His collaborators in these efforts include Klaus Conrad (1975) on West Germany, Laurits Christensen and Dianne Cummings (1980, 1981) on productivity in nine countries—Canada, France, West Germany, Italy, Japan, South Korea, the Netherlands, the U.K. and the U.S., Mitsuo Ezaki (1973) and Mieko Nishimishu (1978) on Japan, Barbara Fraumeni (1980a, 1980b) on sectoral productivity and Alvaro Pachon (1983a, 1983b) on human capital.

Technology and Producer Behavior
During this decade, Jorgenson pioneered (with Ernst Berndt, 1973 and Edward Hudson, 1974a) the study of multi-sectoral production mod-

els with variable input-output coefficients which depend on relative prices and technological change.[28] Berndt and Jorgenson (1973) initiated what was subsequently known as the "KLEM" approach to the modeling of technology at the individual industrial sector level. In Hudson and Jorgenson (1974a, 1978), nine sectors are explicitly distinguished. This research on the structure of inter-industry technology is partially related to Jorgenson's earlier work on the stability of multisector models. His new approach frees inter-industry analysis from the severe restrictions imposed by the assumptions of fixed input-output coefficients as originally formulated by Wassily Leontief (1941). It also provides the first practical alternative to the purely algebraic RAS method, first proposed by Richard Stone, for the updating and projection of input-output coefficients over time. Subsequently, Jorgenson expanded the model to include thirty-five sectors (with Barbara Fraumeni, 1980a, 1981). These models form the basis of the general equilibrium work to be discussed below. Jorgenson (1983) discusses the modeling of production for general equilibrium analysis.

(BIII)   The Effects of Government Policies

The Concept of the Marginal Effective Tax Rate
Jorgenson initiated the second phase of his research on the modeling of the effects of government policies by introducing the concept of a marginal effective tax rate in a joint article with Alan Auerbach published in 1980. This concept is derived by comparing the "cost of capital" before and after taxes. Auerbach and Jorgenson (1980) calculated effective tax rates under the 1980 U.S. tax law and demonstrated the existence of substantial differences in the marginal effective tax rates across assets. They also presented a proposal for reform of capital income taxation, the First Year Capital Recovery System, that would have equalized marginal effective tax rates for all assets.

The concept of the marginal effective tax rate has also spawned a large literature, both theoretical and empirical. The marginal effective tax rate has now become the standard measure for the evaluation of the effects of taxation on capital.[29]

(BIV)   Preferences and Consumer Behavior

Jorgenson's research on the preferences and consumer behavior block was initiated with his joint article with Christensen and Lau, pub-

lished in 1975. In Christensen, Jorgenson, and Lau (1975), the transcendental logarithmic functional form was used as both a direct and
an indirect utility function to derive flexible complete systems of consumer demand functions that allow arbitrary degrees of substitution
among commodities and taste changes over time. A more detailed
implementation of this approach is presented in a series of joint articles
published in 1975, 1977, 1979 and 1986 by Jorgenson and Lau. These
articles provide an exhaustive treatment of the econometric modeling
of consumer behavior within a representative consumer framework.
Concepts of full income and full consumption are employed in these
models. These concepts require imputations of income from and consumption of leisure and consumer durables, including housing. As
indicated earlier, proper measurements of the imputed flows of income
and consumption services require knowledge of not only the quantities
of the capital stocks but also the "costs of capital."

Jorgenson and Lau, together with Thomas Stoker, developed a new
starting point for the modeling of aggregate consumer behavior in a
series of articles published in 1980, 1981 and 1982. This new approach
contains the following original contributions: (1) implementation of
Lau (1982)'s concept of exact aggregation, making it possible to dispense with the notion of a representative consumer; (2) development
of statistical methods for combining aggregate time series data with
individual cross-section data; (3) the identification from aggregate
consumption data of individual utility functions that can be used as
the basis for social welfare measurements; and (4) the formulation of
exact measures of individual welfare based on the notions of compensating and equivalent variations originated by John Hicks (1942).

(BV)   Saving Behavior

As mentioned earlier, while the importance of saving behavior for
intertemporal general equilibrium was long recognized by Jorgenson,
it is not until the third decade that he returned to undertake research
on this block with Kun-Young Yun.

(MI)   Aggregation

Progress was made on aggregation on several fronts. With regard to
investment and production, the aggregation problem was solved
through disaggregation of the production sectors. Thus, from the

two-sector (Consumption and Investment) model of Christensen, Jorgenson and Lau (1971, 1973), we have, progressively, the nine-sector model of Hudson and Jorgenson (1974a, 1978), and then the thirty-five-sector model of Fraumeni and Jorgenson (1981). Within each sector distinguished, the outputs and inputs are aggregated based on separability assumptions, employing essentially the Törnquist implementation of Divisia index numbers, which turn out to be exact for the transcendental logarithmic function.

With regard to consumer demand, the aggregation across commodities was also carried out based on separability assumptions for each commodity group. The problem of aggregation across consumer units was solved through the empirical implementation of Lau (1982)'s exact aggregation approach in Jorgenson, Lau and Stoker (1980a, 1981 and 1982).

(MII)   Econometric Methods

Jorgenson further refined statistical methods for systems of nonlinear simultaneous equations with Ronald Gallant (1979).

(MIII)   The Measurement of Economic Variables

The Measurement of the Price and Quantity of Factor Inputs
Jorgenson, together with Laurits Christensen and Dianne Cummings, developed the same system of national income and product accounts as implemented earlier for the United States by Jorgenson and Laurits Christensen for Canada, France, Germany, Italy, Japan, Korea, the Netherlands, and the U.K. in 1980 and 1981. The data were used as the basis for an international comparison of the levels of rates of growth of productivity.

The Measurement of National Income
Similar sets of national income, product, and expenditure account data were also developed by Jorgenson and his collaborators for the same set of countries. These data form the bases of his extensive empirical studies of technology and preferences of these countries.

The Reconciliation of Sectoral Consumption and Production
A special data problem arises in general equilibrium analysis, in the sense that the sectoral disaggregation of the data on production is in

general incompatible with the sectoral disaggregation of the data on consumption. For example, aggregate consumer expenditure on food, even in the absence of net change in stocks and international trade, is not necessarily equal to (and in general will be greater than) the total revenue of the food production sector. This is because the actual aggregate consumer expenditure on food includes transportation costs and other distribution margins that are not considered to be the output of the food production sector but rather the output of the transportation and distribution sectors.[30] It is therefore necessary to net out the transportation and distribution margins from the consumption side before equilibrium is to be realized in the food market through the equilibration of supply and demand. The same holds for all of the other sectors.[31] This reconciliation of the production and consumption data was achieved by Jorgenson and his collaborators prior to the general equilibrium analysis.

The Econometric Modeling of Intertemporal General Equilibrium

Computation of general equilibrium was carried out for production in Hudson and Jorgenson (1974a), using a nine-sector model of the U.S. economy. This was followed by a thirty-five sector model of production for the U.S. economy by Jorgenson and Fraumeni in 1981. Jorgenson's 1980 and 1981 articles with Lau and Stoker represent general equilibrium computations based on their econometric model of aggregate consumer behavior and the multi-sector model of production of Hudson and Jorgenson (1974a) combined. During this decade, however, the general equilibria achieved are not yet truly intertemporal but rather consist of a sequence of single-period general equilibria.

Jorgenson's progress in the Second Decade is presented in Figure 1.2.

1.6   The Third Decade (1983–1993)

(BI)   Investment Behavior

Jorgenson and Yun (1986a, 1986b) revisited the question of investment and capital accumulation.

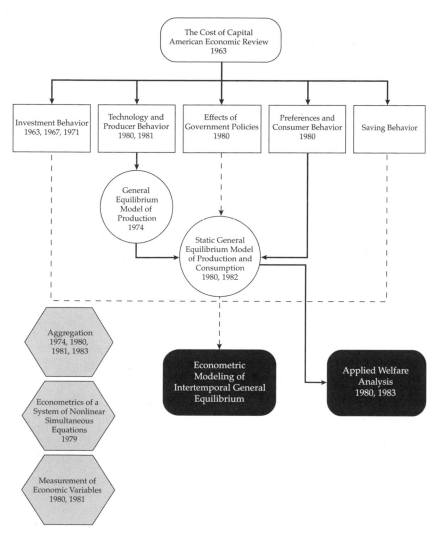

Figure 1.2
The Second Decade (1974–1983).

(BII)   Technology and Producer Behavior

The Measurement of Productivity and Technical Progress
Jorgenson's research on productivity at the disaggregated level of
individual industries culminated in his 1987 book with Frank Gollop
and Barbara Fraumeni, *Productivity and U.S. Economic Growth,*

published by the Harvard University Press. This book contains by far the most detailed and refined data ever compiled on productivity in the U.S. economy. For example, the data on labor input distinguish among 81,600 categories of labor input, broken down by age, sex, education, occupation, class of employment, and industry. Jorgenson's research on productivity is summarized in this book and in his invited lecture commemorating the 50th Anniversary of the Conference on Research in Income and Wealth. This lecture has appeared in a volume entitled, *Fifty Years of Economic Measurement*, published by the University of Chicago Press in 1990.

Technology and Producer Behavior
By the Third Decade, the technology and producer behavior block is essentially complete. Jorgenson's research on modeling technology and producer behavior is summarized in his survey article (Jorgenson, 1986).

(BIII)   The Effects of Government Policies

Jorgenson's contributions to this block include an analysis of the economic impact of the Tax Reform Act of 1986 in the United States, co-authored with Kun-Young Yun and published in the Journal of Political Economy in 1990. Jorgenson's extensive research on marginal effective tax rates is summarized in his Lindahl Lectures at Uppsala University, which have been published by the Oxford University Press in 1991 in a book entitled, *Tax Reform and the Cost of Capital*, also co-authored with Yun.

(BIV)   Preferences and Consumer Behavior

By the Third Decade, the preferences and consumer behavior block is also essentially complete. Jorgenson's research on consumer behavior is summarized in his Presidential Address to the Econometric Society (Jorgenson (1990a)).

(BV)   Saving Behavior

In Jorgenson and Yun (1986), consumption-saving decisions are modeled as an intertemporal optimization problem, with intertemporally additive preferences. The solution takes the form of an "Euler equation," an approach pioneered by Hall (1978). Expectations play an important role in this approach and Jorgenson and Yun implement their model based on the assumption of "rational expectations" or "perfect foresight."[32] With the addition of the saving behavior block, and the adoption of the "rational expectations" assumption, true intertemporal general equilibrium is finally achieved.

(MI)   Aggregation

An important new development is Jorgenson's research on the aggregation of utilities across consumer units with Daniel Slesnick (1983, 1984a, 1985b and 1987b). In this series of articles, Jorgenson and Slesnick introduce cardinal and interpersonally comparable measures of individual welfare, based on empirically estimated and appropriately normalized indirect utility functions for all households. By contrast the measures of individual welfare developed by Hicks are ordinal and not interpersonally comparable. Jorgenson and Slesnick have formulated social welfare functions that are essentially sums of such individual utility functions. The concept of a social welfare function was originated by Abram Bergson. These social welfare functions have applications in applied welfare analysis.

(MII)   Econometric Methods

Jorgenson further refined statistical methods for systems of nonlinear simultaneous equations with Thomas Stoker (1986).

(MIII)   The Measurement of Economic Variables

By the Third Decade, the specification and measurement of economic variables for the purpose of econometric modeling of intertemporal general equilibrium has been essentially perfected. Jorgenson, with Barbara Fraumeni (1989a, 1989b, 1992a and 1992b), successfully incorporated human capital into the national income, product, expenditure and wealth accounts.

The Econometric Modeling of Intertemporal General Equilibrium

By the Third Decade, Jorgenson has completed the different building blocks required for an econometrically estimated intertemporal general equilibrium model and has begun to combine them together in various ways. His objective has finally come to fruition. Jorgenson is the originator of the econometric approach to intertemporal general equilibrium modeling. His approach, as we have attempted to outline above, is to construct separate econometric models of producer and consumer behavior, including investment and saving behavior, and to combine them to form empirical general equilibrium models.

The organizing principle of Jorgenson's approach to intertemporal general equilibrium modeling is the notion of an intertemporal price system. This price system balances supply and demand for products and factors of production. In addition, the price system links the prices of assets in every time period to the discounted value of future prices of capital services, that is, future "costs of capital." This forward-looking feature of an intertemporal price system is combined with backward linkages among investment, capital stock, and capital services in modeling the dynamics of long-run economic growth empirically.

Jorgenson and Yun (1986) present an example of one implementation of an intertemporal general equilibrium model based on rational expectations. The model was used to analyze the impact of tax policy on U.S. economic growth through a very detailed representation of the "cost of capital" for individual assets. Alternative tax policies generate different costs of capital and different growth paths. These alternative growth paths are evaluated in terms of their impact on the time path of present and future consumption for the economy.

The model of producer behavior employed by Jorgenson and Yun is a direct outgrowth of the model originated by Christensen, Jorgenson, and Lau in 1971 and 1973. The model of consumer behavior employed by Jorgenson and Yun is a representative consumer model of the type presented by Christensen, Jorgenson, and Lau in 1975. Saving behavior is modeled with an "Euler equation" approach that was introduced by Hall (1978). The combined model was also used to analyze economic policies in terms of their impact on social welfare in a series of joint articles by Jorgenson and Slesnick, published between 1983 and 1987. Jorgenson's article, "Environmental Regulation and U.S. Economic Growth," co-authored with Peter Wilcoxen and published in the Rand Journal of Economics in 1990, provides an example of another implementation of his econometric approach to intertemporal general equilibrium modeling. This article presents a highly disaggregated model of the impact of environmental regulations on U.S.

economic growth. Detailed data on the costs of compliance imposed on individual industries by these regulations are utilized in modeling the impact of environmental policy. Alternative policies generate different costs of production for these industries and different growth paths for the economy.

The general equilibrium model of production employed by Jorgenson and Wilcoxen is based on the thirty-five sector model of production originated by Jorgenson and Fraumeni in 1981. The model of consumer behavior included in the Jorgenson-Wilcoxen model is based on the work of Jorgenson, Lau, Slesnick, and Stoker and dispenses with the notion of a representative consumer. The difference between the Jorgenson-Wilcoxen model and the Jorgenson-Yun model lies in the assumption of whether the economy can be represented by a single representative consumer or by many heterogeneous consumers.

Jorgenson's econometric approach to intertemporal general equilibrium modeling is summarized in his survey article with Peter Wilcoxen (1993c). Jorgenson's progress in the Third Decade is presented in Figure 1.3.

1.7   Future Research Opportunities

The Econometric Modeling of Intertemporal General Equilibrium

The five building blocks, investment behavior, technology and producer behavior, the effects of government policies, preferences and consumer behavior and saving behavior, have all been completed. The methodological problems of aggregation, econometrics of a system of nonlinear simultaneous equations, and the measurement of economic variables, have all been satisfactorily, and in some cases, more than satisfactorily solved. Jorgenson has finally achieved his goal of constructing an econometrically estimated intertemporal general equilibrium model, a major milestone in the annals of economics. In fact, Jorgenson and his collaborators have constructed more than one such model and have applied them very successfully for the analysis of social welfare. Are there any remaining challenges left?

Three promising directions of research can be identified. The first consists of the addition of an explicit international block, incorporating exports and imports of goods and services disaggregated by

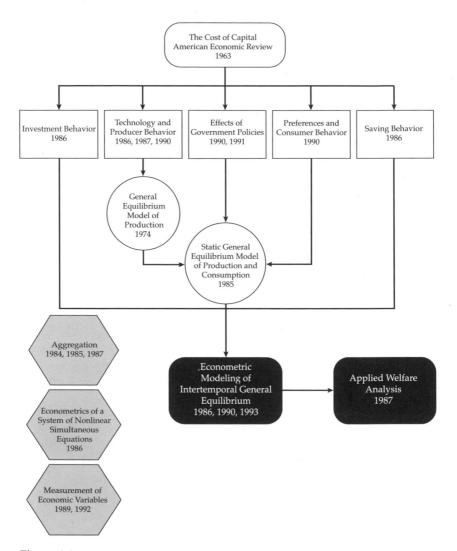

Figure 1.3
The Third Decade (1984–1993).

sector, to the intertemporal general equilibrium model. This appears reasonably straightforward and readily achievable, although compatibility of the import-export data with the production data and the consumption data can be a potential difficulty. The second is more challenging. It consists of attempting to replace the representative agent model by a model that recognizes explicitly the existence of heterogeneous agents, with different tastes and risk and time preferences and possibly even diverse expectations.[33] The difficulty lies in implementing such a model under the assumptions of forward-looking behavior—what does the "rational expectations" hypothesis mean in this context? The traditional Euler equation approach does not appear to work in this case. However, it is also possible that even with diverse subjective prior probability distributions an intertemporal general equilibrium can still be sustained because of the presence of market imperfections, risk aversion, and transactions costs.[34] The third consists of the addition of a financial block, including possibly money. This last task is likely to be the most challenging but also potentially the most rewarding. However, it is also possible that in contrast to static single-period general equilibrium models, which normally cannot find a meaningful role for money, an intertemporal general equilibrium model with intrinsic uncertainty may find a real, significant role for money. All of this awaits further research.

The Future of the "Cost of Capital"

What extensions are possible to the very fruitful concept of the "Cost of Capital," which Jorgenson introduced thirty years ago?

A natural extension of the concept, which is also related to the task of adding a financial block, is to integrate it with the concept of the "cost of capital" as used in the theory of corporate finance. Under this theory, the "cost of capital" depends on the capital structure, that is, the relative proportions of debt and equity finance. The capital structure, however, ought to be determined endogenously, together with the payout policy (including dividends as well as systematic repurchases of shares), through general equilibrium in the market of financial assets. In an intertemporal general equilibrium model with assets, the demand for new gross fixed investment is derived from the demand for physical capital and the existing stock of capital, as well as the Jorgensonian "cost of capital." The finance "cost of capital" may be identified as the rate of interest in the Jorgensonian "cost of capital" formula. In general equilibrium, the supply of investable funds, both debt and equity, should be equal to the value of the new investment goods demanded. The market will be cleared through the equilibration of the rate of interest/finance "cost of capital."

A second extension is the explicit recognition of risk and uncertainty in production in the "cost of capital" formula. A third extension is the incorporation of the effect of technical progress, including embodied technical progress in the "cost of capital." We can also consider the "cost of capital" under increasing returns and/or irreversibility of fixed investment,[35] or distinguish between the private and the social "costs of capital" in the presence of externalities. In short, the Jorgensonian "cost of capital" is such a central concept in economic analysis that its possible extensions are limited only by one's time and imagination.

1.8   Concluding Remarks

Dale Jorgenson is clearly one of the few visionary leaders in the economics profession. His contributions to the science of economics have been enormous and his influence is felt in every field. The time for large-scale econometrically estimated "intertemporal general equilibrium" models, especially their application to applied welfare analysis, has finally arrived, thanks to the quantum leap in our computational ability. The concept of the "cost of capital," is critical to the theoretical specification, the measurement of data, the econometric estimation and the general equilibrium computation of an intertemporal general equilibrium model. In another decade, the use of intertemporal general equilibrium models will become as common as the use of input-output analysis. Econometrically estimated intertemporal general equilibrium models will be the new techniques of choice for applied welfare analysis and Dale Jorgenson will be remembered as the pioneer.

Notes

1. D.W. Jorgenson, "Capital Theory and Investment Behavior," (1963), pp. 247–259.
2. This article has been identified as a Citation Classic based on the Social Sciences Citation Index.
3. See Jorgenson (1963), p. 249.
4. The assumption of exponential depreciation is not critical to the concept of a "cost of capital" although the precise form of the "cost of capital" formula will differ with the form of the mortality density function of capital.
5. Thus, the higher the rate of appreciation of the investment good is, the lower the user cost of capital will be.
6. In the case of constant returns to scale in production, the level of output is not determinate, even though the capital-output and labor-output ratios are determinate. However, it remains true that only the prices of the current period matter.
7. On this point, see also Arrow (1964).

8. For a discussion of the relationship between Jorgenson's "cost of capital" and Tobin (1969)'s "q", see Hayashi (2000), this volume.

9. See Hall and Jorgenson (1967). Of course, the exact "cost of capital" formula will vary, depending on the exact provisions of the income tax laws.

10. This concept of "cost of capital" should not be confused with the concept of the "cost of capital" used in the theory of finance, as, for example, by Modigliani and Miller (1958). Of course, in general equilibrium, the two concepts of "cost of capital" must be such that the market for investment goods as well as the market for finance are simultaneously cleared.

11. This research was cited as the primary justification for Jorgenson's award of the John Bates Clark Medal by the American Economic Association in 1971.

12. See, e.g., Barro (1974).

13. For a discussion of the problems of the "calibration" approach, see Lau (1984).

14. It is of course true that one can use sensitivity analysis to mitigate the potential error that may result from reliance on a single observation. However, ultimately, for applied analysis, one needs to know what is likely to be the best representation of the real situation. A series of conditional statements will not be very helpful.

15. That saving (investment) or the "cost of capital" must be exogenous is a consequence of the fact that in a one-period model, there is, technically, no future, and any positive saving, or investment, cannot be optimal within the model.

16. Strictly speaking, on the probability distribution of relative factor prices in future periods.

17. The assumptions necessary for the economy to behave as if it were a single consumer are identical and homothetic preferences for all households.

18. See Jorgenson and Lau (1977).

19. Ideally, in a proper measurement of real GDP, one should also include the depletion of natural resources, the degradation of the environment, and the increase in the stock of knowledge.

20. Of critical importance are the quantities of the terminal period capital stocks.

21. The problem of sensitivity to the terminal conditions does not disappear, but can be minimized by lengthening the time horizon. When the terminal time is sufficiently far away the solution near the initial time will be virtually insensitive to the terminal conditions.

22. See Jorgenson (1963).

23. These studies include Hall and Jorgenson (1967, 1969), Jorgenson and Siebert (1968a, 1968b, 1972), and Jorgenson and Stephenson (1967a, 1967b, 1969).

24. Christensen, Jorgenson and Lau (1971, 1973).

25. On this point, see, for example, Lau (1978).

26. Christensen, Jorgenson and Lau (1973) has also been identified as a Citation Classic based on the Social Science Citation Index.

27. While the model itself was never published, parts of it found their way into the Ph.D. dissertation of Richard Parks (1971).

28. This is a difficult undertaking. See the attempt by Arrow and Hoffenberg (1959).

29. See, e.g., Auerbach (1983a, 1983b, 1984, 1987), Bradford and Fullerton (1981), Fullerton (1984, 1989) and King and Fullerton (1984).

30. Indirect taxes are an additional complication.

31. It is, of course, also possible to add the transportation and distribution margins back to the production side. In principle, that is probably preferred, because consumer demand is really for food actually delivered to the market, and not separately for food at the point of production and for transportation and distribution services. However, that will require a major change in the way the sectors are defined and input-output data are collected in inter-industry analysis.

32. Unfortunately, the Euler equation approach does not generalize easily to the case of more than one distinct type of consumer units.

33. More properly, with possibly diverse subjective prior probability distributions on future prices.

34. The analogy is that in the abstraction of a frictionless world, an object is either at rest or once it begins moving horizontally, it will continue moving at the same velocity for ever. It takes the existence of friction to make it possible for the object to come to rest again.

35. Arrow (1968) considered the case of irreversible investment.

2

The International Consequences of the Leading Consumption Tax Proposals

Robert E. Hall

2.1 Introduction

Economists have long advocated that the general revenue requirements of the federal government should be met through a national
consumption tax. Recently, consumption taxes have begun to receive
serious consideration in Washington. As we move toward a major tax
reform based on the consumption tax principle, economists need to
pay more attention to practical issues of the reform. Some important
issues relate to the relation of the U.S. and world economies, some
relate to the transition from the current tax system to a consumption
tax, and in fact there is a good deal of overlap—the international
issues are largely transitional issues.

I start by describing the various consumption tax systems that are
under consideration. These are three variants of the value-added tax
(including the Hall-Rabushka flat tax), the sales tax, and the personal
consumption tax. Then I lay out the basic effects of the taxes in an
open economy and draw certain conclusions about the transition,
including the effects on the real exchange rate and trade deficit.
Finally, I consider the implications of nominal wage rigidity in order
to describe the effects of tax reform on nominal prices and the nominal
exchange rate.

2.2 Taxes Considered

A central topic in the design of taxes in open economies is border
adjustment. Under GATT, it is permissible to rebate some taxes for
exports and impose taxes on imports. These border adjustments are
seen as aspects of the tax system and not as barriers to trade. Border
adjustment is immensely popular among lawmakers because they are

thought to convey an advantage to domestic producers. I will discuss the substance of border adjustments in a later section.

The taxes I will consider are all equivalent or close to equivalent. They take a number of different approaches to measuring consumption and taxing it. All the taxes drive a wedge between work effort and consumption. None drives a wedge between current consumption and later consumption. The latter wedge is the harmful aspect of an income tax.

A *value-added tax* (VAT) is a tax on firms on the difference between total revenue and purchases of intermediate products from other firms. Purchases of capital goods are counted as intermediate products. The VAT is a consumption tax because it is imposed, in effect, as an excise tax on consumption goods. I will assume that firms quote their prices inclusive of the VAT. With respect to foreign trade, the VAT may include border adjustments. The *VAT without border adjustments* includes revenue from foreign sales in the base and permits deductions for purchases of intermediate products from foreign sources. The *VAT with border adjustments* excludes exports and imports, or, equivalently, imposes an import duty at the VAT rate and pays a rebate on exports. Finally, the *Hall-Rabushka VAT*[1] is a variant of the VAT without border adjustments in which the firm deducts the wages it pays and there is a personal wage tax at the VAT rate. The motivation for this complication is that it permits easy administration of an exemption, in order to make the VAT progressive. The Hall-Rabushka proposal is usually called the "flat tax," although it really has two brackets, one at zero and the other at a single positive rate. Many popular discussions of the flat tax do not refer to the Hall-Rabushka proposal and may not even refer to consumption taxes.

A *consumption sales tax* is a tax imposed on sellers of consumption goods at the point where they go into the hands of final consumers. Again, I assume that firms quote prices inclusive of tax. I will also assume that the tax is adjusted at the border—it is imposed on imported consumption goods, and all exported goods are free from tax.

A *personal consumption tax* measures consumption at the household level on a cash-flow basis. It is a personal income tax with an unlimited deduction for saving. The Nunn-Domenici U.S.A. tax includes a personal consumption tax as well as an eleven percent VAT.

The tax base for the VAT with border adjustment, the consumption sales tax, and the personal consumption tax is literally consumption as measured in the national income accounts, except that housing is treated as a consumer durable. The tax base for the VAT without border adjustment and the Hall-Rabushka tax differs by the amount of the trade surplus. But, since the present discounted value of the trade surplus must be the net indebtedness of the U.S. to the rest of the world, which was determined by history, the VAT without border adjustment differs from a consumption tax only by a lump sum.

2.3   Basic Effects

To explain the basic effects, I will make the simplifying assumption that there is only one kind of output. As numeraire, I will take the consumption good after VAT or sales tax but before personal tax. I assume competition in all markets. I denote the marginal product of labor by λ. The prices I will consider are:

1. The wage paid by the firm,

2. The wage received by the worker,

3. The price of traded goods paid by the export customer or received by the import supplier.

Table 2.1 shows the effects on these relative prices of the various taxes.

Explanations of the entries in the table 2.1:

a. For the two VATs and the sales tax, the goods-work wedge occurs within the firm. The equilibrium wage at zero profit is equal to the net after-tax selling price, $1 - t$, multiplied by the marginal product of labor, λ.

b. For the three taxes where the wage component is collected at the personal level, there is no tax wedge at the firm level.

c. For the two VATs and the sales tax, the wage paid and the wage received are the same.

d. For the three taxes where the wage component is collected at the personal level, there is no tax wedge at that level.

e. Hence all six taxes drive the same wedge between the benefit of working and the price of consumption goods. The wedge is the inescapable inefficiency of taxation when it is impossible to tax the consumption of time at home.

Table 2.1
Prices relative to domestic consumption goods

	VAT with border adjustment	VAT without border adjustment	Consumption sales tax	Hall-Rabushka	Personal consumption tax	Personal income tax
Cost of labor to firm						
note	$(1-t)\lambda$ a	$(1-t)\lambda$ a	$(1-t)\lambda$ a	λ b	λ b	λ b
Benefit of work to worker						
note	$(1-t)\lambda$ c,e	$(1-t)\lambda$ c,e	$(1-t)\lambda$ c,e	$(1-t)\lambda$ d,e	$(1-t)\lambda$ d,e	$(1-t)\lambda$ d,e
Traded goods						
note	$1-t$ f	1 g	$1-t$ f	1 g	1 g	1 g

f. The VAT with border adjustment and the sales tax raise the price of consumption goods above traded goods, because the tax is levied on imports and rebated on exports.

g. Consumption goods and traded goods have the same price for taxes without border adjustments.

As I noted in the introduction, the immediate effects of a move to a consumption tax involve not only the relative price effects displayed in table 2.1, but also issues of wage rigidity and changes in interest rates. Still, some important inferences follow from the table.

First, under either the standard VAT (with or without border adjustment) or under the sales tax, the real product wage must fall by the amount of the tax. Under the existing income tax, wages are set on a pre-tax basis, whereas under the VATs or sales tax, wages are set on an after-tax basis. Wages would remain on a pretax basis under Hall-Rabushka or the personal consumption tax. Most of the issues associated with the lowering of the real product wage have to do with wage rigidity, so I will defer further discussion of this point until the next section.

Second, under the VAT with border adjustment or under the sales tax, the price of traded goods falls below the price of consumption goods by the amount of the tax. These taxes are hugely attractive to politicians because the export subsidy and import tax are thought to improve something called "competitiveness." This idea receives no support from economics. Real exchange rates will change to offset the tax change. Whether this occurs as a change in the nominal rate as well depends on the behavior of the price level, a topic deferred to the next section.

2.3.1   Stock Prices

As a simplification, think of equity as direct ownership of capital goods. The consumption tax depresses the purchasing power of the existing capital stock.[2] Domestic equity holders suffer capital losses from consumption tax reform. The VAT with border adjustment and the sales tax keep foreign equity holders whole because these taxes lower the price of traded goods in terms of domestic consumption goods by the same amount.[3] The original VAT and Hall-Rabushka impose the same loss on foreign equity holders as on domestic ones.

2.4 Nominal Prices and Price Measurement

Prediction of the effects on nominal prices as the result of the transition to a consumption tax enters the tricky territory of price-level economics. Under monetary neutrality, the price level is chosen unilaterally by the central bank. An event such as tax reform affects the price level only to the extent that it makes the central bank choose a different target.

With monetary non-neutrality, there is more to say, though of course the central bank unambiguously chooses the price level in the longer run. The biggest issue is how nominal prices and wages achieve the decline in the real product wage required under a VAT or sales tax. Either the price level must rise or the wage level must fall. If the latter is ruled out as impractical, then the economy needs a quick burst of inflation. If the inflation triggers indexation, there may be further problems. British adoption of the VAT in 1979 put the economy through this type of cycle.

The central problem is the wage contract. Under the income tax, wages are set on a pre-tax basis. Workers pay taxes out of their earnings. The taxes that put wages on an after-tax basis—the VATs and the sales tax—call for either a price change or a wage change to accommodate the switch. One way is for wages to fall by the amount of the tax. Except for effects caused by changes in tax rates, there would then be no change in after-tax wages, and prices would not have to change. Evidence on the nature of the wage contract suggests it would be difficult to bring about the immediate wage cut. The other way to accommodate the change is for prices to rise. Then the wage contract is honored in nominal terms, but real after-tax earnings are kept stable in the face of tax reform by the price increase. In order for a price increase to work, it is essential that there be no feedback from prices to wages. In an economy with full cost-of-living escalation of wages, no price increase would be large enough to get the real after-tax wage back down to its appropriate level.

The best answer would appear to be to encourage firms to reset prices on the day the tax becomes effective by the amount of the tax, and then to define the cost-of-living index to exclude the VAT or sales tax. The goal is to get the price level to rise immediately but not to develop any momentum, and to prevent wages from changing at all.

The taxes that leave wages on a pre-tax basis—Hall-Rabushka and the personal consumption tax—do not encounter this problem at all.

The existing wage and price levels remain the appropriate levels after tax reform.

The assumption I will make in the remainder of the paper is that the standard VATs (but not Hall-Rabushka) and the sales tax cause a one-time increase in the prices of consumption goods and the other taxes leave the price level unchanged. This assumption is stated in the first line of table 2.2.

2.4.1 Nominal Exchange Rates

As I noted in the previous section, the destination VAT and the sales tax drive wedges between domestic consumption goods prices and the prices of traded goods. As a result, they affect real exchange rates in the same way. If, as suggested above, the right accommodation to a VAT or sales tax is an immediate jump in the nominal price level, then nominal exchange rates need not change. However, it will not be possible to introduce a VAT as a complete surprise and raise the price level by twenty percent in the same millisecond. The foreign exchange market will be perturbed by expectations, as I discuss in the next section.

These conclusions are summarized in the second and third lines of table 2.2.

2.4.2 Value of Debt Claims

With respect to debt, the issue is the change in the price level. It is both realistic and desirable for the domestic price of consumption goods to rise by the amount of a VAT or sales tax. Thus, debt holders suffer a loss of purchasing power over domestic consumption goods equal to the amount of the tax, for these taxes. Foreign debt holders come out even in relation to traded goods for the destination-basis VAT and the sales tax and lose under the origin-basis VAT. No changes in any of these nominal variables or in the purchasing power of debt would need to occur under Hall-Rabushka or a personal consumption tax. The conclusions about the purchasing power of debt are summarized in the fourth and fifth lines of table 2.2.

Table 2.2
Effects on nominal measures

	VAT with border adjustment	VAT without border adjustment	Consumption sales tax	Hall-Rabushka	Personal consumption tax
Nominal price of consumption goods	↑	↑	↑	0	0
Nominal price of traded goods	0	↑	0	0	0
Nominal exchange rate	0	↓	0	0	0
Value of dollar debt in relation to consumption goods	↓	↓	↓	0	0
Value of dollar debt in relation to traded goods	0	↓	0	0	0

Notes: ↑ means rise by the amount of the tax;
↓ means fall by the amount of the tax; and 0 means no change.

2.5   Effects of the Anticipation of Tax Reform

The effects of a switch to a consumption tax in a closed economy, announced in advance, are discussed in detail in Hall (1971). At the moment of the switch, there is a discontinuous drop in consumption. Prior to the switch, consumption gradually rises. After the drop caused by the new tax, consumption gradually rises again until it reaches its new steady state. Investment does the opposite—it declines in anticipation of the tax change, jumps upward at the time of the change, and then gradually declines.

There is an incentive for consumers to hoard consumption goods before the consumption tax and then to consume them later. If the consumption tax cannot be imposed on hoarded goods and hoarding is technologically feasible, the equilibrium will be quite different.

For a brief instant surrounding the switch date, the real interest rate, stated in terms of consumption goods after tax, is infinitely negative.[4] That is why consumption falls by a discrete amount. Alternatively, if the interest rate is stated in terms of investment goods (or consumption goods before tax), nothing exciting happens to the interest rate on the switch date. The interest rate gradually rises during the consumption bubble before the switch date and then gradually falls during the investment boom that follows the tax reform.

These conclusions about the interest rate can be restated in nominal terms under the assumptions given earlier. For the VATs and the sales tax, where there is a discontinuous increase in the nominal price of consumption goods, the nominal interest rate will be stable during the period of the switch. There will be an incentive to hoard consumer goods. For Hall-Rabushka and the personal consumption tax, where nominal consumption goods prices do not jump and so the nominal interest rate is stated in terms of after-tax consumption, there will be a brief period of infinitely negative nominal interest rates. A different way to think about the same point is that these two taxes depress the nominal value of existing capital goods. In order to prevent businesses from selling their capital just before tax reform and buying it back just after, the opportunity cost of funds needs to be negative over that brief period.

Note that the incentive to hoard consumer goods is just as strong, in principle, under Hall-Rabushka and the personal consumption tax as under the taxes that cause discontinuous increases in the price of consumer goods. Consumers can take advantage of infinitely negative interest rates to hoard beneficially, even though the price of consumer goods does not go up.

In the real world, these effects between announcement and implementation would not be nearly as dramatic as theory suggests. By making the effect of the tax immediate or even retroactive, most of the shocks can be limited. Under the VATs or sales tax, the public will try to beat the tax-induced price increase as soon it appears likely that the tax reform will occur. Under Hall-Rabushka or the personal consumption tax, businesses will defer investment in order to take advantage of the tax incentives for investment that will be part of the reform. In the resulting weak economy, the interest rate will be low and used capital goods prices will be soft. Consumer hoarding will take the form of borrowing at low rates to purchase consumer goods and also the purchase of used capital goods for consumption purposes.

The extension to an open economy can be divided into three cases:

1. *VAT (with border adjustment) and sales tax.* With these taxes, as shown in table 2.2, the dollar price of tradable goods and the exchange rate do not change as the tax goes into effect. The only potential source of dislocation in the world economy would be the effects from anticipatory hoarding by U.S. consumers. A boom before the tax change followed by a contraction in consumer goods sales would cause an immediate appreciation of the dollar followed by a gradual depreciation.

2. *VAT without border adjustment.* In this case, table 2.2 shows that the dollar price of tradable goods will rise after tax reform and the dollar will depreciate to offset that rise, leaving the foreign-currency price of U.S. goods unchanged. The depreciation will occur upon announcement of the tax reform. From announcement to implementation, the foreign prices of U.S. goods will be unusually low. Foreign demand for U.S. goods will swell at the same time that U.S. consumers are hoarding goods to beat the forthcoming consumption tax. The U.S. interest rate will rise, which will limit the amount of the anticipatory depreciation.

3. *Hall-Rabushka and personal consumption tax.* Table 2.2 shows no effects from these taxes on domestic prices, traded goods prices, or the exchange rate. To the extent that weak investment brings a lower interest rate in the period between announcement and implementation, the dollar will depreciate at the time of announcement and then

gradually appreciate. Exports would be stimulated to make up some of the slack in the economy.

2.6 Interaction of the U.S. Economy and the Rest of the World

U.S. capital markets are tightly integrated with those of other major industrial countries, notably Japan, Britain, and Germany. Those countries rely on a mixture of consumption and income taxation and presumably would not change their tax systems upon U.S. tax reform. The analysis of tax reform in the open U.S. economy has to consider the general equilibrium in a world economy with heterogeneous tax systems.

The general equilibrium analysis encounters a basic problem, as a number of earlier authors have observed. High-growth countries like Japan should have chronically higher interest rates, according to the life-cycle theory of consumption. In fact, real interest rates seem to be roughly equal among the major countries with open capital markets. Although expected changes in real exchange rates can support differences in real interest rates in the short run, neither theory nor actual experience suggests that this mechanism works in the long run.

Tax reform in the United States would encounter the same paradox. How can the U.S. interest rate fall if interest rates in Japan and elsewhere remain locked in place by the life-cycle principle? The answer to both the growth and tax paradoxes appears to be that real interest rates for equivalent traded securities are equalized in world markets but households see rewards for saving that are sufficiently different to satisfy the life-cycle model separately for each country's parameters.

Differences in internal capital markets among countries may be an important part of the resolution of the paradox. For example, direct controls on borrowing may prevent Japanese households from the high levels of debt that would be needed to satisfy the life-cycle model's prescription for scheduling consumption in a high-growth, low-interest economy. On the other hand, the U.S. consumer is in fairly direct contact with world capital markets. Interest rates in the most important credit market for households, the mortgage market, are tightly linked to world rates.

In world equilibrium, firms and intermediaries in countries with naturally high interest rates (with high growth rates and high income tax rates) will be net suppliers of bonds in world markets. Equilibrium occurs where the marginal cost of issuing more bonds is equated, after risk adjustment, to the costs of other sources of funds and to the marginal benefit from investing the funds. Patterns of specialization in the issuance of securities should track differences in fundamental interest.

In the resulting equilibrium, there may be scope for a considerable effect of tax reform on U.S. interest rates. In the first place, the United States is about a third of the total world capital market. Second, relatively modest changes in the pattern of specialization in world securities markets may be enough to reach the new equilibrium in which the world interest rates have moved most of the way to the point predicted by the life-cycle model for the United States.

Notes

1. Hall and Rabushka (1995).
2. See Hall (1996).
3. This point may be easier to see if one supposes that the price of domestic consumption goods rises by the amount of the tax. Neither the price of equity nor the price of traded goods changes at all. Domestic shareholders suffer a loss of purchasing power, but foreign equity holders can still buy the same volume of goods with their shares as they could before tax reform.
4. See Hall (1971), p. 235.

3   The Cost of Capital and Regulation

Laurits R. Christensen

3.1   Introduction

Dale W. Jorgenson's work has spawned advances in numerous areas of economic research, including investment, productivity, econometrics, and consumer behavior. The unifying theme for all of this work has been Dale's careful treatment of capital as a factor of production, which dates back at least to his pioneering 1963 paper, "Capital Theory and Investment Behavior" (Jorgenson, 1963). Like many economists at this conference, I was profoundly influenced by Dale early in my career. I began my graduate studies at Berkeley in 1964, and I became Dale's thesis advisee in 1965. My entire academic career, including virtually all of my professional publications, was spent developing themes that were motivated by Dale's seminal contributions to economic literature.

During the first half of my academic career I was heavily involved in developing capital accounts at the national level for the United States and other countries. This work was presented in Christensen and Jorgenson (1969, 1970, 1973a, 1973b), Christensen, Cummings, and Jorgenson (1978, 1980, 1981), and Christensen and Cummings (1981). During the second half of my academic career my work included development of capital accounts for numerous firms and industries in the U.S. economy. This work included Caves, Christensen, and Swanson (1980), Caves, Christensen, and Tretheway (1981), Christensen, Cummings, and Schoech (1983), and Christensen, Christensen, Degen, and Schoech (1989).

In 1987 I completed my academic career, but through my consulting activities I have continued to be concerned with the proper measurement of capital. My work has focused on the measurement of productivity, as well as providing proper incentives for the improvement of productivity, for regulated industries. The proper treatment of capital as a factor of production is a key element of this work.

Traditional rate-of-return (cost-of-service) regulation in the United States consists of establishing a revenue requirement based on the actual or forecasted cost of service, including an allowed return on invested capital. As I discuss below, regulatory agencies have adopted simplified measures of capital costs that are not necessarily consistent with true economic capital costs. This can lead to improperly measured capital costs, resulting in mismeasured revenue requirements and prices that do not mimic those that would hold in a competitive environment. Specifically, regulatory agencies have used the nominal cost of capital rather than the real cost of capital in establishing revenue requirements. This means that during inflationary times capital costs for any particular asset are too high early in the asset's useful life and too low late in its useful life. This has been called a "front-end load" in capital charges.

During the 1970s and 1980s, years of high inflation, the electric utility industry invested heavily in new generating stations. Because of the traditional procedure for measuring capital costs, electric utilities had artificially high revenue requirements and prices, which simultaneously decreased demand and led to initiatives that fostered and subsidized competition from new energy sources. These developments have weakened the financial prospects for many electric utilities in the United States.

Competition in the U.S. electric power industry is an ever-increasing reality. Traditional investor-owned electric utilities are most likely to be competitive if they are not encumbered by measures of capital cost that do not reflect economic reality. I will discuss below steps that are being taken that will gradually free electric utilities from the improper measurement of capital cost.

3.2   Capital Costs for Unregulated and Regulated Firms

Dale Jorgenson's research has always reflected his view that understanding observed data on firm behavior requires a detailed representation of the cost of capital services as perceived by the firm's management. Dale's papers that focused primarily on development of such a representation include Hall and Jorgenson (1967) and Christensen and Jorgenson (1969). An important part of the representation is the recognition that revaluations (capital gains and losses) on existing assets can have a material impact on capital costs.

Prices for firms subject to rate-of-return regulation are set based on the total costs of the firm, as defined by the regulatory agency. The opportunity cost portion of capital service costs is typically defined by regulatory commissions to exclude revaluations; thus defined costs will differ from actual costs when revaluation are significant. For unregulated industries, failure to properly measure capital costs can vitiate research intended to explain firm behavior based on true economic capital costs. For regulated industries, the improper specification of capital costs by the regulatory agency can actually distort the behavior of the firm by forcing it to base its prices on measured costs that differ from actual costs. This violates the principle that regulation causes the regulated firm to behave as if it were operating in a competitive market.

The issue of appropriate capital charges has been discussed in the literature in terms of the measure to use for the rate base on which the regulated utility can earn a return. Traditional regulation allows a return to be earned on depreciated original cost of assets in the rate base. The alternative is often formulated as "trended original cost," in which the rate base is "written up" from original cost to reflect inflation. In essence this would allow regulators to provide for an inflation-adjusted (real) return on those assets. Myers, Kolbe, and Tye (1985) provide an analysis of the economic issues from this literature, including an extensive discussion of the front-end load problem arising from the traditional treatment of capital costs by regulatory commissions.

It is rare, if not unheard of, for regulatory agencies to recognize that the nominal opportunity cost of invested capital reflects the current and expected level of inflation. This will introduce distortions in pricing of the products of the regulated firm that will be more severe the greater is the rate of inflation, the greater is capital intensity of the firm, and the greater is current investment in fixed assets. All of these factors were presents in the 1970s and 1980s for the U.S. electric power industry, which make this industry a prime example of the distortions that can result from a disparity between regulatorily-defined costs and economic costs.

3.3   The Legacy of Improperly Measured Capital Costs for Regulated Electric Utilities in the United States

The 1970s and 1980s was a period in which the U.S. electric utility industry was adding rapidly to its capital stock, especially in the form of large generating stations. During this period the United States economy was experiencing the highest rates of inflation of the twentieth century. This resulted in interest rates that were correspondingly higher than previous experience. The traditional costing methods employed by the state commissions regulating the electric utilities produced large front-end loaded capital costs. As a result, these additions to rate base yielded substantial increases in the measured cost of service (the revenue requirement).

The regulatory commissions found that they could not simply proceed with business as usual, increasing rates to reflect the increased revenue requirements. The political backlash to the rate increases required to cover apparent cost increases was too great. A natural outcome would have been revision of the traditional capital costing procedures, which would have reduced the front-end load and better matched measured costs with economic costs. I am not aware of any state in which this outcome ensued. Instead, there were numerous instances in which the commissions decided that the investments themselves had been imprudent. Portions of the investments were thereby excluded from the rate base, lessening the required increases in revenue requirement.

Notwithstanding the prudence disallowances, the increases in the revenue requirements were in many cases substantially in excess of the general rate of inflation. This gave rise to the notion that perhaps firms other than the investor-owned utilities (IOUs) with monopoly franchises could produce electric power more cheaply. This notion was the basis for "reform" legislation in the 1980s that allowed for participation in electric power markets by "non-utility generators" (NUGs).

This marked the advent of competition in electric power markets. The IOUs were required to buy power from NUGs at their avoided cost, the theory being that if the NUGs could produce at or below the IOUs costs, then society would presumable be better off. All this was happening at a time when the conventional wisdom was that energy prices would indefinitely rise more rapidly than inflation in general.

The result was that many states defined avoided costs in ways that would turn out to be far higher than warranted by economic costs. For example, New York made one of the most extreme interpretations of avoided cost and arbitrarily set the rate at 6¢ per kilowatt-hour. In the event, the true avoided IOU costs were much lower than the mandated levels. The result was an exacerbation and prolongation of the high revenue requirements of the IOUs.

Declines in inflation and interest rates in the late 1980s and early 1990s have diminished the distortion caused by the improper measurement of capital costs. But the distortions remain, nonetheless, and they continue to be important. The reason is that competition is well on its way to becoming a fact of life in the electric power industry. The regulated IOUs are being forced to face competitors who are not handicapped by a wide range of regulations—including the improper measurement of capital costs. I believe it is time for regulators to think seriously about ways to level the playing field, such that efficiency will ultimately determine the electric power producers that thrive and survive in the market.

It is probable that in the not-too-far distant future the generation portion of the electric power industry will be deregulated. At that point the issue of how to measure capital costs will disappear. Firms will account for the true economic costs of their capital assets as well as or as poorly as unregulated firms in other industries, and they will compete accordingly. In the interim period prior to the deregulation of electric power generation, it will be desirable to have a regulatory model that emulates the incentives of a competitive market.

3.4 Incentive Regulation for U.S. Electric Utilities Based on the True Cost of Capital

As the electric power industry continues toward deregulation of the generation portion of the business, what is needed is a regulatory model that will provide a smooth transition from rate-of-return regulation. Attempts to provide such a regulatory model have been discussed under the general heading of "incentive regulation." In this section I present my conception of the most attractive transitional regulatory model.

Rate-of-return regulation can be approximated by specifying that revenues ("the revenue requirement") are equal to total costs of production ("the cost of service"):

Revenues = Costs   (3.1)

Revenues can be decomposed into price and quantity components of output:

Revenues = Price of Output × Output   (3.2)

Similarly costs can be decomposed into price and quantity components of input:

Costs = Price of Input × Input   (3.3)

Substituting (3.2) into (3.1), we have:

Price of Output × Output = Costs   (3.4)

Traditional rate-of-return rate cases can be thought of as setting the Price of Output to satisfy equation (3.4), viz:

Price of Output = Costs/Output = Unit Cost .   (3.5)

Substituting (3.3) into (3.5), we obtain:

Price of Output = Price of Input/TFP   (3.6)

where

TFP = Total Factor Productivity = Output/Input .

Thus the process of setting retail rates for consumers of electricity has been based on the Unit Cost actually experienced by the regulated firm (equation (3.5)). Combining (3.5) and (3.6) we see that Unit Cost can be decomposed into the Price of Input and TFP.[1]

Unit Cost = Price of Input/TFP.   (3.7)

Embedded in the Price of Input is the rate of return on capital that is allowed by the regulatory commission. Insofar as this is the only portion of Unit Cost that is directly controlled by regulators (views differ widely as to how much direct control regulators exert over the rest of the components of Unit Cost), the incentive for electric utilities to control Unit Cost is weak. Various approaches have been proposed to strengthen the cost-control incentive.

Regulators have experimented for many years with narrowly-based reward-penalty mechanisms. For example, a target heat rate may be set with a financial reward or penalty applying to performance that exceeded or fell short of the target. The problem with this approach is the lack of comprehensiveness. Unless all items of cost are subject to a reward mechanism, there is an incentive to increase costs in areas lacking a reward-penalty mechanism, in order to improve performance in areas where there are reward-penalty mechanisms. The only approach that can guarantee improved Unit Cost performance is one that bases the reward-penalty mechanism on the performance of Unit Cost.

As long as regulators maintain equation (3.5), setting prices to cover actual costs, cost control will be difficult. The solution appears to be the violation of equation (3.5), and this is an approach that is now being tried in various forms for several regulated industries, under the general rubric of incentive regulation. The term "price cap regulation" is generally used to describe incentive regulation plans involving the greatest departures from (3.5), in which the Price of Output is largely or completely divorced from actual costs.

Whatever the degree of departure from rate-of-return regulation, the primary challenge is how to establish a Unit Cost target that is external to (not based upon) the firm's own actual costs. One of the earliest approaches adopted is also the most sophisticated approach of which I am aware. This is the Railroad Cost Adjustment Factor (RCAF) that has been used by the Interstate Commerce Commission (ICC) to set the maximum tariff rates that U.S. railroads can charge to shippers who lack competitive alternatives. The approach relies on equation (3.6) (in rate-of-growth form) by utilizing observed changes in input prices and TFP for the entire industry.[2] The resulting index is called the RCAF, and changes in the RCAF apply equally to all railroads regardless of their individual changes in Price of Input and TFP (and hence their Unit Cost). Other industries have thus far adopted various approximations to the ICC approach. State regulatory commissioners have only recently begun to experiment with comprehensive incentive regulation plans for the electric power industry. One of the first such plans was the ECI (external cost index) plan that was instituted for Niagara Mohawk Power Corporation by the New York Public Service Commission in 1993.

The Niagara Mohawk ECI plan was conceived and designed by me and my colleagues at Christensen Associates. The external cost target is based on the contemporaneous Unit Cost performance by a group of approximately twenty utilities that (on average) have characteristics similar to Niagara Mohawk. To lessen dependence on business conditions beyond management control, the ECI plan is based on rates of change of Unit Cost, rather than its level. The measurement of Unit Cost for the ECI plan relies on a capital costing approach that approximates formulas proposed by Christensen and Jorgenson (1969).

Since the ECI plan for Niagara Mohawk was viewed as experimental by the NYPSC, externally measured Unit Cost changes have been used to determine only a small portion of the change in Niagara Mohawk's revenue requirement. But it appears that this will be true only for a brief transition period. Both Niagara Mohawk and the Commission Staff have recently proposed a move to price-cap regulation, in which virtually the entire change in the revenue requirement would be based on indexes external to Niagara Mohawk.

3.5   Concluding Remarks

The California Public Utilities Commission has recently taken the initiative to move toward what it calls Performance Based Ratemaking. It is too early to tell how quickly the Commission will move the California electric power industry away from rate-of-return regulation. But many observers believe that the CPUC initiative will move the industry inexorable toward deregulation of the generation portion of the industry. I believe that any transition plans that are instituted will better serve the industry, as well as the public welfare, if cost measurement reflects the true cost of capital services—as developed and practiced by Dale Jorgenson.

Notes

1. For ease of exposition, equations (3.1) through (3.7) have been presented as levels. They could all equally well be presented in terms of rates of change. For example, equation (3.1) would state that the rate of growth of Revenues is equal to the rate of growth of Costs, and so on.
2. The TFP portion is based on a multi-year moving average with a two-year lag to avoid a zero-sum game situation for the entire industry.

4   The Cost of Capital, Q, and the Theory of Investment Demand

Fumio Hayashi

This chapter reviews the theory of investment demand since the publication of Jorgenson (1963). The emphasis is on the essential role played by the cost of capital in all the existing models of investment. Topics covered are: derivation of the cost of capital, corporate taxes and the cost of capital, the Q theory of investment, the Euler equation approach, multiple capital goods, uncertainty, investment irreversibility, and investment finance.

4.1   Introduction

This chapter reviews the theory of investment demand by individual firms. Since it is an act of sacrificing current resources for future rewards, investment can best be modelled as a dynamic choice made by a firm to maximize shareholders' wealth. The first explicit modelling of a firm's dynamic decision problem for investment is in Jorgenson (1963), where he showed that the construct called the *cost of capital* is the key variable affecting investment. Our review is limited to the developments over the last three decades since the appearance of his celebrated article.

We will start out in section 4.2 by deriving the cost of capital for a firm acting to maximize its share price. Our derivation is rather unconventional. We will show that the share price maximization is equivalent to maximizing the rent which is defined as the difference between the value of the firm and its reproduction cost. It serves to highlight the rather paradoxical result that the objective of the forward-looking firm is best served by the myopic rule (to be referred to as the *Jorgenson condition*) of setting the marginal profits to the cost of capital at every moment in time. The import of the Jorgenson condition is that it, along with the marginal productivity condition for other inputs, allows us to identify the parameters characterizing the profit function, which is a complete summary of the firm's technology. In the following section we will formally derive the result of Hall and Jorgenson (1967) that all the aspects of the corporate tax law relevant for investment can be incorporated in the cost of capital.

If there are costs in changing the level of the capital stock, the Jorgenson condition will not hold in the short run. We will review two approaches for identifying the profit function when the Jorgenson condition does not hold in the short run. The first is the Q theory of investment which provides an alternative first-order condition for the profit function in terms of the stock market valuation of the firm. The other utilizes the Euler equation regarding the second derivatives of the profit function. The following two sections are extensions of the adjustment cost models. Section 4.5 is a compact exposition of the Q theory with multiple capital goods. Section 4.6 shows that the Q theory remains valid under uncertainty. Our exposition of the adjustment cost models is hopefully more transparent than existing ones due to our use of the equivalence between value maximization and rent maximization.

Another possible reason for the Jorgenson condition to fail is the irreversibility of investment. If assets once acquired have a low resale value, there will be instances in which the firm is stuck with too much capital. Section 4.7 examines the consequence of investment irreversibility under uncertainty. It will be shown that the Jorgenson condition does not generally hold, even when the firm is actively investing. The marginal condition will be affected by the parameters describing the uncertain environment, so the profit function cannot be identified without specifying the environment the firm is in. This is in contrast to the Q theory and the Euler equation approach. Also, we will provide some evidence that irreversibility may not be empirically important.

In section 4.8, we will explicitly take into account the financing side of investment. We will show how the cost of capital should be modified when investment can be financed by either debt, retention, or new share issues. The model we consider is deterministic yet sufficiently rich so that the choice of investment finance is nontrivial. A special case of the model will serve to justify the popular practice of calculating the cost of capital as a weighted average of the equity rate of return and the corporate bond rate.

This review does not consider the effect of the personal tax code on the cost of capital to avoid any further notational complications.[1] Also, it is important to keep in mind that all the models examined in this review are regarding the *demand* for investment and hence the usual caveat of identification applies here.[2] A model of investment demand implies a relationship between investment demand and its observable and unobservable determinants. Since actual investment is determined by the intersection of supply and demand, there may not be a stable relationship between actual investment and the observable determinants of investment demand. A model of investment demand provides a testable restriction on actual investment and the observable determinants of investment demand only if one imposes an identifying assumption that the unobservable determinants are unrelated to a set of observables affecting investment supply. This review does not deal with the identification issue, and as a result is silent on the empirical performance of the models of investment demand.

4.2   The Cost of Capital

We consider a firm acting to maximize its share price p_E. If E is the number of existing shares and DIV total dividends, then the rate of return on equity, ρ, satisfies the arbitrage condition:

$$\rho = \frac{\text{DIV}/E + \dot{p}_E}{p_E} = \frac{\text{DIV} + \dot{p}_E \cdot E}{p_E E} . \tag{4.2.1}$$

For the time being we ignore corporate taxes and debt, so DIV equals the sum of net cash flow (profits less investment expenditure) and new share issues ($p_E \cdot \dot{E}$):

$$\text{DIV} = \Pi(K) - p_I I + p_E \cdot \dot{E} . \tag{4.2.2}$$

Here K is the capital stock owned by the firm, $\Pi(K)$ is the nominal profit function, p_I is the price of investment goods, and I is investment. Combining (4.2.1) and (4.2.2) and noting $d/dt(p_E \cdot E) = \dot{p}_E \cdot E + p_E \cdot \dot{E}$, we obtain

$$\rho p_E E = \Pi(K) - p_I I + \frac{d}{dt}(p_E E) . \tag{4.2.3}$$

Under the "no-bubble" condition, that

$$\lim_{t \to \infty} \exp\left(-\int_0^t \rho(s)\, ds \right) p_E E = 0,$$

this differential equation can be solved for the equity value of the firm, $p_E E$, which at time 0 is

$$p_E(0)E(0) = \int_0^\infty \exp\left(-\int_0^t \rho(s)\,ds\right)[\Pi(K(t)) - p_I(t)I(t)]\,dt$$

$$\equiv PV[\Pi(K) - p_I I]. \tag{4.2.4}$$

Since at time 0 the number of existing shares, $E(0)$, is given, maximizing the share price is equivalent to maximizing the equity value of the firm, $p_E(0)E(0)$. The decision problem for the firm at time 0, therefore, is to maximize the present value of net cash flow (4.2.4) over time paths of capital, $\{K(t)\}$, subject to the capital accumulation constraint:

$$\max_{\{K(t)\}} PV[\Pi(K) - p_I I] \text{ subject to } \dot{K} = I - \delta K \tag{4.2.5}$$

where δ is the physical depreciation rate.

We note here that financial policy of the firm, represented by the time path of new share issues, $\{p_E(t)\dot{E}(t)\}$, is irrelevant for the share price. Thus it does not matter whether investment expenditure is financed by retention (cutting dividends) or new share issues. This is because, as assumed in (4.2.1), shareholders value dividends and capital gains equally. This would not be the case if we took into account personal taxes discriminating between dividends and capital gains. Throughout the paper we will ignore personal taxes.

The fundamental insight of Jorgenson (1963) is that the relevant price for the firm's investment decisions is not the investment goods price *per se* but the construct called the *cost of capital*. The investment goods price is relevant only so long as it affects the cost of capital. For our purposes the most useful way to formalize this insight is to rewrite the expression for the equity value of the firm, $p_E(0)E(0)$, as follows.

Let $V = p_E E - p_I K$ be the difference between the market valuation and the reproduction cost of the firm. Using the capital accumulation constraint in (4.2.5) to eliminate investment I in (4.2.3) and noting that $d/dt(p_I \cdot K) = \dot{p}_I \cdot K + p_I \cdot \dot{K}$, we obtain

$$\rho V = \Pi(K) - cK + \frac{d}{dt}V, \tag{4.2.6}$$

where

$$c = \rho p_I - \dot{p}_I + p_I \delta = \left(\rho - \frac{\dot{p}_I}{p_I} + \delta\right)p_I. \tag{4.2.7}$$

This c is the *cost of capital*. The differential equation (4.2.6) for V can be solved under the "no-bubble" condition to yield

$$V(0) \equiv p_E(0)E(0) - p_I(0)K(0) = PV[\Pi(K) - cK] . \qquad (4.2.8)$$

Since the initial capital stock, $K(0)$, is given, maximizing the equity value of the firm is equivalent to maximizing the present value of excess profits, $V(0) \equiv p_E(0)E(0) - p_I(0)K(0)$, which can be interpreted as the *rent* accruing to the access to the profit opportunity represented by the profit function.

In the rent maximization problem, the capital accumulation constraint is already embedded in the objective function. Thus the firm's decision problem, which apparently looked dynamic when written as (4.2.5), is really the same as one that would be faced by a fictitious firm which rents, rather than owns, capital for a rental price of c. Since capital is effectively a variable factor input, the optimal policy is entirely *myopic*: maximize the current return, $\Pi - cK$, every moment in time without regard to the future besides the instantaneous capital gain needed to compute the cost of capital. The necessary condition for optimality is the Jorgenson condition that the marginal profit be equal to the cost of capital:

$$\Pi_K(K) = c , \qquad (4.2.9)$$

which is also sufficient if the profit function Π is concave in K.

For later reference we note the implication of this for the value function. The value function associated with the rent maximization problem when the initial time is t is

$$V(K(t), t) = \max_{\{K(s)\}} \int_t^\infty \exp\left(-\int_t^s \rho(v)\, dv\right)[\Pi(K(s)) - c(s)K(s)]\, ds . \quad (4.2.10)$$

We also define the *marginal rent* $Q(K(t), t)$ as $V_K(K(t), t)$. In the present model, since capital is effectively a variable factor input, the firm can choose the optimal capital stock given by the Jorgenson condition without being constrained by the historically given initial capital stock $K(t)$. So the value function does not depend on the initial capital stock and hence the marginal rent $Q(K, t)$ is zero.

4.3   Detour: Corporate Taxes

The derivation of the cost of capital can be extended to account for a proportional tax on business income and depreciation write-offs for tax purposes. It turns out that the effect of taxes on the capital stock operates only through the tax-adjusted cost of capital. In this section we carry out the tax adjustment more detailed than in Hall and Jorgenson (1967), by first modifying the expression for the value of the firm and then indicating how it affects the subsequent derivation.

Let $D(x,t)$ be the depreciation formula, in effect at time t, which gives the fraction of the original cost of an asset of age x deductible from income. If u is the corporate tax rate, the depreciation for tax purposes that can be deducted from income at time t is:

$$\text{DEP}(t) = \int_0^\infty D(x, t-x) p_I(t-x) I(t-x) \, dx \ . \tag{4.3.1}$$

If, in addition, there is an investment tax credit at rate k, then net cash flow equals $\Pi - u \cdot (\Pi - \text{DEP}) - p_I I + k \cdot p_I I$. Thus the equity value of the firm is given by

$$p_E(0) E(0) = PV[(1-u)\Pi + u \cdot \text{DEP} - (1-k)p_I I] \ . \tag{4.3.2}$$

A rather tricky manipulation included in the Appendix, which involves changes of variables in double integrations, can be used to show:

$$p_E(0) E(0) = A(0) + PV[(1-u)\Pi - (1-k-z)p_I I] \ , \tag{4.3.3}$$

where

$$z(t) = \int_0^\infty \exp\left(-\int_t^{t+x} \rho(s) \, ds\right) u(t+x) D(x,t) \, dx \ , \tag{4.3.4}$$

$$A(0) = PV\left[u\left[\int_{-\infty}^0 D(t-v, v) p_I(v) I(v) \, dv\right]\right] \ . \tag{4.3.5}$$

One dollar of investment at time t entitles the firm to a tax deduction of $u(t+x)D(x,t)$ dollars x years hence. The z in (4.3.4) is the present value of this benefit at time t.[3] Thus the price of investment goods is effectively $(1-k-z)p_I$. The firm also benefits from a tax deduction due to depreciation on assets acquired prior to time 0. The value of tax saving at time t on those assets is

$$u(t) \int_{-\infty}^{0} D(t-v, v) p_I(v) I(v) \, dv.$$

$A(0)$ in (4.3.5) is the present value of that benefit, which is a hidden claim on the tax authority that would be reflected in the share price.

Performing the same operation as in the previous section on the second term on the right-hand side of (4.3.3), we obtain the expression for the rent:

$$p_E(0)F(0) - p_I(0)K(0) - A(0) = PV\{(1-u)[\Pi - cK]\}, \tag{4.3.6}$$

where c here is the tax-adjusted cost of capital given by

$$c = \frac{1-k-z}{1-u}\left(\rho + \delta - \frac{d[(1-k-z)p_I]/dt}{(1-k-z)p_I}\right) p_I. \tag{4.3.7}$$

If the tax rate u and the tax-adjusted investment price $(1-k-z)p_I$ are constant, then this expression reduces to the Hall-Jorgenson cost of capital.

Having shown how taxes can be incorporated, we will ignore taxes for most of the remainder of the chapter in order to focus on other issues.

4.4 Models with Strictly Convex Adjustment Costs

4.4.1 Need for Introducing Frictions

The level of investment implied by the theory can be calculated by differentiating the Jorgenson condition (4.2.9) with respect to time and solving for $\dot{K}$. Is this a good theory of investment? One can raise several objections. First, at a formal mathematical level, investment cannot be defined at points in time where the capital stock changes discontinuously (which will happen, for example, when the cost of capital does so). This, while bothersome to some, does not seem a serious flaw. It simply means that the firm should be viewed as solving the problem of maximizing (4.2.8), which is well defined, rather than solving (4.2.4), which presumes the capital stock to be a smooth function of time.

The second and more important objection to the model is the general notion that it may not be feasible to set the capital stock at the level dictated by the Jorgenson condition at all times. We observe firms making losses. If all factors of production were variable, this would never happen, and capital is the factor of production most likely to be fixed in the short run.

Third, the model exhibits indeterminacy in the benchmark case of perfect competition with constant returns to scale. Since all inputs are variable, there is no distinction between the long-run and short-run cost curves, and under constant returns to scale the marginal cost and average cost curves are the same horizontal line. If the level of technology differs across firms in the industry, the entire market would be captured by the most efficient firms. If all firms are identical in technology, the division of total industry supply between firms is indeterminate. To obtain determinacy under a horizontal demand curve for the firm's output, one needs a theory in which the short-run marginal cost is increasing even though the long-run marginal cost curve is horizontal. As observed by Lucas (1967), such theory obtains if the capital stock is costly to change.

There are several ways to model the fixity of capital, all of which can be viewed as different specifications of adjustment costs. The most tractable and popular is strictly convex adjustment costs. The cost of changing the capital stock accelerates as the change gets larger, and so the firm, rather than instantaneously adjusting the capital stock to meet the Jorgenson condition, would spread the change over time. There is a large theoretical literature on this,[4] which we review in this and the next two sections. The second specification is that the adjustment cost rises proportionately with the change but it is more costly to reduce rather than increase the capital stock. We will examine its extreme case of investment irreversibility in section 4.7. The third specification of concave adjustment costs is hard to analyze; the only attempt to date is Rothschild (1971) which assumes static expectations.

4.4.2   Convex Adjustment Costs

In our exposition of the convex adjustment cost model, we assume that the adjustment cost applies to net, rather than gross, investment. This makes very little difference to the structure of the model. We take the "net" specification because it has a natural extension to the case of multiple capital goods (to be examined in the next section). Thus the profit function now depends on net investment $N(\equiv \dot{K})$ as well as on the capital stock: $\Pi(K, N)$. It is costly to change K, so Π is decreasing in N if $N > 0$ and increasing if $N < 0$. The convexity of adjustment costs requires that $\Pi(K, N)$ be strictly *concave* in N.[5] If Π is differentiable, $\Pi_N < 0$ if $N > 0$, $\Pi_N > 0$ if $N < 0$, $\Pi_N = 0$ if $N = 0$, and $\Pi_{NN} < 0$ for all N. Since K is no longer a choice variable, the profit function as a function of K need to be only weakly concave.

Just by replacing the Π in (4.2.8) by this new Π, we obtain the expression for the rent component of the value of the firm:

$$V(0) = PV[\Pi(K, N) - cK].\tag{4.4.1}$$

So, as before, value maximization amounts to maximizing the rent, but now the problem is truly dynamic because of the presence of $N(\equiv \dot{K})$. We can use calculus of variations on the problem, which we will do later on, but to pave way to the Q theory of investment we employ dynamic programming to characterize the solution. The Bellman equation is[6]

$$\rho V(K, t) = \max_N \left[\Pi(K, N) - cK + \frac{dV(K, t)}{dt} \right].\tag{4.4.2}$$

Since $dV/dt = V_t + V_K \dot{K} = V_t + V_K N = V_t + QN$ where $Q = V_K$ is the marginal rent, the Bellman equation becomes

$$\rho V - V_t = \max_N H(K, N, Q)\tag{4.4.3}$$

where

$$H \equiv \Pi(K, N) - cK + Q \cdot N.$$

This H is the Hamiltonian in the theory of optimal control.

Assuming that the profit function is differentiable, the first-order condition is

$$-\Pi_N(K, N) = Q,\tag{4.4.4}$$

which says that the marginal cost of investing, $-\Pi_N$, be set equal to the incremental contribution of additional capital to the rent. Strict convexity of Π in N implies that this can be solved uniquely for N to obtain the investment equation:[7]

$$N = N(K, Q) .$$ (4.4.5)

The convexity also implies that net investment N is increasing in Q. Note that the functional form of $N(.,.)$ depends only on the profit function. All the relevant information about future (future values of the cost of capital, the investment goods price, etc.) are summarized in Q.

We can derive from the Bellman equation a differential equation for Q. Substitute (4.4.5) into (4.4.3), differentiate both sides of (4.4.3) with respect to K, and use (4.4.4) and the fact that $V_K = Q$ and $\dot{Q} = V_{Kt} + V_{KK}\dot{K} = V_{tK} + Q_K N$ to obtain

$$\dot{Q} = \rho Q - \partial H / \partial K = \rho Q - (\Pi_K - c) .$$ (4.4.6)

Under the transversality condition that

$$\lim_{t \to \infty} \exp\left(-\int_0^t \rho(s)\, ds\right) Q(t) K(t) = 0,$$

the differential equation Q can be solved to yield:

$$Q(t) = \int_t^\infty \exp\left(-\int_t^s \rho(v)\, dv\right) [\Pi_K(K(s)N(s)) - c(s)]\, ds ,$$ (4.4.7)

which highlights the close connection between the Jorgensonian cost of capital and the Q theory: Q is a long-run average of the gap between the marginal profit and the cost of capital. In the steady state in which both $\dot{K} = 0$ and $\dot{Q} = 0$ (if it exists), $\Pi_K - c = Q/\rho$ by (4.4.6) and $Q = \Pi_N(K, 0) = 0$ by (4.4.4). So the Jorgenson condition $\Pi_K = c$ holds in the steady state in which no further adjustment in the capital stock is called for.

4.4.3   The Q Theory and the Euler Equation

The theory presented so far is vacuous because the key variable in the investment equation (4.4.5), Q, is not observable. There are two directions to pursue from here. The first approach, often referred to as the Q theory of investment, is to relate Q to the stock market valuation of the firm. The second is to apply the calculus of variations directly to the rent maximization problem.

As shown in Hayashi (1982), the condition under which Q can be made observable is that (1) the firm is perfectly competitive and (2) the adjustment cost is homogeneous in that the profit function is homogeneous in (K, N). Under these two conditions the profit function Π can be written as

$$\Pi(K, N) = p \cdot K \cdot \pi(g) , \tag{4.4.8}$$

where p is the output price, $g \equiv N/K = \dot{K}/K$ is the growth rate of capital. A straightforward manipulation shows that the optimality conditions can be written as:

$$-\pi_g(g) = Q^R , \tag{4.4.4'}$$
$$\dot{Q}^K = (r - g)Q^R - [\pi(g) - c/p] , \tag{4.4.6'}$$

where $r \equiv \rho - \dot{p}/p$ is the real interest rate and $Q^R \equiv Q/p$ is the "real" Q. Formula (4.4.6') immediately implies that the investment equation takes a more specific form:

$$(\dot{K}/K =) g = g(Q^R) . \tag{4.4.5'}$$

To understand the structure of the model, we consider the stationary environment where the real interest rate r and the profit function $\pi(g)$ do not change over time. Then the system of two differential equations, (4.4.5') and (4.4.6'), is an autonomous system which can be analyzed by the phase diagram. Since the growth equation (4.4.5') does not involve K and since g is increasing in Q^R, there is a unique Q^R such that $\dot{K} = 0$. So the $\dot{K} = 0$ locus (set of (K, Q^R) for which $\dot{K} = 0$) is a horizontal line, as drawn in Figure 4.1. The $\dot{Q}^R = 0$ locus can be obtained by substituting (4.4.5') into (4.4.6') and setting $\dot{Q}^R = 0$. The concavity of π and the monotonicity of $g(Q^R)$ implies that there is a unique Q^R consistent with $\dot{Q}^R = 0$. In the figure this horizontal $\dot{Q}^R = 0$ locus is drawn above the $\dot{K} = 0$ locus. Since Q^R is increasing (decreasing) if (K, Q^R) is above (below) the $\dot{Q}^R = 0$ locus and since K is increasing (decreasing) if (K, Q^R) is above (below) the $\dot{K} = 0$ locus, typical trajectories are as illustrated in the figure. Of these the only one that satisfies the transversality condition is the horizontal trajectory *on* the $\dot{Q}^R = 0$ locus.

This diagrammatic analysis shows, first, that the firm responds to the stationary environment by growing at a constant rate (so there is no such thing as an equilibrium capital stock), and, second, that Q^R

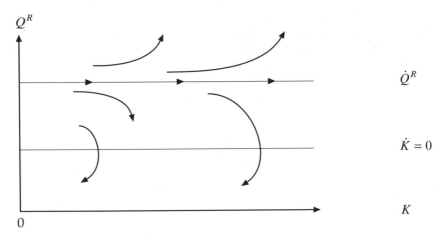

Figure 4.1
Phase diagram under constant returns to scale.

and hence g are independent of the initial capital stock. It turns out that this second property is not specific to the stationary case. It is reasonably obvious that the optimal investment policy $\{g(t)\}$ does not depend on the initial capital stock $K(t)$,[8] so the rent, $V(K(0),0)$, is proportional to the initial capital stock $K(0)$. Clearly, this is true if the current time is t, not 0. So the value function $V(K,t)$ is proportional to K. Since $Q^R(t) = Q(t)/p(t)$ and $Q(t) = V_K(K(t),t)$ is the marginal rent at time t, it follows that the marginal and average rents are equal:

$$Q^R = \frac{p_E E - p_I K}{pK} = (q-1) \cdot \frac{p_I}{p} \qquad (4.4.9)$$

where

$$q = \frac{p_E E}{p_I K} \ .$$

The q thus defined is the so-called *Tobin's q*, the ratio of the value of the firm to the reproduction cost of capital which is in principle observable.

With data on g and Q^R, we can uncover the firm's technology from the first-order condition (4.4.4′). To make explicit the dependence of profits on real variable factor prices denoted w and a technology shock ε, write the profit function π in (4.4.8) as $\pi(g, w, \varepsilon)$. If L is the quantity of variable factor inputs, the duality theorem yields

$$\pi_w(g, w, \varepsilon) = L \ . \tag{4.4.10}$$

Equations (4.4.4') and (4.4.10) can be jointly estimated by some appropriate econometric techniques to identify the parameters characterizing the profit function.[9]

The second way to describe investment in terms of observables is to use calculus of variations directly.[10] The Euler equation for the problem of maximizing the rent given in (4.4.1) is

$$\Pi_K - c = -\rho\Pi_N + \Pi_{KN}N + \Pi_{NN}\dot{N} \ . \tag{4.4.11}$$

This investment equation can also be derived from (4.4.4) and (4.4.6) by eliminating Q. Note the re-emergence of the cost of capital, c.

Neither approach dominates the other. The Q theory requires (1) perfect competition, (2) homogeneous adjustment costs, and (3) that the stock market provide an accurate valuation of the firm, none of which is required by the investment Euler equation. On the other hand, if the three conditions are met, the Q theory embodies more information because it exploits the transversality condition, which should lead to a more efficient estimation of the parameters characterizing the profit function. Furthermore, it is generally not possible to estimate the parameters by the investment Euler equation if the profit function involves an error term in the form of an unobservable technology shock. This is because the stochastic version of the investment Euler equation will have an additional error term arising from forecast error about the future, and only by accident the two error terms enter the investment equation through a single term.

4.5   Multiple Capital Goods

If the firm owns a collection of different capital goods, the information provided by the share price is concerning the market valuation of the entire collection of capital, not of each individual capital stock. Thus it is in general impossible to derive a functional relationship between investment and Q for each capital good; different distribution of investments between capital goods can be associated with the same value of Q. Our goal here is to impose a plausible restriction on the profit function so that some summary statistic of the distribution of investments is a function of Q.[11]

With multiple capital goods, the expression for the rent is

$$V(0) = p_E(0)E(0) - \sum_{j=1}^{n} p_j(0)K_j(0) = PV\left[\Pi(\mathbf{K}, \dot{\mathbf{K}}) - \sum_{j=1}^{n} c_j K_j\right], \qquad (4.5.1)$$

where p_j, K_j, and c_j are the price, the capital stock, and the cost of capital of the j-th capital good, respectively, and $\mathbf{K} \equiv (K_1, \ldots, K_n)$. The restriction we impose on the profit function is the weak separability of capital in the sense that

$$\Pi(\mathbf{K}, \dot{\mathbf{K}}) = \Pi(\phi(K), \dot{\phi}(K)) \qquad (4.5.2)$$

for some homogeneous function $\phi(.)$, where $\dot{\phi}(\mathbf{K}) = d\phi(\mathbf{K})/dt$.

The firm's problem is to choose the capital accumulation path $\{\mathbf{K}(t)\}$ to maximize the rent $V(0)$. The set of capital accumulation paths can be divided into subsets, each of which is indexed by a scalar path $\{\Phi(t)\}$. All capital accumulation paths belonging to the subset indexed by $\{\Phi(t)\}$ satisfies $\Phi(t) = \phi(\mathbf{K}(t))$ for all t. So the rent maximization problem can proceed in two steps. Step 1 chooses within each subset $\{\Phi(t)\}$ the capital accumulation path that maximizes the rent, while Step 2 picks from among the subsets the best capital accumulation path.

Since by weak separability Π is constant across all capital accumulation paths in the subset $\{\Phi(t)\}$, Step 1 is equivalent to minimizing

$$PV\left(\sum_{j=1}^{n} c_j K_j\right),$$

which in turn is equivalent to the static problem of minimizing the capital cost for any given point in time:

Step 1: $\min_K \sum_{j=1}^{n} c_j K_j$ subject to $\phi(K) = \Phi$. $\qquad (4.5.3)$

The first-order condition is

$$\phi_j(\mathbf{K}) = \lambda_\Phi c_j \quad (j = 1, 2, \ldots, n), \qquad (4.5.4)$$

where λ_Φ is the (inverse of) Lagrange multiplier which can depend on Φ. Since ϕ is homogeneous, the minimized capital cost can be written as $\gamma(\mathbf{c})\Phi$ where $\mathbf{c} = (c_1, \ldots, c_n)$. The second step, therefore, is

Step 2: $\max_{\{\Phi(t)\}} PV[\dot{\Pi}(\Phi, \dot{\Phi}) - \gamma(\mathbf{c})\Phi] \qquad (4.5.5)$

which is exactly the same as the single capital good problem (4.4.1).

The derivation of the Q theory under perfect competition and homogeneous adjustment costs proceeds just as before. One only need to repeat the argument starting with equation (4.4.8) to show that the growth rate of the capital aggregate Φ, $\dot{\Phi}/\Phi$, is a function of Q^R ("real" Q), as in (4.4.5'), where Q^R is now defined as

$$Q^R = \frac{p_E E - \sum_{j=1}^{n} p_j K_j}{p\Phi} . \tag{4.5.6}$$

To make this real Q observable, we have to be able to calculate the index of capital aggregate Φ. In the productivity literature, the capital aggregate is calculated using the marginal condition $\phi_j(\mathbf{K}) = c_j$.[12] Here, ϕ_j is only proportional to the cost of capital, but it does not prevent us from carrying out the standard index number construction (introduced by Griliches and Jorgenson, 1966) because:

$$\frac{\dot{\Phi}}{\Phi} = \frac{\sum_{j=1}^{n} \phi_j(\mathbf{K})\dot{K}_j}{\sum_{j=1}^{n} \phi_j(\mathbf{K})K_j} = \frac{\sum_{j=1}^{n} \lambda_\Phi c_j \dot{K}_j}{\sum_{j=1}^{n} \lambda_\Phi c_j K_j} = \frac{\sum_{j=1}^{n} c_j \dot{K}_j}{\sum_{j=1}^{n} c_j K_j} , \tag{4.5.7}$$

where the first equality is by the Euler's theorem and the second equality is by (4.5.4). Given a base year value for Φ, the value of Φ for time t can be obtained by integrating the growth rate given by (4.5.7) to t, which is exactly how the capital aggregate series are constructed in the productivity literature. If one so desires, the base year value of Φ can be set to satisfy $p\Phi = \sum_j p_j K_j$ so that the implied value of Q^R for the base year is equal to $q - 1$, where q is the ratio of the market value of the firm, $p_E E$, to the reproduction cost $\sum_j p_j K_j$.

4.6 Uncertainty

Once we allow for uncertainty, it is much less clear what the objective of the firm should be. If markets are complete, every shareholder's welfare is maximized when the share price is maximized. This is not the case if markets are incomplete, for reasons expounded in Kreps (1979). We sidestep this unresolved issue by assuming risk-neutrality. Under risk-neutrality, the share price is the expected present value of dividends and maximizing the share price is unanimously agreed to by shareholders.

It turns out that the investment theory with convex adjustment costs in continuous time under risk-neutrality can be straightforwardly extended to encompass uncertainty by the use of stochastic calculus.[13] As an illustration, we consider a simplest possible case in which a scalar technology shock ε affecting the profit function is the only source of uncertainty, with the rate of return ε and the investment goods price p_I remaining to be deterministic function of time. We assume that $\varepsilon(t)$ evolves according to the diffusion process:

$$d\varepsilon(t) = \mu(\varepsilon)dt + \sigma(\varepsilon)dz , \qquad (4.6.1)$$

where dz is the increment of a Brownian motion, a continuous time analogue of the discrete-time white noise process. Here, μ is the instantaneous expected change in ε while σ is the standard deviation of the change in ε. This is by far the most widely studied continuous-time stochastic process in the literature.

Under risk-neutrality, the required rate of return equals the sum of dividend yield and expected capital gains:

$$\rho p_E E = \Pi(K, N, \varepsilon) - p_I I + \frac{E[d(p_E E)]}{dt} . \qquad (4.6.2)$$

As in section 4.2, we define the rent to be $V = p_E E - p_I K$ and substitute the capital accumulation equation in (4.2.5) into (4.6.2) to derive

$$\rho V = \Pi(K, N, \varepsilon) - cK + \frac{E(dV)}{dt} . \qquad (4.6.3)$$

Since $\{\varepsilon(t)\}$ is a Markov process with the current value of ε providing all the information about the future course of ε, the triplet $(K(t), \varepsilon(t), t)$ is a complete summary of the current state and is the arguments of the value function V. So the Bellman equation is:

$$\rho V(K, \varepsilon, t) = \max_N \left[\Pi(K, N, \varepsilon) - cK + \frac{E[dV(K, \varepsilon, t)]}{dt} \right], \qquad (4.6.4)$$

which should be compared to (4.4.2).

By Ito's lemma, $E(dV) = V_K dK + [V_t + \mu(\varepsilon)V_\varepsilon + 1/2\ \sigma^2(\varepsilon)V_{\varepsilon\varepsilon}]dt$. Substituting this into (4.6.4) gives

$$\rho V - V_t = \max_N [\Pi(K, N, \varepsilon) - cK + V_K N + \mu(\varepsilon)V_\varepsilon + 1/2\ \sigma(\varepsilon)^2 V_{\varepsilon\varepsilon}] . \qquad (4.6.5)$$

As before, define $Q(t)$ to be the marginal rent $V_K(K(t), \varepsilon(t), t)$. The investment first-order condition is exactly the same as before:

$$-\Pi_N(K, N, \varepsilon) = Q , \tag{4.6.6}$$

which can be solved for N to obtain the investment equation

$$N = N(K, Q, \varepsilon) . \tag{4.6.7}$$

As clear from the derivation, the functional form $N(.,.,.)$ depends on neither μ, the expected rate of change of ε, nor the degree of uncertainty measured by σ. As in the deterministic case, Q summarizes all the information relevant to current investment.

The differential equation for Q can be derived in much the same way as before. Substitute (4.6.7) into the Bellman equation, take the derivative of both sides with respect to K, and use Ito's lemma for Q, $E(dQ) = [V_{Kt} + V_{KK} N + \mu(\varepsilon) V_{\varepsilon K} + 1/2 V_{\varepsilon\varepsilon K} \sigma^2(\varepsilon)] dt$, to obtain:

$$E(dQ) = [\rho Q - (\Pi_K - c)] dt . \tag{4.6.8}$$

Under an appropriate transversality condition, this can be solved to yield

$$Q(t) = E_t \left[\int_t^\infty \exp \left(- \int_t^s \rho(v) \, dv \right) \left[(\Pi_K(s) - c(s) \right) ds \right] , \tag{4.6.9}$$

which is the generalization of (4.4.7).

The equality of marginal rent and average rent carries over to the stochastic case. Under perfect competition and constant returns to scale, (4.4.5′) is the investment equation. It is easy to show that the optimal policy for the growth of the capital stock does not depend on the initial capital stock; the proof is exactly as in footnote 8. This invariance to the scale of the firm implies that the firm's rent, V, is proportional to the initial capital stock. Hence average rent, V/K, equals marginal rent, Q.

4.7   Irreversibility

4.7.1   Theory

We now turn to the second specification of the proportional but asymmetric adjustment cost in which the proportional adjustment cost is

higher for decreases than increases in the capital stock. We only consider the special case of investment irreversibility: gross investment, I,
cannot be negative because the resale value of assets is zero.[14] Thus
the capital stock can be reduced only through attrition (depreciation)
of existing assets. We remove the convex adjustment cost from the
model, so the profit function no longer depends on (net) investment.
The investment goods price, p_I, should now be interpreted as inclusive of the proportional adjustment cost associated with positive gross
investment (if it exists) in increasing the capital stock. We continue to
suppose for simplicity that the technology shock, ε, is the only source
of uncertainty.

The qualitative property of the solution can be described as follows.
For a given time t, let $K^d(t)$ be the capital stock that the firm would
hold if irreversibility were temporarily lifted. By construction it does
not depend on the existing capital stock. Since $\varepsilon(t)$ is a complete summary of the uncertain future, $K^d(t)$ is a function of $\varepsilon(t)$ and t:
$K^d(t) = K^d(\varepsilon(t), t)$.[15] It does not necessarily satisfy the Jorgenson condition (4.2.9), because investment is irreversible in the future and so the
firm may regret to have invested too much if business condition dete-
riorates in the future. Now consider the implication of the current
irreversibility constraint. If $K^d(t) \geq K(t)$, then the constraint does not
bind, so the capital stock will be set to $K^d(t)$. If $K^d(t) < K(t)$, there is
too much capital but the firm is forced to hold $K(t)$ due to investment
irreversibility. Therefore, $K(t) \geq K^d(t)$ for all t and $K(t) = K^d(t)$ if
$I(t) > 0$.

Since the existing capital stock is relevant only when the irre-
versibility is binding, the marginal rent, $Q(K(t), \varepsilon(t), t) = V_k(K(t), \varepsilon(t),$
$t)$, is zero when $K(t) \leq K^d(t)$. The logic here is exactly the same as in
the model without adjustment costs in section 4.2. On the other hand,
when $K(t) > K^d(t)$, the capital stock at the margin only contributes to
reduce the rent, so $Q < 0$. The graph of Q as a function of K for some
given value of (ε, t) is drawn in figure 4.2. To calculate K^d, one needs
to explicitly solve for $Q(K, \varepsilon, t)$. As clear from figure 4.2, $K^d(\varepsilon, t)$ is
such that $Q(K, \varepsilon, t) = 0$ for all $K \leq K^d(\varepsilon, t)$. To solve for Q, one derives a
partial differential equation for $Q(K, \varepsilon, t)$ for region $K > K^d$ from the
Bellman equation and chooses a particular solution and the value of
K^d such that the solution as a function of K touches the horizontal
axis at K^d in a smooth fashion as in figure 4.2.[16]

The K^d thus calculated does not in general satisfy the Jorgenson
condition in that there is no suitably defined cost of capital indepen-

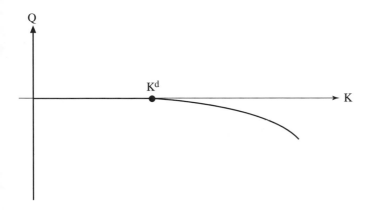

Figure 4.2
Marginal rent under irreversibility.

dent of ε such that it is equal to $\Pi_K(K^d, \varepsilon)$. An exception occurs when the profit function is Cobb-Douglas (so $\Pi(K, \varepsilon) = K^\alpha \varepsilon$ with $0 < \alpha < 1$) and the diffusion process (4.6.1) is geometric (so $\mu(\varepsilon) = \mu \cdot \varepsilon$, $\sigma(\varepsilon) = \sigma \cdot \varepsilon$ for some constant μ, σ). Bertola (1988) shows that for this particular case $K^d(\varepsilon, t)$ satisfies the Jorgenson condition:

$$\Pi_K(K^d(\varepsilon, t), \varepsilon) = \tilde{c}(t) \equiv \tilde{c}\left(\rho + \delta - \frac{\dot{p}_I}{p_I} + \frac{1}{2}\sigma^2 A\right) \cdot p_I , \qquad (4.7.1)$$

where $\dot{p}_I/p_I$ is a constant expected growth rate of the investment goods price, and A is the positive solution to the quadratic equation

$$\frac{1}{2}\sigma^2 A^2 + \left[\mu + (1 - \alpha)\delta - \frac{\dot{p}_I}{p_I} - \frac{1}{2}\sigma^2\right]A - \left(\rho + \delta - \frac{\dot{p}_I}{p_I}\right) = 0 . \qquad (4.7.2)$$

Thus A depends on ρ, μ (expected growth rate of ε), and σ^2 (variance of the growth rate of ε). Equation (4.7.1) should be compared to (4.2.9) with (4.2.7). It is easy to verify that

$$\partial \tilde{c}/\partial \rho > 1, \quad \partial \tilde{c}/\partial \mu < 0, \quad \partial \tilde{c}/\partial \sigma^2 > 0 . \qquad (4.7.3)$$

Thus the desired capital stock with investment irreversibility is more sensitive to the interest rate than without irreversibility.[17] As one would expect, better business prospects in the sense of higher μ or lower σ reduces the modified cost of capital and increases the desired capital and hence investment.

4.7.2   Evaluation of the Theory

Is there any basis for preferring the model of investment irreversibility to the adjustment cost model? Both are consistent with the elementary observation that firms can make negative profits. The irreversibility model still contains indeterminacy if placed in the environment of perfect competition and constant returns to scale because the desired capital stock cannot be defined if the profit function is linear in the capital stock. On the other hand, many researchers find adjustment costs an *ad hoc* way of modelling the fixity of capital.

To examine the empirical relevance of irreversibility, I calculated the frequency of zero gross investment among Japanese publicly traded manufacturing firms. The data set is the one used in Hayashi and Inoue (1991) which includes 687 firms for the ten-year period of 1977–1986, providing 6,870 firm-year observations. Nominal gross investment is divided into five assets: nonresidential buildings, structures, machinery, transportation equipment, and instruments and tools. Figure 4.3 shows the frequency distribution of the ratio of nominal investment to the beginning-of-period capital stock. Figure 4.3a is for the overall ratio (the ratio of total nominal investment $\Sigma_j p_j I_j$ to total nominal capital stock $\Sigma_j p_j K_j$, while figures 4.3b–4.3f are for each individual ratio of $p_j I_j$ to $p_j K_j$ $(j = 1, \ldots, 5)$. As clear from figure 4.3a, cases of zero total nominal investment is negligible (only 10 cases out of 6,870 are zeros). Figures 4.3b–4.3f show that zero gross investment is infrequent except for transportation equipment, but this asset type is only a tiny fraction (1%) of the capital stock.[18]

That firms actively invest almost always is not necessarily inconsistent with irreversibility *per se*. In the present formulation, new information about profitability of capital arrives continuously. In contrast, in Zeira's (1987) model the firm does not know the size of the market for its output and can discover it only by changing the level of output. Because of investment irreversibility, the experiment starts with a low level of output and hence a low level of the capital stock, followed by a sequence of positive investments. This model of learning with irreversibility can explain why the capital stock adjusts only gradually and why the adjustment is almost always on the expansion phase.[19]

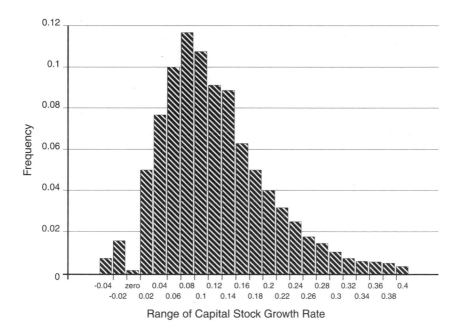

Figure 4.3a
Gross investment in all five assets.

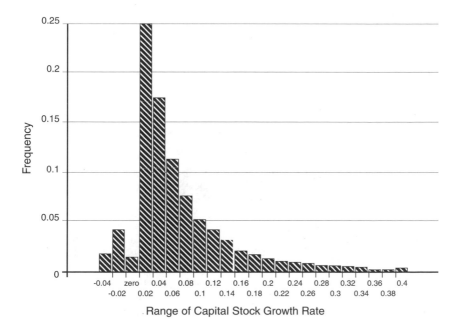

Figure 4.3b
Buildings.

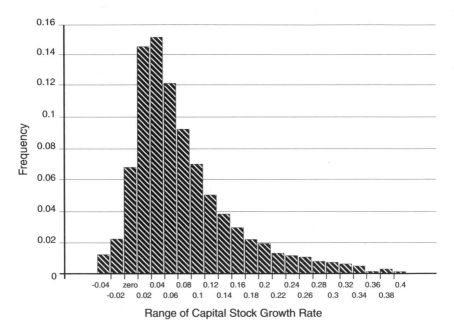

Figure 4.3c
Structures.

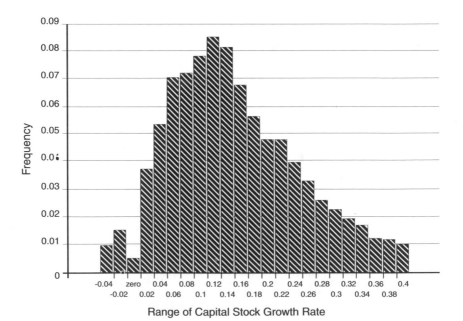

Figure 4.3d
Machinery.

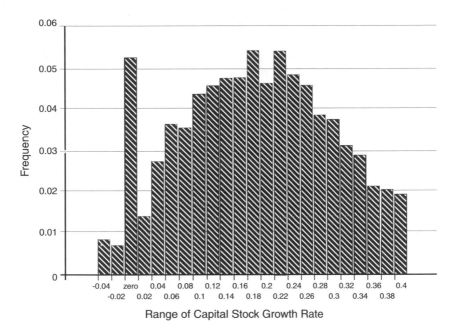

Figure 4.3e
Transportation equipment.

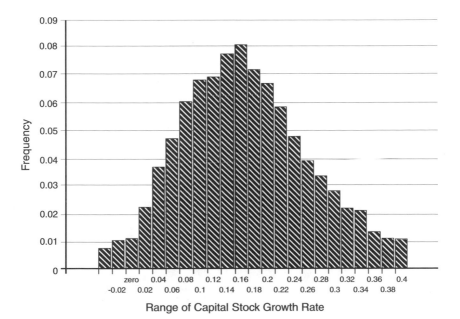

Figure 4.3f
Instruments and tools.

4.8   Capital Structure

So far we have ignored debt and assumed that the firm is completely
equity financed. We now allow for debt and examine the interaction
between the cost of capital and corporate capital structure. Without
taxes, the debt-equity ratio is indeterminate by the Modigliani-Miller
theorem, so corporate taxes have to be figured in to have a theory of
capital structure. In the model we present below, the borrowing rate
for the firm increases with debt, which has to be traded off against the
tax advantage of debt (due to the tax deductibility of interest costs
from corporate income). We develop this model in a deterministic
framework.[20]

To avoid the unessential complication arising from depreciation
accounting, we assume that the depreciation deductible from corporate income coincides with economic depreciation $\delta p_I K$. If B is debt
and i is the associated borrowing rate, interest costs of iB, too, are
deductible. So the expression for dividends becomes

$$\text{DIV} = \Pi - u \cdot (\Pi - \delta p_I K - iB) - p_I I + P_E \dot{E} + \dot{B} - iB , \tag{4.8.1}$$

where u is the corporate tax rate. As before, we define the rent, V, to
be the difference between the value of the firm and its reproduction
cost, but now the value of the firm is the sum of equity and debt. So
$V = p_E E + B - p_I K$. Again as in section 4:2, we can substitute the capital accumulation equation into (4.8.1) to eliminate I and then use the
arbitrage equation (4.2.1) to derive the differential equation for V:

$$\rho V = (1-u)(\Pi - cK) + [\rho - (1-u)i]B + \dot{V} , \tag{4.8.2}$$

where the cost of capital, c, is now given by

$$c = \frac{\rho - \dfrac{\dot{p}_I}{p_I}}{1-u} + \delta . \tag{4.8.3}$$

Under the "no-bubble" condition (4.8.2) can be solved for V to yield

$$V(0) \equiv p_E(0)E(0) + B(0) - p_I(0)K(0)$$

$$= PV\{(1-u)(\Pi - cK) + [\rho - (1-u)i]B\} , \tag{4.8.4}$$

which says that the firm's rent is the present value of: after-tax excess
profits, $(1-u)(\Pi - cK)$, and the subsidy to corporate debt, $[\rho - (1-u)i]B$.

For the borrowing rate, i, we assume that it increases with debt to reflect a risk premium for bankruptcy. It will also be decreasing with the capital stock because a higher level of the capital stock makes bankruptcy less likely. Thus:

$$i = i(B, K) \text{ with } i_B > 0, \quad i_K \le 0 . \tag{4.8.5}$$

This specification includes as a special case *credit rationing* where the interest rate schedule becomes vertical at some maximal debt.

No Adjustment Costs
With no adjustment costs, it is optimal to follow the myopic rule of maximizing the instantaneous return:

$$\max_{\{K,B\}} (1-u)[\Pi(K) - cK] + [\rho - (1-u)i(K, B)]B . \tag{4.8.6}$$

Since K affects the borrowing rate schedule, the firm's financial decision of choosing the optimal debt level cannot be made independent of the real decision of choosing the optimal capital stock in general. However, there are two cases of interest in which the real and financial decisions can be made separately. Obviously, if the borrowing rate schedule is unaffected by the firm size measured by the capital stock, the optimal debt level maximizes the subsidy to debt finance, $[\rho - (1-u)i(B)]B$, and the optimal capital stock will be determined by the Jorgenson condition $\Pi_K = c$ where c is the tax-adjusted cost of capital given by (4.8.3). Financing the capital stock at the margin (i.e., investment) comes exclusively from either new shares or cutting dividends.

The second case of real and financial separability occurs when the borrowing rate schedule $i(K, B)$ depends on the capital stock only through the debt/capital ratio, i.e., when $i(B, K) = i(B/K)$. This includes a case of credit rationing where the maximal debt is proportional to K. Since the debt subsidy term in (4.8.6) can be written as $[\rho - (1-u)i(B/K)](B/K)K$, the choice of debt/capital ratio can be made independent of K. Let γ be the optimal debt/capital ratio that maximizes $[\rho - (1-u)i(B/K)](B/K)$. The current return (4.8.6) can be written as

$$(1-u)[\Pi(K) - c] \tag{4.8.7}$$

with

$$c = \frac{(1-\gamma)\rho + \gamma(1-u)i - \dfrac{\dot{p}_I}{p_I}}{1-u} + \delta \, .$$

Since a constant fraction, $1-\gamma$, of investment is financed by equity or dividend while the remaining fraction financed by debt, the relevant cost of capital involves the weighted average of the equity rate of return, ρ, and the after-tax borrowing rate, $(1-u)i$. This is how the cost of capital is usually calculated.[21] Our discussion here clarifies what assumptions are needed to justify the usual practice.

So far, we have not paid any attention to the constraint that dividends be nonnegative. The constraint is never binding because the firm can always issue new shares to alleviate the constraint.[22] If there is some additional costs in issuing new shares in the form of commissions charged by underwriters or the "lemon" premium, the nonnegativity constraint becomes relevant, which has two consequences. First, when the constraint is binding, the Jorgenson condition does not hold. Second, since dividends depend on the rate of investment which affects $\dot{K}$, the firm's decision problem becomes truly dynamic. In the deterministic case, the Jorgenson condition will hold when the constraint is not binding. However, with uncertainty, the situation is analogous to the case of irreversible investment. There is an incentive to acquire more capital stock than warranted by the Jorgenson condition when the firm is not constrained in order to alleviate future constraints.

Strictly Convex Adjustment Costs
Finally, we very briefly examine the interaction of investment and debt with strictly convex adjustment costs. We only consider the case in which the borrowing rate schedule depends on B and K only through the debt/capital ratio. Then the rent to be maximized is the same as (4.4.1) provided that the cost of capital is the c given in (4.8.7) and current return, $\Pi - cK$, is understood to be after-tax. Therefore, all the results in section 4.4 are valid when the firm can borrow to finance investment. Since the borrowing rate schedule considered here includes credit rationing, it follows that the Q theory holds even if the firm is credit rationed as long as the firm has the option of issuing new shares.

4.9   Conclusion

We have reviewed a number of approaches to modelling investment demand by an individual firm. In each model, the cost of capital is not only the key variable affecting investment but also the sole channel through which tax parameters exert incentive effects.

It remains an open question which model is empirically most relevant. Most recent micro-studies utilize the adjustment cost model to address specific issues.[23] Very few attempts have been made to compare the adjustment cost model with other competing models on micro-data.[24] It is also important to note that the model best suited to investment demand may not be capable of explaining aggregate investment, because aggregate investment is determined by the interaction of supply and demand. Explaining aggregate investment requires in principle a general equilibrium modelling as in Jorgenson and Yun (1991a) and Kydland and Prescott (1982).

Appendix

The present value of tax saving due to depreciation, $PV(u \cdot DEP)$, can be divided into two pieces, one having to do with past investment and the other with current and future investment. We show this formally in this appendix.

Using (4.3.1), the present value can be written as

$$PV(uDEP) = \int_0^\infty \exp\left(-\int_0^t \rho(s)\, ds\right) u(t)\left[\int_0^\infty D(x, t-x)Y(t-x)\, dx\right] dt$$

$$= \int_0^\infty \left[-\int_0^\infty \exp\left(\int_0^t \rho(s)\, ds\right) u(t)D(x, t-x)Y(t-x)\, dt\right] dx, \qquad \text{(A.1)}$$

where $Y(t) = p_I(t)I(t)$. This can be divided into two integrals:

$$\int_0^\infty \left[\int_0^x \exp\left(-\int_0^t \rho(s)\, ds\right) u(t)D(x, t-x)Y(t-x)\, dt\right] dx$$

$$+ \int_0^\infty \left[\int_x^\infty \exp\left(-\int_0^t \rho(s)\, ds\right) u(t)D(x, t-x)Y(t-x)\, dt\right] dx. \qquad \text{(A.2)}$$

For the first integral, define $v = t - x$ and note that in terms of (t, v) the integration becomes

$$\int_0^\infty \left[\int_{-\infty}^0 \exp\left(-\int_0^t \rho(s)\,ds \right) u(t)D(t-v,v)Y(v)dt \right] dv$$

$$= \int_0^\infty \exp\left(-\int_0^t \rho(s)\,dt \right) u(t)\left[\int_{-\infty}^0 D(t-v,v)Y(v)\,dv \right] dt \ . \qquad \text{(A.3)}$$

The second integral in (A.2) can be written in terms of (t, v) as follows:

$$\int_0^\infty \left[\int_0^\infty \exp\left(-\int_0^{v+x} \rho(s)\,ds \right) u(v+x)D(x,v)Y(v)\,dx \right] dv$$

$$= \int_0^\infty \exp\left(-\int_0^v \rho(s)\,ds \right)\left[\int_0^\infty \exp\left(-\int_v^{v+x} \rho(s)\,ds \right) u(v+x)D(x,v)Y(v)\,dx \right] dv$$

$$= \int_0^\infty \exp\left(-\int_0^v \rho(s)\,ds \right) z(v)Y(v)\,dv \qquad \text{by (3.4)}$$

$$= \int_0^\infty \exp\left(-\int_0^t \rho(s)\,ds \right) z(t)Y(t)\,dt \ . \qquad \text{(A.4)}$$

Notes

1. For the treatments of personal taxes in the literature, see Auerbach's (1983b) survey.
2. A standard theory of investment supply assumes "external" adjustment costs or the imperfect substitutability of consumption and investment demand. See Mussa (1977) and Jorgenson and Yun (1991a).
3. If the tax rate u is constant over time, it equals u times the z in Hall and Jorgenson (1967).
4. See the literature cited in, e.g., Hayashi (1982).
5. A popular special case is that the profit function can be written as: $[F(K)-G(K,N)]$, where F is profit gross of adjustment costs, and G is increasing in N if $N>0$ and decreasing if $N<0$. The convexity of adjustment costs requires that G be strictly convex in N.
6. See, e.g., Kamien and Schwartz (1981, part II, section 20) for a derivation of the Bellman equation. The term ρV enters the Bellman equation because $V(K,t)$ is a current value, discounted only to the current time t.

7. In order to derive the investment equation (4.5) we do not require the profit function $\Pi(K, N)$ to be differentiable in N, because the strict concavity of Π in N guarantees that there is a unique N that maximizes the Hamiltonian. For example, there can be a kink at $N = 0$, so that $\lim_{N \downarrow 0} \Pi_N < 0$ and $\lim_{N \uparrow 0} \Pi_N > 0$. In particular, if $\lim_{N \uparrow 0} \Pi_N = \infty$, (net) investment is irreversible. It is therefore trivial to superimpose irreversibility on the convex adjustment cost structure, but this generality is illusory: if the strict convexity of adjustment cost is replaced by proportional adjustment costs but the irreversibility is kept intact, one gets a very different theory of investment, as we will see in section 4.7.

8. Consider otherwise identical two firms, firm 1 and firm 2, with different initial capital stocks K_1 and K_2, respectively. Let $\{g_j(t)\}$ be the optimal path for the growth rate for firm $j (j = 1, 2)$, with associated path of the capital stock denoted by $\{K_1(t)\}$ and $\{K_2(t)\}$, and the rent denoted by V_1 and V_2. If firm 2 adopts $\{g_1(t)\}$, the associated capital path is $K_1(t) \cdot (K_2/K_1)$, resulting the rent of $V = V_1 \cdot (K_2/K_1)$. Since V_2 is the maximized rent, we have $V_2 \geq V_1 \cdot (K_2/K_1)$ or $V_2/K_2 \geq V_1/K_1$. Similarly for firm 1, $V_1/K_1 \geq V_2/K_2$. So $V_1/K_1 = V_2/K_2$. This type of argument case can be found in the NBER Working Paper No. 3326 which underlies Hayashi and Inoue (1991).

9. The estimation technique must take into account that Q^R, g, and L are all endogenous because they are functions of the unobservable technology shock ε.

10. A recent example of the Euler equation approach is Hubbard and Kashyap (1992).

11. The material that follows is the deterministic, continuous-time version of the stochastic, discrete time model of Hayashi and Inoue (1991).

12. See, e.g., Griliches and Jorgenson (1966), Jorgenson, Gollop, and Fraumeni (1987).

13. Merrill's (1982) dissertation seems to be the first to realize this. See Abel and Eberly (1993) for a recent thorough treatment. The necessary mathematical tools, including Ito's lemma, are contained in e.g., Kamien and Schwarz (1981, part II, section 21).

14. The exposition of the theoretical model draws on Bertola (1988) and Bertola and Caballero (1994).

15. If the rate of return, ρ, and the investment goods price, p_I, are constant, then K^d depends only on ε.

16. This condition is the so-called "smooth pasting" condition. See Dixit and Pindyck (1994).

17. This does not necessarily mean that the actual capital stock $K(t)$ is more sensitive to the interest rate under irreversibility.

18. Values of nominal investment are reported in million yen. For most firms reporting zero investment in transportation equipment, the capital stock is in single digits. Probably for firms reporting zero investment, the true value is positive but less than one million yen.

19. Rob (1991) extends Zeira's single-firm model to study industry equilibrium with many firms. Zeira's model is in discrete time. I do not present Zeira's model in more detail because it is not clear to me what the continuous-time analogue of the model would be.

20. If risk-neutrality is assumed, it is fairly straightforward to extend the model to a stochastic environment where the assumption of the upward-sloping borrowing rate schedule can be made slightly less *ad hoc* by deriving it from bankruptcy costs. See Hayashi (1985).

21. See, e.g., Jorgenson and Yun (1991a).

22. If personal taxes favoring capital gains over dividends are taken into account, cutting dividends and new share issues are no longer equivalent, so that the nonnegativity constraint on dividends becomes relevant even if the firm can issue new shares to finance investment. See, e.g., Hayashi (1985).

23. A sample includes Hubbard and Kashyap (1992), Whited (1992).

24. An exception is Demers, Demers, and Schaller (1993).

5   The Cost of Capital and the Measurement of Productivity

Frank M. Gollop

Productivity analysts today take for granted not only that capital input has a rightful place in the production function underlying measures of productivity growth but also that there is a well-defined and measurable cost of capital services corresponding to capital input. This, of course, was not always the case.

The link between capital as an input in the production function, the demand for investment, and the corresponding cost of capital was first formalized by Jorgenson (1963) in his seminal paper "Capital Theory and Investment Behavior." Soon thereafter, Jorgenson (1967b) focused squarely on the relationship between investment and the cost of capital. The blueprint for total factor productivity accounting was finally in place.

Jorgenson and Griliches (1967) were the first to exploit this intellectual innovation. Not only was capital positioned as an input in a model of production but Jorgenson's contributions to the cost of capital literature permitted a disaggregated treatment of capital input in the production function.

Christensen and Jorgenson (1969, 1973b) soon introduced an indirect approach to measuring capital's service price based on the dual to the perpetual inventory method. They demonstrate how the service price can be derived from the correspondence between the price of an investment good at a point in time and rental prices of capital services from that point forward. The service price is shown to depend on the asset price, the rate of return, the rate of replacement, and the tax structure.

The Christensen and Jorgenson (1969, 1973b) model spawned debate about, among other things, the appropriate treatment of depreciation, the proper incorporation of tax considerations, aggregation bias resulting from the use of asset prices instead of service prices, and the proper adjustment for capacity utilization.[1] Sound productivity measurement depended on the resolution of these issues.

The economic literature records the consensus that has formed on these issues. There is little need to repeat that history here. Let it suffice to say that the fact that the original Jorgenson (1963, 1967b) and Christensen and Jorgenson (1973b) model has survived with only minor amendment is a testimonial to the importance of the work.

There is, however, an issue related to the measurement of capital input and its service price that continues to be debated: The role of input "quality" or "compositional shift effects" in the proper measurement of productivity growth. Most economists agree that changes in input quality are a measureable source of economic growth. The disagreement, however, centers on where to assign the contribution of input quality. Kendrick (1973) and Denison (1957, 1969, 1989), among others, are steadfast in their position that input quality is a component of productivity growth. Changing input quality should not affect measured input. Alternatively, Jorgenson and Griliches (1967), Christensen and Jorgenson (1973b), and Jorgenson, Gollop, and Fraumeni (1987) consider changing input quality to be a proper component of input growth.

This paper focuses on input quality and its proper treatment in a model of productivity growth. Section 5.1 formally develops the production model of economic growth. Following Jorgenson and Griliches (1967), the model defines input quality and presents the formal basis for including input quality in a model of productivity growth. Section 5.2 offers a context within which to settle the continuing debate about the proper role of input quality in a model of growth. Whether changing input quality should be incorporated into the measure of input growth or the measure of productivity growth is shown to depend on the distinctly different conceptual requirements of welfare and production models of economic growth. Inputs in a welfare analysis must be measured in units unadjusted for changing input quality. An analysis of productivity growth properly based in a model of production, however, requires that input quality be captured in the measure of input growth. Failing to do so leads to a biased measure of productivity growth. Section 5.3 quantifies the contribution of input quality and especially capital quality to sectoral economic growth over the 1947–1985 period. The bias in total factor productivity resulting from either ignoring quality change or misidentifying it as a source of productivity growth is quantified as well.

Interestingly, an important conclusion of this paper is little different from the original insight stated more than thirty years ago in Jorgenson and Griliches (1967): Properly measured, input growth is more important than productivity growth as a source of economic growth.

5.1 Input Quality

Jorgenson and Griliches (1967) exploit the equilibrium conditions of economic theory to give formal foundation to the notion of changing input quality within an input aggregate. A model of productivity growth is developed. The model begins with a homogeneous production function for each of n sectors:

$$Y_i = F^i(M_i, K_i, L_i, E_i, T) \qquad (i = 1, 2, \ldots, n), \tag{5.1}$$

where Y_i is output and M_i, K_i, L_i, and E_i are material, capital, labor, and energy inputs, respectively, in the i-th sector and T is time.

Necessary conditions for producer equilibrium require that each input is paid its marginal value product. These conditions are represented by equalities between the share of the j-th input (v^i_j) in the value of output and the elasticity of output with respect to that input:

$$v^i_M = \frac{p^i_M M_i}{q_i Y_i} = \frac{\partial \ln Y_i}{\partial \ln M_i}$$

$$v^i_K = \frac{p^i_K K_i}{q_i Y_i} = \frac{\partial \ln Y_i}{\partial \ln K_i}$$

$$v^i_L = \frac{p^i_L L_i}{q_i Y_i} = \frac{\partial \ln Y_i}{\partial \ln L_i}$$

$$v^i_E = \frac{p^i_E E_i}{q_i Y_i} = \frac{\partial \ln Y_i}{\partial \ln E_i} \qquad (i = 1, 2, \ldots, n) \tag{5.2}$$

where q_i, p^i_M, p^i_K, p^i_L, and p^i_E represent the prices of output and material, capital, labor, and energy inputs, respectively. Under constant returns to scale, both the output elasticities and the input shares sum to unity.

The model yields the rate of productivity growth (v_T^i) defined as the growth in output with respect to time holding constant all inputs:

$$v_T^i = \frac{\partial \ln Y_i}{\partial T}$$

$$= \frac{d \ln Y_i}{dT} - v_M^i \frac{d \ln M_i}{dT} - v_K^i \frac{d \ln K_i}{dT} - v_L^i \frac{d \ln L_i}{dT}$$

$$- v_E^i \frac{d \ln E_i}{dT} \qquad (i = 1, 2, \ldots, n). \tag{5.3}$$

Jorgenson and Griliches (1967) address the aggregation bias that results from ignoring significant differences in the marginal productivities of disaggregated inputs within the above input aggregates M_i, K_i, L_i, and E_i. Their analysis begins by recognizing that each input is an aggregate that depends on distinct material, capital, labor, and energy inputs:

$$M_i = M_i(M_{1i}, M_{2i}, \ldots, M_{ni})$$

$$K_i = K_i(K_{1i}, K_{2i}, \ldots, K_{si})$$

$$L_i = L_i(L_{1i}, L_{2i}, \ldots, L_{mi})$$

$$E_i = E_i(E_{1i}, E_{2i}, \ldots, E_{ni}) \qquad (i = 1, 2, \ldots, n), \tag{5.4}$$

where M_{ji} and E_{ji} represent the material and energy inputs, respectively, from the j-th sector to the i-th sector and K_{ki} and L_{li} represent individual capital and labor inputs, respectively.

Modeled in this way, the input aggregates infer that the production function (5.1) is separable in material, capital, labor, and energy inputs. Furthermore, assuming the input aggregates (5.4) are homogeneous of degree one in their input components, the production function is homothetically separable.

Necessary conditions for producer equilibrium underlying (5.4) lead to equalities between the share (v^i) of each individual input in the value of its corresponding aggregate and the elasticity of the aggregate with respect to that individual input:

$$v_{Mj}^i = \frac{p_{Mj}^i M_{ji}}{p_M^i M_i} = \frac{\partial \ln M_i}{\partial \ln M_{ji}} \qquad (j = 1, 2, \ldots, n)$$

$$v_{Kk}^i = \frac{p_{Kk}^i K_{ki}}{p_K^i K_i} = \frac{\partial \ln K_i}{\partial \ln K_{ki}} \qquad (k = 1, 2, \ldots, s)$$

$$v_{Ll}^i = p_{Ll}^i \frac{L_{li}}{p_L^i L_i} = \frac{\partial \ln L_i}{\partial \ln L_{li}} \qquad (l = 1, 2, \ldots, m)$$

$$v_{Ej}^i = \frac{p_{Ej}^i E_{ji}}{p_E^i E_i} = \frac{\partial \ln E_i}{\partial \ln E_{ji}} \qquad (j = 1, 2, \ldots, n) \quad (i = 1, 2, \ldots, n) \qquad (5.5)$$

where p_{Mj}^i, p_{Kk}^i, p_{Ll}^i, and p_{Ej}^i are prices corresponding to individual material, capital, labor, and energy inputs, respectively. Given linear homogeneity of the input aggregates, the individual input elasticities and their corresponding value shares both sum to unity. In addition, the value of each input aggregate equals the sum of the values of its component inputs.

The above formulation makes clear that an input aggregate formed as the simple sum of disaggregated components is free of aggregation bias if and only if the disaggregated inputs have identical marginal products. For example, logarithmically differentiating aggregate capital services K_i in (5.4) with respect to time makes explicit the role of marginal product based weights in forming the measure of capital services.

$$\frac{d \ln K_i}{dT} = \sum_k \frac{\partial \ln K_i}{\partial \ln K_{ki}} \frac{d \ln K_{ki}}{dT} \qquad (i = 1, 2, \ldots, n). \qquad (5.6)$$

Equilibrium conditions suggest that relative differences in marginal productivity are reflected by relative factor prices p_{Kk}^i, leading to the now familiar share-weighted transformation of (5.6)

$$\frac{d \ln K_i}{dT} = \sum_k \left(\frac{p_{Kk}^i K_{ki}}{p_K^i K_i} \right) \frac{d \ln K_{ki}}{dT} \qquad (i = 1, 2, \ldots, n), \qquad (5.7)$$

where p_K^i is the service price corresponding to aggregate services K_i and $\partial K_i / \partial K_{ki} = p_{Kk}^{il} p_K^i$. Material, labor, and energy input analogues of (5.7) follow directly:

$$\frac{d \ln M_i}{dT} = \sum_j \left(\frac{p_{Mj}^i M_{ji}}{p_M^i M_i} \right) \frac{d \ln M_{ji}}{dT}$$

$$\frac{d \ln L_i}{dT} = \sum_l \left(\frac{p_{L_{li}} L_{li}}{p_L^i L_i} \right) \frac{d \ln L_{li}}{dT}$$

$$\frac{d \ln E_i}{dT} = \sum_j \left(\frac{p_{Ej}^i E_{ji}}{p_E^i E_i} \right) \frac{d \ln E_{ji}}{dT} \qquad (i = 1, \ldots, n), \qquad (5.8)$$

where conditions for producer equilibrium yield $\partial M_i / \partial M_{ji} = p_{Mj}^i / p_M^i$, $\partial L_i / \partial L_{li} = p_{Ll}^i / p_L^i$, and $\partial E_i / \partial E_{ji} = p_{Ej}^i / p_E^i$.

Equation (5.7) is important for a number of reasons. First, it formalizes the proper way in which capital services should be defined. The capital input aggregate K_i introduced by Jorgenson and Griliches (1967) eliminated the error that previously arose through the assumption that service prices were simply proportional to asset prices. A source of aggregation error was eliminated. Second, given the role of asset-specific service prices in (5.7), the practical importance of correctly measuring service prices by asset category and legal form of organization became clear. The need for work that was soon to be accomplished by Christensen and Jorgenson (1969) was clear. Measures of aggregate capital input had to incorporate through factor price based weights the differing marginal products of the underlying disaggregated inputs.

The growth of aggregate capital services is no longer equal to the growth in the simple constant dollar sum of capital stocks. Changes in the composition of the stocks matter as well. The separate contributions of growth in arithmetically summed capital stocks (A_K^i) and the changing quality of aggregate input can be identified by adding and subtracting to (5.7) the growth rate of the constant dollar sum of the individual capital stocks

$$\frac{d \ln K_i}{dT} = \sum_k \left(\frac{p_{Kk}^i K_{ki}}{p_K^i K_i} \right) \left[\frac{d \ln K_{ki}}{dT} - \frac{d \ln A_K^i}{dT} \right] + \frac{d \ln A_K^i}{dT}, \qquad (5.9)$$

where $A_K^i = \sum_k K_{ki}$.

The share-weighted difference in (5.9) quantifies the contribution of changing input quality to the growth in aggregate capital services. If all K_{ki} grow at the same rate and/or all K_{ki} have identical marginal products, then quality change takes a zero value in (5.9). If, however, those K_{ki} that grow faster (slower) than the overall average growth in unweighted stocks A_K^i also have higher (lower) than average marginal products, then the first term in (5.9) takes a positive value inferring that, quite independent of the simple growth rate in stocks, capital quality has contributed to the overall growth in capital services. Only if input growth is dominated by K_{ki} that have below average marginal products will the contribution of quality change be negative.

Measures of the growth in the quality of capital input (Q_K^i) can be derived directly from (5.9):

$$\frac{d \ln Q_K^i}{dT} = \frac{d \ln K_i}{dT} - \frac{d \ln A_K^i}{dT} \qquad (1 = 1, 2, \ldots, n). \qquad (5.10)$$

Corresponding growth rates of input quality for material, labor, and energy inputs have the following form:

$$\frac{d \ln Q_M^i}{dT} = \frac{d \ln M_i}{dT} - \frac{d \ln A_M^i}{dT}$$
$$\frac{d \ln Q_L^i}{dT} = \frac{d \ln L_i}{dT} - \frac{d \ln A_L^i}{dT}$$
$$\frac{d \ln Q_E^i}{dT} = \frac{d \ln E_i}{dT} - \frac{d \ln A_E^i}{dT} \qquad (1 = 1, 2, \ldots, n). \qquad (5.11)$$

where A_M^i, A_L^i, and A_E^i are, analogous to A_K^i, unweighted sums of material, labor, and energy stocks, respectively.

Excluding changing input quality from measures of aggregate input growth leads to biased measures of input growth and, worse, productivity growth. Recall, productivity growth is defined as the difference between properly measured rates of output and input growth. The next section of this paper provides a context for addressing the continuing debate about the proper treatment of changing input quality in models of economic growth.

5.2 Welfare versus Productivity Growth

The formal derivation by Jorgenson and Griliches (1967) of a source of growth originating through the changing composition of capital assets was quite novel. Solow (1957) and Denison (1962) had employed a pure stock concept of capital input (as defined by A_K^i above) wholly ignoring changes in the quality of capital services due to changes in the composition of the capital stock. Kendrick (1961) had adjusted capital input for the effects of changing industrial composition but ignored shifts in asset mix or legal form of organization.

Jorgenson and Griliches (1967) identified and quantified the changing quality of capital input as a unique source of economic growth. Given the established method for measuring productivity growth, the effect of changing capital quality had previously been buried in the productivity "residual." Jorgenson and Griliches (1967) effected the transfer of capital quality from its status as an unmeasurable component of the residual to its role as a source of growth flowing through the growth of capital services.

The Jorgenson-Griliches (1967) paper did much to focus on measurement issues and sources of aggregation bias and prepared detailed blueprints for the measurement of both capital input and productivity growth—blueprints that were soon to be followed by Christensen and Jorgenson (1969, 1970). More importantly, since substitution possibilities reflected through differing marginal products are appropriately the domain of movements along the production function rather than shifts in the function, Jorgenson and Griliches (1967) clearly positioned the effect of changing input quality as an element in the measure of aggregate input.

The argument for treating input quality as part of input growth is simple and mathematically persuasive given the precepts of the economic theory of production, yet disagreement persists about whether to assign changing input quality to the input growth or productivity growth categories. Kendrick (1973) continues to treat all laborers within an industry as homogeneous.[2] He ignores differences in the marginal products of various categories of employed persons. Any influence of changing input quality effectively remains in the productivity residual. Symmetrically, Kendrick (1973) specifically treats any growth in output resulting from a change in the composition of capital stock by asset type or legal form of organization as part of productivity growth.[3]

Denison (1957, 1969) objects to measuring investment goods in constant quality units. He specifically argues the point in his response to Jorgenson and Griliches (1972a) and, even later, Denison (1989) objects to the proposed use by the Bureau of Economic Analysis of constant quality price indexes for computers. Asymmetrically, however, Denison (1962, 1974, 1979, 1985) takes great effort to incorporate changes in the age, sex, and education composition of the labor force into his measure of labor input.

One way to explain the source of disagreement in the above studies regarding the treatment of input quality is to consider the different conceptual requirements of production and welfare models of economic growth. The production approach adopted by Jorgenson (1966b), Jorgenson and Griliches (1967), and Christensen and Jorgenson (1973b) is based on the production possibility frontier. It begins with a production account preserving an accounting identity equating the values of outputs and inputs. As in section 5.1, the production-based data can be used to decompose the growth of output into distinct sources associated with input growth and productivity growth.

The welfare approach to economic growth begins from an income and expenditure account. The underlying accounting identity equates income with the sum of consumption and saving. Growth in income (welfare) is allocated between the growth rates of consumption and saving.

The different implications of the two approaches for the measurement of inputs and output becomes clear when examined in the context of the "net versus gross" output controversy between Denison (1969) and Jorgenson and Griliches (1972a). Denison (1962) clearly follows the welfare approach of Solow (1957) by defining output net of depreciation. Clearly, welfare is not improved by that part of an increase in gross output that is due to an increase in the rate of capital consumption. This simply represents trading future consumption for current consumption. "Net" output becomes the appropriate measure of output for welfare analysis. This is precisely the definition of output adopted by Denison in all his research and by Kendrick (1973) when he measures output net of depreciation.[4]

Jorgenson (1966b), Jorgenson and Griliches (1967), and Christensen and Jorgenson (1973b), however, focus on production—gross production. After all, any increase in inputs or productivity leads to an increase in gross production. If output were modeled as output net of depreciation, what would account for the production of replacement investment and precisely which inputs should be deleted from the production accounts? Replacement investment has to be produced somehow and must be incorporated in a model of production. Moreover, there is no basis for asserting that productivity growth augments only "net" output and not output destined for replacement. Put simply, the formal modeling of production and the pure measurement of productivity growth have their own conceptual integrity and are not constrained by welfare considerations. Gross output becomes the appropriate measure of output for productivity analysis.

Hulten (1992) formally derives a model of optimal economic growth that encompasses both production and welfare approaches to growth accounting. The model is similar to one proposed earlier by Weitzman (1976). Income, appropriately measured net of depreciation and thereby often labeled "net product," measures the welfare resulting from the intertemporal optimization of consumption. The growth in net product is allocated between the growth in current consumption and future consumption (saving). Production, however, is appropriately measured as gross output whose growth rate is a function of the growth in inputs and productivity growth. By combining an aggregate production function and an explicit social welfare function within a model of optimal economic growth, Hulten (1992) has shown that gross output and net output are not substitutes vying for position in growth models but complementary concepts in a larger model of optimal growth.

The complementary nature of welfare and production approaches to growth accounting has clear implications for the treatment of input quality. In explaining the growth in gross output a model of production must distinguish betweeen movements along and shifts of the production frontier. "Shifts" correspond to productivity growth. "Movements along" the frontier are the domain of aggregate input and incorporate both changes in the levels of inputs as well as pure substitution possibilities among the inputs. This production criterion clearly positions input quality within the definition of input growth.

In particular, if one were interested in aggregating material, capital, labor, and energy inputs into a single index of aggregate input to model movements along a production function, the growth rate of the aggregate index would have to reflect changes in the levels of its component inputs (M, K, L, and E) as well as substitution possibilities among these inputs. The familiar cost-share weights on input growth rates in the TFP formula (5.3) explicitly account for these substitution possibilities.

The corollary is equally important. A properly formed measure of aggregate input must incorporate substitution possibilities not only among the broadly defined input categories of material, capital, labor, and energy but also among disaggregated input classes within the material, capital, labor, and energy aggregates. Treating one constant dollar of durable equipment as equivalent to one constant dollar of structures violates the same economic principle as would the assumption that one constant dollar of labor input equals one constant dollar of capital input.

The role and therefore the appropriate measure of "input" in the context of a welfare model is quite different. A welfare analysis views labor not as an input into production but as a measure of human effort. Focus shifts from substitution among various workers having different marginal productivities to substitution between labor and leisure. In an analysis of welfare, an increase in social welfare that results not from an increase in hours worked but from a recomposition of hours to a higher marginal productivity content does not connote a movement along the welfare function but an unambiguous shift in the function. Welfare will have increased without any corresponding increase in labor effort. In the context of welfare analysis, the contribution of labor quality belongs in the welfare residual.

An analogous distinction applies to the proper treatment of capital quality. In a pure model of production, recomposition of aggregate capital stock resulting from producers having taken advantage of substitution possibilities among detailed capital inputs clearly indicates a movement along the production frontier. There has been no technical change leading to a shift of the frontier. Movements in capital quality thereby properly belong in the measure of capital input.

In a welfare context, however, investment dollars, regardless of their allocation to specific asset types, represent equal opportunity cost claims on scarce savings. Any recomposition of the capital stock that does not alter the overall dollar commitment to capital simply does not affect substitution between current consumption and saving. Social welfare may well be impacted but the effect of any change in capital quality should be modeled as a shift of the welfare function.

The conceptually distinct roles of input quality in welfare and production models of economic growth are really quite straightforward. The continuing controversy over the treatment of input quality stems from the fact that Denison (1962, 1989), Kendrick (1973), Weitzman (1976), and others adopt production-based terminology in their welfare analyses. Measured shifts in welfare functions are confounded with productivity-induced shifts of the production possibilities frontier.

Weitzman (1976), for example, carefully derives the concept of national income and equates it with the flow of consumer welfare. He then renames national income "net product" and thereby connotes a production context for his analysis. "Productivity growth" in his analysis really connotes the residual in a welfare function and is thereby confounded with the true measure of productivity growth that describes a shift of the production frontier.

John Kendrick is best known for his "productivity" research, yet his resolute stand against incorporating either labor or capital quality within the boundaries of input growth positions his treatment of labor and capital clearly within a welfare framework. Labor and capital as measured by Kendrick (1973) for either aggregate or sectoral applications do not conform to the conceptual criteria required by a model of production but rather conform to the standards of welfare analysis. Labor and capital are measured in terms of their opportunity costs in terms of leisure and savings, respectively.

Denison (1962, 1974, 1979, 1985, 1989) adopts a net income measure of output as discussed above and, like Kendrick, remains steadfast in his refusal to account for the changing quality of capital input as part of his measure of aggregate capital. He clearly adopts a welfare approach to growth accounting. Denison (1989) even goes so far as to propose measuring investment, for productivity accounting purposes, as foregone consumption. Except for his inconsistent treatment of labor, which incorporates the changing age, sex, and education composition of the labor force, Denison clearly adopts a welfare approach to growth accounting.

In the final analysis, the concept of productivity growth has precise meaning. It corresponds to the shift in the production frontier. It is not, however, to be confused with the shift in the welfare function. Productivity analysis is concerned with a society's ability to transform inputs into output. Applying a productivity interpretation to the residual of the welfare function leads to a bias in the measurement of productivity growth.

In the context of a model designed to quantify the contribution of productivity growth to economic growth and indirectly to social welfare, sums over disaggregated input categories that fail to adjust for changing input quality lead to biased measures of aggregate inputs and, worse, productivity growth. The next section of this paper examines the extent of this bias and therefore the importance of properly accounting for changing input quality.

5.3 Input Growth and Productivity Bias

The analysis developed in this paper is based on the model of sectoral production developed in Jorgenson, Gollop, and Fraumeni (1987) and on data updated through 1985 as described in Jorgenson, Gollop, and Fraumeni (1987). For purposes of this paper, the U.S. economy is decomposed into the ten sectors listed in table 5.1.[5] Each is formed as an aggregate over the relevant disaggregated sectors listed in Jorgenson, Gollop, and Fraumeni (1987).[6]

The relevant inputs for this study are capital, labor, energy, and materials. Each input is itself an aggregate formed over distinct quantities of, respectively, capital stocks, labor hours, energy inputs, and material inputs. Capital stocks are differentiated within each industry by six asset types and four forms of legal organization. Labor hours in each industry are categorized by sex (2), age (8), education level (5), occupation (10), and employment class (2). Energy and material inputs in each industry are distinguished into disaggregated deliveries from thirty-five energy and non-energy producing sectors, respectively.

Constructing measures of sectoral inputs using data identified with discrete points in time requires transforming the model derived in section 5.1 from continuous to discrete time. For this purpose, the production function (5.1) is given the translog form introduced by Christensen, Jorgenson, and Lau (1971, 1973). The sectoral inputs L_i, K_i, M_i, and E_i thereby become translog aggregates of their individual input components. The growth rate of each input aggregate is a weighted average of the growth rates of its detailed input components. The growth rate of capital input K_i, for example, is formed as the translog aggregate over its twenty-four capital components (six asset types and four forms of legal organization):

$$\ln K_i(T) - \ln K_i(T-1)$$
$$= \sum \bar{v}_{Kk}^i [\ln K_{ki}(T) - \ln K_{ki}(T-1)], \quad (i = 1, 2, .., n), \qquad (5.12)$$

where weights $\bar{v}_{Kk}^i$ are given by average shares of each K_{ki} in the value of the i-th sector's property compensation:

$$\bar{v}_{Kk}^i = \frac{1}{2}\left[v_{Kk}^i(T) + v_{Kk}^i(T-1)\right] \quad (i = 1, 2, \ldots, n; \, k = 1, 2, \ldots, s). \qquad (5.13)$$

Table 5.1
Capital input and its source decomposition

Sectors	Average annual rates of growth									Quality change as percent of input growth		
	1947–1985			1947–1966			1966–1985			1947–1985	1947–1966	1966–1985
	Input	Stocks	Quality	Input	Stocks	Quality	Input	Stocks	Quality			
Agriculture	.0083	−.0047	.0130	.0082	−.0097	.0179	.0083	.0000	.0083	156	218	100
Mining	.0341	.0313	.0027	.0305	.0287	.0018	.0377	.0339	.0038	8	6	10
Construction	.0366	.0306	.0061	.0448	.0332	.0116	.0285	.0280	.0005	17	26	2
Manufacturing	.0338	.0285	.0053	.0366	.0289	.0077	.0310	.0280	.0030	16	21	10
Transportation	.0134	−.0021	.0155	.0094	−.0066	.0160	.0174	.0025	.0149	116	170	86
Communication	.0695	.0563	.0132	.0819	.0630	.0189	.0571	.0496	.0075	19	23	13
Public utilities	.0381	.0341	.0040	.0446	.0365	.0081	.0316	.0317	−.0001	10	18	(−)
Trade	.0394	.0270	.0124	.0342	.0189	.0153	.0446	.0351	.0095	31	45	21
Finance, insurance and real estate	.0371	.0287	.0084	.0363	.0284	.0079	.0379	.0289	.0090	23	22	24
Other services	.0498	.0379	.0118	.0582	.0461	.0121	.0413	.0298	.0115	24	21	28

The value shares, defined above in (5.5), are calculated from data on detailed capital input (K_{ki}) and service prices (p^i_{Kk}) cross-classified by asset type and legal form of organization.

Translog indexes of aggregate labor, material, and energy inputs are formed analogously. The corresponding translog price index for each input aggregate is formed as the ratio of the value of the aggregate to its quantity index.

The discrete representation of input quality follows directly from (5.10) and (5.11). The growth in the quality of capital input (Q^i_K) is defined as the difference between the growth in aggregate capital services (K_i) and the growth in aggregate capital stock (A^i_K):

$\ln Q^i_K(T) - \ln Q^i_K(T-1)$

$$= [\ln K_i(T) - \ln K_i(T-1)] - \left[\ln A^i_K(T) - \ln A^i_{K(T-1)}\right]$$

$$= \sum \bar{v}^i_{Kk}\left[\ln K_{ki}(T) - \ln K_{ki(T-1)}\right] - \left[\ln A^i_K(T) - \ln A^i_{K(T-1)}\right]$$

$$(i = 1, 2, \ldots, n). \tag{5.14}$$

Aggregate capital stock, recall, is defined as the unweighted sum of capital stocks. Consequently, if and only if all K_{ki} grow at the same rate and/or all K_{ki} have identical marginal products, will quality change take a zero value in (5.14). Quality change for material, labor, and energy inputs is defined symmetrically:

$$\ln Q^i_M(T) - \ln Q^i_M(T-1) = \sum \bar{v}^i_{Mj}[\ln M_{ji}(T) - \ln M_{ji}(T-1)]$$

$$- \left[\ln A^i_M(T) - \ln A^i_M(T-1)\right]$$

$$\ln Q^i_L(T) - \ln Q^i_L(T-1) = \sum \bar{v}^i_{Ll}\left[\ln L_{li}(T) - \ln L_{li}(T-1)\right]$$

$$- \left[\ln A^i_L(T) - \ln A^i_L(T-1)\right]$$

$$\ln Q^i_E(T) - \ln Q^i_E(T-1) = \sum \bar{v}^i_{Ej}\left[\ln E_{ji}(T) - \ln E_{ji}(T-1)\right]$$

$$- \left[\ln A^i_E(T) \ln A^i_E(T-1)\right] \quad (i = 1, 2, \ldots, n) \tag{5.15}$$

where

$$\sum \bar{v}^i_{Mj} = \frac{1}{2}\left[v^i_{Mj}(T) - v^i_{Mj}(T-1)\right]$$

$$\sum \bar{v}^i_{LI} = \frac{1}{2}\left[v^i_{LI}(T) - v^i_{LI}(T-1)\right]$$

$$\sum \bar{v}^i_{Ej} = \frac{1}{2}\left[v^i_{Ej}(T) - v^i_{Ej}(T-1)\right].$$

Table 5.1 focuses on the growth in capital input and its source decomposition into unweighted stock (A^i_K) and quality (Q^i_K) components. Following the formulation in equation (5.9), the average annual rate of growth in capital input in each sector is defined as the sum of the growth rate of unweighted capital stock in that sector and the effect of changes in the composition or quality of the capital stock.

The first important observation from Table 5.1 is that the contribution of quality change to the growth in capital input is positive in every sector over the full 1947–1985 period. That pattern persists when the full period is divided into pre- and post-1966 periods.[7] The contribution of quality change is positive for every sector in the pre-1966 period and for all but public utilities in the post-1966 period. The important conclusion is that ignoring compositional shifts leads to downward biased measures of growth in capital input, a result wholly consistent with the findings of Jorgenson and Griliches (1967) nearly thirty years ago.

The importance of evaluating the changing composition of a sector's capital stock is perhaps best illustrated by the agriculture and transportation sectors. Ignoring quality change, the average annual rates of growth in capital input in these sectors would have been found to have been negative, −0.47 and −0.21 percents, respectively. Incorporating compositional shifts shows that true average annual capital input growth rates in agriculture and transportation were in fact positive at 0.83 and 1.34 percent rates, respectively.

Trends in the agriculture sector underscore the point. Unweighted stocks decline at a −0.97 percent annual rate in the 1947–1966 period. The post-1966 rate is zero implying that, relative to the pre-1966 period, a negative trend is reversed. If one disregards quality change, the trend in capital input would be inferred from this trend in capital stocks. However, once compositional shifts are introduced into the analysis, not only do the negative rates of growth disappear but the trend over time becomes quite different. Instead of inferring that input growth moves from a nearly −1.0 percent annual rate pre-1966 to a zero rate post-1966, true capital input growth is seen to have remained constant at a positive 0.8 percent rate throughout the full 1947–1985 period.

Ignoring quality change not only biases inferences within sectors but across sectors as well. In the 1947–1985 period, for example, the average annual contribution of quality change in capital input varied from 0.27 percent in mining to 1.55 percent in transportation. The range is even wider in the 1947–1966 subperiod. Mining again exhibits the lowest contribution of quality change with an average annual 0.18 percent rate while communication has the highest rate at a 1.89 percent level.

The potential for biased inferences over time is also evident from table 5.1. From the pre- to post-1966 subperiods, two sectors (mining and finance, insurance and real estate) reveal increasing contributions from quality change while the remaining eight exhibit decreasing contributions. The differential trends are significant. The average annual contribution of quality change in communications falls from 1.16 percent in the 1947–1966 period to 0.05 percent in the 1966–1985 period. In contrast, mining's compositional shifts in capital increased their contributions to input growth from 0.18 to 0.38 percent.

The last three columns of table 5.1 summarize well the varying importance of quality change both across sectors and over time. Inferences about the growth in capital input within sectors, across sectors and over time would be biased unless quality change is correctly incorporated as defined in equations (5.9) through (5.11).

It is important to emphasize that identifying and quantifying the effects of compositional shifts within capital were made possible only through the careful modeling and later measuring of the cost of capital by industry, asset type, and legal form of organization. Without the early work on investment in Jorgenson(1963), the cost of capital in Jorgenson (1967b) and Hall and Jorgenson (1967), and the later measurement work in Jorgenson and Griliches (1967) and Christensen and Jorgenson (1969, 1973b), an important source of growth in capital input would have been masked, leading to biased inferences both across sectors and over time.

Table 5.2 widens the focus from capital input to aggregate input whose growth rate is defined as the cost-share weighted growth rates of quality-adjusted capital, labor, energy, and material inputs. The measures of aggregate input growth reported in table 5.2 therefore correctly account for all substitution possibilities—not only among but

Table 5.2
Aggregate input and its source decomposition

Sectors	Average annual rates of growth, 1947–1985			Quality decomposition			
	Input	Stocks	Quality	Capital	Labor	Energy	Materials
Agriculture	.0034	−.0014	.0048	.0023	.0026	.0001	−.0002
Mining	.0262	.0249	.0013	.0010	.0009	−.0003	−.0003
Construction	.0279	.0264	.0015	.0005	.0006	.0000	.0004
Manufacturing	.0220	.0202	.0018	.0005	.0013	.0001	−.0001
Transportation	.0128	.0093	.0035	.0025	.0010	−.0002	.0002
Communication	.0433	.0368	.0065	.0039	.0024	.0000	.0001
Public utilities	.0388	.0378	.0010	.0016	.0009	−.0015	.0000
Trade	.0264	.0224	.0040	.0025	.0014	.0001	.0001
Finance, insurance and real estate	.0381	.0330	.0051	.0028	.0020	.0000	.0003
Other services	.0416	.0350	.0066	.0047	.0017	.0000	.0002

within the capital, labor, energy, and material subaggregates. The contribution to aggregate input growth of each unweighted stock and input quality is measured as the product of each component and its input cost share. Table 5.2 reports the contribution of quality change associated with each input as well as total contributions arising through aggregate stocks and overall quality change.

The overall contribution of quality change reported in column 3 of table 5.2 can be interpreted as the magnitude of bias that is introduced in the measure of aggregate input in each sector if quality change is ignored. It ranges from one-tenth of a percent per year in mining and public utilities to annual percentage rates greater than or equal to one-half percent in agriculture, communication, other services, and finance, insurance and real estate. Excluding agriculture for the moment, the bias stated in percentage terms ranges from 2.5 percent in public utilities to 27 percent in transportation with a 13 percent median value. Quality change is an important dimension of input measurement.

The importance of properly accounting for compositional shifts within each input aggregate is clearly illustrated in agriculture. Input stocks in agriculture grew at an average annual rate equal to −0.14 percent over the 1947–1985 period. The net effect of quality change in all four inputs, however, made a positive 0.48 percent annual contribution leading to a measured growth rate in quality-adjusted aggregate input of 0.34 percent per year.

Table 5.3
Contributions to economic growth

Sectors	Average annual rates of growth, 1947–1985				
	Output	Input			TFP
		Input	Stocks	Quality	
Agriculture	.0192	.0034	−.0014	.0048	.0158
Mining	.0147	.0249	.0249	.0013	−.0114
Construction	.0308	.0279	.0264	.0015	.0029
Manufacturing	.0292	.0220	.0202	.0018	.0072
Transportation	.0223	.0128	.0093	.0035	.0096
Communication	.0637	.0433	.0368	.0065	.0204
Public utilities	.0475	.0388	.0378	.0010	.0087
Trade	.0354	.0264	.0224	.0040	.0090
Finance, insurance and real estate	.0405	.0381	.0330	.0051	.0024
Other services	.0403	.0416	.0350	.0066	−.0013

The additional disaggregation of aggregate quality change into its input-specific components makes clear that compositional shifts within capital and labor inputs have made significant contributions to input growth. Interestingly, the cost-share weighted contribution of changing quality among capital stocks exceeds the corresponding contribution through any of the other three inputs in seven of ten sectors—again pointing to the importance of properly measuring the cost of capital associated with each capital stock.

Table 5.3 further broadens the analysis by summarizing the sources of growth in each of the ten economic sectors. Output growth is decomposed into its input and TFP components. Input growth is further disaggregated into its stock and quality change contributions. Stated as annualized rates, output growth over the full 1947–1985 period has been positive in every sector as have been the growth rates of aggregate inputs and input quality.

The contribution of changing input quality is a nontrivial component of output growth, contributing approximately one-half percent per year or more to economic growth in four sectors—agriculture, communication, other services, and finance, insurance and real estate. Stated in percentage terms, quality change explains no less than 10 percent of economic growth in six of the 10 sectors. It accounts for as much as 25 percent of economic growth in agriculture.

Table 5.4
Measurement bias: TFP growth

Sectors	Average annual rates of growth , 1947–1985		
	TFP	Quality change	TFP if ignore quality change
Agriculture	.0158	.0048	.0206
Mining	−.0114	.0013	−.0101
Construction	.0029	.0015	.0044
Manufacturing	.0072	.0018	.0090
Transportation	.0096	.0035	.0131
Communication	.0204	.0065	.0269
Public utilities	.0087	.0010	.0097
Trade	.0090	.0040	.0130
Finance, insurance and real estate	.0024	.0051	.0075
Other services	−.0013	.0066	.0053

It is also the case that the contribution of quality change is larger than total factor productivity growth in three sectors—mining, other services, and finance, insurance and real estate. Among the remaining seven sectors, the ratios of the contributions of quality change to TFP growth range from 11 percent (public utilities) to 52 percent (construction). Excluding only public utilities, the contribution of quality change is at least 25 percent of the TFP growth rate. Quality change is an important dimension of the economic growth story.

The results in table 5.3 also confirm one of the novel findings first reported in Jorgenson and Griliches (1967): the growth in inputs is a more important determinant of economic growth than is productivity change. This result holds true for all non-agricultural sectors. The identification of the contribution of quality change as an important source of input growth simply reinforces this general result.

The measurement bias introduced by ignoring changes in input quality is made evident in table 5.4. When ignored, the effect of compositional shifts within each capital, labor, energy, and materials aggregate remains hidden within the productivity residual leading to the measured rates of TFP growth reported in the last column of table 5.4. When input growth rates correctly incorporate the effects of quality change among disaggregated components within each input aggregate, TFP growth rates take the measured values reported in the first column.

Since input quality has improved in every sector over the 1947–1985 period, the conclusion is straightforward. If input quality is either ignored or inappropriately assigned to productivity growth, the average annual postwar rates of TFP growth in all 10 sectors would be upward biased. However, while the direction of bias is unambiguous, the magnitude is not. The bias ranges from 0.1 (public utilities) to 0.66 (other services) percentage points across the 10 sectors identified in this study. There is no substitute for careful productivity accounting, in particular measuring the impact of the changing composition of disaggregated input components within the capital, labor, energy, and material aggregates.

Inspection of the measured rates of TFP growth and quality change reported in tables 5.5 and 5.6 reinforces this point. The potential TFP bias resulting from ignoring input quality change not only can be substantial but can be expected to vary considerably across industries and over time. In the 1947–1953 subperiod, for example, the average contribution of quality change as reported in table 5.6 was a full 1.33 and 1.46 percentage points per year in communication and other services, respectively. During the same period, it was a negative 0.17 percentage points in mining. Absent measured quality change, TFP growth in the postwar period in communications and other services would have been upward biased by more than one and one-quarter percentage points per year. Mining TFP would have been downward biased by two-tenths of a point.

The variation over time within industries is equally dramatic. While compositional shifts within input categories contributed 1.33 percentage points to economic growth in the communications sector over the 1947–1953 subperiod and 0.93 percentage points per year in 1953–1957, this contribution turned negative (–0.18) between 1957 and 1960. Careful measurement of quality-adjusted input growth is essential to not only unraveling the sources of economic growth but also producing unbiased measures of productivity growth.

5.4 Conclusion

Capital services in the economy are compensated at rental rates, just as labor services are compensated at wage rates. Unfortunately, even to this day, very little effort has been expended on compiling data from rental transactions. Meaningful progress in productivity measurement had to await a framework linking capital as an input in the

Table 5.5
Total factor productivity growth

Sectors	Average annual rates of growth								
	1947–1985	1947–1953	1953–1957	1957–1960	1960–1966	1966–1969	1969–1973	1973–1979	1979–1985
Agriculture	.0158	.0137	.0233	.0135	.0063	.0119	-.0067	.0206	.0358
Mining	-.0114	.0056	-.0039	.0075	.0097	.0062	.0029	-.0675	-.0264
Construction	.0029	.0129	.0170	.0266	.0022	-.0119	-.0114	-.0111	.0032
Manufacturing	.0072	.0051	.0011	.0107	.0099	.0080	.0110	.0021	.0115
Transportation	.0096	.0049	.0200	.0100	.0185	.0026	.0257	.0098	-.0093
Communication	.0204	.0175	.0170	.0407	.0194	.0248	.0208	.0393	-.0007
Public utilities	.0087	.0289	.0167	.0147	.0169	.0198	.0017	-.0173	-.0029
Trade	.0090	.0098	.0126	.0105	.0215	-.0008	.0126	-.0042	.0080
Finance, insurance and real estate	.0024	.0014	.0066	.0100	.0088	.0097	.0028	.0076	-.0187
Other services	-.0013	-.0011	-.0036	-.0020	.0031	-.0025	.0011	.0003	-.0065

Table 5.6
Quality change

Sectors	Average annual rates of growth								
	1947–1985	1947–1953	1953–1957	1957–1960	1960–1966	1966–1969	1969–1973	1973–1079	1979–1985
Agriculture	.0048	.0102	.0068	.0032	.0055	.0077	.0014	.0027	.0012
Mining	.0013	-.0017	.0005	.0019	.0041	.0036	-.0009	.0046	-.0012
Construction	.0015	.0036	.0012	.0008	.0026	.0014	.0004	.0006	.0003
Manufacturing	.0018	.0019	.0036	.0011	.0041	-.0002	.0003	.0012	.0010
Transportation	.0035	.0037	.0034	.0024	.0085	.0061	.0017	.0018	.0007
Communication	.0065	.0133	.0093	-.0018	.0081	.0052	.0040	.0065	.0024
Public utilities	.0010	.0013	.0058	-.0027	.0018	.0047	.0015	-.0004	-.0024
Trade	.0040	.0079	.0055	.0013	.0054	.0053	.0004	.0019	.0029
Finance, insurance and real estate	.0051	.0091	.0074	.0028	.0040	.0060	.0029	.0037	.0040
Other services	.0066	.0146	.0070	.0034	.0045	0062	.0040	.0061	.0043

production function with a model of rental prices. Jorgenson's early work provided that breakthrough and set in motion a wave of interest in productivity measurement.

Measurement was not the only beneficiary, however. Jorgenson (1963, 1967b) permitted a disaggregated treatment of capital input in the production function. Measures of capital input now could incorporate through factor price based weights the differing marginal products of the underlying disaggregated capital stocks. The effect on capital input of changes in the composition of the disaggregated stocks could be identified. The effect of this quality change in capital input on economic growth could be removed from the productivity residual and identified and quantified as a unique source of economic growth. Jorgenson's work enhanced the analysis of the sources of economic growth as well as productivity measurement.

The empirical results reported in this paper make clear that quality change is a nontrivial component in the sources of growth story. Stated in percentage terms, quality change explains no less than ten percent of economic growth in six of the ten sectors examined in this study. It is also the case that the contribution of quality change is larger than total factor productivity growth in three sectors and, in six of the remaining seven sectors, the contribution of quality change is at least 25 percent of the TFP growth rate. Quality change is an important dimension of the economic growth story.

Perhaps more importantly, properly accounting for quality change has removed a significant source of bias from measured productivity growth. This study shows that TFP growth over the 1947–1985 period would have been upward biased in all ten sectors if changing input quality had been ignored. The extent of the bias would have ranged across the sectors from 0.1 to nearly 0.7 percentage points.

The measure of our ignorance is now smaller thanks to the intellectual innovations introduced by Jorgenson (1963). That is the good news. The even better news is that the productivity residual is still large enough to keep those of us committed to productivity measurement and analysis fully employed for the indefinite future.

Notes

1. Christensen and Jorgenson (1969, 1973b) discuss both the aggregation bias due to using asset prices rather than service prices in measuring capital input and the method by which to incorporate tax structure considerations. The issues involving the proper

treatment of depreciation and the role of utilization adjustments can be found in the lengthy Jorgenson-Griliches (1967, 1972a, 1972b) versus Denison (1969, 1972) debates.

2. Kendrick (1973), p.12.

3. *Ibid*, p. 146.

4. See Denison (1962, 1974, 1979, 1985, 1989) and Kendrick (1973), p. 17.

5. The "Other Services" sector includes private households and government enterprises.

6. Operationally, this means that transactions in energy and material goods and services among individual sectors within each of the nine non-farm aggregates enter the calculation of TFP growth reported for the representative non-farm sector.

7. The year 1966 marks the beginning of the 1966–1969 cycle and roughly divides the full 1947–1985 period in half.

6

The Jorgenson System of
National Accounting

Barbara M. Fraumeni

6.1 Introduction

The Jorgenson system of national accounting, with the cost of capital formulation at its core, has made a singular contribution to economic analysis. Economists depend on data that accurately reflect the situation of the whole economy as well as the situation of individual agents: consumers and businesses. Economic data allow for comparisons to be made across time for a particular country as well as across countries. The importance of national accounting was clearly recognized by the awarding of the Nobel Prize in Economics to Richard Stone. The Jorgenson system of national accounts is a complete and integrated set of national accounts with a production account, income and expenditure account, an accumulation account and a wealth account in current and constant dollars. This set of accounts taken together forms a complete and consistent set of accounts suitable for economic analysis.

The purpose of this chapter is to present and examine the features of the Jorgenson system of national accounts, with an emphasis on the human and nonhuman capital accounts. The Jorgenson system of national accounts is comprised of three major components: 1) the Christensen-Jorgenson national accounts (1969, 1970, 1973a, 1973b), 2) the Jorgenson-Gollop-Fraumeni sectoral accounts (1987),[1] and 3) the Jorgenson-Fraumeni human capital and nonmarket accounts (1989a, 1989b, 1992a, 1992b). Section 6.2 compares national accounting systems and discusses their historical development. The national accounting systems covered include the U.S. National Income and Product Accounts (NIPA), the United Nations System of National Accounts (SNA) and the Jorgenson system of national accounts. Section 6.3 presents definitional tables. Section 6.4 describes the human capital and nonmarket accounts, the most recent additions to the Jorgenson system of national accounts, and presents selected time series from those accounts. Section 6.5 concludes.

6.2   National Accounting Systems

The major national accounting systems of today were all developed during the 20th century. The collaboration of Meade and Stone in Great Britain in 1940 was the beginning of the work that eventually resulted in the SNA. After World War II development of the SNA, which became the international model for a system of national accounts, accelerated. It culminated in the late sixties with the publication of the 1968 version of the SNA (United Nations, 1968). Simon Kuznets began work on a national accounting system for the U.S. in the thirties. After World War II, the U.S. government developed a system of national accounts (Ruggles and Ruggles, 1971), led by Milton Gilbert and later George Jaszi. Griliches and Jorgenson debated national accounting constructs with Denison in the context of productivity measurement in the late sixties and early seventies (Griliches and Jorgenson, 1966; Jorgenson and Griliches, 1972; Denison, 1969, 1972). Christensen and Jorgenson presented their system of national accounts in a series of papers in the late sixties and early seventies (Christensen and Jorgenson 1969, 1970, 1973a, 1973b). The earliest version of the Christensen-Jorgenson U.S. Worksheets, implementing their accounting system, existed by this time.

The NIPA accounts of today and the SNA accounts until recently are in basic format the same as the NIPA and SNA accounts of the late sixties. There have been a number of other data sets created or more clearly related to the NIPA accounts since then, such as the Capital Stock Study and the input output tables of BEA, and the Flow of Funds Accounts (FFA) of the Federal Reserve Board, but they have not been completely integrated into the national accounting system.[2] The SNA, in contrast to NIPA, integrates national income and product accounts with inter-industry and flow of funds accounts. The revision of the SNA accounts has just been completed (United Nations, 1993), with the emphasis on the addition of satellite accounts rather than a major revision of the general format or definitions and concepts included.

By contrast, the Christensen-Jorgenson national accounts of the late sixties were just a starting point for the current system. Beginning with theses completed in the late sixties and early seventies (Barger, 1972; Chinloy, 1974; Fraumeni, 1980; Gollop, 1974; Ho, 1989; Hulten, 1973; Wilcoxen, 1989), modeling work begun in the seventies (Hudson and Jorgenson, 1974a, 1974b; Jorgenson-Yun, 1986a, 1986b), and ongoing work by Christensen, Jorgenson and others, the system was greatly expanded. Barger, Chinloy, Gollop and Hulten developed disaggregated production accounts consistent with the Christensen-Jorgenson aggregate national accounts. The Chinloy and Gollop theses involved development of a labor data base, with detail classifying labor into over 70,000 categories. Fraumeni incorporated a disaggregated production account and a disaggregated set of capital accounts into a complete accounting system. The 1987 book by Jorgenson, Gollop and Fraumeni linked sectoral productivity to aggregate productivity. Ho (1989) incorporated individual data from the Census of Population. Wilcoxen (1988) constructed a complete and improved set of input-output matrices. Most recently, human capital and nonmarket accounts were added to the integrated accounting framework (Jorgenson and Fraumeni, 1989a; 1989b, 1992a, 1992b). Throughout, the basic concepts and philosophy of building a completely integrated set of accounts have been a constant.

The U.S. national accounts main weakness is the strength of Jorgenson's (1980) set of accounts. Jorgenson's system is a complete system that looks at asset flows, stocks and inputs, production, outlays, receipts, expenditures, income, and wealth. First, BEA produces estimates of investment in reproducible tangible assets and the stocks of nonhuman capital created, but these estimates are not directly linked to the production account in NIPA via the services they produce. Jorgenson, by contrast, estimates the capital service flows or productive contribution of nonhuman capital assets (in both current and constant dollars). Similarly, labor services in both current and constant dollars are incorporated into the production account. In his most recent work on human capital (Jorgenson and Fraumeni, 1989a), human capital flows and stocks are estimated in a manner that is parallel to the estimation of nonhuman capital flows and stocks and their productive input. Second, BEA does not include a set of balance sheets or revaluation accounts in its set of national accounts. While estimates of fixed reproducible wealth exist with information from BEA and from the FFA for other components such as land, they do not exist as part of a national balance sheet. The FFA provide financial accounts, balance sheets and revaluation accounts, but these differ conceptually and statistically from the NIPA. The Christensen-Jorgenson set of national accounts define national wealth as human and nonhuman saving minus depreciation plus revaluation of assets. In addition, the income and wealth accounts are linked through investment and saving in the capital accumulation accounts. Third, the U.S. national accounts do not include a complete production account, as in the Jorgenson accounts, that describe how output is produced using capital (including inventories and land), labor, and intermediate inputs.[3] Information on gross product originating by fourteen individual components is generated by BEA, but there is not a complete allocation of these components to labor versus capital.[4] Fourth, BEA does not allocate income between labor and property, where the Jorgenson accounts make this allocation. Finally, BEA does not treat consumer durables as investment goods; the Jorgenson accounts do so.

The SNA accounts and the Jorgenson accounts are much more similar than the U.S. national accounts and the Jorgenson accounts. Nonetheless, differences still exist. The major differences are threefold. First, in order to reconcile the identity that the value of initial stocks, minus capital consumption, plus capital formation and revaluation of stocks should be equal to the value of ending stocks a reconciliation entry is frequently used. The value of beginning and ending stocks is estimated, the resulting flow therefore being determined. The identity holds directly in the Jorgenson accounts, using estimates of each component. Second, there are differences in coverage. The SNA will include an environmental satellite account, but not include a human capital or nonmarket satellite accounts. The former is not yet part of the Jorgenson accounts, the latter two are a part of the Jorgenson accounts.[5] The SNA does include a more complete set of government accounts, for example services of nonmilitary reproducible assets are estimated as the value of capital consumption allowances.[6]

Finally, there are differences in the accumulation and wealth account. The Jorgenson accounts recognize consumer durables as an investment item, the SNA do not. However the SNA accounts have both assets and liabilities in their wealth accounts, the Jorgenson accounts include only assets.

6.3 Definitional Tables

I will now turn my attention to a specific description of the Jorgenson system of national accounts.

The Jorgenson system includes a production account, income and expenditure account, an accumulation account, and a wealth account. The set of accounts are described by the eight tables which follow. The aggregates in these tables are constructed when appropriate from the industry level sectoral accounts.

Table 6.1 presents the production account. In the NIPA accounts, GNP is divided among durable and nondurable goods, services and structures. Durables include consumer durables and producer durables used by nonprofit institutions, yet property compensation does not include services from these durables. In the Jorgenson accounts all durables are treated as an investment expenditure, therefore services from these durables are included in the product and factor outlay account (lines 4 and 5 of the product account, included in line 3 of the factor outlay account).

In NIPA, services from owner-occupied residential structures and land are imputed as the sum of net rent, interest, taxes and capital consumption allowances. A similar imputation is made for services from real estate held by nonprofit institutions, except that net rent is excluded. The Jorgenson accounts impute the services from owner-occupied real estate as in NIPA and net rent from institutional real estate (line 6 of the product account, included in line 3 of the factor outlay account). Nondurables and structures are treated in a parallel fashion in NIPA and in the Jorgenson accounts.

There are differences between the two accounts in the treatment of taxes, subsidies and surplus. NIPA includes all indirect taxes and the current government surplus (deficit). The Jorgenson accounts include only property-type indirect business taxes: capital stock taxes, property taxes, motor vehicle licenses, severance taxes and other taxes (lines 9 through 13). Excise and sales taxes, custom duties, and nontaxes are excluded. Government subsidies are included and current surplus (deficit) are excluded (lines 14 and 15).

In addition in the latest set of Jorgenson accounts reported here, further imputations are made to GNP to adjust for negative property compensation in certain industries, notably the motor vehicle industry.

Finally, in the Jorgenson accounts, imputations are made for the product of the nonmarket sector. These include the value of nonmarket time, investment in infants and education (lines 17, 18 and 19). Full gross private domestic product is equal to gross private domestic

Table 6.1
Production account, gross private domestic product and factor outlay, United States, 1982 (billions of current dollars)[ab]

	Product	
1.	Private gross national product (table 1.7, 1.1–1.12)	2822.1
2.	– Compensation of employees in government enterprises (tables 6.4, 1.81 and 1.86)	39.6
3.	– Rest-of-the-world gross national product (table 1.7, 1.15)	51.2
4.	+ Services of consumer durables (Christensen-Jorgenson)	290.0
5.	+ Services of durables held by institutions (Christensen-Jorgenson)	8.0
6.	+ Net rent on institutional real estate (Christensen-Jorgenson)	4.8
7.	+ GNP imputations (Fraumeni-Jorgenson)	20.7
8.	– Indirect business tax and nontax accruals (table 3.2, 1.9)	258.8
9.	+ Capital stock tax (table 3.1, footnote 2)	---
10.	+ Business property taxes (table 3.3, 1.9)	85.3
11.	+ Business motor vehicle licenses (table 3.5, 1.25)	2.1
12.	+ Business severence taxes (table 3.5, 1.26)	7.8
13.	+ Business other taxes (table 3.5, 1.26,27)	14.8
14.	+ Subsidies less current surplus of federal government enterprises (table 3.2, 1.27)	16.0
15.	+ Subsidies less current surplus of state and local government enterprises (table 3.3, 1.22)	–7.3
16.	= Gross private domestic product	2906.8
17.	+ Time in household production and leisure (Jorgenson-Fraumeni)	4706.9
18.	+ Investment in infants (Jorgenson-Fraumeni)	2597.9
19.	+ Investment in education (Jorgenson-Fraumeni)	2834.9
20.	= Full gross private domestic product	13046.4

	Factor outlay	
1.	Compensation of employees (GPO)	1523.6
2.	+ Income of self-employed persons allocated to labor compensation (Fraumeni-Jorgenson)	135.7
3.	+ Property compensation before taxes (Fraumeni-Jorgenson)	1247.6
4.	= Gross private domestic factor outlay	2906.8
5.	+ Imputations for human capital services (1.17, 18 and 19 above)	10139.6
6.	= Full gross private domestic factor outlay	13046.4

[a]All table references unless otherwise noted are to the NIPA tables in the *Survey of Current Business*, July 1986, with the exception of capital stock tax which refers to the *National Income and Product Accounts of the United States, 1929–1965, Statistical Tables, A Supplement ot the Survey of Current Business*, 1966. The Christensen-Jorgenson series come from the Christensen-Jorgenson *National Income Accounts* (1969, 1970, 1973b, 1973c). The GPO series come from the Bureau of Economic Analysis Study, "Gross Product Originating by Industry, 1977–1989," U.S. Department of Commerce, National Income and Wealth Division, BEA-NIW-91-406, May 6, 1991. The Fraumeni-Jorgenson series come from an update of the study by Fraumeni and Jorgenson (1980c). The Jorgenson-Fraumeni series come from the studies by Jorgenson and Fraumeni (1989, 1992a, 1992b, 1993).

[b]Totals listed may differ from a summation of table entries due to rounding.

product plus these imputations. As a balancing item, these imputations are included in the factor outlay account (line 5). NIPA does not make any such imputations.

Table 6.2 presents the income and expenditure accounts. Gross private national income includes property compensation (line 1) and labor compensation. Labor compensation includes compensation of both wage and salaried and self-employed workers, in the private, government, and rest of world sectors (lines 2 through 5, part of line 6). Other income originating in the rest of world, net interest paid by government and investment income of social insurance funds less transfers are also added in (lines 6 through 8). Finally, tax adjustments are made: corporate profits taxes, indirect business taxes allocated to capital assets, and personal taxes are subtracted (lines 9 through 12).

Full gross private national income is gross private national income plus nonmarket labor income (line 14), where as noted before the latter is not included in NIPA. Finally, the difference between consumer receipts and income is government transfer payments to persons other than benefits from social insurance funds (line 16).

Table 6.3 indicates the difference between the NIPA concept of personal disposable income and the Jorgenson concept of gross private national income (table 6.2, line 13). The two concepts differ in the treatment of social insurance funds and government transfer payments (lines 2 and 3). The statistical discrepancy (line 6) and the imputed capital services and GNP imputation (line 7) are included to preserve consistency between accounts and to insure that accounting identities are satisfied. Other definitional differences include the inclusion of undistributed corporate profits, capital consumption allowances, personal nontax payments and the exclusion of interest paid by consumers to business.

In the expenditure account (table 6.2), expenditures include personal consumption expenditures, except for expenditures on durables (lines 1 and 2). To preserve consistency with the product and accumulation accounts, services of consumer and institutional durables, net rent on institutional real estate and the GNP imputation are included (lines 3 through 6). Full gross private national income (line 9) is gross private national income plus consumption of nonmarket goods and services or time in household production and leisure. Personal transfer payments to foreigners and personal non-tax payments (lines 10 and 11) are included in full private national consumer outlays. Finally,

Table 6.2
Gross private national receipts and expenditures, 1982 (billions of current dollars)

	Receipts	
1.	Property compensation before taxes (Fraumeni-Jorgenson)	1247.6
2.	+ Compensation of employees (GPO)	1523.6
3.	+ Income of self-employed persons allocated to labor compensation (Fraumeni-Jorgenson)	135.7
4.	+ Compensation of employees in general government (GPO)	343.9
5.	+ Compensation of employees in government enterprises (GPO)	39.6
6.	+ Income originating in rest of world (table 6.1, 1.82)	51.2
7.	+ Investment income of social insurance funds less transfers to general government (table 3.13, 1.7 and 1.18 minus 1.9 and 1.20)	33.0
8.	+ Net interest paid by government (table 1.9, 1.16 minus 1.12 table 3.1, 1.18 and table 2.1, 1.28)	39.0
9.	− Corporate profits tax liability (table 6.20B, 1.1)	63.1
10.	− Indirect business taxes allocated to capital assets (Fraumeni-Jorgenson, see above table 1, sum of items 9–13)	102.2
11.	− Personal tax and nontax payments (table 3.4, 1.2 and 1.9)	409.4
12.	+ Personal nontax payments (table 3.4, 1.8 and 1.15)	43.5
13.	= Gross private national income	2882.4
14.	+ Nonmarket labor income (see above table 1, sum of items 17–19)	10139.6
15.	= Full gross private national income	13022.0
16.	+ Government transfer payment to persons other than benefits from social insurance funds (table 3.11, 1.1 minus 1.3 and 1.29)	99.6
17.	= Full gross private national consumer receipts	13121.7

	Expenditures	
1.	Personal consumption expenditures (table 1.1, 1.2)	2050.7
2.	− Personal consumption expenditures, durable goods (table 1.1, 1.3)	252.7
3.	+ Services of consumer durables (Christensen-Jorgenson)	290.0
4.	+ Services of institutional durables (Christensen-Jorgenson)	8.0
5.	+ Net rent on institutional real estate (Christensen-Jorgenson)	4.8
6.	+ GNP imputation (Fraumeni-Jorgenson)	20.7
7.	= Private national consumption expenditure	2121.5
8.	+ Consumption of nonmarket goods and services (see above table 1, 1.17)	4706.9
9.	= Full private national consumption expenditure	6828.4
10.	+ Personal transfer payments to foreigners (table 2.1, 1.29)	1.3
11.	+ Personal nontax payments (table 3.4, 1.5 and table 3.3, 1.4)	43.5
12.	= Full private national consumer outlays	6873.2
13.	+ Full gross private national saving (see below table 6.6, 1.13)	6248.5
14.	= Full private national expenditures	13121.7

Table 6.3
Reconciliation of personal disposable income and gross private national income, 1982 (billions of current dollars)

1. Personal disposable income (table 2.1, 1.31)	2261.5
2. + Surplus of social insurance funds (table 3.13, 1.11 and 1.22)	6.1
3. – Government transfer payments to persons other than social insurance funds (table 3.11, 1.2 and 1.28 minus 1.3 and 1.29)	99.6
4. + Undistributed corporate profits with inventory valuation and capital consumption adjustment (table 5.1, 1.4)	20.0
5. + Capital consumption allowances with capital consumption allowances (table 1.9, 1.2)	383.2
6. + Statistical discrepancy (table 1.9, 1.8)	–.1
7. + Expenditure (items 3, 4, 5, and 6 from table 2, expenditures, above)	323.5
8. + Government and private wage accruals less disbursements (table 3.1, 1.22 and table 5.1, 1.10)	0.0
9. – Interest paid by consumers to business (table 2.1, 1.27)	55.5
10. + Personal nontax payments (table 3.2, 1.5 and table 3.4, 1.4)	43.5
11. = Gross private national income	2882.4

full private national expenditures is full private national consumer outlays plus full gross private national saving (line 13).

Table 6.4 splits gross private national income into labor income and property income. The NIPA accounts do not make a similar division. Personal income taxes are split between labor and property income (line 6 of labor income, line 8 of property income). The allocation of other receipts items in table 6.2 to labor or property income is obvious.

Table 6.5 defines property compensation after taxes by legal form of organization. The sum of property compensation before taxes for the corporate, noncorporate, household and institutional sectors is equal to property compensation before taxes, table 6.1, line 3 of the factor outlay account. In table 6.5, information for the government and rest of world sectors is presented as well. Compensation from net claims on government include net interest paid by government domestically and investment income of social insurance funds less transfers to general government (lines 1 and 2 of compensation from net claims on government and rest of world). Compensation from net claims on rest of world include corporate profits and net interest (lines 5 and 6). All taxes are deducted in the accounts for property compensation by legal form of organization. These include corporate profits taxes, property taxes, indirect business and personal income taxes allocated to

Table 6.4
Gross private national labor and property income, 1982 (billions of current dollars)

	Labor income	
1.	Compensation of employees (GPO)	1523.6
2.	+ Income of self-employed persons allocated to labor compensation (Fraumeni-Jorgenson)	135.7
3.	+ Compensation of employees in general government (GPO)	343.9
4.	+ Compensation of employees in government enterprises (GPO)	39.6
5.	+ Compensation of employees, rest of world (GPO)	0.0
6.	− Personal income taxes attributed to labor income (Christensen-Jorgenson)[a]	263.1
7.	= Private national labor income	1779.6
8.	+ Nonmarket labor income (see above table 1, sum of items 17–19)	10139.6
9.	=Full private national labor income	11919.2
	Property income	
1.	Property compensation before taxes (Fraumeni-Jorgenson)	1247.6
2.	+ Corporate profits, rest of world (GPO)	23.2
3.	+ Net interest, rest of the world (GPO)	28.0
4.	+ Investment income of social insurance funds less transfers to general government (table 3.13, 1.7 and 1.18 minus 1.9 and 1.20)	33.0
5.	+ Net interest paid by government (table 1.9, 1.16 minus 1.12, table 3.1, 1.18 and table 2.1, 1.28)	39.0
6.	− Corporate profits tax liability (table 6.20, 1.1)	63.1
7.	− Indirect business taxes allocated to capital assets (Fraumeni-Jorgenson, see above table 1, sum of items 9–13)	102.2
8.	− Personal income taxes attributed to property income (Christensen-Jorgenson)[a]	85.4
9.	− Federal estate and gift taxes (table 3.4, 1.7)[a]	7.6
10.	− State and local estate and gift taxes (table 3.4, 1.11)[a]	2.6
11.	− State and local personal motor vehicle licences, property taxes, and other taxes (table 3.4, 1.12, 13, and 14)	7.3
12.	= Gross private national property income	1102.8

[a]The sum of line 6 under labor income plus lines 8, 9, 10, and 11 under property income is equal to table 6.2 above, line 11 minus line 12 under receipts.

Table 6.5
Gross private national property compensation after taxes by legal form of
organization, 1982 (billions of current dollars)

	Corporate property compensation	
1.	Corporate property compensation before taxes (Fraumeni-Jorgenson)	528.6
2.	− Corporate profits tax liability (table 6.20B, 1.12) (Fraumeni-Jorgenson)	63.1
3.	− Indirect business taxes allocated to corporate capital assets (Fraumeni-Jorgenson)	36.3
4.	− Personal income taxes attributed to corporate property income	119.0
5.	− Wealth taxes attributed to corporate (Fraumeni-Jorgenson)	3.1
6.	= Corporate property compensation after taxes	307.1

	Noncorporate property compensation	
1.	Noncorporate property compensation before taxes (Fraumeni-Jorgenson)	205.9
2.	− Indirect business taxes allocated to noncorporate capital assets (Fraumeni-Jorgenson)	28.4
3.	− Personal income taxes allocated to noncorporate property income (Fraumeni-Jorgenson)	38.7
4.	− Wealth taxes attributed to noncorporate assets (Fraumeni-Jorgenson)	2.5
5.	= Noncorporate property compensation after taxes	136.3

	Household property compensation	
1.	Household property compensation before taxes (Fraumeni-Jorgenson)	480.3
2.	− Property taxes, owner-occupied dwellings (table 8.3, 1.65 and 1.67)	37.6
3.	− Personal property taxes, consumer durables (table 3.4, 1.12, 1.13, and 1.13)	7.3
4.	− Personal income taxes attributed to household and property income (Christensen-Jorgenson)[a]	−14.2
5.	− Wealth taxes attributed to household assets (Fraumeni-Jorgenson)	3.4
6.	= Household property compensation after taxes	446.2

	Institutional property compensation	
1.	Institutional property compensation after taxes (Fraumeni-Jorgenson)	32.8
2.	− Wealth taxes attributed to institutional assets (Fraumeni-Jorgenson)	0.3
3.	= Institutional property compensation after taxes (Fraumeni-Jorgenson)	32.5

Table 6.5 (continued)

	Compensation from net claims on government and rest of world	
1.	Net interest paid by government domestically (table 1.9, 1.16 minus table 3.1, 1.18 and table 2.1, 1.28)	39.0
2.	+ Investment income of social insurance funds less transfers to general government (table 3.13, 1.7 and 1.18 minus 1.9 and 1.20)	33.0
3.	+ Corporate profits, rest of the world (GPO)	23.2
4.	+ Net interest, rest of world (GPO)	28.0
5.	− Personal income taxes attributed to compensation from net claims (Fraumeni-Jorgenson)	28.6
6.	− Wealth taxes attributed to net claims (Fraumeni-Jorgenson)	0.7
7.	= Compensation from net claims	93.9

[a]The negative tax reflects deductibility of interest and property taxes for owner-occupied dwellings.

property income, and wealth taxes. The NIPA accounts identify property compensation broken out by legal form of organization.

Table 6.6 presents the accumulation account. As shown in table 6.7, saving includes the components of gross private saving as defined in NIPA, as well as personal consumption expenditure, durable goods, surplus (deficit) of social insurance funds, government wage accruals less disbursements and the statistical discrepancy. Full gross private national saving includes human capital saving, a substantial addition to national saving (table 6.6, line 12). Depreciation includes imputations for depreciation of consumer durables, institutional durables and human capital, as well as the assets for which depreciation is defined in NIPA. The NIPA accounts do not estimate revaluation, therefore NIPA change in private national wealth cannot be calculated. An important link between the accumulation and the wealth account is missing. The Jorgenson savings account estimates both.

Gross private national capital formation includes similar items for durables, government deficits, less deficits of social insurance funds, and wage accruals as well as gross private domestic investment and net foreign investment. Full gross private national capital formation includes human capital formation, where in the human capital accounts saving is equal to investment (line 12 under saving and line 11 under capital formation).

Table 6.6
Gross private national capital accumulation, 1982 (billions of current dollars)

	Savings	
1.	Personal saving (table 5.1, 1.3)	153.9
2.	+ Undistributed corporate profits (table 5.1, 1.5)	39.6
3.	+ Corporate inventory valuation adjustment (table 5.1, 1.6)	−10.4
4.	+ Corporate capital consumption allowances (table 6.24B, 1.1)	225.7
5.	+ Noncorporate capital consumption allowances with capital consumption adjustment (table 5.1, 1.9)	148.2
6.	+ Private wage accruals less disbursements (table 5.1, 1.10)	0.0
7.	+ Personal consumption expenditures, durable goods (table 1.1, 1.3)	252.7
8.	+ Surplus, social insurance funds (table 3.13, 1.11 and 1.22)	6.1
9.	+ Government wage accruals less disbursements (table 3.1, 1.17)	0.0
10.	+ Statistical discrepancy (table 1.9, 1.8)	−0.1
11.	= Gross private national saving	815.7
12.	+ Human capital saving (see above table 6.1, line 18 plus line 19)	5432.7
13.	= Full gross private national saving	6248.5
14.	− Nonhuman depreciation (Fraumeni-Jorgenson)	565.5
15.	− Human depreciation (Jorgenson-Fraumeni)	2827.8
16.	= Net private national saving	2855.2
17.	+ Human revaluation (Jorgenson-Fraumeni)	9610.7
18.	+ Nonhuman revaluation (Fraumeni-Jorgenson)	480.7
19.	= Change in private national wealth	12946.6
	Capital formation	
1.	Gross private domestic investment (table 1.1, 1.6)	447.3
2.	+ Personal consumption expenditures, durable goods (table 1.1, 1.3)	252.7
3.	+ Deficit of federal government (table 3.23, 1.31)	145.9
4.	+ Deficit of state and local governments (table 3.3, 1.26)	−35.1
5.	− Deficit, federal social insurance funds (table 3.13, 1.11)	30.8
6.	− Deficit, state and local social insurance funds (table 3.13, 1.22)	−36.9
7.	+ Wage accruals less disbursement, federal government (table 3.2, 1.30)	0.0
8.	+ Wage accruals less disbursement, state and local government (table 3.3, 1.25)	0.0
9.	+ Net foreign investment (table 5.1, 1.17)	−1.0
10.	= Gross private national capital formation	815.8
11.	+ Gross private national human capital formation (1.12 above)	5432.7
12.	= Full gross private national capital formation	3173.5

Table 6.7
Reconciliation of gross private saving and gross private national saving, 1982 (billions of current dollars)

1.	Gross private saving (table 5.1, 1.2)	557.1
2.	+ Personal consumption expenditures, durable goods (table 1.1, 1.3)	252.7
3.	+ Surplus, social insurance funds (table 3.13, 1.11 and 1.22)	6.1
4.	+ Government wage accruals less disbursements (table 3.1, 1.22)	0.0
5.	+ Statistical discrepancy (table 1.9, 1.8)	−0.1
6.	= Gross private national saving	815.7

Table 6.8 presents the wealth account. The wealth account gives the value of the stock of assets, human and nonhuman, for the private national economy. Change in national wealth from year to year is equal to the change in private national wealth (table 6.6, line 19). Private national human wealth, which is not measured by BEA, is clearly the largest component of full private national wealth (table 6.8, line 5), followed by private domestic tangible assets (line 1), net claims on government (line 2) and net claims on the rest of world (line 3).

6.4   Human Capital and Nonmarket Accounts

The most recent expansion of the Jorgenson system of national accounts is the integration of human capital and nonmarket accounts to form a more complete set of accounts (Jorgenson and Fraumeni, 1989a). The incorporation of human capital accounts has a tremendous effect on the magnitude of such numbers as gross private domestic product, investment, labor outlay and wealth. Adding an education sector which produces a human capital stock of educated individuals who may enter the labor force reduces measured productivity significantly (Jorgenson and Fraumeni, 1992a).

The following tables present time series from the expanded set of accounts.

The human capital and nonmarket accounts depend upon the measurement of lifetime income for all individuals in the U.S. population and the allocation of their time between work, school, maintenance and other nonmarket activities. Individuals are cross-classified by sex, age and education. Labor market information, including wages and hours worked, comes from the labor data base of Gollop and Jorgenson (1980, 1983) and Ho (Ho, 1989; Jorgenson, Ho, and Fraumeni, 1994).[7] Maintenance, including sleep, is assumed to take on average

Table 6.8
Private national wealth, 1982 (billions of current dollars)

1. Private domestic tangible assets (Fraumeni-Jorgenson)			13128.5
2. + Net claims on the federal, state, and local governments			867.9
a. Federal, monetary		182.6	
(i) + Vault cash of commercial banks[a]	19.5		
(ii) + Member bank reserves[a]	26.5		
(iii) + Currency outside banks[a]	136.6		
(iv) − Book to market value adjustment (Christensen-Jorgenson)	11.3		
b. Federal, nonmonetary		669.6	
(i) US govt. total liabilities[a]	1139.1		
(ii) − US govt. financial assets[a]	278.5		
(iii) + Net liabilities, federally-sponsored credit agencies[a]	0.5		
(iv) + Assets of social insurance funds[b]	65.7		
(v) − US govt. liabilities to rest of world[c]	172.0		
(vi) + US govt. credits and claims abroad[c]	97.4		
(vii) − Federal, monetary liabilities[d]	182.6		
(viii) − Book to market value adjustment (Christensen-Jorgenson)	41.4		
c. State and local			86.0
(i) State and local government total liabilities[a]	351.5		
(ii) − State and local government financial assets[d]	265.5		
(iii) + Assets of cash sickness compensation fund (Christensen-Jorgenson)	0.1		
(iv) − Book to market value adjustment (Christensen-Jorgenson)	17.6		
3. + Net claims on the rest of world			253.9
a. Private US assets and investments abroad[c]	716.2		
b. − Private US liabilities to foreigners[c]	516.1		
c. Adjustment for US territories and Puerto Rico (Christensen-Jorgenson)	53.7		
4. = Private national nonhuman wealth			14250.3
5. + Private national human wealth (Jorgenson-Fraumeni)		198538.3	
6. = Full private national wealth			212788.6

[a] Board of Governors of the Federal Reserve System, *Flow of Funds Accounts*, 1966–1989, September 1990.

[b] US Department of Treasury, *Treasury Bulletin*, Fall issues.

[c] *Survey of Current Business*, June issues, "The International Investment Position of the United States."

[d] From a above.

ten hours per day.[8] For those currently enrolled in school, education is assumed to take on average 1300 hours per year, or approximately three and one-half hours per day. Information on market hours worked comes from the labor database. Other nonmarket time is therefore equal to fourteen hours per day, minus school and work time. Other nonmarket time is evaluated at the corresponding after tax market wage for an individual of the same sex, age and education. Individuals go to school, work, and have valuable nonmarket time depending on their stage in the life cycle. From birth through age five, individuals neither go to school[9] or work and the value of their time is assumed to be zero. From age six through thirteen, individuals can go to school. The value of their nonmarket non-school time is assumed to be zero.[10] From age fourteen though thirty-four,[11] individuals may work and go to school; their nonmarket non-school time has a positive value. From age thirty-five through seventy-four, individuals may work. Starting at age seventy-five, we assume that individuals do not work and that the value of their nonmarket time is zero.[12]

Lifetime income is constructed assuming that individuals will follow the pattern of cohorts currently alive. For example, in 1980 the lifetime income of someone who is twenty depends on the lifetime income in 1980 of someone of the same sex who is twenty-one, but possibly having one more year of education, plus the lifetime income in 1980 of someone of the same sex who is twenty-two, but possibly having one more year of education, and so on. Adjustments are made for expected mortality. In practice, the construction of lifetime income begins with individuals who are seventy-four, having only one year of potential lifetime income left and proceeds backwards to accumulate a lifetime income for infants.

Investment in infants or the expected lifetime income of an infant can therefore be probabilistically determined depending on the average probabilities of cohorts alive in the year of the birth of the infant to work, to go to school and to die. Investment in education by an individual currently enrolled in school is determined as the difference in lifetime income of two individuals in a given year who are of the same sex and age, but with one having completed one more year of school. The increase in lifetime income due to an additional year of education is investment in education.

There are four tables (tables 6.9 through 6.12) giving details corresponding to the production account (table 6.1). Gross private domestic product can be allocated between full consumption and full invest-

Table 6.9
Full investment (billions of constant dollars)

Year	Full Investment Quantity	Price	Human Investment Quantity	Price	Nonhuman Investment Quantity	Price	Human Current Dollar Share	Nonhuman Current Dollar Share
1949	3503.3	0.185	3231.5	0.178	281.9	0.259	0.887	0.113
1950	3650.4	0.195	3280.4	0.188	353.7	0.269	0.866	0.134
1951	3823.9	0.208	3410.0	0.200	389.0	0.284	0.861	0.139
1952	3858.4	0.222	3435.3	0.217	396.6	0.280	0.870	0.130
1953	4003.9	0.239	3562.0	0.236	413.8	0.281	0.878	0.122
1954	3905.1	0.254	3477.9	0.253	400.2	0.282	0.886	0.114
1955	4112.5	0.266	3631.0	0.265	449.9	0.294	0.879	0.121
1956	4227.8	0.286	3751.0	0.285	446.0	0.310	0.006	0.114
1957	4359.5	0.310	3889.8	0.311	439.2	0.321	0.895	0.105
1958	4258.3	0.327	3816.3	0.330	412.2	0.320	0.905	0.095
1959	4262.2	0.338	3776.1	0.341	457.8	0.330	0.895	0.105
1960	4371.1	0.345	3889.4	0.349	451.9	0.333	0.900	0.100
1961	4450.6	0.356	3964.9	0.361	455.1	0.332	0.905	0.095
1962	4519.5	0.357	3993.1	0.361	497.9	0.339	0.895	0.105
1963	4693.4	0.362	4138.6	0.367	525.7	0.341	0.895	0.105
1964	4741.7	0.373	4158.2	0.379	556.2	0.344	0.892	0.108
1965	4867.4	0.385	4235.8	0.391	606.9	0.354	0.885	0.115
1966	4889.6	0.402	4214.1	0.411	655.6	0.362	0.879	0.121
1967	4941.1	0.422	4263.4	0.432	656.8	0.368	0.884	0.116
1968	4960.3	0.441	4259.5	0.452	683.4	0.385	0.880	0.120
1969	5446.1	0.468	4723.7	0.480	695.0	0.406	0.889	0.111
1970	5331.3	0.522	4642.0	0.539	658.5	0.424	0.900	0.100
1971	5366.6	0.552	4653.5	0.570	687.4	0.448	0.896	0.104
1972	5253.5	0.579	4497.2	0.599	747.2	0.466	0.886	0.114
1973	5268.0	0.605	4445.1	0.627	833.0	0.481	0.874	0.126
1974	5345.6	0.634	4550.3	0.654	794.2	0.520	0.878	0.122
1975	5315.6	0.676	4581.7	0.692	720.5	0.586	0.882	0.118
1976	5364.7	0.699	4565.4	0.712	794.8	0.627	0.867	0.133
1977	5631.0	0.724	4761.5	0.734	868.4	0.667	0.858	0.142
1978	5842.0	0.758	4905.9	0.765	937.7	0.718	0.848	0.152
1979	5940.7	0.809	4995.0	0.813	947.0	0.783	0.846	0.154
1980	6181.6	0.854	5303.0	0.854	878.0	0.854	0.858	0.142
1981	6177.5	0.934	5284.9	0.933	892.0	0.941	0.855	0.145
1982	6217.8	1.000	5432.7	1.000	785.1	1.000	0.874	0.126
1983	6213.7	1.057	5361.8	1.065	853.8	1.006	0.869	0.131
1984	6386.1	1.105	5384.3	1.117	1012.8	1.026	0.853	0.147
1985	6471.7	1.167	5448.7	1.190	1035.1	1.032	0.859	0.141
1986	6676.1	1.250	5618.1	1.288	1071.1	1.034	0.867	0.133

Table 6.10
Full gross private domestic product (billions of constant dollars)

Year	Full Product Quantity	Price	Full Consumption Quantity	Price	Full Investment Quantity	Price	Consumption Current Dollar Share	Investment Current Dollar Share
1949	6685.0	0.186	3116.9	0.190	3503.3	0.185	0.478	0.522
1950	6853.9	0.193	3137.8	0.194	3650.4	0.195	0.461	0.539
1951	7100.7	0.203	3208.0	0.202	3823.9	0.208	0.449	0.551
1952	7228.5	0.213	3301.8	0.207	3858.4	0.222	0.444	0.556
1953	7550.8	0.225	3478.0	0.214	4003.9	0.239	0.438	0.562
1954	7317.8	0.239	3343.1	0.226	3905.1	0.254	0.432	0.568
1955	7697.3	0.246	3510.8	0.228	4112.5	0.266	0.423	0.577
1956	7935.2	0.260	3633.4	0.235	4227.8	0.286	0.414	0.586
1957	8155.6	0.278	3716.6	0.247	4359.5	0.310	0.405	0.595
1958	7946.5	0.292	3608.0	0.258	4258.3	0.327	0.401	0.599
1959	8161.5	0.299	3848.1	0.261	4262.2	0.338	0.411	0.589
1960	8334.9	0.309	3906.4	0.272	4371.1	0.345	0.413	0.587
1961	8483.9	0.318	3974.5	0.281	4450.6	0.356	0.414	0.586
1962	8588.9	0.323	4006.5	0.291	4519.5	0.357	0.419	0.581
1963	9021.0	0.328	4273.7	0.295	4693.4	0.362	0.426	0.574
1964	9167.5	0.342	4376.8	0.312	4741.7	0.373	0.436	0.564
1965	9425.1	0.356	4508.7	0.329	4867.4	0.385	0.442	0.558
1966	9548.5	0.375	4616.0	0.349	4889.6	0.402	0.450	0.550
1967	9699.1	0.393	4718.3	0.367	4941.1	0.422	0.454	0.546
1968	9823.7	0.413	4829.6	0.387	4960.3	0.441	0.460	0.540
1969	10644.7	0.438	5151.7	0.409	5446.1	0.468	0.452	0.548
1970	10515.2	0.484	5145.1	0.448	5331.3	0.522	0.453	0.547
1971	10560.1	0.514	5152.5	0.478	5366.6	0.552	0.454	0.546
1972	10635.9	0.538	5364.9	0.500	5253.5	0.579	0.468	0.532
1973	10824.3	0.568	5549.9	0.534	5268.0	0.605	0.482	0.518
1974	10981.1	0.604	5628.9	0.576	5345.6	0.634	0.489	0.511
1975	11068.4	0.645	5753.3	0.617	5315.6	0.676	0.497	0.503
1976	11198.7	0.676	5835.6	0.655	5364.7	0.699	0.505	0.495
1977	11742.7	0.706	6113.0	0.690	5631.0	0.724	0.509	0.491
1978	12106.6	0.751	6264.7	0.744	5842.0	0.758	0.513	0.487
1979	12324.7	0.807	6384.1	0.806	5940.7	0.809	0.517	0.483
1980	12658.3	0.861	6477.4	0.867	6181.6	0.854	0.516	0.484
1981	12922.9	0.932	6745.3	0.930	6177.5	0.934	0.521	0.479
1982	13046.3	1.000	6828.5	1.000	6217.8	1.000	0.523	0.477
1983	13095.2	1.055	6881.6	1.052	6213.7	1.057	0.524	0.476
1984	13537.2	1.101	7151.4	1.097	6386.1	1.105	0.527	0.473
1985	13799.7	1.162	7328.6	1.157	6471.7	1.167	0.529	0.471
1986	14390.3	1.231	7716.2	1.215	6676.1	1.250	0.529	0.471

Table 6.11
Full labor outlay (billions of constant dollars)

Year	Full Labor Outlay		Market Labor Outlay		Nonmarket Labor Outlay		Market Current Dollar Share	Nonmarket Current Dollar Share
	Quantity	Price	Quantity	Price	Quantity	Price	Share	Share
1949	6705.1	0.169	906.7	0.154	5797.4	0.171	0.124	0.876
1950	6797.0	0.176	957.7	0.161	5842.6	0.178	0.129	0.871
1951	7026.6	0.185	1043.7	0.170	5990.9	0.188	0.136	0.864
1952	7144.5	0.196	1076.8	0.177	6077.4	0.199	0.136	0.864
1953	7435.9	0.209	1099.1	0.186	6344.4	0.213	0.132	0.868
1954	7164.1	0.224	1052.8	0.195	6117.7	0.229	0.128	0.872
1955	7498.6	0.230	1109.9	0.197	6396.7	0.236	0.127	0.873
1956	7762.0	0.245	1153.9	0.207	6617.1	0.251	0.126	0.874
1957	7964.6	0.264	1146.8	0.221	6820.4	0.271	0.120	0.880
1958	7725.0	0.280	1089.4	0.234	6633.9	0.287	0.118	0.882
1959	7891.3	0.286	1146.9	0.236	6749.1	0.294	0.120	0.880
1960	8060.4	0.295	1155.5	0.245	6906.5	0.304	0.119	0.881
1961	8169.9	0.306	1149.4	0.253	7018.0	0.315	0.116	0.884
1962	8218.4	0.311	1184.0	0.259	7037.3	0.319	0.120	0.880
1963	8604.9	0.316	1204.5	0.265	7396.8	0.324	0.118	0.882
1964	8667.5	0.331	1223.4	0.279	7442.4	0.340	0.119	0.881
1965	8841.9	0.346	1264.6	0.287	7578.7	0.356	0.119	0.881
1966	8869.4	0.367	1292.0	0.307	7583.2	0.377	0.122	0.878
1967	8986.0	0.388	1303.5	0.324	7687.3	0.398	0.121	0.879
1968	9077.9	0.409	1342.1	0.348	7745.1	0.419	0.126	0.874
1969	9894.9	0.434	1385.0	0.369	8506.9	0.445	0.119	0.881
1970	9709.6	0.486	1318.0	0.410	8381.5	0.498	0.115	0.885
1971	9676.1	0.518	1290.9	0.444	8371.3	0.531	0.114	0.886
1972	9683.7	0.544	1358.4	0.465	8322.3	0.557	0.120	0.880
1973	9799.8	0.577	1404.7	0.510	8396.5	0.588	0.127	0.873
1974	10003.0	0.613	1417.9	0.555	8584.6	0.622	0.128	0.872
1975	10051.0	0.653	1368.4	0.610	8676.9	0.660	0.127	0.873
1976	10108.2	0.684	1436.7	0.653	8669.5	0.689	0.136	0.864
1977	10570.7	0.712	1500.9	0.690	9067.8	0.716	0.138	0.862
1978	10859.6	0.757	1576.9	0.743	9281.5	0.759	0.143	0.857
1979	11092.6	0.813	1645.3	0.806	9446.7	0.814	0.147	0.853
1980	11438.5	0.866	1638.9	0.884	9799.4	0.863	0.146	0.854
1981	11682.5	0.933	1679.9	0.948	10002.2	0.930	0.146	0.854
1982	11798.9	1.000	1659.3	1.000	10139.6	1.000	0.141	0.859
1983	11727.1	1.056	1674.1	1.039	10053.2	1.059	0.140	0.860
1984	12059.8	1.104	1806.8	1.079	10255.2	1.108	0.146	0.854
1985	12231.7	1.173	1841.4	1.130	10392.8	1.180	0.145	0.855
1986	12754.9	1.256	1862.8	1.204	10892.2	1.266	0.140	0.860

Table 6.12
Full gross domestic factor outlay (billions of constant dollars)

Year	Full Factor Outlay Quantity	Price	Property Outlay Quantity	Price	Full Labor Outlay Quantity	Price	Property Current Dollar Share	Labor Current Dollar Share
1949	6705.8	0.171	110.6	0.265	6606.7	0.169	0.026	0.974
1950	6842.7	0.179	124.3	0.291	6723.0	0.176	0.030	0.970
1951	7059.4	0.188	138.4	0.306	6919.2	0.186	0.033	0.967
1952	7135.5	0.199	137.7	0.293	6997.3	0.197	0.029	0.971
1953	7328.1	0.212	143.8	0.296	7182.7	0.210	0.028	0.972
1954	7253.0	0.226	143.3	0.284	7107.8	0.225	0.025	0.975
1955	7521.9	0.233	166.4	0.327	7347.4	0.231	0.032	0.968
1956	7716.6	0.247	163.0	0.312	7547.9	0.246	0.027	0.973
1957	7920.3	0.266	169.1	0.310	7745.0	0.265	0.026	0.974
1958	7836.0	0.281	163.9	0.286	7666.2	0.281	0.022	0.978
1959	7879.9	0.288	191.3	0.336	7680.1	0.287	0.029	0.971
1960	8065.7	0.297	191.6	0.324	7865.9	0.297	0.027	0.973
1961	8213.4	0.308	199.6	0.329	8005.2	0.308	0.027	0.973
1962	8332.5	0.313	221.8	0.358	8099.7	0.312	0.031	0.969
1963	8585.9	0.318	240.9	0.381	8331.6	0.317	0.035	0.965
1964	8688.9	0.334	261.6	0.405	8409.9	0.332	0.038	0.962
1965	8892.2	0.349	297.5	0.443	8569.5	0.347	0.044	0.956
1966	8961.9	0.370	325.0	0.457	8605.0	0.368	0.047	0.953
1967	9095.2	0.389	332.3	0.447	8729.9	0.389	0.044	0.956
1968	9194.1	0.410	346.2	0.448	8813.4	0.410	0.043	0.957
1969	9811.1	0.434	361.7	0.446	9413.0	0.435	0.039	0.961
1970	9765.0	0.483	369.0	0.430	9360.1	0.487	0.035	0.965
1971	9881.1	0.515	409.6	0.460	9439.5	0.519	0.038	0.962
1972	9873.3	0.541	459.2	0.502	9386.8	0.545	0.045	0.955
1973	9940.1	0.573	498.4	0.517	9417.5	0.578	0.047	0.953
1974	10164.1	0.607	505.2	0.504	9633.5	0.614	0.043	0.957
1975	10331.7	0.648	577.2	0.558	9738.9	0.654	0.051	0.949
1976	10522.9	0.681	658.8	0.630	9856.1	0.685	0.062	0.938
1977	10956.3	0.712	766.0	0.709	10185.1	0.713	0.075	0.925
1978	11336.2	0.758	870.0	0.769	10460.2	0.757	0.085	0.915
1979	11618.1	0.810	930.6	0.785	10681.7	0.813	0.084	0.916
1980	12087.1	0.860	987.2	0.804	11094.9	0.866	0.083	0.917
1981	12350.7	0.932	1145.1	0.927	11205.4	0.933	0.102	0.898
1982	12712.3	1.000	1247.6	1.000	11464.8	1.000	0.109	0.891
1983	12928.3	1.064	1419.2	1.130	11503.5	1.057	0.132	0.868
1984	13303.0	1.121	1591.2	1.262	11691.8	1.104	0.156	0.844
1985	13582.6	1.184	1689.1	1.282	11865.4	1.173	0.156	0.844
1986	13874.0	1.252	1703.4	1.242	12142.9	1.256	0.139	0.861

ment, similarly full investment can be allocated between human investment and nonhuman investment.[13] On the outlay side, factor outlay is either for property or labor. Full labor outlay is composed of market labor outlay and nonmarket labor outlay. Nonmarket labor outlay is the value of all nonmarket activities (excluding sleep and other maintenance activities).

In table 6.9, human investment is the sum of investment in infants and investment in education. Nonhuman investment is investment in reproducible assets such as buildings and equipment. Human investment is far larger than nonhuman investment, although the growth in nonhuman investment in constant dollars, 1949–1986, 3.6%, is considerably greater than that for human investment, 1.5%. By contrast, the price of human investment grows more rapidly than that for nonhuman investment, reflecting increases in wages and the return to education. As shown in table 6.10, full consumption is larger than full investment by the end of the period. This occurs primarily because of the slower growth in the quantity of human investment during the postwar period. Nonmarket labor outlay in table 6.11 includes investment in human capital plus the value of time spent in household production and leisure. As a result, nonmarket labor outlay accounts for the majority of full labor outlay. Market labor outlay grows at a faster rate than nonmarket labor outlay (1.9% versus 1.7%). The most marked production account differences, shown in table 6.12, are between property outlay and full labor outlay. Full property outlay is less than 10% of full factor outlay in current or constant dollars until the eighties, but grows at a much faster rate than full labor outlay (7.4% versus 1.7% in constant dollars).

There are three tables (tables 6.13 through 6.15) giving details corresponding to the expenditures part of the income and expenditure account (table 6.2). Full consumer outlays can be allocated between market consumer outlays and nonmarket consumer outlays. Nonmarket consumer outlays are the value of time spent in household production and leisure. The difference between full private national expenditures and full private national consumer outlays is full gross private national saving. Full gross private national saving is the sum of nonhuman saving and human saving.

The division of full consumer outlays between market and nonmarket components is given in table 6.13. The rate of growth for constant dollar market consumer outlays (3.5%) is approximately double the rate of growth for constant dollar nonmarket consumer outlays (1.7%).

Table 6.13
Full consumer outlay (billions of constant dollars)

Year	Full Consumer Outlays		Market Consumer Outlays		Nonmarket Consumer Outlays		Market Current Dollar Share	Nonmarket Current Dollar Share
	Quantity	Price	Quantity	Price	Quantity	Price		
1949	3147.1	0.190	692.6	0.262	2521.7	0.165	0.304	0.696
1950	3187.2	0.194	725.8	0.266	2515.3	0.169	0.312	0.688
1951	3220.7	0.202	747.2	0.281	2526.9	0.175	0.322	0.678
1952	3320.9	0.207	774.6	0.288	2591.6	0.180	0.324	0.676
1953	3484.2	0.215	802.5	0.293	2735.2	0.187	0.315	0.685
1954	3376.4	0.226	822.2	0.295	2583.1	0.201	0.318	0.682
1955	3552.2	0.227	871.6	0.299	2708.0	0.202	0.323	0.677
1956	3676.6	0.234	898.4	0.302	2808.3	0.210	0.315	0.685
1957	3752.5	0.247	919.8	0.312	2862.1	0.223	0.310	0.690
1958	3651.0	0.257	929.1	0.317	2737.9	0.235	0.313	0.687
1959	3895.8	0.260	979.8	0.326	2937.2	0.236	0.315	0.685
1960	3952.1	0.271	1001.4	0.332	2969.7	0.249	0.310	0.690
1961	4011.1	0.280	1027.1	0.336	2999.9	0.259	0.307	0.693
1962	4046.4	0.289	1068.7	0.343	2984.5	0.269	0.313	0.687
1963	4311.0	0.294	1110.4	0.350	3215.5	0.273	0.306	0.694
1964	4413.5	0.311	1176.2	0.356	3243.0	0.294	0.305	0.695
1965	4549.6	0.328	1248.3	0.364	3300.5	0.315	0.304	0.696
1966	4649.2	0.348	1311.5	0.374	3332.3	0.338	0.303	0.697
1967	4751.2	0.365	1355.9	0.382	3388.4	0.359	0.298	0.702
1968	4873.0	0.385	1408.3	0.396	3456.9	0.381	0.297	0.703
1969	5209.1	0.407	1458.7	0.412	3743.2	0.405	0.284	0.716
1970	5213.4	0.446	1504.7	0.431	3702.3	0.453	0.279	0.721
1971	5225.5	0.475	1543.6	0.450	3677.6	0.486	0.280	0.720
1972	5441.7	0.497	1631.4	0.469	3807.7	0.509	0.283	0.717
1973	5639.6	0.529	1687.5	0.495	3949.1	0.544	0.280	0.720
1974	5706.9	0.573	1669.5	0.543	4031.2	0.587	0.277	0.723
1975	5821.5	0.614	1722.5	0.588	4094.1	0.625	0.283	0.717
1976	5924.1	0.652	1818.9	0.624	4104.2	0.664	0.294	0.706
1977	6213.7	0.686	1905.3	0.665	4307.2	0.695	0.298	0.702
1978	6359.1	0.740	1984.2	0.712	4375.4	0.753	0.300	0.700
1979	6476.2	0.803	2025.4	0.775	4451.5	0.815	0.302	0.698
1980	6536.1	0.868	2038.9	0.856	4497.6	0.874	0.308	0.692
1981	6801.4	0.931	2084.3	0.939	4717.6	0.927	0.309	0.691
1982	6873.1	1.000	2166.3	1.000	4706.9	1.000	0.315	0.685
1983	6950.0	1.051	2258.6	1.047	4691.5	1.053	0.324	0.676
1984	7238.6	1.096	2366.6	1.093	4872.2	1.097	0.326	0.674
1985	7405.1	1.155	2460.5	1.129	4945.6	1.168	0.325	0.675
1986	7795.0	1.211	2513.7	1.154	5278.5	1.238	0.307	0.693

Table 6.14
Full gross private national saving (billions of constant dollars)

Year	Full Saving Quantity	Price	Nonhuman Saving Quantity	Price	Human Saving Quantity	Price	Nonhuman Current Dollar Share	Human Current Dollar Share
1949	3464.4	0.186	236.9	0.288	3231.5	0.178	0.106	0.894
1950	3605.7	0.192	302.4	0.256	3280.4	0.188	0.112	0.888
1951	3730.5	0.207	301.5	0.296	3410.0	0.200	0.115	0.885
1952	3731.0	0.224	284.7	0.321	3435.3	0.217	0.109	0.891
1953	3871.7	0.242	297.4	0.326	3562.0	0.236	0.104	0.896
1954	3785.8	0.258	294.7	0.327	3477.9	0.253	0.099	0.901
1955	4004.2	0.267	350.1	0.312	3631.0	0.265	0.102	0.898
1956	4114.6	0.287	342.8	0.328	3751.0	0.285	0.095	0.905
1957	4243.1	0.313	334.5	0.354	3889.8	0.311	0.089	0.911
1958	4145.0	0.332	312.2	0.366	3816.3	0.330	0.083	0.917
1959	4155.2	0.340	359.6	0.349	3776.1	0.341	0.089	0.911
1960	4261.7	0.348	352.6	0.357	3889.4	0.349	0.085	0.915
1961	4334.9	0.360	350.1	0.368	3964.9	0.361	0.082	0.918
1962	4403.9	0.361	389.7	0.373	3993.1	0.361	0.091	0.909
1963	4577.2	0.365	416.5	0.370	4138.6	0.367	0.092	0.908
1964	4631.9	0.377	451.1	0.382	4158.2	0.379	0.099	0.901
1965	4761.7	0.388	503.1	0.379	4235.8	0.391	0.103	0.897
1966	4780.1	0.407	544.6	0.392	4214.1	0.411	0.110	0.890
1967	4829.2	0.428	543.8	0.414	4263.4	0.432	0.109	0.891
1968	4848.0	0.446	567.8	0.416	4259.5	0.452	0.109	0.891
1969	5332.3	0.471	581.6	0.421	4723.7	0.480	0.097	0.903
1970	5235.4	0.527	566.1	0.459	4642.0	0.539	0.094	0.906
1971	5293.0	0.558	619.1	0.481	4653.5	0.570	0.101	0.899
1972	5178.1	0.583	672.7	0.482	4497.2	0.599	0.107	0.893
1973	5195.1	0.610	757.9	0.505	4445.1	0.627	0.121	0.879
1974	5263.4	0.640	711.2	0.553	4550.3	0.654	0.117	0.883
1975	5254.8	0.687	667.0	0.661	4581.7	0.692	0.122	0.878
1976	5300.0	0.705	731.5	0.669	4565.4	0.712	0.131	0.869
1977	5556.3	0.727	793.1	0.688	4761.5	0.734	0.135	0.865
1978	5761.3	0.761	855.2	0.738	4905.9	0.765	0.144	0.856
1979	5855.2	0.812	859.7	0.804	4995.0	0.813	0.145	0.855
1980	6117.0	0.857	814.3	0.880	5303.0	0.854	0.137	0.863
1981	6137.7	0.936	852.2	0.954	5284.9	0.933	0.142	0.858
1982	6248.5	1.000	815.8	1.000	5432.7	1.000	0.131	0.869
1983	6252.2	1.056	892.7	1.005	5361.8	1.065	0.136	0.864
1984	6416.8	1.103	1044.0	1.016	5384.3	1.117	0.150	0.850
1985	6508.1	1.165	1072.8	1.021	5448.7	1.190	0.144	0.856
1986	6714.9	1.249	1111.4	1.033	5618.1	1.288	0.137	0.863

Table 6.15
Full gross private national savings (billions of constant dollars)

Year	Full Expenditures		Full Consumer Outlays		Full Saving		Outlays Current Dollar Share	Saving Current Dollar Share
	Quantity	Price	Quantity	Price	Quantity	Price	Share	Share
1949	6679.8	0.186	3147.1	0.190	3464.4	0.186	0.481	0.519
1950	6862.3	0.191	3187.2	0.194	3605.7	0.192	0.471	0.529
1951	7028.6	0.203	3226.7	0.202	3730.5	0.207	0.458	0.542
1952	7121.6	0.214	3320.9	0.207	3731.0	0.224	0.452	0.548
1953	7426.6	0.227	3484.2	0.215	3871.7	0.242	0.444	0.556
1954	7233.2	0.240	3376.4	0.226	3785.8	0.258	0.438	0.562
1955	7632.8	0.246	3552.2	0.227	4004.2	0.267	0.430	0.570
1956	7867.4	0.260	3676.6	0.234	4114.6	0.287	0.422	0.578
1957	8078.3	0.279	3752.5	0.247	4243.1	0.313	0.411	0.589
1958	7878.5	0.294	3651.0	0.257	4145.0	0.332	0.406	0.594
1959	8103.5	0.300	3895.8	0.260	4155.2	0.340	0.417	0.583
1960	8273.2	0.309	3952.1	0.271	4261.7	0.348	0.419	0.581
1961	8407.5	0.319	4011.1	0.280	4334.9	0.360	0.419	0.581
1962	8516.0	0.324	4046.4	0.289	4403.9	0.361	0.424	0.576
1963	8945.3	0.329	4311.0	0.294	4577.2	0.365	0.431	0.569
1964	9098.1	0.343	4413.5	0.311	4631.9	0.377	0.440	0.560
1965	9364.4	0.357	4549.6	0.328	4761.7	0.388	0.447	0.553
1966	9476.3	0.376	4649.2	0.348	4780.1	0.407	0.454	0.546
1967	9623.8	0.395	4751.2	0.365	4829.2	0.428	0.456	0.544
1968	9757.1	0.414	4873.0	0.385	4848.0	0.446	0.464	0.536
1969	10591.6	0.437	5209.1	0.407	5332.3	0.471	0.457	0.543
1970	10490.7	0.485	5213.4	0.446	5235.4	0.527	0.457	0.543
1971	10564.3	0.514	5225.5	0.475	5293.0	0.558	0.457	0.543
1972	10639.4	0.538	5441.7	0.497	5178.1	0.583	0.472	0.528
1973	10841.4	0.567	5639.6	0.529	5195.1	0.610	0.485	0.515
1974	10977.5	0.605	5706.9	0.573	5263.4	0.640	0.493	0.507
1975	11077.0	0.648	5821.5	0.614	5254.8	0.687	0.497	0.503
1976	11222.4	0.677	5924.1	0.852	5300.0	0.705	0.508	0.492
1977	11768.1	0.706	6213.7	0.686	5556.3	0.727	0.513	0.487
1978	12120.2	0.750	6359.1	0.740	5761.3	0.761	0.518	0.482
1979	12331.0	0.807	6476.2	0.803	5855.2	0.812	0.522	0.478
1980	12652.5	0.863	6536.1	0.868	6117.0	0.857	0.520	0.480
1981	12939.1	0.933	6801.4	0.931	6137.7	0.936	0.524	0.476
1982	13121.7	1.000	6873.1	1.000	6248.5	1.000	0.524	0.476
1983	13202.1	1.054	6950.0	1.051	6252.2	1.056	0.525	0.475
1984	13655.0	1.099	7238.6	1.096	6416.8	1.103	0.529	0.471
1985	13912.6	1.160	7405.1	1.155	6508.1	1.165	0.530	0.470
1986	14507.9	1.228	7795.0	1.211	6714.9	1.249	0.529	0.471

This higher growth rate is almost offset by a deflator growth rate that is lower than the corresponding deflator growth rate for nonmarket consumer outlays (4.0% versus 5.4%). By the end of the period in current dollars market consumer outlays account for one-third of full consumer outlays. As shown in table 6.14, nonhuman saving in constant dollars grows much more rapidly than human saving (4.2% versus 1.5%), but the deflator grows at a slower rate (3.4% versus 5.3%). The current dollar share of human saving in full saving drifts downward during the seventies and eighties. The trends for full consumer outlays and full saving given in table 6.15 are not significantly different. Neither series dominates in current or constant dollars, although until sometime in the seventies full saving is larger than full consumer outlays. The current dollar shares for full consumer outlays vary from 39.8% to 51.7%; those for full saving vary from 48.3% to 60.2%.

There are two tables (tables 6.16 and 6.17) giving details corresponding to the income account (table 6.4). Full private national income is broken out between full labor income and property income; full labor income is broken out further between market labor income and nonmarket labor income.

Table 6.16 shows that in constant dollars, market labor income grows at a rate that is about one-third faster than nonmarket labor income (2.1% versus 1.6%). The deflators show very similar trends, reflecting the importance of wages in both calculations. Table 6.17 again demonstrates that when a set of human capital accounts are incorporated into a national accounting system, labor plays the predominate role. The property income current dollar share at no time reaches 10% of full income. The pattern observed in earlier tables again appears. Labor income in constant dollars grows at a relatively slow rate (1.8%); the deflator grows at a relatively rapid rate (5.4%). Constant dollar property income grows at 4.2% per year, the deflator at 3.4%.

There are three tables (tables 6.18 through 6.20) giving details corresponding to the accumulation and wealth accounts (tables 6.6 and 6.8). Table 6.18 shows that constant dollar full net saving grew very slowly primarily because of the nearly four-fold higher rate of growth in constant dollar full depreciation (0.7% versus 2.6%). During the seventies and eighties, the current dollar share of full depreciation in full gross saving tended to increase, while the current share of full net saving correspondingly decreased. Table 6.19 gives the saving and depreciation series in current dollars and shows how revaluation affects

Table 6.16
Full labor income (billions of constant dollars)

Year	Full Labor Income Quantity	Price	Market Labor Income Quantity	Price	Nonmarket Labor Income Quantity	Price	Market Current Dollar Share	Nonmarket Current Dollar Share
1949	6682.7	0.171	878.9	0.172	5797.4	0.171	0.132	0.888
1950	6764.3	0.178	915.0	0.182	5842.6	0.178	0.138	0.862
1951	7007.2	0.187	1008.9	0.187	5990.9	0.188	0.143	0.857
1952	7138.2	0.198	1053.8	0.192	6077.4	0.199	0.143	0.857
1953	7417.5	0.211	1064.6	0.203	6344.4	0.213	0.138	0.862
1954	7175.5	0.226	1051.0	0.210	6117.7	0.229	0.136	0.864
1955	7490.0	0.233	1085.1	0.215	6396.7	0.236	0.134	0.866
1956	7743.9	0.247	1117.9	0.227	6617.1	0.251	0.132	0.868
1957	7951.6	0.266	1119.1	0.240	6820.4	0.271	0.127	0.873
1958	7751.7	0.281	1108.2	0.248	6633.9	0.287	0.126	0.874
1959	7902.4	0.288	1145.6	0.253	6749.1	0.294	0.128	0.872
1960	8078.8	0.297	1163.3	0.261	6906.5	0.304	0.126	0.874
1961	8211.7	0.307	1185.0	0.265	7018.0	0.315	0.124	0.876
1962	8255.7	0.312	1213.0	0.273	7037.3	0.319	0.128	0.872
1963	8646.6	0.317	1239.7	0.279	7396.8	0.324	0.126	0.874
1964	8710.8	0.333	1259.7	0.298	7442.4	0.340	0.129	0.871
1965	8881.8	0.348	1295.7	0.307	7578.7	0.356	0.129	0.871
1966	8917.9	0.369	1331.4	0.326	7583.2	0.377	0.132	0.868
1967	9050.7	0.390	1361.4	0.342	7687.3	0.398	0.132	0.868
1968	9145.0	0.411	1401.3	0.365	7745.1	0.419	0.136	0.864
1969	9958.9	0.436	1442.4	0.384	8506.9	0.445	0.127	0.873
1970	9807.3	0.487	1415.7	0.422	8381.5	0.498	0.125	0.875
1971	9793.7	0.519	1412.0	0.456	8371.3	0.531	0.127	0.873
1972	9791.0	0.545	1466.1	0.477	8322.3	0.557	0.131	0.869
1973	9889.5	0.579	1491.7	0.531	8396.5	0.588	0.138	0.862
1974	10104.1	0.614	1517.5	0.569	8584.6	0.622	0.139	0.861
1975	10209.5	0.653	1530.4	0.611	8676.9	0.660	0.140	0.860
1976	10243.8	0.685	1574.2	0.659	8669.5	0.689	0.148	0.852
1977	10686.4	0.714	1617.9	0.702	9067.8	0.716	0.149	0.851
1978	10949.9	0.760	1667.7	0.762	9281.5	0.759	0.153	0.847
1979	11164.1	0.816	1716.5	0.826	9446.7	0.814	0.156	0.844
1980	11539.0	0.867	1739.6	0.891	9799.4	0.863	0.155	0.845
1981	11784.3	0.933	1781.9	0.949	10002.2	0.930	0.154	0.846
1982	11919.2	1.000	1779.6	1.000	10139.6	1.000	0.149	0.851
1983	11853.6	1.058	1800.6	1.048	10053.2	1.059	0.150	0.850
1984	12128.1	1.110	1873.0	1.124	10255.2	1.108	0.156	0.844
1985	12299.7	1.179	1906.9	1.175	10392.8	1.180	0.154	0.846
1986	12814.4	1.263	1921.9	1.255	10892.2	1.265	0.149	0.851

Table 6.17
Full private national income (billions of constant dollars)

Year	Full Income Quantity	Price	Property Income Quantity	Price	Full Labor Income Quantity	Price	Current Dollar Share	Current Dollar Share
1949	6982.1	0.177	318.6	0.290	6682.7	0.171	0.075	0.925
1950	7081.4	0.184	331.2	0.290	6764.3	0.178	0.074	0.926
1951	7330.1	0.193	339.6	0.308	7007.2	0.187	0.074	0.926
1952	7471.3	0.203	348.6	0.303	7138.2	0.198	0.070	0.930
1953	7760.6	0.216	360.2	0.305	7417.5	0.211	0.065	0.935
1954	7540.0	0.230	372.5	0.300	7175.5	0.226	0.064	0.936
1955	7867.1	0.238	386.3	0.334	7490.0	0.233	0.069	0.931
1956	8131.3	0.251	397.5	0.312	7743.9	0.247	0.061	0.939
1957	8348.5	0.269	407.5	0.318	7951.6	0.266	0.058	0.942
1958	8162.0	0.282	418.0	0.301	7751.7	0.281	0.055	0.945
1959	8324.0	0.291	429.1	0.343	7902.4	0.288	0.061	0.939
1960	8509.4	0.299	438.3	0.335	8078.8	0.297	0.058	0.942
1961	8650.4	0.309	446.4	0.340	8211.7	0.307	0.057	0.943
1962	8708.7	0.316	459.3	0.374	8255.7	0.312	0.062	0.938
1963	9112.0	0.322	473.5	0.395	8646.6	0.317	0.064	0.936
1964	9193.7	0.338	488.4	0.421	8710.8	0.333	0.066	0.934
1965	9386.9	0.355	508.0	0.464	8881.8	0.348	0.071	0.929
1966	9448.5	0.376	528.0	0.487	8917.9	0.369	0.072	0.928
1967	9608.9	0.394	551.6	0.476	9050.7	0.390	0.069	0.931
1968	9733.7	0.413	578.7	0.458	9145.0	0.411	0.066	0.934
1969	10575.0	0.436	606.8	0.450	9958.9	0.436	0.059	0.941
1970	10444.6	0.484	628.8	0.453	9807.3	0.487	0.056	0.944
1971	10456.8	0.517	656.3	0.485	9793.7	0.519	0.059	0.941
1972	10470.3	0.543	673.3	0.528	9791.0	0.545	0.063	0.937
1973	10593.8	0.577	698.9	0.556	9889.5	0.579	0.064	0.936
1974	10836.4	0.609	727.8	0.536	10104.1	0.614	0.059	0.941
1975	10966.2	0.650	753.8	0.610	10209.5	0.653	0.065	0.935
1976	11055.2	0.682	811.7	0.646	10243.8	0.685	0.070	0.930
1977	11547.9	0.714	862.2	0.713	10686.4	0.714	0.075	0.925
1978	11844.9	0.762	895.5	0.790	10949.9	0.760	0.078	0.922
1979	12102.0	0.816	937.8	0.818	11164.1	0.816	0.078	0.922
1980	12520.4	0.865	981.6	0.838	11539.0	0.867	0.076	0.924
1981	12820.5	0.934	1036.6	0.948	11784.3	0.933	0.082	0.918
1982	13021.9	1.000	1102.8	1.000	11919.2	1.000	0.085	0.915
1983	13068.8	1.056	1215.9	1.043	11853.6	1.058	0.092	0.908
1984	13444.4	1.108	1318.3	1.084	12128.1	1.110	0.096	0.904
1985	13700.4	1.169	1406.2	1.078	12299.7	1.179	0.095	0.905
1986	14296.7	1.238	1491.5	1.013	12814.4	1.263	0.085	0.915

Table 6.18
Full gross private national savings (billions of constant dollars)

Year	Full Gross Saving		Full Net Saving		Full Depreciation		Net Current Dollar Share	Depreciation Current Dollar Share
	Quantity	Price	Quantity	Price	Quantity	Price		
1949	3464.3	0.186	2316.8	0.160	1383.7	0.198	0.575	0.425
1950	3605.6	0.192	2428.3	0.161	1407.7	0.214	0.566	0.434
1951	3730.4	0.207	2527.7	0.171	1437.6	0.237	0.560	0.440
1952	3730.8	0.224	2531.8	0.184	1442.2	0.257	0.557	0.443
1953	3871.5	0.242	2666.2	0.196	1439.6	0.288	0.557	0.443
1954	3785.7	0.258	2626.6	0.208	1436.3	0.300	0.558	0.442
1955	4004.0	0.267	2808.9	0.213	1460.6	0.323	0.559	0.441
1956	4114.5	0.287	2876.7	0.228	1479.4	0.355	0.556	0.444
1957	4242.9	0.313	2982.5	0.249	1500.9	0.390	0.559	0.441
1958	4144.9	0.332	2894.6	0.262	1522.0	0.405	0.552	0.448
1959	4155.1	0.340	2890.6	0.272	1536.8	0.408	0.556	0.444
1960	4261.6	0.348	2941.7	0.283	1555.4	0.419	0.561	0.439
1961	4334.8	0.360	2990.8	0.300	1583.2	0.419	0.574	0.426
1962	4403.7	0.361	2973.3	0.306	1646.1	0.411	0.574	0.426
1963	4577.0	0.365	3035.5	0.314	1705.7	0.423	0.569	0.431
1964	4631.7	0.377	3020.6	0.330	1761.4	0.427	0.570	0.430
1965	4761.4	0.388	3040.4	0.341	1821.1	0.445	0.561	0.439
1966	4779.8	0.407	2957.0	0.360	1889.6	0.466	0.547	0.453
1967	4828.9	0.428	2891.4	0.384	1977.9	0.485	0.537	0.463
1968	4847.7	0.446	2813.8	0.405	2067.1	0.495	0.527	0.473
1969	5332.1	0.471	3170.5	0.411	2131.0	0.568	0.518	0.482
1970	5235.1	0.527	3032.7	0.476	2200.8	0.598	0.523	0.477
1971	5292.7	0.558	3035.2	0.510	2278.5	0.616	0.524	0.476
1972	5177.9	0.583	2805.6	0.549	2377.4	0.623	0.510	0.490
1973	5194.9	0.610	2712.3	0.592	2477.2	0.632	0.506	0.494
1974	5263.3	0.640	2661.8	0.629	2579.0	0.657	0.497	0.503
1975	5254.8	0.687	2561.4	0.700	2678.1	0.678	0.497	0.503
1976	5300.0	0.705	2512.0	0.730	2781.3	0.685	0.490	0.510
1977	5556.3	0.727	2656.4	0.761	2892.4	0.699	0.500	0.500
1978	5761.3	0.761	2741.0	0.803	3014.2	0.724	0.502	0.498
1979	5855.1	0.812	2717.2	0.872	3136.6	0.760	0.499	0.501
1980	6116.9	0.857	2879.2	0.883	3234.2	0.835	0.485	0.515
1981	6137.7	0.936	2817.6	0.963	3317.8	0.913	0.473	0.527
1982	6248.5	1.000	2855.2	1.000	3393.3	1.000	0.457	0.543
1983	6252.2	1.056	2814.0	1.079	3440.0	1.037	0.460	0.540
1984	6416.7	1.103	2906.8	1.112	3514.0	1.094	0.457	0.543
1985	6508.1	1.165	2917.0	1.184	3594.3	1.148	0.456	0.544
1986	6714.8	1.249	3038.0	1.228	3682.5	1.264	0.445	0.555

Table 6.19
Gross private national capital accumulation (billions of current dollars)

Year	Full Gross Saving	Full Depreciation	Net Capital Formation	Full Revaluation	Change in Wealth
1949	643.3	273.3	369.9	548.6	918.5
1950	692.9	300.7	392.2	790.2	1182.4
1951	772.5	340.2	432.3	807.6	1239.9
1952	835.9	370.4	465.5	936.5	1402.0
1953	936.7	414.5	522.2	1464.1	1986.2
1954	976.5	431.1	545.4	249.5	794.9
1955	1070.4	472.2	598.1	1116.1	1714.2
1956	1182.3	525.5	656.8	1763.7	2420.5
1957	1327.3	585.0	742.4	1836.1	2570.4
1958	1375.0	616.4	758.6	225.1	983.8
1959	1414.2	627.5	786.7	1251.0	2037.8
1960	1484.2	651.0	833.2	1478.3	2311.5
1961	1560.6	664.0	896.5	1281.3	2177.9
1962	1588.2	677.1	911.1	459.0	1370.1
1963	1672.7	721.0	951.7	2205.3	3157.1
1964	1747.6	751.9	995.7	2069.8	3065.5
1965	1848.4	810.5	1037.9	3085.9	4123.8
1966	1944.0	880.4	1063.5	2827.7	3891.3
1967	2067.6	958.3	1109.2	3362.2	4471.5
1968	2161.9	1022.6	1139.3	3310.8	4450.2
1969	2513.5	1210.3	1303.2	7556.3	8859.5
1970	2760.9	1316.5	1444.4	5442.4	6886.9
1971	2951.4	1403.5	1547.9	3821.5	5369.4
1972	3019.2	1480.4	1538.9	6467.3	8006.2
1973	3170.2	1565.6	1604.6	7351.7	8956.3
1974	3371.1	1695.6	1675.5	8378.4	10053.9
1975	3609.9	1816.9	1793.0	7481.9	9274.8
1976	3738.7	1906.0	1832.7	6087.3	7920.0
1977	4041.3	2020.7	2020.6	10219.1	12239.7
1978	4383.9	2183.2	2200.6	12061.5	14262.2
1979	4753.4	2383.7	2369.8	12535.8	14905.6
1980	5244.0	2701.1	2542.8	10168.8	12711.6
1981	5743.1	3028.8	2714.3	14191.6	16905.9
1982	6248.5	3393.3	2855.2	10091.4	12946.6
1983	6605.2	3568.8	3036.4	9003.9	12040.2
1984	7075.2	3842.8	3232.3	12676.1	15908.4
1985	7580.7	4127.0	3453.7	14677.5	18131.2
1986	8386.1	4656.4	3729.7	23026.5	26756.1

Table 6.20
Full private national wealth (billions of constant dollars)

Year	Full Wealth Quantity	Price	Human Wealth Quantity	Price	Nonhuman Wealth Quantity	Price	Human Current Dollar Share	Nonhuman Current Dollar Share
1949	120985.7	0.150	114433.8	0.148	6436.4	0.189	0.933	0.067
1950	123330.7	0.157	116610.8	0.155	6593.5	0.197	0.933	0.067
1951	125737.0	0.163	118856.2	0.161	6745.0	0.211	0.931	0.069
1952	128228.9	0.171	121207.7	0.169	6881.7	0.217	0.932	0.068
1953	130758.7	0.183	123598.2	0.181	7018.2	0.222	0.935	0.065
1954	133550.4	0.185	126242.9	0.183	7163.2	0.226	0.935	0.065
1955	136370.7	0.194	128885.4	0.192	7333.8	0.233	0.935	0.065
1956	139196.8	0.207	131549.3	0.206	7491.6	0.244	0.937	0.063
1957	142203.2	0.221	134417.4	0.220	7630.5	0.255	0.938	0.062
1958	145500.7	0.223	137589.0	0.221	7760.6	0.259	0.938	0.062
1959	148658.2	0.232	140602.6	0.230	7905.0	0.264	0.939	0.061
1960	151826.4	0.242	143645.0	0.241	8033.1	0.272	0.941	0.059
1961	155164.2	0.251	146834.9	0.250	8181.0	0.275	0.942	0.058
1962	158651.0	0.254	150142.7	0.253	8357.5	0.281	0.942	0.058
1963	161871.4	0.269	153163.0	0.268	8552.4	0.285	0.944	0.056
1964	165115.1	0.282	156181.4	0.282	8772.2	0.291	0.945	0.055
1965	168178.5	0.301	158985.0	0.302	9027.8	0.299	0.947	0.053
1966	171169.2	0.319	161712.1	0.320	9290.3	0.311	0.947	0.053
1967	174065.3	0.339	164348.9	0.341	9551.1	0.321	0.948	0.052
1968	176900.5	0.359	166921.4	0.361	9818.2	0.336	0.948	0.052
1969	179508.7	0.403	169284.1	0.406	10072.1	0.354	0.951	0.049
1970	182407.5	0.434	171945.0	0.438	10319.5	0.372	0.952	0.048
1971	185525.1	0.456	174813.8	0.460	10577.9	0.395	0.951	0.049
1972	188204.5	0.492	177195.8	0.497	10898.3	0.419	0.951	0.049
1973	190759.5	0.532	179433.3	0.538	11245.1	0.455	0.950	0.050
1974	193152.0	0.578	181556.6	0.583	11534.2	0.507	0.948	0.052
1975	195597.8	0.618	183740.5	0.622	11810.6	0.558	0.945	0.055
1976	198080.1	0.650	185914.8	0.653	12133.2	0.605	0.943	0.057
1977	200478.6	0.704	187985.3	0.707	12474.5	0.659	0.942	0.058
1978	202818.8	0.766	189947.0	0.768	12867.4	0.730	0.940	0.060
1979	205182.6	0.830	191961.4	0.831	13224.3	0.811	0.937	0.063
1980	207710.6	0.881	194175.5	0.880	13539.3	0.890	0.934	0.066
1981	210324.6	0.950	196439.1	0.949	13887.2	0.965	0.933	0.067
1982	212788.6	1.000	198538.3	1.000	14250.3	1.000	0.933	0.067
1983	215432.0	1.044	200776.4	1.045	14657.6	1.026	0.933	0.067
1984	218035.4	1.104	202876.3	1.108	15173.4	1.048	0.934	0.066
1985	220596.1	1.173	204969.7	1.182	15664.9	1.065	0.936	0.064
1986	222906.9	1.281	206833.3	1.296	16154.8	1.088	0.938	0.062

wealth. Revaluation fluctuates a great deal. For all but three years revaluation is larger than net capital formation. Given the larger magnitude of human saving versus nonhuman saving, it is not surprising that, as table 6.20 shows, human wealth totally dominates nonhuman wealth. The current dollar share of nonhuman wealth is always less than 7% for the period covered. Constant dollar nonhuman wealth does grow at approximately a 1% per annum faster rate than constant dollar human wealth (2.5% versus 1.6%).

The integration of human capital and nonmarket accounts into the Jorgenson system of national accounts by Jorgenson and Fraumeni demonstrates the importance of including these accounts in a national accounting system. The added components are large in magnitude and therefore shpould not be ignored. For example, the human investment and nonmarket consumption components of full gross private domestic product taken together are three times the nonhuman investment and market consumption components. In addition, given the notable differences in the rates of growth between market and nonmarket components on the one hand and human and nonhuman components on the other, analysis done using national accounts without such components will be misleading and inaccurate (Jorgenson and Fraumeni, 1992a). As Jorgenson and Fraumeni continue to explicitly value human capital and nonmarket components as part of their goal to improve the Jorgenson national accounting system, the importance of these features will become even more obvious. The next feature that is being integrated into the Jorgenson national accounts are components related to children beyond the infant investment feature already developed. These features include investment in children, inputs into child rearing, standard costs such as food, housing, and clothing, as well as reductions in parent's lifetime income due to child rearing activities, as part of a family production sector. It is expected that these improvements will have an effect as significant on our understanding of our economy as the human capital and nonmarket features already incorporated.

6.5 Conclusion

This chapter indicates the extent of the contribution of the Jorgenson system of national accounts. It summarizes the differences between the Jorgenson system, NIPA and SNA, by outlining the Jorgenson system with a set of definitional tables and by showing the details of one contribution, the incorporation of human capital and nonmarket activities into the Jorgenson system. The differences between the Jorgenson system and other major accounting systems are significant and lead to differences in economic analysis. It is clear that the incorporation of human capital and nonmarket activities results in aggregates that are higher by an order of magnitude and growth rates that are significantly lower. Other Jorgenson modifications, such as the treatment of consumer durables as an investment item, may not have such an obvious effect, but their impact is equally important.

The Jorgenson system of national accounts is one that continually evolves and expands. Particularly when looking at the seventies and eighties and beyond, when economic change proceeds quickly and the dimensions of economic markets are expanding, the impact of Jorgenson's system on economic analysis will continue to be felt.

Notes

1. The Jorgenson-Gollop-Fraumeni system of sectoral accounts include the Jorgenson-Gollop-Ho sectoral labor accounts (Gollop and Jorgenson, 1980, 1983; Ho, 1989; Jorgenson-Ho-Fraumeni, 1994) and the Fraumeni-Jorgenson capital accounts (1980c, 1986).
2. Currently, the Bureau of Economic Analysis (BEA) is considering changes in NIPA to bring it into closer conformity with the SNA.
3. The Jorgenson accounts do not yet include intangible assets or inputs (such as service flows from R&D) or nonproducible assets or inputs (such as natural resources).
4. Of the fourteen components, proprietors income is the component that includes both a labor and capital component.
5. Environmental modeling is being done by Jorgenson and his associates. See Jorgenson and Wilcoxen (1990a, 1990b, 1991) for example.
6. The SNA does not allow for a return on nonmilitary reproducible assets, therefore the value of services from these assets is clearly understated.
7. Modifications to the Gollop-Jorgenson labor data base by Ho are described in Jorgenson (1990b) and Jorgenson, Ho and Fraumeni (1994).
8. The value of maintenance time is assumed to be zero.
9. We count education from the point at which you enter grade one.
10. The Bureau of Labor Statistics (BLS) does not record labor market participation for individuals under age fourteen. As market wages are the basis for our valuation of nonmarket time not spent in school, we do not impute a positive value for nonmarket time until individuals turn fourteen.
11. The endpoint age for education is determined by data availability.
12. Again this assumption is made because of data availability.
13. The use of the qualifier "full" indicates that both human and nonhuman components or market and nonmarket components are included, when appropriate. Investment is made in human capital (births and education) and nonhuman capital (buildings, equipment and consumer durables). For consumption, the division is between nonmarket (time in household production and consumption, excluding investment activities) and market (personal consumption expenditure for nondurables, being one component).

7

Does Infrastructure Investment Increase the Productivity of Manufacturing Industry in the U.S.?

Charles R. Hulten and Robert M. Schwab

7.1 Introduction

The American South started the post–World War II era as the poorest region of the country. Per capita disposable income was less than 70 percent of the national level and the South produced less than 13 percent of national manufacturing output. Over the ensuing 40 years, the South grew much faster than the most of the rest of the nation. As a result, incomes in the South are now 90 percent of the national average and the South now produces 22 percent of all manufacturing output.

Our previous studies of regional manufacturing examined the sources of this differential growth and concluded that the superior growth rate of the Sun Belt region was explained entirely by the more rapid growth in capital and labor input (Hulten and Schwab, 1984, 1991). Differences in the regional growth rates of total factor productivity (TFP) were found to be negligible. This led to the further conclusion that regional differences in factors like infrastructure investment did not translate into differences in the productive efficiency of manufacturing industry. This conclusion is of some interest for the debate over the adequacy of the nation's infrastructure capital, since it suggests that there were no technological spillovers among manufacturing industries associated with infrastructure investment. Thus our findings in those earlier papers lend no support for the very high rates of return to infrastructure found by Aschauer (1989, 1990) and others.[1]

Equal growth rates of regional TFP do not, however, imply equal levels of TFP, and our findings are thus consistent with different hypotheses about the nature of regional growth. For example, the Sun Belt manufacturing industry may have been initially more backward than the older Snow Belt regions and the gap continued despite TFP growth in all regions. Deficient infrastructure capital is one possible reason for a low level of TFP, although the failure to adopt best-practice technologies or an industry mix at the low end of the "technology ladder" are other explanations (factors often cited when discussing the growth of developing countries).[2] On the other hand, the equality of regional TFP growth rates is also consistent with the equality of TFP levels. In this alternative view, the Sun Belt states produced manufactured goods with exactly the same technological efficiency as elsewhere despite differences in infrastructure endowment.

We attempt to sort out these possibilities by extending our original analysis in the direction pioneered by Jorgenson and Nishimizu (1978). Prior to Jorgenson and Nishimizu, studies of the sources-of-growth of different countries or regions had to be content with Solow's residual measure of TFP growth. The contribution of Jorgenson and Nishimizu was to show how to convert the Solow (1957) residual into a measure of the level of TFP. We implement this approach using 1970–1986 data from the Census and Annual Survey of Manufactures for the nine Census divisions of the U.S. and national data from the Bureau of Labor Statistics and Bureau of Economic Analysis. We then perform a modified version of the Hall (1988b) invariance test using the regional levels of TFP and check to see if there is a statistically significant correlation between these levels and the level of infrastructure capital in each region. Combining the Hall methodology with the Jorgenson-Nishimizu model allows us to avoid one of the main problems associated with the analysis of TFP: an untested assumption of perfect competition and constant returns to scale.

The remainder of the chapter has the following organization. Section 7.2 sets out the sources of growth framework and our proposed tests of several alternative models of regional growth. In section 7.3 we present the data we use in our study and in section 7.4 we set forth our econometric results. Section 7.5 includes a brief summary and conclusions.

7.2   Testing the Alternative Models

Our extension of the Jorgenson-Nishimizu model starts with the assumption that there is a Hicks-neutral production function for manufacturing industry within each region. We assume that manufactured goods in region i in year t, Q_{it}, are produced using privately owned capital K_{it}, labor L_{it}, intermediate inputs M_{it}, and public capital B_{it}:

$$Q_{it} = A_{i0}B_{it}^{\gamma_i}e^{\lambda_i t}F^i(K_{it}, L_{it}, M_{it}, B_{it}).\tag{7.1}$$

Our specification of the public capital variable follows Meade (1952) and Berndt and Hansson (1992) in identifying two ways that public capital influences output. First, it yields direct productive services and thus appears as an argument of $F^i(\cdot)$ (as, for example, when trucks and drivers are combined with public highways to produce transportation services). Second, public capital acts as an "environmental" factor or "systems spillover" which enhances the productivity of some or all of the private inputs. This is represented by the B_{it} component of the technical efficiency term. The infrastructure variable is assumed to enter (1) in constant elasticity form, and the parameter γ_i thus measures the strength of the within-region spillover effect.[3] The other arguments of technical efficiency include the level of regional technical efficiency in some initial year 0, A_{i0}, and the growth rate of technical change, λ_i. The product of these three terms defines the level of total factor productivity.

Regional differences in the level TFP can arise, in this framework, from variations in the quantity of infrastructure capital, different initial levels of TFP, or regional differences in the growth rate of technical change. If some regions are relatively backward for any of these reasons, this backwardness may (in and of itself) give rise to convergence in TFP levels, as in Dowrick and Nguyen (1989). This convergence may be enhanced if there is an infrastructure gap that can be closed. However, under the circumstances posited in endogenous growth theory, regional differences in TFP levels may lead to divergent growth rates among regions.

One mechanism through which infrastructure investment may promote divergent growth is analyzed in Barro (1990). The Barro framework is a variant of the Lucas-Romer-Rebelo endogenous growth model in which public infrastructure capital is fixed by policy at a constant fraction of the private capital stock, i.e., $B_{it} = \tau_i K_{it}$. The production function in this case can then be written as

$$Q_{it} = [A_{i0}B_{it}^{\gamma_i}]K_{it}^{\alpha_i}L_{it}^{\beta_i}M_{it}^{\eta_i} = A_{i0}\tau_i K_{it}^{\alpha_i+\gamma_i}L_{it}^{\beta_i}M_{it}^{\eta_i}.\tag{7.2}$$

If direct input elasticities ($\alpha_i + \beta_i + \eta_i$) sum to one, private producers believe that production takes place under constant returns to scale and a competitive equilibrium may be established. However, the true elasticity of output with respect to total capital ($\alpha_i + \gamma_i$) exceeds the direct elasticity, implying increasing returns to scale and the possibility of endogenous growth.

The Sources of Growth Framework

One major advantage of the Solow-Jorgenson-Nishimizu framework is that it is unnecessary to estimate all of the parameters of the production function. Instead, the measurement of TFP can be based on a two stage procedure that makes use of nonparametric index number techniques. The first step involves the computation of the Solow residual under the assumption that public capital has no effect on private output growth.[4] The continuous time version of the Solow residual has the form:

$$\dot{A}_{it}^{S} = \dot{Q}_{it} - \pi_{it}^{K} \dot{K}_{it} - \pi_{it}^{L} \dot{L}_{it} - \pi_{it}^{M} \dot{M}_{it} \tag{7.3}$$

where dots over variables denote rates of growth and the π_{it}^{X} are income shares. Each term in (7.3), except the growth rate of the Solow residual, can in principle be measured directly, and the growth rate of the technology index can thus be estimated as a residual.

We link the regional Solow level index numbers to the technical efficiency terms in the underlying production function (7.1) in the second stage of the analysis. The true growth rate of efficiency is derived from (7.1) and equals

$$\dot{A}_{it} = \dot{Q}_{it} - \varepsilon_{it}^{K} \dot{K}_{it} - \varepsilon_{it}^{L} \dot{L}_{it} - \varepsilon_{it}^{M} \dot{M}_{it} - \varepsilon_{it}^{B} \dot{B}_{it} = \gamma_i \dot{B}_{it} + \lambda_i \tag{7.4}$$

where ε_{it}^{X} is the elasticity of output with respect to input X.

A comparison of the Solow residual $\dot{A}_{it}^{S}$ with the true efficiency term $\dot{A}_{it}$ reveals two major differences: in the Solow residual, public capital's contribution to output has been ignored and the income shares π_{it}^{X} are assumed equal to the corresponding output elasticities ε_{it}^{X}. The second issue does not pose a problem for estimating the income shares of the variable private factors (labor and intermediate input) when the economy is in competitive equilibrium and they are paid the value of their marginal products. However, it is not generally true that $\varepsilon_{it}^{K} = \pi_{it}^{K}$, even under competitive assumptions, and the wedge between the two can introduce a bias into the Solow residual.[5] The bias can, however, be given an explicit form and, with some manipulation, it can be shown that the Solow residual is related to the underlying parameters of the problem by

$$\dot{A}_{it}^{S} = \lambda_{it} + [\varepsilon_{it} - 1]\dot{K}_{it} - [\gamma_{it} + \varepsilon_{it}^{B}]\dot{B}_{it} \tag{7.5}$$

where $\varepsilon_{it} = \varepsilon_{it}^{K} + \varepsilon_{it}^{L} + \varepsilon_{it}^{M}$ is the scale elasticity. This expression indicates that the growth rate of the measured Solow residual is the sum of three factors: (i) the rate of growth of public capital weighted by the indirect and direct contributions of public capital, (ii) the growth rate of private capital weighted by a correction for any error that is introduced by the assumption of constant returns to scale in private inputs, and (iii) the true growth rate of technical progress. Variants of (7.5) are also the basis for the marginal cost mark-up model of Hall (1988b) and the externality model of Caballero and Lyons (1990, 1992).

Equation (7.5) relates the growth of the Solow residual to its component elements. However, since the goal of this paper is to examine the level of technical efficiency rather than its growth rate, one final step is needed to complete the second stage our analysis. By assuming that γ, ε, ε^{B}, and λ are constant over time, we can integrate (7.5) to obtain[6]

$$A_{it}^{S} = \ln A_{i0} + \lambda_{i}t + [\varepsilon_{i} - 1]\ln K_{it} + [\gamma_{i} + \varepsilon_{i}^{B}]\ln B_{i} . \tag{7.6}$$

A stochastic version of (7.6) in the empirical work is presented below.

Equation (7.6) is expressed in continuous time. The empirical application of (7.6) requires the discrete time analogue developed by Jorgenson and Nishimizu, and extended by Denny, Fuss, and May (1981) and Christensen, Cummings, and Jorgenson (1981). In this framework, the difference between the level of technology in region i at time t and region j at time s equals the logarithmic differences in output minus the share weighted logarithmic differences in inputs, where the shares are the simple averages of the shares in the two regions. The resulting levels indexes, A_{it}^{S}, are expressed relative to the efficiency of the "base" region in the base year, $A_{00}^{S} = 1$. We use the U.S. total and 1970 as the base region and year, and thus all of the productivity index numbers should be interpreted as a proportion of national productivity in 1970.

7.3   Data

The data needed to estimate the parameters of equation (7.6) are described in full in our earlier papers (Hulten and Schwab, 1984,

1991). Our analysis is restricted to manufacturing industries, and most of our regional data are obtained from the Census of Manufactures and the Annual Survey of Manufactures and then reconciled to Bureau of Labor Statistics national totals. We use gross output as our measure of output in this paper, and thus our private inputs include capital, labor, and intermediate inputs (corrected for the purchased services problem). Since regional output deflators are not available from any source, we have used the national deflators from the U.S. Bureau of Labor Statistics. This introduces a potential bias in our results, since any error in the price deflator translates directly into an error in measuring real output and thus into an error in measuring the left-hand side of (7.6).[7]

Our data on public capital are the same as those used in Munnell (1990), and a full description of the data are included in Appendix A of that paper. Briefly, Munnell used annual data on state capital outlays to allocate BEA estimates of the national stock of public capital among the states. Her data set includes estimates of total public capital for each state as well as separate estimates of state stocks of highways and water and sewer facilities.

Since the Munnell data are available only for the period 1970–1986, our analysis is limited to those years.

Table 7.1 presents summary statistics on our measures of manufacturing input, output, and the Solow residual for the various regions, as well as statistics on regional output per worker, private capital per worker, and public capital. It is clear from this table that the manufacturing sector grew much faster in the South and West. Gross output rose 3.75 percent per year in the Sun Belt during the 1970–1986 period as compared to only 1.53 percent per year in the Snow Belt.[8] Labor input grew by more than 1 percent per year in the Sun Belt but fell in the Snow Belt. Public capital grew more rapidly in the Sun Belt (2.19 versus 1.30 percent).

It is apparent in the last two columns of table 7.1 that regional differences in the growth rates of the Solow residual (TFP) were relatively small, while the trends in output, capital, and labor showed a strong convergence. Moreover, table 7.1 indicates that the growth rates of capital per worker and output per worker were roughly the same in the Sun Belt and Snow Belt regions over this period. Our conclusions about the lack of TFP convergence during the years 1970–1986 can thus be extended to the convergence in output per worker due to capital-deepening.[9]

Table 7.1
Summary of the level and growth rate of manufacturing gross output, 1970–1986 (U.S. 1970 = 1.000)

	NE	MA	ENC	WNC	SA	ESC	WSC	M	PAC	Total	Snow Belt	Sun Belt
Gross Output												
1970	0.0590	0.1979	0.2767	0.0764	0.1234	0.0573	0.0780	0.0220	0.1094	1.0000	0.6100	0.3900
1986	0.0851	0.2106	0.3623	0.1212	0.2201	0.0978	0.1564	0.0428	0.1935	1.4897	0.7792	0.7105
Growth Rate	0.0229	0.0039	0.0169	0.0289	0.0362	0.0334	0.0435	0.0416	0.0357	0.0249	0.0153	0.0375
Labor												
1970	0.0773	0.2205	0.2620	0.0633	0.1325	0.0579	0.0618	0.0187	0.1053	1.0000	0.6227	0.3767
1986	0.0753	0.1626	0.2198	0.0684	0.1551	0.0628	0.0765	0.0310	0.1353	0.9868	0.5254	0.4611
Growth Rate	−0.0017	−0.0190	−0.0110	0.0049	0.0099	0.0050	0.0134	0.0314	0.0156	−0.0008	−0.0106	0.0126
Private Capital												
1970	0.0580	0.1890	0.2877	0.0552	0.1261	0.0597	0.0898	0.0199	0.1136	1.0000	0.5894	0.4106
1986	0.0902	0.2210	0.3456	0.1004	0.2122	0.0921	0.1727	0.0458	0.1995	1.4812	0.7571	0.7240
Growth Rate	0.0275	0.0098	0.0115	0.0374	0.0325	0.0271	0.0409	0.0521	0.0352	0.0246	0.0157	0.0354
Intermediate Input												
1970	0.0506	0.1838	0.2772	0.0859	0.1258	0.0578	0.0875	0.0245	0.1069	1.0000	0.5976	0.4024
1986	0.0640	0.1757	0.3428	0.1204	0.2003	0.0945	0.1677	0.0371	0.1722	1.3749	0.7030	0.6719
Growth Rate	0.0147	−0.0028	0.0133	0.0211	0.0291	0.0308	0.0407	0.0259	0.0298	0.0199	0.0102	0.0320

Table 7.1 (continued)

	NE	MA	ENC	WNC	SA	ESC	WSC	M	PAC	Total	Snow Belt	Sun Belt
Total Factor Productivity												
1970	0.9113	0.9777	1.0192	1.1095	0.9576	0.9839	1.0226	1.0504	1.0202	1.0000	1.0027	0.9945
1986	1.1639	1.1966	1.2869	1.3137	1.2122	1.2285	1.2531	1.2069	1.2285	1.2386	1.2505	1.2251
Growth Rate	0.0153	0.0128	0.0146	0.0106	0.0147	0.0139	0.0127	0.0087	0.0116	0.0134	0.0138	0.0130
Labor Productivity												
1970	0.7630	0.8976	1.0561	1.2075	0.9315	0.9896	1.2630	1.1726	1.0383	1.0000	0.9795	1.0353
1986	1.1303	1.2948	1.6481	1.7721	1.4192	1.5572	2.0444	1.3815	1.4304	1.5096	1.4831	1.5409
Growth Rate	0.0246	0.0229	0.0278	0.0240	0.0263	0.0283	0.0301	0.0102	0.0200	0.0257	0.0259	0.0249
Capital Labor Ratio												
1970	0.7510	0.8570	1.0981	0.8724	0.9522	1.0307	1.4541	1.0622	1.0780	1.0000	0.9464	1.0899
1986	1.1984	1.3592	1.5719	1.4675	1.3687	1.4669	2.2570	1.4790	1.4745	1.5010	1.4411	1.5701
Growth Rate	0.0292	0.0288	0.0224	0.0325	0.0227	0.0221	0.0275	0.0207	0.0196	0.0254	0.0263	0.0228
Public Capital												
1970	0.0516	0.1820	0.1893	0.0847	0.1235	0.0620	0.0920	0.0497	0.1652	1.0000	0.5076	0.4924
1986	0.0645	0.2268	0.2219	0.1119	0.1949	0.0793	0.1364	0.0816	0.1959	1.3132	0.6251	0.6881
Growth Rate	0.0139	0.0138	0.0099	0.0174	0.0285	0.0154	0.0247	0.0310	0.0106	0.0170	0.0130	0.0209
Rate of Return												
1970	13.7%	14.8%	12.8%	19.7%	15.8%	19.7%	15.8%	17.5%	13.2%	15.9%	15.3%	16.4%
1986	8.5%	8.5%	8.5%	13.1%	13.6%	13.6%	8.7%	10.2%	7.5%	10.3%	9.7%	10.7%
Divisia Wage Index												
1970	0.955	1.016	1.097	0.979	0.851	0.842	0.924	0.962	1.103	0.970	1.012	0.937
1986	3.198	3.272	3.607	3.207	2.822	2.790	3.139	3.139	3.416	3.177	3.321	3.061

NE = New England, MA = Middle Atlantic, ENC = East North Central, WNC = West North Central, SA = South Atlantic, ESC = East South Central, WSC = West South Central, M = Mountain, PAC = Pacific

The last two rows of table 7.1 present estimates of regional wage rates and rates of return to private capital. Inspection of this table indicates that the average manufacturing wage rate in the Sun Belt regions was less than the corresponding wage rate in the Snow Belt, while the average rate of return was persistently higher in the Sun Belt.[10] This is could be interpreted as evidence of a persistent disequilibrium in the factor markets. However, it should be noted that we have not standardized either the regional wage or rate of return for regional differences in industry mix, nor have we adjusted the wage for regional differences in the cost of living or skill differentials. Such adjustments might eliminate the observed regional differentials, so this interpretation is at best a surmise.

We note, finally, that table 7.1 covers a fairly short period 1970–1986, and it is possible that convergence (in terms of TFP or capital per worker) was essentially complete by that time. Regional gross output data are not available prior to the mid-1960s, but regional value added data are available beginning in 1951. In table 7.2, we briefly shift the focus to value added as a measure of output in order to extend the analysis back in time. Out data show that there has been no significant compression (or divergence) in TFP, in output per worker, or in capital-deepening since 1951.

7.4   Econometric Results

While the data shown in tables 7.1 and 7.2 suggest that TFP levels in the various regions are approximately equal, they do not constitute a formal test of alternative hypotheses about regional growth. We carried out a standard econometric analysis by estimating the basic model (7.6) using ordinary least squares. This procedure yields the usual parameter estimates and hypothesis tests, but it is subject to a potential bias arising from the possibility that private capital (and possibly public capital as well) are endogenously determined by the level of TFP and may thus be correlated with the error term in the regression. However, the direction of the bias is unclear, since the feedback effect of TFP on capital formation may be positive or negative. Instrumental variables might be used to avoid simultaneous equations bias, but a set of valid regional instruments is hard to find.

Another problem arises from the fact that the estimation of the parameters of (7.6) produces an estimate of $\gamma + \varepsilon^B$, so that these key parameters are not separately identified. However, since most public

Table 7.2
Summary of the growth rate of manufacturing value added, 1951–1986

	NE	MA	ENC	WNC	SA	ESC	WSC	M	PAC	Total	Snow Belt	Sun Belt
Value Added	0.0258	0.0164	0.0215	0.0388	0.0451	0.0445	0.0473	0.0570	0.0445	0.0308	0.0222	0.0459
Labor	0.0002	−0.0074	−0.0026	0.0111	0.0190	0.0193	0.0238	0.0368	0.0230	0.0065	−0.0025	0.0219
Private Capital	0.0272	0.0183	0.0207	0.0370	0.0404	0.0428	0.0474	0.0526	0.0443	0.0309	0.0223	0.0442
Total Factor Productivity	0.0182	0.0166	0.0175	0.0197	0.0192	0.0173	0.0160	0.0538	0.0155	0.0171	0.0176	0.0170
Labor Productivity	0.0256	0.0238	0.0241	0.0277	0.0261	0.0252	0.0235	0.0202	0.0216	0.0244	0.0246	0.0240
Capital Labor Ratio	0.0270	0.0257	0.0233	0.0259	0.0213	0.0235	0.0236	0.0158	0.0214	0.0245	0.0248	0.0223

NE = New England, MA = Middle Atlantic, ENC = East North Central, WNC = West North Central, SA = South Atlantic, ESC = East South Central, WSC = West South Central, M = Mountain, PAC = Pacific capital enters the production function of the manufacturing sector indirectly as a purchased intermediate good and not as a direct input, the elasticity ε^B is likely to be of negligible importance in manufacturing and can be assumed to equal zero, thus identifying the spillover parameter, γ.[11]

Our least-squares estimates are reported in table 7.3. The first column of that table shows the results obtained from the estimation of (7.6) under the assumption that the initial level of TFP and the growth rate of TFP are equal across regions (i.e., there are no regional fixed effects). Interestingly, the results are similar to those found in the earlier literature on public capital: the coefficient on public capital is statistically significant and reasonably large given that the direct effect of public capital is already accounted for in the purchased service component of the production function. The private capital coefficient suggests that there are mildly decreasing returns to scale and the point estimate of the time parameter implies a rate of TFP growth of 0.8 percent per year.

It is common in this literature to include a measure of capacity utilization in order to control for the cyclical effect of demand fluctuations on the Solow residual. We have followed this procedure in order to maintain comparability with other studies, even though there is no theoretical justification for including capacity utilization in a productivity model (Berndt and Fuss, 1986; Hulten, 1986), and despite the fact that capacity utilization is particularly problematical in regional studies since regional capacity utilization measures are not available. Thus, column (5) in table 7.3 adds the Federal Reserve Board's national capacity utilization data for manufacturing to the model in column (1). It is apparent that this does not change the picture very much, though the error-sum-of-squares does fall significantly.

One of the central results in the infrastructure literature is that the inclusion of regional fixed effects causes the estimated coefficient on infrastructure to become insignificant from zero (Holtz-Eakin, 1991; Garcia-Mila, McGuire, and Porter, 1992; Eisner, 1991; though Morrison and Schwartz, 1966, reach a different conclusion). In column (2) we allow for separate regional intercepts (New England is taken as the base region). As shown, the addition of these regional fixed effects causes the public capital spillover variable to become insignificant (and negative as well). Our finding are thus consistent with those of previous research. The estimated plausible result, and it casts doubt on the usefulness of using an aggregate capacity utilization adjustment.

Table 7.3
Parameter estimates of alternative restricted models

	Without adjustment for capacity utilization				With adjustment for capacity utilization			
	(1)	(2)	(3)	(4)	(5)	(6)	(7)	(8)
Intercept	0.102214	-0.315016	0.126697	-0.660555	-0.378122	-0.910440	-0.351948	-1.42213
	(3.988)	(1.681)	(3.533)	(2.037)	(3.880)	(5.912)	(4.979)	(5.846)
MA	—	0.174645	—	0.361255	—	0.223457	—	0.476241
		(2.133)		(2.504)		(3.579)		(4.560)
ENC	—	0.245769	—	0.423950	—	0.283020	—	0.522270
		(3.015)		(2.729)		(4.558)		(4.653)
WNC	—	0.200081	—	0.278372	—	0.227019	—	0.335459
		(5.137)		(4.846)		(7.635)		(8.046)
SA	—	0.120506	—	0.215552	—	0.156855	—	0.288187
		(1.911)		(2.253)		(3.263)		(4.163)
ESC	—	0.087153	—	0.127440	—	0.094803	—	0.140694
		(5.088)		(4.225)		(7.266)		(6.466)
WSC	—	0.195922	—	0.245046	—	0.215640	—	0.288537
		(4.797)		(4.018)		(6.930)		(6.542)

Table 7.3 (continued)

	Without adjustment for capacity utilization				With adjustment for capacity utilization			
	(1)	(2)	(3)	(4)	(5)	(6)	(7)	(8)
MT	—	0.060219 (1.591)	—	0.065613 (0.945)	—	0.078654 (2.728)	—	0.081865 (1.636)
PAC	—	0.191201 (2.653)	—	0.338488 (2.787)	—	0.237179 (4.313)	—	0.454201 (5.155)
Time	0.008445 (8.241)	0.010567 (7.225)	0.006314 (3.755)	0.015121 (5.448)	0.009906 (9.993)	0.012336 (10.959)	0.007492 (5.225)	0.016974 (8.461)
Time*MA			-0.002131 (0.859)	-0.005766 (1.976)			-0.001712 (0.814)	-0.005071 (2.412)
Time*ENC			0.007321 (3.439)	-0.003467 (1.235)			0.007512 (4.163)	-0.003097 (1.532)
Time*WNC			0.008035 (4.117)	-0.003878 (1.465)			0.008342 (5.041)	-0.003497 (1.833)
Time*SA			-0.002247 (1.058)	0.001049 (0.332)			-0.001937 (1.076)	0.003106 (1.359)
Time*ESC			0.004258 (2.824)	-0.002564 (0.987)			0.004339 (3.396)	-0.002015 (1.076)

Table 7.3 (continued)

	Without adjustment for capacity utilization				With adjustment for capacity utilization			
	(1)	(2)	(3)	(4)	(5)	(6)	(7)	(8)
Time*WSC	—	—	0.009938	0.002267	—	—	0.010056	0.003223
			(5.925)	(0.746)			(7.073)	(1.472)
Time*MT	—	—	-0.000853	-0.002950	—	—	-0.000488	-0.000488
			(0.393)	(0.867)			(0.266)	(0.538)
Time*PAC	—	—	0.001227	-0.004016	—	—	0.001630	-0.004545
			(0.520)		(1.515)		(0.814)	(2.379)
Ln Public Capital	0.081694	-0.036604	0.158439	-0.117309	0.079613	-0.094269	0.150372	-0.244341
	(3.526)	(0.472)	(4.704)	(1.034)	(3.711)	(1.590)	(5.263)	(2.961)
Ln Private Capital	-0.044530	-0.046562	-0.105826	-0.076725	-0.043099	-0.024187	-0.100638	-0.040135
	(2.606)	(1.029)	(4.556)	(1.094)	(2.724)	(0.702)	(5.109)	(0.793)
Capacity Utilization	—	—	—	—	0.005806	0.005961	0.005731	0.006087
					(5.082)	(10.191)	(7.501)	(11.150)
R^2	0.3661	0.7689	0.6801	0.7906	0.4603	0.8673	0.7718	0.8922
SSE	0.53478	0.19494	0.26987	0.17668	0.45531	0.11192	0.19250	0.09098
F-statistic	16.8480	1.7182	8.7689	—	33.0372	3.7976	18.4115	—

t statistics in parentheses

Hypothesis Testing

The implied hypothesis tests of table 7.3 can be generalized by putting them into a nested hypothesis testing framework. The nesting procedure is somewhat complicated from an expositional standpoint, since there are four sets of restrictions that are of interest, and these restrictions can be imposed one at a time, in pairs, three at a time, or all together. The four restrictions include:[12]

(1) the intercepts, interpreted as the levels of TFP in 1970, do not vary across regions (common productivity starting point).

(2) the time coefficients, interpreted as the growth rate of TFP, do not vary across regions (no convergence or divergence).

(3) the coefficient on public capital equals zero in all regions (no infrastructure spillovers).

(4) the coefficient on private capital equals zero in all regions (constant returns to scale).

The results of the various tests of the formally nested hypotheses confirm our basic conclusions. We found that the data do not reject any of the constraints imposed singly or in pairs. When we impose the restrictions three at a time, we find that we can reject the simultaneous equality of the initial levels of TFP (restriction (1)), a zero elasticity of TFP with respect to public capital (restriction (2)), and constant returns to the private inputs (restriction (3)). However, all of the other three-way restriction do hold jointly. Finally, the simultaneous imposition of all equality restrictions simultaneously is also rejected.

Some Econometric Extensions

We tested several variants of our models using several alternatives suggested in the infrastructure literature. Following Fernald (1992), we carried out an analysis of (7.6) using deviations from time trend rather than the log-level of variables in order to control for demand fluctuations and to reduce any simultaneous equation bias resulting from the endogeneity of public and private capital. The results of this exercise were similar to the results obtained using the capacity utilization variable.

We also tested the assumption of perfect competition using a Hall (1988b) marginal cost markup model. In an imperfectly competitive market where the ratio of price to marginal cost is a constant μ, the income shares of labor and intermediate input are equal to the true output elasticities divided by μ (i.e., $\pi_{it}^L = \varepsilon_{it}^L/\mu$ and $\pi_{it}^M = \varepsilon_{it}^M/\mu$). If capital's share is calculated as a residual so the shares sum to one, then it follows from Hall's model that (7.6) becomes

$$\ln A_{it}^S = \ln A_{i0} + \lambda_i t + [\gamma_i + \varepsilon_i^B] \ln B_{it} + [\varepsilon_i^B - 1] \ln K_{it} \qquad (7.7)$$
$$+ (\mu - 1)[\pi_{it}^M \ln(M_{it}/K_{it}) + \pi_{it}^L \ln(L_{it}/K_{it})].$$

We estimate this model by adding the share-weighted log of the intermediate input-capital and the labor-capital ratios to the model underlying table 7.3, thus obtaining an estimate of $(\mu - 1)$. Under perfect competition price equals marginal cost, μ equals 1, and the coefficient on $[\pi_{it}^M \ln(M_{it}/K_{it}) + \pi_{it}^L \ln(L_{it}/K_{it})]$ is zero; if firms have market power then price will exceed marginal cost and this coefficient will be positive.

Estimates of different versions of the Hall model are shown in table 7.4. In those specifications where we exclude capacity utilization variable, our estimate of $(\mu - 1)$ is always positive and significant. This implies that the usual competitive pricing assumption of the Solow residual model is not appropriate, and non-competitive pricing must be taken into account (as in (7.7)). However, our estimate of $(\mu - 1)$ is always insignificant in those specifications where we exclude capacity utilization variable, providing support for applying the competitive model to the measurement of TFP. Estimates of all of the other parameters in table 7.4 are quite similar to the corresponding estimates in table 7.3.

7.5 Summary and Conclusions

The key result of this paper is that the path of productive efficiency has been essentially parallel across regions in recent decades. This finding, which is consistent with our earlier work, suggests that manufacturing technology and organizational practice had already diffused widely throughout the country before the start of this period. By implication, this leaves little room for convergence explanations of regional growth that rely on the technological diffusion or learning-by-doing, or for endogenous growth explanations that rely on increasing returns to scale or the differential growth of public capital.[13] These alternatives have been widely discussed as mechanisms for explaining the convergence of output per capita in middle and high income countries, and while it was reasonable to postulate that they might be "imported" to explain the compression of regional incomes within the U.S., they do not seem to generalize in this way.[14]

What, then, does explain the pattern of regional manufacturing growth in the U.S.? Our results are consistent with a model of regional growth in which the location and scale of economic activity are strongly influenced by historical evolution and geographical factors: i.e., the U.S. developed from East to West, with the South initially specialized in agriculture, the North in commerce and manufacturing, and the Midwest, with its resource endowments, in manufacturing and agriculture. In this paradigm, the overall growth and structural changes in the economy (e.g., the huge increase in output per worker in the economy as a whole between 1880 and 1930, and the decline in the importance of the agricultural sector) unleashed forces that, at the level of regional economies, created significant factor market disequilibria: an excess supply of labor in the agricultural and resource regions of the South and West, but also opportunities for capital formation in those regions, which, in turn, raised the demand for manufacturing labor.

There is, however, an important caveat to this "explanation." Our finding that public capital externalities were not an important source of regional TFP differentials, but this does not mean that public capital formation is irrelevant. Indeed, it is likely to have played an essential role in facilitating the movement of capital, labor, and intermediate inputs among regions, and thus enabled the main sources of differential regional growth. The direct return to infrastructure investments may have been quite large, as Nadiri and Mamuneus (1995) found for the Interstate Highway System in the 1950s and 1960s. However, our results argue that excess returns due to spillovers are not an important component of the overall rate of return, at least for manufacturing industry, and therefore cannot be used to rationalize the very large rates of return to infrastructure found by Aschauer and others.

Table 7.4
Parameter estimates of Hall price marginal cost model

	Without adjustment for capacity utilization				With adjustment for capacity utilization			
	(1)	(2)	(3)	(4)	(5)	(6)	(7)	(8)
Intercept	0.111867	-0.366781	0.131674	-0.501104	-0.287737	-0.89163	-0.332772	-1.435805
	(4.651)	(2.061)	(3.744)	(1.604)	(2.999)	(5.803)	(4.504)	(5.641)
MA	—	0.198808	—	0.296728	—	0.228430	—	0.480014
		(2.556)		(2.137)		(3.673)		(4.497)
ENC	—	0.280831	—	0.360785	—	0.292247	—	0.525848
		(3.615)		(2.417)		(4.710)		(4.602)
WNC	—	0.166374	—	0.222000	—	0.214389	—	0.338376
		(4.404)		(3.903)		(6.997)		(7.582)
SA	—	0.136925	—	0.184615	—	0.184615	—	0.290149
		(2.287)		(2.013)		(3.344)		(4.130)
ESC	—	0.091689	—	0.146818	—	0.095827	—	0.139978
		(5.638)		(5.018)		(7.375)		(6.314)
WSC	—	0.215901	—	0.271294	—	0.220988	—	0.287790
		(5.538)		(4.626)		(7.098)		(6.475)

Table 7.4 (continued)

	Without adjustment for capacity utilization				With adjustment for capacity utilization			
	(1)	(2)	(3)	(4)	(5)	(6)	(7)	(8)
MT	—	0.065067 (1.814)	—	0.119396 (1.760)	—	0.079134 (2.759)	—	0.079699 (1.547)
PAC	—	0.216643 (3.160)	—	0.314981 (2.712)	—	0.242739 (4.428)	—	0.456220 (5.122)
Time	0.011850 (9.893)	0.014131 (8.663)	0.008220 (4.575)	0.019052 (6.682)	0.012374 (10.858)	0.013394 (10.263)	0.008034 (5.162)	0.016821 (7.749)
Time*MA	—	—	-0.001958 (0.806)	-0.006045 (2.169)	—	—	-0.001675 (0.796)	-0.005053 (2.392)
Time*ENC	—	—	0.007331 (3.516)	-0.004480 (1.663)	—	—	0.007508 (4.158)	-0.003050 (1.492)
Time*WNC	—	—	0.006203 (3.052)	-0.004394 (1.735)	—	—	0.007768 (4.376)	-0.003472 (1.809)
Time*SA	—	—	-0.002491 (1.197)	-0.001665 (0.536)	—	—	-0.002023 (1.122)	0.003241 (1.348)
Time*ESC	—	—	0.004061 (2.748)	-0.005407 (2.084)	—	—	0.004276 (3.339)	-0.001888 (0.946)

Table 7.4 (continued)

	Without adjustment for capacity utilization				With adjustment for capacity utilization			
	(1)	(2)	(3)	(4)	(5)	(6)	(7)	(8)
Time*WSC	—	—	0.009572	-0.003909	—	—	0.009939	0.003497
			(5.807)	(1.171)			(6.957)	(1.327)
Time*MT	—	—	0.000358	-0.005130	—	—	-0.000130	-0.001214
			(0.165)	(1.555)			(0.069)	(0.480)
Time*PAC	—	—	0.001595	-0.006534	—	—	0.001729	-0.004441
			(0.689)	(2.495)			(0.862)	(2.227)
π_{Ln} (L/K)	(4.737)	(4.139)	(2.652)	(3.732)	(3.893)	(1.579)	(0.899)	(0.188)
Ln Public	0.078704	-0.042892	0.150455	-0.083582	0.077584	-0.092869	0.148217	-0.246897
Capital	(3.632)	(0.583)	(4.542)	(0.769)	(3.784)	(1.575)	(5.166)	(2.941)
Ln Private	-0.032747	-0.052971	-0.093573	-0.044749	-0.033935	-0.027622	-0.097066	-0.041188
Capital	(2.026)	(1.235)	(4.032)	(0.663)	(2.218)	(0.804)		
Capacity	—	—	—	—	0.004806	0.005603	0.005520	0.006140
Utilization					(4.287)	(8.977)	(6.901)	(9.959)
R^2	0.4496	0.7941	0.6954	0.8106	0.5108	0.8697	0.7732	0.8922
SSE	0.46436	0.17369	0.25696	0.15982	0.41275	0.10994	0.19139	0.09096
F-statistic	14.2204	1.2953	9.0718	—	28.9586	3.4161	18.0759	—

t statistics in parentheses

Notes

1. The literature on infrastructure investment has grown voluminously since the papers by Aschauer (indeed, because of these papers). Gramlich (1994), Nadiri and Mamuneus (1995), and Pfahler *et al.* (1996) provide extensive reviews of this literature.

2. See for example, Krugman (1990).

3. The formulation of technology also assumes that the spillover effect is separable from the pure technical effect, as represented by the parameter λ_i. This specification of the public capital externality also assumes that the only source of spillovers in each region is the quantity of public capital within that region. This implies, for example, that the highway system of one region may give rise to spillovers among manufacturing firms within the region, but the highways of an adjacent region have no effect at all. This is consistent with our interpretation of the region specific externalities as an engine of regionally endogenous growth.

4. This mode of analysis is termed "sources of growth analysis." For a review of the relevant literature, see U.S. Bureau of Labor Statistics (1983). It is worth noting, here, that the sources of growth analysis has, for the most part, ignored the role of public capital as a source of output growth.

5. This problem arises because the price of capital services, P_{it}^K, can rarely be observed directly. Capital income is usually imputed from the "adding-up" condition that factor payments exhaust total income, with capital income measured as the residual. The residual measurement of capital income thus imposes the condition that income shares sum to one (i.e., $\pi_{it}^K = 1 - \pi_{it}^L - \pi_{it}^M$). Thus whenever the elasticity of scale of private inputs $\varepsilon_{it} = \varepsilon_{it}^K + \varepsilon_{it}^L + \varepsilon_{it}^M$ is different from 1, π_{it}^X misstates capital's true output elasticity.

6. The constancy of these parameters imposes restrictions on the underlying technical efficiency terms of the production function (1). Note, however, that the multiplicative restrictions on the form of the efficiency function does not impose restrictions on the rest of the technology. In particular, they do not imply that the production function has the Cobb-Douglas form.

7. If the Law of One Price does not hold for manufactured goods within the U.S. market and there is in fact regional variation in output prices, our assumption of one price will overstate real output in those regions where prices are higher than average. This, in turn, overstates the level index of the Solow residual. If, in addition, the regional output prices are changing relative to the average, a bias is introduced into the growth rate of the Solow residual as well.

8. Throughout the paper, we define the Snow Belt as the New England, Middle Atlantic, East North Central, and West North Central Census divisions. The Sun Belt includes the South Atlantic, East South Central, West South Central, Mountain, and Pacific divisions.

9. This impression is reinforced by decomposing the total variation of TFP into variation across time within in regions and variation across regions. Slightly less than one-half of the variation in the level of TFP is due to cross-sectional variation, with the balance due to variation over time. For the growth rates of TFP, however, virtually all of the variation is variation over time, i.e., there is almost no variation in the growth rate of TFP across regions. Given the substantial differences in the growth rates of public capital stock in different regions, the lack of variation in the growth rate of TFP suggests that the two variables are essentially uncorrelated.

10. The internal rate of return in table 7.2 is that rate such that, given the stock of capital, payments to factors of production exhaust revenue. Thus, as we noted above, this calculation assumes implicitly a constant returns to scale technology. We return to this issue in a subsequent section of the paper.

11. According to BLS data, trucks and autos accounted for approximately eight percent of the income accruing to equipment in manufacturing, and thus about one percent of the total income, over the period 1949—1983, and that communications and electricity generation equipment, which account for about nine percent of income accruing to equipment, and, again, about one percent of total income. This low share reflects the fact that public capital is mainly an input to the transportation and communication sectors, to public utilities, and to some service industries, and these sectors pass along their services (and thus the services of public capital) by selling their output to manufacturing industries. Thus, public capital is at best a marginal contributor to the gross output of many such industries.

12. All of the models in table 7.3 implicitly impose the restriction that the public and private capital elasticities are the same across regions, though not necessarily all equal to zero. Here we allow the public and capital coefficients to vary across regions unless we restrict these coefficients to equal zero.

13. E.g., Barro (1991), Baumol (1986), Baumol *et al.* (1989), and De Long (1988).

14. Moreover, an inspection of the trends in output per worker and capital per worker tor the 1970–1986 and the 1951–1986 periods using different output concepts does not offer any encouragement for the capital-deepening variant of the convergence hypothesis (Barro and Sala-i-Martin, 1991; Holtz-Eakin, 1991).

8   The Cost of Capital and Consumer Behavior

Thomas M. Stoker

8.1   Introduction

It is quite appropriate to look anew at Dale Jorgenson's productive career, if only to catalog the sheer magnitude of the contributions he has made to economic science. Some may regard the "Cost of Capital" as Jorgenson's most important innovation. However, Jorgenson's imprint is unmistakable in many other areas of economic research.

This chapter covers work in "Consumer Behavior." Work in this area is in some sense more distant from the "Cost of Capital" than work on productivity, national accounts and producer behavior, yet it is not unrelated. One obvious connection concerns how consumers evaluate capital in relation to other spending categories. Consumers spend on housing, buy cars, refrigerators and other appliances, for instance; and it is silly to account for the value of these items by their initial purchase price. These items are valuable in terms of their ongoing service, and a purchase involves a multiyear commitment to such services. As such, durable goods are best priced in terms of service flows, involving value of ongoing service as compared to opportunity cost and depreciation, as with capital employed by business. Durable aspects can be found with many goods, and in each case, the market value of the service represents the correct economic measure of the original purchase. This notion is embodied in the data series used in the construction of Jorgenson's models of the U.S. and world economies. We could explore the "Cost of Capital and Consumer Behavior" in the context of how a clear view of the nature of durability affects how one measures budget allocations by individual households.

This tact, however, would miss the point of Jorgenson's main contributions to modeling consumer behavior, and would represent a classical mistake in the reading of Jorgenson's work. All of Jorgenson's work is a part of a focused research program, and to consider bits and pieces in isolation is analogous to detailing features of a booster rocket on a space shuttle. While Jorgenson's work contains many contributions to individual areas of economics, including consumer behavior, there is a grand theme to his contributions that we must bring out at the outset.

There are many ways to build a model of an economy. First, there are nonstatistical methods, where researchers invent a package of equations, plug in numbers drawn here and there, and simulate their invented economy. Various "black-box" engineering and calibration approaches have this character. Second, there are purely statistical approaches, where researchers regard values of economic variables as resulting from a stable stochastic process, with simulation amounting to extensions of past data patterns. Time series modeling of business cycle fluctuations and elaborate co-integration schemes come to mind. Finally, there are approaches based on econometric modeling of economic behavior, with interactions among consumers and producers captured through markets. This latter kind of model represents the grand aim envisioned for econometric methods in the 1940s and 1950s. Jorgenson is a classic economic modeler in the econometric tradition.

Moreover, there are many reasons for building a model of an economy—for instance, to forecast future values of economic quantities. Jorgenson's primary motivation is to analyze economic policy. In particular, Jorgenson's models are constructed so as to capture the essence of the policy under study, such as tax policy or environmental policy. Ultimately, the aim is to see how the welfare of individuals is affected by the policy under study. Whether one is studying growth and productivity (where individuals' welfares are increased without tough trade-offs) or studying distributional impacts of relative price shifts, this aim is evident. It is especially evident to those of us who have witnessed Jorgenson's research program first hand. The number of contributions from Jorgenson's research program is testimony to his skills as a superb manager; while he has nurtured and worked with many talented individuals, there is never a departure from the theme of analyzing economic policy.

This feature places a practical proviso on each of Jorgenson's innovations in economics; namely they have to be useful to an economy-wide model. With the above analogy, we could easily debate what kind of booster rocket would work best in "general applications," or what color of fuel to use, but the bottom line is that the rocket has to work to deliver the shuttle to orbit. The rules for innovation in Jorgenson's modeling involve a strict adherence to interpretable economic theory, and implementation via econometric methods. This combination; adherence to theory and practical workability; underly the strength and durability of Jorgenson's contributions to economics at large. At the time when many of his innovations were developed, alternatives were proposed, but few have stood the test of time as delivered by adherence to Jorgenson's main theme. The only way to see his work is in the context of this unified research program.

Consequently, we adopt a liberal tact toward discussing Jorgenson's work on consumer behavior and the "cost of capital." As an early major contribution of his research program, we take the "cost of capital" as a pseudonym for the research program itself. The work we discuss involves demand modeling of continuous expenditure levels, which require "cost of capital" flow concepts to be applicable to durable goods. However, we leave the task of detailing research on the valuation of capital to the other papers in the conference, as well as how it fits with the modeling of productivity and growth. Instead, we focus on Jorgenson's work on consumer behavior as oriented toward modeling demands from the household sector, for use in a broader modeling context. Our aim is to spell out Jorgenson's innovations in demand modeling through the window of contributions to economics, econometric modeling and econometric estimation.

The work to be discussed ranges over the period from the early 1970s to the mid-1980s. We cover three main blocks of contributions—those involving flexibility in the modeling of consumer demands, those involving accommodation of consumer heterogeneity, and the associated work on econometric methods. For each area, we give some treatment to the basic motivation for the work, and where it has impacted on subsequent developments. As with the papers covering other areas, we will be lax in detailing the separate contributions of each of Jorgenson's numerous co-authors and associates.

8.2   Modeling Demands with Flexible Functional Forms

8.2.1   Prelude

Two traditions exist for the modeling of economic behavior of consumers, and prior to the late 1970s, these traditions evolved independently of one another. The first tradition involved the analysis of economy-wide aggregate consumer expenditures over time, as they are related to aggregate income and relative prices. This "time series" tradition is the most relevant for the discussion of this section, which is on modeling the demand allocations of the household sector. The second tradition involved the analysis of budget allocations by individual households, as they were related to household income and demographic make-up, typically based on surveys of households during a short time period. This "cross-section" tradition will concern us later.

The time series tradition focused directly on the measurement of aggregate expenditures on goods and services, producing equations that are used to represent the adjustments of the household sector to changing relative prices and aggregate income. The foundation of this approach rests on the notion that the household sector as a whole makes predictable adjustments to price and income influences, and the equations summarizing these reactions are based on econometric modeling of observed aggregate data patterns.

By the early 1960s, models of the time series tradition were built in accordance with the "representative agent paradigm." This paradigm was an interpretive vehicle, that held that models of aggregate expenditures were to be designed in a fashion consistent with the behavior of a single optimizing individual. This paradigm served to structure of development of household sector demand models in three ways. First, it gave instructions for how to introduce economic theory into econometric models—use equations appropriate for a single individual. Second, it gave instructions for how to interpret empirical estimates— judge estimates as "reasonable" if the associated individual behavior were "reasonable." Third, it gave instructions for what constituted an improvement to an econometric model—one that accommodated a richer set of behavioral reactions by an individual consumer. This paradigm is still in force in various research programs today for the same reasons; for instance the modeling of consumption and savings decisions under uncertainty.

For example, consider the simplest model of expenditure application, that based on fixed expenditure shares. Suppose that we are studying aggregate budget allocation among K commodities at time t, with aggregate quantities denoted $Q_{1t}, \ldots, Q_{Kt}$. Prices are $p_t = (p_{1t}, \ldots, p_{Kt})$ and total expenditure is M_t. The household sector could be modeled as maintaining constant budget shares $W_{kt} = p_{kt}Q_{kt}/M_t$, or more formally as

$$W_{kt} = \alpha_k \quad k = 1, \ldots, K, \quad t = 1, \ldots, T \tag{8.2.1}$$

where the α_k's are the share levels to be estimated from aggregate data observed over time. The "representative agent" interpretation of this model arises from the fact that equations (8.2.1) are implied by maximizing a Cobb-Douglas utility function

$$\ln U_{CD} = \sum_k \alpha_k \ln Q_{kt} \tag{8.2.2}$$

subject to the budget constraint $\sum_k p_{kt}Q_{kt} = M_t$. From duality theory, an equivalent "representative agent" foundation of (8.2.1) arises from applying Roy's identity to the indirect utility

$$\ln V_{CD} = \sum_k \alpha_k \ln\left(\frac{M_t}{p_{kt}}\right),$$

where $\sum_k \alpha_k = 1$ here as above.

The problem with (8.2.1) as a general household sector model arises from its simplicity; by design it prohibits variation in aggregate budget shares. Aside from the levels of budget shares, which can be estimated, all other behavioral reactions are imposed by the model: income (total expenditure) elasticities for all goods are 1, own price elasticities are -1 and cross price elasticities are 0. While a simple model of this sort gives great advantages in the process of simulating an economy-wide model (prices must adjust to keep budget shares constant), its use involves many artificial impositions. In other words, the model makes use of very few aspects of the observed patterns in the data used for estimation.

During the 1960s, various generalizations of the Cobb-Douglas model were applied in practice. Foremost among these was the Stone-Geary Linear Expenditure System (LES). The LES arises from assuming the representative agent has (direct) utility,

$$\ln U_{LES} = \sum_k \alpha_k \ln(Q_{kt} - b_k), \tag{8.2.3}$$

which is maximized subject to the budget constraint $\sum_k p_{kt}Q_{kt} = M_t$. This gives aggregate expenditure equations of the form

$$W_{kt} = \alpha_k + p_{kt}b_k\left(\frac{p_{kt}}{M_t}\right) - \alpha_k \sum_j b_j\left(\frac{p_{jt}}{M_t}\right); \quad k = 1, \ldots, K, \ t = 1, \ldots, T. \tag{8.2.4}$$

These equations exhibit constant marginal effects of income and prices on expenditures.

While the LES has served as a real workhorse of aggregate demand modeling, it likewise involves imposing extremely strong conditions on price and income elasticities. With zero b's, the LES reduces to a Cobb-Douglas model, and with non-zero b's, it involves many of the same impositions as the Cobb-Douglas model. In particular, under the familiar interpretation that b_k is a required "subsistence level" of good k, we have that all expenditures in excess of $b_1, \ldots, b_K$ are allocated in accordance with fixed budget shares; in particular, $p_{kt}[Q_{kt} - b_k]/[M_t - \sum_j b_j p_{jt}] = \alpha_k$. Since the b's are valued by prices, the overall price effects do depend on estimates of the parameters: the income elasticity of good k is α_k/W_{kt}, the own price elasticity is $b_k(1 - \alpha_k)/Q_{kt} - 1$ and the cross price elasticity of good k with regard to p_j is $-\alpha_k b_j/Q_{kt}$. While determined by estimates, these values are tightly constrained, with many restrictions implied between them. As such, the full array of observed price and income reactions are necessarily straight-jacketed into these formulations, with the reactions implied by the LES based on minimal use of the observed aggregate data patterns.

8.2.2   The Translog Demand Model

The realization that many empirical effects were artificially determined by the LES gave rise to a great amount of research devoted to finding demand models that could more accurately depict a full array of price and income elasticities, and the work of Jorgenson and his associates was at the forefront of this effort.[1] The original concept of a "flexible functional form" denoted a model that had the ability of measure effects, or derivatives, without constraint at a given price and income level. One could propose flexible approximation of demand functions directly, but because of the value of economic properties (e.g., integrability), this research focused on approximation of the primitive structure of choice models, namely preferences. The prime example of such models were "transcendental logarithmic" or translog models, introduced by Christensen, Jorgenson and Lau (1975). Here, the indirect utility function of the representative agent is given as a quadratic function in log normalized prices as

$$\ln V_{TL}(p_t, M_t) = \sum_k \alpha_k \ln\left(\frac{M_t}{p_{kt}}\right) + \left(\frac{1}{2}\right)\sum_k \sum_j \beta_{kj} \ln\left(\frac{M_t}{p_{kt}}\right)\ln\left(\frac{M_t}{p_{jt}}\right) \tag{8.2.5}$$

where for simplicity, we have imposed the implication of utility theory that utility is homogeneous of degree zero in prices and total expenditure. We can further take $\sum_k \alpha_k = 1$, and $\beta_{jk} = \beta_{kj}$ for all j, k without loss of generality, and consider parameter values subject to the convexity properties of indirect utility (either at a point or over a range of price and income values). Relative to flexibility, it is not hard to see that any array of first and second derivatives of indirect utility can be matched by appropriate choice of the α's and β's; accordingly (8.2.5) is "second-order flexible" in the terminology of this genre.[2]

The translog specification (8.2.5) of preferences of a representative agent gives household sector demand equations that generalize the Cobb-Douglas model in a different way than the LES. Aside from noting that (8.2.5) is a quadratic generalization of Cobb-Douglas preferences, the translog model allows interpretable variations in budget shares. Consider first the case where $\sum_j \beta_{jk} = 0$ for each k, which coincides with homothetic preferences (or unitary income elasticities for each good). Roy's identity applied to (8.2.5) gives the share equations

$$W_{kt} = \alpha_k - \sum_j \beta_{jk} \ln p_{jt}. \tag{8.2.6}$$

The homothetic translog demand model fits the levels (α_k) in budget shares, and permits a linear effect of each log price on budget shares. Since budget shares and log prices are each in percentage terms, the $-\beta_{kj}$ parameters can be regarded as constant "share elasticities," namely $-\beta_{jk} = \partial W_k / \partial \ln p_j$.

The general nonhomothetic translog preferences give a demand model in ratio form, that permits a general set of price and income elasticities at any evaluation point. In particular, Roy's identity applied to the general form of (8.2.5) gives

$$W_{kt} = \frac{\alpha_k - \sum_j \beta_{jk} \ln p_{jt} + \sum_j \beta_{jk} \ln M_t}{1 - \sum_k \sum_j \beta_{jk} \ln p_{jt} + \sum_k \sum_j \beta_{jk} \ln M_t}. \tag{8.2.7}$$

The ability of this system to match any set of values of income and price elasticities is easy to see: if $D(p_t, M_t)$ denotes the denominator of (8.2.7), then the own-price elasticity of good k is $-1 + [-\beta_{kk}/W_{kt} + \sum_j \beta_{kj}]/D(p_t, M_t)$, the cross price elasticity of good k for the lth price is $[-\beta_{jl}/W_{kt} + \sum_j \beta_{kl}]/D(p_t, M_t)$ and the income elasticity of good k is $-1 + [\sum_j \beta_{jk}/W_{kt} - \sum_k \sum_j \beta_{kj}]/D(p_t, M_t)$.

Because of the budget constraint, the ratio form of flexible demand systems is essentially unavoidable. Alternatives to the translog model, from contemporaneous proposals like the Generalized Leontief model of Diewert to the more recent AIDS model of Deaton and Muellbauer, all involve ratios of expressions in parameters and prices. Jorgenson and Lau (1977, 1979) give a theoretical argument that the only integrable demand systems that can arbitrarily approximate all income and price elasticities are models of the translog form.

While introducing a more general tool, Jorgenson and his associates did not lose sight of the reason for introducing flexibility in econometric modeling. The problem with the LES was not that measured price and income elasticities were related to one another, but rather that such restrictions were imposed by the choice of model at the outset. A flexible form permits such restrictions to be checked for empirical adequacy; and if such tests are passed, those restrictions can be imposed with proper scientific foundation.

In Jorgenson and Lau (1977, 1986) and Conrad and Jorgenson (1978, 1979), the application of the translog models were carried out hand-in-hand with a battery of statistical tests to determine the empirically adequate restrictions on household sector demands. These tests involved two blocks of hypotheses on the structure of the preferences of a representative agent. The first block involved detailed questions of functional structure under the assumption that representative agent demands were integrable. The second block involved the basic question of whether the integrability conditions could be verified for representative agent demands.

One might ask how it makes sense to separate these blocks of restrictions and consider them in the order depicted above. The reason comes again from Jorgenson's research program, since the aggregate demand equations are an essential part of a larger general equilibrium model of the economy. As is clear from the simplest "Robinson Cru-soe" economy, the integrability conditions serve to greatly facilitate solving for the equilibrium prices and quantities. Consequently, a practical aim is served by maintaining the integrability conditions and searching for subsequent functional structure.

The kinds of functional structure of interest to model building involve homotheticity restrictions and separability restrictions. Homo-theticity restrictions refer to simplifications of income effects that per-mit budget shares to be determined without reference to income level. Separability restrictions refer to grouping restrictions on goods; such as whether different energy types can be combined into a single energy aggregate. While some level of grouping is required at the start for an economy-wide model, functional structure tests are designed to ask whether further grouping is in conflict with the aggregate data pattern. Combining homotheticity and separability restrictions for a group of goods permits the beneficial structure of multistage budgeting - goods are grouped into an aggregate, an aggre-gate group price can be constructed without reference to overall group expenditure, so that allocation occurs between the group and other goods, and then among the goods within the group. This structure gives a justifiable breakdown of a demand system into smaller, more manageable pieces. The restrictions involved in testing local and global versions of these kinds of functional structure for a translog are cataloged in Jorgenson and Lau (1975), and applied to a three category model of demand of the U.S. household sector.

Another block of hypotheses involve the basic integrability condi-tions, or the conditions under which the demand equations could have arisen from the maximization of preferences of a representative agent. Since the demand equations were originally derived from indi-rect utility (8.2.5), the integrability restrictions refer to the parameter restrictions that make (8.2.5) an indirect utility function, such as $\alpha_k \geq 0$ for all k. Also, the presence of (8.2.5) implies that $\beta_{jk} = \beta_{kj}$ for all j, k in the systems (8.2.6) and (8.2.7), or in words, that the coefficient β_{kj} of $\ln p_j$ in the jth share equation matches the coefficient β_{jk} of $\ln p_k$ in the kth share equation. Further restrictions involve imposing the quasi-convexity of indirect utility (8.2.5). Testing these restrictions check the basic underpinnings of the representative agent model of aggregate demand. The reason it is important to use a flexible system for this kind of testing is for interpreting rejections. For example, rejection of the LES could arise from the rejection of integrability or from the rejection of imposed constraints between price and income elasticities. Rejection with a flexible system lessens the possibility of that the integrability conditions would actually hold with a different model.

The translog models were among the first to be used to test integrability restrictions with aggregate data. The broad conclusion of the results from the translog and many subsequent systems was that the integrability conditions do not hold in many aggregate data series. This constituted an opening salvo of the argument that the representative agent paradigm just did not have a useful foundation in economic theory or observed data. As discussed later, there are no valid theoretical grounds for basing an economy-wide demand model on a representative consumer, and the empirical rejections of integrability removed any statistical justification as well. In essence, the development of flexible methods of studying aggregate demand patterns served to reveal the representative agent as a house of cards, with no foundation to stand on. At best, a representative agent model was a flawed "reduced form" depiction of aggregate expenditure patterns, whose value was limited to giving data-based summary equations of reactions of the household sector as a whole.

By the late-1970s, Jorgenson and his associates had recognized this situation. One possible approach could have been to seek further methods of justifying the representative agent, but there were other reasons not to do this. In particular, finding a justification for a representative agent approach would not help in the welfare analysis of economic policy. The preferences of a representative agent, or less refined notions of aggregate consumer surplus, could not answer questions about policy impacts on the welfare of individual households; save to verify that "more is better." This realization led Jorgenson and his associates to pursue a brand new approach to modeling the consumption sector. The new approach needed to retain feasibility of modeling aggregate demand patterns, use economic theory in a defensible fashion to aid simulation, but dispense with the representative agent. We discuss this new approach in the next section.

The original work on flexible functional forms avoided the most basic types of artificial impositions on household sector demand models. However, the notion of "flexibility" as providing approximation of derivatives at a point is itself limited, as it does not provide a useful notion of approximation over a range of price and income values. This work served as one of two important stimuli[3] for the extensive development of nonparametric and semiparametric methods of econometrics that began in the early 1980s. One of the first applications of nonparametric methods in econometrics was the use of Fourier series by Eldawabi, Gallant, and Souza (1983), which was focused on whether elasticities could be measured consistently.[4] Subsequent work has used derivatives as a starting point for developing semiparametric modeling methods, such as described in Stoker (1992). While there has not yet been a full integration of integrability properties and nonparametric demand equations, there have been proposals of demand systems that are more flexible in terms of approximating concave preference relations over ranges of prices and incomes.[5]

8.3 Aggregate Demand and Heterogeneous Households

8.3.1 Heterogeneity of Household Demand Behavior and Aggregation

The basic problem with representative agent modeling is that different households choose budget allocations that are markedly different. This means that an economy-wide policy may impact households differently, and will cause different reactions from those households. For example, we cannot usefully speak of the "effect of increased aggregate income" on aggregate demand, since it matters which households get the additional income. A well crafted representative agent model could, in principle, capture observed aggregate demand-price-aggregate income patterns, but its only use for application would be to replicate those historical patterns. One cannot expect future aggregate data to match choices from preferences of a representative agent, because there is no basis for thinking that such choices would be consistently obeyed. Further, measuring economic welfare on the basis of representative agent preferences involves yet a further leap of faith without foundation. Even the concept of market consumer surplus is ambiguous when the marginal utility of income varies across households.

This means that household differences must be captured in a model of the household sector, for either realistic simulation or welfare analysis. But what method of capturing differences is practical for building a household sector demand model? One possibility is to regard every household as having unique, idiosyncratic features; in line with looking at one's neighbors for evidence of individual heterogeneity. This method, as embodied in fixed effects analysis of panel data, is not practical for modeling the household sector as a whole, as it would require detailed accounting for every household in the economy over time. An alternative is to focus on broad reasons for differences in demand behavior; looking at differences between rich and poor households, large and small households, households with older children versus younger ones, etc. This approach characterizes differences along a few observable dimensions of income and attributes, and requires accounting for the distribution of households relative to their income and attributes.

The latter view was adopted by Jorgenson and his associates. Facilitating this approach was the extensive literature on the "cross section" tradition of demand analysis. This work had shown the necessity of modeling individual budget allocations as nonlinear in income (or total expenditure), as well as the necessity for incorporating many differences associated with demographic attributes.

But this connection did not serve to completely solve the problems of incorporating heterogeneity into aggregate demand. To spell this out, consider a flexible, demographically-varying household demand model along the lines discussed above. Suppose households in the economy are indexed by i, with M_{it} denoting total expenditure of household i. Suppose further that the observed demographic differences relevant to demand are denoted by a set of S variables; $A_{it} = (A_{1it}, \ldots, A_{Sit})$. The foundation of a household demand model is a specification of preferences; say in indirect form as $V(p_t, M_{it}, A_{it})$; from which household-specific demand equations $q_{ikt} = q_k(p_t, M_{it}, A_{it})$ can be derived. For instance, a translog model that permitted demographic variation could be based on a quadratic function of log prices, log total expenditure and demographic attributes; as in

$$\ln V(p_t, M_{it}, A_{it}) = \sum_k \alpha_k \ln\left(\frac{M_{it}}{p_{kt}}\right) + \left(\frac{1}{2}\right)\sum_k \sum_j \beta_{kj} \ln\left(\frac{M_{it}}{p_{kt}}\right)\ln\left(\frac{M_{it}}{p_{jt}}\right)$$
$$+ \sum_s \beta_{Aks} A_{sit} \ln\left(\frac{M_{it}}{p_{kt}}\right) \tag{8.3.1}$$

where we include only the terms that depend on price and total expenditure, because the other terms do not impinge on demands. This preference specification gives the budget share model

$$w_{kit} = \frac{p_{kt}q_{kit}}{M_t} = \frac{p_{kt}q_k(p_t, M_{it}, A_{it})}{M_t}$$

$$= \frac{\alpha_k - \sum_j \beta_{jk} \ln p_{jt} + \sum_j \beta_{jk} \ln M_t - \sum_s \beta_{Aks} A_{sit}}{1 - \sum_k \sum_j \beta_{jk} \ln p_{jt} + \sum_k \sum_j \beta_{jk} \ln M_t + \sum_k \sum_s \beta_{Aks} A_{sit}}.$$ (8.3.2)

The parameters of a model of this kind could be estimated with data on household expenditures, prices and demographic attributes. One problem, however, is that such data are not readily available for individual households. The work in the cross section tradition analyzed household surveys over single time periods. Detailed evidence on income and demographic influences are available from this work, but there is little information on which to base the measurement of price effects. Even though some household surveys observed limited variation in prices, it is impossible to measure household reactions to broad-based trends in relative prices, such as those that occur over a few years. For example, results from the U.S. Consumer Expenditure Survey of 1972 are not informative as to household reactions to the energy price shocks of 1973–1974.

The second problem arises from the basic motivation for the work, which is to build a realistic model of the entire household sector. In particular, the aggregate demands implied by (8.3.2) involve a complicated addition across the distribution of households by income and demographic class. Even with a small number of demographic dimensions accounted for, this is a daunting prospect for simulation of the resulting demand model.

The natural recourse to dealing with these problems is to appeal to aggregation theory. The overall aim was to produce a single model that account for demographic differences in households as well as a practically simple specification of aggregate demands. With one model applicable to both individual and aggregate expenditure data, all relevant effects could be measured: in essence, price effects are measured with aggregate data, and income and demographic effects measured with individual household data; with all measurements made consistently, under the rubric of a single model. The practical simplicity of the aggregate model would facilitate is use in simulation and policy analysis.

However, up until the mid-1970s, there did not exist practical solutions to these problems. In particular, the main result governing the expression of aggregate demands as a function of aggregate income was Gorman's (1953) insight that all households must have the same marginal responses to new income. In other words, for aggregate demand to depend only on aggregate income, household Engel curves must be linear, and have the same slope for all households. If a Cobb-Douglas model (or a Linear Expenditure System) were applicable for each household (with the same parameter values for all households), this structure would obtain, giving aggregate equations of the form (8.2.1) (or (8.2.4), respectively). But more complicated income structures were ruled out from the basic Gorman theory. An important generalization of this theory at the time was enacted by Muellbauer (1975), who characterized when aggregate budget shares could be written as a function of a single "representative income" value, or when

$$W_{kt} = W(p_t, S_t) \tag{8.3.3}$$

where S_t was a symmetric statistic of the distribution of total expenditure values. He showed how budget share equations had to be linear in a single function of income, which could be further restricted to a power of total expenditure or log-total expenditure. While this permitted nonlinear Engel curve structures, this development was still constrained by the requirement that aggregate allocations must be determined by a single, representative income value.

Jorgenson and his associates reacted to this state of affairs by developing a new aggregation theory that dispensed with the concept of a representative agent, or dependence of aggregate allocations on a representative income value. With economy-wide demand allocations recognized as aggregates of individual demands, one immediately confronts the practical problems of how to carry along the entire expenditure-attribute distribution in the construction of aggregate demand. The solution to these problems was developed by Lau, who studied the question of when aggregate demand could be formulated with just a few statistics of the expenditure-attributed distribution. In particular, of interest was the conditions under which one could write aggregate demand as

$$Q_{kt} = Q(p_t, \mathcal{M}_{1t}, \dots, \mathcal{M}_{Rt}) \tag{8.3.4}$$

where the $\mathcal{M}$'s were R symmetric statistics of the distribution;

$$\mathcal{M}_{rt} = \mathcal{M}[(M_{1t}, A_{1t}), \dots, (M_{Nt}, A_{Nt})] \, ,$$

with "symmetric" meaning that the (M, A) values for any two households could be interchanged without changing the value of the M_{rt}'s. Since no further distributional structure is maintained, Lau showed how demands must be intrinsically linear in functions of (M, A), the elements that varied over households; with sample averages for the M statistics. This solution was tailor-made for econometric modeling, since it recognized the need for modeling demographic influences in demands, as well as the practical need for generating a parsimonious model for aggregate demand.[6] We now describe the model of demand that grew out of this work; Jorgenson, Lau and Stoker (1980, 1981, 1982) give the whole body of research developments that surrounded it.

8.3.2 The Translog Model of Aggregate Consumer Behavior

The individual translog household model (8.3.2) is too general to permit parsimonious aggregation as above; the problem is that log-total expenditure and attributes appear nonlinearly in demand, because of their appearance in the denominator of (8.3.2). To facilitate the construction of aggregate demand, restrictions must be applied to invoke intrinsic linearity; the obvious restrictions are $\sum_j \sum_k \beta_{jk} = 0$ and $\sum_k \beta_{Aks} = 0$ for all s. Applying these restrictions gives the budget share system

$$w_{kit} = \frac{1}{D(p_t)}\left[\alpha_k - \sum_j \beta_{jk} \ln p_{jt} + \sum_j \beta_{jk} \ln M_t - \sum_s \beta_{Aks} A_{sit} \right] \qquad (8.3.5)$$

where $D(p_t) = 1 - \sum_k \sum_j \beta_{jk} \ln p_{jt}$.

Aggregate budget shares can then be derived immediately as

$$W_{it} = \frac{1}{D(p_t)}\left[\alpha_k - \sum_j \beta_{jk} \ln p_{jt} + \sum_j \beta_{jk} \mathcal{E}_t - \sum_s \eta_{Aks} A_{st} \right] \qquad (8.3.6)$$

where $\mathcal{E}_t$ is an entropy statistic

$$\mathcal{E}_t = \frac{\sum_i M_{it} \ln M_{it}}{\sum_i M_{it}} \qquad (8.3.7)$$

and A_{st} is a demographic statistic

$$A_{st} = \frac{\sum_i M_{it} A_{sit}}{\sum_i M_{it}}.$$ (8.3.8)

Model (8.3.6) relates aggregate demands to prices and the joint distribution of total expenditure and attributes through the statistics $\mathcal{E}_t$ and A_{st}, $s = 1, \ldots, S$. The entropy statistic $\mathcal{E}_t$ represents the size distribution of total expenditure; relatively rich populations have different budget allocations than relatively poor ones. The demographic statistics A_{st} represent the distribution of total expenditure by demographic categories. For instance, if A_{sit} is a qualitative (dummy) indicator, say for large families, then A_{st} is the proportion of total expenditure accounted for by large families. Populations of differing demographic composition have different budget allocations, to the extent that the demographic differences affect preferences or basic needs. This model achieves the aggregate demand-expenditure distribution connection needed, requiring observations on only the aggregate statistics (8.3.7) and (8.3.8) for each time period.

What can be said about the budget share model (8.3.5)? First, it is not as flexible as a general translog specification (8.3.2), which reflects the costs of accommodating feasible aggregation. However, it does have many desirable structural aspects relative to previous empirical work. The fact that budget shares are linear in log total expenditure reflects the Working-Leser Engel curve structure, that had been validated in many budget studies. The fact that the attributes A_{sit} can be specified quite generally, for instance as indicators of ranges of demographic variables, means that the model can accommodate a wide range of demographic effects in budget shares. The price structure involves a generalization of the "constant share elasticity" case discussed before. As such, the model accommodates fairly flexible budget share patterns with a single cross section budget study and aggregate time series data. The main restrictions involve commonality between the shapes of Engel curves in different periods, and some restrictiveness in the price responses across families.

The aggregate model of budget allocation requires observations on the distributional statistics $\mathcal{E}_t$ and A_{st} for each time period—these are constructed in Jorgenson, Lau and Stoker (1982) for application to the U.S. household sector. Even if the demographic statistics A_{st} are each constant over time, this model is in no way based on the representative agent paradigm.[7] Yet it exhibits the strongest virtue advocated by more recent "representative agent" modelers. In particular, the parameters in (8.3.5) are the same parameters as in (8.3.6), and represent the basic structural parameters of household preferences (8.3.1). All the integrability restrictions applicable to (8.3.1) are immediately applicable to the individual model (8.3.5), and more importantly, to the aggregate demand model (8.3.6). As such, the connection through aggregation provides a proper foundation for translating restrictions of individual economic behavior to aggregate demand, or the overall model of the household sector. While the aggregate equations are not integrable, they do carry a justifiable amount of regularity from the foundation of the model.

An additional application of this modeling paradigm arose from Jorgenson's continuing research on the energy sector of the U.S. economy. This work combined structure for aggregation over individual households with aggregation over individual energy types. Jorgenson and Stoker (1984) give a household model of expenditures on individual energy types, and Jorgenson, Slesnick and Stoker (1987, 1988) give a two-stage budgeting model of allocation across broad expenditure categories (including energy), and to individual energy types. These models included specification of a (demographically varying) energy price index for each household, as well as aggregation in the presence of the varying price indexes.

As a prelude to the work discussed in the conference on welfare measurement, we note a final point regarding basic translog model (8.3.5). A primary reason for modeling preferences of individual households is for welfare analysis. The preferences (8.3.1) provide the connection between the utility level of household i, price levels and their total expenditure. Likewise, these preferences permit the computation of compensating and equivalent variation measures of consumer surplus associated with price changes. This requires a bridge between expenditure and utility level (i.e., the expenditure function); from which one can hold utility constant and see how much expenditure change compensates for a price change. However, the general formulation of (8.3.1) expresses utility in terms of a quadratic function of log total expenditure, so that solving out for total expenditure is difficult or at best awkward. But notice how the exact aggregation restrictions delete the quadratic term in ln total expenditure. Consequently, for preferences underlying model (8.3.5) it is easy to solve for the expenditure function. Under these restrictions, indirect utility appears as

$$\ln V(p_t, M_{it}, A_{it}) = C(p_t, A_{it}) + D(p_t) \ln M_{it} \tag{8.3.9}$$

where

$$C(p_t, A_{it}) = -\sum_k \alpha_k \ln \ p_{kt} - (1/2)\sum_j \sum_k \beta_{kj} \ln p_{jt} \ln p_{kt}$$
$$- \sum_s \sum_s \beta_{Aks} A_{kit} \ln p_{kt}.$$

Minimum required expenditure for a given utility level is easily derived as

$$\ln M = \frac{1}{D(p_t)} [C(p_t, A_{it}) - \ln V_{it}]. \tag{8.3.10}$$

For an example, consider how to compute the compensating variation associated with a change in prices from p_0 to p_1 for a family with total expenditure M_0 and attribute configuration A_0. First, solve for initial utility $\ln V_0$ using p_0, M_0 and A_0 substituted into (8.3.9). Solve for necessary expenditure M_1 by inserting $\ln V_0$, A_0 and p_1 in (8.3.10). The compensating variation is $M_1 - M_0$. I mention this connection because welfare measurement was always a primary motivation in Jorgenson's research program, and has a central role in the development of this aggregate demand model from the outset.

The translog model (8.3.5)–(8.3.6) stood for nearly a decade as the only model in use that captured price, income and demographic effects in a consistent fashion that is valuable to modeling household sector demand. Other methods were proposed in this time that allowed for differences in income across households, in the same fashion as above. Recently, more detailed methods have been applied to repeated cross section data sets that suggest the income and demographic effects in (8.3.5) need to be augmented with quadratic terms in log-total expenditure, and interaction terms between demographic attributes and prices.[8] Nevertheless, the scope of the innovation of the basic translog model is large, and on it stands the most recent developments of demand analysis in economics.

Also, I have spent a substantive amount of my career studying topics related to the ideas basic connections outlined above. This work includes some detailed study of micro-macro connections (recoverability of basic preference parameters, as above) and general connections between cross section estimates and (time series) macroeconomic effects. This work, and other related developments, are surveyed in Stoker (1993).

8.4   Related Innovations to Econometric Methods

Our coverage of the work of Jorgenson and his associates on consumer behavior has focused on modeling, without explicit discussion of the econometric methods for estimating the models. However, each of the innovations discussed above was sufficiently novel to require new developments to econometric methods, which we mention now.

Econometric approaches often differ in terms of how the systematic part of a model is treated relative to the unobserved, stochastic part. One kind of research starts with a simple linear model, and considers detailed variations on the distribution of the unobserved stochastic terms. Another kind focuses attention on a detailed structure of the systematic part of the equation, with less attention to the source of the stochastic disturbance. While each style has its merits, Jorgenson's work is clearly in the latter format, since his aim is to produce more realistic equations (the systematic part) for simulation.

The models discussed in section 8.2 involve estimation of nonlinear systems of equations. Because these are demand systems, the classical demand-supply identification problem suggests using instrumental variables methods for estimation and inference on the basic parameters. In conjunction with the modeling efforts discussed above, Jorgenson and his associates carried out a systematic development of efficient estimation and inference for equation systems, culminating in complete methods for nonlinear simultaneous equations models. Brundy and Jorgenson (1971, 1973, 1974) develop efficient methods for estimating linear simultaneous equations models, as well as comparing various competing estimation methods. Jorgenson and Laffont (1974) give efficient methods for estimating nonlinear simultaneous equation systems using instrumental variables methods. Gallant and Jorgenson (1979) give general methods for carrying out specification tests in nonlinear simultaneous equation systems, such as required for the analysis of functional form discussed earlier.

This work provided a complete set of tools for estimation and inference of virtually all kinds of representative agent models of consumer or producer behavior. Each of the developments of Jorgenson and his associates can be seen as a step in the standard line of developments in econometric methods; evolving from known instrumental variables methods for linear systems through to fully developed methods of inference for nonlinear systems. While straightforward, one should not discount the value of the overall development. For instance, consider the estimation method of Jorgenson and Laffont (1974). Suppose one adds a correction for heteroskedasticity, renames the estimating equations "orthogonality conditions," and renames the overall method the "generalized method of moments." You would have arrived at the premier econometric method used for estimating rational expectations models of Hansen (1982).

For estimating the translog demand model (8.3.5) and (8.3.6), Jorgenson, Lau and Stoker (1982) combined traditional data pooling methods with methods for nonlinear simultaneous systems. Jorgenson and Stoker (1986) cover how to generally apply this method for estimating exact aggregation model, including adjustments for heteroskedasticity appropriate for comparing individual and aggregate data. This work provides the basis for estimation of any model with a consistent aggregation structure, using all available data sources.

Finally, it is worthwhile noting that Jorgenson's research program also involved overcoming many of the practical obstacles inherent to complicated estimation of nonlinear systems, and his research program may have given rise to the largest practical estimation project to date. For instance, the software package Time Series Processor (TSP) was developed in conjunction with the estimation of many of Jorgenson's production and consumption models. Refinements to numerical algorithms and the discovery of practical problems (such as failures of numerical convergence) were studied as a matter of course in the maintenance of Jorgenson's various general equilibrium and growth models.

8.5   A Closing Note

In winning the John Bates Clark Medal in 1971, Jorgenson's work on the cost of capital and investment was cited as "one of the finest examples of the marriage of theory and practice in economics." The purpose of this chapter was to provide a glimpse of Jorgenson's subsequent work on consumer behavior in the same light. Each of Jorgenson's innovations involves developments in modeling, economic theory and econometric methods that are blended together to produce frontier models of household sector demand behavior. Applications of these innovations to analysis of the household sectors of United States and other countries accompanied their introduction at every stage.

The unique thing about all of Jorgenson's work is the marriage of theory and practice. It would be wrong to characterize Jorgenson as either an economic theorist trying to do empirical work, or an empirical economist trying to use some economic theory. Intrinsic to Jorgenson's research program is the simultaneous development of theory, modeling and econometric methods. To focus on one aspect of his work without considering the others misses the essential features and the lasting character of his contributions.

The research frontier of economics has always, at any particular time, been characterized by pockets of intense activity devoted to very narrow questions and current issues. The development of the field of economics occurs through the long-term process of sifting out what theoretical insights have empirical validity, and what empirical facts are relevant for revising the current theoretical paradigm. While we have only looked at a small facet of Jorgenson's work, it is fair to say that no other researcher has done more to keep economic theory and empirical research developing together toward a useful end, namely to address important questions of economic policy.

This view is not based on the large number of professionals who were students of Jorgenson, nor on the many professionals who have, after hearing about this conference, relayed stories to me of how their work had been directly inspired by Jorgenson. Rather, it is based on the fact that during my professional career, I have witnessed a few research areas rise and then peter out; and what has survived from them are the theoretical and empirical aspects that apply to several areas of economics. The multi-area integration of new ideas is the central tenet of Jorgenson's research approach. Consequently, while one can cite the importance of many of the individual parts of Jorgenson's work, from the cost of capital through consumer behavior, I view Jorgenson's greatest contributions to have arisen from his approach itself, which insists that all innovations must work toward the greater aim of addressing real economic problems.

Notes

1. Lau (1986) gives a useful survey of flexible functional forms.
2. We note in passing that Jorgenson and his associates also considered second-order translog specifications of direct utility, which add quadratic terms to the Cobb-Douglas direct utility function. Roy's identity here leads to relationships between budget shares and quantities, which are difficult to solve out for demands as a function of prices and income. Nevertheless, if quantities are constrained, or their endogeneity can be accounted for, this approach leads to a similar study of functional forms and related aspects. We have focused on translog systems that give demand functions immediately, in line with traditional approaches to demand analysis. All of our later remarks on testing functional structure, etc., apply in this case.

3. The other important stimuli was the recognition that models of limited dependent variables were extremely sensitive to arbitrary distributional assumptions.

4. The issues this chapter addressed were a common theme of discussions that occurred during Gallant's visits to Cambridge in the late 1970s, as part of his collaboration with Jorgenson on testing problems (Gallant and Jorgenson, 1979).

5. For example, see Barnett and Lee (1985) for one such proposal, as well as references to this literature.

6. Lau's aggregation theory is covered in Lau (1977, 1982). Lau's visit to Harvard University during this period lead to the simultaneous development of the translog aggregate demand model along with tenets of his basic theory.

7. Unless one defines "representative" to refer to households as distinguished by income and demographic configuration; in which case we have many kinds of "representative" households.

8. See Blundell, Pashardes and Weber (1993), for instance.

9

Innovations in Applied Welfare Economics

Daniel T. Slesnick

9.1 Introduction

Does the standard of living of the elderly, relative to younger generations, warrant funding Social Security at current levels? How have the poor fared relative to the rest of the population as the economy has grown? Does governmental regulation increase the welfare of consumers? Topical issues such as these indicate that the measurement of welfare is a fundamental element of public policy analysis. A full consideration of taxes, subsidies, transfer programs, health care reform, regulation, environmental policy, the Social Security system, and educational reform must ultimately address the question of how these policies affect the welfare of individuals.

While centrally important to many problems of economic analysis, confusion persists concerning the relationship between commonly used indicators of welfare and well-established theoretical formulations. Indeed, theoretical and empirical research on welfare economics has largely developed along parallel lines with little cross-fertilization. For example, social welfare is often measured using real median family income even though there is no basis for this in the voluminous social choice literature. Consumer's surplus is the method of choice for policy evaluation despite theoretical results, presented as many as five decades ago, that have shown that it is not an indicator of the change in utility.

As with his work in capital theory, Dale Jorgenson has set the standard in applied welfare economics for empirical work painstakingly linked with established micro-theory. The measurement of individual well-being is tied explicitly to the theory of consumer behavior to obtain an exact welfare indicator that increases if and only if utility rises. More unusual, the measurement of social welfare is founded on the basic principles of social choice that have long been the exclusive domain of micro-theorists.

An examination of econometric approaches to welfare economics is best organized by the level of aggregation at which they are applied. In section 9.2, I contrast consumer's surplus with a model which measures changes in utility using information on expenditure patterns. In section 9.3, I use this approach to estimate household equivalence scales, measure the cost of living and conclude with an application to the measurement of welfare in an intertemporal setting.

Of course, the primary concern is the welfare effect of policy at the macro level. The analysis of social welfare requires solving a difficult aggregation problem that has troubled economists, political scientists and philosophers for at least a century. In section 9.4 I review previous efforts to measure social welfare and present an empirically implementable alternative that is founded on social choice theory. This is utilized to investigate the aggregate welfare impact of alternative tax proposals, and has the added feature of providing a theoretical foundation for social welfare statistics such as standard of living indexes, aggregate price indexes as well as inequality and poverty measures.

9.2 Welfare Economics at the Individual Level

9.2.1 Historical Context

The empirical methods used to measure welfare depend critically on the level of aggregation at which they are applied. We begin with the ubiquitous micro-formulation which can be described using the following notation:

$\mathbf{p} = (p_1, p_2, \ldots, p_N)$—a vector of prices of all commodities.

x_{nk}—the quantity of the n-th commodity group consumed by the k-th household ($n = 1, 2, \ldots, N; k = 1, 2, \ldots, K$).

$M_k = \sum_{n=1}^{N} p_n x_{nk}$—total expenditure, or the dollar value of consumption of the k-th household ($k = 1, 2, \ldots, K$).

$\mathbf{A}_k$—the vector of household attributes of the k-th household ($k = 1, 2, \ldots, K$).

Consumer's surplus, largely associated with Marshall (1920), was originally developed 150 years ago by Dupuit (1844). It remains the most frequently used method of welfare measurement despite having several problems. To illustrate, consider the simplest case of a change in the price of a single good, say commodity 1, from p_1^0 to p_1^1. The change in consumer's surplus is the negative of the change in the area under the demand curve and can be interpreted as the change in the individual's willingness to pay:

$$\Delta CS_k = - \int_{p_1^0}^{p_1^1} x_1(t, p_2, \ldots, p_N, M_k, A_k) \, dt \,, \tag{9.1}$$

where $x_1(\mathbf{p}, M_k, A_k)$ is the demand function for good 1.

The popularity of consumer's surplus can largely be attributed to the ease with which it is implemented. In its simplest form, a linear demand function is specified:

$$x_1 = \gamma_1 + \gamma_p \mathbf{p} + \gamma_3 M_k + \gamma_A A_k,$$

and the unknown parameters, γ_1, γ_p, γ_3, and γ_A are estimated by fitting the demand function to expenditure data. Using the fitted demand function, the change in welfare resulting from the change in the price of commodity 1 is calculated using equation (9.1).

Is consumer's surplus an exact measure of the change in welfare? To answer this question note that, by Roy's Identity:

$$x_1(\mathbf{p}, M_k, A_k) = - \frac{\partial V(\mathbf{p}, M_k, A_k)/\partial p_1}{\partial V(\mathbf{p}, M_k, A_k)/\partial M_k}, \tag{9.2}$$

where $V(\mathbf{p}, M_k, A_k)$ is the individual's indirect utility function. If the marginal utility of income is constant, substituting (9.2) into (9.1) reveals that consumer's surplus is an exact representation of the change in utility and can be represented as:[1]

$$\Delta CS_k = \frac{V(\mathbf{p}^1, M_k, A_k) - V(\mathbf{p}^0, M_k, A_k)}{\partial V/\partial M_k} \,.$$

While the assumption of constant marginal utility of income is restrictive, the problems become more serious in the general setting of changes in more than one price. In this case, the change in consumer's surplus must be evaluated using a line integral:

$$\Delta CS_k = - \int_{\mathbf{p}^0}^{\mathbf{p}^1} \Sigma x_i(\mathbf{p}, M_k, \mathbf{A}_k) \, dp_i. \tag{9.3}$$

The generalization is conceptually straightforward but suffers from the problem that line integrals typically depend on the path over which they are evaluated. Since we do not observe the paths of price movements but only the initial and final values, consumer's surplus defined in (9.3) is multiple-valued unless the integral is path independent. Path independence, in turn, is achieved if the uncompensated price effects are symmetric:

$$\frac{\partial x_i}{\partial p_j} = \frac{\partial x_j}{\partial p_i} \quad \text{for all } i \neq j.$$

A rational consumer will exhibit compensated price effects that are symmetric but uncompensated demands will have this property if and only if preferences are homothetic.[2] From a practitioners perspective, this is a fatal flaw since homotheticity has been shown repeatedly to be inconsistent with empirical evidence based on demand patterns.[3]

An alternative approach, originally developed by Hicks (1942), is to measure welfare using individuals' compensated demands:

$$\Delta HS_k = - \int_{\mathbf{p}^0}^{\mathbf{p}^1} \Sigma x_i^c(\mathbf{p}, V, \mathbf{A}_k) \, dp_i,$$

where $x_i^c(\mathbf{p}, V, \mathbf{A}_k)$ is the compensated demand for the i-th good evaluated at utility level V. Compensated price effects are symmetric, so the line integral is path independent and the surplus measure is single-valued. If the integral is evaluated at V^0 (the utility attained at prices $\mathbf{p}^0$), the Hicksian index is the well-known compensating variation:

$$CV_k = M(\mathbf{p}^1, V^0, \mathbf{A}_k) - M(\mathbf{p}^0, V^0, \mathbf{A}_k), \tag{9.4}$$

where $M(\mathbf{p}, V, \mathbf{A}_k)$ is the individual's expenditure function. The equivalent variation is obtained if the surplus measure is evaluated at $V^1 = V(\mathbf{p}^1, M_k, \mathbf{A}_k)$:

$$EV_k = M(\mathbf{p}^1, V^1, \mathbf{A}_k) - M(\mathbf{p}^0, V^1, \mathbf{A}_k). \tag{9.5}$$

Unlike consumer's surplus, both the compensating and equivalent variations provide exact measures of the change in individual welfare for binary comparisons of social states since each is nonnegative if and only if $V(\mathbf{p}^0, M_k, \mathbf{A}_k) \geq V(\mathbf{p}^1, M_k, \mathbf{A}_k)$.[4] This resolves the conceptual problem of welfare measurement at the micro-level but, it was originally thought, does not help the practitioner because compensated demands and, therefore, Hicksian surplus measures are unobservable.

Willig (1976) made the first attempt to solve this problem by demonstrating that, in the case of a single price change, it is possible to use (observable) estimates of consumer's surplus to bracket the Hicksian surplus measures. He presents several examples illustrating that, in practice, the bounds can be very tight. Of course, Willig's approach is unusable in the more general setting of multiple price and income changes because consumer's surplus is not single-valued and, therefore, is of no use in setting bounds on the change in welfare.

9.2.2 Exact Welfare Measures: Static Formulation

An empirical approach to the measurement of welfare that does not suffer from the deficiencies of consumer's surplus and its variants was developed independently by Jorgenson, Lau and Stoker (1980, 1981, 1982) and Hausman (1981).[5] This model is almost as easy to implement as consumer's surplus and has exactly the same data requirements. The first step is to estimate the unknown parameters of a demand system subject to the integrability conditions implied by utility maximization. The indirect utility function as well as the expenditure function are recovered using the fitted demands to solve the implied system of partial differential equations.

To illustrate, consider the following demand system specified by Jorgenson, Lau and Stoker:

$$\mathbf{w}_k = \frac{1}{D(\mathbf{p})} (\alpha_p + B_{pp} \ln \mathbf{p} - \imath B_{pp} \ln M_k + B_{pA}\mathbf{A}_k), \tag{9.6}$$

where $D(\mathbf{p}) = -1 + \imath B_{pp}' \ln \mathbf{p}$ and $\mathbf{w}_k$ is the vector of budget shares of all goods consumed by the k-th household. The unknown parameters α_p, B_{pp} and B_{pA} can be estimated by fitting the system of share equations to data on consumer expenditures.

Given these estimates, it is possible to integrate backwards to obtain the household's indirect utility function:

$$\ln V(\mathbf{p}, M_k, \mathbf{A}_k) = C(\mathbf{A}_k) + \alpha_p' \ln \mathbf{p} + 1/2 \ln \mathbf{p}' B_{pp} \ln \mathbf{p}$$
$$- D(\mathbf{p}) \ln M_k + \ln \mathbf{p}' B_{pA}\mathbf{A}_k. \tag{9.7}$$

Solving (9.7) for total expenditure as a function of utility yields the expenditure function:

$$\ln M(\mathbf{p}, V_k, \mathbf{A}_k) = \frac{1}{D(\mathbf{p})} (C(\mathbf{A}_k) + \alpha_p' \ln \mathbf{p} + 1/2 \ln \mathbf{p}' B_{pp} \ln \mathbf{p}$$
$$+ \ln \mathbf{p}' B_{pA} \mathbf{A}_k - \ln V_k). \tag{9.8}$$

With prices, total expenditure and the attributes of the household, one has all of the variables needed to estimate an exact welfare measure. No approximations, such as those presented by Willig, are needed since the Hicksian surplus measures can be determined exactly.

Consider the most general scenario in which both prices and total expenditure change from $(\mathbf{p}^0, M_k^0)$ to $(\mathbf{p}^1, M_k^1)$. The change in welfare, evaluated at the initial prices $\mathbf{p}^0$, is:[6]

$$\Delta W_k = \Delta M_k - EV_k$$
$$= M(\mathbf{p}^0, V^1, \mathbf{A}_k) - M(\mathbf{p}^0, V^0, \mathbf{A}_k), \tag{9.9}$$

where EV_k is the Hicksian equivalent variation defined in (9.5), $V^0 = V(\mathbf{p}^0, M_k^0, \mathbf{A}_k)$, and $V^1 = V(\mathbf{p}^1, M_k^1, \mathbf{A}_k)$. ΔW_k is positive (negative) if and only if V^1 is greater (less) than V^0 so that (9.9) provides an exact measure of the change in welfare.

Note that this model facilitates welfare comparisons across a broad range of household types. One would expect policies to have different effects on large versus small households, the young versus the elderly as well as the rich versus the poor. In their original formulation of the model, Jorgenson, Lau and Stoker distinguished households by size, age of the head of the household, region of residence, race of the head of the household, farm versus nonfarm residence and welfare calculations could be made for almost 700 different types of households.

As important, it was recognized from the outset that welfare analysis of this type requires the maintained hypothesis of utility maximization. Unless consumers are fully rational, there is no basis for the comparisons of utility as prices and total expenditure change. This fact is usually ignored by practitioners but is a central element of the Jorgenson, Lau and Stoker model. In particular, the demand system is estimated subject to all of the integrability conditions implied by static utility maximization such as homogeneity of degree zero in prices and total expenditure, nonnegativity, summability, symmetry and negative semidefiniteness of the matrix of compensated price effects.[7]

The econometric approach to the measurement of welfare has been extended in a number of directions. Small and Rosen (1981) developed a model to measure individual welfare when some of the choices made by the consumer are discrete such as labor supply decisions or the decision to buy a home. More recent efforts have focused on obtaining a better fit for the demand curves that form the foundation for the welfare calculations. The demand model in (9.6) is, in Gorman's (1981) terminology, a rank two demand system. Banks, Blundell and Lewbel (1993) estimated a rank three model using UK data and found that the resulting welfare calculations were different from less flexible specifications. Deaton (1989) and Hausman and Newey (1995) went to another level of generality and performed welfare calculations using fully nonparametric specifications of the underlying demand functions.

9.2.3   Exact Welfare Measures: Dynamic Formulation

To this point I have considered the measurement of welfare in a static, single-period framework. This approach could provide a misleading picture of the change in welfare since the effects of policies often last more than one period. Poterba (1989, 1991b) discussed the need to develop a framework for welfare analysis that focuses on the "lifetime incidence" of policies rather than on their short-run impact.

The most common approach to intertemporal welfare analysis is to represent the lifetime equivalent variation as the discounted sum of the within-period changes in welfare. Blackorby, Donaldson, and Moloney (1984) and Keen (1990) have demonstrated that the intertemporal equivalent variation will diverge from the discounted sum of the within-period equivalent variations to the extent that households have the ability to substitute intertemporally.

To illustrate, let V_d be the maximum level of lifetime utility of an infinitely-lived household when the profiles of prices and interest rates are $\{\mathbf{p}_t\}$ and $\{r_t\}$, respectively. If the (optimal) time path of utility corresponding to V_d at these prices and interest rates is $\{V_{dt}\}$, the lifetime expenditure function can be represented as:

$$\Omega_d(\{\mathbf{p}_t\}, \{\gamma_t\}, V_d) = \sum_{t=0}^{\infty} \gamma_t \, M(\mathbf{p}_t, V_{dt}, A_d),$$

where

$$\gamma_t = \prod_{s=0}^{t} (1 + r_s)^{-1},$$

and r_0 is equal to zero.

Let V_d^1 be the maximum level of lifetime welfare when the profile of prices and interest rates are $\{\mathbf{p}_t^1\}$ and $\{r_t^1\}$, respectively and denote the corresponding time path of utility as $\{V_{dt}^1\}$. In the reference scenario, prices and interest rates are $\{\mathbf{p}_t^0\}$ and $\{r_t^0\}$ resulting in a lifetime utility level of $\{V_d^0\}$ and within period utilities $\{V_{dt}^0\}$. An exact measure of the change in lifetime welfare, evaluated at the reference prices, is:

$$\Delta W_d = \Omega_d(\{\mathbf{p}_t^0\}, \{\gamma_t^0\}, V_d^1) - \Omega_d(\{\mathbf{p}_t^0\}, \{\gamma_t^0\}, V_d^0) \tag{9.10}$$

$$= \sum_{t=0}^{\infty} \gamma_t^0 \, [M(\mathbf{p}_t^0, V_{dt}^1, \mathbf{A}_d) - M(\mathbf{p}_t^0, V_{dt}^0, \mathbf{A}_d)]$$

$$+ \sum_{t=0}^{\infty} \gamma_t^0 \, [M(\mathbf{p}_t^0, V_{dt}^3, \mathbf{A}_d) - M(\mathbf{p}_t^0, V_{dt}^1, \mathbf{A}_d)], \tag{9.11}$$

where $\{V_{dt}^3\}$ is the optimal time path of utility required to attain lifetime welfare level V_d^1 when prices and interest rates are $\{\mathbf{p}_t^0\}$ and $\{r_t^0\}$, respectively.

The first term in (9.11) is the discounted sum of the within period changes in welfare. The second term represents the gain to the household that results from its ability to adjust the time path of consumption as the profile of prices and interest rates change. This is nonpositive since the "rational" household minimizes the cost of attaining a given level of lifetime welfare, implying that the discounted sum of the intraperiod changes in utility overstates the change in lifetime welfare. The magnitude of the bias is dictated by the extent to which the household can adjust consumption intertemporally.

Since the present value of the within-period changes results in a distorted assessment of lifetime well-being, an alternative empirical model is required to measure the change in welfare accurately. Such a model was developed by Jorgenson, Slesnick and Wilcoxen (1991) in which households are assumed to be infinitely-lived and linked to similar households in the future through intergenerational altruism in preferences.[8] This household, referred to as a "dynasty," is assumed to maximize an additive intertemporal utility function of the form:

$$V_d = \sum_{t=0}^{\infty} \delta^t \ln V_{dt}, \tag{9.12}$$

where $\delta = 1/(1 + \rho)$ and ρ is the subjective rate of time preference. The intratemporal indirect utility function V_{dt} is taken to be of the form:

$$\ln V_{dt} = \alpha_p' \ln \mathbf{p}_t + \frac{1}{2} \ln \mathbf{p}_t \, B_{pp} \ln \mathbf{p}_t - D(\mathbf{p}_t) \ln (M_{dt}/N_{dt}), \tag{9.13}$$

where $N_{dt} = K_{dt} \, m_0(\mathbf{p}_t, \mathbf{A}_d)$ is the number of household equivalent members in the dynasty at time t. Dynasties are distinguished by a vector of attributes $\mathbf{A}_d$ which allows for differences in preferences among households.

The dynasty maximizes (9.12) over the time path of utility levels $\{V_{dt}\}$ subject to the budget constraint:

$$\sum_{t=0}^{\infty} \gamma_t \, M_{dt}(\mathbf{p}_t, V_{dt}, \mathbf{A}_d) = \Omega_d,$$

where Ω_d is the wealth of the dynasty and the intratemporal expenditure function is:

$$\ln M_{dt}(\mathbf{p}_t, V_{dt}, \mathbf{A}_d) = \frac{\alpha_p' \ln \mathbf{p}_t + 1/2 \ln \mathbf{p}_t' B_{pp} \ln \mathbf{p}_t - \ln V_{dt}}{D(\mathbf{p}_t)} + \ln(N_{dt}). \tag{9.14}$$

The necessary conditions for a maximum of the lifetime utility function are given by the discrete time Euler equations:

$$\ln V_{dt} = \frac{D_t}{D_{t-1}} \ln V_{dt-1} + D_t \ln \left(\frac{D_{t-1} \gamma_t N_{dt} P_t}{\delta D_t \gamma_{t-1} N_{dt-1} P_{t-1}} \right), \tag{9.15}$$

where I have used D_t to denote $D(\mathbf{p}_t)$ and:

$$P_t = \exp \left(\frac{\alpha_p' \ln \mathbf{p}_t + 1/2 \ln \mathbf{p}_t \, B_{pp} \ln \mathbf{p}_t}{D_t} \right).$$

The Euler equation implies that the maximum level of lifetime welfare for the dynasty can be represented as:

$$V_d = S \ln R - S \ln \Omega_d + \sum_{t=0}^{\infty} \delta^t D_t \ln \left(\frac{\gamma_t N_{dt} P_t D_0}{\delta^t D_t P_0} \right), \tag{9.16}$$

where

$$S = \sum_{t=0}^{\infty} \delta^t \, D_t \quad \text{and} \quad R = \frac{P_0}{D_0} \left(\sum_{t=0}^{\infty} \delta^t D_t \right).$$

Solving for wealth as a function of prices and utility yields the intertemporal expenditure function of the dynasty:

$$\ln \Omega_d(\{\mathbf{p}_t\}, \{\gamma_t\}, V_d) = \frac{1}{S} \left\{ S \ln R + \Sigma \delta^t D_t \ln \left(\frac{\gamma_t N_{dt} P_t D_0}{\delta^t D_t P_0} \right) - V_d \right\}. \qquad (9.17)$$

This expenditure function can be used to measure the monetary equivalent of a change in lifetime utility that results from a policy change using equation (9.10). In the next section, I illustrate this approach to intertemporal welfare analysis by evaluating the impacts of carbon taxes on individuals.

9.2.4 Index Numbers and Welfare Analysis

The models described to this point are based on explicit parametric representations of the utility function and the unknown parameters are estimated econometrically using demand data. An alternative approach is to forgo functional form assumptions for the utility function and evaluate the relative levels of welfare using the principle of revealed preference developed by Samuelson (1948). For example, let $\mathbf{x}^0$ and $\mathbf{p}^0$ be the quantity and price vector in the reference period and define $\mathbf{x}^1$ and $\mathbf{p}^1$ to be the corresponding vectors in the current period. Assuming consistent preferences, the individual is better off in the base period if $\mathbf{p}'^0\mathbf{x}^0 \geq \mathbf{p}'^0\mathbf{x}^1$ and is better off in period 1 if $\mathbf{p}'^1\mathbf{x}^1 \geq \mathbf{p}'^1\mathbf{x}^0$. If neither condition holds, nothing can be said about the relative welfare levels in the two periods.

Clearly, the fact that the ordering of consumption vectors is incomplete is a serious impediment to the use of index numbers to assess relative welfare levels. More recent efforts have focused on developing index numbers for which tighter bounds can be obtained. For example, Diewert (1990) developed bounds on a Malmquist (1953) index defined as:

$$Q_M(\mathbf{x}^1, \mathbf{x}^0, u) = \frac{D(u, \mathbf{x}^1)}{D(u, \mathbf{x}^0)},$$

where D is a distance function defined as:

$D(u, \mathbf{x}) = \max_d \{d : U(\mathbf{x}/d) \geq u, d > 0\}.$

This index has the correct ordinal properties of being greater than unity if and only if utility is higher in period 1 but is inherently unobservable. Diewert showed that $Q_M(\mathbf{x}^1, \mathbf{x}^0, u^0)$ is bounded from below by the minimum relative quantity and bounded from above by the Laspeyres quantity index.

However, there is no *a priori* reason why these bounds need to be tight. Afriat (1967) and, more recently, Varian (1982) have relied on multiple observations of price-quantity combinations to further tighten the bounds on the unobserved quantity index, while Manser and McDonald (1988) impose the condition of homotheticity for the same purpose. Each effort, however, highlights the problems associated with an index number approach compared to econometric methods.

In particular, the data requirements for index numbers are higher since at least two price-quantity data points are required for each individual. Repeated observations on the consumption levels of individuals are rare and, in fact, unavailable in the United States. This contrasts with the econometric approach which requires only one observation per person. In many instances, welfare analysis requires an assessment of alternative policies, one of which is hypothetical and unobserved. For example, we may want to assess the welfare impact of a reduction in taxes relative to the status quo. Clearly, the former outcome is not observed so its effects must be simulated which is impossible using the index number approach. Lastly, after all is said and done, index numbers do not provide a complete ordering of outcomes which is wholly unsatisfactory from a practical perspective.

9.3   Applications: The Measurement of Individual Welfare

9.3.1   Policy Analysis: Static Formulation

The model described in section 9.2.2 provides a framework for a large body of empirical work designed to answer many questions facing public policy analysts. Prominent among these applications is the evaluation of the impact of policies on different types of households. A base case is simulated using a computable general equilibrium model to yield equilibrium prices $\mathbf{p}^0$ and an expenditure level of M_k^0 for the k-th household. This is compared with the outcome of an alternative policy characterized by prices $\mathbf{p}^1$ and expenditure levels M_k^1. Defining the utility levels attained in the reference and policy simulations as, respectively, V_k^0 and V_k^1, the welfare impact on the k-th household is:

$$\Delta W_k = M(\mathbf{p}^0, V_k^1, \mathbf{A}_k) - M(\mathbf{p}^0, V_k^0, \mathbf{A}_k).$$

This general procedure has been used in a number of contexts such as the analysis of the impact of petroleum price deregulation by Jorgenson, Lau and Stoker (1980), petroleum taxation by Jorgenson and Slesnick (1985b) and natural gas price deregulation by Jorgenson and Slesnick (1985a). King (1983) has used a similar model to investigate the impact of housing tax reforms in the United Kingdom.

9.3.2   Deadweight Loss of Taxation

Perhaps the most common application of this framework is to the measurement of the efficiency losses attributable to taxation. The excess burden is defined as the amount, in excess of the tax revenue collected, the consumer would be willing to pay for the removal of all taxes. Using the framework developed by Diamond and McFadden (1974), the deadweight loss of commodity taxation can be represented as:[9]

$$DWL_k = M(\mathbf{p}^1, V^1, \mathbf{A}_k) - M(\mathbf{p}^0, V^1, \mathbf{A}_k) - \sum_{i=1}^{N} t_i x_i(\mathbf{p}^1, M_k, \mathbf{A}_k),$$

where $p_i^1 = p_i^0 + t_i$ $(i = 1, 2, \ldots, N)$, t_i is the tax on the i-th good, and V^1 is the post-tax utility level.

Empirical estimates of the deadweight loss attributable to labor income taxation are presented by Hausman (1981) and Rosen (1978), while Slesnick (1991a) estimated the excess burden due to commodity taxes in the U.S. Using simulations from computable general equilibrium models, Ballard (1988) evaluated the efficiency losses of redistributional programs, while Ballard, Shoven and Whalley (1985), Fullerton and Rogers (1993) and Jorgenson and Yun (1991b) considered the larger question of the inefficiencies of the entire U.S. tax system.

9.3.3   Cost of Living Indexes

Changes in prices can have different impacts on individuals with different expenditure patterns. An increase in the price of necessities, for example, will have a larger impact on the poor relative to the rich. Household-specific cost of living indexes were introduced by Konus (1939) and defined as the ratio of the (minimum) expenditure required to attain a given level of utility, say V, at current prices $\mathbf{p}^1$ to that needed to attain the same level of utility at base prices $\mathbf{p}^0$:

$$P_k(\mathbf{p}^1, \mathbf{p}^0, V_k) = \frac{M(\mathbf{p}^1, V, \mathbf{A}_k)}{M(\mathbf{p}^0, V, \mathbf{A}_k)} .$$

While the theory was established years ago, as with the Hicksian surplus measures, the empirical implementation of household-specific cost of living indexes was hindered by the presumption that the expenditure function could not be recovered from the observable behavior of households.[10] The empirical model described in section 9.2.2, however, can be used to estimate cost-of-living indexes for a wide variety of household types.

Household-specific price indexes and the accompanying estimates of inflation were computed by Jorgenson and Slesnick (1990b) using the expenditure function in (9.8). We found variation in inflation rates across households with different expenditure levels as well as for households with different demographic characteristics. This suggests that the common practice of using a single aggregate price index to adjust transfers to the poor or Social Security benefits to the elderly likely results in a biased assessment of the amount by which transfers must increase to maintain a constant standard of living.

9.3.4   Household Equivalence Scales

To this point, we have compared the welfare levels of the *same* household as prices and incomes change. Empirical estimates are derived solely from demand patterns that are invariant to monotonic transformations of the underlying utility functions. No assumptions of cardinality or interpersonal comparability are required for the analysis.

In contrast, consider the determination of the appropriate benefit levels for transfer programs such as the Food Stamp Program or Aid to Families with Dependent Children (AFDC). This requires an assessment of the extent to which "needs" change with household composition and injects a normative element to the analysis that was previously absent. In the case of AFDC, a principle of horizontal equity is invoked in which it is assumed that all poor women with children should receive benefits sufficient to attain the same subsistence standard of living. More important, interpersonal comparisons of the relative welfare levels of heterogeneous households are required.[11] Interpersonal comparability has, in the past, been dismissed by theorists as being "meaningless" because it cannot be inferred from observable behavior. This critique has been universally ignored by policy makers since comparisons of well-being are the essence of virtually every issue of practical concern. Assessments of this type are needed not only to index transfer payments but also to evaluate the cost of children for various purposes and to adjust the poverty line for households with different characteristics.

Welfare comparisons of households with different characteristics, such as family size, are made using the concept of household equivalence scales. Formally, these scales are defined as the minimum expenditure required, relative to a reference household, to attain a given level of welfare at fixed prices:[12]

$$m_0(\mathbf{p}, V_k, \mathbf{A}_k) = \frac{M(\mathbf{p}, V_k, \mathbf{A}_k)}{M(\mathbf{p}, V_k, \mathbf{A}_R)},$$

where $\mathbf{A}_R$ is the vector of attributes of a reference household. Note that this definition is exactly analogous to the definition of the household-specific price index described in the previous subsection. The price index is the relative cost of attaining a given level of well-being as prices change, while the equivalence scale is the relative cost of attaining a given level of utility as demographic characteristics change with prices fixed.

The key element in estimating equivalence scales is the recovery of the expenditure function for different types of households. Therefore, the empirical model used to analyze the change in welfare can be applied to this problem as well. This type of model has been used to estimate U.S. scales by van der Gaag and Smolensky (1982), Jorgenson and Slesnick (1987a), Lazear and Michael (1980) and Nelson (1988). General surveys of the voluminous literature on equivalence scale estimation are presented by Deaton and Muellbauer (1980b), Browning (1992), and Lewbel (1989a).

With the assumption of interpersonal comparability comes objections. The most eloquent critique of the use of household equivalent scales for welfare comparisons was put forward by Pollak and Wales (1979). The essence of the argument is that expenditure patterns provide information only on the household's well-being conditional on their demographic characteristics whereas welfare must be based on their unconditional preferences. The two assessments will typically diverge because conditional estimates do not take into account how the household feels about having the observed characteristics.[13] For example, suppose that the attribute of interest is family size. The equivalence scales derived from household expenditure patterns do not take into account the utility derived from having children. Therefore, a couple that has been trying to have children for years and is finally successful will, with no change in expenditure, be judged to have a decrease in well-being.

9.3.5 Policy Analysis: Dynamic Formulation

I conclude this section by illustrating the econometric approach to welfare analysis using the intertemporal formulation described in section 9.2.3. I compare the impact of a carbon tax on households to the alternative of no carbon tax. To make the comparison revenue neutral, the imposition of carbon taxes is accompanied by a reduction in the marginal tax rate on capital. An intertemporal general equilibrium model is used to project commodity prices, interest rates and total expenditure for each dynasty under the two scenarios.[14] Given these projections, the changes in welfare induced by the imposition of a carbon tax can be measured at a disaggregated level.

Consider, for example, dynasties distinguished by the following demographic characteristics:

1. *Family Size:* 1, 2, 3, 4, 5, 5, 6, and 7 or more persons.

2. *Age of Household Head:* 16–24, 25–34, 35–44, 45–54, 55–64 and 65 and over.

3. *Region of Residence:* Northeast, Midwest, South and West.

4. *Race:* White, Nonwhite.

5. *Type of Residence:* Nonfarm, Farm.

6. *Gender of Household Head:* Male, Female.

I examine 1,344 distinct types of households and twelve wealth categories within each household type for a total of 16,128 household groups.

Since it is difficult to present equivalent variations for each of the more than sixteen thousand household types, a single reference household of size four, white, male head of household, age 35–44, living in the urban Northeast is chosen. I present equivalent variations corresponding to the imposition of a carbon tax for this household type and others that differ in one of the demographic characteristics. I also evaluate these equivalent variations for different levels of wealth. The results are presented in table 9.1.

The "medium" and "high" wealth levels correspond to time paths of total expenditure corresponding to the average and double the average wealth levels. Households with low wealth have a time path of expenditure that is one-half the average. Table 9.1 shows that the equivalent variation is positive for some households and negative for others. For a household of size one with low wealth, the carbon tax results in a welfare gain of $1,399. The equivalent variations increase with wealth and, usually, more than proportionately. For example, a household of size one with a medium level of wealth has an equivalent variation that is more than twice that of low wealth households but less than half that of high wealth households.

The demographic pattern of the equivalent variations is also of interest. For a medium level of wealth, households of size one have an equivalent variation of $3,673 while households of size seven with the same level of wealth have an equivalent variation of $-1,208. The magnitude of the equivalent variation decreases with the age of the head of the household. For a medium wealth household, the equivalent variation is $1,625 for the youngest head of household and $-202 for the oldest. Households living in the West gain the most from the carbon tax, while those living in the South have the greatest loss. Farm households experience losses while nonfarm households gain from a carbon tax.

Although the demographic pattern of the equivalent variations resulting from the imposition of a carbon tax is interesting, an important feature of table 9.1 is that all of the gains and losses are small. This can be seen more clearly in table 9.2 where the equivalent variations are divided by the corresponding levels of wealth. For our reference dynasty—size four with a medium level of wealth—imposition of a carbon tax is equivalent to a gain of 0.01 percent of lifetime wealth.

9.4   Welfare Economics at the Aggregate Level

While the measurement of individual welfare is an essential first step, analysts are primarily concerned with the impact of policies on groups of individuals. For welfare economics to be useful to practitioners, a

Table 9.1
Life equivalent variations (1990 dollars). Reference Dynasty: Size 4, age 35–44, northeast, nonfarm, white, male, head of household

Wealth	Size 1	Size 2	Size 3	Size 4	Size 5	Size 6	Size 7+
Low	1399	371	-121	-391	-511	-778	-1039
Medium	3673	1614	630	89	-151	-686	-1208
High	9095	4974	3005	1923	1442	371	-673
	Age 16–24	Age 25–34	Age 35–44	Age 45–54	Age 55–64	Age 65+	
Low	376	-133	-391	-810	-937	-537	
Medium	1625	605	89	-750	-1004	-202	
High	4996	2954	1923	243	-266	1340	
	Northeast	Midwest	South	West	White	Nonwhite	
Low	-391	-882	-1178	106	-391	-670	
Medium	89	-894	-1486	1084	89	-469	
High	1923	-46	-1230	3914	1923	805	
	Nonfarm	Farm	Male	Female			
Low	-391	-1650	-391	345			
Medium	89	-2431	89	1562			
High	1923	-3121	1923	4870			

Table 9.2
Lifetime equivalent variations as a percent of wealth. Reference Dynasty: Size 4, age 35–44, northeast, nonfarm, white, male

Wealth	Size 1	Size 2	Size 3	Size 4	Size 5	Size 6	Size 7+
Low	0.26	0.07	-0.02	-0.07	-0.10	-0.15	-0.19
Medium	0.34	0.15	0.06	0.01	-0.01	-0.06	-0.11
High	0.43	0.23	0.14	0.09	0.07	0.02	-0.03

	Age 16–24	Age 25–34	Age 35–44	Age 45–54	Age 55–64	Age 65+
Low	0.07	-0.02	-0.07	-0.15	-0.18	-0.10
Medium	0.15	0.06	0.01	-0.07	-0.09	-0.02
High	0.23	0.14	0.09	0.01	-0.01	0.06

	Northeast	Midwest	South	West	White	Nonwhite
Low	-0.07	-0.17	-0.22	0.02	-0.07	-0.13
Medium	0.01	-0.08	-0.14	0.10	0.01	-0.04
High	0.09	-0.005	-0.06	0.18	0.09	0.04

	Nonfarm	Farm	Male	Female
Low	-0.07	-0.31	-0.07	0.06
Medium	0.01	-0.23	0.01	0.15
High	0.09	-0.15	0.09	0.23

method of aggregating the effects of policies on different individuals is essential. An all too common approach is to assume the existence of a representative agent and apply the techniques described in the previous section to aggregate data. This is unappealing because the representative agent assumption has been shown repeatedly to be inconsistent with empirical evidence on demand patterns.[15]

A more sophisticated solution to the aggregation problem is to measure the change in social welfare by summing the equivalent variations across the population.[16] This is unsatisfactory because the procedure is *ad hoc*, has no obvious link to social choice theory, and has no obvious interpretation as an index of social welfare. The sum of equivalent variations, moreover, is typically represented as a positive measure of aggregate welfare even though it is no less normative than an explicit social welfare function.

Using equivalent variations to make social welfare judgments suffers from an additional problem. The equivalent variation is an exact measure of the change in individual welfare for a specific reference price vector. In aggregating the equivalent variations into a measure of social welfare, the ordinal ranking of social states need not be invariant to the choice of reference prices. Let $\mathbf{m}(\mathbf{p},\mathbf{u}) = (M_1(\mathbf{p},W_1)$, $M_2(\mathbf{p},W_2),\ldots,M_K(\mathbf{p},W_K))$ be the vector of individual expenditure functions of all individuals. A social welfare function, say Ψ, defined over the distribution of expenditure functions can be represented as $E(\mathbf{p},\mathbf{u}) = \Psi(m(\mathbf{p},\mathbf{u}))$ where $\mathbf{u} = (W_1,W_2,\ldots,W_K)$. The ordinal ranking of social states must be invariant to the choice of reference prices so that the social welfare function satisfies the condition:

$$E(\mathbf{p},\mathbf{u}) \geq E(\mathbf{p},\mathbf{u}') \quad \text{if and only if} \quad E(\mathbf{p}',\mathbf{u}) \geq E(\mathbf{p}',\mathbf{u}'),$$

for all possible $\mathbf{u}$, $\mathbf{u}'$, $\mathbf{p}$ and $\mathbf{p}'$. This is the property of "price independence" introduced by Roberts (1980a) and it holds only under very restrictive conditions.[17] Given that adding up equivalent variations is an inappropriate basis for policy analysis, it is necessary to develop a suitable measure of social welfare.

9.4.1 Historical Context

By the end of the 1930s economists began to reject welfare judgments founded on (normative) interpersonal comparisons of utility.[18] As a result, the focus of attention returned to the use of the Pareto principle as the foundation for policy prescriptions. If every individual is better off under policy A relative to policy B, then it is socially preferred as well. In this fortuitous circumstance, normative judgments concerning trade-offs in welfare levels are unnecessary. Unfortunately, the Pareto principle can only rarely be applied in practice as the results displayed in table 9.1 illustrate.

To obtain a complete ranking of social states, efforts were made to use the Pareto principle in conjunction with compensation mechanisms. Formulated by Kaldor (1939), Hicks (1940) and Scitovsky (1941) among others, this approach judges policy A to be preferred to policy B if the gainers can compensate the losers to make every individual better off. The fundamental flaw with the "New Welfare Economics" is that many compensation schemes yield inconsistent or intransitive orderings of policies. In addition, Chipman and Moore (1971, 1973) have shown that even transitive compensation mechanisms will yield valid assessments of the relative levels of (potential) welfare only if individual preferences are restricted to be identical and homothetic.[19] As a final nail in the coffin, Sen (1979) points out that the "New Welfare Economics" is, in a sense, irrelevant. If the compensation is not provided, its impact on welfare is never realized and should not influence public policy. If it is provided, one can simply apply the Pareto principle.

Despite these problems, compensation principles remained the method of choice among welfare economists due, in part, to the parallel development of the Arrow (1963) impossibility theorem. This famous result states that, under a set of "reasonable" conditions, the only feasible social welfare function is a dictatorship. To describe it more fully, define R to be the set of complete, reflexive and transitive orderings over the set of social states X. A social welfare functional f is a mapping from the set of individual welfare functions to the set of social orderings so that $f(\mathbf{u}) = f(\mathbf{u}')$ implies $R = R'$ where $\mathbf{u}$ and $\mathbf{u}'$ are vectors of individual welfare functions. Let L_k be the set of admissible individual welfare functions for the k-th individual and define L to be the Cartesian product of all such sets. Finally, let Λ be the partition of L such that all elements of Λ yield the same social ordering. Using this notation, the Arrovian axioms are:

Unrestricted Domain: The social welfare functional f is defined for all possible vectors of individual welfare functions $\mathbf{u}$.

Independence of Irrelevant Alternatives: For any subset A contained in X, if $\mathbf{u}(\mathbf{x}) = \mathbf{u}'(\mathbf{x})$ for all x in A, then $R: A = R': A$, where $R = f(\mathbf{u})$ and $R' = f(\mathbf{u}')$ and $R: A$ is the social ordering over the subset A.

Weak Pareto Principle: For any x, y in X, if $W_i(x) > W_i(y)$ for all individuals i, then xPy.

Ordinal Noncomparability: The set of individual welfare functions that yield the same social ordering Λ is defined by

$$\Lambda = \{\mathbf{u}': \ W_k' = \phi_k(W_k)\},$$

where ϕ_k is increasing and $f(\mathbf{u}) = f(\mathbf{u}')$ for all $\mathbf{u}$ in Λ.

The axiom of unrestricted domain is self-explanatory. Independence of irrelevant alternatives requires the social ranking of any two social states to be independent of a third state. The Pareto principle implies that a social state is socially preferred if every individual (strictly) prefers it. The axiom of ordinal noncomparability implies that the social welfare functional must be invariant to monotonic transformations of individual welfare functions that vary across individuals.

The Arrow impossibility theorem spawned a subfield of economic theory that examined the robustness of the impossibility result. Theorem after theorem demonstrated that modest changes to the axioms left the dictatorial result intact. The inescapable conclusion was that if one precludes interpersonal comparisons of welfare, the *only* logically consistent foundation for welfare analysis was the Pareto principle. Therefore, for economic theorists, welfare economics was (and is) concisely summarized by the two Fundamental Theorems of Welfare Economics relating competitive equilibria to Pareto optimality.

Of course, all of this was bad news for practitioners. The Pareto principle can only rarely be applied in practice and most would agree that a dictatorship is an inappropriate basis for the formation and evaluation of public policy. This, in conjunction with the problems associated with compensation principles, left a gap between what theorists felt was an appropriate foundation for applied welfare economics and what policy analysts felt was needed to provide a complete and consistent assessment of policies.

What additional information is required for policy analysis? While theorists published literally hundreds of papers focusing on impossibility, this fundamental question remained unanswered. The breakthrough occurred with a series of seminal books and papers by Sen (1970, 1973, 1977) who approached the problem of collective choice in

a less nihilistic light. Sen viewed the Arrovian axioms as restrictive
since they rule out by assumption the ability of the analyst to weigh
the gains of the winners against the losses of the losers in ranking
social states. He demonstrated that relaxing the measurability and
comparability assumption expands the spectrum of possible social
welfare functions dramatically. "Possibility" results were synthesized
and extended in a series of important papers by Roberts (1980b,c,d)
and, by the early 1980s, theoretical results demonstrating the existence
of logically consistent, nondictatorial social welfare functions had
been established but remained unexploited empirically.

9.4.2   Applied Social Welfare Analysis

Where does the additional information required to develop a social
welfare function come from? Is it possible to infer interpersonal comparability from household expenditure patterns? The answer is clearly
no. We have known since the Ordinalist Revolution that demand
functions enable us to identify utility functions that are unique up to
monotonic transformations that can differ across individuals. With
ordinal noncomparability, we return to the Arrovian framework with
its limited scope for policy analysis.[20]

Therefore, practical application of welfare economics requires information based, either implicitly or explicitly, on the analyst's assessment of the relative impacts of policies on different households. The
greater the (assumed) ability to measure and compare welfare levels,
the wider the set of possible social welfare functions. Suppose, for
example, that policy makers are able to rank the welfare levels of individuals but cannot measure the magnitudes of the differences in well-
being. In this instance, preferences are ordinally comparable and the
set of possible social welfare functions is a member of the class of positional dicatorships.[21] If the analyst is unable to rank welfare levels, but
can determine that a change in policy hurts individual A twice as
much as individual B, then utilitarian social welfare functions provide
consistent rankings of social states.[22]

Jorgenson and Slesnick (1984a,b) developed a framework that links
the social choice theoretic results of Sen, Roberts and others with an
empirical model designed to measure aggregate welfare. The assumptions of unlimited domain, independence of irrelevant alternatives
and the weak Pareto principle are retained but ordinal noncomparability is replaced with the assumption that *both* levels and differences

in welfare across social states are meaningfully compared across individuals.[23] More formally:

Cardinal Full Comparability: The set of individual welfare functions that yield the same social ordering Λ is defined by:

$$\Lambda = \{\mathbf{u}': W_k' = \alpha + \beta(W_k)\},$$

where $\beta > 0$ and $f(\mathbf{u}) = f(\mathbf{u}')$ for all $\mathbf{u}$ in Λ.

Roberts (1980c) has shown that, under these conditions, the real-valued representation of the social ordering must be of the form:

$$W(\mathbf{u}, x) = \bar{W}(x) + g(W_1 - \bar{W}, W_2 - \bar{W}, \dots, W_K - \bar{W}),$$

where

$$\bar{W} = \sum_{k=1}^{K} a_k W_k,$$

and $g(.)$ is a linearly homogeneous function. To satisfy this condition and maintain as much flexibility as possible, the function g is taken to be a mean value function of order ρ so that the social welfare function is the sum of the mean welfare level and an index of deviations from the mean:

$$W(\mathbf{u}, x) = \sum_{k=1}^{K} a_k W_k - \gamma \left[\sum_{k=1}^{K} a_k |W_k - \bar{W}|^{-\rho} \right]^{-1/\rho}. \tag{9.18}$$

The parameter γ is chosen to ensure that the ranking of social states satisfies the Pareto principle. The curvature of the social welfare function is determined by ρ which can be interpreted as an inequality aversion parameter.

The specification is completed by choosing an explicit representation of the individual welfare function as well as a set of weights $\{a_k\}$ for each individual. The welfare function is represented as a linear function of the logarithm of per equivalent total expenditure:

$$W_k = \alpha_p' \ln \mathbf{p} + 1/2 \ln \mathbf{p}' B_{pp} \ln \mathbf{p} - D(\mathbf{p}) \ln (M_k/m_0(\mathbf{p}, \mathbf{A}_k)). \tag{9.19}$$

The linearity property is preserved only by affine transformations of the welfare function and, in this sense, provides a cardinal representation of individual welfare. This general canonical form, which arises from the exact aggregation conditions, is substantially less restrictive than previous cardinalizations of utility. For example, under the expected utility hypothesis, cardinality is achieved by assuming that utility is additively separable across states of nature. An analogous condition could also be imposed in this context but would be substantially more restrictive than (9.19). The assumption of linear homogeneity of the utility function would provide yet another cardinalization at the cost of imposing unrealistic conditions on the form of preferences.

Since the welfare function is unique up to linear transformations that are the same for every individual, it is possible to compare welfare levels of two individuals facing a common price system. As important, the relative magnitudes of changes in the welfare levels across social states can also be compared. To reiterate, this assumption is absolutely critical to the development of a well-behaved social welfare function since, for any application, it is important to be able to weigh the magnitudes of the gains of the winners against the losses of the losers. Without such comparability, distributional issues can play only a minor role in the formation and evaluation of alternative policies.

The weights $\{a_k\}$ of the social welfare function are chosen to ensure that a transfer from a "rich" individual to a "poor" individual, that does not reverse their relative position, increases social welfare.[24] To satisfy the equity principle the weights must be:

$$a_k = \frac{m_0(\mathbf{p}, \mathbf{A}_k)}{\sum\limits_{k=1}^{K} m_0(\mathbf{p}, \mathbf{A}_k)}.$$

The assumption that progressive transfers increase social welfare implies that the maximum level of social welfare for a fixed level of aggregate expenditure $M = \Sigma M_k$ is attained at the perfectly egalitarian distribution of individual welfare:

$$W_{\max} = \alpha_p' \ln \mathbf{p} + 1/2 \ln \mathbf{p}' B_{pp} \ln \mathbf{p} - D(\mathbf{p}) \ln (M/\Sigma m_0(\mathbf{p}, \mathbf{A_k})). \qquad (9.20)$$

Social welfare is converted into monetary equivalents using the social expenditure function introduced by Pollak (1981). Exactly analogous to the individual expenditure function, it is defined as the minimum level of aggregate expenditure required to attain a specified social welfare contour:

$M(\mathbf{p}, W) = \min \{M : W(\mathbf{u}, x) \geq W, \Sigma M_k = M\}.$

For the social welfare function (9.18), the expenditure function is:

$$\ln M(\mathbf{p}, W) = \frac{1}{D(\mathbf{p})} (\alpha_p' \ln \mathbf{p} + 1/2 \ln \mathbf{p}' B_{pp} \ln \mathbf{p} - W)$$
$$+ \ln(\Sigma m_0(\mathbf{p}, \mathbf{A}_k)). \tag{9.21}$$

I conclude by summarizing the appealing features of this approach to applied welfare analysis. First, the social welfare function is a real-valued representation of a social ordering that is consistent with the fundamental principles of social choice theory. By construction it satisfies the Arrovian axioms of unlimited domain, independence of irrelevant alternatives and the weak Pareto principle. Second, the normative basis of the ranking of states is made explicit through the measurability and comparability assumptions of the individual welfare functions as well as through the equity principle describing the impact of transfers on social welfare. Third, in contrast with *ad hoc* representations of aggregate well-being such as real GNP or national income, this approach incorporates both efficiency and equity concern in ranking outcomes. Fourth, the measures of individual welfare are indirect utility functions that are fully consistent with the theory of consumer behavior. This implies that well-being is a function of prices, consumption and the attributes of the consumer in contrast with the standard procedure of representing welfare by current income alone.

9.5 Applications: The Measurement of Social Welfare

9.5.1 Policy Analysis

Using the framework described in section 9.4, the aggregate welfare impact of alternative policies can be analyzed in a manner exactly analogous to the method used to examine the change in welfare at the micro-level. Let W^0 be the level of social welfare attained under the base case when the distribution of individual welfare is $u^0 = (W_1(\mathbf{p}^0, M_1^0, \mathbf{A}_1), \ldots, W_K(\mathbf{p}^0, M_K^0, \mathbf{A}_K))$. If W^1 is the level of social welfare attained under the policy scenario when the distribution is $u^1 = (W_1(\mathbf{p}^1, M_1^1, \mathbf{A}_1), \ldots, W_K(\mathbf{p}^1, M_K^1, \mathbf{A}_K))$, the change in social welfare, evaluated at base prices, is:

$$\Delta W = M(\mathbf{p}^0, W^1) - M(\mathbf{p}^0, W^0). \tag{9.22}$$

This is an exact monetary measure of the change in social welfare that is positive if and only if social welfare is higher under the policy relative to the base case.

Jorgenson and Slesnick (1985a,b) present a decomposition of the change in welfare into the sum of the change in efficiency and the change in equity. Money metric potential welfare, evaluated at base case prices, is $M(\mathbf{p}^0, W_{max})$ so that the change in potential welfare or efficiency is:

$$\Delta EFF = M(\mathbf{p}^0, W_{max}^1) - M(\mathbf{p}^0, W_{max}^0).$$

Likewise, $[M(\mathbf{p}^0, W) - M(\mathbf{p}^0, W_{max})]$ can be interpreted as a monetary measure of the loss in social welfare attributable to an inequitable distribution of welfare. Thus, a measure of the change in equity is:

$$\Delta EQ = [M(\mathbf{p}^0, W^1) - M(\mathbf{p}^0, W_{max}^1)]$$
$$- [M(\mathbf{p}^0, W^0) - M(\mathbf{p}^0, W_{max}^0)].$$

The change in social welfare is the sum of the change in efficiency and the change in equity:

$$\Delta W = \Delta EFF + \Delta EQ.$$

To illustrate this approach to policy analysis, I evaluate the social welfare impact of carbon taxes with concomitant reductions in taxes on capital. Rather than use the static measure of individual welfare in (9.19), W_k is taken to be the lifetime utility of an infinitely-lived dynasty given in (9.16). Social welfare is represented by (9.18) where the weights a_k are chosen to ensure that progressive transfers of wealth among dynasties increase social welfare. The social welfare impact of carbon taxes is given in table 9.3 for two different representations of the social welfare function. The egalitarian specification corresponds to a social welfare function with the inequality aversion parameter equal to minus one. This gives the greatest weight to efficiency relative to equity in ordering policies. The utilitarian social welfare function places the least weight on equity and corresponds to an inequality aversion parameter equal to minus infinity.

For both specifications, the imposition of carbon taxes reduces social welfare. For the egalitarian welfare function, carbon taxes reduce social welfare by $105 billion (in 1990 dollars) while the loss is $76 billion when the inequality aversion parameter is equal to minus

Table 9.3
Change in Social Welfare

Inequality Aversion	Change in Welfare (billions of 1990 dollars)			Change in Welfare as a Proportion of Wealth (percent)		
	Social Welfare	Efficiency	Equity	Social Welfare	Efficiency	Equity
Egalitarian	−105	241	−345	−0.084	0.193	−0.277
Utilitarian	−76	241	−317	−0.061	0.193	−0.254

infinity. These losses are small proportions of aggregate wealth; 0.084 percent and 0.061 percent, respectively. The decomposition into changes in efficiency and equity shows that carbon taxes (accompanied by a decrease in capital taxes) increase efficiency by $241 billion, or 0.193 percent of total wealth. However, for both social welfare functions, this gain is outweighed by the change in equity which falls $345

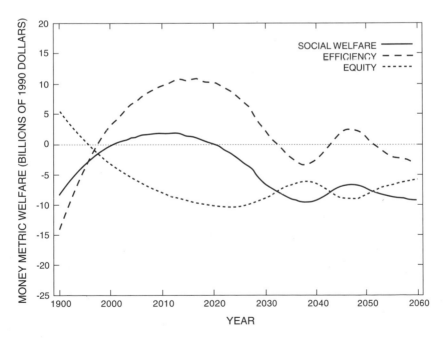

Figure 9.1
Carbon taxes and Social Welfare.

billion and \$317 billion for the egalitarian and utilitarian specifications respectively.

The importance of looking at the intertemporal impacts of policies is illustrated in figure 9.1 which plots the static, single period measures of social welfare, efficiency and equity over the period from 1990 through 2060. There is substantial fluctuation in each measure over time which suggests that a snapshot view of the impact of carbon taxes on social welfare can be misleading. In the early years, for example, the change in equity is positive while efficiency is negative; exactly the opposite result that is obtained using measures of social welfare based on lifetime utility.

9.5.2   Social Welfare Statistics

This general framework can be used to develop social welfare statistics such as indexes of the standard of living or measures of inequality. The advantage of the approach described in section 9.4 is that the statistics are founded on well-developed theoretical models of individual and social choice. This facilitates a meaningful interpretation of the indexes, which contrasts sharply with the *ad hoc* statistics that are frequently used. In what follows, I present examples of statistics founded on economic theory and show that they diverge from the indexes published by governmental statistical agencies.

Social Cost of Living Indexes
One cannot overstate the importance of measuring the cost of living accurately. Not only are price indexes critical inputs to the calculation of social welfare statistics, they are also used to adjust wages, pensions, welfare payments and other government expenditures as prices change. In virtually every application, the key issue is the amount by which nominal wages, benefits, or expenditures must be adjusted to ensure a constant level of well-being. The aggregate price index most commonly used for this purpose is the CPI.

There are a number of reasons why the CPI is ill-suited for this exercise.[25] First, it is a Laspeyres index that is calculated as a fixed, weighted average of price changes and, therefore, does not incorporate adjustments made by households in response to changes in relative prices.[26] A widely recognized defect of the CPI is related to its treatment of housing. Prior to 1983, the weight corresponding to the budget share devoted to owner-occupied housing was inaccurately measured using investment expenditures made by homeowners rather than the flow of services or rental equivalent of the home.[27] This resulted in a permanent upward bias in the price level due to a sharp rise in interest rates in the late 1970s. Perhaps the most serious conceptual problem is that the CPI is a statistical measure of price changes developed in the tradition of Fisher (1922) and does not provide a consistent basis for welfare comparisons.[28]

Jorgenson and Slesnick (1983) developed a social cost-of-living index (SCOLI) as an alternative to the CPI. Using the social welfare function (9.18) and the social expenditure function (9.21), the SCOLI is defined as the ratio of the cost of attaining a given level of social welfare at current prices to that needed to attain the same welfare at base prices:

$$P(\mathbf{p}^1, \mathbf{p}^0, W) = \frac{M(\mathbf{p}^1, W)}{M(\mathbf{p}^0, W)}.$$

The normative basis of this index is made explicit through the choice of the social welfare function and, by design, is meaningfully employed for comparisons of well-being across groups of individuals. If, for example, the SCOLI takes the value 1.5 between 1980 and 1990, this implies that in 1990 society needs 1.5 times the expenditure required in 1980 to attain a constant level of social welfare.

Does the SCOLI yield dramatically different estimates of inflation in the United States? In figure 9.2 I compare the inflation rates measured using the SCOLI with those obtained using the CPI over the period from 1947 to 1995. While the same qualitative pattern of movements in prices is found for each index, there are sizable differences in the magnitudes of the inflation rates in some years. Over the entire sample period the average annual inflation rate measured by the CPI was 4.0 percent compared to 3.8 percent obtained using the SCOLI. Over subperiods the differences were amplified. From 1970–1980 the average annual inflation rate based on the CPI is 7.5 percent per year compared to 6.7 percent per year for the SCOLI. Between 1979–1980 the CPI inflation rate was 12.7 percent compared to 9.9 percent obtained using the SCOLI.[29]

The Standard of Living
Jorgenson and Slesnick (1990a) have used this framework to measure the aggregate standard of living in the United States using the index:

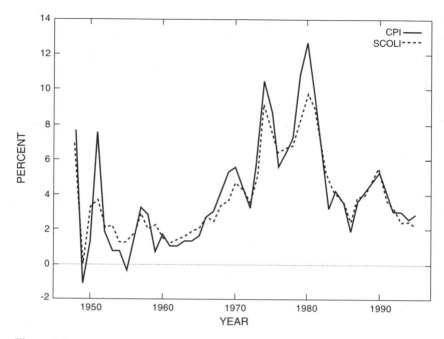

Figure 9.2
Inflation rates.

$$Q(\mathbf{p}^0, W) = \frac{M(\mathbf{p}^0, W)}{\Sigma m_0(\mathbf{p}^0, \mathbf{A}_k)} , \tag{9.23}$$

where $\mathbf{p}^0$ is a vector of reference prices and W is the level of social welfare. Evaluated at the potential level of welfare, the index can be interpreted as the level of consumption per adult equivalent member:

$$Q(\mathbf{p}^0, W) = \frac{\Sigma M_k}{P(\mathbf{p}^1, \mathbf{p}^0, W) \, \Sigma m_0(\mathbf{p}^0, \mathbf{A}_k)} .$$

There are several features of this index that distinguish it from more familiar indexes of the standard of living. First, it is a function of total expenditure and is based on consumption rather than income. Second, nominal expenditures are deflated by the SCOLI rather than a statistical price index such as the CPI. Finally, changes in the demographic composition of the population are incorporated through estimates of the total number of household equivalent members.

The logarithm of the consumption-based standard of living index is presented in figure 9.3 and exhibits an average annual growth rate of

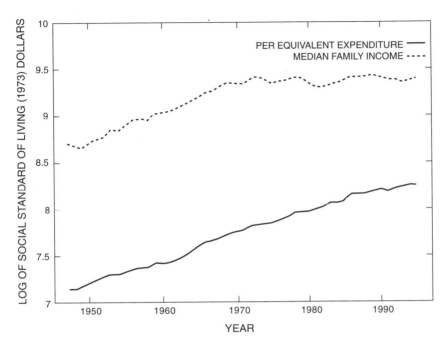

Figure 9.3
Standard of living in the U.S.

2.3 percent per year over the period from 1947 through 1995. From 1947 to 1971 the average growth rate was 2.6 percent per year compared to 1.9 percent per year over the latter half of the sample period. The lower growth rate can be attributed to several deep recessions in the mid-1970s, the early 1980s and the beginning of the 1990s. The average annual growth rate by decades was 2.1 percent in the 1950s, 3.4 percent in the 1960s, 2.1 percent in the 1970s, 2.3 percent in the 1980s, and 0.8 percent in the first half of the 1990s.

The consumption-based measure of the standard of living contrasts sharply with real median family income, also presented in figure 9.3, which is frequently used as an indicator of living standards.[30] This index grew at roughly the same rate as per equivalent consumption between 1947 and 1971 but subsequently diverged. Over the first half of the sample period real median family income grew at a rate of 2.6 percent per year but exhibited little net change from 1971 to 1995. This suggests that real median family income presents a biased picture of the trend of the standard of living in the United States.[31]

Daniel T. Slesnick

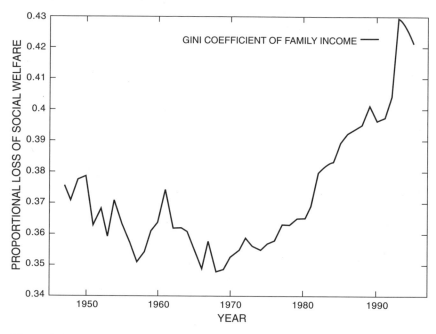

Figure 9.4
Income inequality in the U.S.

Inequality

A casual examination of the menu of government programs indicates that distributional considerations play a central role in the formation of public policy in the United States. There are enormous expenditures on social insurance and transfer programs that are designed both to provide a minimal standard of living for the poor as well as to reduce the level of inequality. Given this fact, it is troubling and surprising that government statistics have indicated a reversal in the general downward trend in the level of income inequality. Figure 9.4 shows that the Gini coefficient of family income fell from a level of 0.376 in 1947 to 0.348 in 1968. Subsequently, income inequality increased to 0.429 in 1993.[32] The attention of researchers has been directed towards obtaining an explanation for the infamous *U*-turn in inequality.

While an examination of income inequality could reveal interesting and important features of labor markets,[33] it is not particularly informative about the distribution of well-being in the United States. Interpreting the Gini coefficient of family income as a measure of dispersion in welfare implicitly assumes that families with the same

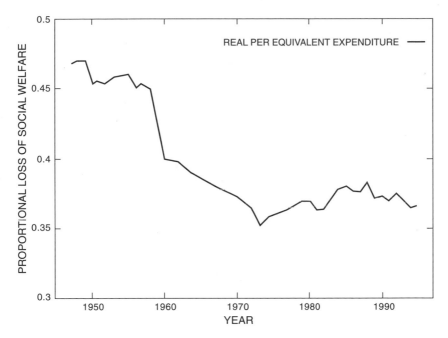

Figure 9.5
Inequality in the U.S.

level of before-tax income are equally well-off. Utility, however, is derived from the consumption of goods and services and there is ample evidence, emanating from Friedman's (1957) permanent income hypothesis, which suggests that the distribution of total expenditure is likely to be quite different from the distribution of income.

Jorgenson and Slesnick (1984a,b) developed a measure of inequality in which individual welfare is represented by (9.19). Following Atkinson (1970), Kolm (1969) and Sen (1973), inequality is defined as the proportional loss in social welfare attributable to an inequitable distribution of well-being. If W is the actual level of social welfare and $W_{\max}$ is the potential level of social welfare attained at the perfectly egalitarian distribution of household welfare, a monetary measure of relative inequality is given by:

$$I(\mathbf{p}, W, W_{\max}) = 1 - \frac{M(\mathbf{p}, W)}{M(\mathbf{p}, W_{\max})} . \tag{9.24}$$

Using the social expenditure function (9.21), this simplifies to:

$$I(\mathbf{p}, W, W_{\max}) = 1 - \exp\left(\frac{1}{D(\mathbf{p})}(W - W_{\max})\right).$$

In figure 9.5 I present a consumption-based measure of inequality and observe that its trend is quite different from the income inequality index.[34] The level of inequality fell from 0.47 in 1947 to 0.40 in 1961, decreased through 1973, and subsequently changed very little over the remainder of the sample period. Since 1970 there has been very little net change in inequality; the widely reported U-turn in inequality in the United States is not found using a consumption-based index.

Poverty

The general framework for applied welfare analysis can also be used to measure the extent of poverty. Again, largely inspired by the work of Sen (1976), a line of theoretical work has developed to measure the level of aggregate poverty.[35] Jorgenson and Slesnick (1989) have contributed to this literature by extending their approach to inequality measurement to the evaluation of poverty. Specifically, poverty is measured as the social welfare loss that results from the existence of individuals living below the poverty line. So defined, it can be interpreted as the gain to society that would result from redistributional policy that eliminates poverty.

The importance of a coherent framework for welfare analysis lies not so much in the specific poverty index but in the choice of the individual welfare measure. To illustrate, I measure poverty using the widely-criticized head count ratio which is defined as the proportion of individuals with welfare levels less than an exogenously chosen threshold. The Bureau of the Census publishes poverty statistics for the United States based on income data from the *Current Population Surveys*. If W_z is the threshold level of welfare, the Census index is the proportion of individuals belonging to households with $W_k < W_z$ where:

$$W_k = \frac{Y_k}{\Pi m_f(A_k)}, \tag{9.25}$$

where Y_k is the before-tax income of the k-th household, $m_f(A_k)$ is a nutritional equivalence scale and Π is the CPI.

The Census' estimates of poverty are presented in figure 9.6. Between 1959 and 1973 the Census reports that the proportion of persons below the poverty line fell from 0.224 to a postwar low of 0.111. Between 1973 and 1979 the head-count ratio increased slightly. There was a surge in the level of poverty over the recession years of the early 1980s and then a modest decline. The level of poverty in 1993 exceeded the level in 1965 implying that little progress has been made in rectifying the plight of the poor.

The Census' poverty measure is plagued by three problems. First, household welfare is evaluated using before-tax income even though poverty is defined using the concept of consumption. I have shown (Slesnick, 1993) that income is a poor proxy for consumption, even for those below the poverty line. Second, the needs of the household are represented solely through a nutritional equivalence scale rather than through an equivalence scale defined over all commodities in the budget. Finally, only absolute price effects are incorporated in evaluating well-being using (9.25) even though relative price changes could have a substantial impact on the well-being of the poor. For a given absolute change in the price level, an increase in the price of necessities relative to luxuries will have a different impact on the level of poverty than would an increase in the relative price of luxuries. Furthermore, as demonstrated in figure 9.2, the CPI provides an upward biased estimate of inflation, particularly in the early 1980s.

A poverty index that does not have these shortcomings can be obtained by determining the proportion of individuals belonging to households with $W_k < W_z$ where household welfare is defined by (9.19). Such an index is based on consumption, incorporates relative price effects and uses an equivalence scale defined over the entire budget. When poverty is evaluated using this consumption-based welfare function, a completely different picture emerges. Figure 9.6 reveals that the poverty rate decreased from 0.308 in 1947 to 0.102 in 1978. As with the income-based index, the head count increased in 1980 but, unlike the Census measure, decreased over the remainder of the sample period. While the Census reports no net change in the poverty rate over the last thirty years, the consumption-based head-count ratio decreased from 0.145 in 1966 to 0.095 in 1995. Furthermore, the official income-based index overstates the level of poverty in every year. In 1995 the Census poverty rate was 0.138 compared to 0.095 for welfare functions based on total expenditure.

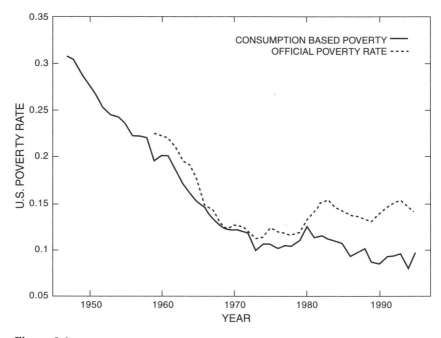

Figure 9.6
Poverty in the U.S.

9.6   Conclusions

The volume of research devoted to welfare economics is evidence of its central importance to applied economics. For years, there was a division between the state of art as described by theorists and the methods used by policy analysts. Jorgenson's research has bridged this gap, demonstrating that empirical work in welfare economics can have a solid theoretical foundation. At the micro-level, consumer's surplus remains the proverbial workhorse for practitioners in spite of repeated demonstrations of its inadequacy as an indicator of individual welfare. The approach developed by Jorgenson provides an exact representation of well-being with no increase in data requirements.

In retrospect, this was the easy part of the general problem of welfare measurement. The more important and difficult issue was the aggregation of the impacts of price and income changes across the population. As is typical in dealing with empirical macroeconomic issues, this problem is most often finessed by assuming the existence of a representative agent and applying microeconomic principles to make statements about social welfare. Ignoring the overwhelming empirical evidence against the representative consumer model, this common approach to the measurement of aggregate welfare suffers from a number of additional shortcomings.

There is an implicit assumption that aggregate demand patterns can, in some way, be used to make normative judgements concerning the ranking of alternative policies. In fact, social welfare judgments require considerably more information than can be revealed from aggregate demand. In section 9.4 it was demonstrated that assumptions of measurability and, most important, comparability of individual welfare levels are required in order to meaningfully aggregate the individual welfare effects into a social welfare function. This information is not revealed through consumer behavior, even if the data are consistent with a representative agent. As important, the welfare judgments based on a representative consumer do not include the distributional effects of policies.

The econometric approach to the measurement of individual and social welfare overcomes many of the obstacles that were considered insurmountable. The welfare measures are tied explicitly to the theory of consumer behavior so that indicators of the change in well-being have a consistent and meaningful interpretation. The measures of social welfare are based on the basic principles of social choice ensuring consistent rankings of alternative policies. The normative judgments that are inevitable in the analysis of social welfare are made explicit in comparing social states. The models are flexible and have the same data requirements as commonly used methods. This is not to suggest that these methods are easy to use; complicated questions often call for complicated answers. Jorgenson has not only shown us that these questions have answers, he has shown us how to answer them.

Notes

1. This was pointed out over fifty years ago by Samuelson (1947).
2. For a proof of this result and further discussion, see Chipman and Moore (1976, 1980). They also demonstrate that if incomes change along with prices, there are no conditions under which consumer's surplus will provide an exact measure of the change in welfare.
3. See, for example, the survey by Houthakker (1957) marking the *centennial* anniversary of Engel's Law.
4. Note, however, that only the equivalent variation provides consistent rankings of more than two states. See Chipman and Moore (1980) for further elaboration.

5. See, also, Muellbauer (1974). Rosen (1978) developed a similar approach to the measurement of the excess burden of taxation.

6. This measure of welfare was later termed the equivalent gain by King (1983).

7. See Jorgenson (1990) for more details.

8. Barro (1974) demonstrates the equivalence between a household with an infinite time horizon and generations linked by intergenerational altruism. Laitner (1991) show how similar household types are linked through time by assortative mating.

9. Diamond and McFadden (1974) actually present the compensating variation definition of the deadweight loss. The equivalent variation version presented below was originally developed by Mohring (1971). Excellent surveys and syntheses of the measurement of the excess burden of taxation are presented by Auerbach (1985), Diewert (1985) and Kay and Keen (1988).

10. Diewert (1990) provides an excellent synthesis of the theoretical issues involved with price indexes.

11. See Blackorby and Donaldson (1988b) and Lewbel (1989a) for a formal statement of the degree of comparability required to assess the needs of households using household equivalence scales.

12. Pashardes (1991) and Banks, Blundell and Preston (1994) have extended this general approach to equivalence scale estimation by considering the cost of children in an intertemporal context.

13. For additional elaboration, see the excellent discussion in Pollak (1991). Blundell and Lewbel (1991) represent this issue as an econometric identification problem.

14. The general equilibrium model of the U.S. economy is described in detail by Jorgenson and Wilcoxen (1990b).

15. See, for example, the surveys by Kirman (1992) and Stoker (1993).

16. This approach is advocated by Harberger (1971), Diewert (1981) and King (1983).

17. Other limitations associated with the use of money metric utility functions as arguments of social welfare functions are described by Blackorby and Donaldson (1985, 1988a). See, also, Slesnick (1991a).

18. Robbins (1938) critique of this approach to welfare economics has been taken to be the watershed event that shifted the focus from the prevalent use of utilitarianism to an exclusive reliance on the Pareto principle.

19. Ruiz-Castillo (1987) has extended these results to the sum of the equivalent and compensating variations as indicators of potential welfare. Blackorby and Donaldson (1990) present a survey of this approach to welfare economics.

20. It is possible to have a nondictatorial social welfare function without interpersonal comparability if other axioms are relaxed. However, the possibilities remain quite limited. For example, if preferences are single-peaked (i.e., unrestricted domain is relaxed) the social welfare function is majority rule and aggregate preferences are those of the median voter. Thus, a dictatorial social welfare function is replaced by a "positional" dictatorship in which the median voter is decisive.

21. This assumes that the other Arrovian axioms are maintained. Hammond (1976), Roberts (1980b), and Sen (1977) refer to this degree of comparability as ordinal level comparability and demonstrate the axiomatic basis for Rawls (1971) difference principle.

22. This is the assumption of cardinal unit comparability. For further details, see Maskin (1978) and Roberts (1980c).

23. This implies that individual welfare can be measured in the same way as thermal temperature. That is, using either the Fahrenheit or Centigrade scales, it is possible to indicate that one day is colder than another and to measure the relative magnitude of changes in the temperature.

24. This equity principle was originally introduced by Hammond (1977).

25. The problems with the CPI are summarized by Boskin *et al.* (1997).

26. The empirical magnitude of this "substitution bias" has been estimated by Braithwait (1980) and Manser and McDonald (1988).

27. A more comprehensive discussion of the biases in the CPI is presented by Gillingham and Lane (1982).

28. Pollak (1990) demonstrates that a fixed weight price index, such as the CPI, has a welfare-theoretic interpretation only under extremely restrictive and unrealistic circumstances that a representative consumer exists and has Leontief preferences.

29. I have found (Slesnick, 1991b) that the estimated inflation rates obtained from the SCOLI are generally insensitive to the normative basis of the cost-of-living index. That is, SCOLI for different social welfare functions give virtually identical estimates of inflation.

30. The estimates of median family income are obtained from the *Current Population Surveys* and are reported in various issues of the Current Population Reports, Series P–60.

31. Slesnick (1991c) reports that mean household income exhibits the same biases in trends at all levels of aggregation.

32. See table 12 in the Current Population Reports, Series P-60, No. 162, p. 42 and table B-7, Current Population Reports, Series P-60, No. 180, p. B-11.

33. See, for example, Levy and Murnane (1992).

34. An explanation for these differences is provided by Slesnick (1994).

35. See Foster (1984) for a survey.

10

The Cost of Capital and Intertemporal General Equilibrium Modeling of Tax Policy Effects

Kun-Young Yun

10.1 Introduction

Since Dale Jorgenson's seminal paper on capital theory and investment behavior (1963), the cost of capital has served as a central concept for explaining investment behavior and capital allocation. There are a number of reasons why Jorgenson's theory of capital has been so successful. One is that it is derived from explicit optimization of firm behavior. Another is that it provides an elegant and convenient conceptual framework for measuring the effects of various tax policy instruments such as tax rates, investment tax credit, depreciation, and interest deduction. It is also versatile enough to incorporate firm's financial behavior concerning capital structure and dividend payment.

In the 1960s and early 1970s, the cost of capital approach provided a new perspective for national income and product accounting, and was used in the analyses of investment behavior and productivity change. Later, it was also employed in the analyses of technological change and economic growth, consumer behavior, producer behavior, tax reform, energy and resources, environmental regulation, etc. As the originator of the cost of capital approach, Jorgenson was one of the most intensive users of it.

In 1980, Auerbach and Jorgenson extended the cost of capital approach by introducing the concept of effective tax rate. Ever since, the cost of capital and the effective tax rate have been widely used in the analysis of capital income taxation. For example, in the policy debates which preceded the two major tax reforms of the Reagan Administration,[1] the cost of capital and effective tax rate were routinely computed to evaluate alternative reform proposals for capital income taxation. The cost of capital approach was also proved to be useful for international comparison of capital income taxation.[2]

Since cost of capital represents the price of capital services, it plays important roles in resource allocation at the intratemporal and intertemporal margins. Thus an intertemporal general equilibrium model (IGEM) is an ideal place to implement the cost of capital approach. In this sense, Jorgenson's work in intertemporal general equilibrium modeling is a natural extension of his earlier work on the cost of capital. In addition, IGEM opened a new area of research for Jorgenson where most of his earlier work can be tied together to form a theoretically consistent and practical framework.

We have four objectives in this chapter: first, we present a recent version of the cost of capital formula. In particular, we extend the standard expression for the cost of capital by incorporating most of the current policy instruments for capital income taxation. We also model those tax policy instruments which were considered in the process of the 1981 and 1986 tax reforms in the U.S. Second, we present an IGEM developed by Jorgenson and Yun. This model incorporates the cost of capital approach and is employed for the analyses of fiscal policies, especially tax policies. Third, we present an analytical framework for welfare analysis. A special feature of the analytical framework is the use of an intertemporal expenditure function which enables us to express differential welfare effects of policy changes in terms of the Hicksian variations in full wealth. Finally, we present some interesting summary results from three sets of simulations employing the Jorgenson and Yun model.

The chapter is organized as follows. In section 10.2, we derive a set of expressions for the cost of capital in the corporate, noncorporate, and household sectors. In addition, we present an aggregation scheme for the effects of asset specific tax policy and the rate of economic depreciation. This method is useful for implementing the cost of capital approach in general equilibrium models in which asset classifications are more aggregated in the model than in the tax provisions. We also discuss two alternative ways of representing of the cost of capital in general equilibrium models.

Section 10.3 describes basic structure of the IGEM developed by Jorgenson and Yun. The model consists of the household, producer, government, and the rest of the world sectors. In the household sector, the representative consumer is endowed with perfect foresight and infinite time horizon. He maximizes intertemporal welfare through optimal allocation of lifetime wealth intertemporally across time periods, and intratemporally among leisure, nondurable goods, and capital services. The producer maximizes the wealth of share-holders. He employs capital and labor services to produce consumption and investment goods. Government collects taxes, issues debts to finance budget deficits, and pays interest on outstanding debts. The rest of the world trades with the U.S. in consumption goods, investment goods, and labor, and receives transfer payments.

In section 10.4, we present the analytical framework for welfare analysis in the context of the Jorgenson and Yun model. We also present some interesting results from three applications of the model. In the applications, we analyze the welfare effects of various tax reforms, excess burden of taxation, and marginal cost of public spending. Section 10.5 concludes the chapter with a few remarks.

10.2   The Cost of Capital

10.2.1   Measuring the Cost of Capital

In the absence of capital income taxation, the cost of capital is simply equal to the sum of the equilibrium rate of return on investment and the rate of economic depreciation. However, with taxation of income from capital, the expressions for the cost of capital become quite complicated. In the following, we present the expressions for the cost of capital derived by Jorgenson and Yun (1991). Since the taxation of capital income originating from the corporate sector is the most complicated, we begin with the corporate sector. Then we obtain the expressions for the noncorporate and household sectors by analogy.

10.2.1.1   *Corporate Cost of Capital*
In the absence of uncertainty, the shareholder of a corporate firm is in a portfolio equilibrium if the expected rate of return on his wealth is equal to the required nominal rate of return, r:

$$(1-t_c^e)D + \frac{dV}{ds} - S - t_c^g\left(\frac{dV}{ds} - S - DC \cdot \pi \cdot V\right) = r \cdot V \tag{10.1}$$

where t_c^e is the marginal tax rate of dividend, D is dividend, V is the market value of the firm's shares, S is the value of new share issues, t_c^g is the accrual based marginal tax rate of capital gains on corporate equity, DC is the fraction of nominal asset revaluation to be excluded for the individual income tax purposes, π is the rate of inflation in the price of assets, and s denotes time.[3] If nominal capital gains are fully taxed, $DC = 0$, and if capital gains are perfectly indexed against inflation, $DC = 1$. Equation (10.1) implies that the nominal returns to corporate equity is equal to the sum of dividend received and nominal capital gains, both measured after individual income taxes. Solving (10.1) for V under the appropriate transversality condition, we obtain:

$$V_t = \int_t^\infty \left[\frac{1-t_c^e}{1-t_c^g} D - S \right] e^{-(r-DC\pi t_c^g)(s-t)/(1-t_c^g)} \, ds \, . \tag{10.2}$$

Under the traditional view on dividend behavior, dividend may be expressed as a constant fraction of the after-tax corporate profits:

$$D = \alpha\{p \cdot F(K, L) - w \cdot L - (1 - ITC - t_c \cdot z)qK[\beta_c(i - \pi) + \delta] \\ - R_c^y - R_c^p\} \tag{10.3}$$

where α is the dividend payout ratio, p is the price of output, $F(\cdot)$ is the production function of the firm, K is capital input, L is labor input, w is wage rate, ITC is the rate of investment tax credit, t_c is the statutory rate of corporate income tax, z is the present value of tax depreciation, q is the price of capital good, β_c, is the debt/asset ratio of the firm, i is the nominal rate of interest on debt, δ is the rate of economic depreciation, R_c^y is the Federal and state and local corporate income tax liabilities, and R_c^p is the property tax liabilities.[4]

Assume that a fraction DI of interest paid and a fraction DD of dividend paid are deductible for Federal and state and local income tax purposes, and that a fraction DSL_i of the state and local income taxes are deductible for Federal income tax purposes. Further assume that property taxes are fully deductible for the state and local income tax purposes but only a fraction DSL_c is deductible for the Federal income tax purposes. Then R_c^y can be written

$$R_c^y = t_c[p \cdot F(\cdot) - wL - (1 - ITC - t_c \cdot z)\beta_c qK(1 - DI)i - DD \cdot D] \\ - [t_c^s + t_c^f(DSL_c - DSL_i \cdot t_c^s)]R_c^p \, , \tag{10.4}$$

where t_c^f and t_c^s are the Federal and state and local corporate income tax rates, respectively, and $t_c \equiv t_c^f + t_c^s - DSL_i \cdot t_c^f \cdot t_c^s$ is the corporate income tax rate reflecting both the Federal and the state and local income taxes.

Under the Fisher's law, where inflation raises nominal interest rate point for point, a complete indexing of interest deduction is represented by $DI = \pi/i$. If $DI > \pi/i$, tax deduction of interest payment exceeds the real interest cost and part of the inflation premium included in the nominal interest payment is also deducted. As a result, the effective tax burden on capital is reduced by inflation. On the other hand if $DI < \pi/i$, interest deduction does not cover total real interest payment and part of the inflation premium is taxed. The result is that effective tax burden is increased by inflation.

Making use of (10.3), (10.4), and the relationship $R_c^p = q \cdot K \cdot t_c^p$, where t_c^p is property tax rate, we can express dividend as:

$$D = \frac{\alpha}{1 - \alpha \cdot DD \cdot t_c} \{(1 - t_c)(p \cdot F(\cdot) - wL)$$
$$- (1 - ITC - t_c \cdot z)qK[\beta_c((1 - (1 - DI)t_c)i - \pi) + \delta]$$
$$- qK[1 - (t_c^s + t_c^f(DSL_c - DSL_i \cdot t_c^s))]t_c^p \} . \tag{10.5}$$

Under the traditional view on dividend behavior, marginal source of equity financing is new share issue, and the firm maximizes market value of its shares (V) subject to the cash flow constraint

$$D + (1 - ITC - t_c \cdot z)q[K\delta + (1 - \beta_c)I]$$
$$= p \cdot F(\cdot) - wL - (1 - ITC - t_c \cdot z)\beta_c qK(i - \pi) - R_c^y - R_c^p + S \tag{10.6}$$

and the dynamic equation

$$\frac{\partial K}{\partial s} = I \tag{10.7}$$

where I is net investment.

The present value Hamiltonian for the firm's dynamic problem can be written (suppressing time subscripts):

$$H = \left[\frac{1 - t_c^e}{1 - t_c^g} D - S + \lambda I \right] e^{-(r - DC \cdot \pi \cdot t_c^g)(s-t)/(1-t_c^g)} \tag{10.8}$$

where λ is the multiplier associated with (10.7). Making use of (10.5), (10.6), and the first-order conditions

$$\frac{\partial H}{\partial I} = 0$$
$$\frac{\partial H}{\partial K} + \frac{d}{ds} \left(\lambda e^{-(r - DC \cdot \pi \cdot t_c^g)(s-t)/(1-t_c^g)} \right) = 0$$

and invoking the equality between the cost of C_c, and the marginal value product of capital, $p \cdot \partial F / \partial k$, we obtain the following expression for the cost of capital in the corporate sector:

$$\frac{C_c}{q} = \frac{1 - ITC - t_c z}{1 - t} (r_c + \delta) + \gamma_c t_c^p \tag{10.9}$$

where r_c is the after-tax discount rate for corporate investments and γ_c adjusts the effect of property taxes on the cost of capital for the deduction of property taxes for Federal and state and local income tax purposes and for the deduction of state and local income taxes for Federal income tax purposes. r_c and γ_c are defined as:

$$r_c = (1 - \beta_c) \frac{[r - \pi(1 - (1 - DC)t_c^g)](1 - \alpha \cdot DD \cdot t_c)}{1 - [\alpha \cdot t_c^e + (1 - \alpha)t_c^g]}$$
$$+ \beta_c[(1 - (1 - DI)t_c)i - \pi] \tag{10.10}$$

and

$$\gamma_c = \frac{1 - \left[t_c^s + t_c^f (DSL_c - DSL_i \cdot t_c^s) \right]}{1 - t_c}. \tag{10.11}$$

Equation (10.10) shows that γ_c is a weighted average of the discount rates for the purely equity financed ($\beta_c = 0$) and the purely debt financed ($\beta_c = 1$) investments. It also shows how indexing of capital gains and interest payments against inflation and deduction of dividends-paid affect the discount rate and the cost of capital.

As an illustration, consider the case in which $DC = DD = DI = 0$. Then (10.10) corresponds to the discount rate for corporate equity under the current U.S. law. Alternatively, if $DC = DD = \alpha = 1$ and $DI = \pi/i$, capital gains and interest payments are perfectly indexed against inflation and the entire equity share of the capital income is paid out as dividend, which is deductible for corporate tax purposes. In this case, the tax treatment of equity income is formally identical with that of interest income in the sense that, both for equity and debt financing, real financial costs are fully deductible for corporate income tax purposes.

Equation (10.11) shows how the deduction of state and local income and property taxes for Federal income tax purposes and the deduction of property taxes for state and local income tax purposes affect the effect of property taxes on the cost of capital. If the state and local income and property taxes are fully deductible for Federal income tax purposes, as they are under the current U.S. tax law, $DSL_i = DSL_c = 1$, $\gamma_c = 1$, and property taxes increase the cost of capital point for point. If the state and local taxes are not deductible for the Federal income tax purposes, then the property taxes are deductible only for the state and local income tax purposes. In this case $DSL_i = DSL_c = 0$ and $\gamma_c = (1-t_c^s)/(1-t_c)$.

It is useful to note that the after corporate tax real rate of return, say r_c^{cr}, can be written:

$$r_c^{cr} = (1-\beta_c)\frac{r-\pi[1-(1-DC)t_c^g]}{1-[\alpha \cdot t_c^e + (1-\alpha)t_{i.}^g]} + \beta_c(i-\pi) \qquad (10.12)$$

and the private real rate of return on corporate assets, r_c^{pr}, can be written:

$$r_c^{pr} = (1-\beta_c)(r-\pi)+\beta_c\left[(1-(1-DI)t_c^i)i-\pi\right] \qquad (10.13)$$

where t_c^i is the marginal tax rate of interest income originating from the corporate sector, and the superscripts cr and pr stand for "after corporate tax real" and "private real," respectively.

10.2.1.2 Noncorporate Cost of Capital

The expression for cost of capital in the noncorporate sector can be derived in a similar way. It can also be inferred directly from (10.9), (10.10), and (10.11):

$$\frac{C_n}{q} = \frac{1-ITC-t_n^e \cdot z}{1-t_n^e}(r_n+\delta)+\gamma_n t_n^p \qquad (10.14)$$

where r_n is the after-tax discount rate for noncorporate investments and γ_n adjusts for the deduction of the property taxes and state and local income taxes. r_n and γ_n are defined as:

$$r_n = (1-\beta_n)\lfloor r-\pi(1-(1-DC)t_n^g)\rfloor+\beta_n\lfloor(1-(1-DI)t_n^e)i-\pi\rfloor \qquad (10.15)$$

$$\gamma_n = \frac{1-\left[t_n^{es}+t_n^{ef}(DSL_n - DSL_i \cdot t_n^{es})\right]}{1-t_n^e} \qquad (10.16)$$

where t_n^{ef} and t_n^{es} are the Federal and the state and local marginal tax rates of noncorporate equity income, respectively, and $t_n^e \equiv t_n^{ef}+t_n^{es}-DSL_i \cdot t_n^{ef} \cdot t_n^{es}$ is the marginal income tax rate reflecting both Federal and state and local income taxes.

The private real rate of return on noncorporate assets, r_n^{pr}, can be inferred from (10.13):

$$r_n^{pr} = (1-\beta_n)(r-\pi)+\beta_n\left[(1-(1-DI)t_n^i)i-\pi\right]. \tag{10.17}$$

10.2.1.3 Household Cost of Capital

As in the case of the noncorporate sector, we can also infer from (10.9), (10.10), (10.11) and (10.13) the expressions for the cost of capital, discount rate, and the private real rate of return for the assets in the household sector. The cost of capital can be written:

$$\frac{C_h}{q} = (r_n+\delta)+\gamma_h t_h^p \tag{10.18}$$

where r_h is the after-tax discount rate for household investments and γ_h adjusts for the deduction of the property taxes and state and local income taxes. The expressions for r_h and γ_h are

$$r_h = (1-\beta_h)\left[r-\pi(1-(1-DC)t_h^g)\right]+\beta_h\left[(1-DHI\cdot(1-HDI)t_h^e)i-\pi\right] \tag{10.19}$$

and

$$\gamma_h = 1-\left[t_h^{es}+t_h^{ef}(DSL_h-DSL_i\cdot t_h^{es})\right] \tag{10.20}$$

where t_h^{ef} and t_h^{es} are the Federal and the state and local marginal tax rates of household equity owners, respectively, and $t_h^e \equiv t_h^{ef} + t_h^{es} - DSL_i\cdot t_h^{ef}\cdot t_h^{es}$ is the marginal income tax rate reflecting both Federal and state and local income taxes. HDI is the fraction of nominal interest payment deductible for individual income tax purposes and DHI is the fraction of the indexed interest expenses deductible for individual income tax purposes.[5] The private real rate of return on household assets, r_h^{pr}, can be written:

$$r_h^{pr} = (1-\beta_h)(r-\pi)+\beta_h\left[(1-(1-DI)t_h^i)i-\pi\right]. \tag{10.21}$$

10.2.2 Aggregation of the Cost of Capital over Assets

In the U.S., asset classifications for investment tax credit and tax depreciation are substantially more detailed than those in any practical IGEM. Therefore, in order to represent the cost of capital in an

IGEM, it is necessary to aggregate tax parameters to the level of asset classification in the model.

Suppose that one class of asset in the model corresponds to J types of assets in the tax code. The cost of capital for one dollar's worth of asset type j can be written:

$$\frac{C_j}{q_j} = \frac{1 - ITC_j - t \cdot z_j}{1-t}[R + \delta_j] + t_j^p \qquad j = 1, \dots, J \qquad (10.22)$$

where R is the after-tax discount rate of the firm, and the subscript j denotes the asset type j. We assume that R is the same for all assets in the firm.

The value of capital services generated from asset type j, say, VKS_j, is

$$VKS_j = C_j \cdot VK_j \qquad (10.23)$$

where $VK_j \equiv K_j \cdot q_j$ is the value of capital stock in asset type j and K_j is the corresponding quantity of asset. Since the total value of capital services from the class of assets in consideration should not be affected by the aggregation,

$$\sum_{j=1}^{J}\left[\left\{\frac{1 - ITC_j - t \cdot z_j}{1-t}(R + \delta_j) + t_j^p\right\}VK_j\right]$$
$$= \left[\frac{1 - ITC - t \cdot z}{1-t}(R + \delta) + t^p\right]\sum_{j=1}^{J} VK_j \qquad (10.24)$$

must hold, where the tax policy variables without subscript, i.e., ITC, z, δ, t^p on the right-hand side of (10.24) correspond to the aggregate class of asset in the model. Equation (10.24) suggests that the appropriate weights for aggregation are $(R + \delta_j)VK_j$ for ITC_j and z_j and VK_j, for δ_j and t_j^p.

Notice that the weights for ITC_j and z_j depend upon the after-tax discount rate of the investor and the rate of economic depreciation. Since a less durable asset is replaced more frequently, a heavier weight is applied to an asset with a higher depreciation rate.

10.2.3 Representation of the Cost of Capital in IGEMs

In applied IGEMs, there are two alternative ways of representing the cost of capital. One is to use the effective tax rate introduced by

Auerbach and Jorgenson (1980) and the other is to use the cost of capital expression like the ones derived above.

The effective tax rate is defined as:

$$E \equiv \frac{r^s - r^p}{r^s} \tag{10.25}$$

where r^s is the marginal social rate of return to the capital asset and r^p is the corresponding marginal private rate of return. The marginal productivity of capital, gross of depreciation, may be written as:

$$F_k = q(r^s + \delta) \tag{10.26}$$

where output is used as the numeraire. In a producer equilibrium, marginal productivity of capital is equal to the cost of capital, i.e., $F_k = C$. Combining (10.25), (10.26) and the producer equilibrium condition, we can express the cost of capital as

$$\frac{C}{q} = \left[\frac{r^p}{(1-E)} + \delta \right]. \tag{10.27}$$

Equation (10.27) is simpler than the expression for the cost of capital. In addition, there can be situations where information on some of the determinants of the cost of capital is not available, although there is a short cut to calculate the effective tax rate. For these reasons, (10.27) is frequently used in empirical works.

In a static situation, (10.27) does not present any serious problem as the cost of capital can be represented accurately. However a serious pitfall emerges if the approach is used in an IGEM in which the rate of return to capital varies as the economy moves along a transition path. Suppose tax policy is held fixed along the transition path of the economy in the sense that the statutory tax rate, investment tax credit, and depreciation schedules, etc. remain fixed. As the economy moves from an initial state toward a new steady state, the rate of return to capital varies unless the initial state itself is the steady state. Consequently, the effective tax rate also varies along the transition path.[6]

In practical application of IGEMs where formulas like (10.27) are used to represent the cost of capital, taxation of income from capital is summarized by the effective tax rate at a reference point and a fixed tax policy is typically represented by a constant effective tax rate. Since the true effective tax rate changes as the economy moves along the transition path, a constant effective tax rate fails to represent the tax policy properly.

Although effective tax rate representation of the cost of capital is simple and convenient in a static context, it fails to represent the tax policy accurately in a dynamic context. We conclude that, in an IGEM, complete expression for the cost of capital formula is better suited to represent the tax policy on income from capital. This point is important because, in many applied IGEMs for tax policy analysis, the cost of capital is represented by some measure of effective tax rates.

10.3   Intertemporal General Equilibrium Model

Based on Jorgenson's eariler work, Jorgenson and Yun developed an IGEM which can be used for analyses of U.S. tax policy. In many ways, the model is similar to the Hudson and Jorgenson model (1974a).[7] At the same time, the Jorgenson-Yun model is different from the Hudson and Jorgenson model in a number of important ways. Building upon Hudson and Jorgenson's work, Jorgenson and Yun introduced a number of innovations.

First, myopic expectation on the part of the consumer in the Hudson and Jorgenson model is replaced with perfect foresight. Compared with myopic expectation, perfect foresight may be theoretically more satisfactory although it makes the model computationally more expensive.

Second, the Jorgenson and Yun model has a detailed representation of the U.S. tax system. For example, average and marginal tax rates are distinguished and the expressions for the cost of capital derived in section 10.2 are incorporated. Third, Jorgenson and Yun distinguish capital services in the corporate, noncorporate, and household sectors. In addition, they distinguish capital services from short-lived and long-lived assets in each of the three sectors. The distinction of the corporate, noncorporate, and household capital services is important for realistic representation of the U.S. tax system. So is the distinction between the services from short-lived and long-lived assets as most of tax preferences are concentrated on short-lived assets. An obvious advantage of these distinctions is that intersectoral and interasset capital allocation can be analyzed.[8]

Among the IGEMs used for tax policy analysis, the Jorgenson and Yun model is unique in that key parameters of the household and the business behavior are econometrically estimated using a consistent time series data of the U.S. economy covering the period 1947–1986. We now describe the basic structure of the Jorgenson and Yun model.

10.3.1   Household

10.3.1.1   Intertemporal Allocation
The household sector is represented by a consumer who is endowed a
perfect foresight and infinite time horizon. He maximizes intertemporal welfare function which is iso-elastic and additively separable. Formally, the consumer maximizes

$$
V = \left[\begin{array}{ll}
\dfrac{1}{1-\sigma} \displaystyle\sum_{t=0}^{\infty} \left(\dfrac{1+n}{1+\rho}\right)^{t} U_{t}^{1-\sigma} & \sigma \neq 1 \\[3ex]
\displaystyle\sum_{t=0}^{\infty} \left(\dfrac{1+n}{1+\rho}\right)^{t} \ln U_{t} & \sigma = 1
\end{array} \right.
\tag{10.28}
$$

where $1/\sigma$ is intertemporal elasticity of substitution, n is the rate of
population growth, ρ is the rate of time preference, U is per capita full
consumption with population measured in natural unit, and t is time.
Felicity of the consumer is $U_{t}^{1-\sigma}$, if $\sigma \neq 1$, and $\ln U_{t}$, if $\sigma = 1$. Intertemporal welfare is measured as a discounted sum of per capita felicity
weighted by the size of population.

In general, welfare of the consumer is affected by the consumption
of both public and private goods (and services). However, it is
difficult to measure the value of public consumption and there is no
reliable estimate of the elasticity of substitution between private and
public consumption. We simplify the model by assuming that the
welfare effects of public consumption are additively separable from
private consumption, intertemporally and intratemporally. We sup-
press consumption of public goods from the welfare function and
interpret U as per capita private consumption.

We assume that technological change is of the Harrod neutral type
which improves the efficiency of labor at the rate of μ. Thus the welfare level may be expressed as a function of full consumption per
capita, F_{t}, with population measured in efficiency unit where

$$
U_{t} = F_{t}(1+\mu)^{t}.
\tag{10.29}
$$

The representative consumer maximizes the welfare function
(10.28), subject to the intertemporal budget constraint:

$$\sum_{t=0}^{\infty} \frac{F_t \cdot PF_t(1+\mu)^t(1+n)^t}{\prod_{j=0}^{t}(1+r_j^{pn})} \leq W \tag{10.30}$$

where PF_t is the price of full consumption in period t, r_j^{pn} is the after-tax (private) rate of return to capital, W is the sum of human and non-human wealth,[9] respectively. We refer to W as full wealth.

Since the intertemporal welfare function is additively separable in full consumption, consumer problem may be separated into two stages. In the first stage, the consumer allocates full wealth among full consumption of different time periods. In the second stage, full consumption is allocated among consumption goods, leisure, and household capital services.

The necessary condition for the maximization of intertemporal welfare subject to the intertemporal budget constraint is given by the Euler equation:

$$\frac{F_t}{F_{t-1}} = \left[\frac{PF_{t-1}}{PF_t} \frac{1+r_t^{pn}}{(1+\rho)(1+\mu)^\sigma} \right]^{\frac{1}{\sigma}}. \tag{10.31}$$

Given the future paths of the price of full consumption and private nominal interest rate, the Euler equation determines the optimal growth rate of full consumption per capita.

In a steady state, the level of full consumption per capita, with population measured in efficiency unit, is constant. With no inflation, the steady-state condition for full consumption implies that the steady-state private real rate of return on wealth, say $r*$, is

$$r* = (1+\rho)(1+\mu)^\sigma - 1. \tag{10.32}$$

We denote the rate of inflation in the price of full consumption by π_t^F, where

$$\pi_t^F = \frac{PF_t}{PF_{t-1}} - 1.$$

In a steady state with a constant rate of inflation, $\pi*$, $\pi^F = \pi*$ and the nominal private rate of return on wealth is

$$r* = (1+\rho)(1+\mu)^\sigma(1+\pi*) - 1. \tag{10.33}$$

Notice that the steady-state private rate of return depends upon the pure rate of time preference, rate of technological change, and the elasticity of intertemporal substitution in consumption. However it is independent of production technology and any government policy including tax policy.

Equation (10.31) indicates that, to a first-order approximation, the growth rate of full consumption is proportional to the difference between the current and the steady-state private real rates of return. In order to determine the complete path of full consumption, we need to find the level of full consumption. Conceptually, this can be done by combining the Euler equation and the intertemporal budget constraint. In practice, we solve for the initial level of full consumption, F_0, which is consistent with (10.30).

10.3.1.2 Intratemporal Allocation

Allocation of Full Consumption

Once full consumption of period t is determined, it is further allocated among consumption goods, leisure, and household capital services. This intratemporal allocation of full consumption is based on the maximization of a homothetic translog indirect utility function[10] (suppressing time subscripts):

$$\ln V = \alpha_0 + \alpha' \ln\left(\frac{P}{VF}\right) + \ln\left(\frac{P}{VF}\right)' B \ln\left(\frac{P}{VF}\right) \tag{10.34}$$

where $VF \equiv F \cdot PF = PCD \cdot CD + PLJ \cdot LJ + PHD \cdot HD$ is the value of full consumption, PCD, PLJ, and PHD are the price indexes of consumption good, leisure, and household capital services, respectively, CD, LJ, and HD are the corresponding quantity indexes, α_0 is a constant, $\alpha = [\alpha_1, \alpha_2, \alpha_3]'$

$$\ln\left(\frac{P}{VF}\right) = \begin{bmatrix} \ln(PCD/VF) \\ \ln(PLJ/VF) \\ \ln(PHD/VF) \end{bmatrix}, \qquad \beta = \begin{bmatrix} \beta_{cc} & \beta_{cl} & \beta_{ch} \\ \beta_{lc} & \beta_{ll} & \beta_{lh} \\ \beta_{hc} & \beta_{hl} & \beta_{hh} \end{bmatrix},$$

and the subscripts c, l, and h denote the three components of full consumption. Making use of the logarithmic form of Roy's identity, we obtain the expenditure share equations:

$$\begin{bmatrix} PCD \cdot CD/VF \\ PLJ \cdot LJ/VF \\ PHD \cdot HD/VF \end{bmatrix} = \alpha + \beta \ln P \qquad (10.35)$$

where

$$\ln P = \begin{bmatrix} \ln PCD \\ \ln PLJ \\ \ln PHD \end{bmatrix}.$$

The consumer budget constraint implies that the shares of the three components of full consumption add up to 1. In addition, since the indirect utility function (10.34) is twice differentiable, the matrix β is symmetric. It follows that

$$\alpha'l = 1, \quad \beta' = \bar{0}, \quad \beta = \beta',$$

where $l = (1\ 1\ 1)'$ and $\bar{0} = [0\ 0\ 0]'$.

Labor Supply

Total time endowment, in natural unit, of the consumer is fixed and labor supply, say LS, is the difference between total time endowment and leisure:

$$LS = LH - LJ. \qquad (10.36)$$

where LH is the total time endowment.

Demand for Household Capital Services

The demand for household capital services is obtained from the allocation of full consumption among consumption good, leisure, and household capital services. We refer to the demand for household capital services at this stage as the aggregate demand for household capital services. The aggregate demand for household capital services is further allocated between the services from the short-lived and long-lived assets. The allocation of aggregate demand for capital services between the short-lived and long-lived assets is similar to the allocation of full consumption among its three components.

Formally, we introduce a time invariant translog price function for the aggregate household capital service which depends upon the prices of capital services from the short-lived and long-lived assets:

$$\ln PHD = A_0 + A \ln P + 1/2 \ln P'B \ln P \qquad (10.37)$$

where A_0 is a constant,

$$A = \begin{bmatrix} A_s \\ A_l \end{bmatrix}, \quad B = \begin{bmatrix} B_{ss} B_{sl} \\ B_{ls} B_{ll} \end{bmatrix}, \quad \ln P = \begin{bmatrix} \ln PHD_s \\ \ln PHD_l \end{bmatrix},$$

PHD is the price index of aggregate capital services, and the subscripts s and l stand for short-lived and long-lived assets, respectively.

Allocation of the aggregate demand for capital services is determined according to the share equations:

$$\begin{bmatrix} PHD_s \cdot HD_s / VHD \\ PHD_l \cdot HD_l / VHD \end{bmatrix} = A + B \ln P \qquad (10.38)$$

where $VHD \equiv PHD \cdot HD = PHD_s \cdot HD_s + PHD_l \cdot HD_l$ is the value of aggregate demand and HD_s and HD_l are the quantities of capital services from the short-lived and long-lived assets, respectively. Since the shares add up to 1, $l'A = 1$, $l'B = \bar{0}$, where $l' = [11]$ and $\bar{0} = [00]'$, and differentiability of the price function (10.37) implies symmetry of the matrix B.

In empirical implementation of the model, the price of capital services from the short-lived and long-lived assets are computed with the discrete time versions of (10.18), i.e.,

$$PHD_j = \left[(r_k + (1+\pi)\delta_{hj}) + \gamma_h t_h^p \right] PKL_{hj}, \quad j = s, l. \qquad (10.18')$$

where the subscript h denotes the household sector, π is the rate of inflation in the price of assets, and PKL is the price of asset at the beginning of the period. Equation (10.18') is the same as (10.18) except that the rate of economic depreciation is multiplied by $(1+\pi)$ and the short-lived ($j = s$) and long-lived ($j = l$) assets are distinguished. The discount rate, r_h, and the adjustment factor for the property tax rate, γ_h are defined by (10.19) and (10.20), respectively.

10.3.2   Producer

10.3.2.1   Aggregate Production Function

In modeling the producer behavior, we distinguish two legal forms of organization: corporate and noncorporate firms. This distinction is essential for capturing the differential tax treatments of income from capital in the two business sectors. However, we do not model the corporate and noncorporate sectors as separate production units. Instead, we simplify the representation of production technology by employing an aggregate production function where the capital services from the corporate and noncorporate assets enter as separate inputs. In order to model the effects of taxation on the allocation of capital between assets with different durability, we further disaggregate the demand for the corporate and noncorporate services into the demands for capital services from the short-lived and long-lived assets. The production technology of business sector is represented by a price possibility frontier (*PPF*) which is defined in terms of the producer prices of inputs and outputs, and time. The inputs are labor services and corporate and noncorporate capital services, and the outputs are consumption and investment goods. An advantage of defining the *PPF* in time varying form is that we can represent the rate of technical change in a form similar to the share equations of the inputs and outputs. The *PPF* is defined by a translog price function of labor services in natural units:

$$\ln PLD_n = A_0 + A' \ln P + A_T T + 1/2 \ln P'B \ln P + B_T'T \ln P$$
$$+ 1/2\, B_{TT} T^2 \tag{10.39}$$

where A_0, A_T, and B_{TT} are constants, $A' = \begin{bmatrix} A_c A_i A_q A_m \end{bmatrix}$

$$\ln P = \begin{bmatrix} \ln PCS \\ \ln PIS \\ \ln PQD \\ \ln PMD \end{bmatrix}, \quad B = \begin{bmatrix} B_{cc} & \cdots & B_{cm} \\ \cdot & \cdots & \cdot \\ \cdot & \cdots & \cdot \\ B_{mc} & \cdots & B_{mm} \end{bmatrix}, \quad B_T = \begin{bmatrix} B_{cT} \\ B_{iT} \\ B_{qT} \\ B_{mT} \end{bmatrix}$$

and PLD_n, PCS, PIS, PQD and PMD are the producer prices of labor services in natural unit, consumption goods, investment goods, corporate capital services, and noncorporate capital services, respectively.

Taking derivatives of (10.39) with respect to logarithms of the prices, and making use of the zero-profit condition underlying the *PPF*, we have

$$\begin{bmatrix} PCS \cdot CS/VLD \\ PIS \cdot IS/VLD \\ -PQD \cdot QD/VLD \\ -PMD \cdot MD/VLD \end{bmatrix} = A + B \ln P + B_T T \tag{10.40}$$

where $VLD \equiv PLD_n \cdot LD_n$, LD_n is the demand for labor services in natural unit, CS and IS are the supplies of consumption and investment goods, QD and MD are the demands for corporate and noncorporate capital services, respectively.

Under the zero-profit condition, the rate of technological change, μ, is defined as the rate of change in the price of labor services in natural unit when all other prices are held constant:

$$\mu = \frac{\partial \ln PLD_n}{\partial T} = A_T + B_T' \ln P + B_{TT}T . \tag{10.41}$$

Equations (10.40) and (10.41) can be combined and expressed conveniently in a matrix form

$$w = \begin{bmatrix} A \\ A_T \end{bmatrix} + \begin{bmatrix} B & B_T \\ B'_T & B_{TT} \end{bmatrix} \begin{bmatrix} \ln P \\ T \end{bmatrix} \tag{10.42}$$

where $w \equiv [w_c \ w_i \ w_q \ w_m \ \mu]'$ is a vector with the first four elements equal to the the left-hand side of (10.40), and the matrices B and B_T are conformable with the vector $\ln P$. Under zero-profit condition,

$$PLD_n \cdot LD_n + PQD \cdot QD + PMD \cdot MD = PCS \cdot CS + PIS \cdot IS$$

and

$$l'A = 1, \qquad l'B = \bar{0}$$

where $l = [1, 1, 1, 1]'$ and $\bar{0} = [0, 0, 0, 0]'$. Since the matrix

$$\begin{bmatrix} B & B_T \\ B_T' & B_{TT} \end{bmatrix}$$

is the Hessian of the logarithmic price function, it is symmetric.

Finally, we require that the PPF be consistent with balanced growth where technological change is Harrod neutral and the rate of technological change is constant over time. It follows that

$$B_T = \bar{0}, \qquad B_{TT} = 0 .$$

These are referred to as the *balanced growth* conditions. Given the balanced growth conditions, we can easily convert the time dependent PPF into a time invariant one by redefining the unit of labor services in efficiency terms. In econometric implementation of the model, we use (10.42) to estimate the parameters including the rate of technological change. However, in applications of the IGEM, we use the time invariant *PPF*.

10.3.2.2   Demand for Capital Services
The demands for capital services in the corporate and noncorporate sectors are allocated between the short-lived and long-lived assets. We model the allocation of capital services in the corporate and noncorporate sectors in exactly the same way as in the household sector. Since the structure of the allocation process is the same as in the household sector, we simply present the expressions for the cost of capital in the corporate and noncorporate sectors.

In the corporate sector, discrete time version of the cost of capital is:

$$PQD_j = \frac{1 - ITC_{cj} - t_c Z_{cj}}{1 - t_c} \, [(r_c + (1+\pi)\delta_{cj}) + \gamma_c t_c^p]PKL_{cj}, \qquad j = s, l \quad (10.9')$$

where the subscript c denotes the corporate sector. Equation (10.9') is the same as (10.9) except that the rate of economic depreciation is multiplied by $(1+\pi)$ and the short-lived ($j = s$) and the long-lived ($j = l$) assets are distinguished. The after-tax discount rate for corporate investment, r_c, is defined by (10.10) and the adjustment factor for the property tax rate, γ_c, by (10.11). A translog price function like (10.37) is used to compute the price of aggregate capital services in the corporate sector, *PQD*.

In the noncorporate sector, discrete time version of the cost of capital is:

$$PMD_j = \frac{1 - ITC_{nj} - t_n Z_{nj}}{1 - t_n} \, [(r_n + (1+\pi)\delta_{nj})\gamma_n t_n^p]PKL_{nj} \qquad j = s, l \quad (10.14')$$

where the subscript n denotes the noncorporate sector. Equation (10.14') is the same as (10.14) except that the rate of economic depreciation is multiplied by $(1+\pi)$ and that the short-lived ($j = s$) and long-lived ($j = l$) assets are distinguished. The after-tax discount rate for noncorporate investment, r_n, is defined by (10.15) and the adjustment factor for the property tax rate, $\gamma_{n'}$, by (10.16). As in the corporate sector, a translog price function is used to compute the price of aggregate capital services in the noncorporate sector, *PMD*.

10.3.3   Government Behavior

We consolidate the accounts of the Federal and the state and local governments into a single account of the general government. Similarly, we consolidate the accounts of government enterprises into a single account. The government is allowed to run budget deficits and borrow from the household sector in order to finance expenditures in excess of total tax revenue. We ignore the social security system.

The government collects taxes from the household and business sectors, issues debts to finance deficits, spends the revenues on consumption goods, investment goods, and labor services, pays interest on government debts, and makes transfer payments to the households and the rest of the world. Public enterprises employ labor to produce consumption goods and turn over the surpluses to the general government. We assume that the government objectives underlying the allocation of public spending among consumption goods, investment goods, labor, transfers to households and foreigners can be represented by a Cobb-Douglas utility function.

10.3.3.1   Tax System

Sales Taxes

Sales taxes on consumption and investment goods are treated as *ad valorem* taxes based on the producer prices. The revenues are:[11]

$$R^c = PCS \cdot CS \cdot t^c \tag{10.43}$$

and

$$R^i = PIS \cdot IS \cdot t^i \tag{10.44}$$

where R^c and R^i are the tax revenues and t^c and t^i are the tax rates.

Property Taxes

Property taxes are levied on the lagged values of capital stock. We assume that the tax rates on the short-lived and long-lived assets are the same. Total amount of property taxes, R^p, is equal to the sum of the property taxes on the corporate, noncorporate, and household assets:

$$R^p = R^p_c + R^p_n + R^p_h \tag{10.45}$$

where

$$R_c^p = VQL \cdot t_c^p$$
$$R_n^p = VML \cdot t_n^p$$
$$R_h^p = VHL \cdot t_h^p$$

and VQL, VML, and VHL are the lagged values of assets, t_c^p, t_n^p and t_h^p are the property tax rates in the corporate, noncorporate, and household sectors, respectively.

Wealth Tax

Wealth tax includes federal estate and gift taxes and state and local death and gift taxes. The tax revenue, R^w, is defined by

$$R^w = WL \cdot t^w \tag{10.46}$$

where t^w is the tax rate, and WL is the lagged value of total wealth:

$$WL = VQL + VML + VHL + VGL + VRL \tag{10.47}$$

VGL and VRL are the lagged values of the claims on the government and the rest of the world, respectively.

Corporate Income Tax

Income from corporate capital is taxed at two levels; first at the corporate level and then at the individual level. The base of corporate income tax is defined as the corporate property compensation less depreciation allowances. It is further reduced by the tax deduction of interest expenses, dividends-paid, property taxes, and state and local taxes for Federal tax purposes. After the tax rate is applied to the tax base, tax liability is reduced by the amount of investment tax credit.

For an accurate accounting of depreciation allowances, we need to keep vintage accounts of all depreciable assets. Similarly, for an accurate accounting of investment tax credits, we need to know the composition of investment by asset types in every sector, in every period. Modeling actual allowances for depreciation and investment tax credit not only requires a detailed representation of the tax law, vintage accounting system of capital stock, and a mechanism to allocate investment spending among various categories of assets. It also complicates the intertemporal optimization problem. We take a short cut by employing the concepts of imputed depreciation and imputed investment tax credit.[12]

The revenue of corporate income tax, R_c^y, can be written:

$$R_c^y = t_c \cdot BQ - ITC_c \tag{10.48}$$

where BQ is the tax base and ITC_c is the imputed corporate investment tax credit. ITC_c is defined as

$$ITC_c = \sum_{j=s,l} ITC_{cj}[r_c + (1+\pi)\delta_{cj}]PKL_{cj} \cdot KL \tag{10.49}$$

where KL_{cj} is the quantity of corporate asset in category j. The base of corporate income tax, BQ, is defined as:

$$BQ = PQD \cdot QD - DQ - [\beta_c(1-DI)i + \alpha \cdot DD(1-\beta_c)r^e]VQL$$
$$- [t_c^s + t_c^f(DSL_c - DSL_i t_c^s)]R_c^p/t_c \tag{10.50}$$

where DQ is the imputed depreciation allowances:

$$DQ = \sum_{j=sl} z_{cj}[r_c + (1+\pi)\delta_{cj}]PKL_{cj} \cdot KL_{cj} \tag{10.51}$$

and r^e is the real rate of return to corporate equity, after corporate income tax:

$$r^e = \frac{r - \pi\lfloor 1 - (1-DC)t_c^g \rfloor}{1 - [\alpha t_c^e + (1-\alpha)t_c^g]} . \tag{10.52}$$

Notice that, since QD represents domestically employed corporate assets, (10.50) implies that foreign assets employed in U.S. corporations pay U.S. corporate income tax. Symmetrically and implicitly, we assume that U.S. corporations pay corporate income taxes for their assets employed abroad to their host countries.

Individual Income Tax

In modeling the taxation of individual income, we treat labor income, interest income, and income from equities separately. In addition, we distinguish between average and marginal tax rates. Average tax rates are used to generate tax revenues and marginal tax rates are used to guide resource allocation.

Labor income, BL, includes all the compensation for labor services:

$$BL = PLD \cdot LD + PLG \cdot LG + PLE \cdot LE + PLR \cdot LR \tag{10.53}$$

where *PLD*, *PLG*, *PLE*, and *PLR* are the prices of labor employed in the business, government, government enterprises, and the rest of the world sectors and *LD*, *LG*, *LE*, and *LR* are the corresponding quantities, respectively.

Interest income, *BD*, includes all the interests earned on various debt claims:

$$BD = [\beta_c(VQL + VRL) + \beta_n VML + \beta_h VHL + VGL](1 - DI)i \qquad (10.54)$$

where we assume that the claims on the rest of the world are owned by the households through U.S. corporations, and that they have the same debt/equity ratio and after-tax rate of return as domestically employed corporate capital.

Equity income, *BE*, includes all the individual income from equity claims on the corporate and noncorporate assets. The imputed income from household equities is not taxable, but interest expenses and property taxes on household assets are deductible for the equity owner's income tax purposes. Since nominal capital gains on assets are taxed on a realization basis, we convert the realization based taxation to accrual based taxation by assuming that the fraction of accrued nominal capital gains effectively included in the ordinary income tax base is equal to the ratio of the accrual based marginal tax rate of capital gains and the tax rate of other equity income.

The total equity income taxable on an accrual basis is broadly defined as the after-tax corporate profits (dividends, retained earnings and earnings on the equity claims on the rest of the world), plus noncorporate property compensations net of interest expenses, property taxes and depreciation allowances, less property taxes and interest expenses on household assets, plus nominal capital gains on private assets adjusted for realization based taxation:

$$
\begin{aligned}
BE = {}& PQD \cdot QD - R_c^p - R_c^y + (1 - \beta_c)r^e VRL - \beta_c(i - \pi)VQL - VDQ \\
& + PMD \cdot MD - DM - \beta_n(1 - DI)VML \cdot i \\
& - [t_n^{es} + t_n^{ef}(DSL_h - DSL_t \cdot t_n^{es})]R_n^p/t_n^e \\
& - DHI \cdot \beta_h(1 - HDI)VHL \cdot i - [t_h^{es} + t_h^{es}(DSL_h - DSL_i \cdot t_h^{es})]R_h^p/t_h^e \\
& + [(1 - \beta_c)(VQL + VRL)t_c^g/t_c^e + (1 - \beta_n)VMLt_n^g/t_n^e \\
& + (1 - \beta_h)VHLt_h^g/t_h^e](1 - DC)\pi \qquad (10.55)
\end{aligned}
$$

where *VDQ* is the economic depreciation of corporate assets:

$$VDQ = \sum_{j=s,l} (1+\pi)\delta_{cj} PKL_{cj} \cdot KL_{cj} \tag{10.56}$$

and DM is the imputed noncorporate depreciation allowances:

$$DM = \sum_{j=s,l} z_{nj}[r_n + (1+\pi)\delta_{nj}] PKL_{nj} \cdot KL_{nj} . \tag{10.57}$$

The tax revenue from individual income is:

$$R_p^y = BL \cdot t_l^a + BD \cdot t_d^a + \lfloor BE \cdot t_e^a - ITC_n \rfloor \tag{10.58}$$

where t_l^a, t_d^a and t_e^a are the average tax rates of labor income, interest income, and equity income, respectively, and ITC_n is the imputed investment tax credit for noncorporate investment:

$$ITC_n = \sum_{j=s,l} ITC_{nj}[r_n + (1+\pi)\delta_{nj}] PKL_{nj} \cdot KL_{nj} . \tag{10.59}$$

Non-tax Payments
The federal and state and local personal non-tax payments, R^{nt}, are assumed to be a constant fraction of the before tax labor income:

$$R^{nt} = BL \cdot t^{nt} \tag{10.60}$$

where t^{nt} is the rate of non-tax payments.

10.3.3.2   Government Enterprises
Government enterprises employ labor and produce consumption goods. The consumption goods produced by government enterprises, CE, is assumed to be a constant fraction, SCE, of the consumption goods produced in the private sector:

$$CD = SCE \cdot CS . \tag{10.61}$$

Similarly we assume that government enterprises employ a fixed fraction, SLE, of the total value of labor supplied:

$$PLE \cdot LE = SLE(PLH \cdot LH - PLJ \cdot LJ)/(1-t_l^m) \tag{10.62}$$

where PLE is the producer price of labor employed in government enterprises, PLH, and PLJ are the consumer prices of time endowment and leisure, and t_l^m is the marginal tax rate of labor income. The surplus, R^g, is turned over to the general government, where:

$$R^g = PCD \cdot CE - PLE \cdot LE .$$

(10.63)

10.3.3.3 Government Budget

Expenditures

We assume that total government expenditure, *XPND*, is a constant fraction of the gross private national income net of after-tax interest income from government debts:

$$XPND = \left[Y - (1 - (1 - DI) \cdot t_g^d) \cdot VGL \cdot i \right] \cdot SGOV$$

(10.64)

where *SGOV* is a constant, Y is private national income defined below, and t_g^d is the marginal tax rate of interest income from government debts.

Total government expenditure, net of interest payment, is allocated in constant proportions among consumption goods, investment goods, labor services, and transfers to the household and the rest of the world:

$$PCD \cdot CG = SCG \cdot (XPND - VGL \cdot i)$$ (10.65a)
$$PID \cdot IG = SIG \cdot (XPND - VGL \cdot i)$$ (10.65b)
$$PLG \cdot LG = SLG \cdot (XPND - VGL \cdot i)$$ (10.65c)
$$EL = SEL \cdot (XPND - VGL \cdot i)$$ (10.65d)
$$ER = SER \cdot (XPND - VGL \cdot i)$$ (10.65e)

where *CG*, *IG*, *LG* are government demands for consumption goods, investment goods, and labor, and *PCD*, *PID*, and *PLG* are the corresponding prices; *EL* and *ER* are the transfer payments to households and foreigners; *XPND* is total expenditure; and finally, *SCG*, *SIG*, *SLG*, *SEL*, and *SER* are constants.

Under the assumption that government maximizes a Cobb-Douglas objective function, we can aggregate the five categories of government expenditures. Price index of aggregate government expenditures, *PGS*, may be written:

$$\log(PGS) = SCG \cdot \log(PC) + SIG \cdot \log(PI) + SLG \cdot \log(PLG)$$

(10.66)

where we implicitly set the price of the transfers to households and foreigners at unity. The index of real government expenditure, net of interest payments, is implicitly defined as:

$$GS = (XPND - VGL \cdot i)/PGS. \tag{10.67}$$

Revenues

Government revenue, REV, consists of tax revenues and non-tax receipts including the surplus of the government enterprises:

$$REV = R^c + R^i + R_c^y + R_p^y + R^p + R^w + R^{nt} + R^g + R^{lum} \tag{10.68}$$

where R^{lum} represents a lump sum tax which is used in policy simulations to control total government revenue.

Budget Balance

Since the government can run budget deficit, the government budget constraint can be written:

$$XPND = REV + DG \tag{10.69}$$

where DG is the budget deficit.

10.3.3.4   Rest of the World

The U.S. trades with the rest of the world in consumption goods, investment goods, and labor services. In addition, U.S. makes transfer payments to the rest of the world. U.S. trade with the rest of the world is not necessarily balanced and the value of net export and the earnings from the claims on the rest of the world, net of the government transfer to foreigners, are added to the U.S. claims on the rest of the world. Deficit of the rest of the world, or surplus of the U.S., can be written:

$$\begin{aligned}
DR = PC \cdot CR + PI \cdot IR + PLR \cdot LR + \lfloor (1 - \beta_c) r^e \\
+ \beta_c (i - \pi) \rfloor \cdot VRL - ER
\end{aligned} \tag{10.70}$$

where CR, IR, and LR are net exports of consumption goods, investment goods, and labor services, respectively. CR, IR, and LR are determined according to

$$CR = SCR(C + CG) \tag{10.71a}$$
$$IR = SIR \cdot IS \tag{10.71b}$$
$$PLR \cdot LR = SLR(PLH \cdot LH - PLJ \cdot LJ)/(1 - t_l^m) \tag{10.71c}$$

where SCR, SIR, and SLR are constants.

10.3.3.5 National Income and Wealth

Gross national product, GNP, is defined to be equal to the sum of total labor and capital inputs, earnings on the claims on the rest of the world, and indirect taxes:

$$GNP = PLD \cdot LD + PLG \cdot LG + PLE \cdot LE + PLR \cdot LR + PQD \cdot QD$$
$$+ PMD \cdot MD + PHD \cdot HD + [(1 - \beta_c)r^e + \beta_c(i - \pi)]VRL$$
$$+ R^c + R^I \tag{10.72}$$

The gross private national income, Y, is the sum of after-tax labor and capital income:

$$Y = PLD \cdot LD + PLG \cdot LG + PLE \cdot LE + PLR \cdot LR + PQD \cdot QD$$
$$+ PMD \cdot MD + PHD \cdot HD + [(1 - \beta_c)r^e + \beta_c(i - \pi)]VRL$$
$$+ VGL \cdot i - (R_p^y + R_c^y + R^p + R^w + R^{nt} + R^{lum}). \tag{10.73}$$

Gross private domestic saving, S, is disposable income less household expenditures on consumption goods and capital services:

$$S = (Y + EL) - (PC \cdot C + PHD \cdot HD). \tag{10.74}$$

Gross private domestic saving is used to finance private investment and the deficits of government and the rest of the world:

$$S = PID \cdot ID + DG + DR \tag{10.75}$$

where ID is the private demand for investment goods.

The demand for private investment is allocated among the six categories of assets. However we assume that all tangible assets are perfectly malleable and they can be transformed from one category into another in accordance with the rate of transformation implied by the relative price of the assets. Under this assumption, it is sufficient to represent the accumulation of capital stock with the change in total capital stock.

The value of capital stock at the end of the current period (VK) is equal to the value of capital stock at the beginning of the period (VKL), plus the value of gross investment, less depreciation (DEP), plus revaluation (RV):

$$VK = VKL + PID \cdot ID - DEP + RV \tag{10.76}$$

where

$$VK = \sum_{i,j} PK_{ij} \cdot K_{ij} \quad (i = c, n, h; \ j = s, l)$$

$$VKL = VQL + VML + VHL$$

$$DEP = \sum_{i,j} PK_{ij} \cdot KL_{ij} \cdot \delta_{ij} \quad (i = c, n, h; \ j = s, l)$$

$$RV = \sum_{i,j} [PK_{ij} - PKL_{ij}] KL_{ij} \quad (i = c, n, h; \ j = s, l).$$

The accumulation of nominal government debts is represented by:

$$VG = DG + VGL \tag{10.77}$$

where VG is the value of outstanding government debts at the end of the current period. Similarly, the accumulation of the claims on the rest of the world is represented by:

$$VR = DR + (1 + \pi)VRL \tag{10.78}$$

where VR is the value of the claims on the rest of the world at the end of the current period.

10.3.3.6 Market Equilibrium

There are four markets in the economy corresponding to the four goods and services traded in the economy: consumption goods, investment goods, labor services, and capital services. Each market is cleared in every period.

Consumption Goods Market

Equilibrium in the consumption goods market is characterized with the market clearing condition

$$CS + CE = CD + CG + CR \tag{10.79}$$

and the relationship between the producer and consumer prices:

$$PCD = (1 + t^c)PCS. \tag{10.80}$$

Investment Goods Market

Similarly, equilibrium in the investment goods market is characterized with the market clearing condition

$$IS = ID + IG + IR \tag{10.81}$$

and the relationship between the producer and consumer prices:

$$PID = (1 + t^i)PIS.$$ (10.82)

Since private savings are used to finance private investment and the deficits of government and the rest of the world, private demand for investment good is given by (10.75), i.e., $PID \cdot ID = S - DG - DR$.

Labor Market

Equilibrium in the labor market is characterized by the equality between the values of supply and demand:

$$\frac{PLH \cdot LH - PLJ \cdot LJ}{1 - t_l^m} = PLD \cdot LD + PLG \cdot LG + PLE \cdot LE$$
$$+ PLR \cdot LR.$$ (10.83)

The relative prices among time endowment, leisure, and labor employed in various sectors are fixed.

Capital Service Market

Since capital is perfectly malleable, a given amount of capital stock is consistent with more than one pattern of demands for capital services. Market equilibrium is reached when the total value of capital stock necessary to meet the demands for all the six categories of capital services is equal to the total value of capital stock available. With an accounting system in which one unit of capital stock in each of the six asset categories generates one unit of service in the corresponding category, equilibrium of the capital service market is characterized by:

$$\sum_{i,j} PKL_{ij} \cdot KL_{ij} = VKL \quad (i = c, n, h; \; j = s, l).$$ (10.84)

10.4 Welfare Analysis of Tax Policy

10.4.1 Analytical Framework

In order to evaluate alternative tax policies, we need to consider the intertemporal general equilibrium associated with each policy. Under perfect foresight, the intertemporal equilibrium is unique and has a saddle point configuration. Once equilibrium is found, making use of the intertemporal welfare function (10.28), we can easily compute the level of welfare, V. Making use of the Euler equation (10.31) we can express per capita full consumption in period t, with population measured in efficiency unit, in terms of the full consumption in period 0 and the private real rates of return between periods 0 and t:

$$\frac{F_t}{F_0} = \prod_{s=0}^{t} \left[\frac{1+r_s}{(1+\rho)(1+\mu)^\sigma} \right]^{1/\sigma}, \quad t = 1, 2, \cdots \tag{10.85}$$

where r_s is the private real rate of return in period s.[13] Substituting (10.85) into the intertemporal welfare function, we obtain the level of intertemporal welfare:

$$V = \frac{F_0^{1-\sigma}}{1-\sigma} D \tag{10.86}$$

where

$$D = \sum_{t=0}^{\infty} \left[\frac{1+n}{(1+\rho)^{1/\sigma}} \right]^t \prod_{s=0}^{t} (1+r_s)^{(1-\sigma)/\sigma}.$$

Due to the additive separability of the intertemporal welfare function, D is a function of the real rates of return only. However, since r_s is adjusted for the inflation in the price of full consumption, D in fact summarizes the effects of all future prices and rates of return on the initial level of full consumption associated with a given level of welfare V.

Since the optimal path of full consumption satisfies the intertemporal budget constraint, total present value of full consumption per capita multiplied by the size of population must be equal to the full wealth at the beginning of the transition path. We have:

$$F_0 = \frac{W}{PF_0} \frac{1}{D}. \tag{10.87}$$

Substituting (10.87) in (10.86) and rearranging terms, we obtain

$$W(PF_0, D, V) = PF_0 \left[\frac{(1-\sigma)V}{D^\sigma} \right]^{\frac{1}{1-\sigma}}. \tag{10.88}$$

Given PF_0 and D, (10.88) gives the minimum value of full wealth required to attain intertemporal welfare of V. Equation (10.88) is equivalent to the expenditure function in a static context. Thus we refer to (10.88) as the *intertemporal expenditure function*. Note that the expression in the square bracket raised to the power of $1/(1-\sigma)$ measures the minimum amount of full wealth in the unit of full consumption in the initial period.

The intertemporal expenditure function gives a measure of welfare in terms of what Paul Samuelson calls a "wealth-like" magnitude.[14] Given D, there is a unique level of minimum full wealth required to attain any given level of intertemporal welfare. Thus intertemporal expenditure function can be employed to compare the levels of intertemporal welfare in terms of the amounts of full wealth at a reference price. We employ the intertemporal expenditure function in the welfare analyses with our IGEM.

Suppose we consider a policy change and want to know the welfare effects of the policy change. We begin by solving for the intertemporal equilibria under the reference and the alternative policies, and compute the level of intertemporal welfare under each policy. Let the subscripts 0 and 1 denote the cases with the reference and the alternative policies, respectively. Then we can write the equivalent variation in full wealth of the policy change as:

$$\Delta W = W(PF_0, D_0, V_1) - W(PF_0, D_0, V_0)$$
$$= W(PF_0, D_0, V_1) - W_0. \tag{10.89}$$

Similarly we can employ the intertemporal expenditure function to compute the compensating variation. Since equivalent variation is transitive, while compensating variation is not, we use equivalent variation for welfare analysis.[15]

10.4.2   Simulation

10.4.2.1   Base Case Simulation

Economic analysis of tax policy is mostly concerned with the differential effects of policy change. The analysis may focus on the resources allocation in various parts of the economy, or it may concentrate on a summary measure of the differential effects of a policy change. In any case, in order to measure the differential effects of a policy change, we need to establish a reference for comparison in the first place. We refer to the simulation under the reference policy as the base case simulation.

In the base case simulation, we adjust some parameters of the model so that the overall configuration of the steady-state allocation, or the balanced growth equilibrium, under the reference policy looks reasonable. In particular we adjust the share of government expenditure, net of interest payments on government debts, in the private national income ($SGOV$) so that the ratio between government debt and private national income has a plausible value in the steady state. Similarly, we adjust the coefficients of net exports for consumption goods, investment goods, and labor (SCR, SIR, SLR) so that the ratio between the claims on the rest of the world and private national income has a plausible value in the steady state. The capital intensity in the balanced growth equilibrium is determined endogenously.

Once the configuration of the balanced growth equilibrium is determined under the reference policy, we construct the transition paths of government debt (VG) and the claims on the rest of the world (VR). Since, in most cases, the economy comes very close to the balanced growth equilibrium within thirty-five years from the initial period, we assume that the gap between the level of government debt in the initial period and that in the balanced growth equilibrium is closed at a constant rate over a period of thirty-five years. After that, the level of government debt remains at its balanced growth level. The path of the claims on the rest of the world is determined similarly.

The transition path of government debt implies the path of government budget deficit (DG). Then the dynamic budget constraint of the government requires that either total government expenditure or total tax revenue be determined endogenously in each period. We choose to allow total government expenditure to be determined endogenously so that government deficit is consistent with the path of government debt. Similarly, in order to make the total value of net export to be consistent with the path of the claims on the rest of the world, we adjust the coefficients of net exports (SCR, SIR, SLR) every period.

The fact that the paths of government debt and the claims on the rest of the world are set exogenously may appear to be restrictive. However, it does not pose any serious problem for our purposes, because we are interested in the differential effects of policy changes and the paths of government debt and the claims on the rest of the world are set to be the same across all the policies to be compared.

10.4.2.2 *Alternative Case Simulation*
In the simulations under alternative policies, we impose a number of restrictions so that the welfare analyses become meaningful. First of

all, in our IGEM, all the taxes except for the lump sum tax are distortionary and the Ricardian Equivalence does not hold. In order to control the welfare effects of debt-tax choice of the government, we constrain the path of government debt under alternative policies to be the same as that under the reference policy.

Second, we set the path of the claims on the rest of the world to be the same as in the base case simulation because, in our IGEM, the rest of the world sector serves mainly to close the model and the model is not intended for the analysis of trade policy or balance of payment dynamics.

Third, we set the path of real aggregate government expenditure net of interest payments on outstanding public debt (GS) to be the same as in the base case. This procedure is necessary because the intertemporal welfare function of the consumer does not reflect the welfare effects of government expenditure. Given the real aggregate government expenditure net of interest payments on government debt, its allocation among the five components of government spending is determined endogenously in such a way that maximizes a Cobb-Douglas objective function of the government.

Fourth, since the dynamic paths of real aggregate government expenditure and government budget deficit are held fixed, government budget constraint implies a constraint on the amount of tax revenue. In order to satisfy the government budget constraint under alternative policies, we adjust tax revenues. We consider four alternative methods for adjusting tax revenue. They are the adjustments of lump sum tax, labor income tax, sales tax, and individual income tax.

When labor income tax is adjusted, the average and marginal tax rates are adjusted by the same percentage points. Under the individual income tax adjustment, where both the labor and capital income taxes are adjusted, the average tax rates of labor and capital income and the marginal tax rates of capital income are adjusted by the same percentage point. Then the marginal tax rates of capital income are adjusted by the same proportion as the marginal tax rate of labor income.

Finally, for any given path of the claims on the rest of the world, there is a unique path of the balance of payment deficit. Since the path of the claims on the rest of the world is constrained to be the same as in the base case simulation, we need to adjust the level of balance of payment deficit every period. We adjust the net exports of consumption goods, investment goods, and labor services in the same proportion.

10.4.3   Application of the IGEM

10.4.3.1   Tax Reform

Application of the model to the analysis of alternative tax reform proposals is straightforward. Jorgenson and Yun (1990) applied the model to the welfare analysis of alternative tax policies in the U.S. They compared the tax policy which was effective in 1985, Tax Reform Act of 1986, and two alternative tax reform proposals, the Treasury proposal and the President's proposal, both of which emerged in the process of the 1986 tax reform.

Table 10.1 summarizes welfare effects of the four alternative tax policies which were assumed to be put into effect at the beginning of 1987. In the table, the tax policy under the 1985 tax law and an annual rate of inflation of 6% is taken as the reference of comparison. Some interesting conclusions may be drawn from the table. One remarkable finding is that the Treasury and the President's Proposals would have generated substantial welfare gains: Under an annual inflation rate of 6%, the welfare gains from the Treasury proposal would have been in the range of $1.6 trillion and $1.9 trillion in 1987 dollars. These figures may be compared with the private national wealth of $15,920 billion or with gross national product of $4,488 billion in 1987. Somewhat larger gains would have been generated under the President's proposal.

It is also interesting that, under the 1985 tax law or the 1986 Tax Act, welfare gains are sensitive to the rate of inflation. For example, in the case of the 1986 Tax Act, the welfare gain is about $1,560 billion dollars when there is no inflation. But the welfare gains are quickly dissipated as the rate of inflation rises. In contrast, the welfare gains from the Treasury proposal and the President's proposals tend to increase with the rate of inflation due to the various indexing provisions.[16] It appears that appropriate indexing of the current U.S. tax system against inflation would generate substantial welfare gains even at a moderate rate of inflation.

Jorgenson and Yun (1990) also analyzed eight hypothetical tax reforms in which various combination of the interasset, intersector, and intertemporal distortions in the taxation of capital income are eliminated. Table 10.2 summarizes the welfare effects of the tax reforms. Not surprisingly, elimination of the tax wedges tend to increase the welfare of the economy. In particular, approximately revenue neutral elimination of the intersectoral tax wedges among the

Table 10.1
Welfare effects of tax reform (billions of 1987 dollars)

Revenue Adjustment	1985 Tax Law	Treasury Proposal	President's Proposal	1986 Tax Act
		0 Percent Inflation		
Lump-sum tax	724.0	1,489.6	1,691.4	1,561.8
Labor income tax	478.2	1,468.8	1,642.4	1,565.0
Sales tax	400.3	1,452.9	1,614.2	1,558.7
Individual income tax	374.5	1,456.1	1,619.1	1,563.1
		6 Percent Inflation		
Lump-sum tax	0.0	1,907.6	2,452.2	448.4
Labor income tax	0.0	1,771.4	2,170.4	746.9
Sales tax	0.0	1,600.7	2,104.9	901.2
Individual income tax	0.0	1,595.8	2,007.9	999.4
		10 Percent Inflation		
Lump-sum tax	−477.1	2,060.4	3,015.6	−200.8
Labor income tax	−333.7	1,791.6	2,584.7	267.3
Sales tax	−285.2	1,623.5	2,356.4	517.0
Individual income tax	−221.9	1,604.8	2,353.1	748.6

Note: The 1987 national wealth (beginning of the year) and gross national product were $15,920.2 billion and $4,488.5 billion.

Source: Jorgenson and Yun (1990).

corporate, noncorporate, and household sectors would generate a welfare gain in excess of $2 trillion dollars. If interasset tax wedges in each of the three private sectors is eliminated as well, the welfare gains would exceed $2.5 trillion dollars.

Replacing the distortionary capital income taxes of the 1985 laws with a lump sum tax would have generated a welfare gain of $3,854 billion. However, if realistic and distortionary taxes are used to replace the existing capital income taxes, welfare gains are reduced approximately by half. For example, under labor income tax adjustment, the welfare gain is only $2,045 billion. If the sales tax on investment goods is eliminated as well, the welfare gain under the lump sum tax adjustment increases to $4,128 billion, but it becomes only $1,988 billion under the labor income tax adjustment.

These findings suggest that revenue neutral elimination of the interasset and intersector tax distortions can generate as much welfare gains as the complete elimination of intertemporal distortions. Part of the reason is that income taxes on existing capital are lump sum taxes.[17] Another part is that the welfare gains from eliminating the

Table 10.2
Welfare effects of tax distortions (billions of 1987 dollars)

		1985 Law
1.	Within-sector interasset distortion:	
	Lump-sum tax adjustment	443.9
	Labor income tax adjustment	248.1
	Sales tax adjustment	168.7
	Individual income tax adjustment	70.2
2.	Intersector distortion: corporate and noncorporate sectors:	
	Lump-sum tax adjustment	−93.3
	Labor income tax adjustment	−416.7
	Sales tax adjustment	−523.8
	Individual income tax adjustment	−715.5
3.	Intersector distortion: all sectors:	
	Lump-sum tax adjustment	2,262.6
	Labor income tax adjustment	2,156.9
	Sales tax adjustment	2,118.6
	Individual income tax adjustment	2,067.7
4.	No tax distortion: corporate and noncorporate sectors, all assets:	
	Lump-sum tax adjustment	326.4
	Labor income tax adjustment	69.2
	Sales tax adjustment	−29.1
	Individual income tax adjustment	−169.7
5.	No tax distortion: all sectors, all assets:	
	Lump-sum tax adjustment	2,663.7
	Labor income tax adjustment	2,603.9
	Sales tax adjustment	2,572.4
	Individual income tax adjustment	2,547.2
6.	Corporate tax integration:	
	Lump-sum tax adjustment	1,313.1
	Labor income tax adjustment	493.4
	Sales tax adjustment	238.1
	Individual income tax adjustment	−274.5
7.	Consumption tax rules (zero effective tax rates):	
	Lump-sum tax adjustment	3,853.9
	Labor income tax adjustment	2,045.4
	Sales tax adjustment	1,749.3
	Individual income tax adjustment	2,045.4
8.	Consumption tax rules (zero effective tax rates: no sales tax on investment goods)	
	Lump-sum tax adjustment	4,128.1
	Labor income tax adjustment	1,988.0
	Sales tax adjustment	1,722.1
	Individual income tax adjustment	1,988.0

Note: Inflation is fixed at 6 percent per year.

Source: Jorgenson and Yun (1990).

distortions caused by the taxation of income from capital is partly offset by the increase in the distortion of the taxes which are used for revenue adjustment.

10.4.3.2   Excess Burden of Taxation

The model can also be applied to the analysis of excess burden of taxation. Suppose we want to measure the excess burden of a distortionary tax. In order to measure the excess burden, we replace a segment of the tax with a lump sum tax in such a way that total tax revenue is not affected. Then the welfare change is measured in terms of equivalent variation in full wealth. For this purpose we employ the intertemporal expenditure function. Let the equivalent variation be ΔW. Then,

$$\Delta W = W(PF_0, D_0, V_1) - W_0$$

where the subscripts 0 denotes the base case and V_1 is the level of intertemporal welfare under the alternative policy with lump sum tax.

It is convenient to compare the equivalent variation with the present value of the tax revenue replaced by the lump sum tax. In order to compute the present value of the lump sum tax revenue, we first convert the time path of the lump sum tax in the unit of full consumption and add it to the time path of full consumption in the base case. We then evaluate the level of intertemporal welfare, say, V_2, attainable with the composite path of lump sum tax and full consumption in the base case. The present value of lump sum tax, T, is:

$$T = W(PF_0, D_0, V_2) - W_0. \tag{10.90}$$

We define the average efficiency cost, AEC, of the taxes we have replaced with lump sum tax as:

$$AEC = \frac{\Delta W}{T}. \tag{10.91}$$

We can increase the scale of the tax replacement and define the marginal efficiency cost of taxation, MEC, as:

$$MEC = \frac{\Delta(\Delta W)}{\Delta T}. \tag{10.92}$$

Jorgenson and Yun (1991b) implemented this approach to measure the excess burden of various segments of the U.S. tax system. In this analysis, we reduce the rates of relevant distortionary taxes incrementally. At first we reduce the tax rates by 5% of those under the reference policy. Then we reduce the tax rate by 20%, 30%, and so forth. Eventually, the entire segment of the distorting taxes is replaced by lump sum tax. Some of the results are reproduced in Table 10.3, where the tax policy under the tax reform act of 1986 and an annual rate of inflation of 6% is taken as the reference. We find, for example, that the marginal efficiency cost of corporate income tax is 44.8 cents per one dollar's worth of tax revenue. If we replace the corporate income tax with a lump sum tax with equal revenue, welfare gain would be 37.4% of the present value of the tax revenue.

10.4.3.3   Marginal Cost of Public Spending
This analysis of the excess burden of taxation is in the tradition of differential incidence in which expenditure side of government budget is not affected. The model can also be employed in economic analyses in the tradition of balanced budget incidence in which both the revenue and expenditure sides of government budget are affected.

Jorgenson and Yun (1992) used the model to measure the social cost of public spending.[18] In this application of the IGEM, we consider a marginal spending program which is financed with an increase in existing taxes. Since the revenue and expenditure sides of government budget are affected by the marginal spending program, we are in the tradition of balanced budget incidence.

The marginal program raises funds by increasing taxes and spends it on consumption goods, investment goods, labor services, and transfer payments. The consumption goods, investment goods, and labor services purchased with the marginal fund are used to produce goods and services which are provided to the public free of charge. Transfer payments benefit the consumers directly by augmenting their disposable income.

In general, the goods and services provided by the marginal program are imperfect substitutes with private consumption. But we consider two polar cases. In one extreme, we assume that the goods and services provided by the marginal spending program is additively separable from full consumption. Hence private consumption is not affected by the marginal program. In the other extreme, the output of the marginal program is assumed to be perfect substitute with full consumption.

Table 10.3
Efficiency cost of U.S. Tax Revenues: Tax Reform Act of 1986

Tax Bases		Reduction in Tax Rates (%)										
		5	10	20	30	40	50	60	70	80	90	100
1. Corporate Income	MEC	.448	.435	.418	.397	.379	.363	.348	.334	.322	.310	.301
	AEC	.448	.442	.431	.421	.412	.404	.397	.391	.384	.379	.374
2. Ind. Cap. Income	MEC	1.017	.989	.951	.904	.853	.812	.767	.727	.688	.650	.613
	AEC	1.017	1.003	.977	.953	.928	.906	.884	.863	.842	.822	.803
3. Property Value	MEC	.176	.174	.171	.168	.164	.160	.157	.153	.149	.145	.142
	AEC	.176	.175	.173	.171	.169	.168	.166	.164	.162	.160	.158
4. All Cap. Income	MEC	.675	.650	.616	.573	.533	.498	.466	.435	.407	.382	.359
	AEC	.675	.663	.640	.619	.600	.582	.566	.551	.537	.524	.512
5. Labor Income	MEC	.376	.358	.333	.303	.276	.253	.237	.216	.201	.190	.183
	AEC	.376	.367	.350	.334	.320	.307	.296	.285	.275	.266	.259
6. 1+2+5 =4+5	MEC	.497	.462	.414	.355	.301	.254	.212	.175	.142	.114	.091
	AEC	.497	.480	.448	.418	.391	.366	.343	.323	.304	.287	.271
7. Ind. Income	MEC	.520	.490	.449	.396	.349	.305	.265	.229	.196	.167	.140
	AEC	.520	.505	.477	.451	.426	.403	.381	.361	.342	.325	.308
8. Sales Value	MEC	.262	.259	.254	.249	.242	.236	.230	.224	.218	.211	.205
	AEC	.262	.261	.257	.254	.251	.248	.245	.242	.239	.236	.232
9. All Tax Bases	MEC	.391	.346	.308	.249	.197	.151	.113	.082	.063	.048	.040
	AEC	.391	.374	.342	.312	.285	.260	.238	.220	.204	.190	.180

Source: Jorgenson and Yun (1991b).

In the latter case of perfect substitute, we further assume that the value of output is equal to the value of inputs. Under these assumptions, the benefit of the marginal spending program is the same as that of a transfer program of equal size. It does not follow, however, that the marginal spending program is equivalent to the transfer program. The difference is that the marginal spending program affects the demands for consumption goods, investment goods, and labor, while a transfer program simply turns over purchasing power to the households.

The effects of the marginal spending program on the welfare of the consumer may be written as:

$$\Delta V(q, G, T) = \frac{\partial V}{\partial q} \Delta q + \frac{\partial V}{\partial G} \Delta G + \frac{\partial V}{\partial T} \Delta T \tag{10.93}$$

where V is indirect utility function of the consumer, q is the vector of consumer prices, G is the vector of government outputs which are provided to the public free of charge, and T is exogenous income including, among others, transfer payments. Since consumer price of a commodity (or a factor) is equal to the sum of producer price and tax,

$$q = p + t \tag{10.94}$$

where p is the vector of producer prices and t is the corresponding vector of taxes. In the accounting framework of cost-benefit analysis, social cost of the marginal spending program may be identified with the first term of (10.93), and the benefits, with the two remaining terms. Accordingly, social cost of the marginal spending program may be expressed in monetary terms as:

$$MC = - \frac{\frac{\partial V}{\partial q} \Delta p + \frac{\partial V}{\partial q} \Delta t}{\frac{\partial V}{\partial T}}. \tag{10.95}$$

The marginal cost of public spending, MCS, is measured as the ratio of MC to the tax revenue used to finance the marginal program, ΔR:

$$MCS = \frac{MC}{\Delta R}. \tag{10.96}$$

ΔR can be written as:

$$\Delta R = X(q,G,T)\Delta t + t\Delta X(q,G,T) \tag{10.97}$$

where $X(q,G,T)$ is the vector of consumer demand. Thus MCS is the social cost of one dollar's worth of government spending.

The next step is to measure the social cost of the marginal program and the present value of tax revenue. For this purpose we need to consider the general equilibrium impacts of the program on the resource allocation in the economy. Let $Z(p,G,T,S)$ be the vector of government demands, where S stands for the government policy regarding the allocation of total expenditure among goods and services. Since government does not collect taxes on the goods and services purchased by itself, government expenditure is expressed in producer prices. Further, assume that Δt is predetermined up to a scale factor α in the sense that

$$\Delta t = \alpha \tau \tag{10.98}$$

where τ is a predetermined vector of tax rates.

Net supply of the business sector may be expressed simply as $Y = Y(p)$ where demands for inputs are represented by negative entries. Market equilibrium requires

$$\Delta X(q,G,T) + \Delta Z(p,G,T,S) = \Delta Y(p) \tag{10.99}$$

and budget balance of the marginal spending program requires:

$$X\Delta t + t\Delta X = Z\Delta p + p\Delta Z. \tag{10.100}$$

Once τ, ΔG, ΔT, and ΔS are determined for the marginal program, α and Δp are solved from (10.94), (10.98)–(10.100).

Once the general equilibrium is found, computation of ΔR and MC is straightforward. At this stage, recall that we distinguish two types of benefits from the marginal program. In the case where the benefits are additively separable from private consumption, the social cost of the marginal program is:

$$MC = W(PF_0, D_0, V_0) - W(PF_0, D_0, V_1)$$

where V_1 and V_0 are the levels of intertemporal welfare from private consumption with and without the marginal spending program. In the case where the benefits are perfect substitutes with full consumption, V_1 measures the welfare from full consumption and the public consumption of goods and services provided by the marginal spending program. Thus the social cost of the marginal program is:

$$MC = W(PF_0, D_0, V_0) - [W(PF_0, D_0, V_1) - \Delta T]$$

where ΔT is the present value of the benefits from the marginal program. In the case of lump sum transfer, the value of the transfer is simply equal to the amount of transfer.

Table 10.4 shows some results from Jorgenson and Yun (1992) where the Tax Reform Act of 1986 was taken as the reference tax policy. We find that MCS depends upon the source as well as the use of public funds. It also depends upon the type of benefits. In earlier studies, the source of public fund and the types of benefits were emphasized as the determinants of MCS. We interpret the marginal spending program as a production process in which inputs are transformed into outputs. In this context, general equilibrium consideration leads to the conclusion that MCS depends upon the use of marginal fund as well, which is confirmed in table 10.4.

10.5 Concluding Remarks

We began the chapter by presenting the expressions for the cost of capital in the corporate, noncorporate, and household sectors. The expressions are derived with special attention to the effects of indexing, deduction of interests and dividends, and the deduction of state and local taxes on the cost of capital. These expressions can be employed to measure the cost of capital in the U.S. They can also be used to evaluate the cost of capital under various tax reform proposals.

Closely related to the cost of capital is the effective tax rate of capital income. Effective tax rate is defined as the tax wedge between the before- and after-tax rates of return divided by a reference rate of return. In principle, the cost of capital can be represented in terms of effective tax rate and a reference rate of return. Thus in some general equilibrium models, capital income tax is modeled as an *ad valorem* tax on capital services. Setting the *ad valorem* tax rate is equivalent to fixing the effective tax rate. The problem with this approach is that the effective tax rate depends upon tax policy as well as the reference rate of return at which the effective tax rate is measured.

The problem takes a particularly serious form in the context of an intertemporal general equilibrium model (IGEM) where the rate of

Table 10.4
Marginal cost of public spending (Tax Reform Act of 1986)

Revenue Source	Type of Marginal Public Spending								
	Consumption Goods		Investment Goods		Labor Services		Transfer Payment	Proportional Expansion	
	A	B	A	B	A	B	B	A	B
a. Corporate Income	1.071	1.229	0.980	1.139	1.229	1.458	1.454	1.213	1.350
b. Ind. Cap. Income	1.541	1.726	1.397	1.582	1.877	2.062	2.050	1.750	1.911
c. Property Value	0.850	0.997	0.779	0.926	1.024	1.171	1.170	0.959	1.086
d. All Cap. Income	1.257	1.426	1.146	1.315	1.527	1.696	1.691	1.422	1.568
e. Labor Income	1.026	1.181	0.955	1.110	1.253	1.411	1.408	1.166	1.306
f. $a+b+c = d+e$	1.127	1.289	1.039	1.200	1.372	1.535	1.532	1.277	1.420
g. Individual Income	1.148	1.310	1.060	1.222	1.399	1.564	1.560	1.302	1.447
h. Sales Value	0.921	1.071	0.850	0.999	1.117	1.267	1.266	1.043	1.172
i. All Tax Bases	1.038	1.195	0.956	1.112	1.261	1.418	1.416	1.174	1.311

Notes: 1. Columns A are for additively separable (exhaustive) benefits and columns B are for benefits which are perfect substitute with private consumption. In Columns B, the value (to consumer) of benefits from public spending is assumed to be equal to the amount of marginal government spending.
2. Government spendings are increased by 1% in real terms and the relevant tax rates are adjusted to keep government budget balanced at the margin.
3. Proportional expansion of public spending includes a proportional increase in transfer payment to households and foreigners. Thus Column A: under proportional expansion reflects the effects of type B benefits generated by the transfer component in the spending. Transfer payment to foreigners' accounts for 1.06% of total government spending, net of interest payments.
Source: Jorgenson and Yun (1992).

return to capital changes continuously as the economy moves toward a balanced growth equilibrium. Even under a fixed tax policy, the true effective tax rate varies over time as the economy moves along a transition path and a constant effective tax rate fails to represent the fixed tax policy.

This is an unavoidable consequence of the attempt to represent the tax policy on capital income with a single parameter where the tax policy has more than one instrument. Such difficulties can be avoided if we represent the cost of capital with the expressions like those derived in section 10.2. Since the expressions for the cost of capital captures the effects of each of the tax policy instruments individually, the cost of capital is represented accurately regardless of the reference rates of return.

We also described an IGEM developed by Jorgenson and Yun, which can be used to analyze various fiscal policies, especially tax policies. The model is based on Jorgenson's earlier work in many areas of economics such as national income and product account, consumer theory, econometrics, translog function, productivity, general equilibrium modeling, etc. In particular, the model incorporates the cost of capital approach in representing the resource allocation in the corporate, noncorporate, and household sectors.

The IGEM consists of four main sectors: household, business, government, and the rest of the world. The household sector is represented by a consumer who is endowed a perfect foresight and infinite time horizon. The model distinguishes corporate and noncorporate firms in the business sector, but represents the production technology with a single production function. The government collects taxes, issues debts, pays interests on government debts, makes transfer payments, and spends on goods and labor services. The rest of the world sector closes the model.

The Jorgenson and Yun model captures resource allocation at the intertemporal, intersectoral (corporate vs. noncorporate vs. household), and interasset (short-lived vs. long-lived assets) margins. However the model does not distinguish production in different industries. An obvious direction for the extension of the model is to capture interindustry resource allocations. We can think of still another margin of resource allocation, namely, the intergenerational margin, which is not covered by the model. This margin is particularly important for the analysis of intergenerational distribution issues. In order to amend this shortcoming, one needs to replace the model of the infinitely lived consumer with an overlapping generations model with bequest motives.

We presented an analytical framework for welfare analysis of fiscal policies in the context of the Jorgenson and Yun IGEM. At the core of the analytical framework is the intertemporal expenditure function which determines the minimum value of full wealth required to attain a given level of intertemporal welfare. Formally, this is an extension of the expenditure function approach to the intertemporal context.

Samuelson (1961) noted that "the only valid approximation to a measure of welfare comes from computing wealth-like magnitude not income magnitude (of Haig, Fisher or any other type)." The intertemporal expenditure function computes exactly what Samuelson calls wealth-like magnitude that measures the level of welfare. Application of the intertemporal expenditure function to differential welfare analysis is straightforward. We can easily compute the Hicksian variations of a policy change. In practice, since equivalent variation is transitive, we use equivalent variation measure of welfare change.

The IGEM of Jorgenson and Yun has been employed in the analyses of various fiscal policy issues such as tax reform, excess burden of taxation, marginal social cost of public spending, welfare effects of defense cuts, etc. The analyses focus on the welfare effects of fiscal policies where the intertemporal expenditure function plays a central role. Some of the interesting results are presented in tables 10.1 through 10.4. Overall, we find that the cost of capital approach provides a practical and convenient vehicle for realistic representation of the taxation of income from capital in IGEM.

Notes

1. The Economic Recovery Tax Act of 1981 and the Tax Reform Act of 1986.
2. See King and Fullerton (1984).
3. Measurement of t_c^e, t_c^g, and many other tax parameters for personal income and property ownership are described in Jorgenson and Yun (1991a,b).
4. In contrast, under the alternative view known as the new view, or the trapped equity model, divident payout ratio is endogenous and the marginal source of equity financing is retaining. In this view, new share issue is exogenous. See King (1977), Auerbach (1979), and Bradford (1981).
5. Conceptually HDI is the same as DI for the corporate and noncorporate sectors. However it is distinguished from DI for practical reasons. For example, in the Treasury Proposal of 1984, business interest payments are indexed while household interest payments are not. U.S. Department of Treasury, 1984.
6. Bradford (1981) makes essentially the same point in a different context.
7. The Hudson and Jorgenson model is a dynamic general equilibrium model with nine industrial sectors. (Later it was expanded to a thirty-six sector model by Richard J.

Goettle, IV and Hudson). It implemented the cost of capital approach consistently from model building and parameter estimation to simulation of policy effects. The model provided an important stepping stone for Jorgenson's students who were interested in general equilibrium modeling. Yun, Wilcoxen, and Ho are among the principle beneficiaries.

8. In resource allocation, we can think of five important margins of resources allocation: intertemporal, intersectoral (corporate vs. noncorporate vs. household), interasset (short-lived and long-lived assets), interindustry, and intergenerational margins. Of these, we capture the resource allocation at the first three margins.

9. Human wealth is defined as the sum of the present values of labor income and personal transfer payment.

10. Christensen, Jorgenson, and Lau (1975)

11. In the following, R stands for revenues, t for tax rates, and the subscripts c, n, and h, for the corporate, noncorporate, and household sectors, respectively.

12. The imputed depreciation converts the present value of tax depreciation into a flow which is proportional to the flow of capital services from the asset, net of property taxes. The imputed investment tax credit is similarly defined. See the definition of DQ and ITC_c below.

13. Recall that $r_s \equiv (1 + r_s^{pn})PF_{s-1}/PF_s - 1$. Thus the rate of inflation associated with r_s is the rate of inflation in the price of full consumption. In contrast, the rate of inflation in the expressions for the cost of capital measures the inflation in the price of assets.

14 Samuelson, Paul A. (1961).

15. See Kay (1980).

16. For details, see Jorgenson and Yun (1990).

17. Chamley (1981, 1986)

18. The cost of public spending has been an area of active research in recent years. For details, see Jorgenson and Yun (1992) and the papers listed there.

11 Progress in Measuring the Price and Quantity of Capital

W. Erwin Diewert and Denis A. Lawrence[1]

11.1 Introduction

The fundamentals of capital measurement for production function and productivity estimation were laid out by Dale Jorgenson (1963) over 35 years ago. This theory, which lays out the relationships between asset prices, rental prices, depreciation and the relative efficiencies of vintages of durable inputs, has been refined and extended by a large number of authors, including Jorgenson and Griliches (1967, 1972a), Christensen and Jorgenson (1969, 1970), Jorgenson (1973, 1989, 1996), Diewert (1980), Hulten and Wykoff (1981a, 1981b, 1996), Hulten (1990, 1996) and Triplett (1996). Unfortunately, the United Nations (1993) System of National Accounts has not yet incorporated this well established theory into its production accounts, partly because the SNA regards interest as an income transfer rather than being a productive reward for postponing consumption and partly because capital gains are also regarded as being unproductive.[2] Thus from some points of view, there has been little official progress in measuring the price and quantity of capital in a form that would be suitable for production and productivity accounts.

However, the above paragraph presents a picture that is a bit too gloomy for two reasons: Several statistical agencies, starting with the U.S. Bureau of Labor Statistics,[3] have introduced productivity accounts that are based on user costs[4]; An international group of statistical agencies has set up a Working Group (the Canberra Group) under the direction of Derek Blades of the OECD whose mandate is to construct a handbook of capital measurement that would be used by national income accountants around the world. Hopefully, the user cost of capital will make its national income accounting debut in this document.

After delivering the above brief progress report, is there anything new that we can say in the remainder of the paper? We believe that there is. In the remainder of the paper, we flesh out a suggestion that dates back to Jorgenson: "According to the neo-classical theory of capital, as expounded for example by Irving Fisher, a production plan for the firm is chosen so as to maximize utility over time. Under certain well-known conditions this leads to maximization of the net worth of the enterprise as the criterion for optimal capital accumulation. Capital is accumulated to provide capital services, which are inputs into the productive process. For convenience the relationship between inputs, including the input of capital services, and output is summarized in a production function." Dale Jorgenson (1963, reprinted in Jorgenson, 1996; 1).

Following up the suggestion of Christensen and Jorgenson (1973, reprinted in Jorgenson, 1995a; 175–272), we will treat each vintage of a particular capital good as a separate vintage specific input into production and construct a separate rental price for that vintage. Then we will form a capital aggregate over vintages by using a superlative index number formula[5] that does not restrict *a priori* the substitution possibilities between the various vintages of that type of capital.[6] Thus instead of aggregating over vintages using an assumed pattern of relative efficiencies, we use the theory of exact index numbers to do the aggregation. However, as we shall see, the use of Hicks' (1946; 312–313) Aggregation Theorem (applied in the producer context) leads to the emergence of some familiar capital aggregates in the end.

In the following section, we lay out the basic relationships between depreciation (the decline in value of an asset due to age) and the asset and rental prices of each vintage of a durable input. We look at the relationships between each of these three profiles of prices (or depreciation amounts) as functions of age, assuming that we can observe a cross section of asset prices by age of asset. It turns out that any one of these profiles determines the other two profiles.

In sections 11.3, 11.4 and 11.5, we specialize the general model of section 11.2 to work out the implications of three specific models of depreciation or relative efficiency that have been proposed in the literature. In section 3, we consider *the declining balance or geometric depreciation* model while in section 11.5, we consider the *straight line depreciation* model. In section 11.4, we consider the *one hoss shay model of depreciation* which assumes that the efficiency and hence rental price of each vintage of the capital good is constant over time (until the good is discarded as completely worn out after N periods). This model is sometimes known as the *gross capital stock* model. Note that these models all assume that the real rate of interest r is constant at any point in time.

The models derived in sections 11.3–11.5 imply different measures for the aggregate service flow of capital. Hence, the use of these different capital flow measures will lead to different measures of total factor productivity growth. In sections 11.6–11.8, we use Canadian data for the private business sector for the years 1962–1996 to construct alternative capital flows and productivity measures using the alternative capital concepts developed in sections 11.3–11.5. Thus we ask the question: does the use of these alternative capital measures *empirically matter* for the purpose of productivity measurement?[7] In sections 11.6–11.8, we also address some of the complications associated with the measurement of real interest rates when rates of inflation for asset prices differ.

Section 11.9 offers some concluding comments while the Data Appendix briefly describes and lists the Canadian data that we use.

11.2   The Relationship between Asset Prices, Depreciation, and Rental Prices

Consider a new durable input that is purchased at the beginning of a period at the price P_0. At this same point in time, older vintages of this same input can be purchased at the price P_t for a unit of the asset that is t years old, for $t = 1, 2. \ldots$. Generally speaking, these vintage asset prices decline as the age of the asset increases. This sequence of vintage asset prices at a particular point in time,

$$P_0, P_1, \ldots, P_t, \ldots \tag{11.1}$$

is called the *asset price profile* of the durable input.

Depreciation for a unit of a new asset, D_0, is defined as the difference in the price of a new asset and an asset that is one year old, $P_0 - P_1$. In general, *cross-section depreciation* for an asset that is t years old is defined as

$$D_t = P_t - P_{t+1}; \quad t = 0, 1, 2, \ldots. \tag{11.2}$$

Obviously, given the asset price profile, the profile of depreciation allowances, D_t, can be calculated using equations (11.2). Conversely, given the sequence of depreciation allowances, the asset price profile can be calculated using the following equations:

$$P_t = D_t + D_{t+1} + D_{t+2} + \ldots; \qquad t = 0, 1, 2, \ldots. \tag{11.3}$$

In addition to the asset price sequence $\{P_t\}$ and the depreciation sequence $\{D_t\}$, there is a sequence of rental payments to the vintage assets or the sequence of *vintage user costs*, $\{U_t\}$, that an asset of age t can earn during the current period, $t = 0, 1, 2, \ldots$. If the real interest rate in the current period is r, then economic theory suggests that the price of a new asset, P_0, should be equal to the rental for a new asset, U_0, plus the discounted stream of rentals or user costs that older vintage assets can earn. In general, the price of an age t asset, P_t, should be approximately equal to a discounted stream of rental revenues that the asset can be expected to earn for the remaining periods of its useful life:

$$P_t = U_t + (1+r)^{-1}U_{t+1} + (1+r)^{-2}U_{t+2} + ; \qquad t = 0, 1, 2, \ldots. \tag{11.4}$$

Equation (11.4) can be manipulated (use the equation for t and $t+1$) to give us a formula for U_t in terms of the asset prices:

$$P_t = U_t + (1+r)^{-1}P_{t+1}; \qquad t = 0, 1, 2, \ldots. \tag{11.5}$$

Equations (11.5) then yield the following formula for the user cost of a t year old asset:

$$U_t = P_t - (1+r)^{-1}P_{t+1}; \qquad t = 0, 1, 2, \ldots. \tag{11.6}$$

The interpretation of (11.6) is clear: the net cost of buying an asset that is t years old and using it for one period and then selling it at the end of the period is equal to its purchase price P_t less the discounted end of the period price for the asset when it is one year older, $(I+r)^{-1}P_{t+1}$. User cost formulae similar to (11.6) date back to the economist Walras (1954; 269) and the early industrial engineer Church (1901; 907–908). In more recent times, user cost formulae adjusted for income taxes have been derived by Jorgenson (1963, 1989) and by Hall and Jorgenson (1967). A simple method for deriving these tax adjusted user costs may be found in Diewert (1980, 471; 1992, 194).

The above equations show that the sequence of vintage asset prices $\{P_t\}$, the sequence of vintage depreciation allowances $\{D_t\}$, and the sequence of vintage rental prices or user costs $\{U_t\}$, *cannot be specified independently*; given any one of these sequences, the other two sequences are completely determined.[8] This is an important point since capital stock researchers usually specify a pattern of depreciation rates and *these alternative depreciation assumptions completely determine the sequence of vintage specific rental prices which should be used as weights when aggregating across vintages to form an aggregate capital stock component.*

In what follows, we consider three alternative patterns of depreciation: (a) declining balance or exponential depreciation (the amount of depreciation for each vintage is assumed to be a constant fraction of the depreciated asset value at the beginning of the period); (b) one hoss shay depreciation (or light bulb depreciation) where the efficiency of the asset is assumed to be constant until it reaches the end of its life when it completely collapses and (c) straight line depreciation where the amount of depreciation is assumed to be a constant amount for each vintage until the asset reaches the end of its life.

11.3 The Declining Balance Depreciation Model

In terms of the sequence of vintage asset prices, this model can be specified as follows:

$$P_t = (1-\delta)^t P_0; \quad t = 1, 2, \ldots \tag{11.7}$$

where δ is a positive number between 0 and 1 (the constant depreciation rate). Thus from (11.7), we see that the vintage asset price declines geometrically as the asset ages. If we substitute (11.7) into (11.2), we see that:

$$D_t = [1-(1-\delta)](1-\delta)P_0 = \delta(1-\delta)^t P_0 = \delta P_t; \quad t = 0, 1, 2, \ldots \tag{11.8}$$

i.e., depreciation for a t year old asset is equal to the constant depreciation rate δ times the vintage asset price at the start of the period, P_t. Note that the second equality in (11.8) tells us that D_t declines geometrically as t increases.

Substituting (11.7) into (11.6) yields the following sequence of vintage rental prices:

$$U_t = (1-\delta)^t P_0 - (l+r)^{-1}(1-\delta)^{t+1} P_0$$
$$= (1-\delta)^t (l+r)^{-1}[r+\delta]P_0; \quad t = 0, 1, 2, \ldots. \tag{11.9}$$

Thus the rental price for a new asset is (set $t = 0$ in the above equation):

$$U_0 = (1+r)^{-1}[r+\delta]P_0. \tag{11.10}$$

Now substitute (11.10) into (11.9) and we find that the rental price for a t year old asset is a geometrically declining fraction of the rental price for a new asset:

$$U_t = (1-\delta)^t U_0; \quad t = 1, 2, \ldots . \tag{11.11}$$

The above equations imply that the vintage specific asset rental prices vary in fixed proportion over time. This means that we can apply Hicks' (1946; 312–313) Aggregation Theorem to aggregate the capital stock components across vintages.[9] If I_0 is the new investment in the asset in the current period and I_t is the vintage investment in the asset that occurred t periods ago for $t = 1, 2, \ldots$, then the current period value of the particular capital stock component under consideration, aggregated over all vintages is:

$$U_0 I_0 + U_1 I_1 + \cdots = U_0[I_0 + (1-\delta)I_1 + (1-\delta)^2 I_0 + \cdots]. \tag{11.12}$$

Thus (11.12) gives us the value of capital services over all vintages of the capital stock component under consideration. It can be seen that this value flow can be decomposed into a price term U_0 which is the user cost for a new unit of the durable input, times an aggregated over vintages capital stock K defined as

$$K = I_0 + (1-\delta)I_1 + (1-\delta)^2 I_2 + \cdots . \tag{11.13}$$

This is the standard net capital stock model that has been used extensively by Jorgenson and his associates; see Jorgenson (1963, 1983, 1984), Jorgenson and Griliches (1967, 1972a) and Christensen and Jorgenson (1969).

Note that in this model of depreciation, it is not necessary to use a superlative index number formula to aggregate over vintages in this model since its use would just reproduce the decomposition into price and quantity components that is on the right-hand side of (11.12); i.e., in this model, Hicks' Aggregation Theorem makes the use of a superlative formula superfluous.

We turn now to the one hoss shay model of depreciation.

11.4   The Gross Capital Stock Model

In this model, it is assumed that the efficiency of the asset remains constant over its life of say N years and then the asset becomes worthless. This means that the rental price for the asset remains *constant* over its useful life; i.e., we make the following assumption:

$$U_t = U_0 \text{ for } t = 1, 2, \ldots, N-1 \text{ and } U_t = 0 \text{ for } t = N, N+1, N+2, \quad (11.14)$$

We need a formula for the user cost of a new unit of the asset, U_0. Substituting (11.14) into equation (11.4) when $t = 0$ yields:

$$P_0 = U_0 + (1+r)^{-1}U_0 + (1+r)^{-2}U_0 + \cdots + (1+r)^{-N+1}U_0$$
$$= U_0(1+r)r^{-1}[1 - (1+r)^{-N}]. \quad (11.15)$$

Now use (11.15) to solve for U_0 in terms of P_0:

$$U_0 = P_0 r(1+r)^{-1}[1 - (1+r)^{-N}]^{-1}. \quad (11.16)$$

The capital aggregate in this model is simply the sum of the current period investment I_0 plus the vintage investments going back $N-1$ periods:

$$K = I_0 + I_1 + \cdots + I_{N-1}. \quad (11.17)$$

The corresponding price for this capital aggregate is U_0 defined by (11.16). Because the rental price is constant across vintages, we can again apply Hicks' Aggregation Theorem to aggregate across vintages; i.e., we do not have to use a superlative index number formula to aggregate over vintages in this model since the user costs of the vintages will vary in strict proportion over time. This is the standard gross capital stock model that is used by the OECD and many other researchers. The only point that is not generally known is that there is a definite rental price that can be associated with this gross capital stock and the corresponding quantity aggregate is consistent with Hicks' Aggregation Theorem.

For comparison purposes, it may be useful to have explicit formulae for the profile of vintage asset prices P_t and the vintage depreciation amounts D_t. In terms of U_0, these formulae are:

$P_t = U_0(1+r)r^{-1}[1-(1+r)^{-(N-t)}]$ for $t = 0, 1, 2, \ldots, N-1$ and

$P_t = 0$ for $t = N, N+1, \ldots$ (11.18)

and

$D_t = U_0(1+r)^{1-N+t}$ for $t = 0, 1, 2, \ldots, N-1$ and

$D_t = 0$ for $t = N, N+1, \ldots$ (11.19)

Of course, P_t declines as t increases (for t less than N) but D_t *increases* as t increases (for t less than N), which is quite different from the pattern of depreciation in the declining balance model where depreciation *decreases* as t increases.

It is important to use the above gross capital stock user costs as price weights when aggregating over different components of a gross capital stock in order to form an aggregate flow of services that can be attributed to the capital stock in any period. Many researchers who construct gross capital stocks for productivity measurement purposes use formula (11.17) above to construct gross capital stock components but then when they construct an overall capital aggregate, they use the stock prices P_0 as price weights instead of the user costs U_0 defined by (11.16). This will typically lead to an aggregate capital stock which grows too slowly since structures (which usually grow more slowly than machinery and equipment components) are given an inappropriately large weight when stock prices are used in place of user costs as price weights; see Jorgenson and Griliches (1972a) for additional material on this point.

We turn now to our final alternative model of depreciation.

11.5   The Straight Line Depreciation Model

In this model of depreciation, the depreciation for an asset which is t years old is set equal to a constant fraction of the value of a new asset P_0 over the life of the asset; i.e., we have

$D_t = (1/N)P_0$ for $t = 0, 1, 2, \ldots, N-1$ and

$D_t = 0$ for $t = N, N+1, N+2, \ldots$ (11.20)

where N is the useful life of a new asset. Using (11.3) and (11.20), we can deduce that the sequence of vintage asset prices is

$P_t = [1 - t/N]P_0$ for $t = 0, 1, 2, \ldots, N - 1$ and

$P_t = 0$ for $t = N, N + 1, N + 2, \ldots$ (11.21)

Using (11.6) and (11.21), we can calculate the sequence of vintage user costs:

$U_t = [1 - t/N]P_0 - (1 + r)^{-1}[1 - (t + 1)/N]P_0$

$\quad = (1 + r)^{-1}[r + N^{-1} - tN^{-1}r]P_0$ for $t = 0, 1, \ldots, N - 1$ and (11.22)

$U_t = 0 \quad$ for $t = N, N + 1, \ldots$ (11.23)

Recall that in the declining balance model, depreciation *decreased* as the asset aged (see (11.8) above) and in the gross capital stock model, depreciation *increased* as the asset aged (see (11.19) above). In the present model, depreciation is *constant* over the useful life of the asset. Also recall that in the declining balance model, the vintage asset prices *decreased* as the asset aged (see (11.7) above) and in the gross capital stock model, the vintage asset prices also *decreased* as the asset aged (see (11.18) above). In the present model, the vintage asset prices also *decrease* over the useful life of the asset (see (11.21) above). Finally, recall that in the declining balance model, the vintage rental prices *decreased* as the asset aged (see (11.11) above) and in the gross capital stock model, the vintage rental prices *remained constant* as the asset aged (see (11.14) above). In the present model, the vintage asset prices also *decrease* over the useful life of the asset (see (11.22) above); i.e., U_t decreases from $(1 + r)^{-1}[r + (1/N)]P_0$ when $t = 0$ to $(1/N)P_0$ when $t = N - 1$.

How can we empirically distinguish between the three depreciation models? We know of only three methods for doing this: (a) engineering studies; (b) regression models, which utilize profiles of used asset prices;[10] and (c) regression models where production functions or profit functions are estimated where vintage investments appear as independent inputs.[11] In practice, it is difficult to distinguish between the declining balance and straight line models of depreciation since their price and depreciation profiles are qualitatively similar.

We now encounter a problem with the straight line depreciation model that we did not encounter with our first two models: the rental prices of the vintage capital stock components *will no longer vary in strict proportion over time unless the real interest rate r is constant over time*. Thus in order to form a capital services aggregate over the different vintages of capital, we can no longer appeal to Hicks'

Aggregation Theorem to form the aggregate using minimal assumptions on the degree of substitutability between the different vintages.

The aggregate value of capital services over vintages is:

$$U_0 I_0 + U_1 I_1 + \cdots + U_{N-1} I_{N-1} = (1+r)^{-1}[r + (1/N)]P_0 I_0$$
$$+ \cdots + (I/N)P_0 I_{N-1} \qquad (11.24)$$

It can be seen that the price of a new unit of the capital stock, P_0, is a common factor in all of the terms on the right hand side of (11.24); this follows from the fact that P_0 is a common factor in all of the user costs U_t defined by (11.23). Thus we could set the price of the aggregate equal to P_0 and define the corresponding capital services aggregate as the right-hand side of (11.24) divided by P_0. However, to justify this procedure, we have to assume that each vintage of the capital aggregate is a perfect substitute for every other vintage with efficiency weights proportional to the user costs of each vintage. The problem with this assumption is if the real interest rate is not constant, then we are implicitly assuming that efficiency factors are changing over time in accordance with real interest rate changes. This is a standard assumption in capital theory *but it is not necessary to make this restrictive assumption.* Instead, we can use standard index number theory and use a superlative index number formula (see Diewert, 1976, 1978b) to aggregate the N vintage capital stock components: in each period, the quantities are $I_0, I_1, \ldots, I_{N-1}$ and the corresponding prices are the user costs $U_0, U_1, \ldots, U_{N-1}$ defined by (11.23). If we use the Fisher (1922) Ideal index, then this formula is consistent with the vintage specific assets being perfect substitutes but the formula is also consistent with more flexible aggregator functions.

We conclude these theoretical sections of our paper by noting that there was no need to use an index number formula to aggregate over vintages in the first two depreciation models considered above since under the assumptions of these models, the vintage rental prices will vary in strict proportion over time. Thus if we did use an index number formula that satisfied the proportionality test, then the resulting aggregates would be the same as the aggregates that were exhibited in sections 11.3 and 11.4 above. Most models of depreciation do not have vintage rental prices that vary in strict proportion over time so those two models are rather special. More complicated (but more flexible) models of depreciation are considered in Hulten and Wykoff (1981a).[12] The aggregation of the vintage capital stocks that correspond to these more complicated models of depreciation could also be accomplished using a superlative index number formula.

We turn now to an empirical illustration of the above aggregation procedures using Canadian data for the market sector of the economy for the years 1962–1996.

11.6   Construction of the Alternative Reproducible Capital Stocks for Canada

From the Data Appendix below, we can obtain beginning of the year net capital stocks for nonresidential structures, K_{NS}, and machinery and equipment, K_{ME}, in Canada for 1962 and 1997. We also have data on annual investments for these two capital stock components, I_{NS} and I_{ME}, for the years 1962–1996. Adapting equation (11.13) in section 11.3 above, it can be seen that if the declining balance model of depreciation is the correct one for Canada, then the 1997 beginning of the year capital stock for each of the above two components should be related to the corresponding 1962 stock and the annual investments as follows:

$$K^{1997} = (1-\delta)^{35} K^{1962} + (1-\delta)^{34} I^{1962} + (1-\delta)^{33} I^{1963}$$
$$+ \cdots + (1-\delta) I^{1995} + I^{1996} \tag{11.25}$$

where δ is the constant geometric depreciation rate that applies to the capital stock component. Substituting the data listed in the Data Appendix into (11.25) for the two reproducible capital stock components yields an estimated depreciation rate of $\delta_{NS} = 0.058623$ for nonresidential structures and $\delta_{ME} = 0.15278$ for machinery and equipment. Once these depreciation rates have been determined, the year to year capital stocks can be constructed (starting at $t = 1962$) using the following equation:

$$K^{t+1} = (1-\delta)K^t + I^t. \tag{11.26}$$

The resulting beginning of the year declining balance capital stock estimates for nonresidential construction may be found in the second column of table 11.1 below. However, for machinery and equipment, when we compared the stocks generated by equation (11.26) to the net stocks tabled in the Data Appendix, we found that the two series started to diverge around 1991. Hence we used variants of equation (11.25) above to fit two separate geometric depreciation rates for

Table 11.1
Alternative capital stocks for nonresidential structures in Canada

Year	Declining Balance	Straight Line	Gross
1962	30006.6	30006.6	50410.1
1963	30807.5	30828.3	51912.2
1964	31649.0	31685.7	53466.5
1965	32854.3	32902.7	55397.6
1966	34266.5	34330.7	57568.5
1967	36088.6	36176.4	60193.1
1968	37604.7	37732.6	62578.4
1969	39001.9	39176.3	64892.1
1970	40321.1	40544.3	67166.7
1971	41912.9	42183.7	69746.9
1972	43536.1	43858.8	72405.9
1973	45047.2	45425.4	75000.6
1974	46790.4	47223.2	77867.1
1975	48699.9	49190.6	80951.4
1976	51106.5	51660.7	84592.5
1977	53250.5	53883.7	88057.9
1978	55579.4	56297.8	91778.2
1979	57913.1	58724.9	95582.1
1980	60829.7	61740.6	100046.0
1981	64294.4	65321.5	105167.5
1982	68091.1	69260.8	110760.3
1983	70977.3	72319.3	115599.4
1984	73125.6	74642.4	119801.9
1985	75081.2	76753.7	123867.4
1986	77236.7	79039.4	128174.8
1987	78886.4	80797.0	132027.7
1988	80678.2	82660.8	136042.0
1989	83016.6	85037.6	140627.7
1990	85435.0	87473.4	145347.7
1991	87728.5	89763.4	149999.2
1992	89651.3	91656.7	154504.9
1993	90358.7	92291.9	157820.4
1994	91054.5	92842.7	160752.6
1995	92237.8	93820.6	163935.5
1996	93303.7	94640.8	166577.8
1997	94586.6	95649.3	169698.6

machinery and equipment; the first rate applies to the thirty years 1962–1991 and is $\delta_{ME} = .12172$ and the second rate applies to the six years 1991–1997 and is $\delta_{ME} = .16394$. Using these two depreciation rates in equation (11.26) led to the beginning of the year *declining balance* capital stock estimates for machinery and equipment that are found in the second column of table 11.2 below.

Table 11.2
Alternative capital stocks for machinery and equipment in Canada

Year	Declining Balance	Straight Line	Gross
1962	17983.7	17983.7	30017.3
1963	18162.7	17850.3	30606.6
1964	18522.0	17869.8	31291.0
1965	19291.3	18286.0	32316.0
1966	20494.5	19144.4	33748.5
1967	22229.6	20561.7	35732.0
1968	23845.6	21905.9	37672.9
1969	24966.0	22789.3	39171.7
1970	26331.1	23929.0	40900.1
1971	27615.1	25009.7	42552.9
1972	28876.9	26086.8	44169.5
1973	30361.5	27405.5	45981.9
1974	32785.0	29692.8	48722.4
1975	35687.4	32525.6	53247.5
1976	38628.9	35373.7	57962.8
1977	41530.2	38146.7	62542.3
1978	44060.1	40519.8	66575.8
1979	46904.7	43179.5	70553.8
1980	50746.0	46850.6	75782.5
1981	56096.6	52062.8	83287.1
1982	63204.7	59058.4	92819.3
1983	67262.2	63074.3	100081.1
1984	70606.0	66265.2	106988.9
1985	74318.5	69656.2	114296.2
1986	79447.3	74306.4	122352.0
1987	85489.7	79823.3	131171.7
1988	93219.6	87028.0	142022.1
1989	103385.1	96705.1	155931.1
1990	113970.6	106880.4	171515.8
1991	122239.5	114729.0	185449.6
1992	124460.9	121535.7	198159.9
1993	126893.6	127858.7	209468.7
1994	127816.8	132128.5	217258.1
1995	130582.7	137743.2	229226.9
1996	134305.4	143770.9	242825.8
1997	138467.1	149714.6	256698.2

We turn now to the construction of the capital stocks that correspond to the straight line depreciation assumption. Letting I^t be constant dollar investment in year t as usual, if the length of life is N years, then the beginning of year t *straight line* capital stock is equal to:

$$K^t = (1/N)[NI^{t-1} + (N-1)I^{t-2} + (N-2)^{t-3} + \cdots + (1)I^{t-N}] . \qquad (11.27)$$

Our investment data begin at 1962. In order to obtain straight line

capital stocks that start at the year 1962, we require investment data
for the previous N years. We formed an approximation to this missing investment data by assuming that investment grew in the pre-1962
period at the same rate as the net capital stock grew in the 1962–1997
period. The net capital stock for nonresidential structures, K_{NS} in the
Data Appendix, grew at the annual (geometric) rate of 1.033347 for the
1962–1997 period while the net capital stock for machinery and equipment, K_{ME}, grew at the annual (geometric) rate of 1.060053. Thus for a
given length of life N say for machinery and equipment capital, we
took the 1961 investment for machinery and equipment to be the
unknown amount I_{ME}^{1961}, and then defined the investment for 1960 to be
$I_{ME}^{1961}/1.060053$, the investment for 1959 to be $I_{ME}^{1961}/(1.060053)^2$, etc. We
then substituted these values into (11.27) with $t = 1962$ and solved the
resulting equation for I_{ME}^{1961}, assuming that $K_{ME}^{1962} = \$17{,}983.7$ billion
dollars, the starting value taken from the net capital stock listed in the
Data Appendix. We could construct the straight line capital stock for
machinery and equipment using our assumed life N, the artificial
pre-1962 investment data and the actual post 1962 investment data
using formula (11.27). We then repeated this procedure for alternative
values for N. We finally picked the N, which led to the straight line
capital stock which most closely approximated the net capital stock
listed in the Data Appendix. For machinery and equipment, the best
fitting length of life N was 12 years while for nonresidential structures, the best length of life was 29 years. These straight line capital
stocks are reported in column 3 of tables 11.1 and 11.2.

Once the "best" length of lives N for nonresidential structures (29
years) and machinery and equipment (12 years) have been determined, these lives can be used (along with our pre-1962 artificial
investment data and our post-1962 actual investment data) to construct the one hoss shay or gross capital stocks using the following for- ·
mula:

$$K^t = I^{t-1} + I^{t-2} + I^{t-3} + \cdots + I^{t-N}.\tag{11.28}$$

These gross capital stocks are reported in column 4 of tables 11.1 and
11.2.

In the following sections, we use the above capital stock and investment information to construct alternative aggregate capital services
measures along with total primary input and productivity measures
for Canada.

11.7 Alternative Productivity Measures for Canada Using Declining Balance Depreciation

From the Data Appendix, we have estimates for the price and quantity of market sector output in Canada for the years 1962–1996, P_Y and Q_Y; for the price and quantity of market sector labor services, P_L and Q_L; for the price and quantity of business and agricultural land, P_{BAL} and K_{BAL}; and for the price and quantity of beginning of the year market sector inventory stocks, P_{IS} and Q_{IS}. We also have estimates of the operating surplus for the market sector, OS, which is equal to the value of output, $P_Y Q_Y$, less the value of labor input, $P_L Q_L$. From the previous section, we have estimates of the beginning of the year declining balance capital stocks for nonresidential structures K_{NS} and for machinery and equipment K_{ME}. The corresponding prices, P_{NS} and P_{ME}, are listed in the Data Appendix. Thus we have assembled all of the ingredients that are necessary to form the declining balance user costs for each of our four durable inputs (nonresidential structures, machinery and equipment, land and inventories) that were defined by (11.10) in section 11.3 above. The only ingredient that is missing is an appropriate real interest rate, r.

For each year, we determined r by setting the operating surplus equal to the sum of the products of each stock times its user cost. This leads to a linear equation in r of the following form for each period:

$$(1+r)OS = (r+\delta_{NS})P_{NS}K_{NS} + (r+\delta_{ME})P_{ME}K_{ME}$$
$$+ rP_{BAL}K_{BAL} + rP_{IS}K_{IS}. \tag{11.29}$$

Once the interest rate r has been determined for each period, then the declining balance user costs for each of the four assets can be calculated, which are of the following form:

$$(r+\delta_{NS})P_{NS}/(1+r),\ (r+\delta_{ME})P_{ME}/(1+r),\ rP_{BAL}/(1+r),\ rP_{IS}/(1+r). \tag{11.30}$$

Finally, the above four user costs can be combined with the corresponding capital stock components, K_{NS}, K_{ME}, K_{BAL} and K_{IS}, using chain Fisher ideal indexes to form declining balance capital price and quantity aggregates, say $P_K(1)$ and $K(1)$.[13] The resulting aggregate price of capital services is graphed in figure 11.1 below. We also combined the four rental prices and quantities of capital with the price and quantity of labor, P_L and Q_L, to form a primary input aggregate, $Q_X(1)$, (again using a chain Fisher ideal quantity index). Once this

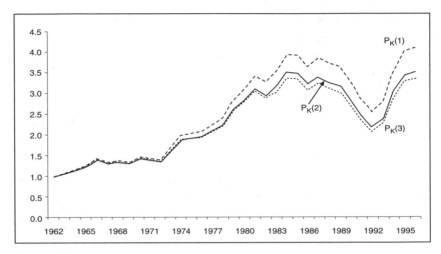

Figure 11.1
Alternative declining balance aggregate capital services prices.

aggregate input quantity index $Q_X(1)$ was determined, we used our aggregate output index Q_Y along with the input index in order to define our first total factor productivity index, $TFP(1)$:

$$TFP(1) \equiv Q_Y/Q_X(1). \tag{11.31}$$

$TFP(1)$ is graphed in figure 11.2 below.

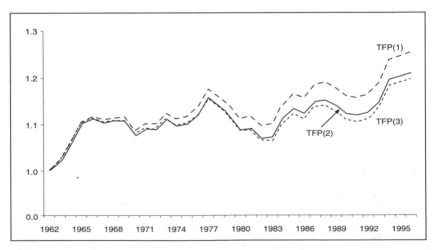

Figure 11.2
Alternative declining balance productivity measures.

Since in many productivity studies (including ours), land is held fixed, it is often neglected as an input into production. However, even though the quantity of land is fixed, its price is not and so neglecting land can have a substantial effect on aggregate input growth. In order to determine this effect empirically, we recomputed the interest rate r for each period by using a new version of equation (11.29) above where the term $rP_{BAL}K_{BAL}$ on the right-hand side of (11.29) was omitted. This omission of land has a substantial effect on the real interest rates: the average r increased from 5.933% to 7.808%. Once the new r's were determined, the three non-land user costs of the form (11.10) were computed. Then these three user costs were combined with the corresponding capital stock components, K_{NS}, K_{ME}, and K_{IS}, using chain Fisher ideal indexes to form new declining balance capital price and quantity aggregates, say $P_K(2)$ and $K(2)$. The resulting aggregate price of capital services $P_K(2)$ is graphed in figure 11.1. We also combine the three new rental prices and quantities of capital with the price and quantity of labor, P_L and Q_L, to form a new primary input aggregate, $Q_X(2)$, (again using a chain Fisher ideal quantity index). Once this aggregate input quantity index $Q_X(2)$ was determined, we used our aggregate output index Q_Y along with the input index in order to define our second total factor productivity index, $TFP(2)$:

$$TFP(2) \equiv Q_Y/Q_X(2) . \tag{11.32}$$

This second declining balance TFP measure (which omits land from the list of primary inputs) is graphed in 11.2.

Many productivity studies also neglect the role of inventories as durable inputs into production. To determine the effects of omitting inventories on TFP in Canada, we recomputed the interest rate r for each period by using a new version of equation (11.29) above where both the land and inventory terms on the right-hand side of (11.29) were omitted. This new omission of inventories has a further substantial effect on the real interest rates: the average r increased from 7.808% (with land omitted) to 10.067% (with land and inventories omitted). Once the new r's were determined, the two reproducible capital user costs of the form (11.10) were computed. Then these two user costs were combined with the corresponding capital stock components, K_{NS} and K_{ME}, using chain Fisher ideal indexes to form new declining balance capital price and quantity aggregates, say $P_K(3)$ and $K(3)$. The resulting aggregate price of capital services $P_K(3)$ is graphed in figure 11.1. We also combine the two new rental prices and quantities of capital with the price and quantity of labor, P_L and Q_L, to form a new primary input aggregate, $Q_X(3)$, (again using a chain Fisher ideal quantity index). Once this aggregate input quantity index $Q_X(3)$ was determined, we used our aggregate output index Q_Y along with the input index in order to define our second total factor productivity index, $TFP(3)$:

$$TFP(3) \equiv Q_Y/Q_X(3).$$ (11.33)

This third declining balance TFP measure (which omits land and inventories from the list of primary inputs) is graphed in figure 11.2.

Once a TFP^t measure has been determined for year t, we can define the total factor productivity growth factor ΔTFP^t and the corresponding TFP growth rate g^t for year t as follows:

$$\Delta TFP^t \equiv TFP^t/TFP^{t-1} \equiv (1 + g^t).$$ (11.34)

The TFP growth factors for the years 1963–1996 for each of the three declining balance TFP concepts that we have considered thus far are listed in the final table of the Data Appendix. However, the arithmetic averages of the three TFP growth rates for the 34 years 1963–1996, $g^t(1)$, $g^t(2)$, and $g^t(3)$, are listed in row 1 of table 11.3 below.

Looking at column 1 of table 11.3, it can be seen that TFP growth over the entire 34 years, 1963–1996 averaged 0.68% per year. However, this average growth rate conceals a considerable amount of variation within subperiods. For the eleven years before the first OPEC oil crisis, 1963–1973, the market sector of the Canadian economy delivered an average growth in TFP of 1.08% per year. During the following eighteen years, 1974–1991, (which were characterized by high inflation, a growing government sector and higher tax levels), average TFP

Table 11.3
Averages of TFP growth rates for declining balance models

	$g(1)$	$g(2)$	$g(3)$	$g(4)$	$g(5)$	$g(6)$
1963–1996	0.68	0.58	0.55	0.57	0.54	0.52
1963–1973	1.08	0.97	0.97	0.98	0.96	0.96
1974–1991	0.18	0.05	−0.01	0.03	0.00	−0.06
1992–1996	1.63	1.60	1.62	1.61	1.60	1.62
average r or R	5.93	7.81	10.07	11.53	12.10	14.41
growth of K	3.89	4.36	4.51	4.42	4.52	4.63

growth fell to 0.18% per year. After the recession in the early 1990s, *TFP* growth made a strong recovery, averaging 1.63% per year during the five years 1992–1996. The final two rows of table 11.3 list the average interest rate that the capital model generated (which was 5.93% for our first declining balance model) along with the (geometric) average growth rate in real capital services (which was 3.89% per year for Model 1).

When land is dropped as a factor of production (see column 2 of table 11.3), the average interest rate increased to 7.89% and the average growth rate for capital services increased from 3.89% to 4.36% per year. This is to be expected: *excluding* land as an input (which does not grow over time) *increases* the overall rate of input growth and hence *decreases* productivity growth. Thus the average rate of *TFP* growth for Model 2 (which excluded land) has *decreased* to 0.58% per year from the Model 1 average rate of 0.68% per year—a drop of 0.1% per year.

Column 3 of table 11.3 reports what happens when *both* inventories and land are dropped as factors of production. Since inventories have grown much more slowly than structures and machinery and equipment, *dropping* inventories further increases the average growth rate for real capital services, from 4.36% to 4.51% per year and further *decreases* the average *TFP* growth rate from 0.58% to 0.55% per year. However, the drop in the average *TFP* growth rate for the "lost" years, 1974–1991, is even greater, from 0.05% to −.01% per year. Note that the average *TFP* growth rates for the recent "good" years, 1992–1996, do not differ much across the three declining balance capital models that we have considered thus far; the average annual *TFP* growth rates were 1.63%, 1.60% and 1.62%, respectively.

The above three declining balance capital models were based on the theory outlined in sections 11.2 and 11.3 above. The analysis in these sections neglected the *inflation problem* or, more accurately, the above analysis implicitly assumed that asset inflation rates were identical across assets. We now want to relax this assumption and allow for differential inflation rates across assets.

The analysis in section 11.2 derived the relationships between vintage asset prices, depreciation and vintage user costs at one point in time, assuming no inflation. Hence the r which appeared in equations (11.4) to (11.6) can be interpreted as a real interest rate. We now want to generalize the fundamental user cost formula (11.6) to allow for asset inflation. We shall now use the superscript t to denote the time period and the subscript s to denote the vintage or age of the asset under consideration. Thus $s = 0, 1, 2, \ldots$ means that asset is new (0 years old), 1 year old, 2 years old, etc. Let P_s^t denote the beginning of year t price of a capital stock component that is s years old and let R^t be the year t nominal interest rate. Then the year t inflation adjusted user cost for an s year old capital stock component, U_s^t, is defined as the beginning of year t purchase cost P_s^t less the discounted value of the asset one year later, P_{s+1}^{t+1}:

$$U_s^t \equiv P_s^t - (1 + R^t)^{-1} P_{s+1}^{t+1} ; \quad s = 0, 1, 2, \ldots . \tag{11.35}$$

We now make the simplifying assumption that the year $t + 1$ profile of vintage asset prices P_s^{t+1} is equal to the year t profile P_s^t times one plus the year t inflation rate for a new asset, $(1 + i^t)$; i.e., we assume that:

$$P_s^{t+1} = P_s^t (1 + i^t) \tag{11.36}$$

where the year t new asset inflation rate i^t is defined as

$$1 + i^t \equiv P_0^{t+1} / P_0^t . \tag{11.37}$$

Substituting (11.36) into (11.35) leads to the following formula for the period t inflation adjusted user cost of an s year old asset:

$$U_s^t = P_s^t - (1 + R^t)^{-1} P_{s+1}^t (1 + i^t) . \tag{11.38}$$

The new user cost formula (11.38) reduces to our old formula (11.6) if the year t nominal interest rate R^t is related to the year t real rate r^t by the following Fisher effect equation:

$$1 + R^t = (1 + r^t)(1 + i^t) . \tag{11.39}$$

Substitution of (11.39) into (11.38) yields our old user cost formula (11.6) using our new notation. Thus is all asset inflation rates are assumed to be the same, our new user cost formula (11.38) reduces to our old formula (11.6). However, in reality, inflation rates differ markedly across assets. Hence, from the viewpoint of evaluating the ex-post performance of a business (or of the entire market sector), it is useful to take ex-post asset inflation rates into account.[14] If a business invests in an asset that has an above normal appreciation, then these asset capital gains should be counted as an inter-temporally productive transfer of resources from the beginning of the accounting period to the end; i.e., the capital gains that were made on the asset should be offset against other asset costs. Thus in the remainder of this section, we use the inflation adjusted user costs defined by (11.38) in place of our earlier no capital gains user costs of the form (11.6).

The profile of year t vintage asset prices in the declining balance model of depreciation will still have the form given by (11.7). Using our new notation, (11.7) may be rewritten as:

$$P_s^t = (1 - \delta)^s P_0^t; \quad s = 0, 1, 2, \ldots. \tag{11.40}$$

Substituting (11.40) into (11.38) yields the following formula for the year t sequence of vintage inflation adjusted user costs:

$$\begin{aligned} U_s^t &\equiv (1 - \delta)^s P_0^t - (1 + R^t)^{-1}(1 - \delta)^{s+1} P_0^t(1 + i^t) \\ &= (1 - \delta)^s (1 + R^t)^{-1} [R^t - i^t + \delta(1 + i^t)] P_0^t \\ &= (1 - \delta)^s U_0^t; \quad s = 0, 1, 2, \ldots \end{aligned} \tag{11.41}$$

where the year t declining balance inflation adjusted user cost for a new asset is defined as

$$\begin{aligned} U_0^t &\equiv P_0^t - (1 + R^t)^{-1}(1 - \delta) P_0^t(1 + i^t) \\ &= (1 + R^t)^{-1} [R^t - i^t + \delta(1 + i^t)] P_0^t. \end{aligned} \tag{11.42}$$

Equations (11.41) show that all of the period t vintage user costs, U_0^t, U_1^t, U_2^t, ..., will vary in strict proportion to the period t user cost for a new asset, U_0^t, and hence we can still apply Hicks' Aggregation Theorem to aggregate over vintage capital stock components. The capital stock aggregates that we used in Models 1–3 above, K_{NS}^t, K_{ME}^t, K_{BAL}^t and K_{IS}^t, can still be used in our new Models 4–6 that allow for differential inflation rates. The only change is that the old user costs defined by (11.30) are now replaced by inflation adjusted user costs of the form given by (11.42) for each of our four capital stock components.

Model 4 is an inflation adjusted counterpart to Model 1. Recall that we used equation (11.29) to solve for the real interest rate r for each year. The Model 4 counterpart to (11.29) is the following equation, which determines the nominal interest rate R for a given year:

$$\begin{aligned} (1 + R)OS &= (R - i_{NS} + \delta_{NS}[l + i_{NS}]) P_{NS} K_{NS} + (R - i_{ME} \\ &\quad + \delta_{ME}[1 + i_{ME}]) P_{ME} K_{ME} + (R - i_{BAL}) P_{BAL} K_{BAL} \\ &\quad + (R - i_{IS}) P_{IS} K_{IS}. \end{aligned} \tag{11.43}$$

Once the nominal interest rates R^t have been determined for each year, then the declining balance user costs for each of the four assets can be calculated, which are of the form defined by (11.42).[15] The above four user costs can be combined with the corresponding capital stock components, K_{NS}, K_{ME}, K_{BAL} and K_{IS}, using chain Fisher ideal indexes to form *inflation adjusted declining balance capital price and quantity aggregates*, say $P_K(4)$ and $K(4)$. The resulting aggregate price of capital services $P_K(4)$ is graphed in figure 11.3 below, along with $P_K(5)$ (where land is dropped as an input) and $P_K(6)$ (where both land and inventories are dropped as inputs). We also combined the four rental prices and quantities of capital with the price and quantity of labor, P_L and Q_L, to form the primary input aggregate, $Q_X(4)$, (again using a chain Fisher ideal quantity index). Once this aggregate input quantity index $Q_X(4)$ was determined, we used our aggregate output index Q_Y along with the input index in order to define the corresponding total factor productivity index, $TFP(4)$:

$$TFP(4) \equiv Q_Y/Q_X(4). \tag{11.44}$$

$TFP(4)$ is graphed in figure 11.4 below, along with $TFP(5)$ and $TFP(6)$. $TFP(5)$ and $TFP(6)$ were defined in an analogous fashion using inflation adjusted user costs but land was dropped as an input for $TFP(5)$ and both land and inventories were dropped for $TFP(6)$.

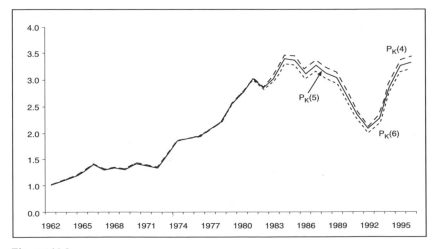

Figure 11.3
Alternative inflation adjusted declining balance aggregate capital services prices.

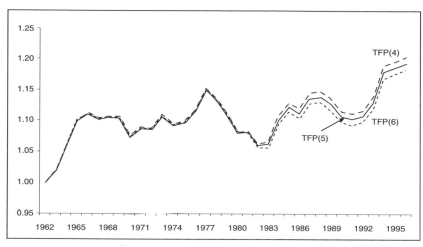

Figure 11.4
Alternative inflation adjusted declining balance productivity measures.

Referring back to the $g(4)$ column in table 11.3 above, it can be seen the inflation adjusted declining balance average rate of growth for real capital services was 4.42% per year which is considerably higher than the corresponding average growth rate for real capital services for Model 1, which was 3.89% per year. What accounts for this major difference? From the Data Appendix, it can be verified that the price of land increased the most rapidly of any of the price series tabled there: the final land price was about 25 times the 1962 level.[16] Hence, the inflation adjusted user cost for land is generally much *lower* than its unadjusted counterpart, so land (which does not grow) gets a much *smaller* price weighting in the inflation adjusted capital services aggregate, leading to a faster growing capital services aggregate. Thus the inflation adjusted declining balance Model 4 has a *faster* growing aggregate input than the unadjusted Model 1 and hence a *lower* average rate of productivity growth (0.57% per year for Model 4 compared with 0.68% per year for Model 1). Since adjusting for inflation reduced the importance of land in Model 4, dropping land (Model 5) made little difference in the average *TFP* growth rate; it decreased from 0.57% per year to 0.54% per year over the entire sample period. The further omission of inventories (Model 6) decreased the average *TFP* growth rate to 0.52% per year. For the "lost" years, 1974–1991, dropping land and inventories from the inflation adjusted declining balance depreciation Model 4 had more of an effect: the average *TFP* growth rate decreased from the barely positive rate of 0.03% per year to the negative average rate of -0.06% per year, a decline of about 0.1 percentage points per year. For the recent "good" years, 1962–1996, all six declining balance models generated an average *TFP* growth rate of about 1.6% per year.

We turn now to our straight line depreciation models.

11.8 Alternative Productivity Measures for Canada Using Straight Line Depreciation

Refer back to section 11.6 above for information on how the vintage capital stocks I_s^t for each year t and each vintage s were constructed for each of the two reproducible capital stocks was constructed. Using equation (11.22) or (11.23) in section 11.5, the straight line depreciation model year t user cost for a reproducible capital stock component s years old can be defined as

$$U_s^t \equiv [1 - s/N]P_0^t - (1 + r^t)^{-1}[1 - (s + 1)/N]P_0^t$$
$$= (1 + r^t)^{-1}[r + N^{-1} - sN^{-1}r]P_0^t \tag{11.45}$$

where N is the assumed length of life for a unit of the new asset (12 years for machinery and equipment and 29 years for nonresidential structures) and P_0^t is the year t price of a new asset. For the nonreproducible assets, we used the same user costs in Models 7 to 9 as we used in Models 1 to 3 in the previous section.

For Model 7, for each year t, we determined the real interest rate r^t by setting the operating surplus equal to the sum of the products of each vintage stock component times its user cost. This leads to a linear equation in r^t of the following form for each year t:

$$(1 + r)OS = \sum_{s=0}^{28}(r + 29^{-1} - s29^{-1}r^t)P_{NSs}^t I_{NSs}^t \tag{11.46}$$

$$+ \sum_{s=0}^{11}(r^t + 12^{-1} - s12^{-1}r^t)P_{MEs}^t I_{MEs}^t + r^t P_{BAL}^t K_{BAL}^t + r^t P_{IS}^t K_{IS}^t.$$

Once the interest rate r^t has been determined for each year t, then the straight-line depreciation user costs for each of the four assets can be calculated, which are of the form (11.45) for the two reproducible vintage capital stock components and of the form (11.30) for land and inventories. Then these vintage user costs can be combined with the corresponding vintage capital stock components, I_{NS}, I_{ME}, K_{BAL} and

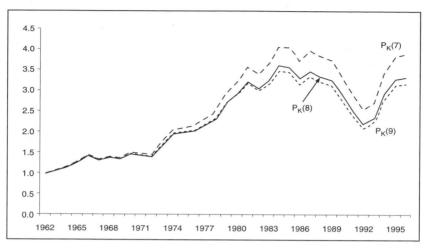

Figure 11.5
Alternative straight line depreciation aggregate capital services prices.

K_{IS}, using chain Fisher ideal indexes to form *straight-line depreciation capital price and quantity aggregates*, say $P_K(7)$ and $K(7)$. The resulting aggregate price of capital services $P_K(7)$ is graphed in figure 11.5 below. We also combined the 43 vintage rental prices and quantities of capital with the price and quantity of labor, P_L and Q_L, to form the primary input aggregate, $Q_X(7)$, (using a chain Fisher ideal quantity index as usual). Once this aggregate input quantity index $Q_X(7)$ was determined, we used our aggregate output index Q_Y along with the input index in order to define the total factor productivity index, $TFP(7)$:

$$TFP(7) \equiv Q_Y/Q_X(7). \tag{11.47}$$

$TFP(7)$ is graphed in figure 11.6 below.

Models 8 and 9 are entirely analogous to Model 7 except that we dropped land from the list of inputs in Model 8 and we dropped land and inventories from Model 9.

The TFP growth factors for the years 1963–1996 for each of the three straight line depreciation models that we have considered thus far in this section are listed in the final table of the Data Appendix. However, the arithmetic averages of the three TFP growth rates for the 34 years 1963–1996, $g'(7)$, $g'(8)$, and $g'(9)$, are listed in row 1 of table 11.4 below.

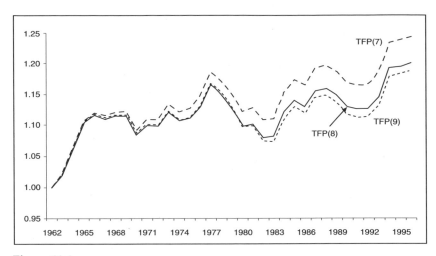

Figure 11.6
Alternative straight line depreciation productivity measures.

When the straight line results in table 11.4 are compared with the corresponding declining balance results listed in table 11.3, we see that the results are fairly comparable for the major subperiods. In both sets of models, dropping land and then dropping inventories tends to *increase* the average growth rate of capital services and hence *decrease* the average rate of *TFP* growth.. However, the capital service aggregates in the straight line depreciation models tend to grow about 0.15% to 0.2% *faster* than the corresponding declining balance models. This leads to somewhat *lower* rates of *TFP* growth in the straight line models. This effect is particularly pronounced for the "good" years 1992–1996: the average *TFP* growth rate falls from about 1.6% per year

Table 11.4
Averages of TFP growth rates for straight line models (%)

	$g(7)$	$g(8)$	$g(9)$	$g(10)$	$g(11)$	$g(12)$
1963–1996	0.66	0.55	0.52	0.55	0.52	0.50
1963–1973	1.16	1.06	1.07	1.07	1.05	1.06
1974–1991	0.16	0.03	−0.04	0.01	−0.02	−0.08
1992–1996	1.35	1.32	1.33	1.32	1.31	1.32
average r or R	5.94	7.84	10.14	11.60	12.20	14.58
growth of K	4.06	4.54	4.69	4.59	4.69	4.80

for the declining balance models to about 1.3 to 1.35% per year for the straight line models. The average real interest rate for the straight line models *increases* from 5.94% to 7.84% when land is dropped and to 10.14% when land and inventories are dropped.

We turn now to Models 10, 11 and 12, which are counterparts to Models 7, 8 and 9 except we now allow for differential rates of asset inflation (as we did with Models 4, 5 and 6 in the previous section). For the reproducible components of the capital stock, we switch to the inflation adjusted vintage user costs defined by (11.38) in the previous section. In the present context where we assume straight line depreciation, this means that the old straight line vintage user cost U_s^t defined earlier by (11.45) is replaced by the following *straight line depreciation inflation adjusted vintage user cost*:

$$U_s^t \equiv [1 - s/N]P_0^t - (1 + R^t)^{-1}[1 - (s+1)/N]P_0^t(1 + i^t) \qquad (11.48)$$

where R^t is now the year t nominal interest rate and it is the year t asset inflation rate for a new unit of the asset.

For Model 10, for each year t, we determined the nominal interest rate R^t by setting the operating surplus equal to the sum of the products of each vintage stock component times its inflation adjusted user cost of the form (11.48). This led to a linear equation in R^t similar to (11.46). Once the interest rate R^t has been determined for each year t, then the inflation adjusted straight line depreciation user costs can be calculated, which are of the form (11.48) for the two reproducible vintage capital stock components and of the form (11.42) (with $\delta = 0$) for land and inventories. Then these vintage user costs can be combined with the corresponding vintage capital stock components, I_{NSS}, I_{Mes}, K_{BAL} and K_{IS}, using chain Fisher ideal indexes to form straight line depreciation inflation adjusted capital price and quantity aggregates, say $P_K(10)$ and $K(10)$. The resulting aggregate price of capital services $P_K(10)$ is graphed in figure 11.7 below. We also combined the 43 inflation adjusted vintage rental prices and quantities of capital with the price and quantity of labor, P_L and Q_L, to form the primary input aggregate, $Q_X(10)$, (using a chain Fisher ideal quantity index as usual). Once this aggregate input quantity index $Q_X(10)$ was determined, we used our aggregate output index Q_Y along with the input index in order to define the total factor productivity index, $TFP(10)$:

$$TFP(10) \equiv Q_Y/Q_X(10). \qquad (11.49)$$

$TFP(10)$ is graphed in figure 11.8 below.

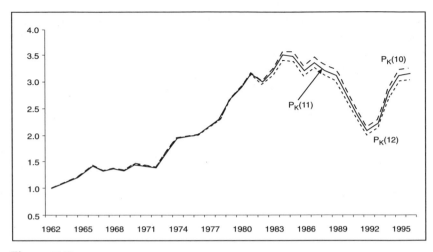

Figure 11.7
Alternative inflation adjusted straight line depreciation aggregate capital.

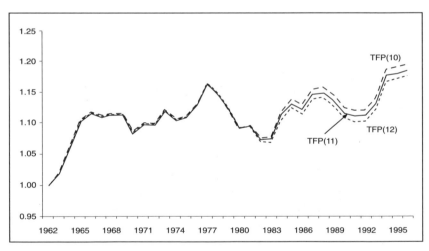

Figure 11.8
Alternative inflation adjusted straight line depreciation productivity
measures.

Models 11 and 12 are entirely analogous to Model 10 except that we dropped land from the list of inputs in Model 11 and we dropped land and inventories from Model 12.

The arithmetic averages of the three straight line depreciation inflation adjusted *TFP* growth rates for the 34 years 1963–1996, $g'(10)$, $g'(11)$, and $g'(12)$, are listed in row 1 of table 11.4 above, along with the average results for the major subperiods. As was the case with the declining balance models described in the previous section, adjusting for inflation tends to *reduce* average *TFP* growth rates. Thus the average *TFP* growth rate for the entire period (with all inputs included) *falls* from 0.66% per year (Model 7) to 0.55% per year when we adjusted our straight line vintage user costs for inflation (Model 10).

We turn now to our gross capital stock models.

11.9   Alternative Productivity Measures for Canada Using One Hoss Shay Depreciation

Refer back to section 11.6 above for information on how the vintage capital stocks I_s^t for each year t and each vintage s were constructed for each of the two reproducible capital stocks was constructed. We now use formula (11.16) in section 11.4 to construct the one hoss shay depreciation model year t user cost for a reproducible capital stock component. For the nonreproducible assets, we used the same user costs in Models 13 to 15 as we used in Models 1 to 3 in section 11.7.

For Model 13, for each year t, we determined the real interest rate r^t by setting the operating surplus equal to the sum of the products of each vintage stock component times its user cost. This leads to a nonlinear equation in r^t of the following form for each year t:

$$(1+r^t)OS = r^t[1-(1+r^t)^{-29}]^{-1}P_{NS}^t K_{NS}^t + r^t[1-(1+r^t)^{-12}]^{-1}P_{ME}^t K_{ME}^t$$
$$+ r^t P_{BAL}^t K_{BAL}^t + r^t P_{IS}^t K_{IS}^t \qquad (11.50)$$

where K_{NS}^t and K_{ME}^t are the year t gross capital stocks tabled in section 11.6 above. The SOLVE option in SHAZAM was used to solve equation (11.50) for the real interest rate r^t. Once the interest rate r^t has been determined for each year t, then the one hoss shay depreciation user costs for each of the four assets can be calculated, which are of the form (11.16) for the two reproducible vintage capital stock components and of the form (11.30) for land and inventories. Then these user costs can be combined with the corresponding capital stock

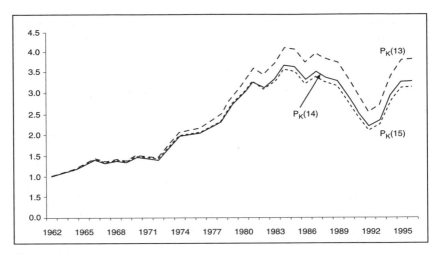

Figure 11.9
Alternative one hoss shay depreciation aggregate capital services prices.

components, K_{NS}, K_{ME}, K_{BAL} and K_{IS}, using chain Fisher ideal indexes to form one hoss shay depreciation capital price and quantity aggregates, say $P_K(13)$ and $K(13)$. The resulting aggregate price of capital services $P_K(13)$ is graphed in figure 11.9. We also combined the one hoss shay rental prices and quantities of capital with the price and quantity of labor, P_L and Q_L to form the primary input aggregate, $Q_X(13)$, (using a chain Fisher ideal quantity index as usual). Once this aggregate input quantity index $Q_X(13)$ was determined, we used our aggregate output index Q_Y along with the input index in order to define the total factor productivity index, $TFP(13)$:

$$TFP(13) \equiv Q_Y/Q_X(13) . \tag{11.51}$$

$TFP(13)$ is graphed in figure 11.10.

Models 14 and 15 are entirely analogous to Model 13 except that we dropped land from the list of inputs in Model 14 and we dropped land and inventories from Model 15.

The TFP growth factors for the years 1963–1996 for each of the three one hoss shay depreciation models that we have considered thus far in this section are listed in the final table of the Data Appendix. However, the arithmetic averages of the three TFP growth rates for the 34 years 1963–1996, $g'(13)$, $g'(14)$, and $g'(15)$, are listed in row 1 of table 11.5 below.

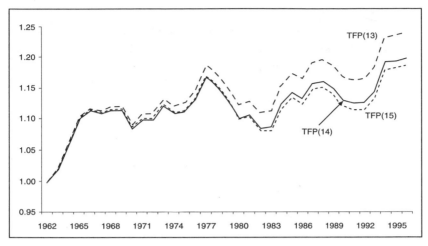

Figure 11.10
Alternative one hoss shay depreciation productivity measures.

When the gross capital stock results in in the first 3 columns of table 11.5 are compared with the corresponding straight line results listed in the first 3 columns of table 11.4, we see that the results are surprisingly close for the major subperiods. In both sets of models, dropping land and then dropping inventories tends to *increase* the average growth rate of capital services and hence *decrease* the average rate of *TFP* growth. The only major difference between the first 3 columns of tables 11.4 and the corresponding columns in table 11.5 are in the average real interest rates: they tended to be lower in the gross capital stock models.

Table 11.5
Averages of TFP growth rates for one hoss shay and other models (%)

	g(13)	g(14)	g(15)	g(16)	g(17)	g(18)
1963–1996	0.65	0.55	0.52	0.59	0.57	0.96
1963–1973	1.16	1.07	1.08	0.99	1.09	1.03
1974–1991	0.16	0.04	-0.02	0.06	0.05	0.71
1992–1996	1.31	1.26	1.26	1.64	1.33	1.73
average r or R	5.72	7.23	8.76	—	—	
growth of K or L	4.08	4.55	4.68	4.29	4.43	2.55

Differential rates of asset inflation can be introduced into the one hoss shay model of depreciation. In the no inflation model of section 11.4 above, the key equation was (11.15), which gave the relationship between the price of a new asset, P_0, and its user cost, U_0. With a constant rate of inflation expected in future periods, so that the ratio of next period's new asset price to this period's price is expected to be $(1+i)$, and with a constant nominal interest rate R, the new relationship between P_0 and U_0 is:

$$P_0 = U_0 + (1+R)^{-1}(1+i)U_0 + (1+R)^{-2}(1+i)^2 U_0$$
$$+ \cdots + (1+R)^{-N+1}(1+i)^{N-1} U_0 \tag{11.52}$$

where N is the length of life of a new asset. Equation (11.52) says that the price of a new asset should be equal to the discounted stream of future expected rentals. Using (11.52) to solve for U_0 in terms of P_0 leads to the following *inflation adjusted one hoss shay user cost*, which replaces formula (11.16):

$$U_0 = P_0[(1+R)(1+i)^{-1} - 1](1+i)(1+R)^{-1}[l - (1+R)^{-N}(1+i)^N]^{-1}. \tag{11.53}$$

It is now possible to repeat Models 13–15, using the inflation adjusted user costs defined by (11.53) for the reproducible capital stock components in place of the earlier user cost formula (11.16). However, given the nonlinearity of (11.53), we did not follow this path. If the one hoss shay model of depreciation were true, then annual rental and leasing rates for reproducible assets would be *constant* across vintages at any given point in time. Thus an old asset would rent for the same price as a new asset. This does not seem to be consistent with the "facts" and thus we do not believe it is worth spending a lot of time on one hoss shay models.

We conclude this empirical part of our paper by computing two additional capital services aggregates. For our first additional capital aggregate, we took our declining balance estimates for the two reproducible capital stock components tabled in section 11.6 above, K_{NS} and K_{ME}, and formed a chained Fisher ideal aggregate of these two stocks, using the investment prices P_{NS} and P_{ME} as price weights in the index number formula. We then divided the resulting stock aggregate, $K(16)$ say, into the operating surplus OS to obtain a corresponding implicit price, $P_K(16)$ say. $P_K(16)$ is graphed in figure 11.11 below, along with our first declining balance aggregate capital services price $P_K(1)$ for comparison purposes. We then combined this capital aggregate with

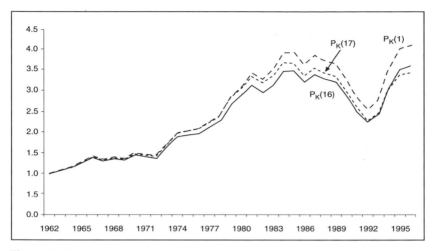

Figure 11.11
Some capital services price aggregates.

the price and quantity of labor, P_L and Q_L, in another chained Fisher ideal aggregation in order to form an input aggregate, $Q_X(16)$. Note that land and inventory stocks are omitted from this input aggregate. Once this aggregate input quantity index $Q_X(16)$ was determined, we used our aggregate output index Q_Y along with this input index in order to define the total factor productivity index, $TFP(16)$:

$$TFP(16) \equiv Q_Y/Q_X(16). \tag{11.54}$$

$TFP(16)$ is graphed in figure 11.12 below along with our first declining balance total factor productivities, $TFP(1)$, for comparison purposes.

For our second additional capital aggregate, we took our gross capital stock estimates for the two reproducible capital stock components tabled in section 11.6 above and formed a chained Fisher ideal aggregate of these two stocks, using the investment prices P_{NS} and P_{ME} as price weights in the index number formula. We then divided the resulting stock aggregate, $K(17)$ say, into the operating surplus OS to obtain a corresponding implicit price, $P_K(17)$. $P_K(17)$ is graphed in figure 11.11 below. We then combined this capital aggregate with the price and quantity of labor, P_L and Q_L, in another chained Fisher ideal aggregation in order to form an input aggregate, $Q_X(17)$. Note that land and inventory stocks are omitted from this input aggregate. Once this aggregate input quantity index $Q_X(17)$ was determined, we used

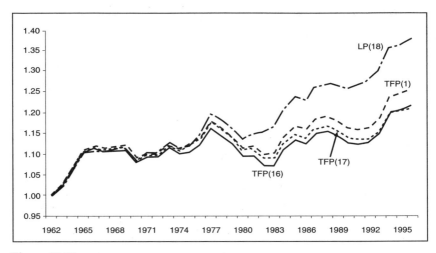

Figure 11.12
Additional productivity measures.

our aggregate output index Q_Y along with this input index in order to define the total factor productivity index, $TFP(17)$:

$$TFP(17) \equiv Q_Y/Q_X(17). \tag{11.55}$$

$TFP(17)$ is graphed in figure 11.12. It can be seen that these last two TFP concepts (with "incorrect" weighting) lead to a somewhat slower rate of TFP improvement over the entire sample compared to the no inflation declining balance concept, $TFP(1)$.

Our final miscellaneous productivity measure is labor productivity $LP(18)$ defined as our output aggregate Q_Y divided by our measure of labor input Q_L.[17] It is graphed in figure 11.12. The final column in table 11.5 shows that the average labor productivity growth rate over the 34 years in our sample was 0.96% per year which is almost twice as big as our typical average TFP growth rate. However, by international standards, this is a rather low rate of growth for labor productivity.

The average rates of TFP growth for our "incorrectly" weighted declining balance productivity measure $TFP(16)$ and our "incorrectly" weighted gross capital stock productivity measure $TFP(17)$ for the entire sample period was 0.59% per year and 0.57% per year respectively; see columns 4 and 5 in table 11.5 above. These average growth rates are between those for the no inflation declining balance Models 1 and 3 (0.68% and 0.55%) and the no inflation gross stock Models 13

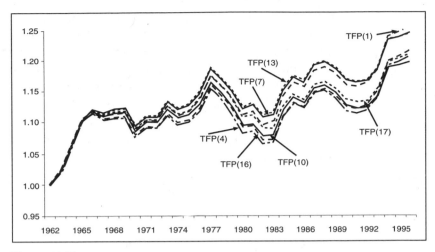

Figure 11.13
Alternative total factor productivity estimates for Canada.

and 15 (0.65% and 0.52%). Thus our incorrectly weighted models led to productivity estimates that were fairly close to the estimates from the "correctly" weighted models.

11.10 Conclusion

We have shown that neglecting land and inventories leads to a decline in average *TFP* growth rates in Canada of about 0.1 percent per year, which is not large in absolute terms, but is large in relative terms, since the average growth rate for total factor productivity in Canada only averaged 0.5 to 0.6% per year over the years 1963–1996. However, once land and inventories are included in the capital aggregate, the differences in average *TFP* growth rates between the various depreciation models (declining balance, one hoss shay and straight line) proved to be surprisingly small, whether we allowed for differential rates of asset inflation or not.

We summarize our results in figure 11.13, where we graph our productivity estimates for Model 1 (declining balance depreciation including all assets), Model 4 (declining balance depreciation including all assets with inflation adjustments), Model 7 (straight line depreciation including all assets), Model 10 (straight line depreciation including all assets with inflation adjustments), Model 13 (one hoss shay depreciation including all assets), Model 16 (declining balance depreciation but with "incorrect" stock weights instead of user cost weights and excluding land and inventories) and Model 17 (one hoss shay depreciation but with "incorrect" stock weights instead of user cost weights and excluding land and inventories). It can be seen that the three "correctly" weighted models with no inflation were relatively close to each other and finished up about 5 percentage points higher than the two "correctly" weighted models with inflation adjustments, $TFP(4)$ and $TFP(10)$, and the two "incorrectly" weighted measures, $TFP(16)$ and $TFP(17)$. We note the highest estimate of TFP in 1996 is given by Model 1 (a 25.29% increase from 1962) and the lowest estimate is given by Model 10 (a 19.63% increase). This is not a huge range of variation.

All of our productivity estimates paint more or less the same dismal picture of Canada's productivity performance. During the pre-OPEC years, 1962–73, TFP growth proceeded at the satisfactory rate of about 1 per cent per year. Then for the 18 "lost" years, 1974–1991, TFP growth was close to 0 on average. Fortunately, there appears to have been a strong TFP recovery in recent years; TFP growth averaged somewhere between 1.6% and 1.3% per year for the 5 years 1992–1996.[18]

There are many problems associated with the measurement of capital that were not discussed in this chapter. Some of these problems are:

• We have discussed only ex-post user costs, which we think is appropriate when measuring the productivity performance of a firm or industry or country. However, for many other purposes (such as econometric modeling), *ex ante* or expected user costs are more relevant.

• The user costs that were defined neglected the complications due to the business income tax and other taxes on capital. Essentially, our user costs assume that these taxes just reduce the pretax real or nominal rate of return.[19]

• We have not related depreciation to the utilization of the asset.

• We have discussed only the easy to measure components of the capital stock. Other components that were not discussed include resource stocks, knowledge stocks and infrastructure stocks.

• We have not modeled the role of research and development expenditures and of knowledge spillovers.

• Finally, we have not discussed the problems involved in measuring capital when there are quality improvements in new units of the capital stock.

However, we hope that our presentation of alternative models of depreciation will be helpful to business and academic economists who find it necessary to construct capital aggregates in the course of their research. We also hope that our exposition will be helpful to statistical agencies who may be contemplating adding a productivity module to their economic statistics. We have shown that it is relatively easy to do this once accurate information on asset lives (or declining balance depreciation rates) are available.

Data Appendix

In this appendix, we will briefly describe our sources and list the data actually used in our capital stock and productivity computations.

We begin by describing the construction of our aggregate output variable. From Tables 52 and 53 of the Statistics Canada publication, *National Income and Expenditure Accounts, Annual Estimates 1984–1995* (and other years), we were able to construct consistent estimates for 19 categories of consumer expenditures for the years 1962–1996. The 19 categories were: (1) food and nonalcoholic beverages; (2) alcoholic beverages; (3) tobacco products; (4) clothing, footwear and accessories; (5) electricity, natural gas and other fuels; (6) furniture, carpets and household appliances; (7) semidurable household furnishings plus reading and entertainment supplies; (8) nondurable household supplies, drugs and sundries, toilet articles and cosmetics; (9) medical care, hospital care and other medical care expenses; (10) new and (net) used motor vehicles plus motor repairs and parts; (11) motor fuels and lubricants; (12) other auto related services plus purchased transportation; (13) communications; (14) recreation equipment, jewelry, watches and repairs; (15) recreational services; (16) educational and cultural services; (17) financial, legal and other services; (18) expenditures on restaurants and hotels and (19) other services (laundry and dry cleaning, domestic and child care services, other household services and personal care). Note that we do not include consumption of housing services in the above list of consumer goods and services. We will also exclude the stock of dwellings from our list of market sector capital inputs. The price series for the above 19 components of consumer expenditure contain various commodity taxes, which are revenues for government but are not revenues for private producers. Thus we attempted to remove these commodity taxes from the above price series using information contained in the Statistics Canada publication, *The Input-Output Structure of the Canadian Economy 1961–1981* and other years. Additional information from the Statistics Canada publication, *The Canadian Economic Observer* for May 1989 and other Statistics Canada sources was used in order to construct final estimates of commodity taxes for the above 19 final demand consumption categories. We note that we were unable to allocate all indirect taxes and subsidies to the appropriate categories so our market sector output aggregate will be subject to some measurement error.

We turn now to a description of our international trade data. In this treatment, exports are produced by the market sector and all imports flow into the market sector as intermediate inputs. These import inputs are either physically transformed by domestic producers or they have domestic value added to them through domestic transportation, storage or retailing activities. When we construct our market sector output aggregate, we index import quantities with a negative sign in keeping with national income accounting conventions.

In forming consistent series for disaggregated export and import components, the principal data source was the Statistics Canada CAN-SIM matrices 6566 and 6541. These matrices provide current and constant price series for 11 export and 11 import components for the years 1971 to 1993.

For exports, the 11 components were aggregated into the following five categories on the basis of similarities in price movements (Hicks aggregation): (1) Forestry; (2) Energy; (3) Equipment; (4) Other goods; and (5) Services. The Forestry and Energy categories were formed directly from the equivalent CANSIM series. The Equipment category is an aggregate of the CANSIM series for Machinery and equipment and Automotive products. The residual Other goods exports category is an aggregate of the CANSIM Agricultural and fish products, Industrial goods and materials and Other consumer goods components. The Services category is an aggregate of the CANSIM Travel services, Transportation services and Commercial services components plus the value of Government services obtained from Statistics Canada's *Canada's Balance of International Payments, 1926 to 1996* and first quarter 1997, Catalogue No. 67–001–XPB, table 13. The Government services variable mainly comprises expenditures by foreign governments in

Canada. It is excluded from the CANSIM series but we assume these purchases are from the Canadian business sector and so should be included in our export series. The eleventh CANSIM component—Financial Intermediation services—was omitted, as it does not accurately represent the movement of goods or services. Rather, it is largely a financial balancing item. Export price indexes were formed using chained Fisher indexes of the component implicit prices from the CANSIM current and constant price matrices. As our complete database runs over the years 1962 to 1996, we had to backdate our five export categories to 1962 using a variety of sources. In order to extend the CANSIM series from 1993 to 1996, again a variety of sources were used. The values and prices of exports of the four goods components were updated from 1993 to 1996 using Statistics Canada's *Canadian Economic Observer*, Catalogue No. 11–010–XPB, tables 18 and 19. The July 1996 and November 1997 issues spanned the four-year period. Values and current weighted price indexes were presented for exports of agriculture and fish, energy, forestry, industrial goods and materials, machines and equipment, automotive and consumer goods. The value of the four services items making up the Services export component were updated from Statistics Canada's *Canada's Balance of International Payments*, 1926 to 1996 and first quarter 1997, Catalogue No. 67–001–XPB, table 13. The price of the overall services export component was updated to 1996 using the price of non-merchandise exports obtained from CANSIM matrix 6628, current and constant dollar estimates of non-merchandise exports and imports from the National Accounts.

The values and price indexes for the five export categories described above are measured at the border and so exclude export taxes paid by producers. To derive exports in producers' prices we needed to estimate export taxes for each of our five export components. The only export components, which had significant export taxes, are Energy and Services exports. Between 1973 and 1985 Canada imposed an Oil Export Charge. Values of this tax were obtained from *Statistics Canada's National Income and Expenditure Accounts, Annual Estimates, 1926–1983*, Catalogue No. 13–531, table 51. For Services exports, we assumed that three of its components were taxed: Travel, Freight and shipping, and Government services. We assumed that Travel and Government services exports were each made up of half expenditure on fuel and half expenditure on hotels and restaurants. Consequently, the commodity tax rates for Fuel and Hotels and restaurants were each applied to half the expenditure in each of these components. We assumed that half of Freight and shipping exports were made up of fuel expenses and subject to the commodity tax rate for Fuel. Other services exports were assumed not to be taxed.

For imports, the 11 components in CANSIM matrices 6566 and 6541 were aggregated into the following four categories on the basis of similarities in price movements (Hicks aggregation): (1) Forestry and other; (2) Energy; (3) Equipment; and (4) Services. The Energy and Equipment categories are formed directly from the equivalent CANSIM series. The Services category is an aggregate of the Travel, Transportation and Commercial services components. The Forestry and other imports category is the aggregate of the Forestry, Agricultural and fish products, Industrial goods and materials, Automotive products and Other consumer goods components. Financial Intermediation services are again omitted. Import price indexes were formed using chained Fisher indexes of the component implicit prices from the CANSIM current and constant price matrices. As was the case with exports, our four import series were backdated to 1962 using a variety of sources. The values and prices of imports of the three goods components were updated from 1993 to 1996 using Statistics Canada's *Canadian Economic Observer*, Catalogue No. 11–010–10XPB, tables 18 and 19. The July 1996 and November 1997 issues spanned the four year period. Values and current weighted price indexes were presented for imports of Agriculture and fish, Energy, Forestry, Industrial goods and materials, Machines and equipment, Automotive and Consumer goods. The value of the three services items making up the Services import component were updated from Statistics Canada's Canada's *Balance of International Payments*, 1926 to 1996 and first quarter 1997, Catalogue No. 67–001–XPB, table 13. The price of the overall Services import component was updated to 1996 using the price of non-merchandise imports obtained from CANSIM matrix 6628, Current and constant dollar estimates of non-merchandise exports and imports from the National Accounts. These import values and prices are measured at the border and so exclude import duties. To derive imports in producers' prices we needed to estimate import duties for each of our four import components. Total import duties for the period 1962–83 were obtained from Statistics Canada's *National Income and Expenditure Accounts, Annual Estimates, 1926–1983*, Catalogue No.

13–531, table 51. Import duties for 1984–1995 were obtained from *National Income and Expenditure Accounts, 1984–1995*, –Catalogue No. 13-201–XP13, table 44. Total import duties for 1996 were estimated by assuming the same aggregate tariff rate applied as that observed in 1995. An estimate of the duty paid on Equipment imports was obtained from various issues of the Canadian Tax Foundation's *The National Finances* for the years 1964–1985. The following categories from the End products, inedible, category were allocated to Equipment imports: General purpose industrial machinery, Special industry machinery, Road motor vehicles, Communication and related equipment, Electric lighting, distribution and control equipment and Office machines and equipment. Values for 1969, 1974 and 1984 were estimated by interpolating implied tariff rates. Equipment import duties for the remaining periods, 1962–1963 and 1986–1996, were estimated by linking the implied Equipment tariff rate to movements in the total imports implied tariff rate. Information in *The National Finances* indicated there were no import duties on Energy imports. We assume there are no tariffs applying to Services imports so the remaining duties are allocated to the Forestry and other imports component. Between 1973 and 1985 Canada subsidized oil imports. The amount of the Oil Import Compensation Charge was obtained from *The National Finances*. This enters as a subsidy, or negative tax, on Energy imports for these years. The subsidy rate for 1982 appeared anomalous and was replaced by an interpolated rate.

The government purchases intermediate inputs and investment goods from the market sector so it is necessary to form estimates for these components of market sector output. We have data on the value and price of total government consumption and government wages payments from the *OECD Economic Outlook* database. We derive the value of government purchases of intermediates by subtracting government wages payments from total government consumption. Having derived the value and price of government purchases of intermediates, we combine this with the value and price of government investment in fixed capital from CANSIM matrices 6828 and 6836, respectively, using a chain Fisher index. Our next task was to derive producers' price series for the two components of government purchases. Indirect taxes paid on total government purchases from the market sector (both intermediates and fixed capital expenditure) were obtained from the final demand matrices of Statistics Canada's *Input-Output Tables* for the years 1962 to 1992. An indirect tax rate was formed by taking the ratio of indirect taxes paid to the value of total government purchases from the market sector. The tax rate for 1992 was assumed to also apply for the remaining four years, 1993 to 1996. Producers' price indexes were then formed by multiplying the government intermediates and investment price indexes by one minus the indirect tax rate.

The final components of our market sector output aggregate are the investment components and the change in inventories. From *The Canadian Economic Observer, Historical Statistical Supplement, 1997/1998,* we obtained investment in nonresidential structures and in machinery and equipment in current and constant dollars for the years 1962–1997. The resulting price (P_{NS} and P_{ME}) and quantity series (I_{NS} and I_{ME}) are listed in table A.1 below.

The construction of price and quantity series for inventory change is not straightforward. From *The Canadian Economic Observer, Historical Statistical Supplement, 1997/1997,* we obtained estimates of inventory in current and constant dollars for the years 1962–1997. The resulting price series is listed in table A.1 below as P_{INA} (price of inventories using national accounts data). It can be seen that this price series for inventory change is not credible as a measure of the average level of inventory prices in a given year. Hence, we will use the Statistics Canada *National Balance Sheet Accounts, Annual Estimates, 1996* for estimates of the total stock of inventories (in current dollars) held at the end of the year for the years 1964 to 1996. This in turn is equal to the beginning of the year stock of inventories held by the market sector (the government's holdings of inventories was negligible) for the years 1965–1997. This series can be extended back to stocks held at the beginning of 1962 using the National Balance Sheet Accounts for an earlier year. Constant dollar stocks of inventories are available for the end of years 1961–1982 from the *National Balance Sheet Accounts, Annual Estimates, 1984* and for the end of years 1984–1993 from the *National Balance Sheet Accounts, Annual Estimates, 1994.* The resulting beginning of the year inventory stock price and quantity series for the years 1962–1994 are listed in table A.1 as P_{IS} and K_{IS}. In order to extend our inventory price series to 1997, we linked P_{IS} to the (erratic) national accounts series P_{INA} at the year 1992, which was the base year for the constant dollar inventory change series. The final three entries in the P_{IS} series reflect this linking procedure. The resulting P_{IS} series looks quite reasonable. Of course, once we have our price series for beginning of the year inventory stocks, P_{IS}, it can be divided into the

Table A.1
Market sector output data for Canada; 1967–1997

Year	P_{NS}	P_{ME}	P_{IS}	P_{INA}	P_Y
1962	1.0000	1.0000	1.0000	1.0000	1.0000
1963	1.0285	1.0280	0.9866	0.9918	1.0241
1964	1.0579	1.0695	1.0288	1.0909	1.0456
1965	1.1168	1.1114	1.0451	1.0445	1.0842
1966	1.1843	1.1476	1.0718	1.0325	1.1422
1967	1.2355	1.1398	1.0970	1.0960	1.1797
1968	1.2492	1.1387	1.1180	1.1506	1.2306
1969	1.3199	1.1692	1.1376	1.0938	1.2936
1970	1.3872	1.2245	1.1618	1.3038	1.3495
1971	1.4713	1.2576	1.1638	1.0937	1.4027
1972	1.5549	1.3077	1.1830	1.2551	1.4800
1973	1.7235	1.3433	1.2974	1.3728	1.6212
1974	2.0439	1.4864	1.5420	1.4454	1.8776
1975	2.2837	1.6650	1.8820	1.7817	2.1021
1976	2.4139	1.7641	1.9290	1.7078	2.2773
1977	2.5428	1.8706	1.9544	2.0536	2.4025
1978	2.7279	1.9467	2.0555	1.6277	2.5687
1979	2.9751	2.0667	2.2834	1.8909	2.8554
1980	3.3367	1.9616	2.6506	4.2658	3.2014
1981	3.7133	1.9860	3.0073	2.5485	3.5656
1982	3.9903	2.1330	3.2945	2.7584	3.8687
1983	3.9631	2.1127	3.3440	2.7320	4.0607
1984	4.1112	2.0873	3.4455	2.9947	4.1719
1985	4.2349	2.0339	3.5308	2.4212	4.2571
1986	4.2977	2.0313	3.5633	2.8847	4.3085
1987	4.4991	1.9851	3.6102	2.7174	4.4881
1988	4.7563	1.9477	3.7149	4.4340	4.6604
1989	4.9655	1.9397	3.8702	2.8741	4.8720
1990	5.1192	1.9237	3.8954	4.2322	5.0121
1991	5.0094	1.7483	3.8846	3.1432	5.0985
1992	4.9730	1.6926	3.7546	3.1024	5.1114
1993	5.0365	1.7181	3.9027	3.9837	5.1431
1994	5.2066	1.7630	4.0362	2.2776	5.2164
1995	5.2717	1.7845	4.1109	3.3968	5.3585
1996	5.2479	1.7719	4.1564	3.4343	5.4999
1997			4.0474	3.3443	

Table A.1 (continued)
Market sector output data for Canada; 1967–1997

Year	I_{NS}	I_{ME}	K_{IS}	Q_{IC}	Q_Y
1962	2560.0	2368.0	13811.3	791.8	32312.7
1963	2647.5	2570.1	14603.1	467.5	33750.7
1964	3060.7	3023.8	15070.7	461.1	36237.1
1965	3338.2	3551.4	15531.8	1145.3	38933.8
1966	3830.9	4229.7	16677.1	1176.2	41905.0
1967	3631.8	4321.8	17853.4	352.7	43435.4
1968	3601.6	4022.9	18206.1	759.0	44962.3
1969	3605.6	4404.0	18965.1	1579.5	46565.0
1970	3955.5	4489.0	20544.6	376.3	48619.9
1971	4080.2	4623.2	20920.9	316.5	50250.7
1972	4063.3	4999.5	21237.5	120.1	51961.9
1973	4384.0	6119.1	21357.5	428.7	55649.0
1974	4652.5	6893.1	21786.2	1546.0	57391.4
1975	5261.6	7285.4	23332.3	650.7	59005.1
1976	5139.9	7603.2	23982.9	1553.2	62302.4
1977	5450.6	7584.9	25536.1	2033.7	65853.2
1978	5591.9	8207.6	27569.8	1059.5	67678.3
1979	6311.6	9550.6	28629.3	1436.1	69943.6
1980	7030.7	11527.5	30065.5	-907.5	70814.5
1981	7565.8	13936.2	29157.9	450.0	73641.7
1982	6877.9	11750.8	29608.0	-2476.4	71606.8
1983	6309.2	11531.0	27131.5	-670.5	72619.0
1984	6242.5	12306.7	26461.1	1428.8	77445.1
1985	6556.9	14174.9	27889.8	790.5	81153.7
1986	6177.5	15712.8	28680.4	570.6	83345.0
1987	6416.4	18135.8	29251.0	929.3	87498.1
1988	7067.9	21512.3	30180.3	699.7	91071.2
1989	7285.1	23169.5	30880.0	1180.8	92786.7
1990	7302.0	22141.5	32060.7	-569.0	92968.8
1991	7065.7	22260.9	31491.8	-613.4	91988.5
1992	5962.9	22836.3	30878.4	-1149.9	92059.5
1993	5992.9	21725.6	29728.5	357.6	95077.8
1994	6521.2	23719.6	30086.1	1820.7	100532.2
1995	6473.1	25129.9	31906.8	2051.4	103633.5
1996	6752.6	26179.2	33958.2	1696.2	104886.0
1997					35654.4

balance sheet value estimates to obtain the quantity series for beginning of the year inventory stocks, K_{IS}, for all 37 years in our sample,
1962–1997. Once K_{IS} has been determined, then inventory change,
Q_{IC} for the 36 years 1962–1996 can be obtained by differencing the
stock series, K_{IS}.

This completes our description of the construction of the components of our market sector output aggregate. The aggregate price of output, P_Y, and the aggregate quantity of output, Q_Y, were constructed as chained Fisher ideal indexes of the nineteen consumption components, the five export components, the four import components, the two government components (investment purchases and purchases of goods and services), the two investment components and the inventory change component. P_Y and Q_Y are listed in table A.1.

We now describe the construction of the primary input components for the market sector of the Canadian economy.

We first describe our labour estimates. From *The Canadian Economic Observer, Historical Statistical Supplement, 1997/1998*, we obtained estimates of the number of self employed workers (including unpaid family workers) from table 8. For the years 1962–1974, we obtained the same information from various *Canada Year Books*. For the year 1975, we interpolated an estimate using the two sources. From table 9 of *The Canadian Economic Observer, Historical Statistical Supplement, 1997/1998*, we obtained estimates of total labor income and labor income paid out to public administration workers. Thus by subtraction, we obtained estimates for market sector employment income. From the Organization of Economic Cooperation and Development's *Economic Outlook* database, we obtained data on the business compensation rate, P_L, which is an annual wage that reflects the full cost of employing a full time worker. We attributed 2/3 of this annual wage rate to the self-employed and we assume that all of the self-employed worked in the market sector rather than the government sector. This gave us a new (bigger) estimate of market sector total labor income. We divided this labor value series by the full time market wage rate P_L in order to obtain market sector labor input, Q_L. The series P_L and Q_L are listed in table A.2. Subtracting P_L times Q_L from the value of market sector outputs (less imports), P_Y times Q_Y, gave us estimates of the market sector's *operating surplus, OS*. This series is also listed in table A.2.

We turn now to the capital components of the input aggregate. We have already described how we used the *National Balance Sheet Accounts* for estimates of the total stock of inventories. The same balance sheets can be used to form estimates of the beginning of the year stocks of nonresidential structures, machinery and equipment and land used by the market sector. We will not go through all of the details of the construction of these series. These beginning of the year

Table A.2
Market sector input data for Canada; 1967–1997

Year	P_L	Q_L	O_S	K_{NS}	K_{ME}	K_{BAL}	P_{BAL}	δ_{NS}	δ_{ME}
1962	1.0000	24118.2	8194.5	30006.6	17983.7	11743.1	1.0000	0.0578	0.0969
1963	1.0422	24657.5	8864.4	30830.7	18609.7	11743.1	1.0695	0.0417	0.1191
1964	1.0984	25555.6	9821.6	32192.4	18964.3	11743.1	1.1647	0.0743	0.1104
1965	1.1795	26382.0	11096.6	32860.3	19894.6	11743.1	1.3126	0.0540	0.1241
1966	1.2272	28284.5	13152.1	34424.6	20977.6	11743.1	1.4529	0.0249	0.0830
1967	1.3048	29314.1	12993.2	37398.8	23465.5	11743.1	1.6315	0.0108	0.0927
1968	1.3729	30086.2	14025.0	40628.4	25611.2	11743.1	1.7998	0.0797	0.1207
1969	1.4799	31107.9	14202.2	40991.6	26542.2	11743.1	1.9647	0.0375	0.1250
1970	1.4660	33670.2	16255.7	43058.0	27627.3	11743.1	2.1581	0.0571	0.1129
1971	1.5833	34141.3	16427.9	44555.9	28997.2	11743.1	2.3732	0.0302	0.1297
1972	1.7062	35323.9	16635.3	47292.0	29860.1	11743.1	2.7360	0.0959	0.1140
1973	1.8592	37185.2	21082.2	46820.1	31455.3	11743.1	3.2506	0.1145	0.1871
1974	2.1251	38782.7	25338.0	45844.7	31689.7	11743.1	4.0754	-0.0113	0.1368
1975	2.4558	39289.9	27545.4	51015.6	34248.6	11743.1	5.1559	-0.0038	0.0829
1976	2.7657	40545.3	29748.1	56471.3	38693.9	11743.1	6.1750	0.0562	0.1249
1977	3.0256	41185.8	33599.6	58439.8	41466.0	11743.1	7.1203	0.0781	0.1078
1978	3.1726	42806.5	38032.9	59325.3	44579.4	11743.1	8.2260	0.0792	0.1219
1979	3.3912	45118.9	46708.6	60218.0	47354.4	11743.1	9.5535	0.0900	-0.0008

Table A.2 (continued)

Year	P_L	Q_L	O_S	K_{NS}	K_{ME}	K_{BAL}	P_{BAL}	δ_{NS}	δ_{ME}
1980	3.7144	46640.3	53461.6	61107.2	56943.2	11743.1	11.4351	0.0697	0.1244
1981	4.1680	47985.3	62573.4	63880.1	61387.2	11743.1	13.7683	0.0304	0.2081
1982	4.5917	46436.4	63803.4	69506.2	62549.6	11743.1	14.9309	-0.0206	0.0557
1983	4.8055	46587.1	71009.0	77816.8	70819.3	11743.1	14.7458	0.1067	0.1246
1984	5.0528	47808.0	81529.4	75826.6	73528.3	11743.1	14.5917	0.0714	0.0990
1985	5.3243	49086.8	84128.0	76652.6	78559.1	11743.1	14.7611	0.0504	0.1711
1986	5.4839	50703.4	81039.4	79349.1	79293.0	11743.1	14.3209	0.0893	0.1154
1987	5.8528	51853.3	89211.6	78437.9	85853.4	11743.1	15.1011	0.0865	0.1538
1988	6.2403	53625.4	89787.8	78070.0	90782.5	11743.1	16.2874	0.0630	0.1670
1989	6.5619	54794.6	92505.0	80220.3	97134.3	11743.1	17.6322	0.0478	0.1502
1990	6.8402	55307.1	87658.5	83670.3	105718.0	11743.1	19.4612	-0.0019	0.0532
1991	7.1797	54288.2	79231.1	91135.2	122239.5	11743.1	19.8549	0.0650	0.1449
1992	7.4056	53822.7	71961.9	92275.7	126789.8	11743.1	20.7385	0.0738	0.1873
1993	7.5141	54492.6	79527.0	91432.1	125878.0	11743.1	21.5174	0.0918	0.1744
1994	7.6295	55303.1	102483.4	89034.4	125654.0	11743.1	22.1142	0.0487	0.1522
1995	7.7065	56783.2	117724.1	91219.3	130249.1	11743.1	23.1090	0.0338	0.1611
1996	7.9883	56848.6	122736.2	94606.3	134392.0	11743.1	23.7180	0.0716	0.1645
1997				94586.6	138467.1	11743.1	25.0208		

balance sheet estimates for constant 1962 dollar net nonresidential structures stocks, K_{NS}, machinery and equipment stocks, K_{ME}, and business and agricultural land stocks, K_{BAL}, are listed in table A.2 below along with the corresponding price of land, P_{BAL}. Note that we have assumed that the stock of business and agricultural land is constant. The price for a unit of the nonresidential structures is assumed to be the same as the corresponding investment price, P_{NS}. The price for a unit of the machinery and equipment stock is assumed to be the same as the corresponding investment price, P_{ME}.[20]

Recall equation (11.13) in section 11.3 above which defined the declining balance capital stock in terms of vintage investments. This equation can be manipulated to yield the following relationship between the capital stock at the beginning and end of year t, K^t and K^{t+1}, respectively, and investment during year t, I^t:

$$K^{t+1} = (1 - \delta)K^t + I^t \tag{A.1}$$

where δ is the declining balance depreciation rate. We can use the information from the national accounts on investment in nonresidential structures listed in table A.1 above, Q_{NS}, along with the information from the national balance sheets on the net stock of nonresidential structures, K_{NS}, and use equation (A.1) to construct implied geometric depreciation rates, δ_{NS}, that are consistent with the two data sources. Similarly, we can use the information from the national accounts on investment in nonresidential structures listed in table A.1 above, Q_{ME}, along with the information from the national balance sheets on the net stock of nonresidential structures, K_{ME}, from table A.2 and use equation (A.1) to construct implied geometric depreciation rates, δ_{ME}, that are consistent with the two data sources.

The resulting depreciation rates are listed in table A.2. Although the arithmetic averages of these annual geometric depreciation rates (0.0555 for nonresidential structures and 0.1256 for machinery and equipment) are very reasonable, it can be seen that the annual fluctuations in these rates are unacceptably large. Thus we regard the balance sheet estimates for the net capital stocks for the two reproducible capital stock components, K_{NS} and K_{ME}, as being "correct" over the entire sample period but not in the year to year movements.

In table A.3, we list the TFP growth rates for each of the 18 Models discussed in the main text for the years 1963–1996.

Table A.3
Productivity growth rates (%) for 18 capital models for Canada

Year	g(1)	g(2)	g(3)	g(4)	g(5)	g(6)	g(7)	g(8)	g(9)
1963	2.20	2.13	2.25	2.14	2.11	2.25	2.18	2.13	2.26
1964	3.96	3.89	3.92	3.91	3.89	3.92	3.99	3.94	3.99
1965	4.02	3.92	3.89	3.95	3.92	3.88	4.14	4.05	4.05
1966	0.99	0.84	0.92	0.85	0.81	0.90	1.16	1.02	1.12
1967	-0.59	-0.77	-0.75	-0.77	-0.79	-0.77	-0.39	-0.56	-0.53
1968	0.38	0.26	0.15	0.28	0.25	0.14	0.50	0.39	0.29
1969	0.09	-0.02	-0.01	0.03	-0.02	-0.02	0.14	0.04	0.05
1970	-2.65	-2.78	-2.66	-2.78	-2.82	-2.67	-2.60	-2.72	-2.60
1971	1.39	1.30	1.23	1.32	1.31	1.22	1.45	1.35	1.29
1972	-0.07	-0.15	-0.21	-0.18	-0.15	-0.22	-0.02	-0.10	-0.16
1973	2.14	2.06	1.97	2.01	2.01	1.94	2.19	2.10	2.02
1974	-1.19	-1.31	-1.39	-1.39	-1.39	-1.42	-1.10	-1.23	-1.31
1975	0.55	0.39	0.43	0.32	0.40	0.43	0.52	0.36	0.39
1976	1.86	1.72	1.65	1.67	1.76	1.66	1.83	1.70	1.62
1977	3.31	3.17	3.19	3.10	3.15	3.19	3.29	3.14	3.16
1978	-1.28	-1.42	-1.36	-1.44	-1.43	-1.38	-1.30	-1.45	-1.39
1979	-1.74	-1.88	-1.90	-1.96	-1.94	-1.95	-1.72	-1.86	-1.89

Table A.3 (continued)

Year	g(1)	g(2)	g(3)	g(4)	g(5)	g(6)	g(7)	g(8)	g(9)
1980	-2.49	-2.68	-2.71	-2.82	-2.79	-2.80	-2.45	-2.64	-2.67
1981	0.48	0.30	0.01	0.24	0.16	-0.04	0.52	0.34	0.04
1982	-1.82	-2.04	-2.19	-1.85	-2.07	-2.20	-1.75	-1.98	-2.14
1983	0.37	0.30	-0.02	0.32	0.23	-0.04	0.28	0.20	-0.13
1984	3.87	3.78	3.63	3.85	3.74	3.60	3.73	3.64	3.48
1985	1.90	1.76	1.81	1.90	1.74	1.79	1.77	1.64	1.69
1986	-0.69	-0.81	-0.83	-0.72	-0.84	-0.87	-0.73	-0.84	-0.87
1987	2.34	2.24	2.20	2.20	2.15	2.11	2.31	2.22	2.18
1988	0.46	0.35	0.33	0.30	0.25	0.23	0.45	0.35	0.33
1989	-0.90	-1.01	-1.06	-1.08	-1.09	-1.14	-0.88	-0.99	-1.03
1990	-1.56	-1.65	-1.67	-1.77	-1.75	-1.77	-1.57	-1.67	-1.68
1991	-0.23	-0.28	-0.34	-0.37	-0.35	-0.40	-0.31	-0.35	-0.41
1992	0.52	0.51	0.48	0.50	0.51	0.48	0.17	0.14	0.10
1993	2.01	2.01	1.99	2.00	1.99	1.98	1.71	1.70	1.66
1994	4.33	4.32	4.32	4.33	4.32	4.32	4.06	4.04	4.04
1995	0.58	0.54	0.59	0.57	0.54	0.59	0.33	0.28	0.33
1996	0.69	0.63	0.71	0.65	0.62	0.71	0.48	0.42	0.49

Table A.3 (continued)

Year	g(10)	g(11)	g(12)	g(13)	g(14)	g(15)	g(16)	g(17)	g(18)
1963	2.12	2.10	2.25	2.08	2.01	2.10	2.22	2.07	2.17
1964	3.95	3.94	3.99	3.90	3.84	3.85	3.90	3.83	3.59
1965	4.08	4.07	4.06	4.11	4.03	4.02	3.89	4.01	4.08
1966	1.04	1.01	1.12	1.20	1.08	1.18	0.95	1.19	0.39
1967	-0.56	-0.57	-0.54	-0.29	-0.42	-0.36	-0.69	-0.34	0.01
1968	0.41	0.38	0.28	0.55	0.45	0.38	0.20	0.40	0.86
1969	0.08	0.04	0.05	0.15	0.05	0.06	0.00	0.07	0.16
1970	-2.72	-2.76	-2.61	-2.58	-2.69	-2.57	-2.63	-2.56	-3.53
1971	1.38	1.38	1.28	1.47	1.38	1.33	1.24	1.33	1.93
1972	-0.12	-0.10	-0.17	-0.01	-0.08	-0.13	-0.20	-0.13	-0.06
1973	2.06	2.06	1.99	2.21	2.13	2.06	2.00	2.07	1.74
1974	-1.30	-1.30	-1.34	-1.03	-1.14	-1.20	-1.33	-1.16	-1.12
1975	0.29	0.37	0.39	0.54	0.39	0.43	0.51	0.52	1.48
1976	1.64	1.73	1.62	1.86	1.73	1.67	1.71	1.75	2.32
1977	3.07	3.12	3.15	3.30	3.16	3.18	3.25	3.25	4.06
1978	-1.46	-1.45	-1.40	-1.29	-1.43	-1.37	-1.34	-1.33	-1.12
1979	-1.93	-1.92	-1.94	-1.70	-1.83	-1.85	-1.87	-1.81	-1.95

Table A.3 (continued)

Year	g(10)	g(11)	g(12)	g(13)	g(14)	g(15)	g(16)	g(17)	g(18)
1980	-2.78	-2.75	-2.77	-2.40	-2.57	-2.58	-2.66	-2.54	-2.06
1981	0.28	0.20	-0.01	0.58	0.42	0.17	0.09	0.24	1.08
1982	-1.78	-2.01	-2.14	-1.67	-1.86	-1.99	-2.09	-1.89	0.48
1983	0.23	0.14	-0.14	0.26	0.17	-0.15	0.02	-0.09	1.09
1984	3.71	3.60	3.46	3.65	3.53	3.37	3.66	3.42	3.92
1985	1.79	1.63	1.68	1.69	1.55	1.57	1.85	1.63	2.06
1986	-0.76	-0.88	-0.90	-0.77	-0.89	-0.92	-0.77	-0.86	-0.57
1987	2.19	2.13	2.10	2.27	2.17	2.13	2.29	2.20	2.65
1988	0.30	0.26	0.24	0.43	0.33	0.31	0.43	0.39	0.64
1989	-1.06	-1.06	-1.11	-0.87	-0.97	-1.02	-0.94	-0.91	-0.29
1990	-1.78	-1.77	-1.78	-1.58	-1.67	-1.68	-1.55	-1.56	-0.73
1991	-0.44	-0.42	-0.47	-0.33	-0.38	-0.45	-0.26	-0.35	0.80
1992	0.12	0.13	0.09	0.14	0.11	0.06	0.47	0.14	0.94
1993	1.69	1.68	1.66	1.68	1.66	1.62	2.02	1.70	2.01
1994	4.05	4.03	4.03	4.02	3.98	3.97	4.32	4.01	4.19
1995	0.31	0.28	0.33	0.28	0.21	0.24	0.62	0.32	0.40
1996	0.43	0.41	0.49	0.42	0.35	0.40	0.75	0.48	1.09

Notes

1. Department of Economics, University of British Columbia, Vancouver, Canada and NBER and Tasman Asia Pacific, Canberra, Australia. The first author thanks the Canadian Donner Foundation for financial support and Michael Harper, Charles Hulten and Dale Jorgenson for helpful comments on an earlier draft.

2. To be fair to national income accountants, defining a coherent set of user costs or rental prices for capital stock components is not a trivial job. As we shall see later in this paper, there are many possible variants for user costs and it is difficult to select any single version. Diewert (1980; 470–486) discusses many of these variants.

3. For descriptions of the BLS multifactor productivity accounts, see Bureau of Labor Statistics (1983) and Dean and Harper (1998).

4. Statistics Canada and the Australian Bureau of Statistics also have multifactor productivity measurement programs.

5. See Diewert (1976, 1978a) for material on superlative index number formulae.

6. We implicitly assume that deterioration and depreciation of the various vintages do not depend on use; only on the age of the input.

7. Thus our study is similar in some respects to the empirical investigation of alternative rental prices made by Harper, Berndt and Wood (1989).

8. This important point was recognized by Hulten (1990; 129) as the following quotation indicates: "One cannot select an efficiency pattern independently of the depreciation pattern and maintain the assumption of competitive equilibrium at the same time. And, one cannot arbitrarily select a depreciation pattern independently from the observed pattern of vintage asset prices P^t_s, (suggesting a strategy for measuring depreciation and efficiency). Thus, for example, the practice of using a straight line efficiency pattern in the perpetual inventory equation in general commits the user to a non straight line pattern of economic depreciation." Hulten's efficiency pattern is our user cost profile.

9. Hicks formulated his aggregation theorem in the context of consumer theory but his arguments can be adapted to the producer context; see Diewert (1978b).

10. See Beidelman (1973, 1976), Hulten and Wykoff (1981a, 1981b) and Wykoff (1989) for studies of this type. An extensive literature review of the empirical literature on depreciation rate estimation can be found in Jorgenson (1996).

11. For examples of this type of study, see Epstein and Denny (1980), Pakes and Griliches (1984) and Nadiri and Prucha (1996).

12. The Bureau of Labor Statistics (1983) has also adopted a more complicated hyperbolic formula to model depreciation.

13. For all of the capital models reported in this paper, the aggregate price of capital services P_K times the corresponding capital services aggregate K will equal the operating surplus OS.

14. From other points of view, ex post user costs of the form defined by (11.38) may not be appropriate. For example, if we are attempting to model producer supply or input demand functions, then producers have to form expectations about future asset prices; i.e., expected asset inflation rates should be used in user cost formulae in this situation rather than actual ex-post inflation rates.

15. It should be noted that the resulting inflation adjusted user costs were negative for inventories in 1992 and negative for land for the years 1971–1972, 1974–1977, 1979–1980 and 1989–1992. This means that for these years, these capital inputs were actually net outputs.

16. Other price growth factors were: 1.8 for machinery and equipment; 4.0 for inventory stocks; 5.2 for nonresidential structures; 5.5 for aggregate output and 8.0 for labor.

17. This measure was normalized to equal 1 in 1962.

18. Diewert and Fox (1999) hypothesized that the worldwide *TFP* slowdown that occurred in OECD countries around 1973 was probably related to the big increase in inflation that occurred around that time. Inflation was high in Canada during the years 1974–1991 and then low in recent years. Thus Canada's recent productivity recovery is consistent with the Diewert and Fox hypothesis.

19. Thus our r^t or R^t are returns that include these business taxes.

20. We could have used the price deflators for nonresidential structures and for machinery and equipment that can be constructed using the constant dollar estimates of these stock components that may be found in the *National Balance Sheet Estimates*, However, we found that the resulting balance sheet price series for machinery and equipment differed substantially from the corresponding investment price deflator for machinery and equipment listed in table A.1, P_{ME}. We feel that the investment price and quantity data are more accurate than the balance sheet price and quantity data with the exception of the national accounts change in inventories series. Thus we used the national accounts investment prices P_{NS} and P_{ME} to deflate the balance sheet capital stock values for nonresidential structures and machinery and equipment, respectively.

12 Modeling Trade Policies and U.S. Growth: Some Methodological Issues

Mun S. Ho

Most analyses of trade policies are now done using dynamic numerical models. These intertemporal equilibrium models have proven very useful in discussing the link between policy and growth. There are, however, many difficult methodological issues that must be confronted in implementing such models, problems that are absent in traditional static models. We discuss these implementation issues and present our approach in dealing with some of them. We report the result of simulating the elimination of tariff and nontariff barriers in the U.S. to illustrate the effects of considering dynamic effects. We also report how different parameter values may affect the estimates of output and welfare.

12.1 Introduction

The continual negotiations over trade liberalization among countries have prompted a large amount of applied research on the impact of changes in trade policies. Traditional approaches to this issue have been purely static.[1] These approaches ignore the effects of trade policy on capital formation and productivity growth.

Recent work has focused on dynamic modeling of the economy. These include Baldwin (1992), Goulder and Eichengreen (1992), Keuschnigg and Kohler (1994), the G-cubed model (McKibbin and Wilcoxen, 1995), and Bohringer, Pahlke and Rutherford (1997). In Ho and Jorgenson (1994) we presented a model for analyzing the effect of trade liberalization on U.S. economic growth. All these models combine intertemporal modeling with detailed disaggregation by commodities (and often by regions) and thus capture the impact of trade policy on imports and exports, the sectoral composition of output, and capital formation. (The main feature that distinguishes our approach is that we utilize all the data available during the sample period rather than a single data point in calibrating our model.)

In Ho and Jorgenson (1994), for example, we reported that if tariffs in the U.S. and rest of the world had been eliminated in 1980, U.S. consumption of goods and services would have risen by only 0.16 percent in the first year. This is similar to the results of static analysis in Deardorff and Stern (1986) and Whalley (1985). However, consumption would have been 0.82 percent higher in the long run. The mechanism underlying this substantial growth in consumption is that trade liberalization reduces the price of capital goods relative to other prices. This leads to an increase in investment and more rapid growth of capital, thereby expanding both output and consumption. If the most significant quantitative restrictions had been eliminated along with tariffs in 1980, the consumption of goods and services would have been 1.08 percent higher in the long run, compared to a first year increase of only 0.36 percent. The difference over time is due to the impact of trade liberalization on U.S. capital formation and productivity growth.

Our results are fairly typical of those generated by intertemporal equilibrium models. Like static models the results here depends on the functional forms used. However, they confront a further difficulty that the results are also affected by the dynamic specification and projections of the exogenous variables. As we show, numerous assumptions have to be made, many of which appear wrong to the most casual observer.

In this chapter we examine the methodological issues of dynamic modeling of trade impacts, whether with a one-country model or with a multi-region one. We then discuss our model's approach to some of these problems and briefly summarize our previous results. Rather than focusing on specific estimates of the effects of policy shocks we discuss how sensitive the results are to alternative specifications and assumptions, and to the use of different parameter values.

12.2   Issues in Numerical Dynamic Models

The importance of considering dynamic aspects in general equilibrium modeling is now well known. It allows a more flexible specification of expectations, it provides a transition path, and it makes clear the link between adjustment specification and the speed of adjustment. Current investment, and hence the structure of the economy, can react to expectations of future policies.

When modelers turn these ideas into numerical models many assumptions regarding the dynamic specification have to be made.

Second, the immense data requirements for a detailed specification of a dynamic model are very daunting. We shall discuss here the specification issues that all builders of dynamic models face. We divide our comments into parts—production, consumer behavior, and trade modeling.

12.2.1 Modeling Production over Time

We write the output of sector j in period t as

$$Q_{jt} = f(KD_{jt}, LD_{jt}, M_{jt}, t) \tag{12.1}$$

where KD_{jt}, LD_{jt} are the capital and labor input demands, and M_{jt} is intermediate input. First, let us consider constant returns to scale models. Many such models employ a Harrod-neutral specification where productivity growth comes from labor augmenting technical change. That is, the production function is written as $f(KD_{jt}, \lambda_t N_{jt}, M_{jt})$ where N is the number of hours worked and λ_t is the index of labor effectiveness. Such a specification is employed, for example, in the G-cubed model.

Harrod-neutrality implies that factor shares change only when prices change. However, many of the movements in input shares over time cannot be explained by price movements alone. Figure 12.1 illustrates this problem for a typical industry in the U.S., Primary Metals.[2] The top graph gives the value ratio of energy to labor input, while the bottom graph gives the (log) ratio of the price of energy to the price of labor. The rapid rise in real wages in the postwar period is not accompanied by any significant change in the energy: labor value ratio, while the oil shocks did lead to a change. (For a more detailed discussion see Jorgenson, Gollop and Fraumeni, 1987, Chap. 7). Simulations over the historical period using a Harrod-neutral form will therefore miss these changes. For simulations of the future, non-neutral production functions are required. Only if there will be no change or the change is completely random can a neutral form be used.

If it is decided to use nonneutral production functions then one must choose the exact formulation. The typical form used in empirical work contains linear and quadratic time terms. (See Diewert and Wales, 1987 for a discussion of flexible functional forms.) A typical cost function, like the translog or Generalized McFadden, have the form:

$$\text{cost}(t) = \alpha_0 + f_1(p) + f_2(p'p) + f_3(p)t + \alpha_1 t + \alpha_2 t^2 \tag{12.2}$$

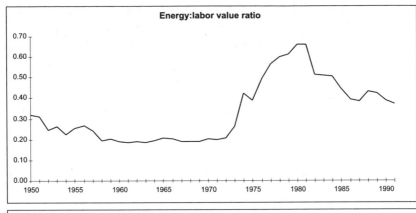

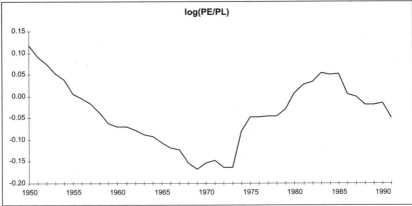

Figure 12.1
Factor inputs and their prices for a typical industry.

where p is the input price vector and t denotes time as the index of the level of technology. $p'p$ denotes the second-order price terms. In the case of the translog, for example, the value shares in input factors (v_t) derived from the above cost function is:

$$v(t) = f_1' + f_2'(p) + f_3't \tag{12.3}$$

The problem of using such a formulation in an infinite horizon model is obvious. The value shares would diverge to plus or minus infinity unless f_3' is zero (which implies neutral technical change). What is reasonable for estimation over a given sample period is unusable for dynamic models. The implementation of nonneutral technical change must therefore be done with nonstandard functional forms.

In our model we deal with this problem by modifying the standard translog and using a logistic time trend instead of a quadratic. That is, the t term above is replaced by a logistic $g(t)$. The coefficient on the price times time term gives the magnitude and direction of the bias. This bias gradually disappears over time. That is, a well defined steady state requires neutral technical change in the long run. Our functional form thus allows biased change in the near term and also satisfies this steady state requirement.

Other forms that allow for such flexibility may of course be used. Such flexibility, however, comes with a cost. The difficulty of estimating such highly parameterized forms are discussed in the econometric literature (Diewert and Wales, 1987). The first difficulty is that time series of output and inputs are required as opposed to a single input-output table. Secondly, numerical models require that production or cost functions have the appropriate curvature. Such curvature may not be produced in unconstrained estimation of the data.

A distinct but related problem is estimating the rate of technical progress. In equation (12.2) this corresponds to the terms involving α_1 and α_2. The formulation in (12.2) produces continual technical progress (or regress). If these functions are estimated separately for the different industries then the different estimates of the α's will cause relative prices to diverge. This is not consistent with a steady state. The long run rate of technical progress must be equal across sectors. In our formulation we express the time term as a logistic function, $\alpha_1 g(t) + \alpha_2 g^2(t)$. This gives us a common long run growth rate of zero while allowing the current rates of technical progress be different across sectors.

In models where there is costly adjustment of capital the econometric difficulties are compounded by the lack of data on the value of "q" (value of installed versus uninstalled capital). Such models have therefore resorted to using *a priori* plausible values of the adjustment parameter instead of estimating it.

These problems are magnified manifold if one wishes to incorporate economies of scale or learning-by-doing. Modeling scale economies and investment over time in a oligopolistic environment is so complex that strong assumptions have to be employed. Keuschnigg and Kohler (1994) is one of the few efforts at this, and they assume that firms engage in monopolistic competition and capital is mobile across all the firms in each industry. Their degree of returns to scale is taken, not from cost functions, but from engineering estimates.

12.2.2   Consumption, Engel Curves and the Steady State

We next discuss the demand for goods and then turn to the demand for leisure and savings. Flexible modeling of household demand for commodities is akin to modeling production under scale economies and biased technical change. It is well known that Engel curves are not linear, that is, expenditure on some goods rise less than proportionally with income while other goods are income elastic.[3]

Most multisector models use simple Cobb-Douglas or LES formulations calibrated to some base year. This includes both Goulder-Eichengreen and some versions of G-cubed. These have unit income elasticity and would be unsuitable for "backcasting" or simulations over the historical period given this observed non-homotheticity.

Empirical work on commodity consumption functions have mostly ignored secular trends and attribute all nonprice changes to income effects. (In the language of production functions this means allowing for scale economies or diseconomies but no technical change.) An example of such estimates is Jorgenson and Slesnick (1987) which is incorporated into our model. In that paper the income elasticity for Food is estimated at 0.8, for Capital 1.0, and for Services 1.3.

Ignoring this feature of consumer behavior would bias the sectoral projections of the economy. The effects of policy shocks that change not just prices but incomes also, will not be captured by usual homothetic models. To illustrate the magnitude of this effect consider a policy shock that changes prices by 5 percent and incomes by 1 percent. Say that in a homothetic model this leads to a 5 percent quantity change due to price effects and a 1 percent change due to income effects. Using our estimates of the income elasticities the gap between Food and Services would then be off by 0.5 percent, that is, an error of about 0.5 out of 6.

Allowing for nonhomothetic demands, however, produces a long run problem similar to the biased technical change issue described above. If incomes rises to infinity due to exogenous productivity growth or endogenous growth, as in many models, then the demand for some commodity will vanish to a zero share and the demand for the most elastic commodity will rise to a 100 percent share. This is clearly unacceptable and there are two ways of dealing with it. One is to have a consumption function that approaches homotheticity. Another is to have zero long run productivity, and hence income, growth. In our model we have chosen the second option, that is, we preserve the functional form in Jorgenson and Slesnick (1987) and the long-run productivity growth is set to zero.

Labor and savings

Many of the numerical dynamic models in use, including ours, feature endogenous labor supplies and endogenous savings. To make this tractable the following specification, or something very similar, is used for aggregate household utility in all the dynamic models cited above:

$$U = \sum_{t=0}^{\infty} \frac{F_t^{\sigma}}{(1+\rho)^t} \tag{12.4}$$

$$F_t = F(CC_t, LEIS_t)$$

$$CC_t = CC(C_{1t}, C_{2t}, \cdots C_{nt})$$

where F_t is full consumption and ρ is the rate of time preference. Full consumption is a function of leisure and a commodity aggregate (CC). The commodity aggregate is a function of the separate commodities (C_{it}).

Unlike some static models which have disaggregated income classes or labor groups, all the infinite-lived models assume an aggregate household as in the theoretical literature. The above formulation means that consumption is assumed to be separable over time despite evidence to the contrary. (See Browning and Lusardi (1996) for a survey.) An exception is the G-cubed model which incorporates liquidity constraints. It also assumes that commodities and leisure are separable. This is rejected by some empirical work, e.g., Browning and Meghir (1991).

Even if we are willing to ignore these rejections of the standard model at both the household and aggregate levels, implementing the above simple system in a numerical model still presents some difficulties. Writing leisure demand (or labor supply) in the above manner implies the existence of an aggregate labor supply curve. However, much of the empirical labor literature estimates labor supplies by demographic groups, e.g., prime age males, married women, and so on. Most do not test that the elasticities of the different groups are different.

What then should one put as the elasticity of labor supply in the aggregate function? Furthermore, how should one treat the secular trends in hours worked? To illustrate this problem figure 12.2 plots the value share of leisure in full consumption and the price of leisure over

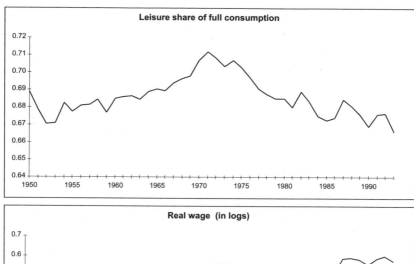

Figure 12.2
Aggregate leisure and wages in the U.S.

time in the U.S. The value of leisure is defined as the after-tax wage multiplied by the nonwork hours of all working age residents.

There are two trends in the U.S. labor supply. First we have the reduction in work hours in the immediate postwar period. Secondly, there is the rise in female participation rates after 1971. The first trend was accompanied by a rapid rise in real wages, the second had a relatively flat wage. Such data could obviously not be explained by a simple aggregate labor supply function. One could disaggregate the data into demographic groups but even this would not be able to capture the secular trend in female labor supply.

The approach that we chose to retain an aggregate labor supply equation and yet be able to track the historical data is to add a time

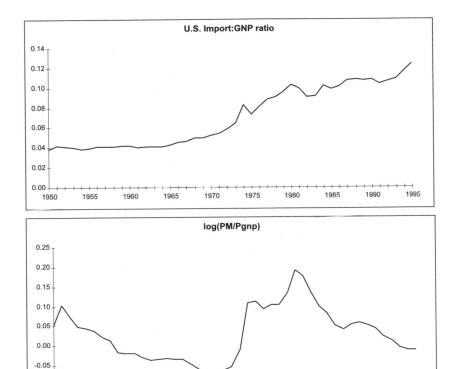

Figure 12.3
Import share and the price of import

term in the full consumption function. Again we choose a logistic form for the time function so that there is no long run change. In conclusion, existing empirical work on labor supply which concentrate on cross-sectional data is not suitable for direct use in dynamic models. The changing behavior of different cohorts have to be taken explicitly into account. Modelers have to take care in interpreting the labor supply elasticities from the empirical literature.

12.2.3 Modeling trade over time

The empirical literature on trade functions—import demands and export supplies—is vast. See, for example, Goldstein and Khan (1984).

These, however, concentrate on finding the price and income elasticities of imports or exports. Estimating functional forms suitable for use in numerical models like those discussed here are not the focus of such research. Like the production and consumption cases above there are special problems in specifying and estimating such trade functions.

The behavior of import and export shares in the U.S. parallels that of the labor supply, that is, there is a secular trend in quantites that is not accompanied by price movements. Figure 12.3 plots the aggregate commodity imports as a share of GNP and the ratio of import prices to the GNP deflator. (While one should, strictly speaking, use the price of domestic tradables, the difference between that and the GDP deflator is small in this context.) Very similar trends exist for data at the 2-digit level that we use in our model.

The import share rose throughout this period with a sharp acceleration in the 1970s. The price of imports relative to domestic goods prices however, showed no particular trend. Any import demand function that has only prices will fail to track these data by a large margin. Much of the empirical work with time series data use an income term, like aggregate activity, in addition to prices to explain these trends. However, we concur with Petri's conclusion (1984, p. 51) that the high income elasticities estimated are probably spurious. We therefore explain the share of imports using a time trend as in Petri (1984).

Here again we confront the problem that specifications that are reasonable for estimating over a given sample is unsuitable for use in dynamic models. Simple time trends would push imports to infinity. We have opted for a simple solution by using a logistic trend. From figure 12.3 it is clear that such a trend would be poorly estimated since U.S. imports seem to be rising with no end in sight. Another way of saying this is that there are fundamental changes in the world's supply of tradable goods over time, and import demand functions are shifting. These shifts do not appear to be converging and we must therefore make some assumption about the maximum possible shift. The assumption we have chosen is to have the logistic curve converging to a point close to the share at the end of the sample period.

Use Table

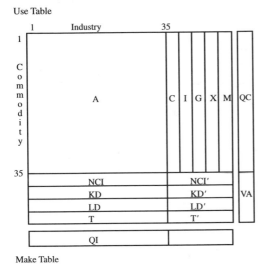

Make Table

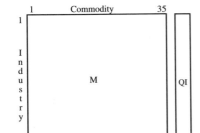

A	Use matrix; commodities used by industries
M	Make matrix; Industries contribution to commodity supply
C	Household consumption of nondurables and services only. Service flow from durables enter in the capital row of that column
I	Investment in the domestic capital stock.
G	Government purchases of goods and services
X	Exports of commodities (interest receipts are accounted separately)
M	Competitive imports (entered as a negative column)
NCI	Non-competitive imports
KD	Capital demanded by producers
LD	Labor demanded by producers
T	Sales tax on industry output
	NCI', KD', LD' are factor inputs allocated directly to final demand
QI	Industry Output
QC	Commodity output of domestic producers
QS	= QC + M = Total commodity supply
VA	Total value added = GDP

Figure 12.4
Intersectoral flows.

12.3   The Structure of the Model

We divide the U.S. economy among four sectors: businesses, households, governments, and the rest of the world. Since trade policy differs substantially among industries, we subdivide the business sector
into the thirty-five industries listed in table 12.1 below. These industries correspond approximately to two-digit industries in the Standard
Industrial Classification. Our model distinguishes the same number
of commodities as industries. Each industry produces a primary
product; this is the commodity group in which the industry is pre-
dominant. Industries also produce secondary products, the primary
products of other industries. The interindustry flows are illustrated in
figure 12.4.

We shall give an overview of the important features of the model
here. The detailed equations are in Appendix A.

12.3.1   Consumer Behavior

Our model of consumer behavior is based on full consumption, comprised of commodities and leisure time, following the structure in
equation 12.4. Full consumption is allocated over time to maximize an
intertemporally additive utility function, subject to an intertemporal
budget constraint. The necessary conditions are expressed as an Euler
equation, giving the growth rate of full consumption as a function of
the discount rate and the growth rate of the price of full consumption.
Current full consumption incorporates expectations about all future
prices that are fulfilled by the solution of the model. This is the first
component of our dynamic model of adjustment to changes in trade
policy.

There is a single, exogenously given, time endowment. The U.S.
population grew substantially during our sample period, 1947–1985.
For later periods we project the population and transform it into a
projection of the time endowment. In each period this endowment is
divided between leisure time and the labor market. Our model allocates full consumption between commodities and leisure. Time in the
labor market is allocated among the thirty-five industries; labor services are also included in final demands for personal consumption
expenditures and public consumption. We assume that labor is perfectly mobile among sectors so that the wage rate in each sector is proportional to a single wage rate for the U.S. economy as a whole.

Table 12.1
Import demand elasticities

Industry	Substitution Elasticities			Import Price Elasticities				
	Stern	Shiells	Ours	Stern	Shiells	Petri	Cline	Ours
Agriculture			0.70				−0.90	−0.68
Metal mining			0.11				−0.22	−0.09
Coal mining							−0.22	
Oil and gas mining							−0.22	
Non-metal mining			0.34				−0.22	−0.34
Construction								
Food & kindred	1.13	0.31	0.65	−1.13	−0.21		−1.13	−0.62
Tobacco	1.13	−16.2	2.60	−1.13	−7.57		−1.13	−2.59
Textile mill	1.15	2.58	1.62	−1.14	−1.41	−1.2	−2.43	−1.54
Apparel	4.27	1.62	1.27	−3.92	−0.52	−1.2	−2.43	−1.01
Lumber and wood	1.76	0.26	1.76	−0.69	−1.32	−1.4	−0.96	−1.60
Furniture	3.10	12.13	1.49	−3.00	−9.56	−1.4	−0.96	−1.36
Paper	1.58	1.80	1.16	−0.55	−1.80	−1.4	−1.44	−1.07
Printing and publish	3.01	2.72	1.22	−3.00	−1.46	−1.4	−1.44	−1.20
Chemicals	2.61	9.85	1.20	−2.53	−6.82	−0.8	−0.97	−1.10
Petroleum refining	2.36	−0.34	1.09	−1.96	−0.79	−0.8	−0.97	−1.00
Rubber and plastic	5.71	2.67	1.76	−5.26	−1.32	−0.8	−3.57	−1.65
Leather	1.81	4.11	1.86	−1.58	−2.01		−2.46	−1.11
Stone Clay and Glass	1.63	4.29	1.86	−1.60	−2.86	−0.8	−1.37	−1.72
Primary metal	1.45	3.05	1.48	−1.42	−2.28	−1.6	−1.99	−1.29
Fabricated metal	3.67	1.54	1.13	−3.59	−0.94	−1.1		−1.08
Machinery	1.02	3.34	1.72	−1.02	−0.88	−0.9	−0.87	−1.53
Electrical machine	2.11	7.46	1.45	−1.00	−3.08	−0.6	−0.87	−1.23
Motor vehicles	3.59	2.01	1.52	−3.28	−1.24	−2.5	−2.53	−1.16
Transport. equipm.	3.59	2.01	1.35	−3.28	−1.24	−2.5	−1.70	−1.28
Instruments	1.98	0.45	0.86	−1.08	0.44	−0.9		−0.77
Misc. manufactures	1.98	3.55	1.52	−2.06	−2.37	−0.8	−4.44	−1.14
Transportation								
Communications								
Electric Utilities								
Gas Utilities								
Trade								
Finance, Insurance								
Services								
Govt Enterprises								

The industrial classification system is different for each study. All entries correspond to the categories used in this study.

Stern: Central tendencies in Stern, Francis and Schumacher (1976).

Shiells: Shiells, Stern and Deardorff (1986), sample period 1962–1978.

Petri: Petri (1985), U.S. imports from rest of the world, excluding Japan, 1960–1080.

Cline: Cline et al. (1978), page 58.

Ours: Elasticities evaluated at 1983 shares, sample period 1964–1995.

Finally, total expenditure on commodities by the household sector is allocated to the thirty-five commodities represented in the model, capital services, and labor services. We estimate price and total expenditure elasticities econometrically for each of 672 types of households.

12.3.2   Producer Behavior

We represent producer behavior by means of econometric models for each of our thirty-five industries. We first express the output of each industry as a function of inputs of intermediate goods, capital services, and labor services. These production functions are characterized by constant returns to scale. The rate of productivity growth in each industry is endogenous and can be expressed as a function of the input prices. The intermediate inputs include the thirty-five commodities produced within the U.S. business sector. Each commodity group is allocated among intermediate demands by the thirty-five industries and final demands for private and public consumption, investment by households and businesses, and exports to the rest of the world.

To implement our econometric approach to modeling producer behavior we have constructed a consistent time series of interindustry transactions tables for the U.S. economy, covering the period 1947–1985 on an annual basis. Empirical evidence on substitutability among inputs is essential in analyzing the impact of trade restrictions. A high degree of substitutability implies that the cost of these restrictions is relatively low, while a low degree of substitutability implies high costs of trade restrictions.

12.3.3   Investor Behavior

In our model a single stock of capital is allocated among the thirty-five industries and the household sector. We assume that capital is perfectly malleable and mobile among sectors, so that the price of capital services in each sector is proportional to a single capital service price for the economy as a whole. The supply of capital available in every year is the result of past investment. This relationship is represented by an accumulation equation, giving capital at the end of each year as a function of investment during the year and capital at the beginning of the year. This backward-looking equation incorporates the whole past history of investment and constitutes the second component of our dynamic model of adjustment to changes in trade policy.

Our model of investor behavior also includes an equation giving the price of capital services in terms of the price of investment goods at the beginning and end of each period. The current price of investment goods incorporates expectations about future prices of capital services and discount rates through the assumption of perfect foresight or rational expectations. Under this assumption the price of investment goods is based on expectations that are fulfilled by the solution of the model. This forward-looking equation incorporates expectations about all future prices and is the third component of our dynamic model of adjustment to trade policy changes.

12.3.4   The Government

The government in this model imposes taxes, buys commodities, make transfers and borrows to finance its deficits. The government deficit is set exogenously since we do not have an equation (e.g., a portfolio choice model) to determine it in the steady state. That leaves us with two possible closures for the model, either endogenizing government purchases given fixed tax rates, or, fixing public spending and adjusting tax rates/lump sum taxes. Both methods are used depending on the simulation.

On the revenue side the government imposes taxes—sales tax, import tariffs, capital income tax, labor income tax, property tax and wealth (estate) tax; and collects fees—"non-tax revenues" and surpluses of government enterprises.

Government spending falls into four major categories—purchases of goods, transfers (to household sector and foreign aid), interest payments on debt (to domestic and foreign bondholders), and subsidies to producers. Transfers and interest payments are included to maintain a realistic set of accounts, they are set exogenously and play no endogenous role.

12.3.5   Total Supply, Imports and the Rest of the World

The total supply of commodities in the U.S. economy comes from the output of domestic industries and "competitive" imports. Competitive imports are defined in the U.S. national income and product accounts as commodities similar to those produced in the U.S. In our model

purchasers of these commodities regard them as imperfect substitutes
for the domestically produced counterparts. Noncompetitive imports
enter directly into the production functions for each industry in the
same way as other inputs. They also enter final demands for consumption by households and governments and investment by businesses and households. Some examples of noncompetitive imports are
tropical agricultural products and tourism.

The demand for competitive imports is derived from a translog cost
function with a logistic time trend to deal with the rising imports as
described in section 12.2.3 above. The share of total supply due to
imports is derived as:

$$\frac{PM_i M_i}{PS_i QS_i} = \alpha_0^i + \frac{\beta_0^i}{1 + e^{-\mu_i(t-\tau_i)}} + B^i \ln \frac{PM^i}{PC_i} \qquad (12.5)$$

where PM and PC are the prices of the imported and domestic commodities, and PS is the price of the total supply. The corresponding
quantities are denoted M, QC and QS. The value of total supply is :

$$PS_i QS_i = PC_i QC_i + PM_i M_i . \qquad (12.6)$$

The above import demand equation is estimated by applying two-
stage least squares to annual data for the period 1960–1985. We present the implied price elasticities of demand for imports in table 12.1.
For comparison we also present elasticities employed in previous
studies. Imports of most manufactured commodities are price elastic,
while imports of most primary commodities are price inelastic. For
eighteen of our twenty-five highly tradable groups the values of R^2
are greater than 0.8.

Our model is limited to the U.S. economy, so that we do not model
production by the rest of the world. Accordingly, we take the prices of
competitive and noncompetitive imports into the U.S. as exogenously
given; during our sample period, 1947–1985, we set these prices equal
to the actual data. Since our model determines prices, both domestic
and foreign, relative to a numeraire given by the U.S. wage rate, we
allow prices of imports from the rest of the world to change through
the terms of trade, say e_t, and through tariffs levied on imports by the
U.S. government, say θ_{it} and θ_{it}^n:

$$PM_{it} = (1 + \theta_{it}) \, e_t \, PM_{it}^*,$$
$$PNCI_{it} = (1 + \theta_{it}^n) \, e_t \, PNCI_{it}^*, \qquad (12.7)$$

where PM_{it} and $PNCI_{it}$ are prices for competitive and noncompetitive imports paid by the U.S. and PM_{it}^* and $PNCI_{it}^*$ are prices received by the rest of the world. The terms of trade e_t is the price of goods in the U.S. relative to the price of goods in the rest of the world.

Exports
Since we do not model production in the rest of the world, we express the demand for U.S. exports, say X_{it}, as a function of rest of the world output Y_t^* and the price of exports PC_{it}:

$$X_{it} = EX_{i0}(Y_t^*)\left[(1 + \theta_{it}^*)\,\frac{PC_{it}}{e_t}\right]^{\eta_i},\tag{12.8}$$

where $EX_{i0}(Y_t^*)$ represents actual U.S. exports during the sample period, 1947–1985, and projected exports outside this period, θ_{it}^* is the rest of the world tariff rate on U.S. exports, and the term in square brackets is the price for U.S. exports faced by the rest of the world. We do not have the data on rest of the world imports from the U.S. required for estimation of the export price elasticities η_i. We take these elasticities as averages of import price elasticities of major trading partners of the U.S. These are given in table 12.2.

The U.S. current account balance is the above commodity exports less commodity imports plus net factor income less transfers. Since the commodity flows are functions of the terms of trade e_t, the current account also depends on e_t. The current account is set exogenously like the government deficit and this constraint is met by the endogenous terms of trade.

12.3.6   The Markets, Equilibrium and Solution of the Model

The intraperiod equilibrium obtains when the markets for goods and factors clear. The first set of markets is for the thirty-five commodities, the supply comes from the producers (via the make matrix) and imports, and the demands are from intermediate users, household consumption, investment, government demand and exports. These markets are cleared by the commodity prices.

Next we have the factor markets. The supply of the malleable capital is equated to the sum of the industry and household demands by an aggregate rental price. The demand for leisure translate into a

Table 12.2
Export price elasticities

Industry	Petri	Stone	Cline
Agriculture		−0.72	−
Metal mining		−0.92	
Oil and gas mining		−0.92	
Non-metal mining		−0.92	
Construction	*		
Food and kindred		−1.975	−0.63
Tobacco		−1.975	−0.63
Textile mill	−1.6	−1.18	−1.57
Apparel	−1.6	−1.18	−1.57
Lumber and wood	−1.0	−1.5	−1.43
Furniture	−1.0	−1.5	−1.43
Paper	−1.0	−1.41	−1.53
Printing and publishing	−1.0	−1.41	−1.53
Chemicals	−0.5	−0.98	−1.47
Petroleum refining	−0.5	−1.72	−1.47
Rubber and plastic	−0.5	−2.10	−2.14
Leather	−1.6	−0.62	−1.49
Stone Clay and Glass	−0.7	−1.26	−1.56
Primary metal	−1.1	−1.65	−1.97
Fabricated metal	−1.1	−1.06	−1.59
Machinery	−0.9	−1.04	−1.59
Electrical machinery	−1.2	−1.05	−1.59
Motor vehicles	−0.9	−2.49	−1.55
Transport. equipment	−0.9	−2.49	−1.55
Instruments	−0.9	−1.18	−1.85
Misc. manufactures	−1.0	−1.55	−1.62
Transportation	*		
Communications	*		
Electric Utilities	*		
Gas Utilities	*		
Trade	*		
Finance, Insurance	*		
Services	*		
Govt Enterprises	*		

*Sectors assumed to have zero price elasticities. Trade and transportation exports are margins on exported goods; other service sectors have only negligible exports.

Petri: Petri (1984).

Stone: Stone (1979), average of import elasticities for EEC and Japan.

Cline: Cline *et al.* (1978), average of Canada, EEC, Japan.

supply of labor. The demand for labor comes from the producers and households and the market is cleared by the wage rate.

We have exogenous government deficits and tax rates. The "revenue, expenditure, deficit" constraint is met by an endogenous level of public spending on goods. Similarly the exogenous current account balance is met by the endogenous terms of trade, e_t.

Finally we have the savings and investment equation. This is determined from the Euler equation linking consumption between adjacent periods.

Our model may be described as a multi-sector Cass-Koopmans model. Intertemporal equilibrium obtains when the two dynamic equations of the model are satisfied—the Euler equation for full consumption, and the capital accumulation equation. The transversality condition must of course also hold.

The economy moves along the saddle path from a given initial capital stock to a steady state defined by two conditions. The first condition is that full consumption is constant (recall that there is no long run technical progress). The second is that investment exactly matches depreciation. The first condition implies that at the steady state the net marginal product of capital is equal to the rate of time preference.

The saddle path is calculated by iterating on a guess of the path of the costate variable until both intraperiod and intertemporal equilibrium conditions are satisfied. The procedure is described in more detail in the Appendix.

12.4 Effects of Trade Barriers

In this section we summarize the results reported in Ho and Jorgenson (1994) where we estimated the impact of trade policy on U.S. economic growth. We constructed a base case for growth of the U.S. economy under actual trade policies, incorporating historical data for all exogenous variables. We then simulated the U.S. economy with a change in trade policy. The economic impact of the policy change is estimated by comparing the results of the two simulations. We initiate both simulations in 1980, immediately after the conclusion of the Tokyo Round negotiations in 1979.

12.4.1   Tariff Reductions

We first describe the effects of multilateral reductions in tariffs with no change in quantitative restrictions on trade. In table 12.3 we present tariff rates on U.S. imports in 1980, following several rounds of tariff reductions under GATT that culminated in the Tokyo Round. The most highly taxed commodity imports were textiles, apparel, leather (mainly footwear), glass, and primary metals (mainly iron and steel). Total customs duties collected on U.S. imports amounted to $7.2 billions or about 2.9 percent of total commodity imports of $251 billions. For comparison the U.S. gross national product in 1980 was $2,732 billions in prices of that year.[4]

To evaluate the economic impact of tariffs, we eliminate all domestic and foreign tariffs, beginning in 1980. In both the base case and alternative case simulations, we set the U.S. capital stock and all other state variables at the beginning of 1980 equal to their historical values. We then simulate the growth of the U.S. economy from 1980 to the year 2100. In the base case the government deficit and tax rates are exogenous, but government spending is endogenous. With all tariffs removed we set government expenditures equal to values from the base case. The exogenous government transfers and interest payments are kept the same in both simulations.

The economic impact of eliminating tariffs is summarized diagrammatically in figures 12.5a and 12.5b. The vertical axis in these figures gives the percentage change in each variable from the elimination of tariffs. The impact of the tariff cut is to raise consumption of goods and services by 0.16 percent in the first year. From the first panel of figure 12.5b we see that the price of capital goods is lower than in the base case and keeps falling. A falling price of capital goods leads to an increase in investment and boosts the growth of capital stock, as shown in figure 12.5b. By the year 2000 the capital stock is 0.49 percent higher than in the base case.

Lower commodity prices and an investment boom induce higher import demands. U.S. exports also increase with reduced tariffs in the rest of the world. From table 12.3 we see that these tariffs are generally higher than those in the U.S. Given the elasticities we have employed, the initial impact is greater for exports than for imports. Since the current account balance is exogenous, the terms of trade e_t must fall to stimulate higher imports. The required decrease of 0.6 percent in the terms of trade is very substantial. The quantity of exports

Table 12.3
Tariff rates in 1980

No.	Sector	Tariff rates ROW	U.S.	Tariff equiv.
1	Agriculture		0.035	
2	Metal mining		0.000	
3	Coal mining		0.000	
4	Oil and gas mining		0.000	
5	Non-metal mining		0.003	
6	Construction		0.000	
7	Food and kindred		0.027	
8	Tobacco		0.111	
9	Textile mill	0.107	0.108	0.030
10	Apparel	0.207	0.218	0.063
11	Lumber and wood	0.027	0.020	
12	Furniture	0.103	0.035	
13	Paper	0.058	0.005	
14	Printing and publishing	0.029	0.008	
15	Chemicals	0.094	0.041	
16	Petroleum refining		0.000	
17	Rubber and plastic	0.058	0.067	
18	Leather	0.045	0.097	0.056
19	Stone Clay and Glass	0.105	0.091	
20	Primary metal	0.058	0.030	0.048
21	Fabricated metal	0.090	0.057	
22	Machinery	0.067	0.041	
23	Electrical machinery	0.096	0.055	
24	Motor vehicles	0.077	0.023	*0.047
25	Transport. equipment	0.077	0.026	
26	Instruments	0.078	0.065	
27	Misc. manufactures	0.078	0.058	
28	Transportation			
29	Communications			
30	Electric Utilities			
31	Gas Utilities			
32	Trade			
33	Finance, Insurance			
34	Services			
35	Govt. Enterprises			

U.S. tariff rates are calculated from International Trade Commission data.

Rest of the world (ROW) tariff rates are from Deardorff and Stern (1986). See Table 12.4b below for tariff equivalents of quotas.

*1981 data.

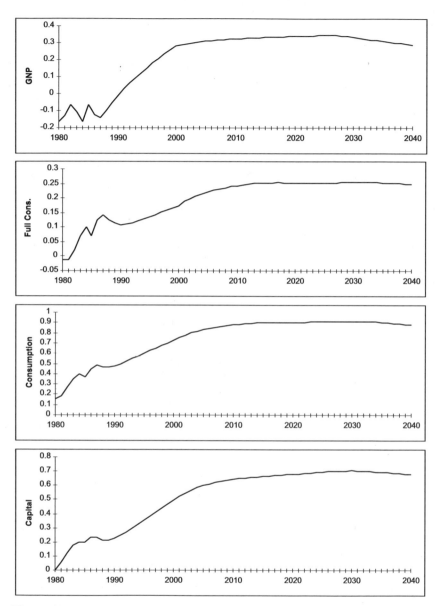

Figure 12.5a
Dynamic effects of tariff elimination.

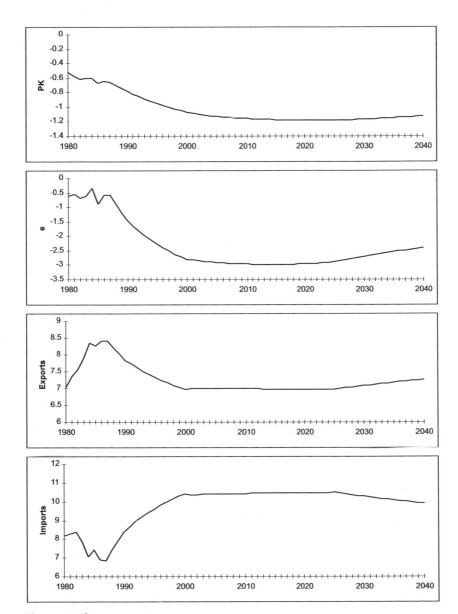

Figure 12.5b
Dynamic effects of tariff elimination.

Table 12.4a
Tariff equivalents of selected quotas

	Textiles	Apparel	Leather	Metals	Autos
1973	0	0	0	0.032	0
1974	0.030	0.063	0	0.032	0
1975	0.030	0.063	0	0	0
1976	0.030	0.063	0	0	0
1977	0.030	0.063	0.056	0	0
1978	0.030	0.063	0.056	0.048	0
1979	0.030	0.063	0.056	0.048	0
1980	0.030	0.063	0.056	0.048	0
1981	0.030	0.063	0.056	0.048	0.047
1982	0.071	0.095	0	0.048	0.047
1983	0.071	0.095	0	0.048	0.047
1984	0.071	0.095	0	0.048	0.047
1985	0.071	0.095	0	0.048	0

Tariff equivalents of "voluntary" export restrictions are calculated from Hufbauer, Berliner, and Elliot (1986) by aggregation to our model's industry classification.

Table 12.4b
Tariff equivalents of quotas on U.S imports from Japan

Sector	1970	1980
Textiles, Apparel	3.5	1.3
Primary Metal	6.0	7.0
Electrical Machinery	-	0.8

Petri (1984), page 138.

increases by 6.7 percent while the quantity of imports rises by 7.5 percent.

Over time the difference between the two simulations increases, due to the growth in capital stock resulting from the elimination of tariffs. By the year 2000 full consumption is 0.17 percent higher; this is comprised of an increase of 0.74 in consumption of goods and services and a decrease of 0.6 percent in leisure. The terms of trade decline over time, since U.S. prices fall but rest of the world prices remain constant, implying an increase in U.S. international competitiveness. As a consequence, the quantity of exports is only 6.5 percent higher in the year 2000, while the quantity of imports is 9.7 percent higher.

Table 12.5 gives the sectoral effects of tariff elimination in the initial year, while table 12.6 shows the effects after twenty years. Raw material industries such as mining have small trade flows; the small decreases in exports are due to the fall in the terms of trade. Agricultural trade is largely governed by quantitative restrictions, including trade embargoes, that we do not explicitly model. The small changes in trade should be interpreted with this in mind. Similarly, the industries producing nontradables—trade, finance, and services—have small declines in exports, due mainly to the terms of trade. Commodities with the highest tariff levels—textiles, apparel, rubber, leather, and glass—show the largest gains in imports. Chemicals, electrical machinery (which includes computers), and instruments have the highest rest of the world tariffs and the most substantial increases in exports.

The output and employment effects of tariff reductions largely parallel the shifts in imports and exports. Chemicals, primary metals, machinery, electrical machinery, and instruments show the largest gains in output and employment. Since the capital stock is initially fixed in supply, capital must be drawn from other sectors to these export oriented industries. Import penetration is so high in the food, furniture, and leather industries that domestic output actually falls. Capital and labor shift from these sectors to sectors that are more competitive internationally.

12.4.2 Quantitative Restrictions

With successive reductions in tariff rates, trade policy has shifted away from tariffs to quantitative restrictions like quotas and "voluntary" export restraints on suppliers of U.S. imports. As a concrete example, world trade in apparel is governed by Multi-Fiber Agreements that allocate quotas to each exporting country. The quotas are highly detailed, covering many categories of apparel. Some countries attain these limits while others are constrained in only a few or even none of the categories. Another example is motor vehicles, where Japanese exports to the U.S. in the 1980s are under "voluntary" export restrictions, while European exports are not.

We have modeled all quantitative restrictions by assuming that the realized import prices reflect the full effects. The primary justification for this approach is simplicity. More specifically, we assume that quotas result in a higher world price of imports PM_{it}^*. Hufbauer, Berliner

Table 12.5
Sectoral effects of eliminating all tariffs in 1980 (% change)

Sector	Output	Capital	Labor	Exports	Imports
Agriculture	−0.32	−0.44	−0.47	−0.34	2.09
Metal mining	2.17	2.08	2.04	−0.43	2.31
Coal mining	0.36	0.26	0.17	−0.44	0.84
Oil and gas mining	0.08	0.00	0.16	−0.56	0.69
Non-metal mining	0.75	0.59	0.35	−0.42	0.97
Construction	0.23	0.05	0.22	−0.14	
Food and kindred	−0.34	−0.45	−0.44	−0.31	1.62
Tobacco	−0.42	−0.47	−0.52	−0.30	20.56
Textile mill	1.42	0.88	0.17	18.94	20.23
Apparel	1.71	−0.26	0.09	29.07	31.06
Lumber and wood	0.25	−0.06	−0.35	3.39	4.59
Furniture	−0.51	−0.66	−0.72	16.25	6.03
Paper	0.85	0.71	0.69	8.64	1.98
Printing and publishing	0.70	0.70	0.57	3.57	2.27
Chemicals	2.47	2.39	2.36	14.58	8.01
Petroleum refining	0.17	0.10	0.12	−0.62	0.75
Rubber and plastic	1.71	1.58	1.45	12.74	15.07
Leather	−1.40	−2.17	−1.75	5.93	16.93
Stone Clay and Glass	0.37	0.23	0.00	18.04	20.38
Primary metal	2.34	1.74	1.74	11.80	7.48
Fabricated metal	1.63	1.17	1.24	15.56	8.67
Machinery	2.51	1.94	1.87	11.11	10.52
Electrical machinery	2.29	1.84	2.06	16.77	11.17
Motor vehicles	1.84	1.44	0.85	13.08	5.76
Transport. equipment	2.93	2.30	2.38	12.65	7.09
Instruments	3.78	3.62	3.50	15.35	9.81
Misc. manufactures	1.44	1.23	1.07	12.94	11.23
Transportation	0.26	0.15	0.15	−0.01	0.78
Communications	0.28	0.26	0.24	−0.05	
Electric Utilities	0.22	0.21	0.13	−0.06	0.09
Gas Utilities	0.40	0.32	0.34	−0.03	
Trade	0.26	0.22	0.22	−0.02	
Finance, insurance	0.08	0.08	0.07	−0.07	0.65
Services	0.02	-0.01	-0.09	−0.11	0.61
Govt. enterprises	0.30	0.31	0.27	−0.10	
Household		−0.54	−0.27		
Government		0.00	−0.82		

Entries are percentage change in the first period from the base case. Output is industry output, not commodity supply. Imports are competitive imports only.

Table 12.6
Eliminating all trade barriers vs. tariffs only after 20 years
(percentage change from base case)

	No tariffs	No barriers
Capital	0.50	0.54
Full consumption	0.17	0.26
Consumption	0.74	0.96
C.P.I.	1.00	1.25
Exports	6.54	7.19
Imports	9.72	10.68
Price of capital	−.72	−1.30

and Elliott (1986) have provided estimates of the tariff equivalents of quantitative restrictions on U.S. imports. While bearing in mind the many limitations of the concept of a tariff equivalent, these tariff rates are consistent with the assumptions of constant returns to scale and perfect competition employed in our model for all industries.

We next consider the economic impact of eliminating all domestic and foreign tariffs and the tariff equivalents of quantitative restrictions for textiles, apparel, shoes, steel and automobiles given in table 12.4. These are the most significant restrictions, but do not exhaust U.S. quotas. We have ignored restrictions on agricultural products and motor vehicles other than autos. We simulate the elimination of quantitative restrictions by reducing the rest of the world price of U.S. imports PM_{it}^*. Under this change in trade policy foreigners lose rents that accrue to them under quotas.

As before, we begin our simulation in 1980 and continue through the year 2100. We have combined tariffs with quantitative restrictions to provide an estimate of the impact of eliminating both types of trade barriers. The results given in figures 12.6a and 12.6b are similar but more substantial in magnitude than those for tariff reductions alone. The only exception is the terms of trade e_t. In our simulations the elimination of quantitative restrictions is unilateral. Given the exogenous trade balance, the terms of trade must rise in some years to cover the increased U.S. imports of textiles, steel, autos, and shoes. In the initial year the fall in the terms of trade is only 0.53 percent compared with 0.61 percent for tariffs alone.

By the year 2000 the economic impacts of eliminating all trade barriers are considerably greater than the effects of tariff cuts alone. The percentage changes at the aggregate level are shown in table 12.6.

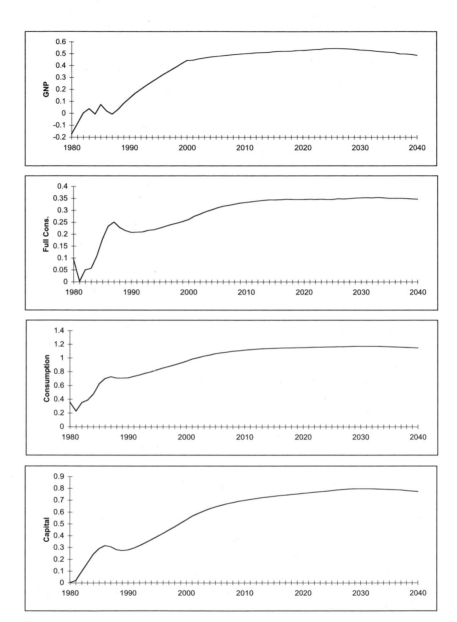

Figure 12.6a
Dynamic effects of eliminating tariffs and quotas.

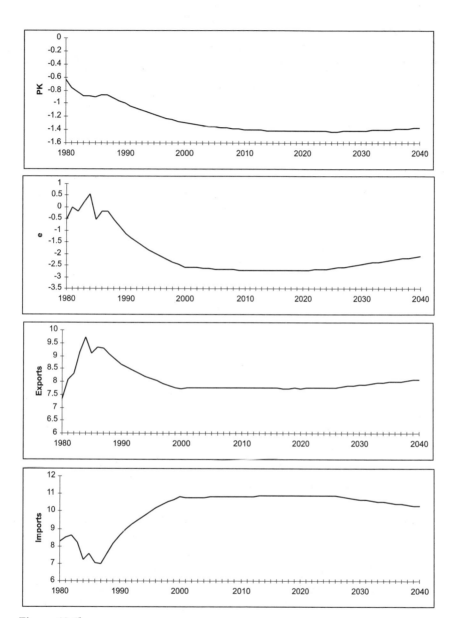

Figure 12.6b
Dynamic effects of eliminating tariffs and quotas.

Table 12.7
Elimination of all trade barriers vs. tariffs:
Effects on GNP growth

	Annual GNP Growth Rate %		
	Base Case	No Tariffs	No Barriers
1980:1990	3.47	3.48	3.50
1980:2000	2.34	2.37	2.38

These impacts arise from reductions in import prices for all the five quota items and the implied reduction in the price of investment goods. Investment goods industries are large consumers of steel; automobiles are included among these industries.

The sharp drop in the price of investment goods due to the elimination of auto quotas raises the U.S. investment level and economic growth rate. These quotas were eliminated in 1985, so that the impact on the growth rate fell. The effects of the elimination of all tariff barriers on growth of the U.S. gross national product is summarized in the table 12.7.

The sectoral effects of eliminating all trade barriers are given in table 12.8. This can be compared with table 12.5 for tariff cuts alone. The sectoral effects are quite similar, except for the commodities subject to quotas. Apparel imports, for example, rise by forty-two percent, compared to a gain of only thirty-one percent for tariff cuts alone. For iron and steel the gain is fifteen percent versus only seven percent; for leather the gain is twenty-eight percent versus seventeen percent. These shifts translate into parallel output changes. The leather industry's output falls by 2.5 percent by comparison with 1.4 percent with tariff cuts alone, while textile output rises by only 1.2 percent compared to 1.4 percent. Resources move out of apparel; since textiles, its main intermediate input, also falls in price, the output of apparel actually rises.

In summary, the economic impact of quantitative restrictions is substantial, even though only a few commodities are affected by them. Elimination of these restrictions on the five items we have considered would produce a gain in U.S. consumption that exceeds the gain from abolishing all remaining tariffs. A multilateral reduction of nontariff barriers would probably have had an even greater impact, given the likelihood that quantitative restrictions in the rest of the world are even higher than those in the U.S.

Table 12.8
Sectoral effects of eliminating tariffs and selected quotas

Sector	Output	Capital	Labor	Exports	Imports
Agriculture	−0.34	−0.43	−0.51	−0.14	1.97
Metal mining	2.10	2.09	1.86	−0.18	2.20
Coal mining	0.30	0.24	0.02	−0.27	0.60
Oil and gas mining	0.07	0.00	0.15	−0.32	0.56
Non-metal mining	0.50	0.32	0.03	−0.23	0.68
Construction	−0.15	−0.30	−0.17	−0.21	
Food and kindred	−0.50	−0.56	−0.62	−0.13	1.37
Tobacco	−0.54	−0.54	−0.73	−0.09	20.06
Textile mill	1.19	0.61	−0.24	19.91	25.64
Apparel	2.01	−0.46	−0.09	33.60	42.31
Lumber and wood	−0.12	−0.45	−0.83	3.81	3.91
Furniture	−1.20	−1.35	−1.49	16.81	4.93
Paper	0.81	0.67	0.62	8.94	1.75
Printing and publishing	0.90	0.93	0.72	3.89	2.29
Chemicals	2.45	2.38	2.31	15.13	7.74
Petroleum refining	0.18	0.19	0.09	−0.44	0.62
Rubber and plastic	1.30	1.21	1.01	13.44	14.38
Leather	−2.52	−3.59	−3.04	11.27	27.56
Stone Clay and Glass	−0.04	−0.16	−0.47	18.83	19.56
Primary metal	2.40	1.33	1.32	13.57	15.09
Fabricated metal	1.66	0.86	0.95	16.42	8.23
Machinery	2.36	1.59	1.45	11.96	9.87
Electrical machinery	2.02	1.46	1.72	17.94	10.52
Motor vehicles	1.58	1.13	0.29	13.95	5.02
Transport. equipment	2.87	2.15	2.10	13.15	6.70
Instruments	3.56	3.40	3.21	16.41	9.42
Misc. manufactures	1.50	1.28	1.02	14.58	10.89
Transportation	0.10	−0.01	−0.03	0.00	0.49
Communications	0.21	0.20	0.14	−0.07	
Electric Utilities	0.23	0.25	0.05	−0.02	0.12
Gas Utilities	0.35	0.31	0.25	−0.03	
Trade	0.10	0.06	0.05	−0.04	
Finance, Insurance	0.04	0.09	−0.01	−0.09	0.46
Services	−0.01	−0.04	−0.15	−0.15	0.45
Govt. Enterprises	0.23	0.28	0.18	−0.14	
Household		−0.40	−0.50		
Government			−0.99		

Entries are percentage change from base case in 1980. Imports are competitive imports only.

12.4.3   Sensitivity Analysis

There are two major issues with the parameters used in this and any other model. The first is the usual variance of estimated parameters due to the error term. The second is the assumption of the functional forms, e.g., our logistic trends. Using quadratic instead of logistic trends would produce different parameter estimates of the price elasticities and other coefficients. This would not be the place to discuss the econometric issues in detail, we would merely follow the sensible practice of using different parameter values and report the sensivity of the results to the various parameters. (A more ambitious project would be to use the estimated variances to give confidence intervals for our estimates, as suggested by a discussant. This is a very involved exercise, as can be seen in the small model used in Pizer, 1996.)

Trade elasticities
For our exercise the most important parameter imprecision is the set of price elasticities in the import demand equations and the export elasticities taken from the literature. The strong feeling in the literature is that these substitution elasticities are biased downwards (Goldstein and Khan, 1985). One problem is that aggregates are dominated by the low elasticity-high price volatility components, which would bias the estimates downwards. Following Deardoff and Stern (1986) we therefore, simply doubled all elasticities in our sensitivity analysis.[5] We used the 1985 shares to calculate the more elastic parameters. The export elasticites η_i are simply doubled.

In the steady state the capital stock gain due to a multilateral tariff elimination is 0.75 percent, in contrast to the 0.59 percent gain for base elasticities. Aggregate commodity consumption is 1.07 percent higher compared to 0.82 percent previously. Leisure falls 0.07 percent with the higher real wage. The real price of capital is 1.36 percent lower vs. 0.68 percent.

The steady-state sectoral results of eliminating tariffs beginning in 1980 for the two sets of parameters are given in table 12.9. The first three columns of numbers are the percent changes in the section 12.4.1 experiment, the last three columns are the changes with the doubled elasticities. The differences are unfortunately large (or fortunately depending on one's emphasis). The elasticities obviously have a significant effect on the estimates of output response, it may even change the sign.

Table 12.9
Sensitivity test using more elastic trade parameters

Sector	Base Elasticities			Doubled Elasticities		
	Output	Exports	Imports	Output	Export	Import
Agriculture	−0.56	−0.88	1.85	−1.59	−2.94	5.71
Metal mining	2.74	−1.13	2.39	2.91	−3.72	2.68
Coal mining	0.29	−1.37	1.83	−0.32	−4.20	3.92
Oil and gas mining	0.08	−1.12	2.19	−0.47	−2.56	3.63
Non-metal mining	1.32	−1.15	2.01	1.23	−3.76	3.12
Construction	−0.05	−0.53	0.00	−0.02	−0.63	0.00
Food and kindred	−0.98	−0.66	2.48	−1.68	−2.27	5.30
Tobacco	−0.83	−0.78	15.08	−1.48	−2.54	32.51
Textile mill	1.04	17.44	22.83	−2.55	34.31	39.56
Apparel	2.54	31.52	24.59	−2.28	66.07	39.73
Lumber and wood	0.22	2.17	4.89	−0.55	2.12	9.60
Furniture	−0.22	15.03	5.55	−0.04	28.84	11.36
Paper	1.00	7.09	3.45	0.87	12.30	7.33
Printing and publishing	0.96	2.18	3.45	1.01	1.83	6.55
Chemicals	3.31	13.56	8.97	4.74	25.76	16.41
Petroleum refining	0.54	−1.70	2.63	0.56	−4.02	5.65
Rubber and plastic	1.99	10.78	13.85	1.23	18.51	23.16
Leather	−1.56	9.09	14.76	−12.87	13.47	22.39
Stone, clay and glass	0.51	17.05	12.38	−0.39	32.60	21.65
Primary metal	2.76	10.23	9.13	2.91	17.73	15.83
Fabricated metal	1.83	13.91	7.00	2.49	26.43	12.40
Machinery	3.54	9.63	11.79	6.43	16.58	40.20
Electrical machinery	3.55	15.84	11.53	4.24	29.95	20.00
Motor vehicles	2.89	12.52	8.93	2.78	23.14	17.94
Transport. equipment	3.77	10.79	7.87	6.10	19.62	17.07
Instruments	4.70	13.82	10.38	8.42	24.65	21.46
Misc. manufactures	1.90	13.21	8.93	−1.11	23.24	13.91
Transportation	0.32	0.01	1.99	0.33	0.02	2.86
Communications	0.55	−0.14	0.00	0.71	-0.17	0.00
Electric utilities	0.76	0.22	0.65	0.86	0.41	0.56
Gas utilities	0.84	0.13	0.00	1.22	0.37	0.00
Trade	0.11	−0.07	0.00	0.11	−0.09	0.00
Finance, Insurance	0.24	−0.12	1.91	0.26	−0.15	2.85
Services	0.02	−0.27	1.82	0.03	−0.34	2.75
Govt. Enterprises	0.45	−0.16	0.00	0.55	−0.20	0.00

Entries are % changes between "no-tariffs" and "base" case. Base trade elasticities are
those estimated in Ho (1989).

Overall, the magnitudes of export and import changes are increased and with no changes in sign. Output responses are different. Despite the increased aggregate labor supply some sectors show a reduction in output in response to the increased import competition. That is, in the more elastic case the Textile, Apparel, Lumber, and Miscellaneous Manufacturing industries have negative output responses to tariff reduction, while in the base elasticities case they are positive due to stronger export effects.

Time preference and labor supply
We now turn to other parameters in the model. The value of ρ, the rate of time preference, estimated over 1948–1985 is 0.0288. In the alternative case we use a value of 0.04. The effect of this is very modest. Trade liberalization in this case produces a slightly smaller long run increase in the capital stock. For a given set of tariff rates, the rate of investment is of course higher in a $\rho = 0.03$ economy than in a $\rho = 0.04$ economy. The *percentage* change in investment due to a reduction in tariffs is, however, roughly the same. (The steady-state capital stock is 29,100 billion dollars in the base parameter case and 26,200 in the $\rho = 0.04$ case.)

Using a different value of the time preference parameter means using a different utility function and therefore utility comparisons must be made carefully. The equivalent variation of the welfare gain in the $\rho = 0.0288$ case is 0.14 percent (i.e., the change in utility value of the discounted stream of consumption as a percentage of initial wealth). The equivalent variation of the welfare gain in the $\rho = 0.04$ case is a similar 0.13 percent as reported in table 12.10. In other words the percentage change is very similar but the levels are different.

As noted in section 12.2.2 above we have tried to track the secular increase in labor supply (i.e., the decrease in leisure per capita) using an exogenous time trend. In the appendix equation (A.8) the estimated values of the time trend parameters are $\beta_0 = 0.04, \mu = 0.585$. To simulate the effect of not tracking this shift we set the value of this β_0 to 0 and repeated the above calculations. That is, the base case with this new value of β_0 is simulated and then the tariffs are set to zero and a new path calculated. The effects of trade liberalization under this "no labor supply shift" scenario is reported in table 12.10.

With no increase in the labor supply the paths of GDP and capital are lower than the base parameter case. The percentage increase in output and work hours due to the elimination of tariffs is, however,

Table 12.10
Sensitivity analyses of different values of time preference and leisure trends

	dK	dY	E.V.
Base case ($\rho = 0.0288$, $\beta_0 = 0.04$, $\beta^{CL} = 0.0375$)	0.65%	0.71%	0.14%
High time preference case ($\rho = 0.04$)	0.64%	0.80%	0.13%
No labor supply shift case ($\beta_0 = 0$)	0.68%	0.46%	0.10%
More inelastic labor supply ($\beta^{CL} = 0.0750$)	0.53%	0.57%	0.12%

dK = Change in steady-state capital stock due to trade liberalization

dY = Change in steady-state GDP due to trade liberalization

$E.V.$ = Equivalent variation as share of Wealth due to liberalization

slightly bigger. This means a bigger percentage reduction in leisure and thus a smaller increase in full consumption and utility. The equivalent variation of trade liberalization is thus smaller, 0.10 percent versus 0.14 percent.

The other problem parameter discussed in section 12.2 is the labor supply price elasticity. We estimate the value of the share elasticity in the goods-leisure tier of the utility function to be 0.0375 (this is the first element of the 2×2 B matrix in appendix equation (A.6)). A value of $B_{11} = 0$ corresponds to the Cobb-Douglas case of unit elasticity, our value estimated from time series aggregate data is a little less elastic than that. To see the effects of a more inelastic labor supply we set the value of B_{11} to twice the base case. The results (also reported in table 12.10) are not surprising, a more inelastic function leads to a smaller increase in labor supply due to a rise in the real wage when the prices of goods fall due to the tariff cuts. This leads to a smaller increase in long run output and capital. The effect on capital accumulation is plotted in figure 12.7. (The bold line gives the effect of trade liberalization on the path of capital stock using original parameters, the dotted line gives the effect using more inelastic parameters.) The welfare effect of trade liberalization, measured in terms of this different utility function, is thus lower than the base parameter case, 0.12 percent versus 0.14 percent.

It is clear from comparing the various rows of table 12.10 that there is no systematic relation between the effect on steady-state capital, output and welfare. These must be calculated separately for a complete sensitivity analysis. There are some parameters that affect the level of the projections but has little effect on the percentage change,

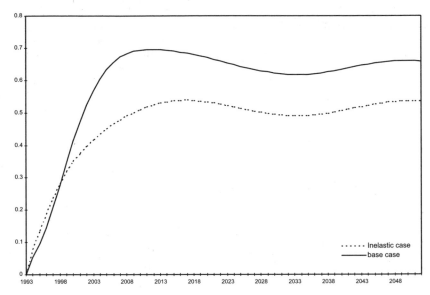

Figure 12.7
More inelastic labor supply. Effect on $dK(t)$.

and hence are less of a worry. These include the rate of time preference, the population growth rate, and the exogenous rate of long-run
neutral technical progress.

12.5   Conclusion

In this chapter we have described some of the issues that must be
addressed in implementing dynamic multi-sector general equilibrium
models of trade policy and economic growth. Such models are useful
in that they can capture dynamic adjustments by businesses and
households to changes in policy. These effects predominate in the
long run, so that economic impacts estimated from static models may
be substantially understated.

Our specific estimate is that a multilateral elimination of tariffs
alone beginning in 1980 raised long run consumption by 0.82 percent
compared to an initial gain of only 0.16 percent. Eliminating both tariffs and nontariff barriers lead to a long-run gain in consumption of
1.08 percent versus 0.36 percent in the first year. The ratio of welfare
cost to the tariffs is about 2. With more comprehensive estimates of

tax equivalents of the quotas that we have ignored here the welfare and growth effects would of course be higher.

These estimates are sensitive to the assumptions of the model and the parameter values used. We have illustrated the magnitude of the effect using different key parameters on welfare, output and capital accumulation. As is well known, using more elastic substitution elasticities will lead to gains that are bigger than the base case ones. We have also performed sensitivity analysis on parameters that are not subsitution elasticities. It is hoped that this is useful for users of numerical models to get a sense of the range of uncertainty.

The degree of sensitivity found here highlights again the need to carefully relate the results of numerical models to the underlying assumptions, of which many must be made in this kind of analysis. Complete Monte Carlo investigations of the sort econometricians do may not be feasible for complicated models like these but even limited sensitivity tests would be very useful.

Appendix

A.1 Household Sector

Stage 1. The aggregate household objective function is written as:

$$\sum_{t=1}^{\infty} \frac{N_t}{(1+\rho)^t} \left(\frac{F_t}{N_t}\right)^{1-\frac{1}{\sigma}} + \lambda \left(WF - \sum_{t=1}^{\infty} \frac{PF_t F_t}{\prod_{s=1}^{t} 1 + r_s} \right) \tag{A.1}$$

where N_t is an index of the number of households, F_t is full consumption and PF_t is its price. WF is full wealth, r is the rate of interest and λ is the Lagrange multiplier on the lifetime budget constraint. Differentiating w.r.t. F_t we obtain the Euler equation :

$$\left[\frac{F_t/N_t}{F_{t-1}/N_{t-1}}\right]^{\frac{1}{\sigma}} = \frac{1+r_t}{1+\rho} \frac{PF_{t-1}}{PF_t}. \tag{A.2}$$

Given last period's F and PF and the current prices the Euler equation gives this period's full-consumption, F_t, and hence savings,

$$S_t = YF_t - PF_t F_t \tag{A.3}$$

where *YF* is full income, the sum of capital income and human income. Capital income is given in equation (A.21) below. Human income is the sum of labor income and net transfers– $\bar{w}LH + Y_{transfer}$. $\bar{w}$ is the after tax wage rate, *LH* is the time endowment which is exogenously calculated from population projections.

Stage 2. Full consumption is allocated to the commodity aggregate and leisure ($F = F(CC, LEIS)$). We use a homothetic translog indirect utility function:

$$-\ln VV = \ln p'\alpha + \tfrac{1}{2}\ln p'B\ln p - \ln MF \tag{A.4}$$

where $\ln p = (\ln PCC, \ln w)'$ is the vector of the (log) price of aggregate commodities and leisure. The budget constraint at this stage is given by:

$$MF = PF.F = PCC.CC + w.LEIS \tag{A.5}$$

We refer the reader to Jorgenson, Lau and Stoker (1982) for details on the derivation and restrictions. Homotheticity implies that $B'\iota = 0$ and Slutsky symmetry gives $B' = B$.

From Roy's identity we can derive the share demand equations:

$$shr = \begin{bmatrix} PCC.CC/MF \\ w.LEIS/MF \end{bmatrix} = \alpha + B\ln p. \tag{A.6}$$

The labor supply is given by time endowment less the leisure demanded:

$$LS_t = LH_t - LEIS_t. \tag{A.7}$$

Given the trends and steady-state requirements as discussed in section 12.2.2 we write α as a logistic function of time *t*:

$$\alpha = \alpha_0 + \frac{\beta_0}{1 + \exp(-\mu(t - \tau))}. \tag{A.8}$$

With the homothetic restriction the price terms of (A.4) correspond to the translog cost function of a constant returns to scale production function:

$$\ln PF = \ln p'\alpha + \tfrac{1}{2}\ln p'B\ln p \tag{A.9}$$

Substituting (A.9) into (A.4) we have $VV = F$. That is, *F* is the level of "static utility" in any given period.

Stage 3. Our methodology for modeling the allocation of total expenditure, $CC(C_1, \ldots, C_{35}, K, L, NCI)$, is discussed by Jorgenson (1990a). The model we have employed was constructed by Jorgenson and Slesnick (1987). Household's utility function over the 35 commodities and 3 non-produced items (capital, labor and noncompeting imports) are assumed to be separable into nested functions.[6] At the top tier we have five commodity groups, $CC(C_1^g, \cdots C_5^g)$ corresponding to Energy, Eood, Nondurables, Services, and Capital. The indirect utility function for this top tier is written as:

$$\ln V^j = \ln\left(\frac{p}{Y_j}\right)'\alpha + \tfrac{1}{2}\ln\left(\frac{p}{Y_j}\right)'B\ln\left(\frac{p}{Y_j}\right) + \ln\left(\frac{p}{Y_j}\right)'B_{pA}A_j \qquad (A.10)$$

where Y_j is the value of total expenditures of household j, p is the vector of prices of the components, and A_j is the vector of dummies for demographic characteristics. Again using Roy's identity we can derive the expenditure share vector :

$$shr^j = \frac{1}{D}(\alpha + B\ln p - B\iota \ln Y_j + B_{pA}A_j) \qquad (A.11)$$

where $shr^j = (p_1 C_1^{gj}/Y_j, \ldots, p_5 C_5^{gj}/Y_j)'$ and the denominator D is:

$$D = -1 + \iota'B\ln p .$$

The above has been derived with the conditions for exact aggregation over the j households imposed (Jorgenson, Lau and Stoker, 1982).

The aggregate share vector is the weighted sum of the individual shares:

$$shr = \frac{1}{D}\left(\alpha + B\ln p - B\iota\frac{\sum Y_j \ln Y_j}{\sum Y_j} + B_{pA}\frac{\sum Y_j A_j}{\sum Y_j}\right)$$

$$\equiv \frac{1}{D}(\alpha + B\ln p - B\iota\xi^d + B_{pA}\xi^L) \qquad (A.12)$$

where $shr = (p_1 C_1^g/PCC.CC, \ldots, p_5 C_5^g/PCC.CC)'$. The value of aggregate commodity consumption expenditures is $PCC.CC = \sum Y_j$. The term ξ^d is a measure of the distribution of expenditures over the households, and ξ^L is the vector of shares of aggregate expenditure spent by each of the 672 demographic groups that are identified. The estimation of these terms and the coefficients are described in Jorgenson and Slesnick (1987), while Ho (1989) describes the projections of the demographic terms ξ^d, ξ^L.

Corresponding to this aggregate share equation we have the price frontier for *PCC* which is written as the social cost-of-living index in Jorgenson (1990a):

$$\ln PCC = \iota B \ln p \ln(PCC.CC/N) - \alpha \ln p + \tfrac{1}{2} \ln p' B \ln p \qquad (A.13)$$

In the tiers below this top one the five commodity groups are allocated to the individual commodities. For example, the energy group is made up of Gasoline, Fuel and Coal, Electricity and Gas, $C_1^g = C(C_{gas}, C_{fuel}, C_{elec}, C_{gas})$ The details of the nested structure is given in Ho (1989 p. 48). For these sub-tiers we use the same functional form as (A.10) and (A.11) but ignore the demographics, i.e., $B_{pA} = 0$. We also impose homotheticity, which implies $B\iota = 0$. The price function and share equations at the *m*th node ($m \neq 1$) thus reduce to a simple:

$$\ln P^m = \ln p^{m'} \alpha^m + \ln p^{m'} B^m \ln p^m \qquad (A.14)$$
$$shr^m = \alpha^m + B^m \ln p^m$$

where P^m is the price of the *m*th group, p^m is the vector of prices of the components of the *m*th node, and shr^m is the vector of value shares. For example, at the second node the price of the energy group is given as a function of the prices of its components, $P_{energy} = P(p_{gas}, p_{fuel}, p_{elec}, p_{gas})$.

A.2 Producer Sector

Each industry produces output using capital, labor and intermediate inputs using a constant returns to scale technology, $QI_{jt} = f(KD_{jt}, LD_{jt}, A_{1j}, \ldots, A_{nj}, t)$. *KD* is the demand for capital, *LD* the demand for labor, and A_{ij} is the demand for the thirty-five intermediate inputs and noncompeting imports. The industry capital is rented from a total stock of malleable capital at a rental price PKD_{jt}. The price of labor is PLD_{jt} while the price of commodity *i* is PS_{it} (this denotes the price of total supply given in A.29 below).

For our model of producer behavior we have modified the usual translog cost function along the lines discussed in section 12.2.1. With the industry superscript suppressed the output price is:

$$\ln PO = \alpha_0 + \alpha_p \ln P + \tfrac{1}{2} \ln P \, B \ln P + \ln P \, B_{pt} \qquad (A.15)$$
$$g(t) + \alpha_t \, g(t) + \tfrac{1}{2} \beta_{tt} g(t)^2$$

where $g(t)$ is a logistic function instead of the original linear trend. P is the vector of input prices. At the top tier the intermediate inputs are aggregated to energy and nonenergy materials, giving four input prices, $P = (PKD, PLD, P_{energy}, P_{material})$. Differentiating w.r.t. the log prices we obtain the input share vector:

$$shr = \alpha_p{}' \ln P + B \ln P + B_{pt} g(t) . \qquad (A.16)$$

The first two elements of this vector are the demands for capital and labor, $shr_K = PKD_j KD_j / PO_j QI_j$, $shr_L = PLD_j LD_j / PO_j QI_j$. The reader is referred to Jorgenson (1986) for details, the restrictions that are imposed are constant returns to scale, symmetry and local concavity. These restrictions imply that:

$$\alpha_p{}' \iota = 1 \qquad B'\iota = 0 \qquad B_{pt}\iota = 0 \qquad B' = B .$$

The vector α_p gives the input value shares at unit relative prices (i.e., shares in the base year), while matrix B is the *share elasticity* matrix which gives the elasticity of substitution between any pair of the four inputs. When B is zero the production function reduces to a Cobb-Douglas one. B_{pt} are the *biases of technical change* that make this a nonneutral production function.

Equations (A.15) and (A.16) characterize the top tier of the production functions with the four inputs—capital, labor, energy and materials. The energy and material inputs are aggregated from the thirty-five commodities and imports. The demands for the individual commodities are derived by cost functions arranged in a nested structure, for example, the energy group is written as $P_{energy} = P(P_{coal}, P_{oil}, P_{refining}, P_{elect}, P_{gas})$.

For the tiers below the top, the cost function used is simplified by dropping the time trend:

$$\ln P_m = \ln P^{m}{}'\alpha^m + \tfrac{1}{2} \ln P^{m}{}' B^m \ln P^m \qquad (A.17)$$

at each node $m \neq 1$. P_m is the price of the input aggregate m, P^m is the vector of prices of the components at node m. The corresponding share equations are:

$$shr^m = \alpha^m + B^m \ln P^m . \qquad (A.18)$$

The submodel embodied in (A.15–A.18) is implemented for each of the thirty-five industries. There is, however, a modification for the Oil and Gas Extraction sector. This industry was tightly regulated for much of the sample period with both price and quantity controls. In particular prices for domestic producers were kept down far below world levels in the 70s. Modelling the complex web of regulations is beyond the scope of the present study, we simplify them by setting the capital stock, which consist mostly of oil wells, equal to the historical data and allow the cost of capital to adjust differently from the other industries. (See Ho (1989) for further details.)

The transformation of industry outputs (*QI*) to commodity supply (*QC*) is done quite simply via a Cobb-Douglas formula:

$$PC_i QC_i = \sum_j M_{ij} PI_j QI_j \qquad i = 1, \ldots, 35 \qquad (A.19)$$

where M_{ij} are the row shares of the "make matrix" in figure 13.4. *PI* is the price after sales taxes

$$PI_j = (1 + t_j) PO_j. \qquad (A.20)$$

A.3   Cost of Capital and Investor Behavior

The cost of capital equation follows the approach in Jorgenson and Yun (1986b). The investor maximizes the discounted stream of net rental income by choosing a path of investment:

$$\max \sum_{t=u}^{\infty} \frac{(1 - tk)[PKD_t K_{t-1} - tpPK_{t-1} K_{t-1}] - PII_t I_t}{\prod\limits_{s=u}^{t} 1 + r_s} \qquad (A.21)$$

subject to

$$K_t = (1 - \delta) K_{t-1} - I_t \qquad (A.22)$$

PKD is the aggregate rental price and *PII* is the price of aggregate capital goods. *K* and *I* are the aggregate capital stock and investment. *tk* is tax rate on capital income, *tp* is the property tax rate, where we have simplified the tax detail by ignoring investment credits and depreciation allowances.

Setting up the Hamiltonian for this dynamic problem, and differentiating, we obtain:

$$(1 + r_t)PII_{t-1} = (1 - tk)[PKD_t - tpPK_{t-1}] + (1 - \delta)PII_t .$$ (A.23)

This equation relates the rental cost of capital to the nominal interest rate and must be satisfied along the dynamic equilibrium path.

Aggregate investment is allocated across the thirty-five commoditites and non-competitive imports via a nested structure of demand functions like the consumer model, $I_t = I(I_{1t}, \ldots, I_{35t})$. At the first tier this is divided into fixed and inventory investment using historical shares. At the nodes of each of the subsequent tiers the disaggregated demands are derived from a translog price frontier:

$$\ln PII_m = \ln P^{m\prime}\alpha^m + \frac{1}{2} \ln P^{m\prime}B^m \ln P^m$$ (A.24)
$$shr^m = \alpha^m + B^m \ln P^m$$

where PII_m is the price of subaggregate m, and P^m is a vector of the component prices, and shr^m is the value shares vector. The tier structure and parameter estimates are reported in Ho (1989 p. 96).

A.4   Government

The government deficits are carefully cumulated into the stock of government debt owned by domestic households (BG_t), and foreigners (BG_t *). The public deficit ΔG_t is financed by issuing these two bonds, and through seignorage ΔP_t^{BG}:[7]

$$BG_t = BG_{t-1} + \Delta G_t + GFI + \Delta P_t^{BG}$$ (A.25)
$$BG_t * = BG_{t-1} * - GFI - \Delta P_t^{BG*}$$

GFI denotes net government foreign investment, i.e., the negative of the flow of government debt to foreigners. The government deficit is expenditures less revenues:

$$\Delta G_t = VGG_t + iBG_{t-1} + iBG_{t-1} * + transfers - \sum t_j PO_j QI_j - tariffs$$
$$- tk(PKD. KD + i. BG + e. i * BF) - tl. w. LS - tp. PK. K - fees - TLUMP$$
(A.26)

where VGG is the expenditures on goods, iBG's are the interest on debt, transfers are transfers to households and foreigners, fees are exogenous government revenues and TLUMP is the lump-sum tax variable used in the simulations. t_j is the sales tax on output j, tk and tl are the taxes on capital and labor income, and tp is the property tax rate.

The total expenditures on goods is allocated to the individual commodities, noncompeting imports and labor via a simple share function. The value of government spending on commodity i is:

$$VG_{it} = \alpha_{it}^G VGG_t .$$ (A.27)

The other public expenditures are set exogenously.

A.5   Rest-of-the-World

We classify imports into two types, competiting and noncompeting following the conventions of the official IO tables. Noncompeting imports enter as an input into the production functions, the price of noncompeting import i is written as:

$$PNCI_{it} = (1 + \theta_{it})e_t PNCI_{it}^*,$$ (A.28)

where θ_{it} is the tariffs and $PNCI^*$ is the world price. The terms of trade, e_t, is the endogenous price of goods in the U.S. relative to the exogenous price of goods in the rest of the world.

The demand for NCI_i comes from the input demands of the producer as given by equation (A.18).

The total supply of commodity i (QS_i) comes from domestic production (QC_i) and competitive imports M_i. We model the allocation between these two sources with a translog cost function:

$$\ln PS_{it} = \ln p_{it}' \alpha_{it} + \frac{1}{2} \ln p_{it}' B_i \ln p_{it} ,$$ (A.29)

where PS_{it} denotes the price of total supply in period t and $\ln p_{it} = (\ln PC_{it}, \ln PM_{it})$ is a vector of logarithms of prices of the domestic commodity PC_{it} and competitive imports PM_{it}.

The price of imports to domestic buyers is the world price plus the tariffs

$$PM_{it} = (1 + \theta_{it}) e_t PM_{it}^*,$$ (A.30)

As discussed in section 12.2.3 the trends in imports cannot be explained by prices alone and we have therefore written α_i as a logistic function of time. The import share demand derived from the above cost function is then:

$$shr^i \equiv \left[\frac{PC_i QC_i / PS_i QS_i}{PM_i M_i / PS_i QS_i} \right] = \alpha_0^i + \frac{\beta_0^i}{1 + e^{-\mu_i(t-\tau_i)}} + B^i \ln p^i . \tag{A.31}$$

The value of total supply to the market is simply $PS_i QS_i = PC_i QC_i + PM_i QM_i$. Equation (A.31) was estimated for all the non-service industries over the sample period 1964:1985 and reported in Ho and Jorgenson (1994).

Since we do not model production in the rest of the world, we express the demand for U.S. exports, X_{it}, as a function of the rest-of-the-world output Y_t^* and the price of exports PC_{it}:

$$X_{it} = EX_{i0}(Y_t^*) \left[(1 + \theta_{it}^*) \frac{PC_{it}}{e_t} \right]^{\eta_i}, \tag{A.32}$$

where $EX_{i0}(Y_t^*)$ represents actual U.S. exports during the sample period and projected exports outside this period, θ_{it}^* is the rest-of-the world tariff rate on U.S. exports, and the term in square brackets is the price for U.S. exports faced by the rest of the world. We do not have the data on rest of the world imports from the U.S. required for estimation of the export price elasticities η_i. We take these elasticities as averages of import price elasticities of major trading partners of the U.S.

The base exports $EX_{i0}(Y^*)$ are set to the historical exports in sample period, and projected out of sample via:

$$\ln EX_{ti} = \alpha_i^x + \lambda_i^x \ln Y_t * \tag{A.33}$$

This equation was estimated for all commodities using our data for the period 1964:1985.[8] World income $Y *$ is assumed to grow initially at 2 percent and slowing down to the presumed steady state of zero growth in 2050.

To complete the current account for the U.S. economy we must determine factor income and payments to the rest of the world. These are interest and dividends on net U.S. private claims on the rest of the world, BF_t , and net U.S. official liabilities, BG_t^*. These net factor incomes, denoted by $i_t^* BF_{t-1}$ and $- i_t BG_{t-1}^*$, are set exogenously. i and i^* are the domestic and rest of the world rates of return. The final exogenous flow is net unilateral transfers or foreign aid, denoted *transfers* *.

Adding foreign trade and noncommodity flows, we obtain the U.S. current account surplus in year t, CA_t:

$$CA_t = \sum PC_{it} X_{it} - \sum PM_{it} M_{it} - \sum PNCI_{it} NCI_{it}$$ (A.34)
$$+ i_t^* BF_{t-1} - i\, BG_{t-1}^* - \mathit{transfers} * \,.$$

From equations (A.31–A.32) we see that U.S. exports X_{it} and imports M_{it} are functions of the terms of trade e_t. This variable is endogenous in our model and adjusts the purchasers' prices of U.S. imports and exports so that the exogenously given current account balance (A.34) is maintained.

The current account surplus goes into the accumulation of private net foreign assets BF, and government net foreign claims $-BG *$:

$$BF_t = BF_{t-1} + CA_t - GFI_t + \Delta P^{BF}$$ (A.35)

where ΔP^{BF} is the capital (exchange rate) gain on the foreign claims.

The allocation of savings among domestic capital formation, acquisition of foreign assets, and investment in government bonds is exogenous in our model. This implies that the public sector deficit and current account balance are exogenous. We allow the public sector deficit to decline gradually to a steady state value in the year 2025, equal to the inflationary gain on the stock of outstanding government debt, which has the effect of holding per capita debt constant in real terms. The current account deficit is allowed to fall to zero by the year 2000. These projections are expressed in terms of the numeraire for our model, the U.S. wage rate.

A.6   The Markets and Equilibrium Conditions

In our model with constant returns to scale and perfect competition all markets clear at zero profits in every period. There are four types of markets and one definitional "market." The first category are the markets for the 35 commodities:

$$PS_i QS_i = \sum_j PS_i A_{ij} + PS_i (C_i + I_i + G_i) + PC_i X_i \quad i = 1, \dots, 35$$ (A.36)

Total supply is allocated to intermediate demands of $j = 1, \dots, 35$ industries and the final demands of the consumer, investor, government and exports. These markets are cleared by the prices of domestically produced commodities PC_i.

The next two markets are the factor markets for capital and labor:

$$PKD_t K_{t-1} = \sum_j PKD_{tj} KD_{tj} \tag{A.37}$$

$$w_t LS_t = (1 - tl^m) \sum_j PLD_{tj} LD_{tj} \tag{A.38}$$

As described in equation (A.5), w is the price of leisure. tl^m is the marginal tax rate. There is only one aggregate capital and one aggregate labor supply in our model. However, the historical factor inputs have varied a great deal across the industries in terms of their compositions (e.g., more or less equipment vs. structures, or highly educated vs. less educated workers). This means that the time series for PKD_j, PLD_j over our sample period have evolved differently among the thirty-five industries. We reconcile the data with our model assumptions in a simple way using adjustment coefficients:

$$PKD_{tj} = \psi_{tj}^K PKD_t \,. \tag{A.39}$$

$$PLD_{tj} = \psi_{tj}^L w_t / (1 - tl_t^m) \,.$$

The ψ coefficients are determined from the data by reversing the above equalities. The aggregate factor prices PKD_t and w_t are of course the ones that clear these markets.

The next two constraints that must be satisfied are for the government and rest of the world. The exogenous government deficit, equation (A.26), is met by an endogenous VGG. The exogenous current account balance (A.34) is met by the "exchange rate" e_t.

The final equality is for savings and investment plus the exogenous deficits:

$$PII_t I_t = S_t - (BG_t - BG_{t-1}) - (BF_t - BF_{t-1}) \tag{A.40}$$

This is not a market as such, savings and investment is the one and same decision derived from the intertemporal optimization behavior of the household. The Household and Investor sections above are two faces of the same optimizing agent, all the capital is owned by the household. We have described the model in the above manner to highlight the market nature of the economy, that there is not a social planner. In this particular model the social planner's decision, given the government constraints, would have been the same as the household's.

All the above intraperiod conditions must be satisfied at every period. Along the transition path the intertemporal conditions for equilibrium is given by equations (A.2) and (A.22). The interest rate in the Euler equation (A.2) is given by equation (A.23).

The steady state is determined by two conditions. The first is that full consumption is constant and the second is that the capital stock is constant. The first condition implies that the net marginal product of capital (or interest rate) at the steady state (ss) is equal to the rate of time preference:

$$r_{ss}k = k\rho.$$ (A.41)

The second condition implies that investment exactly covers depreciation:

$$I_{ss} = \delta K_{ss}$$ (A.42)

Comment

The size of the SS economy is effectively determined by the stationary time endowment. The rate of return r_{SS} is independent of government policies, the capital stock is determined by the cost-of-capital equation linking the marginal product of capital and tax policies with r_t. In this sense the supply of capital is perfectly elastic in the long run. This should be compared with the Cass-Koopmans neoclassical growth model with the same independence of r_{SS}. In our model policies affecting sectoral allocation (e.g., rates of tariffs and quotas) will result in different levels of capital intensity—all corresponding to the same rate of return. This is impossible in the one-sector Cass-Koopmans model.

In the short run the supply of aggregate capital is fixed, however, under our mobility assumptions the sectoral allocation of factors may be affected by government policies within the period. This will result in different prices of the goods, in particular the price of investment. The transition path is thus affected directly, and indirectly through the price of capital goods.

A.7   Solution of Model and Exogenous Variables

For each period, variables regarded as exogenous include the stocks of debt $(BF, BG, BG *)$; public sector deficit, government interest payments and transfers $(\Delta G, iBG)$; the current account balance, foreign factor income, import prices and base exports (CA, $e.i * BF$, PM, $PNCI$, EX); the number of households and time endowment, (N, LH); the composition adjustment coefficients (ψ^K, ψ^L). These variables are set equal to the data during the sample period and projected after that. (The details of the projections are given in Appendix F of Ho, 1989).

The population is projected using a more elaborate version of the Social Security Agency's population projection model. We impose a stationary population in the steady state by adjusting the rate of immigration to fit the base fertility and mortality assumptions of the SSA. From the model we derive the number of households and adjust it by the distribution indices ξ^d, ξ^L from Jorgenson and Slesnick. We also derive a forecast of the population by educational attainment groups and adjust them by relative wages to give the time endowment. Since the population converged rather slowly, and in waves, we simplified by stopping all demographic changes in the year 2050.

In line with this, all exogenous variables reach their targets in 2050. The terminal date for the simulations is 2100, this allows 50 periods for the system to "settle down" (i.e., converge to the steady-state ratios of consumption, investment, etc.).

Projections of government variables are taken in part from Anderson et al. (1987). We assume that the government deficit declines steadily towards πBG in 2025 and remain at this fraction thereafter. From this deficit we obtain the stocks of public debt. The external accounts are projected by setting CA_t to rise gradually to zero by 2000, after which it is set to a surplus so that the steady-state stock of foreign assets bear the same relation to total wealth as that in 1982. Relative import prices are set to the latest data available, the absolute price are these exogenous prices multiplied by the "exchange rate."

We first solve for the steady state as defined by equations (A.41) and (A.42), that is, we solve for F_{ss}, K_{ss}, etc. The model is then solved by iterating on a guess of the path of the costate variable. We choose the value of full consumption $PF_t F_t$ as the costate variable. The transition path is set at 100 periods, i.e., we solve the model for $t = 1, 2, \ldots, 100$. We find that this is sufficiently far out such that K_{100} is very close to K_{ss}. The guess path is set such that $PF_{100}F_{100}$ is equal to the value calculated for the steady state.

Given the initial state variable, $K_{t=0}$, the guess of the costate variable and the exogenous variables we can now solve the intraperiod equilibrium. For each t, we find a set of prices such that the markets as described in (A.36–A.38) clear. Our model is homogenous of degree zero in prices and obeys Walras' Law. The labor supply=demand equation is dropped and we chose the wage rate as the numeraire. The static model is "triangularized" into a small set of 40 basis variables.[9] With the solution of period t we obtain the level of investment and hence the stock of capital available for $t+1$. The whole path of the economy is then calculated.

The value of the F_t's that result from the guess of the whole path of costate variables would not generally satisfy the Euler equation (A.2). We use the residual from this equation to update our guess of the costate variable, always keeping $PF_{100}F_{100}$ at the steady-state value. This is iterated until (A.2) is satisfied.

A.8   Data and Parameters

The data for this model cover the period 1947 to 1985 and follows the methodology of Christensen and Jorgenson (1973b) and Jorgenson, Gollop, and Fraumeni (1987) (JGF). The goal of the exercise is to construct a time series of input-output tables (both "use" and "make" matrices) over which one can estimate the production and demand functions. In addition we also need financial accounts that are not in the I-O tables.

The construction of the I-O matrices are described in Wilcoxen (1988), basically, the official tables published every five years are interpolated using annual industry data.[10] The capital and labor inputs (the value-added rows in the I-O table) are updated with some improvements following the approach in JGF. The detailed investment data from the BEA is cumulated into stocks of capital by Divisia aggregation, the rental price of capital is calculated from National Income Accounts (NIA). Labor input is aggregated over the labor force cross-classified by sex, age, educational attainment and industry. With the Divisia aggregation we take into account the different productivities of the various groups, instead of a simple sum of hours.

The final demand columns are estimated from the NIA and "bridge tables" from the official I-O tables. Imports are aggregated from trade data classified according to the SITC,[11] and price indices from the BLS are used where available (unit values are used otherwise). The financial accounts (stocks of debt, government accounts, tax rates, etc.) are from the US Worksheets which are revised versions of Christensen and Jorgenson.

The top tier of the production functions are estimated using the "use matrix," while the bottom tiers are from Hudson and Jorgenson. The first two stages of the household model are estimated from aggregate data in the *US Worksheets*. The top tier of the Consumption function is from Jorgenson and Slesnick, while the bottom tiers are estimated from the I-O table, as are the invesment functions. The import share equations are estimated from the "import" and "total output" columns of the I-IO table. All estimates are the invesment functions. The import share equations are estimated from the "import" and "total output" columns of the I-O table. All estimates are reported in Chapters 4 and 5 of Ho (1989).

Notes

1. The first of these is based on detailed partial equilibrium models, such as that of Hufbauer, Berliner, and Elliot (1986). The second approach uses multi-country general equilibrium models, such as the "Michigan Model" of Deardorff and Stern (1986) and the world trade model of Whalley (1985).

2. The construction of our data is described in the Appendix.

3. This problem may be quite difficult. There is some evidence that the demand curves are of rank three, i.e., the curves need more than a quadratic term to fit well. (See Lewbel 1991 for estimates using U.S. data.)

4. Tariff rates given in table 12.3 were calculated from data provided by Andrew Parks of the U.S. International Trade Commission, described in detail by Ho (1989), Appendix H. Tariff rates for the rest of the world are taken from Deardorff and Stern (1986).

5. The elasticity of substitution is: $E = \dfrac{B}{\text{share}} + \text{share} - 1$ where B is the price coefficient of equation (5).

6. The household demand functions are estimated over consumption data classified as in the National Accounts. This is different from the IO classification system. There is a bridge that links the NIPA system to the IO system for each official input output table. The latest bridge is used in our model to link the demands estimated in this section to the model's IO categories as given in table 12.1.

7. The notation is meant to suggest the devaluation of the value of government bonds through inflation. The definition of BG is given in Christensen and Jorgenson, it includes money and assets of social insurance funds.

8. The omitted variable bias of λ has the same sign as $\text{corr}(Y^*, P_i * /P_i^{US})$ on which we can put no clear priors. We believe that the magnitude of this bias is small enough for (A.33) to be a usable starting point for the projections.

9. The model as written above has thousands of equations and endogenous variables. Instead of solving $f(x) = 0$ directly for the whole vector x, it is first rewritten as $f(x^1(y), y) = 0$, where y is a small sub-vector of x.

10. I-O data are from the Bureau of Economic Analysis, the latest version is described in the *Survey of Current Business* May 1984. Annual industry output and prices are from the Bureau of Labor Statistics database *Time Series on Output, Prices and Employment*.

11. At the 4-digit level and supplemented by more detailed data where necessary to get a better price index. The former are from the OECD database and the 7-digit data from the Census Bureau's *US Imports by SITC*.

13 The Cost of Capital and the Economics of the Environment

Peter J. Wilcoxen

13.1 Introduction

During the past decade, the economic analysis of environmental policies has undergone a quiet revolution. Prior to the 1990s, empirical studies of environmental regulation were typically static. Many took the total cost of a given regulation in a particular year to be the sum of the regulated firms' direct expenditures on compliance. The most careful studies also included indirect welfare losses caused by changes in the markets upstream and downstream of the point of regulation. Virtually all examined regulation on a year-by-year basis. During the 1990s, however, the pioneering work of Dale Jorgenson on the development and application of large-scale, intertemporal econometric general equilibrium models demonstrated that the most important costs of regulations are often due to their effects on the cost of capital, and hence on economic growth. Regulations can raise the cost of new capital goods and thus slow the rate of capital formation and reduce the rate of growth.[1] At the same time, market-based environmental policies, such as emissions taxes, may raise enough new tax revenue to allow capital income taxes to be reduced, possibly lowering the cost of capital and stimulating growth.[2] On the other hand, tax reforms or policies designed stimulate growth by changing the cost of capital can have unintended effects on environmental problems.[3]

In order to evaluate an environmental policy, therefore, it is essential to determine the effect of the policy on the cost of capital and capital formation. This requires a quantitative model that can capture environmental regulations at a detailed level, trace the effects of those regulations through the economy to determine their influence on the cost of producing new capital goods, and can also determine the effect of the policy on savings and investment. The principal analytical approach possessing these features is large-scale econometric, intertemporal general equilibrium modeling.

Large-scale general equilibrium models divide the economy into many sectors in order to measure policy impacts on narrow segments of the economy. This also makes it possible to model differences among industries in responses to changes in energy prices and the imposition of pollution controls. A second dimension for disaggregation is to distinguish among households by level of wealth and demographic characteristics. This makes it possible to model differences in responses to price changes and environmental controls. It is also useful in examining the distributional effects of energy and environmental policies.

Simply having a large number of sectors or households is not sufficient to capture the effects of environment regulations, however. The behavioral parameters appearing in the optimization models used to represent each agent's behavior must be determined. Under the econometric approach to general equilibrium modeling, pioneered by Jorgenson, these parameters are econometrically estimated from painstakingly-assembled historical data. This attention to the empirical basis of each model is the distinguishing feature of Jorgenson's work; most other general equilibrium models are parameterized by "calibrating" them to a very limited data set, such as a single input-output table. Empirical evidence on substitutability among inputs is essential in analyzing the impact of environmental policies. If it is easy for industries to substitute among inputs, the effects of these policies will be very different than if substitution were limited. Although calibration avoids the burden of data collection required by econometric estimation, it also specifies the substitutability among inputs by assumption rather than relying on empirical evidence. This can easily lead to substantial distortions in estimating the effects of environmental policies.

The remainder of this paper will explore the link between environmental policy and the cost of capital. We begin by presenting an overview of the evolution of large-scale general equilibrium modeling. Following that we discuss the structure and features of one such model in detail and then examine the model's results for a particular simulation: a carbon tax designed to hold U.S. carbon dioxide emissions at 1990 levels with revenues from the tax returned through three alternative instruments: a lump-sum rebate, a reduction in the tax rate on capital income, and a reduction in the tax rate on labor. To explore how these results depend on the estimated behavioral parameters in the model, we next examine one of these policies, the carbon tax with an accompanying cut in capital taxes in a somewhat simpler model that can be used to calculate confidence intervals for results based on the covariance matrix of the parameter estimates. We use the model to calculate the policy's mean equivalent variation (EV) and the corresponding 95% confidence interval. Following this, we conclude with a short summary.

13.2 The Econometric Approach

The roots of large-scale general equilibrium modeling go back to Leontief, who built the first input-output models in the early 1950s.[4] Input-output models are based on the assumption that the behavior of consumers and firms can be represented by fixed-coefficient utility and production functions. This allows technology and preference parameters to be determined from a single inter-industry input-output transactions table. In the 1960s and 1970s the input-output approach was extended to incorporate pollution and the use of natural resources, allowing it to be used to examine environmental policy.[5]

The obvious objection to the fixed coefficients approach to modeling energy and environmental policies is that these policies induce changes in the input-output coefficients. In fact, the explicit objective of many pollution control regulations is to induce producers and consumers to substitute less polluting inputs for more polluting ones. A prime example is the substitution of low sulfur coal for high sulfur coal by electric utilities and manufacturing firms to comply with regulations on sulfur dioxide emissions. Another important example is the shift from leaded to unleaded motor fuels in order to clean up motor vehicle emissions.

The first successful implementation of an applied general equilibrium model without the fixed coefficients assumption is due to Johansen (1960). Johansen retained the fixed coefficients assumption in modeling demands for intermediate goods, but employed linear logarithmic or Cobb-Douglas production functions in modeling the substitution between capital and labor services and technical change. He replaced the fixed coefficients assumption for household behavior by a system of demand functions originated by Frisch (1959).

Linear logarithmic production functions have the obvious advantage that the capital and labor input coefficients respond to price changes. Furthermore, the relative shares of these inputs in the value of output are fixed, so that the unknown parameters characterizing substitution between capital and labor inputs can be estimated from a single data point. In describing producer behavior Johansen employed econometric methods only in estimating constant rates of technical change. Similarly, the unknown parameters of the demand system proposed by Frisch can be determined from a single data point, except for one parameter that must be determined econometrically.

The essential features of Johansen's approach were widely adopted in general equilibrium models built in the 1970s and 1980s.[6] Most used a mixture of fixed coefficients and linear-logarithmic functions to represent preferences and technology. The fixed coefficients approach was generally used to model the demand for intermediate goods while linear-logarithmic functions were used to model substitution between capital and labor This approach avoided some of the restrictions imposed by the input-output approach but still permitted behavioral parameters to be determined by "calibration" to a single data point. However, the oil price shocks of the 1970s provided massive evidence directly contradicting the fixed coefficients assumption for intermediate goods: price-induced energy conservation lead to substantial changes in the ratios of energy to output.[7]

Later models relaxed the unitary substitution elasticity imposed by the linear-logarithmic form by switching to constant elasticity of substitution functions.[8] Such models were usually parameterized by taking substitution elasticities from the literature and then "calibrating" the model by choosing the remaining parameters so that the model would reproduce the given table. The obvious disadvantage of this approach is that highly restrictive assumptions on technology and preferences are required to make calibration feasible. Moreover, calibration causes a model to be affected by peculiarities of the data for the calibration point. By construction, parameters obtained by calibration are forced to absorb all the random errors present in the data for a single benchmark year. This poses a severe problem when the benchmark year is unusual in some respect. For example, parameters calibrated to the year 1973 would incorporate into the model all the distortions in energy markets that resulted from price controls and the rationing of energy during the first oil crisis.

Another important limitation of the Johansen approach is that changes in technology are taken to be exogenous. This rules out another important method for pollution abatement by assumption. This is the introduction of changes in technology by redesigning production methods to reduce emissions. An important example is the introduction of fluidized bed technology for combustion, which results in reduced emissions. Gollop and Roberts (1983, 1985) have constructed a detailed econometric model of electric utility firms based on a cost function that incorporates the impact of environmental regulations on the cost of producing electricity and the rate of productivity growth. They conclude that the annual productivity growth of electric utilities impacted by more restrictive emissions controls declined by 0.59 percentage points over the period 1974–1979. This resulted from switching technologies to meet new standards for air quality.

To represent technologies and preferences that overcome the limitations of the Johansen approach, it is essential to employ econometric methods. Berndt and Jorgenson (1973) pioneered the use of econometric models of producer behavior to generate complete systems of demand functions for inputs of capital, labor, energy, and materials in each industrial sector.[9] Each system gives quantities of inputs demanded as functions of prices and output. The econometric approach was later extended to incorporate endogenous technical change by Jorgenson and Fraumeni (1981).[10] It has been used in general equilibrium modeling by Hudson and Jorgenson (1974a), Longva and Olsen (1983), Hazilla and Kopp (1986), Jorgenson and Wilcoxen (1990b), Glomsrod, Vennemo, and Johnsen (1992), Kildegaard (1994), and McKibbin and Wilcoxen (1999).[11]

Similarly, econometric models of consumer behavior can be used to overcome the limitations of the Frisch model employed by Johansen. Models stemming from the path-breaking contributions of Schultz (1938), Stone (1954), and Wold (1953) consist of complete systems of demand functions, giving quantities demanded as functions of prices and total expenditure. Subsequent work, including Christensen, Jorgenson and Lau (1971), has led to the development of flexible functional forms that impose no restrictions on preferences beyond those implied by economic theory.[12]

A difficult issue in modeling consumer behavior is choosing an appropriate level of aggregation. Most general equilibrium models use the representative consumer approach, in which aggregate demand functions are derived by treating the entire household sector as a single maximizing individual. This is a convenient approach but it imposes strong restrictions on the structure of the underlying optimization problems solved by individual households. For example, the simplest set of restrictions under which the representative consumer approach is appropriate is that preferences are identical and homothetic for all consumers.[13] However, there is abundant empirical evidence rejecting these restrictions. Homothetic preferences are inconsistent with well-established empirical regularities in the behavior of individual consumers, such as Engel's Law, which states that the proportion of expenditure devoted to food is a declining proportion of total expenditure. Identical preferences are inconsistent with empirical findings that expenditure patterns depend on demographic characteristics of individual consumers.[14] Somewhat weaker sets of restrictions for the existence of a representative consumer have been developed but have not been widely used in general equilibrium modeling.[15]

An alternative approach to modeling of aggregate consumer behavior is provided by Lau's (1982) theory of exact aggregation. This approach makes it possible to dispense with the notion of a representative consumer. Under exact aggregation, systems of aggregate demand functions can be shown to depend on statistics of the joint distribution of individual total expenditures and attributes of individuals associated with differences in preferences. A very useful feature of exact aggregation is that systems of demand functions for individuals can be recovered uniquely from the system of aggregate demand functions. This makes it possible to exploit all the implications of the economic theory of the individual consumer in constructing an econometric model of aggregate consumer behavior.

The implementation of an econometric model of aggregate consumer behavior based on the theory of exact aggregation has been carried out by Jorgenson, Lau, and Stoker (1982). Their approach requires time series data on prices and aggregate quantities consumed and cross-section data on individual quantities consumed, individual total expenditures, and attributes of individual households, such as demographic characteristics.[16] By contrast the non-econometric approaches of Leontief and Johansen require only a single data point for prices, aggregate quantities consumed, and aggregate expenditure. A general equilibrium model employing this approach has been constructed by Jorgenson and Wilcoxen (1990), which is discussed in detail in the next section.

13.3   An Econometric General Equilibrium Model

To show how environmental and energy policy are linked to the cost of capital, we now present a brief discussion of the intertemporal general equilibrium model of the U.S. economy constructed by Jorgenson and Wilcoxen (1990). The production portion of the model is based on the approach originated by Jorgenson and Fraumeni (1981). It includes systems of demand functions for capital, labor, energy, and materials inputs and a model of endogenous productivity growth for each of thirty-five sectors of the U.S. economy. The household portion of the model is based on exact aggregation, rather than the representative agent approach, and includes a system of demand functions for five commodity groups—energy, food, nondurable goods, capital services, and other services.

The empirical foundation of the model is a set of U.S. national accounts data developed and refined over many years by Dale Jorgenson and his colleagues.[17] The critical feature of this data is that it includes fully integrated accounts for capital, including investment, capital accumulation, and capital service flows. Unlike conventional national accounts, this approach links the current flow of capital services to the accumulated stock of capital from all past investments. At the same time, the accounts also link the price of investment goods to expected future prices of capital services.

The data set contains annual time-series data on transactions in the U.S. economy over the period from 1947 to 1985. It includes data on sales of intermediate goods between industries at approximately the two-digit SIC level of aggregation (derived from tables produced by the Bureau of Economic Analysis); data on capital and labor income by industry (from the National Income and Product Accounts produced by the Bureau of Economic Analysis extended as described in Jorgenson, Gollop, and Fraumeni (1987)); and integrates the capital accounts described by Jorgenson (1990b) with an accounting system based on the United Nations (1968) System of National Accounts.[18] This extensive data set allows the parameters of the producer and consumer models to be estimated econometrically.

13.3.1   Producers

Production is disaggregated into thirty-five industries. Each industry's behavior is modeled as a two-stage cost minimization problem.[19]

The first stage determines the industry's factor demands for each of four aggregate inputs: capital, labor, energy, and materials. The industry's unit cost is taken to be a transcendental logarithmic function of the prices of each of the aggregates.[20] Each unit cost function must be homogeneous of degree one, non-decreasing, and concave in the input prices. These restrictions are incorporated into the system of input demand functions for each industry.[21] The second stage of each cost minimization problem allocates expenditures on aggregate energy and materials to individual commodities.[22] All parameters in each industry's cost function are estimated using the data set described above.

An important feature of the production model is that each industry's productivity growth can be biased toward some first stage inputs and away from others. Biased productivity growth is a common feature of historical data but is often excluded from models of production. By allowing for biased productivity growth, the model provides a separation between price-induced reductions in energy utilization and those resulting from changes in technology. In addition, the overall rate of productivity growth for each industry in the model is determined endogenously as a function of input prices.[23]

Overall, the key features of the production portion of the model for the purposes of studying environmental and energy policy are that it is disaggregated, econometrically estimated, and includes a model of endogenous technical change. This allows it to capture the effects of regulations falling on narrow segments of the economy and to follow those effects through to changes in key variables: the cost of capital, the rate of investment, and the rate of productivity growth.

13.3.2   Households

To evaluate the effects of a policy on growth and welfare, however, it is also important to account for the effects of the policy on households. Households determine savings, investment in housing and consumer durables, labor supply, and the demand for goods and services, all of which influence overall economic growth.

The econometric approach to modeling consumer behavior has similar advantages over the calibration approach to those described for modeling producer behavior. Moreover, the exact aggregation approach allows the model to incorporate detailed cross-section data on the impact of demographic differences among households and levels of total expenditure on household expenditure patterns. The model takes advantage of this by dividing households into 672 demographic groups.[24] Consumer demands are not required to be homothetic, so that patterns of individual expenditure change as total expenditure varies, even in the absence of price changes. This captures an important characteristic of cross-section observations on household expenditure patterns that is usually ignored in general equilibrium modeling.

The model's specification of consumer demand behavior is based on two-stage allocation.[25] At the first stage, households allocate total expenditure among five broad aggregates: energy, food, nondurable goods, capital services, and other services. At the second stage, expenditure on each aggregate is allocated among labor and capital services and the individual commodities. Preferences are represented by a nested transcendental logarithmic indirect utility function.[26] Exact aggregation requires that the indirect utility function be homothetically separable in the prices of the commodities within the second stage. It must also be homogeneous of degree zero in prices and total expenditure on all commodities. Finally, it must be non-increasing in the prices, non-decreasing in total expenditure, and quasi-convex in prices and expenditure. These restrictions are incorporated into a separate system of demand equations constructed for each of the 672 different household types.[27] All behavioral parameters are estimated using the data set described above.

To determine the level of total expenditure within each period, this system is embedded in a higher-level model that represents consumer preferences between goods and leisure and between saving and consumption. At the highest level, each household allocates "full wealth," defined as the sum of human and non-human wealth, across time periods. This decision is formalized by introducing a representative agent who maximizes an additive intertemporal utility function, subject to an intertemporal budget constraint. The conditions for optimality of the household's intertemporal optimization problem can be expressed in the form of an Euler equation. This equation gives the value of full consumption in one period in terms of the value of full consumption in the next period, the interest rate, the time preference rate, the intertemporal elasticity of substitution and the rate of population growth.[28] The Euler equation is forward-looking, so that the current level of full consumption incorporates expectations about all future prices and discount rates.

The allocation of full wealth to the current time period is "full consumption," defined as an aggregate of goods and leisure. Given this allocation, each household proceeds to a second stage of the optimization process—choosing the mix of leisure and goods. Household preferences at this stage are represented by means of a representative agent with an indirect utility function that depends on the prices of leisure and goods.[29] Demands for leisure and goods are derived as functions of these prices and the wealth allocated to the current period. This implies an allocation of the household's exogenously given time endowment between leisure time and the labor market, so that this stage of the optimization process determines labor supply.[30] In addition, by determining the value of personal consumption expenditures it completes the model for household final demand. Finally, saving is determined by the difference between current income from the supply of capital and labor services and personal consumption expenditures.

In summary, the model of household behavior consists of three stages. First, it includes a system of expenditure share equations derived from maximization of a household utility function and satisfying conditions for exact aggregation. Second, it includes a higher level representative agent model that determines the intertemporal allocation of consumption through an Euler equation derived from maximization of an intertemporal utility function. Third, the representative agent model also allocates full consumption between goods and leisure, determining personal consumption expenditures, labor supply, and saving.

13.3.3   Investment

The model's treatment of investment is based on perfect foresight or rational expectations. Under this assumption the price of investment goods in every time period is based on expectations of future capital service prices and discount rates that are fulfilled by the solution of the model. In particular, the equilibrium price of new investment goods is always equal to the present value of future capital services.[31] The price of investment goods and the discounted value of future rental prices are brought into equilibrium by adjustments in future prices and rates of return. This incorporates the forward-looking dynamics of asset pricing into the model of intertemporal equilibrium.

For tractability, Jorgenson and Wilcoxen assume there is a single capital stock in the economy which is perfectly malleable and mobile among sectors, so that it can be reallocated among industries and final demand categories at zero cost. Under this assumption changes in energy and environmental policy can affect the distribution of capital and labor supplies among sectors, even in the short run. However, the total supply of capital in the model in each time period is perfectly inelastic, since the available stock of capital is determined by past investments. An accumulation equation relates capital stock to investments in all past time periods and incorporates the backward-looking dynamics of capital formation into our model of intertemporal equilibrium.

Since capital is perfectly malleable, the price of capital services in each sector is proportional to a single price of capital services for the economy as a whole. This rental price balances each period's supply with the sum of demands by all thirty-five industrial sectors together with the demand for personal consumption. The model gives the price of capital services in terms of the price of investment goods at the beginning and end of each period, the rate of return to capital for the economy as a whole, the rate of depreciation, and variables describing the tax structure for income from capital. The income from capital in each period is equal to the value of capital services.

New capital goods are produced from the individual commodities included in the model. Each new unit of capital is an aggregate of commodities purchased for investment in producers' and consumers' durables, residential and nonresidential structures, and inventories. The technology for production of new capital goods is represented by means of a price function for investment goods. The parameters of this function were estimated from time series data on gross private domestic investment in the data set discussed above. As with the model of producer behavior, a nested tier structure is used to capture substitution among different inputs in the construction of new capital.[32]

Finally, the total value of investment is constrained to equal the sum of: private savings by households, the government surplus, the capital account surplus, and any revaluation of wealth as the result of inflation.

13.3.4   Government

Final demands for government consumption are determined from the income-expenditure identity for the government sector. The first step is to compute total tax revenue by applying exogenous tax rates to all taxable transactions in the economy. To this is added the capital income of government enterprises and non-tax receipts to obtain total government revenue. Total government spending is equal to total government revenue plus the government budget deficit, which Jorgenson and Wilcoxen take to be exogenous. Spending on government purchases of goods and services, is equal to total spending less interest paid to domestic and foreign holders of government bonds together with government transfer payments to domestic and foreign recipients. Government purchases are allocated among goods and services according to fixed shares constructed from historical data.

13.4   Foreign Trade

Jorgenson and Wilcoxen assume that imports are imperfect substitutes for similar domestic commodities.[33] The goods actually purchased by households and firms reflect substitutions between domestic and imported products. The price responsiveness of these purchases is estimated from historical data. Import prices are assumed to be exogenous. Exports, on the other hand, are modeled by a set of explicit foreign demand equations, one for each commodity, that depend on exogenously given foreign income and the foreign price of U.S. exports. Foreign prices are computed from domestic prices by adjusting for subsidies and the exchange rate. The demand elasticities in these equations are estimated from historical data.

The model incorporates the income-expenditure identity of the rest-of-the world sector. The current account surplus is equal to the value of exports less the value of imports, plus interest received on domestic holdings of foreign bonds, less private and government transfers abroad, and less interest on government bonds paid to foreigners. The current account is taken to be exogenous and the exchange rate is endogenous.

13.4.1   Constructing a Base Case

The first step in analyzing a change in environmental policy is to establish a point of reference by generating a "base case" simulation *without* any changes in policy. Constructing a base case is not trivial because it requires the values of all exogenous variables in every time period. During the historical period, this is straightforward as the variables can easily be obtained from the data set. Beyond that, however, the exogenous variables must be projected. The most important projections are those associated with U.S. population growth and the corresponding change in the time endowment of the U.S. economy. For the years following 1986, Jorgenson and Wilcoxen project population by age, sex and educational attainment through the year 2050, using demographic assumptions consistent with Bureau of the Census projections.[34] After 2050 they hold population constant, which is roughly consistent with Census Bureau projections. They project educational attainment by assuming that future demographic cohorts will have the same level of attainment as the cohort reaching age 35 in the year 1985. They then transform the population projection into a projection of the time endowment used in the model of the labor market by assuming that relative wages across all categories of workers are constant at 1985 levels. Since capital accumulation is endogenous, these population projections effectively determine the size of the economy in the more distant future.

Also important are tax rates and other exogenous components of the government model. Jorgenson and Wilcoxen set all projected tax rates to their values in 1985, the last year in the sample period. The government deficit is projected to decline through the year 2025, after which it is held at four percent of the nominal value of the government debt. This has the effect of maintaining a constant ratio of the value of the government debt to the value of the national product when the inflation rate is four percent, as it is in the model's steady state.

Exogenous international variables include import prices and the current account deficit. Jorgenson and Wilcoxen assume that prices of imports in foreign currency and before tariffs remain constant in real terms at 1985 levels. Projections of the current account deficit fall gradually to zero by the year 2000. After that a small current account surplus is projected sufficient to produce a stock of net claims on foreigners by the year 2050 equal to the same proportion of U.S. national wealth as in 1982.

Given projections of the exogenous variables, the model then is solved for a full intertemporal equilibrium through the year 2050 under the assumption of perfect foresight. The solution provides annual results for a large number of variables: the prices and outputs of each of the thirty-five industries; labor supply; saving; investment; and capital accumulation. The design of the model guarantees that income-expenditure identities for all thirty-five industries and the household, government, and the rest-of-the-world sectors are satisfied. These identities imply that gross private domestic investment is equal to private savings plus the current account deficit less the government budget deficit. Since the government and current account deficits are taken to be exogenous, changes in gross private domestic investment are driven by changes in private savings. Thus, changes in the rate of capital accumulation depend on changes in private savings and the price of investment goods.

13.5   Estimating the Effects of Environmental Regulation

The tight link between environmental regulation, the cost of capital, and economic growth can be seen in an application of the model to the analysis of a carbon tax, as discussed in Jorgenson and Wilcoxen (1992). A carbon tax has often been proposed as a method for reducing carbon dioxide emissions and thereby slowing global warming.[35] It would be applied to fossil fuels used for combustion in proportion to the carbon dioxide the fuels emit when burned, which is shown in table 13.1. From the standpoint of economic efficiency, a carbon tax is an attractive way to reduce carbon dioxide emissions because it is very close to a tax on the externality itself: If firms and individuals must pay to emit carbon dioxide, they will emit less. A carbon tax would stimulate users to substitute other inputs for fossil fuels and to substitute fuels with lower carbon content, such as natural gas, for high-carbon fuels such as coal.

The carbon tax policy which has been debated most widely would impose a tax large enough to limit emissions to 1990 rates. To measure the effect of such a policy on the United States Jorgenson and Wilcoxen constructed a simulation in which the carbon tax rate was allowed to vary from year to year but was always chosen to be exactly enough to hold U.S. carbon dioxide emissions at their 1990 value of

Table 13.1
Relative carbon content of fossil

Characteristic	Fuel		
	Coal (ton)	Oil (bbl)	Gas (mcf)
Million BTU per unit	21.94	5.80	1.03
Tons of carbon per unit	0.649	0.137	0.016
Carbon per million BTU:			
Tons	0.030	0.024	0.016
Relative to coal	100%	80%	54%
Approximate price before tax:			
Per unit of fuel	$22	$21	$2.4
Per million BTU	$1.00	$3.62	$1.36
Tax equal to $10/ton of carbon			
Per unit	$6.49	$1.36	$0.16
Per million BTU	$0.30	$0.24	$0.16
Percentage increase per unit	29.50%	6.48%	6.67%

1576 million tons.[36] As shown in table 13.2, the tax produces significant reductions in carbon emissions relative to what would have happened in the absence of the policy. By 2020, for example, emissions are sixteen percent lower than they would have been without the tax. The tax also produces considerable revenue: $31 billion annually by 2020.[37]

The principal direct effect of the tax is to increase purchasers' prices of coal and crude oil. By 2020, for example, the tax reaches $22.71 per ton of carbon, which is equivalent to a tax of $14.75 per ton of coal, $3.10 per barrel of oil or $0.37 per thousand cubic feet of gas. The tax would increase the prices of fuels but leave other prices relatively unaffected. The price of coal would rise by forty-seven percent, the price of electricity would rise by almost seven percent (coal accounts for about thirteen percent of the cost of electricity), and the price of crude oil would rise by around four percent. The prices of refined petroleum and natural gas utilities would rise because of the tax on the carbon content of oil and natural gas.

Changes in the relative prices for fuels would affect demands for each good and lead to changes in industry outputs. Most sectors show only small changes in output. Coal mining is an exception: its output falls by almost thirty percent. Coal is affected strongly for three reasons. First, coal emits more carbon dioxide than oil or natural gas per unit of energy produced. Thus, the absolute level of the tax per

Table 13.2
Selected 2020 results for the stabilization scenario

Variable	Unit	Value
Carbon Emissions	%Δ	−16.12
Carbon Tax	$/ton	22.71
Tax on Coal	$/ton	14.75
Tax on Oil	$/bbl	3.10
Tax on Gas	$/mcf	0.37
Price of Capital	%Δ	0.40
Capital Stock	%Δ	−0.83
Tax Revenue	$B	31.41
Real GNP	%Δ	−0.55
Coal Price	%Δ	46.99
Coal Output	%Δ	−29.28
Electricity Price	%Δ	6.60
Electricity Output	%Δ	−6.17
Oil Price	%Δ	4.45
Oil Output	%Δ	−3.90

unit of energy content is higher on coal than other fuels. Second, the tax is very large relative to the base case price of coal for purchasers: at the mine mouth, the tax would increase coal prices by around fifty percent. (In contrast, oil is far more expensive per unit of energy so in percentage terms its price is less affected by the tax. The price of crude oil rises only about ten percent.) Third, the demand for coal is relatively elastic. Most coal is purchased by electric utilities, which can substitute other fuels for coal when the price rises. Moreover, the demand for electricity itself is relatively elastic, so when the price of electricity rises, demand for electricity (and hence demand for coal) falls substantially.

From the point of view of firms outside the energy sector, the main result of the tax is to increase the prices of electricity, refined petroleum and natural gas, each by a few percent. This would have two effects. First, higher energy prices would mean that capital goods (which are produced using energy) would become more expensive. Higher prices for capital goods mean a slower rate of capital accumulation and lower GNP in the future. Second, higher energy prices discourage technical change in industries in which technical change is energy-using. Together, these two effects cause the capital stock to drop by 0.7 percent and GNP to fall by 0.5 percent by 2020 (relative to the base case). Average annual GNP growth over the period 1990–2020 is 0.02 percentage points lower than in the base case. About half of this is due to slower productivity growth and half due to reduced capital formation. Thus, the link between environmental regulation and the cost of capital is absolutely fundamental to understanding the effects of the policy.

Because the tax produces 30 to 80 billion dollars of revenue a year, precisely how this revenue is used will have a large effect on the overall economic cost of slowing global warming. In particular, if the revenue were used to reduce distortionary taxes elsewhere in the economy, or if it were used to lower government budget deficits, there would be large welfare gains which would offset some or all of the welfare losses associated with the carbon tax itself.

To determine how large this welfare improvement might be Jorgenson and Wilcoxen constructed three additional simulations in which the revenue from a carbon tax was used to reduce different taxes. In each simulation they imposed a carbon tax of $15 per ton in 1990 with the rate rising by 5% annually in subsequent years. In the first simulation the revenue was returned to households by a lump sum rebate; in the second it was used to lower taxes on labor, such as social security taxes; and in the third it was used to lower taxes on capital, such as corporate income taxes.

Their results, shown in table 13.3, indicate that the disposition of revenue from a carbon tax has a very significant effect on its overall impact on GNP. In the lump sum case, output in 2020 drops by 1.70 percent relative to the base case. When the revenue is returned by lowering the tax on labor the loss of GNP is less than half as much: only 0.69 percent. The improvement is due to an increase in employment brought about by the drop in the difference between before- and after-tax wages. If the revenue were returned as a reduction in taxes on capital, GNP would actually increase above its base case level by 1.10 percent. In this case, the gain is due to accelerated capital formation generated by an increase in the after-tax rate of return on investment. These results suggest that a carbon tax would provide an opportunity for significant tax reform and further emphasize the importance of the cost of capital for understanding the impacts of environmental policies.

Table 13.3
Selected results for revenue experiments in 2020

Variable	Unit	Revenue Policy		
		Lump Sum	Labor Rebate	Capital Rebate
Carbon Emissions	%Δ	−32.24	−32.09	−31.65
Carbon Tax	$/ton	64.83	64.83	64.83
Price of Capital	%Δ	0.97	−1.86	0.23
Capital Stock	%Δ	−2.13	−1.36	1.89
Tax Revenue	$B	79.65	79.82	80.35
Real GNP	%Δ	−1.70	−0.69	1.10
Coal Price	%Δ	143.49	140.57	142.06
Coal Output	%Δ	−54.14	−54.19	−53.45
Electricity Price	%Δ	18.57	15.97	16.99
Electricity Output	%Δ	−15.93	−15.37	−14.66
Oil Price	%Δ	14.20	12.28	14.55
Oil Output	%Δ	−11.92	−11.54	−11.39

13.6   Confidence Intervals

An important benefit of the econometric approach to general equilibrium modeling is that it allows the precision and reliability of model results to be quantified and expressed in the form of confidence intervals. An example is Tuladhar and Wilcoxen (1998), who examined the "double dividend hypothesis" using a small econometric general equilibrium model.

Many market-based policies for controlling environmental problems, such as the carbon taxes discussed above, have the potential to raise large amounts of revenue. The idea that this revenue could be used to lower distorting taxes elsewhere in the economy, hence producing a welfare gain beyond the environmental benefits of the policy, has become known as the "double dividend hypothesis". The hypothesis has appeared in the literature in several forms.[38] The weakest form simply states that using the revenue to lower a distorting tax would be superior to returning the revenue as a lump sum rebate. In this form, the hypothesis is true by construction and generates little controversy.

The strongest form of the hypothesis has been far more controversial. It states that taxing goods that produce externalities (such as fossil fuels) and using the revenue to reduce other taxes (particular those on primary factors) can improve economic welfare even before environmental benefits are considered. In other words, the strong form is really an assertion that the economy would benefit from tax reform.[39] Advocates of stronger environmental regulation have used the strong form to argue that both the economy and the environment would benefit from shifting the tax system toward environmental taxes.[40] The extreme version of this view is that tighter regulations can be a "no regrets" policy—one that can be justified even if its environmental benefits are modest or impossible to quantify. At the same time, however, a large theoretical literature has sprung up challenging the hypothesis and arguing that environmental taxes often exacerbate existing distortions, particularly in the labor market.[41]

Although this theoretical work has made a number of important contributions, it will never completely resolve the debate over the strong double dividend hypothesis because the hypothesis itself is fundamentally empirical rather than theoretical.[42] A simple example makes it clear why. Suppose an economy has two primary factors: capital and labor, and that the supply of capital is elastic while the supply of labor is perfectly inelastic. Now consider what happens under a revenue-neutral shift in taxation that reduces income taxes, which fall on both labor and capital, and increases the tax on energy. Much of the burden of the energy tax will be passed back to the primary factors used in energy production. If energy is more labor-intensive than the rest of the economy, therefore, the shift in taxes would be equivalent to a policy that reduced taxes on capital income while raising taxes on labor income. Since capital is supplied elastically while labor is not, this would stimulate capital formation, raising GDP and producing a strong double dividend. On the other hand, if energy production is more capital-intensive than average, the effect would work in the other direction: the shift would increase the effective tax burden on capital which would reduce capital formation, lower GDP and would fail to generate a double dividend. Finally, if energy production used the two factors in the same proportions they are used in the overall economy, the shift in taxes would have no effect on GDP.

Because the strong form of the hypothesis is an empirical question it must be tested econometrically. In order to do so it is necessary to estimate the mean equivalent variation (EV) for the tax shift *and* its standard error. This would allow the hypothesis to be subjected to standard statistical tests. We could reject the strong double dividend hypothesis if the mean EV is negative and its 95% confidence interval does not include zero. On the other hand, if the estimated EV is positive and its confidence interval again does not include zero we could reject the hypothesis that there is *not* a double dividend. Finally, if the confidence interval includes zero it would be clear why different authors have come to different conclusions: the data simply does not allow us to reject either hypothesis. In that situation, different but equally reasonable choices of parameters would lead to different double dividend results.

Tuladhar and Wilcoxen use a small econometric general equilibrium model of the United States to demonstrate how the mean equivalent variation and its standard error can be calculated for a representative shift from income to energy taxes.[43] They construct a confidence interval for the equivalent variation, which they then use to test the strong form of the double dividend hypothesis. In the remainder of this section we discuss their results.

Tuladhar and Wilcoxen represent the U.S. economy using the smallest possible general equilibrium model that still has enough detail to capture the important features of the double-dividend hypothesis. The production side of the economy is divided into three industries: Energy, E, materials, M, and new capital goods, G. Each industry produces its output according to a constant elasticity of substitution (CES) production function which takes inputs of capital services, labor, energy and materials. The unit cost functions for the industries have the form shown below:

$$c_i = \frac{1}{A_i} \left(\sum_{j \in \{K,L,E,M\}} \gamma_{ji} w_j^{1-\sigma_i} \right)^{\frac{1}{1-\sigma_i}}, \quad i \in \{E, M, G\}$$

where c_i is the unit cost in industry i, w_j is the price of input j, and A_i, γ_{ji} and σ_i are parameteters. Under this specification there are six technology parameters per industry for a total of eighteen in the production model overall.

Household behavior is represented using two-stage budgeting and a single infinitely-lived representative agent. The household supplies all of the economy's labor and capital services. In addition, it demands labor, capital services, energy and materials. The top tier of the household's optimization problem follows Jorgenson and Wilcoxen: The household allocates its wealth over time in order to

Table 13.4
Production parameter estimates with standard errors

Parameter	Estimate	Std. Error
σ_E	1.048	0.0031
A_E	1.187	0.0183
γ_{KE}	0.285	0.0040
γ_{LE}	0.160	0.0024
γ_{EE}	0.393	0.0081
γ_{ME}	0.159	0.0020
σ_M	0.764	0.0048
A_M	0.999	0.0010
γ_{KM}	0.176	0.0012
γ_{LM}	0.356	0.0013
γ_{EM}	0.025	0.0008
γ_{MM}	0.441	0.0016
σ_I	0.990	0.0029
A_I	0.871	0.0199
γ_{KI}	0.041	0.0011
γ_{LI}	0.179	0.0028
γ_{EI}	0.012	0.0013
γ_{MI}	0.767	0.0029

maximize a logarithmic intertemporal utility function. This stage of the model determines the savings rate. At the second tier Tuladhar and Wilcoxen represent preferences over labor, capital services, energy and materials using a Stone-Geary utility function. The utility function is shown below:

$$u = \prod_{j \in \{K,L,E,M\}} (x_j - \mu_j)^{\alpha_j}$$

where x_j is the household's purchase of input j and α_j and μ_j are parameters. The total number of parameters in the household model is eight.

The model's parameters were estimated using the U.S. data set discussed above. The complete production model—all three sectors—was estimated as a single system of simultaneous equations. The resulting estimates are shown in table 13.4 along with standard errors. On the household side, the values of the time preference rate and the depreciation rate were taken from Jorgenson and Wilcoxen (1990). The remaining household parameters were obtained by estimating the household demand functions as system of simultaneous equations. The results are shown in table 13.5.

Table 13.5
Household parameter estimates with standard errors

Parameter	Estimate	Std. Error	Parameter	Estimate	Std. Error
μ_K	55430	20469	α_K	0.205	0.0043
μ_L	110104	20174	α_L	0.125	0.0046
μ_E	52760	23259	α_E	0.044	0.0111
μ_M	670442	79937	α_M	0.623	0.0073

Using the estimates in table 13.4 and table 13.5, Tuladhar and Wilcoxen solved the model for its steady-state equilibrium. They then calculated confidence intervals for the model's endogenous variables using two techniques: The delta method and Monte Carlo simulation.[44] The results for the two techniques were essentially identical and are shown in table 13.6, which gives 95% confidence intervals expressed as percentages of the corresponding variable's base case value.[45] Some of the confidence intervals are quite narrow: the capital stock, for example, is determined within 0.5%.[46] Many of the variables are less precisely determined. The rental price of capital and the price of new capital goods, for example, have confidence intervals of 6.5%. The quantity of energy is the least precise of all with a confidence interval of 11.2%.

In order to examine the double dividend hypothesis Tuladhar and Wilcoxen simulated a shift in tax policy that increased the tax on energy to 10% from an initial value of zero. Simultaneously, the tax rate on capital was reduced (from an initial value of 10%) by exactly enough to leave the lump sum subsidy unchanged.[47]

Figure 13.1 shows the distribution of new capital tax rates resulting from a Monte Carlo simulation using 10,000 draws from the distribution of parameter estimates. The mean of the distribution is 8.46% and the 95% confidence interval runs from 8.11% to 8.81%. Raising the

Table 13.6
Base case confidence intervals as percentages

Variable	%	Variable	%	Variable	%
q	6.5	K	0.5	c_K	6.1
P_G	6.5	Q_E	11.2	c_L	2.1
P_E	4.2	Q_M	1.1	c_E	17.5
P_M	2.2	I	0.5	c_M	1.3

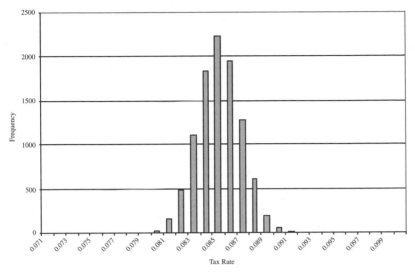

Figure 13.1
Distribution of capital tax rates.

energy tax to 10%, in other words, would allow the capital tax rate to be cut by about 1 to 2 percentage points, with 1.5 being the most likely.

More interesting is the distribution of equivalent variations, shown in figure 13.2. The mean equivalent variation is 0.24% and the 95% confidence interval runs from 0.14% to 0.33%. The key result is that the confidence interval does not include zero. Conditional on the assumptions underlying the model, therefore, it is possible to reject the hypothesis that shifting to energy taxes would not produce a double dividend.

These results are suggestive but should be regarded as preliminary in several respects. First, the model only represents the economy at the steady state. To the extent that the change in policy causes welfare losses along the transition to the new steady state, this equivalent variation will overstate the benefit of the reform. Second, labor supply is fixed. If the energy tax significantly exacerbates distortions in the labor market, these results will also overstate the equivalent variation of the policy. Third, the utility function imposes a unitary intertemporal elasticity of substitution. This will have little effect on the steady state but would have important effects during the transition period in a full intertemporal solution. Finally, Tuladhar and Wilcoxen have examined only the effect of uncertainty in the parameter estimates; it

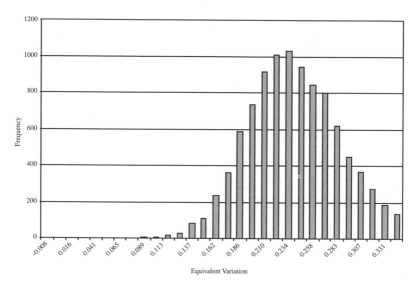

Figure 13.2
Distribution of equivalent variations.

would be useful and straightforward to extend the approach to examine the effect of the residual uncertainty in the estimated equations.

13.7   Conclusion

The shift to intertemporal analysis of environmental policies has emphasized the crucial role played by the cost of capital, which links environmental regulations to overall economic growth. Regulations can raise the cost of new capital goods and hence slow the rate of capital formation and reduce the rate of growth. At the same time, revenue from market-based environmental policies, such as emissions taxes, may raise enough new tax revenue to allow capital income taxes to be reduced, possibly lowering the cost of capital and stimulating growth.

In order to evaluate an environmental policy, therefore, it is essential to determine the effect of the policy on the cost of capital and capital formation. This requires a quantitative model that can capture environmental regulations at a detailed level, trace the effects of those regulations through the economy to determine their influence on the cost of producing new capital goods, and can also determine the effect of the policy on savings and investment.

The principal analytical approach possessing these features is large-scale econometric, intertemporal general equilibrium modeling. The pioneering work of Dale Jorgenson has shown that it is possible to construct large, detailed models without compromising on parameterization. Indeed, intertemporal general equilibrium models can be constructed using econometrically-estimated flexible functional forms, a detailed disaggregation of industries, commodities and households, endogenous technical change, and nonhomothetic consumption. Moreover, the econometric approach allows a further methodological refinement by permitting confidence intervals to be constructed for estimates of the costs and benefits of environmental policies.

Notes

1. Jorgenson and Wilcoxen (1990) show that much of the adverse effect of environmental policy on U.S. economic growth in the 1970s and early 1980s was due to an increase in the price of new capital goods brought about by the regulations.

2. There is a substantial literature on the link between environmental taxes and opportunities for tax reform. We will return to this point below.

3. See Jorgenson and Wilcoxen (1997), for example.

4. See Jorgenson and Wilcoxen (1997), for example.

5. See, for example, Ayres and Kneese (1969), Kneese, Ayres, and d'Arge (1970), or Leontief, Carter, and Petri (1977). Detailed surveys of fixed coefficient input-output models applied to environmental policy, including those of Leontief (1970) and Leontief and Ford (1973), are presented by Forsund (1985) and James, Jansen, and Opschoor (1978).

6. Surveys of such models include Fullerton, Henderson, and Shoven (1984) and Bergman (1985). Johansen's approach has been used in modeling environmental policies for Norway by Forsund and Strom (1976).

7. Reductions in energy use during the 1970s and 1980s has been documented in great detail by Schipper and Meyers (1992). Reductions in energy-output ratios for these activities average 15–20 percent. Price-induced energy conservation in the U.S. has been analyzed in greater detail by Hogan and Jorgenson (1991), Jorgenson (1981, 1984b), Jorgenson and Fraumeni (1981), and Jorgenson and Stoker (1984).

8. The constant elasticity of substitution function was proposed by Arrow, Chenery, Minhas, and Solow (1961).

9. Surveys of functional forms used in modeling producer behavior have been presented by Fuss, McFadden and Mundlak (1978), Jorgenson (1986), and Lau (1986).

10. Alternative models of endogenous productivity growth are surveyed by Jorgenson (1984a, 1990b). A comprehensive survey of models of producer behavior constructed along the lines of Berndt and Jorgenson (1973) is presented by Jorgenson (1986).

11. Surveys of the literature on the econometric approach to general equilibrium modeling are given by Jorgenson (1982), Bergman (1990), and Hazilla and Kopp (1990). Bergman provides detailed comparisons with alternative approaches to general equilibrium modeling.

12. See Fuss, McFadden and Mundlak (1978) for a survey of flexible functional forms.

13. This set of restrictions is implicit in the linear logarithmic demand systems employed by Stone (1954) and Wold (1953), among others.

14. Reviews of the literature are presented by Deaton and Muellbauer (1980b) and Jorgenson (1990a).

15. See, for example, Gorman (1953), Muellbauer (1975) and Lewbel (1989b). Econometric models of aggregate consumer behavior based on the theory of a representative consumer have been constructed by Berndt, Darrough, and Diewert (1977) and Deaton and Muellbauer (1980a, 1980b).

16. The theory of exact aggregation is discussed by Jorgenson, Lau, and Stoker (1982) and Lau (1982). Econometric models based on the theory of exact aggregation are surveyed by Jorgenson (1990a) and Stoker (1993).

17. Conventional systems of national accounts, such as the United Nations (1968) System of National Accounts and the U.S. National Income and Product Accounts are unsatisfactory for modeling purposes, since they do not successfully integrate capital accounts with income and production accounts. An aggregate set of fully integrated accounts for the U.S. was constructed by Christensen and Jorgenson (1973a). Disaggregation to the industry level was done by Fraumeni and Jorgenson (1980). For more information, see Jorgenson (1980) and Jorgenson (1990b).

18. Details are given in Wilcoxen (1988), Appendix C.

19. Two-stage allocation in the context of producer behavior is discussed in more detail by Jorgenson (1986) and Blackorby, Primont, and Russell (1978).

20. This approach was introduced by Christensen, Jorgenson, and Lau (1971, 1973).

21. A more detailed discussion of our econometric methodology is presented by Jorgenson (1984a, 1986).

22. The tier structure used for modeling producer behavior is described by Wilcoxen (1988), Appendix A.

23. This approach follows Hudson and Jorgenson (1974), and Jorgenson and Fraumeni (1980). Other econometric models for analyzing energy and environmental policies, for example, Hazilla and Kopp (1990) and Longva, Lorentsen, and Olsen (1983), exclude biases in productivity growth and take the rate of productivity growth to be exogenous.

24. There are seven categories for family size, six categories for age of head, four categories for region of residence, two categories for race, and two categories for urban versus rural location. For further details, see Jorgenson and Slesnick (1987).

25. Two-stage allocation in the context of consumer behavior is discussed in more detail by Jorgenson, Slesnick, and Stoker (1987, 1988) and Blackorby, Primont, and Russell (1978). The tier structure for our model of consumer behavior is described by Wilcoxen (1988), Appendix A.

26. The translog indirect utility function was introduced by Christensen, Jorgenson, and Lau (1975). Surveys of functional forms employed in modeling consumer behavior have been presented by Blundell (1988), Deaton (1986), and Lau (1986).

27. The particular form of the model follows Jorgenson and Slesnick (1987). For further discussion of our econometric methodology, see Jorgenson (1984a, 1990a).

28. The Euler equation approach to modeling intertemporal consumer behavior was originated by Hall (1978). Our application of this approach to full consumption follows Jorgenson and Yun (1990).

29. The price index for consumption goods follows the approach of Jorgenson and Slesnick (1990b) and is given by the cost of living index generated from the first stage of the model of consumer behavior. The price of leisure time is the wage rate less the marginal tax rate on labor income.

30. Jorgenson and Wilcoxen assume the household has a single exogenous endowment of time which can be used for either labor or leisure. The time endowment is adjusted by educational attainment to reflect changes in the quality of the labor force.

31. The relationship between the price of investment goods and the rental price of capital services is discussed in greater detail by Jorgenson (1989).

32. The tier structure for our model of production for new capital goods is presented by Wilcoxen (1988), Appendix A.

33. This approach was originated by Armington (1969). See Wilcoxen (1988) and Ho (1989) for further details on our implementation of this approach.

34. The breakdown of the U.S. population by age, educational attainment, and sex is based on the system of demographic accounts compiled by Jorgenson and Fraumeni (1989a). The population projections are discussed in detail by Wilcoxen (1988), Appendix B.

35. A carbon tax was first proposed by Nordhaus (1979).

36. A tax which varies from one year to the next in order to keep carbon emissions absolutely constant is a useful analytical device but is not a likely policy. The tax could not be adjusted quickly enough to keep emissions constant in every year.

37. In this simulation, the revenue was returned to households as a lump sum rebate. All dollar amounts are in 1990 prices.

38. For a clear description of the different forms the hypothesis has taken, see Goulder (1995).

39. To put the double dividend debate into terms familiar to tax policy analysts, the strong form asserts that the excess burden of taxation is relatively low on externality-producing goods.

40. Prominent examples include Repetto *et al.* (1992) and Hammond *et al.* (1997).

41. See, for example, Bovenberg and de Mooij (1994).

42. A few studies have attempted to test the strong double dividend hypothesis using computational general equilibrium models; see Jorgenson and Wilcoxen (1993), Ballard and Medema (1993), or Bovenberg and Goulder (1996), for example. These papers have calculated point estimates of the effect of revenue neutral shifts of taxation from primary factors to energy goods. Our work builds on this approach but extends it to allow confidence intervals to be calculated instead of point estimates.

43. Many general equilibrium studies include some degree of sensitivity analysis but only a few studies have gone beyond examining the effects of fairly arbitrary perturbations a handful of parameters. Pagan and Shannon (1985) suggest one approach for systematic sensitivity analysis when the covariance matrix of parameter estimates is unavailable. Harrison *et al.* (1993), propose using a Monte Carlo approach based on drawing parameters from a prior (but not estimated) distribution. Arndt (1996) and Arndt and Pearson (1998) propose a method of sensitivity analysis based on Gaussian quadrature that has much in common with this approach.

44. These techniques are necessary because the endogenous variables are, in general, nonlinear functions of the parameters. In the delta method, confidence intervals are calculated from the covariance matrix of the parameter estimates using a linear approximation to the nonlinear system of equations. This approach is commonly used by econometric software packages. In the Monte Carlo simulation the model was solved for 10,000 draws from the joint distribution of the parameter estimates.

45. These confidence intervals take into account the standard errors of the parameter estimates but not the residual variance of the estimated equations. Including the latter would make the confidence intervals considerably larger.

46. This is an interesting result but it should not be taken too literally since the time preference rate was imposed and thus did not appear in the covariance matrix. Had it been estimated, the confidence interval for K would be considerably larger.

47. These are only very rough approximations to the actual tax rates.

References

Abel, Andrew B., and Olivier J. Blanchard. 1983. An Intertemporal Model of Saving and Investment. *Econometrica* 51, no. 3 (May): 675–692.

Abel, Andrew B., and J. Eberly. 1993. A Unified Model of Investment under Uncertainty. *American Economic Review* 84, no. 5 (December): 1369–1384.

———. 1999. The Effects of Irreversibility and Uncertainty on Capital Accumulation. *Journal of Monetary Economics* 44, no. 3 (December): 339–378.

Abramovitz, Moses. 1956. Resource and Output Trends in the United States since 1870. *American Economic Review* 46, no. 2 (May): 5–23.

Afriat, S. 1967. The Construction of a Utility Function from Expenditure Data. *International Economic Review* 8, no. 1 (February): 67–77.

Anderson, Joseph. 1985. *Updates and Revisions to the NIA Population Model*, ICF Incorporated, Washington.

Anderson, Joseph, Dale W. Jorgenson, John Moeller, and Daniel T. Slesnick. 1987. *A Macroeconomic Demographic Model of Healthcare and Consumer Expenditures*, ICF Incorporated, Washington.

Armington, Paul S. 1969. The Geographic Pattern of Trade and the Effects of Price Changes. *IMF Staff Papers* 16, no. 2 (July): 176–199.

Arndt, Channing. 1966. An Introduction to Systematic Sensitivity Analysis via Gaussian Quadrature. GTAP Technical Paper 2, Global Trade Analysis Project (July): Purdue University.

Arndt, Channing, and K.R. Pearson. 1998. How to Carry out Systematic Sensitivity Analysis via Gaussian Quadrature and GEMPACK. GTAP Technical Paper 3, Global Trade Analysis Project (April): Purdue University.

Arrow, Kenneth J. 1963. *Social Choice and Individual Values.* New Haven, CT: Yale University Press, 2nd ed.

———. 1964. Optimal Capital Policy, the Cost of Capital, and Myopic Decision Rules. *Annals of the Institute of Statistical Mathematics* 16, nos. 1/2: 21–30.

————. 1968. Optimal Capital Policy with Irreversible Investment. In *Value, Capital, and Growth,* Papers in Honor of Sir John Hicks, ed. James N. Wolfe, 1–19. Chicago, IL: Aldine Publishing Company.

Arrow, Kenneth J., and M. Hoffenberg. 1959. *A Time Series Analysis of Interindustry Demands.* Amsterdam: North-Holland.

Arrow, Kenneth J., Hollis B. Chenery, Bagicha S. Minhas, and Robert M. Solow. 1961. Capital-Labor Substitution and Economic Efficiency. *Review of Economics and Statistics* 43, no. 3 (August): 225–250.

Aschauer, David A. 1989. Is Public Expenditure Productive? *Journal of Monetary Economics* 23, no. 2 (March): 177–200.

————. 1990. Why is Infrastructure Important? In *Is There a Shortfall in Public Capital Investment,* ed. Alicia H. Munnell, 21–50. Boston: Federal Reserve Bank of Boston.

Atkinson, Anthony B. 1970. On Measurement of Inequality. *Journal of Economic Theory* 2, no. 3 (September): 244–263.

Auerbach, Alan J. 1979. Wealth Maximization and the Cost of Capital. *Quarterly Journal of Economics* 93, no. 3 (August): 433–446.

————. 1983a. Corporate Taxation in the U.S. *Brookings Papers on Economic Activity,* no. 2: 451–505.

————. 1983b. Taxation, Corporate Financial Policy, and the Cost of Capital. *Journal of Economic Literature* 21, no. 3 (September): 905–940.

————. 1984. Taxes, Firm Financial Policy and the Cost of Capital: An Empirical Analysis. *Journal of Public Economics* 23, nos. 1–2 (February/March): 27–57.

————. 1985. The Theory of Excess Burden and Optimal Taxation. In *Handbook of Public Economics,* vol. 1, eds. Alan J. Auerbach and M. Feldstein, 61–127. Amsterdam: North-Holland Publishing Co.

————. 1987. The Tax Reform Act of 1986 and the Cost of Capital. *Journal of Economic Perspectives* 1 (Summer): 73–86.

Auerbach, Alan J., and Kevin Hassett. 1992. Tax Policy and Business Fixed Investment in the United States. *Journal of Public Economics* 47, no. 2 (March): 141–170.

Auerbach, Alan J., and Dale W. Jorgenson. 1980. Inflation-Proof Depreciation of Assets. *Harvard Business Review* 58, no. 5 (September-October): 113–118.

Auerbach, Alan J., and Lawrence J. Kotlikoff. 1987. *Dynamic Fiscal Policy,* Cambridge: Cambridge University Press.

Auerbach, Alan J., Lawrence J. Kotlikoff, and J. Skinner. 1983. The Efficiency Gains from Dynamic Tax Reform. *International Economic Review* 24, no. 1 (February): 81–100.

Ayres, Robert U., and Allen V. Kneese. 1969. Production, Consumption, and Externalities. *American Economic Review* 59, no. 3 (June): 282–297.

Baldwin, Richard. 1992. Measurable Dynamic Gains from Trade. *Journal of Political Economy* 100, no. 1 (February): 162–174.

Ballard, Charles L. 1988. The Marginal Efficiency Cost of Redistribution. *American Economic Review* 78, no. 5 (December): 1019–1033.

———. 1990. Marginal Welfare Cost Calculations: Differential Analysis vs. Balanced Budget Analysis. *Journal of Public Economics* 41, no. 2 (March): 263–276.

Ballard, Charles L., Don Fullerton, John B. Shoven, and John Whalley. 1985a. *A General Equilibrium Model for Tax Policy Evaluation*, Chicago: The University of Chicago Press.

———. 1985b. General Equilibrium Computation of the Marginal Welfare Costs of Taxes in the United States. *American Economic Review* 75, no. 1 (March): 128–138.

Ballard, Charles L., and Stephen G. Medema. 1993. The Marginal Efficiency Effects of Taxes and Subsidies in the Presence of Externalities: A Computational General Equilibrium Approach. *Journal of Public Economics* 52, no. 2 (September): 199–216.

Ballard, Charles L., John B. Shoven, and John Whalley. 1985. General Equilibrium Computations of the Marginal Welfare Costs of Taxes in the United States. *American Economic Review* 75, no. 1 (March): 128–138.

Banks, James, Richard Blundell, and Arthur Lewbel. 1993. Quadratic Engel Curves and Welfare Measurement, London: Institute for Fiscal Studies.

———. 1996. Tax Reform and Welfare Measurement. *Economic Journal* 106, no. 438 (September): 1227–1441.

Banks, James, Richard Blundell, and Ian Preston. 1994. Life-Cycle Expenditure Allocations and the Consumption Costs of Children. *European Economic Review* 38, no. 7 (August): 1391–1410.

Barger, W. J. 1972. The Measurement of Labor Input: U.S. Manufacturing Industries 1948–1966. Unpublished Ph.D. Dissertation, Harvard University.

Barnett, William A., and Y.W. Lee. 1985. The Global Properties of the Minflex Laurent, Generalized Leontief and Translog Flexible Functional Forms. *Econometrica* 53, no. 6 (November): 1421–1437.

Barro, Robert J. 1974. Are Government Bonds Net Wealth? *Journal of Political Economy* 82, no. 6 (November-December): 1095–1117.

———. 1990. Government Spending in a Simple Model of Endogenous Growth. *Journal of Political Economy* 98, no. 5, part 2 (October): S103–S125.

————. 1991. Economic Growth in a Cross Section of Countries. *The Quarterly Journal of Economics* 106, no. 425 (May): 407–443.

Barro, Robert J., and Xavier Sala-i-Martin. 1991. Convergence Across States and Regions. *Brookings Papers on Economic Activity* 1: 107–158.

Baumol, William J. 1986. Productivity Growth, Convergence, and Welfare: What the Long Data Show, *American Economic Review* 76. no. 4 (September): 1072–1085.

Baumol, William J., Sue A.B. Blackman, and Edward N. Wolff. 1989. *Productivity and American Leadership: The Long View*, Cambridge, MA: The MIT Press.

Beidelman, Carl. 1973. *Valuation of Used Capital Assets*, Sarasota, FL: American Accounting Association.

————. 1976. Economic Depreciation in a Capital Goods Industry. *National Tax Journal* 29, no. 4 (December): 379–390.

Bergman, Lars. 1985. Extensions and Applications of the MSG-Model: A Brief Survey. In *Production, Multi-Sectoral Growth and Planning*, eds. Finn R. Forsund, M. Hoel, and Svein Longva, 127–161, Amsterdam: North-Holland.

————. 1990. The Development of Computable General Equilibrium Modeling. In *General Equilibrium Modeling and Economic Policy Analysis*, eds. Lars Bergman, Dale W. Jorgenson, and Erno Zalai, 3–32, Oxford: Basil Blackwell.

Bergman, Lars, Dale W. Jorgenson, and Erno Zalai, eds. 1990. *General Equilibrium Modeling and Economic Policy*, Oxford: Basil Blackwell.

Berkovec, James, and Don Fullerton. 1992. A General Equilibrium Model of Housing, Taxes and Portfolio Choice. *Journal of Political Economy* 100, no. 2 (April): 390–429.

Bernheim, D., and John B. Shoven, J.B. 1987. Taxation and the Cost of Capital: An International Comparison. In *The Consumption Tax: A Better Alternative*, eds. C.E. Walker and M.A. Bloomfield, 61–85, Cambridge, MA: Harper and Row.

Berndt, Ernst R., and Laurits R. Christensen. 1973. The Translog Function and the Substitution of Equipment, Structures, and Labor in U.S. Manufacturing 1929–1968. *Journal of Econometrics* 1, no. 1 (March): 81–113.

Berndt, Ernst R., Masako N. Darrough, and W. Erwin Diewert. 1977. Flexible Functional Forms and Expenditure Distributions: An Application to Canadian Consumer Demand Functions. *International Economic Review* 18, no. 3 (October): 651–676.

Berndt, Ernst R., and Melvyn A. Fuss. 1986. Productivity Measurement with Adjustments for Variations in Capacity Utilization, and other Forms of Temporary Equilibrium. *Journal of Econometrics* 33, nos. 1–2 (October/November): 7–29.

Berndt, Ernst R., and Bengt Hansson. 1992. Measuring the Contribution of Public Infrastructure Capital in Sweden. *The Scandinavian Journal of Economics* 94 (Supplement): S151–S168.

Berndt, Ernst R., and Dale W. Jorgenson. 1973. Production Structures. In *U.S. Energy Resources and Economic Growth*, eds. Dale W. Jorgenson and Hendrik S. Houthakker, ch. 3, Washington, DC: Energy Policy Project.

Bertola, G. 1988. Adjustment Costs and Dynamic Factor Demands: Investment and Employment under Uncertainty. Unpublished Ph.D. Dissertation, Massachusetts Institute of Technology.

Bertola, G., and R.J. Caballero. 1994. Irreversibility and Aggregate Investment. *Review of Economic Studies* 61(2), no. 207 (April): 223–246.

Bjerkholt, Olav, Svein Longva, Oystein Olsen, and Steinar Strom, eds. 1983. *Analysis of Supply and Demand of Electricity in the Norwegian Economy*, Oslo: Central Bureau of Statistics.

Blackorby, Charles, and D. Donaldson. 1985. Consumers' Surpluses and Consistent Cost-Benefit Tests. *Social Choice and Welfare* 1, no. 4 (December): 251–262.

———. 1988a. Money Metric Utility: A Harmless Normalization? *Journal of Economic Theory* 46, no. 1 (October): 120–129.

———. 1988b. Adult-Equivalence Scales and the Economic Implementation of Interpersonal Comparisons of Well-Being. Discussion Paper 88–27. University of British Columbia: Department of Economics.

———. 1990. A Review Article: The Case against the Use of the Sum of Compensating Variations in Cost-Benefit Analysis. *Canadian Journal of Economics* 23, no. 3 (August): 471–494.

Blackorby, Charles, D. Donaldson, and S. Moloney. 1984. Consumer's Surplus and Welfare Change in a Simple Dynamic Model. *Review of Economic Studies* 51(1), no. 164 (January): 171–176.

Blackorby, Charles, Daniel Primont, and Robert R. Russell. 1978. *Duality, Separability, and Functional Structure*, Amsterdam: North-Holland.

Blundell, Richard. 1988. Consumer Behavior: Theory and Empirical Evidence—A Survey. *Economic Journal* 98, no. 389 (March): 16–65.

Blundell, Richard, and Arthur Lewbel. 1991. The Information Content of Equivalence Scales. *Journal of Econometrics* 50, nos. 1/2 (October/November): 49–68.

Blundell, Richard, Panos Pashardes, and G. Weber. 1993. What Do We Learn about Consumer Demand Patterns from Micro Data. *American Economic Review* 83, no. 3 (June): 570–597.

Boadway, Robin, Neil Bruce, and Jack M. Mintz. 1984. Taxation, Inflation, and the Effective Marginal Tax Rate on Capital in Canada. *Canadian Journal of Economics* 17, no. 1 (February): 62–79.

Bohringer, C., A. Pahlke, and T. Rutherford. 1997. Environmental Tax Reforms and the Prospects for a Double Dividend. Mimeo, University of Colorado.

Borges, Antonio M., and Lawrence H. Goulder. 1984. Decomposing the Impact of Higher Energy Prices on Long-Term Growth. In *Applied General Equilibrium Analysis*, eds. Herbert E. Scarf and John B. Shoven, 319–362, Cambridge, UK: Cambridge University Press.

Boskin, Michael *et al.* 1997. The CPI Commission: Findings and Recommendations. *American Economic Review* 87, no. 2 (May): 78–83.

Bovenberg, A. Lans, and Lawrence H. Goulder. 1966. Optimal Environmental Taxation in the Presence of Other Taxes: General Equilibrium Analyses. *American Economic Review* 86, no. 4 (September): 985–1000.

Bovenberg, A. Lans, and Ruud A. de Mooij. 1994. Environmental Levies and Distortionary Taxation. *American Economic Review* 94, no. 4 (September): 1085–1089.

Box, George, E.P., and Gwilym M. Jenkins. 1970. *Time Series Analysis: Forecasting and Control*, San Francisco, CA: Holden-Day.

Bradford, David F. 1981a. Pitfalls in the Construction and Use of Effective Tax Rates. In *Depreciation, Inflation, and the Taxation of Income from Capital*, ed. Charles R. Hulten, 251–278, Washington, DC: The Urban Institute Press.

———. 1981b. The Incidence and Allocation Effect of a Tax on Corporate Distribution. *Journal of Public Economics* 15, no. 1 (January): 251–278.

———. 1986. *Untangling the Income Tax*, Cambridge, MA: Harvard University Press.

Brainard, William C., and James Tobin. 1968. Pitfalls in Financial Model Building. *American Economic Review* 58, no. 2 (May): 99–122.

Braithwait, S.D. 1980. The Substitution Bias of the Laspeyres Price Index. *American Economic Review* 70, no. 1 (January): 64–77.

Browning, Martin. 1992. Children and Household Economic Behavior. *Journal of Economic Literature* 30, no. 3 (September): 1434–1475.

Browning, Martin, and A. Lusardi. 1996. Household Saving: Micro Theories and Micro Facts. *Journal of Economic Literature* 34, no 4: 1779–1855.

Browning, Martin, and C. Meghir. 1991. The Effects of Male and Female Labor Supply on Commodity Demands. *Econometrica* 59, no. 4 (July): 925–951.

Brundy, James M., and Dale W. Jorgenson. 1971. Efficient Estimation of Simultaneous Equations by Instrumental Variables. *Review of Economics and Statistics* 53, no. 3 (August): 207–224.

———. 1973. Consistent and Efficient Estimation of Simultaneous Equation Systems by Means of Instrumental Variables. In *Frontiers in Econometrics*, ed. Paul Zarembka, 215–244, New York, NY: Academic Press.

———. 1974. The Relative Efficiency of Instrumental Variables Estimators of Simultaneous Equations. *Annals of Social and Economic Measurement* 3, no. 4 (October): 679–700.

Bureau of the Census. 1989. Projections of the Population of the United States, by Age, Sex and Race: 1988–2080. *Current Population Reports*, P-25, no. 1918, Washington, DC: U.S. Department of Commerce.

———. Various annual issues. Pollution Abatement Costs and Expenditures, Washington, DC: U.S. Department of Commerce.

———. Various annual issues. *Current Population Reports, Consumer Income*. Series P-60, Washington, DC: U.S. Department of Commerce.

Bureau of Economic Analysis. 1966. *The National Income and Product Accounts of the United States, 1929–1965: Statistical Tables*, A Supplement to the Survey of Current Business, Washington, DC: U.S. Government Printing Office.

———. 1984. The Input-Output Structure of the U.S. Economy, 1977. *Survey of Current Business* 64, no. 5 (May): 42–79.

———. 1986a. *Survey of Current Business* 66, no. 7 (July), Washington: U.S. Government Printing Office.

———. 1986b. *The National Income and Product Accounts of the United States, 1929–1982: Statistical Tables*, Washington, DC: U.S. Department of Commerce.

———. 1987. *Fixed Reproducible Tangible Wealth in the United States, 1925–1985*, Washington, DC: U.S. Government Printing Office.

Bureau of Labor Statistics. 1983. *Trends in Multifactor Productivity, 1948–1981*, Bulletin no. 2178, Washington, D.C.: U.S. Department of Labor.

Caballero, Ricardo J. 1999. Aggregate Investment. In *Handbook of Macroeconomics*, eds. John B. Taylor and Michael Woodford, vol. 1B, 813–862, Amsterdam: North-Holland.

Caballero, Ricardo J., and R. Lyons. 1992. External Effects in U.S. Procyclical Productivity. *Journal of Monetary Economics* 29, no. 2 (May): 209–225.

———. 1990. Internal and External Economies in European Industry. *European Economic Review* 34, no. 4 (December): 805–826.

Carson, C.S., and Honsa, J. 1990. The United Nations System of National Accounts: An Introduction. *Survey of Current Business* 70, no. 6 (June): 20–30.

Cass, D. 1965. Optimum Growth in an Aggregative Model of Capital Accumulation. *Review of Economic Studies* 32, no. 3 (July): 233–240.

Caves, Douglas W., Laurits R. Christensen, and J. A. Swanson. 1980. Productivity in U. S. Railroads, 1951–1974. *Bell Journal of Economics* 11, no. 1 (Spring): 166–181.

Caves, Douglas W., Laurits R. Christensen, and Michael W. Tretheway. 1981. U.S. Trunk Air Carriers, 1972–1977: A Multilateral Comparison of Total Factor Productivity. In *Productivity Measurement in Regulated Industries*, eds. T. Cowing and R.E. Stevenson, 47–76, Academic Press: New York.

Chamley, Christophe. 1981. The Welfare Cost of Capital Income Taxation in a Growing Economy. *Journal of Political Economy* 89, no. 3 (June): 468–496.

———. 1986. Optimal Taxation of Capital Income in Economies with Identical Private and Social Discount Rates. *Econometrica* 54, no. 3 (May): 607–622.

Chavas, J.-P. 1994. Production and Investment Decisions under Sunk Cost and Temporal Uncertainty. *American Journal of Agricultural Economics* 76, no. 1 (January): 114–127.

Chinloy, Peter T. 1974. Issues in the Measurement of Labor Input. Unpublished Ph.D. Dissertation, Harvard University.

Chipman, J.S., and J. Moore. 1971. The Compensation Principle in Welfare Economics. In *Papers in Quantitative Economics*, eds. A. Zarley and J. Moore, 1–77, Lawrence: University Press of Kansas.

———. 1973. Aggregate Demand, Real National Income and the Compensation Principle. *International Economic Review* 14, no. 1 (February): 153–181.

———. 1976. The Scope of Consumer's Surplus Arguments. In *Evolution, Welfare and Time in Economics: Essays in Honor of Nicholas Georgescu-Roegen*, eds. A.M. Tang *et al.*, 69–123, Lexington: Heath-Lexington Books.

———. 1980. Compensating Variation, Consumer's Surplus, and Welfare. *American Economic Review* 70, no. 5 (December): 933–949.

Christainsen, G.B., and Thomas H. Tietenberg. 1985. Distributional and Macroeconomic Aspects of Environmental Policy. In *Handbook of Natural Resource and Energy Economics*, vol. 1, eds. Allen V. Kneese and James L. Sweeney, 345–395, Amsterdam: North-Holland.

Christainsen, G.B., Frank M. Gollop, and Robert H. Haveman. 1980. *Environmental and Health and Safety Regulations, Productivity Growth, and Economic Performance*, Joint Economic Committee, 96th Congress, 2nd Session, Washington, DC: U.S. Government Printing Office.

Christensen, Laurits R. 1968. Saving and the Rate of Interest. Unpublished Ph.D. Dissertation, University of California, Berkeley.

Christensen, Laurits R., Dianne Cummings, C. G. Degen, and P. E. Schoech. 1989. Capital in the U.S. Postal Service. In *Technology and Capital Formation*, eds. Dale W. Jorgenson and Ralph Landau, 409–450, Cambridge, Massachusetts: The MIT Press.

Christensen, Laurits R., and Dianne Cummings. 1981. Real Product, Real Factor Input, and Productivity in Korea, 1960–1973. *Journal of Development Economics* 8, no. 3 (June): 285–302.

Christensen, Laurits R., Dianne Cummings, and Dale W. Jorgenson. 1978. Productivity Growth, 1947–1973: An International Comparison. In *The Impact of International Trade and Investment on Employment*, ed. W. Dewald, Washington, DC: U.S. Department of Labor.

———. 1980. Economic Growth, 1947–1973: An International Comparison. In *New Developments in Productivity Measurement*, eds. John W. Kendrick and Beatrice Vaccara, 595–698, New York: Columbia University Press.

———. 1981. Relative Productivity Levels, 1947–1973: An International Comparison. *European Economic Review* 16, no. 1 (May): 61–94.

Christensen, Laurits R., Dianne Cummings, and P. E. Schoech. 1983. Econometric Estimation of Scale Economies in Telecommunications. In *Economic Analysis of Telecommunications*, eds. Courville, Leon, Alain de Fontenay and A. Rodney Dobell, 27–53, Amsterdam: North-Holland.

Christensen, Laurits R., and Dale W. Jorgenson. 1969. The Measurement of U.S. Real Capital Input, 1929–1967. *Review of Income and Wealth*, ser. 15, no. 4 (December): 293–320.

———. 1970. U.S. Real Product and Real Factor Input, 1929–1967. *Review of Income and Wealth*, ser. 16, no. 1 (March): 19–50.

———. 1973a. Measuring Economic Performance in the Private Sector. In *The Measurement of Economic and Social Performance*, ed. Milton Moss, 233–251, New York, NY: Columbia University Press.

———. 1973b. U.S. Income, Saving and Wealth, 1929–1969. *Review of Income and Wealth*, ser. 19, no. 4 (December): 329–362.

Christensen, Laurits R., Dale W. Jorgenson, and Lawrence J. Lau. 1971. Conjugate Duality and the Transcendental Logarithmic Production Function. *Econometrica* 39, no. 4 (July): 255–256.

———. 1973. Transcendental Logarithmic Production Frontiers. *The Review of Economics and Statistics* 55, no. 1 (February): 28–45.

———. 1975. Transcendental Logarithmic Utility Functions. *American Economic Review* 65, no. 3 (June): 367–383.

Church, A.H. 1901. The Proper Distribution of Establishment Charges, Part III. *The Engineering Magazine* 21: 904–912.

Cline, W.R. 1992. *The Economics of Global Warming*, Washington, DC: Institute for International Economics.

Cline, W.R., N. Kawanabe, T. Kronsjo, and T. Williams. 1978. *Trade Negotiations in the Tokyo Round*, Washington, DC: The Brookings Institution.

Commission of the European Communities. 1992. Report of the Committee of Independent Experts on Company Taxation, Luxembourg.

Congressional Budget Office. 1990. *Carbon Charges*, January, Washington, DC: U.S. Government Printing Office.

Conrad, Klaus, and Dale W. Jorgenson. 1975. *Measuring Performance in the Private Economy of the Federal Republic of Germany 1950–1973*. Tübingen: J.C.B. Mohr.

———. 1978. The Structure of Consumer Preferences, Federal Republic of Germany, 1950–1973. *Zeitschrift für Nationalökonomie* 38, nos. 1–2 (January): 1–28.

———. 1979. Testing the Integrability of Consumer Demand Functions, Federal Republic of Germany, 1950–1973. *European Economic Review* 12, no. 2 (April): 149–169.

Dasgupta, Partha S., and G.M. Heal. 1979. *Economic Theory and Exhaustible Resources*, Cambridge: Cambridge University Press.

Dean, Andrew. 1992. Costs of Reducing Carbon Dioxide Emission: Evidence from Six Global Models. Economics Department Working Paper, Paris: Organization for Economic Co-Operation and Development.

Dean, E.R., and M.J. Harper. 1998. The BLS Productivity Measurement Program. Paper presented at the CRIW/NBER Conference, *New Directions in Productivity Analysis*, Washington, DC, March 20–21.

Deardorff, A., and R.M. Stern. 1986. *The Michigan Model of World Production and Trade*, Cambridge, MA: The MIT Press.

Deaton, Angus S. 1989. Rice Prices and Income Distribution in Thailand: A Nonparametric Analysis. *Economic Journal* 99, no. 395 (January): 1–37.

———. 1986. Demand Analysis. In *Handbook of Econometrics*, vol. 3, eds. Zvi Griliches and Michael D. Intriligator, 1767–1840, Amsterdam: North-Holland.

Deaton, Angus S., and John S. Muellbauer. 1980a. An Almost Ideal Demand System. *American Economic Review* 70, no. 3 (June): 312–326.

———. 1980b. *Economics and Consumer Behavior*, Cambridge, UK: Cambridge University Press.

De Long, J. Bradford. 1988. Productivity Growth, Convergence, and Welfare: Comment. *American Economic Review* 78, no. 5 (December): 1138–1154.

Demers, Fanny S., Michel Demers, and Huntley Schaller. 1993. Investment Under Uncertainty and Irreversibility. Mimeo: Carleton University.

———. 1994. Irreversible Investment and Costs of Adjustments. Paris, CEPREMAP, no. 9416, June.

Denison, Edward F. 1957. Theoretical Aspects of Quality Change, Capital Consumption, and Net Capital Formation. In *Problems of Capital Formation*, 215–261, Princeton: Princeton University Press.

————. 1962. *Sources of Economic Growth in the United States* Survey of Supplementary Paper No. 13, New York: Committee for Economic Development.

————. 1969. Some Major Issues in Productivity Analysis: An Examination of Estimates by Jorgenson and Griliches. *Survey of Current Business* 49, no. 5, pt. 2 (May): 1–27.

————. 1972. Final Comments. *Survey of Current Business* 52, no. 5, pt. 2 (May): 95–110.

————. 1974. *Accounting for United States Economic Growth, 1929 to 1969*, Washington, DC: The Brookings Institution.

————. 1979. *Accounting for Slower Economic Growth: The United States in the 1970s*, Washington, DC: The Brookings Institution.

————. 1985. *Trends in American Economic Growth, 1929–1982*, Washington, DC: The Brookings Institution.

————. 1989. *Estimates of Productivity Change by Industry*, Washington, DC: The Brookings Institution.

Denny, Michael, Melvyn Fuss, and J.D. May. 1981. Intertemporal Changes in Regional Productivity in Canadian Manufacturing. *Canadian Journal of Economics* 14, no 3 (August): 390–408.

DeWitt, Diane E., Hadi Dowlatabadi, and Raymond J. Kopp. 1991. Who Bears the Burden of Energy Taxes? Discussion Paper QE91–12, Washington, DC: Resources for the Future.

Diamond, Peter A., and Daniel L. McFadden. 1974. Some Uses of the Expenditure Function in Public Finance. *Journal of Public Economics* 3, no. 1 (February): 3–21.

Diewert, W. Erwin. 1976. Exact and Superlative Index Numbers. *Journal of Econometrics* 4, no. 2 (May): 115–146.

————. 1978a. Superlative Index Numbers and Consistency in Aggregation. *Econometrica* 46, no. 4 (July): 883–900.

————. 1978b. Hicks' Aggregation Theorem and the Existence of a Real Value Added Function. In *Production Economics: A Dual Approach to Theory and Applications*, eds. Melvin Fuss and Daniel L. McFadden, vol. 2, 17–51, Amsterdam: North-Holland.

————. 1980. Aggregation Problems in the Measurement of Capital. In *The Measurement of Capital*, ed. Dan Usher, 433–528, Chicago, IL: University of Chicago Press.

———. 1981. The Measurement of Deadweight Loss Revisited. *Econometrica* 49, no. 5 (September): 1225–1244.

———. 1985. The Measurement of Waste and Welfare in Applied General Equilibrium Models. In *New Developments in Applied General Equilibrium Analysis*, eds. J. Piggott and John Whalley, 42–103, Cambridge, UK: Cambridge University Press.

———. 1990. The Theory of the Cost-of-Living Index and the Measurement of Welfare Change. In *Price Level Measurement*, ed. W. Erwin Diewert, 79–147, Amsterdam: North-Holland.

———. 1992. The Measurement of Productivity. *Bulletin of Economic Research* 44, no. 3 (July): 165–198.

Diewert, W. Erwin, and K.J. Fox. 1999. Can Measurement Error Explain the Productivity Paradox? *Canadian Journal of Economics* 32, no. 2 (May): 251–280.

Diewert, W. Erwin, and T.J. Wales. 1987. Flexible Functional Forms and Global Curvature Conditions. *Econometrica* 55, no. 1 (January): 43–68.

Dixit, A., and R. Pindyck. 1994. *Investment Under Uncertainty*, Princeton: Princeton University Press.

Dowrick, Steve, and Duc-Tho Nguyen. 1989. OECD Comparative Economic Growth 1950–1985: Catch-up and Convergence. *American Economic Review* 79, no. 5 (December): 47–58.

Dupuit, Jules. 1969. On the Measurement of the Utility of Public Works. In *Readings in Welfare Economics*, eds. Kenneth J. Arrow and T. Scitovsky, 255–283, Homewood: Richard D. Irwin [originally published in French in 1844].

Eisner, Robert. 1991. Infrastructure and Regional Economic Performance. *New England Economic Review*, Federal Reserve Bank of Boston: 47–58.

Elbadawi, I., A. Ronald Gallant, and G. Sousa. 1983. An Elasticity Can Be Estimated Consistently without *a priori* Knowledge of Functional Form. *Econometrica* 51, no. 6 (November): 1731–1752.

Energy Information Administration. 1990. *Annual Energy Review 1990*, Washington, DC: U.S. Department of Energy.

Englander, A. Steven, and Axel Mittelstadt. 1988. Total Factor Productivity: Macroeconomic and Structural Aspects of the Slowdown. *OECD Economic Studies* 10 (Spring): 7–56.

Environmental Protection Agency. 1988. *The Potential Effects of Global Climate Change in the United States*, Draft Report to Congress, October.

———. 1989. *Policy Options for Stabilizing Global Climate*, Draft Report to Congress, 3 vols., February.

Epstein, Larry G., and Michael Denny. 1980. Endogenous Capital Utilization in a Short Run Production Model; Theory and Empirical Application. *Journal of Econometrics* 12, no. 2 (February): 189–207.

Ezaki, Mitsuo, and Dale W. Jorgenson. 1973. Measurement of Macroeconomic Performance in Japan, 1951–1968. In *Economic Growth: The Japanese Experience Since the Meiji Era*, vol. 1, eds. Kazushi Ohkawa and Yujiro Hayami, 286–361, Tokyo: Japan Economic Research Center.

Felder, Stefan, and Thomas F. Rutherford. 1993. Unilateral CO_2 Reductions and Carbon Leakage: The Effect of International Trade in Oil and Basic Materials. *Journal of Environmental Economics and Management* 25, no. 1 (January): 162–176.

Fernald, John. 1999. Roads to Prosperity? Assessing the Link Between Public Capital and Productivity. *American Economic Review* 88, no. 3 (June): 619–638.

Fisher, Irving. 1922. *The Making of Index Numbers*, Boston: Houghton-Mifflin.

Forsund, Finn R. 1985. Input-Output Models, National Economic Models, and the Environment. In *Handbook of Natural Resource and Energy Economics*, eds. Allen V. Kneese and James L. Sweeney, vol. 1: 325–344, Amsterdam: North-Holland.

Forsund, Finn R., and Steinar Strom. 1976. The Generation of Residual Flows in Norway: An Input-Output Approach. *Journal of Environmental Economics and Management* 3, no. 2 (April): 129–141.

Foster, James E. 1984. On Economic Poverty: A Survey of Aggregate Measures. In *Advances in Econometrics*, vol. 3, eds. Robert L. Basmann and G.F. Rhodes, Jr., 215–251, Greenwich, CO: JAI Press.

Fraumeni, Barbara M. 1980. The Role of Capital in U.S. Economic Growth, 1948–1976. Unpublished Ph.D. Dissertation, Boston College.

Fraumeni, Barbara M., and Dale W. Jorgenson. 1980a. Rates of Return by Industrial Sector in the United States, 1948–1976. *American Economic Review* 70, no. 2 (May): 326–330.

———. 1980b. The Sectoral Sources of Aggregate U.S. Economic Growth, 1948–1976. In *Empirische Wirtschaftsforschung*, eds. J. Frohn and R. Staglin, 27–40, Berlin: Duncker and Humboldt.

———. 1980c. The Role of Capital in U.S. Economic Growth, 1948–1976. In *Capital, Efficiency and Growth*, ed. George M. von Furstenberg, 9–250, Cambridge, MA: Ballinger.

———. 1986. The Role of Capital in U.S. Economic Growth, 1948–1979. In *Measurement Issues and Behavior of Productivity Variables*, ed. Ali Dogramaci, 161–244, Boston, MA: Martinus Nijhoff.

Friedman, Milton. 1957. *A Theory of the Consumption Function*, Princeton: Princeton University Press.

Frisch, Ragnar. 1959. A Complete Scheme for Computing All Direct and Cross Demand Elasticities in a Model with Many Sectors. *Econometrica* 27, no. 2 (April): 177–196.

Fullerton, Don. 1984. Which Effective Tax Rate? *National Tax Journal*, 37, no. 1 (March): 23–41.

————. 1987. The Indexation of Interest, Depreciation, and Capital Gains and Tax Reform in the United States. *Journal of Public Economics* 32, no. 1 (February): 25–52.

————. 1989. The Marginal Excess Burden of Different Capital Instruments. *Review of Economics and Statistics* 71, no. 3 (August): 435–442.

Fullerton, Don, and Yolanda K. Henderson. 1989. A Disaggregate Equilibrium Model of the Tax Distortions Among Assets, Sectors, and Industries. *International Economic Review* 30, no. 2 (May): 391–413.

Fullerton, Don, Yolanda K. Henderson, and John B. Shoven. 1984. A Comparison of Methodologies in Empirical General Equilibrium Models of Taxation. In *Applied General Equilibrium Analysis*, eds. Herbert E. Scarf and John B. Shoven, 367–410, Cambridge, UK: Cambridge University Press.

Fullerton, Don, and D.L. Rogers. 1993. *Who Bears the Lifetime Tax Burden?* Washington, DC: Brookings Institution.

Fuss, Melvyn, Daniel L. McFadden, and Yair Mundlak. 1978. A Survey of Functional Forms in the Economic Analysis of Production. *Production Economics*, vol. 1, eds. Melvyn Fuss and Daniel L. McFadden, 219–268, Amsterdam: North-Holland.

Gallant, A. Ronald, and Dale W. Jorgenson. 1979. Statistical Inference for a System of Simultaneous, Nonlinear, Implicit Equations in the Context of Instrumental Variable Estimation. *Journal of Econometrics* 11, nos. 2/3 (October/December): 275–302.

Garcia-Mila, Theresa, Therese McGuire, and Robert H. Porter. 1993. The Effect of Public Capital in State-Level Production Functions Reconsidered. Working Paper 24: University of Illinois Institute of Government and Public Affairs.

Gillingham, R., and W. Lane. 1982. Changing the Treatment of Shelter Costs for Homeowners in the CPI. *Monthly Labor Review* 105, no. 6 (June): 9–14.

Glomsrud, S., H. Vennemo, and T. Johnson. 1992. Stabilization of Emissions of Carbon Dioxide: A Computable General Equilibrium Assessment. *Scandinavian Economic Journal* 94, no. 1: 53–69.

Goldin, C., and Polacheck, S. 1987. Residual Differences by Sex: Perspectives on the Gender Gap in Earnings, *American Economic Review* 77, no. 2 (May): 143–158.

Goldstein, M., and M. Khan. 1985. Income and Price Effects in Foreign Trade. In *Handbook of International Economics*, eds. R. Jones and P. Kenen, Amsterdam: North-Holland.

Gollop, Frank M. 1974. Modelling Technical Change and Market Imperfections: An Econometric Analysis of U.S. Manufacturing, 1940–1971. Unpublished Ph.D. Dissertation, Harvard University.

Gollop, Frank M., and Dale W. Jorgenson. 1980. U.S. Productivity Growth by Industry, 1947–1973. In *New Developments in Productivity Measurement and Analysis*, eds. John W. Kendrick and Beatrice N. Vaccara, 17–136, Chicago, IL: University of Chicago Press.

———. 1983. Sectoral Measures of Labor Cost for the United States, 1948–1979. In *The Measurement of Labor Cost*, ed. John E. Triplett, 185–235, Chicago, IL: University of Chicago Press.

Gollop, Frank M., and Mark J. Roberts. 1983. Environmental Regulations and Productivity Growth: The Case of Fossil-fueled Electric Power Generation. *Journal of Political Economy* 91, no. 4 (August): 654–674.

———. 1985. Cost-Minimizing Regulation of Sulfur Emissions: Regional Gains in Electric Power. *Review of Economics and Statistics* 67, no. 1 (February): 81–90.

Gordon, Roger H., and Joel Slemrod. 1988. Do We Collect Any Revenue from Taxing Capital Income? In *Tax Policy and the Economy*, vol. 2, ed. Lawrence H. Summers, 89–130. Cambridge, MA: The MIT Press.

Gorman, William M. 1953. Community Preference Fields. *Econometrica* 21, no. 1 (January): 63–80.

———. 1981. Some Engel Curves. In *Essays in the Theory and Measurement of Consumer Behavior in Honor of Sir Richard Stone*, ed. Angus S. Deaton, 7–29, Cambridge, UK: Cambridge University Press.

Goulder, Lawrence H. 1995. Environmental Taxation and the 'Double Dividend': A Reader's Guide. *International Tax and Public Finance* 2, no. 2 (August): 157–183.

Goulder, Lawrence H., and B. Eichengreen. 1992. Trade Liberalization in General Equilibrium: Intertemporal and Interindustry Effects. *Canadian Journal of Economics* 25, no. 2 (May): 253–280.

Gramlich, Edward M. 1994. Infrastructure Investment: A Review Essay. *Journal of Economic Literature* 32, no. 3 (September): 1176–1196.

Green, J.B. 1915. The Perpetual Inventory in Practical Stores Operation. *The Engineering Magazine* 48: 879–888.

Griliches, Zvi. 1963. Capital Stock in Investment Functions: Some Problems of Concept and Measurement. In *Measurement in Economics*, eds. C. Christ *et al.*, 115–137. Stanford: Stanford University Press.

Griliches, Zvi, and Michael D. Intriligator. 1983–1985. *Handbook of Econometrics*, 3 vols., Amsterdam: North-Holland.

Griliches, Zvi, and Dale W. Jorgenson. 1966. Sources of Measured Productivity Change: Capital Input. *The American Economic Review* 56, no. 2 (May): 50–61.

Haavelmo, Trygve. 1960. *A Study in the Theory of Investment*. Chicago, IL: University of Chicago Press.

Hall, Robert E. 1971. The Dynamic Effects of Fiscal Policy in an Economy with Foresight. *Review of Economic Studies* 38(2), no. 114 (April): 229–244.

———. 1978. Stochastic Implications of the Life Cycle-Permanent Income Hypothesis: Theory and Evidence. *Journal of Political Economy* 86, no. 6 (December): 971–987.

———. 1981. Tax Treatment of Depreciation, Capital Gains, and Interest in an Inflationary Economy. In *Depreciation, Inflation, and the Taxation of Income from Capital*, ed. Charles R. Hulten, 149–166, Washington, DC: The Urban Institute Press.

———. 1988a. Intertemporal Substitution in Consumption. *Journal of Political Economy* 96 (April): 339–357.

———. 1988b. The Relation between Price and Marginal Cost in U.S. Industry. *Journal of Politial Economy* 96, no. 2 (April): 921–947.

———. 1996. The Effects of Tax Reform on Prices and Asset Values. In *Tax Policy and the Economy*, 10, ed. James M. Poterba, 71–88, Cambridge, MA: The MIT Press.

Hall, Robert E., and Dale W. Jorgenson. 1967. Tax Policy and Investment Behavior. *The American Economic Review* 57, no. 3 (June): 391–414.

———. 1969. Tax Policy and Investment Behavior: Reply and Further Results. *The American Economic Review* 59, no. 3 (June): 388–401.

———. 1971. Application of the Theory of Optimal Capital Accumulation. In *Tax Incentives and Capital Spending*, ed. Gary Fromm, 9–60, Washington, DC: Brookings Institution.

Hall Robert E., and Alvin Rabushka. 1995. *The Flat Tax*, Hoover Institution Press.

Hammond, M. Jeff, Stephen J. DeCanio, Peggy Duxbury, Alan H. Sanstad, and Christopher H. Stinson. 1977. *Tax Waste, Not Work*, San Francisco: Redefining Progress.

Hammond, Peter J. 1976. Equity, Arrow's Conditions, and Rawls' Difference Principle. *Econometrica* 44, no. 4 (July): 793–804.

————. 1977. Dual Interpersonal Comparisons of Utility and the Welfare Economics of Income Distribution. *Journal of Public Economics* 7, no. 1 (February): 51–71.

Hansen, Lars P. 1982. Large Sample Properties of Generalized Methods of Moments Estimators. *Econometrica* 50, no. 4 (July): 1029–1054.

Harberger, A.C. 1971. Three Basic Postulates for Applied Welfare Economics. *Journal of Economic Literature* 9, no. 3 (September): 785–797.

Harrison, Glenn W., Richard Jones, Larry J. Kimbell, and Randall Wigle. 1993. How Robust is Applied General Equilibrium Analysis? *Journal of Policy Modeling* 15, no. 1 (January): 99–115.

Harper, Michael J., Ernst R. Berndt, and David O. Wood. 1989. Rates of Return and Capital Aggregation Using Alternative Rental Prices. In *Technology and Capital Formation*, eds. Dale W. Jorgenson and Ralph Landau, 331–372, Cambridge, MA: The MIT Press.

Hausman, Jerry A. 1981. Exact Consunmer's Surplus and Deadweight Loss. *American Economic Review* 71, no. 4 (September): 662–676.

Hausman, Jerry A. and Newey, Whitney. 1995. Nonparametric Estimation of Exact Consumers Surplus and Deadweight Loss. *Econometrica* 63, no. 6 (November): 1445–1476.

Hayashi, Fumio. 1982. Tobin's Marginal q and Average q: A Neoclassical Interpretation. *Econometrica* 50, no. 1 (January): 213–224.

————. 1985. Corporate Finance Side of the Q Theory of Investment. *Journal of Public Economics* 27, no. 3 (August): 261–280.

Hayashi, Fumio, and T. Inoue. 1991. The Relation Between Firm Growth and Q with Multiple Capital Goods: Theory and Evidence from Panel Data on Japanese Firms. *Econometrica* 59, no. 3 (May): 731–754.

Hazilla, M., and R.J. Kopp. 1986. Systematic Effects of Capital Service Price Definition on Perceptions of Input Substitution. *Journal of Business and Economic Statistics* 4, no. 2 (April): 209–224.

————. 1990. Social Cost of Environmental Quality Regulations: A General Equilibrium Analysis. *Journal of Political Economy* 98, no. 4 (August): 853–873.

Henderson, Volanda K. 1991. Applications of General Equilibrium Models in the 1986 Tax Reform Act in the United States. *The Economist* 139 (Spring): 147–168.

Hicks, John R. 1940. The Valuation of Social Income. *Economica*, N.S. 7 (May): 105–124.

————. 1942. Consumer's Surplus and Index Number. *Review of Economic Studies* 9, no. 2 (Summer): 126–137.

———. 1946. *Value and Capital*, 2nd edition, Oxford: Oxford University Press (1st ed., 1939).

Ho, Mun Sing. 1989. Effects of External Linkages on U.S. Economic Growth: A Dynamic General Equilibrium Analysis. Unpublished Ph.D. Dissertation, Department of Economics, Harvard University.

Ho, Mun Sing, and Dale W. Jorgenson. 1994. Trade Policy and U.S. Economic Growth. *Journal of Policy Modeling* 16, no. 2: 119–146.

Hogan, William W., and Dale W. Jorgenson. 1991. Productivity Trends and the Cost of Reducing Carbon Dioxide Emissions. *The Energy Journal* 12, no. 1 (January): 67–85.

Holtz-Eakin, Douglas. 1991. Solow and the States: Capital Accumulation, Productivity and Economic Growth. Working Paper: Syracuse University.

———. 1992. Public Sector Capital and the Productivity Puzzle. *Review of Economics and Statistics* 76, no. 1 (February): 12–21.

Hotelling, Harold S. 1925. A General Mathematical Theory of Depreciation. *Journal of the American Statistical Association* 20, no. 151 (September): 340–353.

Houghton, R.A., and G.M. Woodwell. 1989. Global Climate Change. *Scientific American* 260, no. 4 (April).

Houthakker, Hendrik, 1957. An International Comparison of Household Expenditure Patterns Commemorating the Centenary of Engel's Law. *Econometrica* 25, no. 4 (October): 532–551.

Hubbard, G., and A. Kashyap. 1992. Internal Net Worth and the Investment Process: An Application to US Agriculture. *Journal of Political Economy* 100, no. 3 (June): 506–534.

Hudson, Edward A., and Dale W. Jorgenson. 1974a. U.S. Energy Policy and Economic Growth, 1975–2000. *Bell Journal of Economics and Management Science* 5, no. 2 (Autumn): 461–514.

———. 1974b. Tax Policy and Energy Use. In Committee on Finance, United States Senate, *Fiscal Policy and the Energy Crisis*, 1681–1694, Washington, DC: Ninety-Third Congress, First and Second Sessions.

———. 1978. Energy Policy and U.S. Economic Growth. *American Economic Review* 68, no. 2 (May): 118–123.

Hufbauer, G., D.T. Berliner, and K.A. Elliott. 1986. *Trade Protection in the United States*, Washington, D.C.: Institute for International Economics.

Hulten, Charles R. 1973. The Measurement of Total Factor Productivity in United States Manufacturing, 1948–1966. Ph.D. Dissertation, University of California, Berkeley.

————. 1981. The Measurement of Economic Depreciation. In *Depreciation, Inflation, and the Taxation of Income from Capital*, ed. Charles R. Hulten, 81–125, Washington, DC: The Urban Institute.

————. 1986. Productivity Change, Capacity Utilization and the Source of Efficiency Growth. *Journal of Econometrics* 33, nos. 1–2 (October/November): 31–50.

————. 1990. The Measurement of Capital. In *Fifty Years of Economic Measurement*, Erwin R. Berndt and John E. Triplett, 119–158, Chicago, IL: The University of Chicago Press.

————. 1992. Accounting for the Wealth of Nations: The Net versus Gross Output Controversy and its Ramifications. *Scandinavian Economic Journal* 94 (Supplement): 9–24.

————. 1996. Capital and Wealth in the Revised SNA. In *The New System of National Accounts*, ed. J.W. Kendrick, 149–181, Boston, MA: Kluwer Academic Publishers.

Hulten, Charles R., and Robert M. Schwab. 1984. Regional Productivity Growth in U.S. Manufacturing: 1951–1978. *American Economic Review* 74, no. 1 (March): 152–162.

————. 1991. Public Capital Formation and the Growth of Regional Manufacturing Industries. *National Tax Journal* 44, no. 4 (December): 121–134.

Hulten, Charles R., and Frank C. Wykoff. 1981a. The Estimation of Economic Depreciation Using Vintage Asset Prices: An Application of the Box-Cox Power Transformation. *Journal of Econometrics* 15, no. 3 (April): 367–396.

————. 1981b. The Measurement of Economic Depreciation. In *Depreciation, Inflation, and the Taxation of Income from Capital*, ed. Charles R. Hulten, 81–125, Washington, DC: The Urban Institute Press.

————. 1996. Issues in the Measurement of Economic Depreciation, Introductory Remarks. *Economic Inquiry* 34, no. 1 (January): 10–23.

James, D.E., H.M.A. Jansen, and H.P. Opschoor. 1978. *Economic Approaches to Environmental Problems*, Amsterdam: North-Holland.

Johansen, L. 1960. *A Multi-Sectorial Study of Economic Growth*, Amsterdam: North-Holland.

Jorgenson, Dale W. 1963. Capital Theory and Investment Behavior. *American Economic Review* 53, no 2 (May): 247–259.

————. 1964. Minimum Variance, Linear, Unbiased Seasonal Adjustment of Economic Time Series. *Journal of the American Statistical Association* 59, no. 307 (September): 681–724.

————. 1966a. Rational Distributed Lag Functions, *Econometrica* 34, no. 1 (January): 135–149.

————. 1966b. The Embodiment Hypothesis. *Journal of Political Economy* 74, no. 1 (February): 1–17.

————. 1967a. Seasonal Adjustment of Data for Econometric Analysis. *Journal of the American Statistical Association* 62, no. 317 (March): 137–140.

————. 1967b. The Theory of Investment Behavior. In *The Determinants of Investment Behavior*, ed. Robert Ferber, Conference of the Universities—National Bureau of Economic Research, 129–156, New York, NY: Columbia University Press.

————. 1971. Econometric Studies of Investment Behavior: A Review. *Journal of Economic Literature* 9, no. 4 (December): 1111–1147.

————. 1973. The Economic Theory of Replacement and Depreciation. in *Econometrics and Economic Theory*, eds. W. Sellekaerts, 189–221, New York, NY: Macmillan.

————. 1974. Investment and Production: A Review. In *Frontiers in Quantitative Economics*, eds. Michael D. Intriligator and David A. Kendrick, vol. 2, 341–366, Amsterdam: North-Holland.

————. 1980. Accounting for Capital. In *Capital Efficiency and Growth*, ed. George M. von Furstenberg, 251–319, Cambridge: Ballinger.

————. 1981. Energy Prices and Productivity Growth. *Scandinavian Journal of Economics* 83, no. 2: 165–179.

————. 1982a. An Econometric Approach to General Equilibrium Analysis. In *Current Developments in the Interface: Economics, Econometrics, Mathematics*, eds. M. Hazewinkel and A.H.G. Rinooy Kan, 125–157, Dordrecht: D. Reidel.

————. 1982b. Econometric and Process Analysis Models for the Analysis of Energy Policy. In *Perspectives in Resource Policy Modeling: Energy and Minerals*, eds. R. Amit and M. Avriel, 9–62, Cambridge: Ballinger.

————. 1983. Modeling Production for General Equilibrium Analysis. *Scandinavian Journal of Economics* 85, no. 2: 101–112.

————. 1984a. Econometric Methods for Applied General Equilibrium Analysis. In *Applied General Equilibrium Analysis*, eds. Herbert E. Scarf and John B. Shoven, 139–203, Cambridge, UK: Cambridge University Press.

————. 1984b. The Role of Energy in Productivity Growth. *American Economic Review* 74, no. 2 (May): 26–30.

————. 1986. Econometric Methods for Modeling Producer Behavior. In *Handbook of Econometrics*, eds. Zvi Griliches and Michael D. Intriligator, vol. 3, 1841–1915, Amsterdam: North-Holland.

————. 1988. Productivity and Postwar U.S. Economic Growth. *Journal of Economic Perspectives* 2, no. 4 (Fall): 23–42.

————. 1989. Capital as a Factor of Production. In *Technology and Capital Formation*, eds. Dale W. Jorgenson and Ralph Landau, 1–36, Cambridge, MA: The MIT Press.

————. 1990a. Aggregate Consumer Behavior and the Measurement of Social Welfare. *Econometrica* 58, no. 5 (September): 1007–1040.

————. 1990b. Productivity and Economic Growth. In *Fifty Years of Economic Measurement*, eds. Ernst R. Berndt and John E. Triplett, 19–118, Chicago: University of Chicago Press.

————. 1995a. *Postwar U.S. Economic Growth*, Cambridge, MA: The MIT Press.

————. 1995b. *International Comparisons of Economic Growth*, Cambridge, MA: The MIT Press.

————. 1996. Empirical Studies of Depreciation. *Economic Inquiry* 34, no. 1 (January): 24–42.

————. 1996a. *Capital Theory and Investment Behavior*, Cambridge, MA: The MIT Press.

————. 1996b. *Tax Policy and the Cost of Capital*, Cambridge, MA: The MIT Press.

————. 1997a. *Aggregate Consumer Behavior*, Cambridge, MA: The MIT Press.

————. 1997b. *Measuring Social Welfare*, Cambridge, MA: The MIT Press.

————. 1998a. *Econometric General Equilibrium Modeling*, Cambridge, MA: The MIT Press.

————. 1998b. *Energy, the Environment, and Economic Growth*, Cambridge, MA: The MIT Press.

————. 2000. *Econometric Modeling of Producr Behavior*, Cambridge, MA: The MIT Press.

Jorgenson, Dale, W., and Barbara M. Fraumeni, 1981. Relative Prices and Technical Change. in *Modeling and Measuring Natural Resource Substituion*, eds. Ernst R. Berndt and Barry C. Field, 17–47, Cambridge, MA: The MIT Press.

————. 1989a. The Accumulation of Human and Nonhuman Capital, 1948–1984. In *The Measurement of Saving, Investment and Wealth*, eds. Robert E. Lipsey and Helen S. Tice, 227–282, Chicago, IL: University of Chicago Press.

————. 1989b. Investment in Education. *Educational Researcher* 18, no.4 (May): 35–44.

————. 1992a. Investment in Education and U.S. Economic Growth. *Scandinavian Journal of Economics* 94: 51–70.

————. 1992b. The Output of the Education Sector. In *Output Measurement in the Services Sector*, ed. Zvi Griliches, 303–338, Chicago, IL: University of Chicago Press.

Jorgenson, Dale W., Frank M. Gollop, and Barbara M. Fraumeni. 1987. *Productivity and U.S. Economic Growth*, Cambridge, MA: Harvard University Press.

Jorgenson, Dale W., and Zvi Griliches. 1967. The Explanation of Productivity Change. *The Review of Economic Studies* 34(3), no. 99 (July): 249–280.

———. 1972a. Issues in Growth Accounting: A Reply to Edward F. Denison. *Survey of Current Business* 52, no. 5, pt. 2 (May): 65–94.

———. 1972b. Issues in Growth Accounting: Final Reply. *Survey of Current Business* 52, no. 5, pt. 2 (May): 111.

Jorgenson, Dale W., Mun S. Ho, and Barbara M. Fraumeni. 1994. The Quality of the U.S. Work Force, 1948–1990, NBER Summer Institute on Productivity, July 21, unpublished.

Jorgenson, Dale W., and Jean-Jacques Laffont. 1974. Efficient Estimation of Nonlinear Simultaneous Equations with Additive Disturbances. *Annals of Social and Economic Measurement* 3, no. 1 (January): 615–640.

Jorgenson, Dale W., and Ralph Landau, eds. 1989. *Technology and Capital Formation*, Cambridge, MA: The MIT Press.

———, eds. 1993. *Tax Reform and the Cost of Capital*, Washington, DC: The Brooking Institution.

Jorgenson, Dale W., and Lawrence J. Lau. 1975. The Structure of Consumer Preferences. *Annals of Social and Economic Measurement* 4, no. 1 (January): 49–101.

———. 1977. Statistical Tests of the Theory of Consumer Behavior. In *Quantitative Wirtschaftforschung*, eds. H.L. Albach, E. Helmstädter, and R. Henn, 383–394, Tübingen: J.C.B. Mohr.

———. 1979. The Integrability of Consumer Demand Functions. *European Economic Review* 12, no. 2 (April): 115–147.

———. 1986. Testing the Integrability of Consumer Demand Functions, United States, 1948–1971, In *Advances in Econometrics* 5, ed. D. Slottje, 31–48. Greenwich, CT: JAI Press.

Jorgenson, Dale W., Lawrence J. Lau, and Thomas M. Stoker. 1980a. Welfare Comparison under Exact Aggregation. *American Economic Review* 70, no. 2 (May): 268–272.

———. 1981. Aggregate Consumer Behavior and Individual Welfare. In *Macroeconomic Analysis*, eds. D. Currie, R. Nobay, and D. Peel, 35–61, London: Croom-Helm.

———. 1982. The Transcendental Logarithmic Model of Aggregate Consumer Behavior. In *Advances in Econometrics* 1, eds. Robert L. Basmann and G.F. Rhodes, vol. 1, 97–238, Greenwich: JAI Press.

Jorgenson, Dale W., and Mieko Nishimizu. 1978. U.S. and Japanese Economic Growth, 1952–1974: An International Comparison. *The Economic Journal* 88, no. 352 (December): 707–726.

Jorgenson, Dale W., and Alvaro Pachon. 1983a. The Accumulation of Human and Nonhuman Wealth. In *The Determinants of National Saving and Wealth*, eds. R. Hemmings and Franco Modigliani, 302–352, London: Macmillan.

———. 1983b. Lifetime Income and Human Capital. In *Human Resources, Employment and Development*, eds. P. Streeten and H. Maier, vol. 2, 29–90, London: Macmillan.

Jorgenson, Dale W., and Calvin D. Siebert. 1968a. A Comparison of Alternative Theories of Corporate Investment Behavior. *American Economic Review* 58, no. 4 (September): 681–712.

———. 1968b. Optimal Capital Accumulation and Corporate Investment Behavior. *Journal of Political Economy* 76, no. 6 (November/December): 1123–1151.

———. 1972. An Empirical Evaluation of Alternative Theories of Corporate Investment. In *Problems and Issues in Current Econometric Practice*, ed. Karl Brunner, 155–218, Columbus: Ohio State University Press.

Jorgenson, Dale W., and Daniel T. Slesnick. 1984a. Aggregate Consumer Behavior and the Measurement of Inequality. *Review of Economic Studies* 51(3), no. 166 (July): 369–392.

———. 1984b. Inequality in the Distribution of Individual Welfare. In *Advances in Econometrics*, vol. 3, eds. Robert L. Basmann, and G.F. Rhodes, 67–130, Greenwich, CT: JAI Press.

———. 1985a. Efficiency Versus Equity in Natural Gas Price Regulation. *Journal of Econometrics* 30, nos. 1/2 (October/November): 301–316.

———. 1985b. Efficiency versus Equity in Petroleum Taxation. *Energy Journal* 6. Special Issue: 171–188.

———. 1985c. General Equilibrium Analysis of Economic Policy. In *New Developments in Applied General Equilibrium Analysis*, eds. J. Piggott and John Whalley, 293–370, Cambridge: Cambridge University Press.

———. 1987a. Aggregate Consumer Behavior and Household Equivalence Scales. *Journal of Business and Economic Statistics* 5, no. 2 (April): 219–232.

———. 1987b. General Equilibrium Analysis of Natural Gas Price Regulation. In *Public Regulation*, ed. E.E.Bailey, 153–190, Cambridge, MA: The MIT Press.

———. 1989. Redistributional Policy and the Measurement of Poverty. In *Research on Economic Inequality*, vol. 1, ed. D.J. Slottje, 1–48, Greenwich, CT: JAI Press.

————. 1990a. Inequality and the Standard of Living. *Journal of Econometrics* 43, nos. 1/2 (January/February): 103–120.

————. 1990b. Individual and Social Cost of Living Indexes. In *Price, Level Measurement*, ed. W.E. Diewert, 155–234, Amsterdam: North-Holland.

Jorgenson, Dale W., Daniel T. Slesnick, and Thomas M. Stoker. 1987. Two-Stage Budgeting and Consumer Demand for Energy. In *Advances in the Economics of Energy and Resources*, vol 6, ed. John R. Moroney, 125–162, Greenwich: JAI Press.

————. 1988. Two-Stage Budgeting and Exact Aggregation. *Journal of Business and Economic Statistics* 6, no. 3 (July): 313–326.

Jorgenson, Dale W., Daniel T. Slesnick, and Peter J. Wilcoxen. 1991. Carbon Taxes and Economic Welfare. *Brookings Papers on Economic Activity: Microeconomics*: 393–454.

Jorgenson, Dale W., and James A. Stephenson. 1967a. Investment Behavior in U.S. Manufacturing, 1947–1960. *Econometrica* 35, no. 2 (April): 169–220.

————. 1967b. The The Time Structure of Investment Behavior in U.S. Manufacturing, 1947–1960. *Review of Economics and Statistics* 49, no. 1 (February): 16–27.

————. 1969. Anticipations and Investment Behavior in U.S. Manufacturing, 1947–1960. *Journal of the American Statistical Association* 64, no. 325 (March): 67–89.

Jorgenson, Dale W., and Thomas M. Stoker. 1984. Aggregate Consumer Expenditures on Energy. In *Advances in the Economics of Energy and Resources*, vol. 5, ed. John R. Moroney, 1–84, Greenwich, CT: JAI Press.

————. 1986. Nonlinear Three Stage Least-Squares Pooling of Time Series and Cross-Section Data. In *Advances in Statistical Analysis and Statistical Computing*, ed. R.S. Mariano, vol. 1, 87–115, Greenwich, CT: JAI Press.

Jorgenson, Dale W., and Martin A. Sullivan. 1981. Inflation and Corporate Capital Recovery. In *Depreciation, Inflation, and Taxation of Income from Capital*, ed. Charles R. Hulten, 171–238, 311–313, Washington, DC: The Urban Institute.

Jorgenson, Dale W., and Peter J. Wilcoxen. 1990a. Environmental Regulation and U.S. Economic Growth. *The Rand Journal of Economics* 21, no. 2 (Summer): 314–340.

————. 1990b. Intertemporal General Equilibrium Modeling of U.S. Environmental Regulation. *Journal of Policy Modeling* 12, no. 4 (December): 715–744.

————. 1990b. Environmental Regulation and U.S. Economic Growth. *The Rand Journal of Economics* 21, no. 2 (Summer): 314–340.

———. 1991. Global Change, Energy Prices and U.S. Economic Growth. *Structural Change and Economic Dynamics* 3, no. 1 (March): 135–154.

———. 1992. Reducing U.S. Carbon Dioxide Emissions: The Cost of Different Goals. In *Advances in the Economics of Energy and Resources*, ed. John R. Moroney, vol. 7, 125–158, Greenwich: JAI Press.

———. 1993a. Reducing U.S. Carbon Dioxide Emissions: An Assessment of Alternative Instruments. *Journal of Policy Modeling* 15, nos. 5/6 (October/December): 491–520.

———. 1993b. Reducing U.S. Carbon Emissions: An Econometric General Equilibrium Assessment. *Resource and Energy Economics* 15, no. 1 (March): 7–26.

———. 1993c. Energy, the Environment, and Economic Growth. In *Handbook of Natural Resource and Energy Economics*, vol. 3, eds. Allen V. Kneese and James L. Sweeney, 1267–1349, Amsterdam: North-Holland.

———. 1997. Fundamental Tax Reform and Energy Markets. *The Energy Journal* 18, no. 3 (July): 1–30.

Jorgenson, Dale W., and Kun-Young Yun. 1986a. The Efficiency of Capital Allocation. *Scandinavian Journal of Economics* 88, no. 1: 85–107.

———. 1986b. Tax Policy and Capital Allocation. *Scandinavian Journal of Economics* 88, no. 2: 355–377.

———. 1990. Tax Reform and U.S. Economic Growth. *Journal of Political Economy* 98, no. 5, part 2 (October): S151–S193.

———. 1991a. *Tax Reform and the Cost of Capital*, New York, NY: Oxford University Press.

———. 1991b. The Excess Burden of Taxation. *Journal of Accounting, Auditing, and Finance* 6, no. 4 (Fall): 487–509.

———. 1992. Marginal Cost of Public Spending. Mimeo.

Kaldor, Nicholas. 1939. Welfare Propositions of Economics and Interpersonal Comparisons of Utility. *Economic Journal* 49, no. 195 (September): 549–552.

Kamien, M., and N. Schwartz. 1981. *Dynamic Optimization*, New York, NY: North-Holland.

Kay, J.A. 1980. The Deadweight Loss from a Tax System. *Journal of Public Economics* 13, no. 1 (February): 111–119.

Kay, J.A., and M. Keen. 1988. Measuring the Inefficiencies of Tax Systems. *Journal of Public Economics* 35, no. 3 (April): 265–287.

Keen, M. 1990. Welfare Analysis and Intertemporal Substitution. *Journal of Public Economics* 42, no. 1 (June): 47–66.

Kendrick, John W. 1961. *Productivity Trends in the United States*, Princeton, NJ: Princeton University Press.

————. 1973. *Postwar Productivity Trends in the United States, 1948–1969*, New York, NY: National Bureau of Economic Research.

Keuschnigg, C., and W. Kohler. 1994. Commercial Policy and Dynamic Adjustment under Monopolistic Competition, Vienna: Institute of Advanced Studies.

Keynes, John M. 1935. *The General Theory of Employment, Interest and Money*, New York, NY: Harcourt, Brace and Company.

Kildegaard, Arne. 1994. A Dynamic Computable General Equilibrium Analysis of the Stability of the Mexican Financial System in the Wake of Liberal Economic Reforms. Unpublished Ph.D. Dissertation, The University of Texas at Austin.

King, Mervin A. 1974. Taxation and the Cost of Capital. *Review of Economic Studies* 41(1), no. 126 (January): 21–35.

————. 1977. *Public Policy and the Corporation*, London: Chapman and Hall.

————. 1983. Welfare Analysis of Tax Reforms Using Household Data. *Journal of Public Economics* 21, no. 2 (July): 183–214.

King, Mervin A., and Don Fullerton, eds. 1984. *The Taxation of Income from Capital: A Comparative Study of the U.S., U.K., Sweden, and West Germany*, Chicago: University of Chicago Press.

Kirman, Alan P. 1992. Whom or What Does the Representative Individual Represent? *Journal of Economic Perspectives* 6, no. 2 (Spring): 117–136.

Kneese, Allen V., Robert U. Ayres, and R.C. D'Arge. 1970. *Economics and the Environment: A Materials Balance Approach*, Baltimore: Johns Hopkins University Press.

Kneese, Allen V., and James L. Sweeney, eds. 1985. *Handbook of Natural Resource and Energy Economics*, 2 vols., Amsterdam: North-Holland.

Kohli 1978. 1991.

Kolm, Serge C. 1969. The Optimal Production of Social Justice. In *Public Eonomics*, eds. J. Margolis and H. Guitton, 145–200, London: Macmillan.

Konus, A.A. 1939. The Problem of the True Index of the Cost-of-Living. *Econometrica* 7, no. 1 (January): 10–29.

Kravis, Irving, Alan W. Heston, and Robert Summers. 1982. *World Product and Income: International Comparisons of Real Gross Product*, Baltimore, MD: Johns Hopkins Press.

Kreps, D. 1979. Three Essays on Capital Markets. Unpublished Ph.D. Dissertation, Stanford University.

Krishna, Kala. 1985. Rank of Demand Systems: Theory vs. Quotas with Endogenous Quality, NBER Working Paper No. 1535, January.

Krugman, Paul R. 1990. A Technology Gap Model of International Trade. In *Rethinking International Trade*, ed. Paul R. Krugman, 152–164, Cambridge, MA.

Kydland, F., and E. Prescott. 1982. Time-to-build and Aggregate Fluctuations. *Econometrica* 50, no. 6 (November): 1355–1371.

Laitner, John. 1991. Modeling Marital Connections among Family Lines. *Journal of Political Economy* 99, no. 6 (December): 1123–1141.

Lau, Lawrence J. 1977. Existence Conditions for Aggregate Demand Functions. Technical Report 248. Stanford: Stanford University, Institute for Mathematical Studies in the Social Sciences (revised in 1980 and 1982).

———. 1978. Applications of Profit Functions. In *Production Economics: A Dual Approach to Theory and Applications*, eds. Melvyn Fuss and Daniel L. McFadden, vol. 1, 133–216, Amsterdam: North-Holland.

———. 1982. A Note on the Fundamental Theorem of Exact Aggregation. *Economics Letters* 9, no. 2 (February): 119–126.

———. 1984. Comments on Ahsan Mansur and John Whalley, Numerical Specification of Applied General Equilibrium Models: Estimation, Calibration, and Data. In *Applied General Equilibrium Analysis*, eds. Herbert E. Scarf and John B. Shoven, 127–137, Cambridge, England: Cambridge University Press.

———. 1986. Functional Forms in Econometric Model Building. In *Handbook of Econometrics*, eds. Zvi Griliches and Michael D. Intriligator, vol. 3, 1515–1566, Amsterdam: North-Holland.

Lazear, Edward P., and Robert T. Michael. 1980. Family Size and the Distribution of Real Per Capita Income. *American Economic Review* 70, no. 1 (March): 91–107.

Leontief, Wassily W. 1941. *The Structure of American Economy, 1919–1929*, New York: Oxford University Press (second ed., 1951).

———. 1951. *The Structure of the American Economy, 1919–1939*. 2nd ed. (1st ed. 1941), New York: Oxford University Press.

———, ed. 1953. *Studies in the Structure of the American Economy*. New York: Oxford University Press.

———. 1970. Environmental Repercussions and the Economic Structure: An Input-Output Approach, *Review of Economics and Statistics* 52, no. 3 (August): 262–271.

Leontief, Wassily W., Anne P. Carter, and Peter A. Petri. 1977. *The Future of the World Economy*, Oxford: Oxford University Press.

Leontief, Wassily W., and D. Ford. 1972. Air Pollution and the Economic Structure: Empirical Results of Input-Output Computations. In *Input-Output Techniques*, eds. A. Brody, and Anne P. Carter, 9–30, Amsterdam: North-Holland.

Levy, F., and R.J. Murnane. 1992. U.S. Earnings Levels and Earnings Inequality: A Review of Recent Trends and Proposed Explanations. *Journal of Economic Literature* 30, no. 3 (September): 1333–1381.

Lewbel, Arthur. 1989a. Household Equivalence Scales and Welfare Comparisons. *Journal of Public Economics* 39, no. 3 (August): 377–391.

———. 1989b. Exact Aggregation and the Representative Consumer. *Quarterly Journal of Economics* 104, no. 3 (August): 622–633.

———. 1991. Rank of Demand Systems: Theory and Nonparametric Estimates, *Econometrica* 45, no. 3 (May): 711–730.

———. 1997. Consumer Demand Systems and Household Equivalence Scales. In *Handbook of Applied Econometrics*, eds. M.H. Pesaran and P. Schmidt, Oxford: Blackwell.

Longva, Svein, and Oystein Olsen. 1983a. Producer Behavior in the MSG Model. In *Analysis of Supply and Demand of Electricity in the Norwegian Economy*, eds. Olav Bjerkholt, Svein Longva, Oystein Olsen, and Steinar Strom, 52–83, Oslo: Central Statistical Bureau.

———. 1983b. Energy in the Multi-Sectoral Growth Model MSG. In *Analysis of Supply and Demand of Electricity in the Norwegian Economy*, eds. Olav Bjerkholt, Svein Longva, Oystein Olsen, and Steinar Strom, 27–51, Oslo: Central Statistical Bureau.

Lucas, Robert E., Jr. 1967. Adjustment Costs and the Theory of Supply. *Journal of Political Economy* 75, no. 4, part 1 (August): 321–334.

———. 1976. Econometric Policy Evaluation: A Critique. In *The Phillips Curve and Labor Markets*, eds. Karl Brunner and Alan H. Meltzer, 19–46, Amsterdam: North-Holland.

———. 1988. On the Mechanics of Economic Development. *Journal of Monetary Economics* 22, no. 1 (July): 3–42.

Malmquist, S. 1953. Index Numbers and Indifference Surfaces. *Trabajos de Estadistica* 4: 209–242.

Manser, M.E., and R.J. McDonald. 1988. An Analysis of Substitution Bias in Measuring Inflation, 1959–1985. *Econometrica* 56, no. 4 (July): 909–930.

Mansur, Ahsan H., and John Whalley. 1984. Numerical Specification of Applied General Equilibrium Models: Estimation, Calibration, and Data. In *Applied General Equilibrium Analysis*, eds. Herbert E. Scarf and John B. Shoven, 69–127, Cambridge, UK: Cambridge University Press.

Marshall, Alfred. 1920. *Principles of Economics*. London: Macmillan.

Maskin, Eric. 1978. A Theorem on Utilitarianism. *Review of Economic Studies* 42, no. 139 (February: 93–96.

McFadden, Daniel L. 1963. Further Results on CES Production Functions. *Review of Economic Studies* 30(2), no. 83 (June): 73–83.

McKenzie, K.J. 1994. Implications of Risk and Irreversibility for the Measurement of Marginal Effective Tax Rates on Capital. *Canadian Journal of Economics* 27, no. 3 (August): 604–619.

McKibbin, Warwich J., and Peter J. Wilcoxen. 1995. The Theoretical and Empirical Structure of G-cubed, Mimeo: The Brookings Institution.

———. 1999. The Theoretical and Empirical Structure of the G-cubed Model. *Economic Modelling* 16: 123–148.

Meade, James E. 1952. External Economies and Diseconomies in a Competitive Situation. *Economic Journal* 62: 54–67.

Merrill, P. 1982. Adjustment Costs and Industry Investment. Unpublished Ph.D. Dissertation, Harvard University.

Mills, E.S., ed. 1975. *Economic Analysis of Environmental Problems*, New York, NY: Columbia University Press.

Modigliani, Franco, and Merton H. Miller. 1958. The Cost of Capital, Corporation Finance, and the Theory of Investment. *American Economic Review* 48, no. 3 (June): 261–297.

Mohring, H. 1971. Alternative Welfare Gain and Loss Measures. *Western Economic Journal* 9, no. 2 (May): 349–368.

Morrison, Catherine J., and Amy Ellen Schwartz. 1996. State Infrastructure and Productive Performance. *American Economic Review* 86, no. 5 (December): 1095–1111.

Muellbauer, J. 1974. Prices and Inequality: The U.K. Experience. *Economic Journal* 84, no. 333 (March): 32–35.

———. 1975. Aggregation Income Distribution and Consumer Demand. *Review of Economic Studies* 42(3), no. 132 (October): 525–543.

Munnell, Alicia H. 1990. How does Public Infrastructure Affect Regional Economic Performance. In *Is There a Shortfall in Public Capital Investment?* ed. Alicia H. Munnell, 69–103, Boston, MA: Federal Reserve Bank of Boston.

Mussa, M. 1977. External and Internal Adjustment Costs and the Theory of Aggregate and Firm Investment. *Economica* 44, no. 174 (May): 163–178.

Myers, S. C., A. L. Kolbe, and W. B. Tye. 1985. Inflation and Rate of Return Regulation. In *Research in Transportation Economics*, vol. 2, 83–119, Greenwich, CT: JAI Press.

Nadiri, M. Ishaq, and Theofanis P. Mamuneas. 1995. The Effects of Public Infrastructure and RD Capital in the Cost Structure and Performance of U.S. Manufacturing Industries. *Review of Economics and Statistics* 76, no. 1 (February): 22–37.

Nadiri, M. Ishaq, and I.R. Prucha. 1996. Estimation of the Depreciation Rate of Physical and RD Capital in the U.S. Total Manufacturing Sector. *Economic Inquiry* 34, no. 1 (January): 43–56.

Nelson, J.A. 1988. Household Economies of Scale in Consumption: Theory and Evidence. *Econometrica* 56, no. 6 (November): 1301–1314.

Nordhaus, William D. 1979. *The Efficient Use of Energy Resources*, New Haven: Yale University Press.

Organization for Economic Cooperation and Development. 1991. Taxing Profits in a Global Economy: Domestic and International Issues, Paris.

Pagan, Adrian R., and John H. Shannon. 1985. Sensitivity Analysis for Linearized Computable General Equilibrium Models. In *New Development in Applied General Equilibrium Analysis*, eds. John Piggot and John Whalley, 104–118, Cambridge: Cambridge University Press.

Pakes, A., and Zvi Griliches. 1984. Estimating Distributed Lags in Short Panels with an Application to the Specification of Depreciation Patterns and Capital Stock Constructs. *Review of Economic Studies* 51(2), no. 165 (April): 243–262.

Parks, Richard W. 1967. An Econometric Model of Swedish Economic Growth, 1861–1955. Unpublished Ph.D. Dissertation. University of California, Berkeley.

Pashardes, Panos. 1991. Contemporaneous and Intertemporal Child Costs. *Journal of Public Economics* 45, no. 2 (July): 191–213.

Petri, Peter A. 1984. *Modeling Japanese-American Trade*, Cambridge, MA: Harvard University Press.

Pfahler, Wilhelm, Ulrich Hofman, and Werner Bonte. 1996. Does Extra Infrastructure Capital Matter? An Appraisal of Empirical Literature. *Finanzarchiv*: 68–112.

Pizer, William. 1996. Modeling Long-Term Policy under Uncertainty. Unpublished Ph.D. Dissertation, Harvard University.

Pollak, Robert A. 1981. The Social Cost-of-Living Index. *Journal of Public Economics* 15, no. 3 (June): 311–336.

———. 1990. The Theory of the Cost-of-Living Index. In *Price Level Measurement*, ed. W. Erwin Diewert, 5–77m Amsterdam: North-Holland.

———. 1991. Welfare Comparisons and Situation Comparisons. *Journal of Econometrics* 50, nos. 1/2 (October/November): 31–48.

Pollak, Robert A., and T.J. Wales. 1979. Welfare Comparisons and Equivalent Scales, *American Economic Review* 69, no. 2 (May): 216–221.

Poterba, James M. 1989. Lifetime Incidence and the Distributional Burden of Excise Taxes. *American Economic Review* 79, no. 2 (May): 325–330.

———. 1991a. Tax Policy to Combat Global Warming: On Designing a Carbon Tax. In *Global Warming: Economic Policy Responses*, eds. R. Dornbusch, and James M. Poterba, 71–97, Cambridge, MA: The MIT Press.

———. 1991b. Is the Gasoline Tax Regressive? In *Tax Policy and the Economy*, ed. D. Bradford, vol. 5, Cambridge MA: The MIT Press.

Poterba, James M., and Lawrence H. Summers. 1983. Dividend Taxes, Corporate Investment, and Q. *Journal of Public Economics* 22, no. 2 (November): 135–167.

Rawls, J. 1971. *A Theory of Justice*, Cambridge, MA: Harvard University Press.

Rebelo, Sergio T. 1991. Long-Run Policy Analysis and Long-Run Growth. *Journal of Political Economy* 99, no. 3 (June): 500–521.

Repetto, Robert, Roger C. Dower, Robin Jenkins, and Jacqueline Geoghegan. 1992. *Green Fees: How a Tax Shift Can Work for the Environment and the Economy*, Washington, DC: World Resources Institute.

Rob, R. 1991. Learning and Capacity Expansion under Demand Uncertainty. *Review of Economic Studies* 58(4), no. 196 (July): 655–675.

Robbins, L. 1938. Interpersonal Comparisons of Utility: A Comment. *Economic Journal* 43, no. 192 (December): 635–641.

Roberts, K.W.S. 1980a. Price Independent Welfare Prescriptions. *Journal of Public Economics* 13, no. 3 (June): 277–298.

———. 1980b. Possibility Theorems with Interpersonally Comparable Welfare Levels. *Review of Economic Studies* 47, no. 147 (January): 409–420.

———. 1980c. Interpersonal Comparability and Social Choice Theory. *Review of Economic Studies* 47, no. 147 (January): 421–439.

———. 1980d. Social Choice Theory: The Single Profile and Multi-Profile Approaches. *Review of Economic Studies* 47, no. 147 (January): 441–450.

Romer, Paul M. 1986. Increasing Returns and Long-Run Growth. *Journal of Political Economy* 94, no. 4 (November): 1002–1037.

Rosen, H. 1978. The Measurement of Excess Burden with Explicit Utility Function, *Journal of Political Economy* 86, no. 2, part 2 (April): S121–S136.

Rothschild, Michael. 1971. On the Cost of Adjustment. *Quarterly Journal of Economics* 85, no. 4 (November): 605–622.

Ruggles, Richard, and Nancy Ruggles. 1971. The Evolution of National Accounts and the National Data Base. *Survey of Current Business, Anniversary Issue, The Economic Accounts of the United States: Retrospect and Prospect* 51, no. 7, part II (June): 152–161.

Ruiz-Castillo, J. 1987. Potential Welfare and the Sum of the Individual Compensating or Equivalent Variations. *Journal of Economic Theory* 41, no. 1 (February): 34–53.

Samuelson, Paul. 1947. *Foundations of Economic Analysis,* Cambridge, MA: Harvard Univesity.

———. 1948. Consumption Theory in Terms of Revealed Preference. *Economica* 15, no. 60 (November): 243–253.

———. 1951. Abstract of a Theorem Concerning Substitutability in Open Leontief Models. In *Activity Analysis of Production and Allocation,* ed. Tjalling C. Koopmans, 142–146, New York: Wiley.

———. 1953. Prices of Factors and Goods in General Equilibrium. *Review of Economic Studies* 21(1), no. 54: 1–20.

———. 1961. The Evaluation of Social Income: Capital Formation and Wealth. In *The Theory of Capital,* eds. Lutz F.A. and D.C. Hague, 299–324, New York: St. Martin's Press.

Scarf, Herbert E., and John B. Shoven, eds. 1984. *Applied General Equilibrium Analysis,* Cambridge: Cambridge University Press.

Schelling, Thomas C. 1992. Some Economics of Global Warming. *American Economic Review* 82, no. 1 (March): 1–14.

Schillo, Bruce, Linda Giannarelli, David Kelly, Steve Swanson, and Peter J. Wilcoxen. 1992. The Distributional Impacts of a Carbon Tax, mimeo, February.

Schipper, L., and S. Meyers with Richard Howarth, and Ruth Steiner. 1992. *Energy Efficiency and Human Activity: Past Trends, Future Prospects,* Cambridge: Cambridge University Press.

Schultz, Henry. 1938. *The Theory and Measurement of Demand,* Chicago: University of Chicago Press.

Schurr, Sam, and Bruce C. Netschert with Vera E. Eliasberg, Joseph Lerner, and Hans H. Landsberg. 1960. *Energy in the American Economy, 1850–1975,* Baltimore: Johns Hopkins University Press.

Schurr, Sam, C.C. Burwell, W.D. Devine, Jr., and Sidney Sonenblum. 1990. *Electricity in the American Economy: Agent of Technological Progress,* Westport: Greenwood.

Scitovsky, T. 1941. A Note on Welfare Propositions in Economics, *Review of Economic Studies* 9, no. 1 (November): 77–88.

Sen, Amartya K. 1970. *Collective Choice and Social Welfare,* San Francisco, CA: Holden Day.

———. 1973. *On Economic Inequality,* Oxford: Clarendon Press.

———. 1976. Poverty: An Ordinal Approach to Measurement. *Econometrica* 44, no. 2 (March): 219–231.

———. 1977. On Weights and Measures: Informational Constraints in Social Welfare Analysis. *Econometrica* 45, no. 7 (October): 1539–1571.

————. 1979. The Welfare Basis of Real Income Comparisons: A Survey. *Journal of Economic Literature* 17, no. 1 (March): 1–45.

Shiells, C., R.M. Stern, and A. Deardorff. 1986. Estimates of Elasticities of Substitution between Imports and Home Goods for the U.S. *Weltwirtschaftliches Archiv* 3: 497–519.

Slesnick, Daniel T. 1991a. Aggregate Deadweight Loss and Money Metric Social Welfare. *International Economic Review* 32, no. 1 (February): 123–146.

————. 1991b. Normative Index Numbers. *Journal of Econometrics* 50, nos. 1/2 (October/November): 107–130.

————. 1991c. The Standard of Living in the United States. *Review of Income and Wealth* 37, no. 4 (December): 363–386.

————. 1993. Gaining Ground: Poverty in the Postwar United States. *Journal of Political Economy* 101, no. 1 (February): 1–38.

————. 1994. Consumption, Needs and Inequality. *International Economic Review* 35 no. 3 (August).

————. 1998. Empirical Approaches to the Measurement of Welfare. *Journal of Economic Literature* 36, no. 4 (December): 2108–2165.

Small, K.A., and H.S. Rosen. 1981. Applied Welfare Economics with Discrete Choice Models. *Journal of Economic Literature* 49, no. 4 (December): 1827–1874.

Solow, Robert M. 1957. Technical Change and the Aggregate Production Function. *Review of Economics and Statistics* 39, no. 3 (August): 312–320.

Statistics Canada. Various years. *The Input-Output Structure of the Canadian Economy 1961–1981*, Ottawa: Statistics Canada.

————. 1984. *National Income and Expenditure Accounts, Annual Estimates, 1926–1983*, Ottawa: Statistics Canada.

————. 1989. *The Canadian Economic Observer* (May), Ottawa: Statistics Canada.

————. 1996. *National Income and Expenditure Accounts, Annual Estimates 1984–1995*, Ottawa: Statistics Canada.

————. 1997. *Canada's Balance of International Payments, 1926 to 1996*, Ottawa: Statistics Canada.

Stern, R.M., J. Francis, and B. Schumacher. 1976. *Price Elasticities in International Trade: An Annotated Bibliography*, London: Macmillan.

Stiglitz, Joseph E. 1973. Taxation, Corporate Financial Policy, and the Cost of Capital. *Journal of Public Economics* 2, no. 1 (February): 1–34.

Stoker, Thomas M. 1992. *Lectures on Semiparametric Econometrics*. Louvain-la-Neuve: CORE Foundation.

———. 1993. Empirical Approaches to the Problem of Aggregation over Individuals. *Journal of Economic Literature* 31, no. 4 (December): 1827–1874.

Stone, Richard N. 1954. *Measurement of Consumers' Expenditures and Behaviour in the United Kingdom*, vol. 1, Cambridge: Cambridge University Press.

Summers, Lawrence H. 1981. Taxation and Corporate Investment: A Q Theory Approach. *Brookings Papers on Economic Activity* 12: 67–127.

Tobin, James. 1969. A General Equilibrium Approach to Monetary Theory. *Journal of Money, Credit, and Banking* 1, no. 1 (February): 15–29.

Triplett, John E. 1996. Depreciation in Production Analysis and in Income and Wealth Accounts: Resolution of an Old Debate. *Economic Inquiry* 34, no. 1 (January): 93–115.

Tuladhar, Sugandha D., and Peter J. Wilcoxen. 1999. An Econometric Look at the Double Dividend Hypothesis. National Tax Association Proceedings 1998, pp. 57–62.

Turner, C.G. 1981. *Quantitative Restrictions on International Trade of the United States and Japan*, Unpublished Ph.D. Dissertation, Harvard University

U.S. Bureau of Labor Statistics. 1983. *Trends in Multifactor Productivity 1948–1981*, Bulletin 2178, Washington, DC: United States Government Printing Office.

United Nations. 1968. *A System of National Accounts*, New York, NY: United Nations.

United Nations, Eurostat, IMF, OECD and the World Bank. 1993. *System of National Accounts 1993*, New York, Luxembourg, Paris and Washington, DC.

Uzawa, Hirofumi. 1962. Production Functions with Constant Elasticities of Substitution. *Review of Economic Studies* 29(3), no. 81 (October): 291–299.

———. 1975. Optimal Investment in Social Overhead Capital. In *Economic Analysis of Environmental Problems*, ed. E.S. Mills, 9–22, New York, NY: Columbia University Press.

———. 1988. *Optimality, Equilibrium and Growth*, Tokyo: University of Tokyo Press.

van der Gaag, J., and E. Smolensky. 1982. True Household Equivalence Scales and Characteristics of the Poor in the United States. *Review of Income and Wealth* 28, no. 1 (March): 17–28.

Varian, H.R. 1982. The Nonparametric Approach to Demand Analysis. *Econometrica* 50, no. 4 (July): 945–973.

von Furstenberg, George M. 1980. *Capital, Efficiency and Growth*, Cambridge: Ballinger.

Walras, Leon. 1954. *Elements of Pure Economics*, translated by W. Jaffe, London: George Allen and Unwin (first published in French in 1874).

Weitzman, Martin L. 1976. On the Welfare Significance of National Product in a Dynamic Economy. *Quarterly Journal of Economics* 110, no. 1 (February): 156–162.

Whalley, John. 1985. *Trade Liberalization among Major World Trading Areas*, Cambridge, MA: The MIT Press.

Whalley, John, and Randall Wigle. 1990. The International Incidence of Carbon Taxes. In *Global Warming: Economic Policy Responses*, 233–263, Cambridge, MA: The MIT Press.

Whited, T. 1992. Debt, Liquidity Constraints and Corporate Investment: Evidence from Panel Data. *Journal of Finance* 47, no. 4 (September): 1425–1460.

Wilcoxen, Peter J. 1988. The Effects of Environmental Regulation and Energy Prices on U.S. Economic Performance. Unpublished Ph.D. Dissertation, Harvard University.

———. 1992. An Introduction to Intertemporal Modeling. In *Notes and Problems in Applied General Equilibrium Economics*, eds. P.B. Dixon, B.R. Parmenter, A.A. Powell, and Peter J. Wilcoxen, 277–284, Amsterdam: North-Holland.

Willig, R.E. 1976. Consumer's Surplus without Apology. *American Economic Review* 66, no. 4 (September): 589–597.

Wykoff, Frank C. 1989. Economic Depreciation and the User Cost of Business Leased Automobiles. In *Technology and Capital Formation*, eds. Dale W. Jorgenson, and Ralph Landau, 259–292, Cambridge, MA: The MIT Press.

Wold, H.O.A. with Lars Jureen. 1953. *Demand Analysis: A Study in Econometrics*, New York, NY: Wiley.

Zeira, J. 1987. Investment as a Process of Search. *Journal of Political Economy* 95, no. 1 (February): 204–210.

Index